Accessing Transport Networks

McGraw-Hill Series on Computer Communications (Selected Titles)

ISBN	AUTHOR	TITLE
0-07-005147-X	Bates	*Voice and Data Communications Handbook*
0-07-005669-2	Benner	*Fibre Channel: Gigabit Communications and I/O for Computer Networks*
0-07-005560-2	Black	*TCP/IP and Related Protocols, Second Edition*
0-07-005590-4	Black	*Frame Relay Networks: Specifications and Implementation, Second Edition*
0-07-006730-3	Blakeley/Harris/Lewis	*Messaging/Queuing with MQI*
0-07-011486-2	Chiong	*SNA Interconnections: Bridging and Routing SNA in Hierarchical, Peer, and High-Speed Networks*
0-07-020359-8	Feit	*SNMP: A Guide to Network Management*
0-07-021389-5	Feit	*TCP/IP: Architecture, Protocols, and Implementation with IPv6 and IP Security, Second Edition*
0-07-024043-4	Goralski	*Introduction to ATM Networking*
0-07-034249-0	Kessler	*ISDN: Concepts, Facilities, and Services, Third Edition*
0-07-035968-7	Kumar	*Broadbend Communications*
0-07-041051-8	Matusow	*SNA, APPN, HPR, and TCP/IP Integration*
0-07-060362-6	McDysan/Spohn	*ATM: Theory and Applications*
0-07-044362-9	Muller	*Network Planning Procurement and Management*
0-07-046380-8	Nemzow	*The Ethernet Management Guide, Third Edition*
0-07-049663-3	Peterson	*TCP/IP Networking: A Guide to the IBM Environments*
0-07-051506-9	Ranade/Sackett	*Introduction to SNA Networking, Third Edition*
0-07-054991-5	Russell	*Signaling System #7*
0-07-057199-6	Saunders	*The McGraw-Hill High Speed LANs Handbook*
0-07-057639-4	Simonds	*Network Security: Data and Voice Communications*
0-07-060363-4	Spohn	*Data Network Design, Second Edition*
0-07-069416-8	Summers	*ISDN Implementor's Guide*
0-07-063263-4	Taylor	*The McGraw-Hill Internetworking Handbook*
0-07-063301-0	Taylor	*McGraw-Hill Internetworking Command Reference*
0-07-063639-7	Terplan	*Effective Management of Local Area Networks, Second Edition*
0-07-065766-1	Udupa	*Network Management System Essentials*

Accessing Transport Networks

MPTN and AnyNet Solutions

Don Robertson

McGraw-Hill

New York   San Francisco   Washington, D.C.   Auckland   Bogotá
Caracas   Lisbon   London   Madrid   Mexico City   Milan
Montreal   New Delhi   San Juan   Singapore
Sydney   Tokyo   Toronto

Library of Congress Cataloging-in-Publication Data

Robertson, Don.
    Accessing transport networks : MPTN and AnyNet solutions / Don
Robertson.
        p.   cm.
    Includes bibliographical references and index.
    ISBN 0-07-053199-4 (hc : acid-free paper)
    1. Computer network protocols. I. Title.
TK5105.55.R65   1996
004.6′2—dc20   96-22989
                                                      CIP

McGraw-Hill

*A Division of The **McGraw·Hill** Companies*

*The sponsoring editor for this book was Steven Elliot, the editing super-
visor was David E. Fogarty, and the production supervisor was Donald
Schmidt. It was set in Century Schoolbook by Victoria Khavkina of
McGraw-Hill's Professional Book Group composition unit.*

Printed and bound by R. R. Donnelley & Sons Company.

This book is printed on acid-free paper.

AnyNet is a trademark of the IBM Corporation.

Contents

Chapter 10. Multiprotocol Transport Networking: MPTN   239

Chapter 11. The MPTN Access Node   265

Chapter 12. The MPTN Transport Gateway   291

Chapter 13. MPTN Formats   319

Chapter 14. MPTN Address Mapping   349

Part 3   AnyNet

Preface

I was wandering around the display floor at the Spring 1993 Interop Show in Washington, D.C. when I happened upon a little demonstration offered by IBM of something new called multiprotocol transport networking (MPTN). I picked up an *MPTN Fact Sheet* from the table and pondered this latest feat of networking technology. I had already been thinking about IBM's Networking Blueprint, announced a year earlier, and I could see that MPTN was a technical solution for implementing the common transport semantics (CTS) section of the blueprint, to me the blueprint's most interesting feature. As a networking consultant and programmer, I had been contemplating IBM's idea of providing a place in a network protocol stack that would allow programs written with particular network protocols in mind to run on top of the various kinds of transport networks. CTS made complete sense to me. Little did I realize then that three years later I would write the first book on the technology.

I would not have been able to write the material on MPTN and IBM's AnyNet products without the help of some very fine people at IBM. Being a new technology, much of my subject matter was still under development. In fact, I was watching MPTN and AnyNet unfold before my eyes as I wrote the book. Therefore, I was in perpetual contact with the MPTN and Networking Blueprint architects and the folks who were putting together AnyNet while I was writing *Accessing Transport Networks*. The support and help I got from IBM was beyond anything I ever imagined, and I would personally like to extend my warmest thanks to those individuals at IBM Networking Systems, Research Triangle Park, North Carolina, who contributed to this project.

Kathleen Riordan, from AnyNet Planning and Marketing Support, was constantly doing something for me—sending me information, referring me to other individuals, answering questions and reviewing material I was writing. She spent a lot of time dealing with me, and I sincerely appreciate it. Roger Turner was my technical consultant throughout most of the project. Roger, one of the architects of MPTN, tirelessly went through my MPTN chapters as they evolved, correcting errors and misconceptions with numerous detailed drawings and flow control diagrams. He was a fantastic help and has become a good friend. Thanks, Roger, for everything. Burnie Blakeley, another member of the IBM team at Research Triangle Park, and a fellow McGraw-Hill author, was a tremendous asset to this project. As the technical reviewer of the book, he not only provided a tremendous amount of help by suggesting improvements in style and content, but also suggested the title for the book and the final arrangement of the chapters. Diane and Mark Pozefsky, both very busy people, took the time to sit with me answering questions, and were always extremely knowledgeable and helpful.

A number of other people at IBM went through my manuscript, making suggestions, sending me material, and correcting mistakes. I would like to thank Edward Britton, Paul Brown (of the AS/400 Division in Rochester, Minnesota), James Carmichael, Jim Colosimo, Allan Edwards, John Fetvedt, Mathew Hess, Rich Hillman, W. Sands Hobgood, Johny Mathew, Pat Piszczor, Soumitra (Ronnie) Sarkar, and Bart Vashaw. Your time and energy is much appreciated.

Several former IBMers helped me out with the project, and I would like to thank them for their help. They are Steven Smith, Walt Wheeler, and John Walker. Each contributed something special to the project. I would especially like to thank John Walker, former manager of Network Architecture and Development at IBM, and now vice president of development at Ganymede Software, Inc., for allowing me to use two example programs from his book, *CPI-C Programming in C*.

Two other individuals helped me with material for this book. Charles Hights, senior systems analyst at Pacific Bell, explained how AnyNet was being used at Pacific Bell, and Rick Yost, who is in charge of the U.S. Postal Service network, took time from his busy schedule to sit with me and painstakingly explain how the U.S. Postal Service's nationwide network was configured, and how AnyNet was being used to aid in the conversion from SNA to TCP/IP.

At McGraw-Hill, I would like to thank Series Editor J. Ranade, who originally contacted me about writing the book and helped me throughout the project, Jerry Papke, former senior editor at McGraw-Hill, who is now with CRC Press, Dave Fogarty, Steven Elliot, and Donna Namorato.

And finally, I would like to thank my associates of times past at H&A Computer Services: Alan, Nick, "Beeth," Bill Reed (and his wonderful family), Tim, Roger 'n Jacquie, Brock, Howard, Tom, Peg, Louise, Nanzie, Greg, and John ("Who wrote the Greatest Program ever for the Series/1?") Berger. You were a great and inspiring bunch of people to work with, and I owe a lot to you. Also thanks to some of my other computing sidekicks: My pal Al (Masulo), Mike 'n Lisa, Ken Clark, Benoosh, Brian, Barry Hobbs, and Chuck Duerson and his gal Angie ("Hey y'all"). Thanks also to my friends, the Isaacs Family of LaFollete, Tennessee, for the music that healed so many pains, and to Barky. I also want to express my debt of gratitude to my mother, Lois Robertson, and to Ted Boerstler for all the support they gave me during the period of the writing of this book (a difficult time in my life). Thank you! Last and most important, I give all my thanks to our Creator, and to Jesus Christ. I owe it all to You.

Don Robertson

Transport Networks and Transport Network Access

Introduction to Transport Networking

1.1 Introduction

The computer networks of today carry data from one point to another by means of transport networks. The term *transport network* describes a data communications network that transports data from various points within the network and provides a means for the control of the data that flows within it. Transport networks use well-known networking protocols and architectures such as TCP/IP, SNA, IPX, and DECnet and are accessed by application programs that reqvest network services by means of *application programming interfaces* (APIs). Part 1 of this book describes the communications protocols that implement transport networks and presents two popular APIs that are used to access transport networks.

This chapter describes how modern transport networking evolved.

1.2 The Evolution of Networking

Early computers were machines that were located entirely within a single room. If you needed to work with the computer, you had to go into the room where it was located in order to use it. It was not long, however, before people needed to access these computers from other locations. To accomplish this, punch-card readers were installed in remote offices; these enabled personnel located offsite to transfer data to a Sperry, IBM, Honeywell, Burroughs, or DEC computer.

In order to transport data safely from a remote site to a computer, communications protocols were developed. A *communications protocol* is a set of rules, agreed on by all participants, by which data are transferred directly from one computing device to another. Protocols were designed to examine data that were transmitted from one device to another to ensure that it had not been corrupted in transit, and means were devised to control the amount and frequency of data that was transmitted during a particular time period. The earliest communications protocols were very simple in nature. In fact, they would fail frequently, especially if anything other than printable characters was being transmitted.

1.2.1   Systems Network Architecture (SNA)

As the need for various kinds of data entry and retrieval from remote sites grew, and a more flexible system of computer terminal usage became more and more important, it was realized that improved communications protocols would have to be developed. In September 1974, IBM, which had the largest installed base of computers of any manufacturer, introduced a revolutionary communications architecture. This new offering consisted of nothing less than a major overhaul of the entire concept of computer communications and was called *Systems Network Architecture,* or more simply SNA (commonly pronounced *snah*).

SNA was truly a complete networking architecture and not just a replacement for earlier, less robust, communications protocols. It was based on a revolutionary *layered* design that allowed functions allotted to individual parts of the network to be isolated from one another. Additionally, Systems Network Architecture incorporated revolutionary features that controlled the flow of data through complex computer networks. SNA was unlike anything previously introduced by any manufacturer.

The major parts of SNA were implemented by new IBM products: the Virtual Telecommunications Access Method (VTAM), which ran alongside of (and eventually replaced) the Telecommunications Access Method (TCAM); the Network Control Program (NCP), which offloaded terminal and printer communications line control to an IBM 3705 communications controller; and SNA versions of the IBM 3600 and 3650 cluster controllers.

SNA's design was strictly hierarchical. VTAM, residing in the mainframe, controlled the data that flowed to and from the subordinate terminals, printers, and remote data-entry devices. The release of *Systems Network Architecture/Advanced Communications Function* (SNA/ACF) made it possible to interconnect mainframes indirectly by interconnecting their communications controllers.

After the success of IBM's personal computer, the company, beginning in July 1982, introduced a peer-to-peer communications protocol. *Advanced Program-to-Program Communications* (APPC) was an enhancement to SNA that allowed intelligent computing devices (such as personal computers and IBM's System/3x and Series/1 minicomputers) to initiate SNA conversations with other such machines without having to rely on the hierarchical management provided by the mainframe's VTAM.

SNA has been a solid performer for years. Its main limitation, after the introduction of minicomputers and personal computers (PCs), was its design as a hierarchical infrastructure: a primary mainframe with secondary nodes radiating outward. Minicomputers and PCs, being intelligent computing devices, required peer-to-peer networking to its fullest extent. The introduction of APPC in 1982 was the first step in removing this limitation. APPC allowed two minicomputers to communicate with each other using SNA protocols, but there was no provision for handling *nonhierarchical* networking. In other words, if a source computer located in the far reaches of the network somewhere had to communicate with a target computer located at the other end of the SNA network, and the target computer was a personal computer attached to a Series/1 minicomputer, there was no component in place that would route the data from the source computer through many other computers to the target computer. This was because the original design of SNA was tailored to the concept of mainframe computers running application programs which communicated directly with devices such as printers and terminals. IBM first introduced *Advanced Peer-to-Peer Networking* (APPN) on the System/36 minicomputer in June 1986. Basically, APPN provides a means for routing APPC data anywhere in a network. APPN has gradually migrated to other IBM platforms and, at the time of this writing, is still in the process of unfolding. The latest enhancement, at the time of this writing, is the High Performance Routing (HPR) feature. In the early 1990s APPN had not yet been widely implemented because it handled only the newer APPC formats and did not support older terminal and printer sessions. Also, it was not yet available on a wide variety of platforms. However, with the introduction of the APPN Dependent LU Requester/Server Architecture (DLUR/S) in June 1994, the restriction of APPN being provided only for APPC was removed.

SNA is discussed further in Chap. 6.

1.2.2 DECnet

In 1974, the Digital Equipment Corporation (DEC) announced a networking architecture for their computers called Digital Network Architecture (DNA). Digital's implementation of DNA, called DECnet, has, like SNA, undergone major revisions and enhancements over the years. The first version, DECnet Phase I, would not allow two machines to communicate unless they were physically connected with each other. These machines, PDP-11s, ran the Real-time resource-Sharing eXecutive (RSX). Phase II, released in 1976, brought such machines as the DEC-10 and DEC-20 into the picture. In 1980, Phase III allowed these machines to route data in a mesh topology instead of relying only on point-to-point links. DECnet Phase IV arrived two years later and offered Ethernet, X.25, and a SNA gateway. DECnet Phase V, introduced in 1987, includes OSI networking protocols that were implemented in the 1987–1991 time frame. OSI is described in Sec. 1.2.5, and DECnet is discussed further in Chap. 3.

1.2.3   The ARPAnet

The ARPAnet was a very early, revolutionary, and important networking project funded by the Advanced Research Projects Agency of the U.S. Department of Defense. The pioneers of this project were men such as Vinton Cerf and Lawrence Roberts, who have become legendary figures in the computer industry.

ARPA, after 1972 called DARPA (for Defense Advanced Research Projects Agency), provided grants to computer science departments in some U.S. universities and to some private corporations to help stimulate the development of computer networks. Design work on the ARPAnet began as early as 1966. In December 1968, the contract for the initial installation of the network, consisting of switching nodes and interconnecting telephone lines, was awarded to Bolt, Beranek, and Newman (BBN).

In the summer of 1969, Lawrence Roberts organized a meeting at Snowbird, Utah, to begin designing the network, and by the end of that year a network linking four computers was in place. These computers were located at the University of Utah, the Stanford Research Institute (SRI), the University of California at Santa Barbara (UCSB), and the University of California at Los Angeles (UCLA). The computer operating systems at each site were completely different: the Sigma EXecutive (SEX), running on an SDS Sigma 7; the Genie, on an SDS 940; Tenex, on a DEC PDP-10; and OS/MVT or OS/MFT, on an IBM 360.

The ARPAnet project continued and the network gradually grew. When smaller and more affordable minicomputers became available from companies such as DEC, they were used to control communications on the ARPAnet. These communications processors were called *interface message processors* (IMPs).

By 1972 the ARPAnet was composed of 24 nodes. The following year, 12 more nodes were added. In 1975, Lawrence Roberts left the ARPAnet project and went on to originate the world's first data packet switching network, which was called *Telenet.* By 1979, a large network, the *Internet,* was in place. It consisted of interconnected packet radio networks, packet satellite networks, the ARPAnet, and the experimental Ethernets at the Xerox PARC laboratory in Menlo Park, California.

One of the original communications protocols used in the ARPAnet, and the primary one, was the Network Control Program (NCP), developed at UCLA primarily by Steve Crocker. In 1972, Robert Kahn and Vinton Cerf began work on the Kahn-Cerf protocol, which was later renamed Transmission Control Protocol/Internet Protocol (TCP/IP). The IMPs, which were renamed *gateways,* were important to the original design of TCP/IP because of the nature of the Internet. It was a network of interconnected computers without a central reference point of control such as was found in SNA networks. The gateway computers were responsible for the routing of data around this network, and TCP/IP had to work with these gateways in order to get data where it needed to go.

By June 1978, it was agreed that TCP/IP should be implemented on the ARPAnet and work began on the project of replacing NCP with TCP/IP. Simultaneously, the 3Com Company and the University of California at Berkeley started implementing TCP/IP for the Unix operating system. In September 1981, the fundamental specifications were completed and soon the NCP application programs called ftp, sendmail (originally called delivermail), and telnet were rewritten for use with TCP/IP. After years of preparation, the official switchover to TCP/IP on the Internet occurred January 1, 1983.

The Internet grew in size rapidly as it expanded to include more and more sites. The Department of Defense (DOD) disbanded the ARPAnet in 1990, and networks such as the National Science Foundation's NSFNET became the backbone of the Internet.

TCP/IP grew to become a popular network protocol solution. This was because TCP/IP is simple and elegant, and programming with TCP/IP is straightforward. Additionally, TCP/IP was bundled free with many versions of the Unix operating system, and TCP/IP source code has always been easily available.

TCP/IP is discussed further in Chap. 4.

1.2.4 X.25

Besides the work being done with ARPAnet, SNA, and DECnet, many corporations and government agencies had created data communications networks that incorporated their own proprietary communications protocols. Some organizations used the services of *public data networks* that had began appearing in the later 1960s and early 1970s in the United States, Europe, and Canada.

The original concept for public data networks was the creation of data communications network that did for data what the telephone network did for voice—in other words, the ability to send data from a single communications link to any number of recipients located around the globe. The phone network used the principles of *circuit switching*; the data counterpart used *packet switching*. Packet switching used the principle of switching, but instead of switching voice circuits, it switched data packets.

Packet switching networks are comprised of individual computers called *packet switches*. A collection of packet switches that are linked together forms what is often described as a *cloud* because packet switching networks resemble a large, nebulous body like a cloud, into which data are sent that come out somewhere else. Packet switches are tied together using dedicated leased telephone lines, and multiple routes are established between the switches. The switches receive packets of data from one link, then send them out on another. The earliest packet switches were minicomputers such as DEC PDP-11s. Currently, PCs are often used as packet switches.

In the early days of packet switching networks, a standardized method for connecting terminals and computers to the network was needed because many proprietary protocols were already in use. Armed only with ARPAnet experience and a few prototypes in research laboratories, three companies, Tymnet, Datapac, and Lawrence Roberts's Telenet, drew up a proposal for a packet switching protocol. The Consultative Committee for International Telegraphy and Telephony (CCITT), now called the International Telecommunications Union Telecommunications Standardization Sector (ITU-T), worked with the proposal and, in 1974, issued the initial draft of the X.25 packet switching protocol that would be implemented in packet switching networks.. The first standard was issued in 1976 and revisions took place in 1978, 1980, 1984, and 1988.

Because of its incompatibility with existing equipment, the new X.25 interface did not become popular right away. Additionally, the three packet switching networks, Tymnet, Datapac, and Telenet, were not doing well financially and, in 1976, many wondered whether they would survive. Tymnet had a parent company, Tymshare, to fund it, but Telenet's future was in doubt until it was purchased by GTE in 1979. The situation changed in the early 1980s when the use of packet switching skyrocketed in the United States. Telenet had about 18 packet switches in its network when it began operations in 1975. By the end of 1979, there were 92. The end of 1981 saw a network of 264 switches, and by the end of 1983 there were over 800. Packet switching using X.25 also became very popular in Europe. X.25 soon became the communications protocol standard for packet switching networks all over the world. By the late 1980s, however, X.25's momentum began waning with the introduction of frame relay, a more efficient technology developed as a replacement for X.25.

The X.25 standard describes the method for connecting to the network cloud; the routing and relaying functions within that cloud are governed by the network provider. The purpose of X.25 was to define a standard means of connecting devices and computers to a packet switching network in order for the network providers not to have to convert all the various proprietary protocols.

The corporate world was the spawning ground for SNA and the ARPAnet project gave birth to TCP/IP. X.25 was produced by an organization that created standards. Could a standards body also create communications protocols that would replace protocols such as SNA and TCP/IP?

1.2.5 OSI

The *Open Systems Interconnection* (OSI) communications protocol standards were jointly developed by two international standard-making bodies: The CCITT and the International Organization for Standardization (ISO). The OSI standardization effort began in the late 1970s when the need for compatible communications protocols for dissimilar computer architectures became a very important issue. Throughout the 1980s, standards for every aspect of computer networking were published by ISO and CCITT and were known as the OSI protocols. These protocols would provide *open* communications: a nonproprietary, standardized method of linking computers.

During the early 1980s there was a widely held expectation in the business world, in the government, and in research communities that all computer systems would eventually migrate to the OSI standards. The reason for this was that during this period there was an urgent need for *open systems*. IBM mainframe environments were based on SNA, with a mixture of the older bisync protocol, and computer professionals had to depend on IBM for support and expensive software upgrades. TCP/IP was a product of the academic world and not yet known to business computer professionals. Most of the other networks each spoke their own language (that is, had their own proprietary protocols). At that time computer programming languages and operating systems were not *portable,* meaning they could not be moved from one machine type to another. As programmers and administrators went from one machine to another, they were faced with a completely different environment: different languages, different programs, different operating systems, different commands. Computer professionals assumed that OSI was the answer: It would provide a single communications protocol to link dissimilar computers. However, OSI did not arrive quickly enough. While the computer industry waited for OSI to materialize, computers on which the Unix operating system was installed started making inroads into business and government. Unix could be obtained cheaply, or for free, and it had a solid communications protocol, TCP/IP, that came along for the ride. Unix also provided a strong new system programming language called C, and C-language programs and the Unix operating system could easily be moved from one manufacturer's machine to another. As TCP/IP usage became more and more prevalent, it started to be viewed as an interim solution for open communications. Soon, the talk in the industry began to change from talk about TCP/IP as an interim solution to TCP/IP as *the* solution (or at least one of the solutions) for open communications. TCP/IP showed everyone that they did not need OSI. Plus it was free! Unix liberated the computer industry: It now had an operating system and a system programming language that could go just about anywhere, to any machine, and TCP/IP networking was just bundled in there with them.

Even as TCP/IP spread like wildfire in the mid-1980s, many of the TCP/IP developers believed that what they were doing was short-lived, an interim solution while waiting for OSI. The 1990s brought the realization among most of the computer professionals that there would be no migration to OSI. It just was not happening! TCP/IP had become too widespread.

The example of OSI has made it obvious that communications protocols cannot be mandated, but must survive in the marketplace like any other product.

The OSI protocols are discussed further in Chap. 3.

1.2.6   The emergence of local area networks

The idea for *local area networks* (LANs), networks of small computers contained in a small area, came about because of a need to interconnect and interoperate minicomputers. The need for LANs, however, became really pressing with the advent of the personal computer. The turning point for local area networking was IBM's introduction of its first personal computer in 1981.

A number of different kinds of local area networks were developed in the early 1980s. Perhaps the earliest was ARCNET. The *Attached Resource Computer Network* (ARCNET) was developed by a company called Datapoint in the mid-1970s and went on to become a successful LAN solution because it was inexpensive and reliable. Other LANs were Omninet by Corvus, Nestar's Cluster One, Wangnet from Wang Labs, Hyperbus, Cablenet, Z-Net, ConTelNet, Primenet, and Optonet.

1.2.6.1   Ethernet.   The most popular local area network technology is Ethernet, invented by Robert Metcalfe in the 1970s. Metcalfe was an early implementor of the ARPAnet while he was attending graduate school at MIT. After graduation he went to work at the Xerox Palo Alto Research Center (PARC) in Menlo Park, California, and continued to work there on the PARC implementation of the ARPAnet. One day he read a paper about a researcher named Norman Abramson and a project called Aloha. Aloha was a ground radio packet broadcasting system that Abramson was developing at the University of Hawaii. Metcalfe was fascinated. After studying the paper he saw what he considered some flaws in the equation of the Aloha model, and he went to work developing a model of his own, based on the original. He traveled to Hawaii to work with Abramson for a month. On May 22, 1973, Metcalfe wrote a memo outlining his idea for Ethernet. It was based on the ideas of Aloha, but with significant modifications, the main one being Metcalfe's use of a physical cable instead of radio waves. The memo eventually became a paper which appeared in *Communications of the ACM* in July 1976.

In June 1979, DEC, Intel, and Xerox each adopted Ethernet as an internal standard. Specifications for a proposed internet standard were published in September 1980. The Institute of Electrical and Electronics Engineers (IEEE) 802.3 subcommittee worked on it for a few years; then, in December 1982, the standardized version of Ethernet was published.

IEEE 802.3 Ethernet runs at a speed of 10 Mbits/s using coaxial or twisted-pair cabling. Its nodes are connected in a *backplane* fashion and all share the same wire. Control of the medium is maintained by an algorithm called *Carrier Sense Multiple Access / Collision Detection* (CSMA/CD). CSMA/CD was an improvement to Aloha's carrier sense protocol. A higher-speed version of Ethernet, running at 100 Mbits/s, was introduced in the mid-1990s.

1.2.6.2 Token rings. The concept of the token ring network was first developed in 1972 by a man named Von Willemjin. The topology of a token ring network is a ring of interconnected computing nodes on which a *token*—a small, specific packet of data—is circulated. Only a node that *has* received the token can transmit data; therefore, the transmission of data on the network is controlled, not random as in an Ethernet network.

IBM began development of the token ring concept in the early 1980s at its research laboratory in Zurich, Switzerland, and the IEEE 802.5 subcommittee started working on token ring standards about 1982. The work being done with token ring networking was well publicized and the market was hungry for new LAN technology, but IBM was late in releasing the token ring network, so, in 1984, it instead introduced a different LAN technology, the broadband *PC Network* developed by a company called Sytek, Inc. Along with this new local area network IBM supplied a program called the *PC Network Program.*

In 1985, IBM introduced its token ring network. The main elements of the IEEE 802.5 standard were also published in the same year. The token ring network ran at a speed of 4 Mbits/s. Later, an upgraded version, which ran at 16 Mbits/s, was introduced.

1.2.6.3 FDDI. A third, and more recent, local area network type should be mentioned. It employs a much newer technology than either Ethernet or IBM's token ring, but this fiber-optic token-ring LAN filled an industry niche because of its ability to handle higher speeds. Called the *Fiber Distributed Data Interface* (FDDI), it operates at 100 Mbits/s. Originally FDDI could use only fiber optic cabling; later, however, a copper-wire version (CDDI) was developed. FDDI is a point-to-point series of links connected as a ring. There is actually a pair of point-to-point links: One is provided as a backup in case the other fails. FDDI was developed because there was a need for a higher-speed local area network. FDDI was standardized by the American National Standards Institute (ANSI) Committee X3T9.5. Standards development began officially in June 1983, as an outgrowth of earlier work. The first parts of the FDDI standards become available in 1987.

**1.2.7 LAN communications protocols
and network operating systems**

As local area networks appeared, there was a need for efficient, higher-layer communications protocols. The IEEE and ANSI had issued standards that dealt strictly with the protocol layers that worked with the medium. However, full-fledged protocol systems were needed to run on top of these lower layers. Early on, drivers were written to run TCP/IP, which was already associated with Unix, over Ethernet. Other methods of transporting and controlling data that ran on LANs were also introduced.

1.2.7.1 XNS. The *Xerox Network System* (XNS) was developed at Xerox PARC to run over Bob Metcalfe's Ethernet. PARC was literally the cornucopia of modern computing technology, and many of the advances of 1990s computing were developed there. In addition to creating the world's most popular local area network, Ethernet, PARC turned out high-resolution graphics, the concept of the workstation, use of object-oriented programming, the mouse, the graphical user interface, laser printers for LANs, and desktop publishing.

The XNS communications protocol arose from what was originally the PARC Universal Packet (PUP). Released in 1981, it soon became the basis for local area network protocols from such companies as 3Com and Ungermann-Bass. It also is the basis of the popular Banyan VINES local area network and Novell's NetWare.

1.2.7.2 IPX and NetWare. A Provo, Utah, company, Novell, Inc., became the success story of local area networking with its *NetWare* product. Introduced in the early 1980s, NetWare was originally developed for a now long-defunct Z80 file server. It was soon ported to IBM-compatible PCs.

Novell engineers adopted XNS to create their own Internetwork Packet eXchange protocol (IPX) and Sequenced Packet eXchange protocol (SPX). These were incorporated into NetWare to provide the basic communications protocol formats and are described further in Chap. 3.

NetWare's great success was its *network operating system* (NOS), which establishes a NetWare file server (a computing node that provides file access services to individual workstations located throughout a network). The NOS additionally provides print services to client workstations on the LAN. A network operating system is an operating system that must take into consideration not just the operations of the machine on which it resides, the server, but also the client workstations in the network, thus its name.

NetWare has been enhanced continually since its inception and has grown into a very sophisticated, complete, and reliable networking system providing many features, such as file and printer sharing, dial-in access, and global directory objects. NetWare became by far the most popular network operating system in use. Network operating systems from other vendors achieved popularity also. These include Sitka's TOPS, Banyan VINES, AppleTalk, 3Com's 3+, LAN Server, and LAN Manager. The LAN Server and LAN Manager network operating systems use a communications protocol called NetBIOS.

1.2.7.3 NetBIOS. The *Network Basic Input/Output System* (NetBIOS) was developed by IBM and was first introduced in August 1984 as the protocol for the PC Network, IBM's first local area network. NetBIOS ran in the PC network adapter card but later was released as a program named *Netbios.com*. Netbios.com was a complete replacement for the downloaded code running in the adapter. When IBM released its token ring network in October 1985, it provided a NetBIOS programming interface. NetBIOS this time was included in a module called *Netbeui.com*. NetBEUI is an acronym that stands for *NetBIOS Extended User Interface.*

Use of NetBIOS became widespread mostly because of its proliferation by IBM as a part of LAN Server, and by Microsoft in LAN Manager. In the early days of LAN networking, before NetWare and TCP/IP became widespread on LANs, NetBIOS was the standard protocol for LAN networking. It was popular, cheap, easier to configure than other LAN protocols, easy to get, and very fast.

1.3   Summary

This chapter provides an introduction to networking protocols that were developed, widely implemented, and went on to become the various methods which enabled transport networks to become a reality. Chapter 2 describes the OSI reference model, an invaluable tool used to understand the layering techniques that are used in transport networks. Chapter 3 uses the OSI reference model to study some of the transport network protocols (OSI, AppleTalk, IPX, DECnet, and NetBIOS), and Chaps. 4 through 7 are devoted to more detailed descriptions of SNA and TCP/IP and two associated application programming interfaces (APIs): CPI-C and Sockets.

Networking Layers: The OSI Reference Model

2.1 Introduction

The protocols that provide the basis for computer communications became more complex as the science of data communications grew into the science of *networking*. Protocols that were originally developed to enable a computer to communicate effectively with its attached printers, card readers, and terminals were found to be less and less effective as networking developed.

Computer scientists began studying the situation and determined that the way to implement protocols was to use a method of layering of individual protocols that related to different functions, one on top of another. In other words, communications functions that take place at a low level should have a separate protocol to handle that function, and higher-level functions should have their own protocols. Additionally, protocols should be, at least conceptually, stacked one upon the other. The resultant *stack* would consist of protocol layers. The bottom layer would contain the protocol that connected a terminal with a computer and transferred data back and forth, for example. Another layer would then be built on top of that to handle functions more generalized than this, such as routing the data from the original terminal through an intermediate computer back to an originating host.

Computer network architectures such as SNA, DNA, and TCP/IP used this concept of layering of communications protocols in their designs. When protocols are layered, particular functions take place on a conceptual protocol *layer*. However, even though they may be conceptualized as layers, the actual implementations do not really involve completely separate layers. The layers simply represent logical divisions of important communications functions.

This layering of procotols is best described by the reference model created for OSI.

2.2   The OSI Reference Model

When the OSI standardization effort began in the late 1970s, an early OSI document called the *OSI Reference Model* was introduced. It was based on the protocol layering techniques then emerging in the network design for SNA, DNA, and TCP/IP.

The OSI reference model is a seven-layered network model and is shown in Fig. 2.1. At the base of the figure is the lowest layer, the physical layer, that describes the physical media of the network; at the top of the figure is the application layer, where application communication interfaces and services reside. In between these extremities are the layers that represent all functions that come into play when two network endpoints communicate. Each layer of the model represents a particular protocol, or set of protocols. The concept of a set of layered protocols is also referred to as a protocol *stack* because each protocol is stacked on top of the other. The lowest layers involve

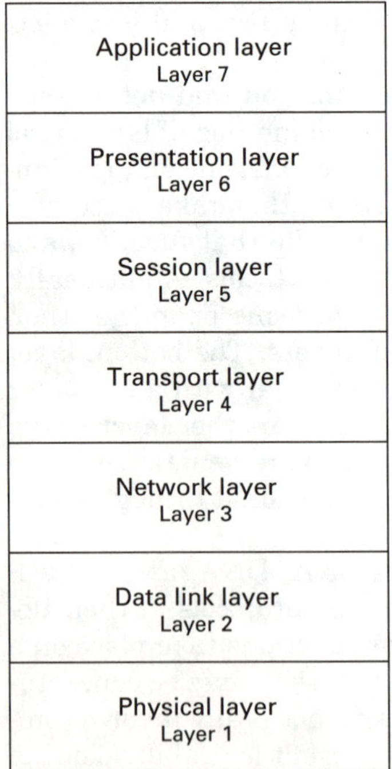

Figure 2.1   The OSI reference model.

point-to-point communication; the highest layers involve end-to-end communication.

The creation of the OSI reference model was an important milestone in the progress of computer networking science because it became the standard reference for dealing with network layering issues. Instead of a hodgepodge of various services, the layers conceptualized functions in such a way that they could be referenced by the name of the layer. This helped simplify and demystify the understanding of complex network architectures.

Each layer in the reference model represents some vertical aspect of the networking picture. Figure 2.2 shows how data flow through a network based on the OSI seven-layer model. On the left, a stream of computer data enters the application layer and cascades down and through the various services that are installed as software programs on that node in the network. As the stream of data travels downward, each layer deals with it according to the functional needs of that layer. As the data are passed down through the layers, headers are added by each layer; as the data pass back up through the layers at the destination node, the corresponding headers for that layer are removed. Headers are attached to the front of the data stream, which, after it has passed through all the layers of the model, is now referred to as a *packet* of data. It is possible that each layer may have its own header to attach to the packet of data that passes through it, so after the packet of data reaches the physical layer, it may have as many as six headers attached to the front of the data. Each one of the headers contains the information concerning the packet that the corresponding layer, residing in the destination node and possibly in other nodes through which the packet will travel, will need know about in order to determine what to do with the data. For example, if the packet of data has a priority, then this priority would be encoded in the packet header. When the packet is processed by another network node, the corresponding layer's software residing on that node will decode the priority from the header representing that particular layer to determine what the class of service for that packet should be.

Continuing with the discussion of Fig. 2.2, when the packet has reached the physical layer, it could have as many as six headers attached to the front of the data. This is shown in Fig. 2.3. At this point, the network services software of the node on which the data stream originated has completed its duties and the steam of data is then encoded onto the physical medium, such as a wire. When the data reach their destination, as depicted on the right side of Fig. 2.2, the physical layer of the destination node decodes it "from the wire" and passes it upward through the layers, where each header is checked, then removed, by the layer corresponding to the layer that attached the

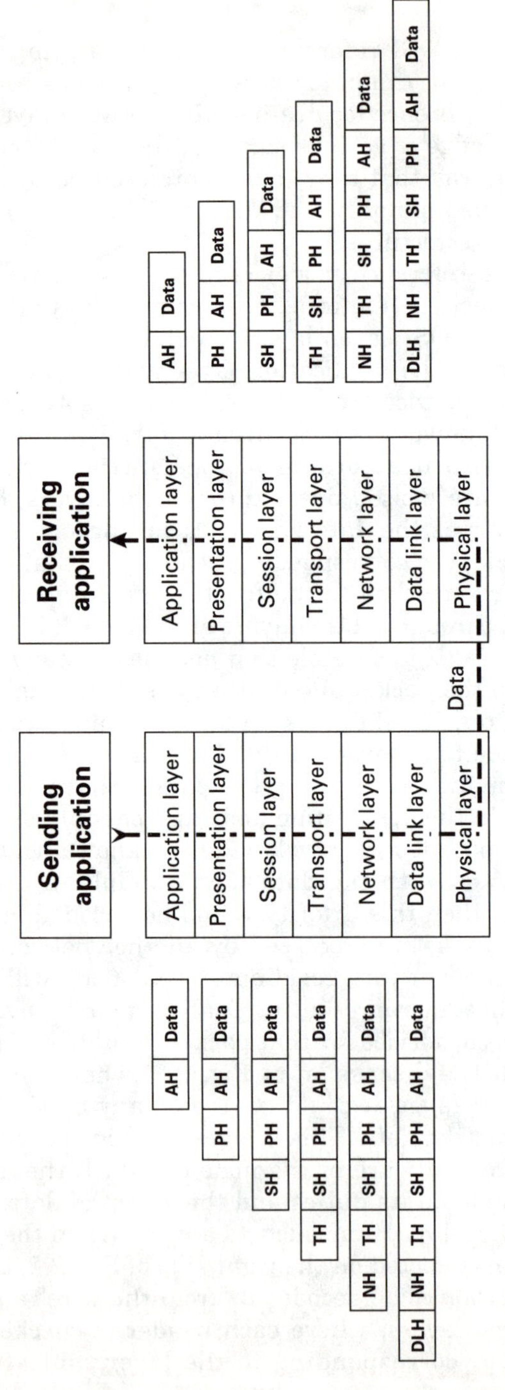

Figure 2.2   The flow of data through a network.

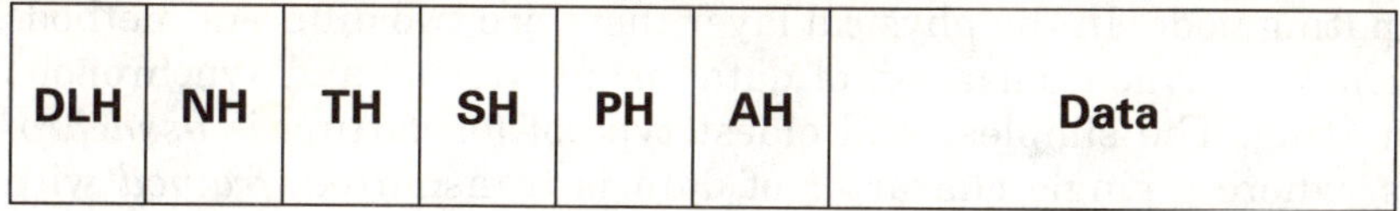

| DLH | NH | TH | SH | PH | AH | Data |

DLH = data link layer header
NH = network layer header
TH = transmission layer header
SH = session layer header
PH = presentation layer header
AH = application layer header

Figure 2.3   A packet of data with six headers attached to it.

header in the beginning. Finally, at the top of the model on the right side of Fig. 2.2, the steam of data is handed to the endpoint recipient application program.

The reference model is conceptual in nature, a helpful way to look at networks, but roles for each layer may not necessarily be strictly adhered to in each type of network architecture. As will be seen, some architectures implement only a few layers, others implement more. Also, many major protocols were precursors to the OSI model. The model is a very helpful tool used to describe the general nature of networks, at least as they were conceived in the 1970s, but it is not a firm and fast requirement. For example, if data were always passed from layer to layer, just like in the model, each time copying it from one buffer to another and each time adding a header, the cost in wasted computing cycles used for all of the copying could possibly be prohibitive.

Each of the seven layers of the OSI reference model will now be described, beginning with the lowest layer, the physical layer.

2.3 The Physical Layer

The lowest of the OSI layers is layer 1, the physical layer. This layer describes the actual physical medium on which the bits and bytes of data travel, be it copper wire, fiber optical cable, or even air (as is the case in wireless transmission). There are no communications protocols at this layer, no headers, only the specifications for the encoding of the bits of data onto the physical medium. The physical layer is responsible for all of the mechanical, electrical, and electronic aspects of data communication: encoding the data onto a baseband or broadband transmission medium and taking care of the clocking and synchronization of the data.

Clocking and synchronization are necessary because data traveling on the physical medium must be interpreted correctly by the recipient computing node. In the physical layer there are two different methods of achieving synchronization of data: asynchronous and synchronous formatting. The simplest and oldest type of formatting is *asynchronous,* where a single character of data is transmitted, *framed* with stop and start bits. *Asynchronous* transmission is familiar to many computer users as the manner in which dial-up connections to bulletin boards and the Internet are established by using modems (modulate/demodulate devices). Asynchronous transmission predates the computer era, having originated in earlier teletype technology.

A revolution in data transfer occurred with the introduction of *synchronous* transmission techniques. Instead of synchronizing a single byte using start and stop bits, serial synchronous transmission methods synchronize by transmitting a clock signal, then sending synchronization characters or a special *flag* sequence to synchronize individual *blocks* of data. This clock signal is embedded within the data sent by a synchronous modem, or travels on a separate signal path in the case of a locally attached device. Synchronous methods vary in the manner in which data are encoded onto the wire, and this is a complex and lengthy subject beyond the scope of the present work.

2.4 The Data Link Layer

The OSI data link layer, layer 2, lies above the physical layer. It defines the data link protocols that delimit the bits of data that are exchanged with the physical layer and performs data flow synchronization and error checking.

The data link layer is the lowest layer in which communications protocols are actually defined. Data link layer protocols govern the transfer of data across the communications path (or link) between adjacent points in the network. The original function of data link protocols was to manage the flow of data between individual adjacent, directly attached devices, such as card readers and printers, and the host computer. In the context of *network* computing and the OSI reference model, however, data link protocols do not just connect a peripheral to a computer; more important, they interconnect individual nodes within networks (Fig. 2.4). When networking principles were

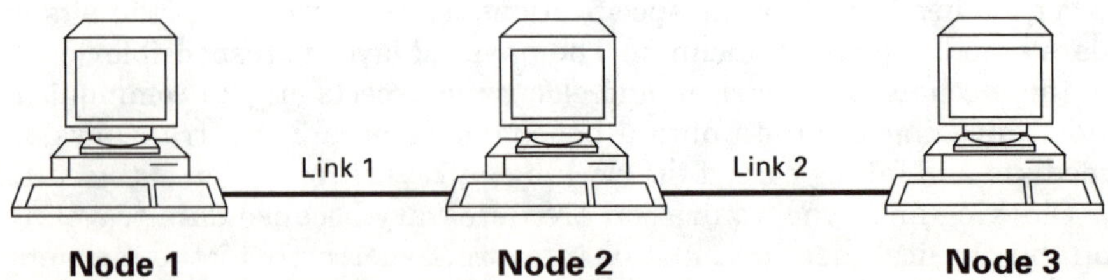

Figure 2.4   A three-node network with two links.

first being applied to computer systems, the original data link protocols were already in place as the links that existed between peripherals and the host computers. The higher layers were simply built on
top of these links.

The great success story, and the major breakthrough in data link
protocols, was *Binary Synchronous Communications* (BSC), also
called *bisync.* Bisync was developed by IBM as a mainframe communications protocol in the mid-1960s. It grew to widespread use all over
the world and became the most popular synchronous data link control
ever developed.

Bisync could be configured to operate either as point-to-point or as
multipoint. In point-to-point mode there is a bisync driver at each end
of the link. Multipoint means that there is a master station at one end
of the wire with tributary stations fanning out from there (Fig. 2.5).
The tributaries are individually *polled,* meaning that they are given
an "invitation to send some data" and *selected,* where they are sent a
"request to receive some data." Bisync uses special binary transmis-

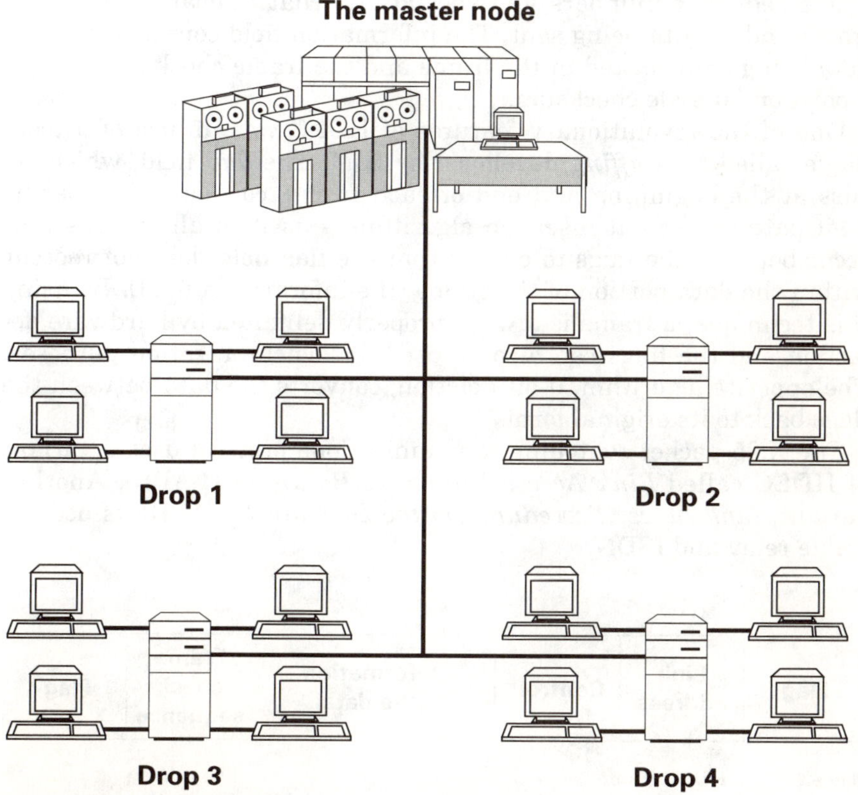

Figure 2.5   A bisync multipoint link.

sion codes to frame each block of data and to send acknowledgments for data that have been received. A checksum sent with each block of data is used to verify if the data were received without error.

The next innovation in data link layer protocols came about when a standard created by the International Organization for Standardization (ISO) called *High-level Data Link Control* (HDLC) was introduced. HDLC is a subset of *Synchronous Data Link Control* (SDLC), which was developed by IBM in the 1960s as a replacement for bisync. Variants of HDLC have become data link layer standards for token ring, Ethernet, Integrated Services Digital Network (ISDN), X.25, Point-to-Point Protocol (PPP), and frame-relay networks.

The basic format of HDLC is called a *frame* and is shown in Fig. 2.6. A frame contains flag fields at either end to delimit the frame. The frame's link address is the address of the secondary station (such as a terminal or printer) or a tributary on a multipoint link. Only one address, the destination address, is used in a frame because it is assumed that all data originate from a single master station, the host computer. The control field is used to send information necessary for proper control of the frame by data link layer drivers. It contains the frame sequence numbers and special bits that indicate the type of frame and/or data being sent. The information field contains the user data being transmitted in the frame and the frame check sequence is a polynomial-style checksum.

One of the revolutionary features of HDLC was its use of a technique called *bit stuffing* developed by IBM. The *flag* field, which occurs at the beginning and end of each frame, consists of a specific 8-bit pattern. A 0-bit insertion algorithm is used on all the bits that occur between the flags to ensure that the flag field does not reoccur within the data portion of the frame (the information field). By using this technique, a frame is always properly delimited by hardware detection and the flags can also be used for synchronization purposes. The opposite algorithm, 0-bit deletion, converts the data between the flags back to its original form.

The X.25 packet switching communications protocol uses a variant of HDLC called *Link Access Procedure Balanced* (LAPB). Another variant, *Link Access Procedures on the D-channel* (LAPD), is used in frame relay and ISDN.

Flag	Link address	Control	Information (the data)	Frame check sequence	Flag

Figure 2.6   An HDLC frame.

The next step in the evolution of data link layer communications protocols was the introduction of local area networks and the creation of new data link layer protocols by the IEEE 802 committee. Since LANs use shared media technology (in contrast to the traditional point-to-point and point-to-multipoint media), a slightly different format for a data link layer frame was needed: An HDLC frame contained only a single address that was used to identify the destination station. A new variant of the tried-and-true HDLC frame was thus created, one that included both the sending and receiving stations' addresses. The new link layer protocol created by the IEEE 802.2 subcommittee was called *Logical Link Control* (LLC).

Chapter 1 discussed the types of LANs that were standardized by the various IEEE 802 subcommittees. Since more than one type of physical medium was being standardized, Ethernet in 802.3, token bus in 802.4, and token ring in 802.5, the IEEE 802.2 subcommittee split the OSI reference model's data link layer into two sublayers. The higher sublayer contains the LLC protocol, which never changes throughout all of the IEEE 802 LANs. The lower sublayer, called the *media access control* (MAC) layer, was defined specifically for the physical medium to be used below it in the physical layer (see Fig. 2.7). A separate MAC protocol has been defined for each of the IEEE 802 local area network protocols. The MAC sublayer appends a header to the data handed to it by LLC, which has already applied an LLC header. The MAC header contains the *MAC* address of the LAN node to which the data are to be sent. It is the MAC address that is looked at by bridges when determining destination network addresses. (Routers operate in the network layer, which is discussed in the next section.)

When the IEEE created LLC, it decided to make three different types available:

- *Type 1: Unacknowledged connectionless service.* Datagrams are sent but not acknowledged.

- *Type 2: Connection-oriented service.* A connection is established between link stations.

- *Type 3: Acknowledged connectionless service.* Datagrams are sent and acknowledged.

Of these three types of LLC service that were designated by the IEEE, one or more can be supported in the same system. The IBM token ring uses both type 1, the unacknowledged connectionless service, and type 2, the connection-oriented service.

The concept of creating a connection-oriented data link layer service was entirely new and extremely controversial. This type of service is usually reserved for layers higher in the protocol stack. (The

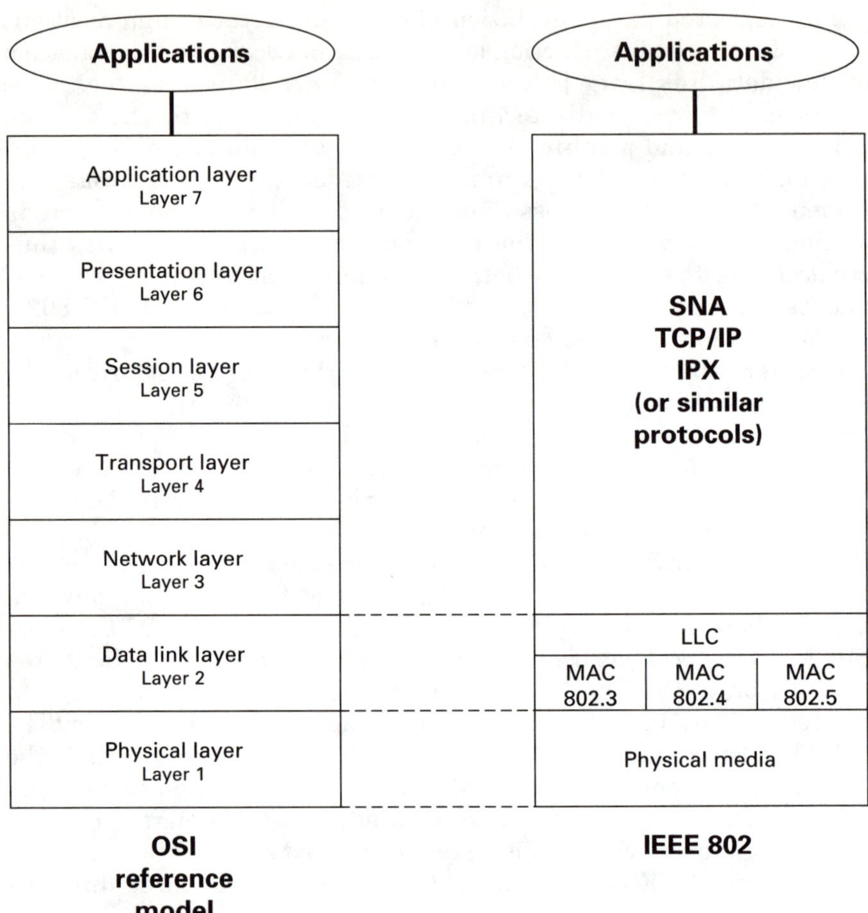

Figure 2.7   The OSI reference model and the IEEE 802 data link layer standards.

terms *connection* and *connectionless* and the term *datagram* are explained in the following section describing the network layer.)

One more data link protocol worth mentioning is the *Point-to-Point Protocol* (PPP) that is defined by RFC (Request For Comments) 1331. PPP is a full-featured data link protocol that is used to transmit multiprotocol datagrams over serial links. One type of serial link is the typical telephone link established using asynchronous transmission and is best known as the typical dial-up connection from a PC, through a serial port and a modem to a bulletin board or similar online service. PPP provides a data link layer service that enables network and transport layers to run on top of a point-to-point serial link. An indicator in the data link layer packets describes the particular higher-level protocol that is being used such as TCP/IP or SNA. PPP is used for dial-up communication that is now no longer restricted to simple bulletin board access, but supports full networking capabilities where the computer dialing into a network becomes a full-fledged network node. PPP, like the other data link layer protocols, is based on the tried-and-true HDLC standard.

2.5   The Network Layer

The OSI network layer, layer 3, manages the routing and relaying of data within a network and between networks. The physical and data link layers transfer data between adjacent nodes on a single link. Direct links are usually not defined between every pair of computers that need to communicate; therefore, networks are made up of computers that route traffic from one node to another until the final destination is reached. The network layer is responsible for maintaining a seamless network over the various segments that are interconnected by the data link layer protocols.

When the data link layer receives frames of data from the network, it removes the data link layer header from the front of the data and then passes the data and the remaining headers to the routines of the network layer. Once the data reach the network layer, the data are no longer referred to as a frame—the name used in the data link layer—but are now referred to as a *packet*. This packet begins with a network layer header. Data link protocols, such as the HDLC and MAC protocols described above, have a header that contains a data link layer address for the destination. Network layer headers have an address also: a network address. A network layer address does not pinpoint the location "on the wire" where the data are destined, as do MAC addresses; it pinpoints an endpoint that is more abstract than that. The network layer can address endpoints that are on an entirely different network, or address endpoints within a specific node, or both. Data link layer addresses are usually numbers, often assigned to attachment cards by the manufacturers of the cards, but a network address can be a human-readable (printable and displayable) name.

A very important aspect of the network layer is *routing*. The network layer is the layer in which routers operate. Routers, and computers with routing software installed, use the network layer to provide the capability for the transfer of data from one network to another. In doing this, they can interconnect networks using dissimilar types of data link layers and, therefore, they can interconnect different types of LANs. A router performs the duty of removing the data link layer header from incoming packets, getting the network address of the destination node from the network layer header, then interrogating the internal routing tables to determine which link to send the packet onto. Before sending the packet on its way, a new data link layer header is attached to the front of the packet.

To understand the addressing concepts being presented here, it is important to relate network layer addresses to the overall concept of internetworking. Four generic address formats can be used in the network layer or above:

- *Network address (NetID).*   Identifies a specific network

- *Subnet address (SubnetID).*   Identifies a subnetwork

- *Host address (HostID).*   Identifies a particular host within a network or subnetwork

- *Local address or port number.*   Identifies a particular software process within a host

The *Internet Protocol* (IP)—the protocol used in the TCP/IP network layer—uses *IP addresses.* IP addresses have two parts. The "higher" part of an IP address is the identifier for the network the data are going to (the NetID), and the lower part is the address of the destination node on that network (the HostID). The lower part (the HostID) can be further divided to produce a HostID and a SubnetID. The local address and port number are not included in the IP network address. IP addresses were designed to be used for *internetworking:* the interconnection of networks. The same basic concept of network layer addressing is used in the Xerox Network System (XNS) and Internetwork Packet eXchange (IPX) network layer protocols and will be described further in Chap. 3.

A different type of network layer address was developed for the SNA and X.25 networks. In these networks, the network layer was designed to intermix data coming from or going to multiple destinations within a node. In other words, data in the network layer could be *multiplexed.* Network layer packet headers in both SNA and in X.25 specify the logical connection endpoint to which data are to be delivered. Using these logical endpoint addresses, data can be demultiplexed and routed to the proper destination within a node. One of the enhancements to SNA that was realized with the introduction of APPN was a change in network layer addressing that enabled internetworking concepts to be applied to SNA networks. X.25 has been upgraded for internetworking with the introduction of the X.75 extensions.

In the X.25 protocol, the network layer is the highest layer in its stack of three layers: physical, data link, and network (Fig. 2.8). There are two implementations of the network layer in X.25: *Permanent Virtual Circuits* (PVC) and *Virtual Calls* (VC). The former is a permanent connection, the latter a switched, or dial-up, connection. The

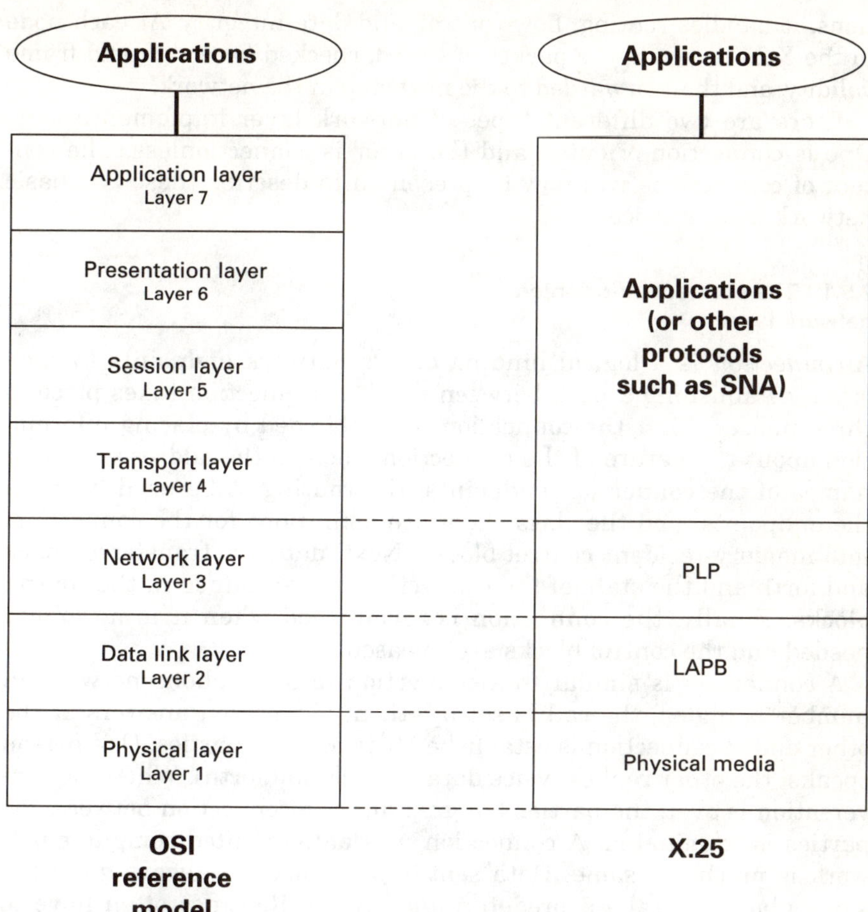

Figure 2.8 The OSI reference model and X.25.

term *virtual circuit* means that a connection appears to be a dedicated connection; however, it is really *multiplexed* with others, meaning that all virtual circuit connections are mixed together into one stream of data and are separated out into their respective connections on the receiving end. More than one PVC or VC can be multiplexed onto a single link layer connection; therefore, flow control techniques must be implemented for both the data link layer and the network layer in X.25. *Flow control* is the term used to describe algorithms that control the flow of data between endpoints to ensure that data do not arrive at the receiving end too quickly, causing buffer overruns.

The protocol for implementing the network layer in X.25 is called the *Packet Layer Protocol* (PLP) and, in addition to establishing connections, it handles routing, flow control, and data integrity. At each node in the X.25 network, the packet is stored, checked for errors and frame validity, and then forwarded to the next stop in the network.

There are two different types of network layer implementations. One is connection-oriented and the other is connectionless. The concept of connections will now be presented to describe these two basic network layer services.

2.5.1   The connection-oriented network layer

A *connection* is a logical binding of two network endpoints to each other, establishing a path between them. A connection takes place in three phases. First the connection is established by placing information about the nature of the connection, such as the addresses and/or names of the connection endpoints, the routing to be used between the endpoints, and the class of service definitions for the connection, into memory-resident control blocks. Next, data are transferred back and forth and the state of the connection is maintained in the control blocks. Finally, the connection is terminated when it is no longer needed and the control blocks are released.

A connection is similar to a connection in a telephone network. A number is dialed, the call is set up, then, if a person answers at the other end, a connection is established between two parties. One person speaks, the other replies (voice data go back and forth). When the conversation is over, the parties hang up and the connection between the parties is terminated. A connection in a data-oriented computer network is much the same. Data sent on a connection always go to the same place and take a predetermined route. Routines often have to manage the connection to ensure that the data arrive in correct order and that the two endpoints take turns sending to each other.

Connections establish a path for data packets to travel through the network. After the connection is established, complete addresses no longer need to be specified for each packet of data, because the packets travel through predefined routes.

2.5.2   The connectionless network layer

Contrasting to a connection is the concept of sending an individual packet of data from one point in the network to another point, or perhaps multiple points, in the network. In this case, a connection is not established and the packet of data is simply sent to the designated target address. These single-minded packets of data are called *datagrams* because they are conceptually similar to a telegram. If, after a datagram is sent, more datagrams are sent to the same endpoint, nothing has been retained in memory to describe the path that was taken by the first datagram between the endpoints; therefore, each transmission of a datagram is always unique.

A datagram is sent individually with the complete address of the recipient in its header. Connectionless services do not provide sequencing of data to ensure that the data arrive in order, and acknowledgments are usually not sent to confirm that the data arrived at the intended destination. Since in a connectionless service each packet is routed individually and can take a different path through the network, each packet must contain a complete destination address.

An analogy for a connectionless service is the postal service. A letter addressed to a friend in Pasqupoke, New Hampshire, is dropped into the mail slot at the local post office in Bismalia, California. A clerk (or perhaps an optical scanner) examines the address on the front of the letter and drops it in a bag to be sent to another post office closer to the destination. That post office is in Chicago. When the bag arrives at the Chicago post office, it is placed on another truck and sent to another large post office in Boston. When the letter arrives at the Boston post office, it is sorted into a bag to be delivered to a small post office in the village in New Hampshire where the party who is to receive the letter lives. If a letter is mailed to the same person the following day, it could perhaps take a different route to the destination. A truck could be loading for a different intermediary office—say, Denver—and from there it could be sent to Detroit, then finally to Boston. In the post office example, each letter or parcel is routed separately.

Connections require a longer setup time and are needed for sending continuous streams of data. Connectionless transfer of data requires no setup time and is adequate for sending only a few packets of data between applications.

Because the network layer is the highest layer in the X.25 protocol suite, it was necessary to establish connections, the virtual circuits, in the network layer. The Internet Protocol, the network layer protocol for the internet suite of protocols and TCP/IP, was designed with a layer on top of the network layer in which the connection could be made. Because the IP network layer can have a connection-oriented transport layer running on top of it, there is no need to establish connections in the network layer. IP's network layer is, thus, connectionless. The IP network layer is described in Sec. 4.4.

2.6 The Transport Layer

The transport layer is responsible for the end-to-end integrity and delivery of data. The basic reason that this layer exists is to provide services for a connection-oriented transport protocol. These services include packet sequencing to ensure arrival of data in the order in which they were sent, quality of service, error correction, and end-to-end flow control. Additionally, the transport layer can have its own addressing, similar to the layers below. A transport address designates the address of a particular end user within a network node.

Quickly reviewing the first four layers of the OSI reference model, it can be seen that the transport layer provides end-to-end connectivity, depending on the network layer to provide a fabric of interconnected network nodes. The network nodes, in turn, depend on the underlying data link layer to transfer data across each particular link connecting (point to point) the adjacent network nodes. The physical layer provides the ultimate transport medium for the data between physical network communication devices.

Just as in the two layers below it, the transport layer has a header and can provide both connection and connectionless varieties of service. A connectionless transport layer, however, has little work to do because the nature of the transport layer is to service end-to-end connections.

The services of the transport layer are typified by the Transmission Control Protocol (TCP), which is described in Chap. 4, and further discussion of the transport layer is continued there.

2.7 The Session Layer

The duty of the session layer is the management of the flow of data between end users. When two endpoints make contact and "connect," a *session* is said to be established. The services of the session layer are as follows:

- *Session establishment and termination.* The concept of a session is almost indistinguishable from that of a connection, established in the transport layer, except that a session can span one or more connections. Like a connection, a session is always between two endpoints. First the session is opened, or established; then it remains open as a dedicated pipeline for the transmittal of data back and forth between the endpoints until the session is closed. One reason that a session layer exists above the transport layer, which usually implements a full connection-oriented service, is because transport layer connections can have more than one session multiplexed into the connection. Additionally, other services, enumerated below, can be offered by a session. Sessions between two endpoints are established before any data are transferred; then they are released when the need for the session is finished. Session establishment is normally accomplished by a negotiation between the endpoints; then the control blocks that contain the session parameters are created. There are three ways to release a session:

1. The session is aborted.
2. There is an orderly release of the session.
3. There is a negotiated release of the session.

- *Dialog management.*   There are two ways to control how data are sent back and forth between the endpoints. One is where only one end of the session can send data at any given time and is called *Two-Way Alternate* (TWA), which is OSI-speak for the more common definition of "half-duplex." The other way is *Two-Way Simultaneous* (TWS), which is a "full-duplex" where both ends of the session can transmit at the same time in different directions.

- *Synchronization.*   Data that are sent on the session are checkpointed so that if there is a system or network failure, data in a session can be recovered after the system is brought back up. Checkpoints are taken at certain intervals in the transmission of data and these checkpoints are stored. When recovery is taking place, the last good set of checkpoints is consulted and data retransmission begins from that point.

- *Expedited data.*   In addition to the normal flow of data in a session, there is an expedited data flow. If for any reason, the normal flow of data is deadlocked, which can happen if both ends of the session are waiting for the other end to send data, then data can still be sent on the expedited flow which has priority over the normal flow.

2.8   The Presentation Layer

The presentation layer in the reference model deals with *data representation* and *interpretation* within a network. Data are represented in different ways on different computing platforms; therefore, this layer, before passing application data to the session layer for transport across the network, formats the data into a network-neutral representation. A network-neutral representation is a standard method used to represent data. When data arrive in a node from another node and are in a network-neutral representation, the data are reformatted into the representation used by the hardware and software for that node.

A network can be made up of many different computer platforms and there are many inconsistencies in these platforms; therefore, the idea of a presentation layer (really a *representation* layer) is an excellent one. Some platforms use 2-byte word lengths in their machine architecture, others use 4-byte word lengths. Some computers store bytes in a word or a doubleword in low-to-high order; others store bytes in high-to-low order. Some computers use EBCDIC encoding rules; others use ASCII. All these differences can be accommodated by using the services of a presentation layer.

2.9 The Application Layer

The application layer provides application programming interfaces (APIs) that enable application programs to communicate with the network. It also provides application services that are made available to application programs for their use in navigating or dealing with the computer network and the distributed application environment. These are services such as electronic mail, file transfer, terminal emulation, and global directory service.

2.10 An Afterthought

The OSI reference model has provided a way to understand how network protocols are layered. In most network protocol stacks, the transport, network, and data link layer are pretty consistent with the OSI model. Above the transport layer there is not a lot of consistency from one protocol stack to another. As will be seen in Chap. 6, SNA has upper layers, but they are not always completely consistent with the OSI reference model. Basically, the OSI reference model has been very useful because it gives the industry a network model, but as dogma it falls short: It really only fully describes the stack of protocols that was developed by OSI itself.

Transport Networks and Protocols

3.1 Introduction

Now that the OSI reference model has been introduced, transport networks will be described using the reference model as a guide. The text will begin with a discussion of the protocols developed for OSI itself, then will continue by describing four other transport network protocols: NetBIOS, IPX, AppleTalk, and DECnet.

3.2 Open Systems Interconnection

The Open Systems Interconnection (OSI) effort for standardization of protocols was mentioned in Chap. 1. Chapter 2 presented the OSI reference model. To continue, the OSI protocols that were designed as an implementation of the model will now be presented.

OSI was the outcome of a massive international effort to standardize communications protocols. Following the creation of the OSI reference model, the international standards bodies involved in the OSI effort, the ISO and the CCITT [now called the International Telecommunications Union-Telecommunications Standardization Sector (ITU-T)], went to work creating communications protocols to be implemented in each of the layers of the reference model (Fig. 3.1). The eventual implementation of OSI protocols for each layer resulted in an OSI network protocol *stack*. In this stack, the physical layer did not employ any protocols and HDLC (chosen for use in the data link layer) was already a recognized standard. It is with the network layer, then, that our description of the OSI communications protocols will begin.

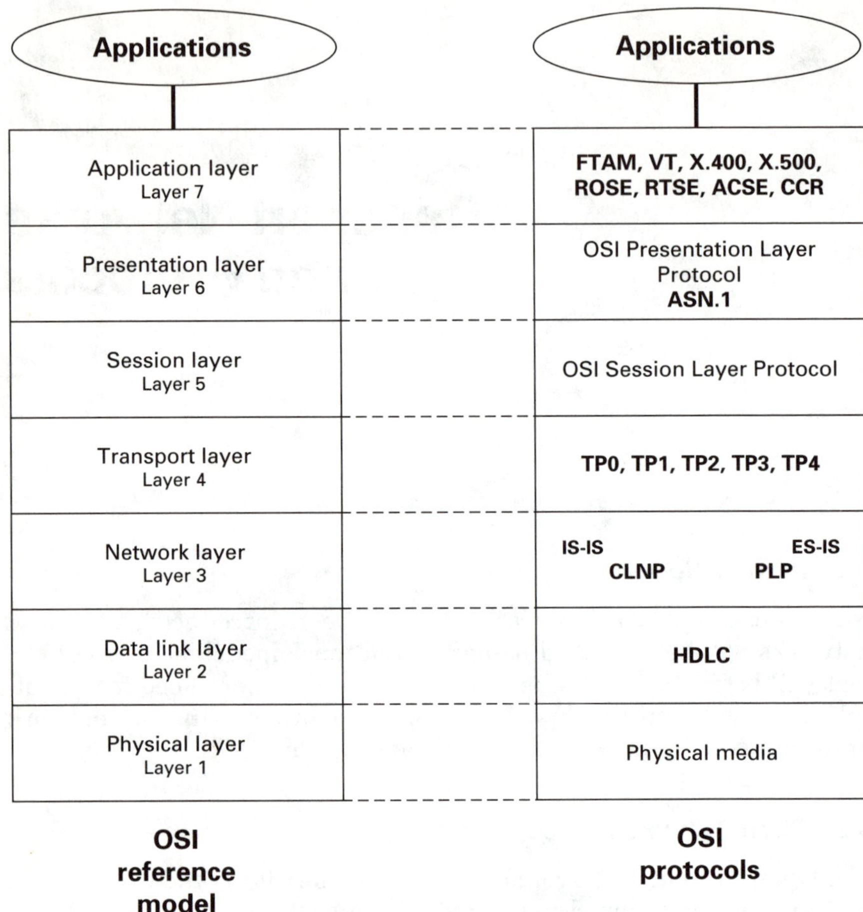

Figure 3.1   The OSI reference model and OSI protocols.

3.2.1   The OSI network layer protocols

Two protocols for the network layer were defined by OSI. The reason
for the definition of two protocols instead of just one was that standardization committees could not agree on a single network layer protocol. The European community favored X.25, which is very widely
implemented in Europe. X.25, as we have seen, has a connection-oriented network layer. The U.S. community, however, was partial to the
Internet Protocol (IP), which, because it supports a connection-oriented transport layer above the network layer, implements a connectionless protocol in its network layer. Therefore, the OSI committees
decided to provide both a connectionless and a connection-oriented
protocol for OSI's network layer.

OSI appointed the already existing X.25 to provide *Connection-Oriented Network Service* (CONS). *ConnectionLess-mode Network Service* (CLNS) was to be provided by a new protocol, similar to IP, which would be called the *ConnectionLess-mode Network Protocol* (CLNP). It was generally assumed that IP would eventually be replaced by CLNP.

Network layer addressing in both protocols uses an address called a *Network Service Access Point* (NSAP, pronounced EN-Sap) address. An NSAP address consists of an *initial domain part* (IDP)—which is further divided into an *authority format identifier* (AFI) and an *initial domain identifier* (IDI)—and a *domain-specific part* (DSP) (see Fig. 3.2). The AFI contains a number between 0 and 99 assigned by ISO that defines the format of the IDI and the syntax of the DSP. The IDI identifies the addressing domain and the authority responsible for assigning addresses in that domain. The DSP contains the network address itself. NSAPs are variable length and can range in length from a few bytes to a maximum of 20 bytes.

3.2.2   The OSI transport layer protocols

Five transport protocols have been defined for OSI to provide multiplexing and single-user service for three network classes:

- *Class A.*   Reliable networks (a low number of errors)
- *Class B.*   Somewhat reliable networks (a higher number of errors)
- *Class C.*   Error-prone networks (an unacceptable number of errors)

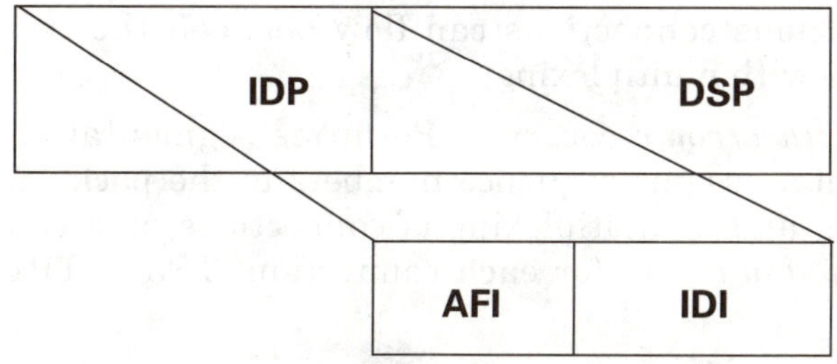

IDP = initial domain part
AFI = authority format identifier
IDI = initial domain identifier
DSP = domain specific part

Figure 3.2   The OSI NSAP address.

TABLE 3.1   OSI Transport Protocols and Network Types

	Class A	Class B	Class C
Single user	TP0	TP1	
Multiple user	TP2	TP3	TP4

The five transport protocols that were created for OSI are called *Transport Protocols* (TP) 0 through 4. TP0 and TP1 were designed for a single-user-per-network connection, and TP2, TP3, and TP4 were designed for multiple users per session (multiplexed). Table 3.1 shows the relationship between transport protocol type and network class.

- *TP0 (simple class).*   Performs segmentation and reassembly of data. If the data passed to the transport layer exceed the maximum transmission unit size, they must be broken into smaller segments; then the segments must be pieced together at the receiving end. TP0 was created to run with telex.

- *TP1 (basic error recovery class).*   Performs segmentation and reassembly of data and additionally assigns sequence numbers to the packets. TP1 was meant to be used for the transport protocol to be implemented on top of X.25, so that if an X.25 RESTART or RESET command was issued in the network layer, the transport layer would know what the last packet number sent was.

- *TP2 (multiplexing class).*   Performs segmentation and reassembly of data, but additionally supports multiplexing and demultiplexing of connections and can perform flow control separately for each connection. Transport connections can be set up between two endpoints, the maximum flow control window can be negotiated, then data belonging to various connections can flow between the two endpoints. TP2 is TP0 with multiplexing.

- *TP3 (multiplexing with error recovery).*   Performs segmentation and reassembly of data, assigns sequence numbers to the packets, supports multiplexing and demultiplexing of connections, and can perform flow control separately for each connection. TP3 is TP1 with multiplexing.

- *TP4 (full error detection and recovery).*   A full-featured, connection-oriented transport protocol similar to TCP. It was designed to run on an unreliable network layer such as one that implements CLNP.

3.2.3   The OSI session layer protocol

The OSI *session layer protocol* implements the session layer features described in Sec. 2.7: dialog management, session initiation and release, synchronization, and expedited data. These features are called *functional units*. Other functional units include activity management and exception reporting. When a session is established between two applications, the set of functional units that will go into effect for the session is negotiated.

The OSI session layer protocol coordinates and manages sessions between applications. It provides synchronization of data by establishing checkpoints which protect the data in case of a failure. If data are being transferred in a session and the network or a system crashes, the transfer of data can be restarted at the last successful checkpoint that was taken. *Two-way alternate* (TWA) dialog management controls how data are passed back and forth in the session and is accomplished by means of an abstraction called a *token*. A token—somewhat like the "hot potato" of children's games—is issued to the endpoint of a session that will be allowed to transmit data. When the holder of the token has completed sending the data, the token is handed to the other end of the session. Only the session endpoint that holds the token is allowed to transmit data. The token can be requested from the other end to turn the session's direction around. The OSI session layer token is used not only in dialog management, but also in session release and synchronization.

The session layer protocol allows expedited data to be sent which is usually considered to be limited to a length of 16 bytes. Expedited data have a higher priority than the normal data that flow in a session.

3.2.4 The OSI presentation layer protocol

The OSI presentation layer protocol has been defined as a part of the OSI standards, but does very little. The major development by OSI in the presentation layer was actually the creation of a data-representation language called *Abstract Syntax Notation One* (ASN.1).

ASN.1 might be described as a programming language for *data*. It is a data declaration language that has the ability to describe complex data structures. ASN.1 can be used for any kind of data representation and is used for the task of creating a network-neutral format for the presentation layer. Along with the ASN.1 language, a set of rules called the *Basic Encoding Rules* (BER) was developed for the actual encoding of the language.

ASN.1, like a lot of today's computer technology, had roots at Xerox PARC, whose *Courier* notation, used in the XNS specification, was an inspiration for ASN.1. ASN.1 was standardized in 1984 by the ITU-T.

ASN.1 is an excellent language for describing data and is used extensively in OSI documents to describe protocols and data structures. The basic encoding rules are rather computation-intensive, but nonetheless have been implemented in middleware products as well as in OSI application systems such as CMIP and X.400. However, ASN.1's greatest claim to fame is its use in the Simple Network Management Protocol (SNMP) that was developed for TCP/IP.

3.2.5   OSI application layer protocols and services

By far the most interesting protocols developed for the OSI effort are those residing in the application layer. The OSI application layer protocols provide services such as electronic mail, virtual terminal support, directory services, file transfer, and network management. The protocols of the application layer are extensive in that they seek to provide all of these services.

3.2.5.1   OSI application layer service elements.   The application layer is implemented with a set of *service elements* that offer services to applications.

- The *association control service element* (ACSE) provides for the establishment and release of an *association,* which is the name OSI uses for an application layer connection.

- The *reliable transfer service element* (RTSE) provides a means for reliable data transfer, meaning that data transfer can resume after a system crash or network failure.

- The *remote operations service element* (ROSE) provides a *remote procedure call* (RPC) function which allows an application program to call procedures that reside and execute on another computer, rather than locally. In other words, the call to the procedure is executed remotely. RPC provides a method for implementing distributed applications, and ROSE is an integral part of many of the OSI applications such as network management services, message handling, and directory services. Actually, ROSE's services are more general than just being a provider of RPC functionality. For example, ROSE also includes data transfer services.

- *Commitment, concurrency, and recovery* (CCR) offers a method for controlling distributed operations, such as the updating of multiple databases, and provides for recovery when system and network failures occur.

3.2.5.2   OSI application layer services.   In addition to the above service elements, OSI also developed standards to implement network application services themselves.

- *X.400 Message Handling System* (MHS) provides an electronic mail application service.

- *X.500 Directory Service* provides a distributed directory function.

- *File Transfer Access and Management* (FTAM) is a full-featured file transfer service.

- *Virtual Terminal Service* (VTS) provides terminal emulation.

- *Transaction Processing* (TP) is a standard for transaction processing in networks.

- *Common Management Information Protocol* (CMIP) is the network management service for OSI. It is listed as an application service but actually permeates more than the application layer.

Now that the protocols that were created for the OSI reference model have been introduced, other transport network protocol standards will be described and the relationship of each to the reference model will be detailed.

3.3 NetBIOS

The Network Basic Input/Output System (NetBIOS) is a communications protocol associated with applications that run on PCs and PS/2s attached to Ethernet and token ring LANs and was introduced in Chap. 1.

By consulting Fig. 3.3, the reader can see that NetBIOS can be roughly mapped into the network, transport, and session layers of the OSI reference model. The NetBIOS architecture, however, does not recognize a separation into three layers.

NetBIOS provides a full-duplex, connection-oriented service and also provides a datagram service. Its sessions use flow control, error recovery, and sequence numbers, and multiple sessions can be multiplexed into one connection. Since there is no separate network layer in NetBIOS, it is not a routable internetworking protocol. To get around this limitation, router manufacturers have devised methods of encapsulating NetBIOS inside other protocols, notably TCP/IP. In order to route NetBIOS on IPX networks, Novell NetWare encapsulates it inside of PEP transport layer packets (PEP will be described shortly). The API for NetBIOS is called the *NetBIOS Extended User Interface* (NetBEUI).

To digress for a moment, there is some confusion in computer-literate circles concerning the use of the names NetBIOS and NetBEUI. Some manufacturers, notably Microsoft, use the name NetBIOS to indicate the API (or user interface) and NetBEUI to describe the protocols. Since there is confusion, this book will use the terms in the manner that they are used by IBM, which created the protocol. NetBIOS is the communications protocol and NetBEUI is the *extended user interface*.

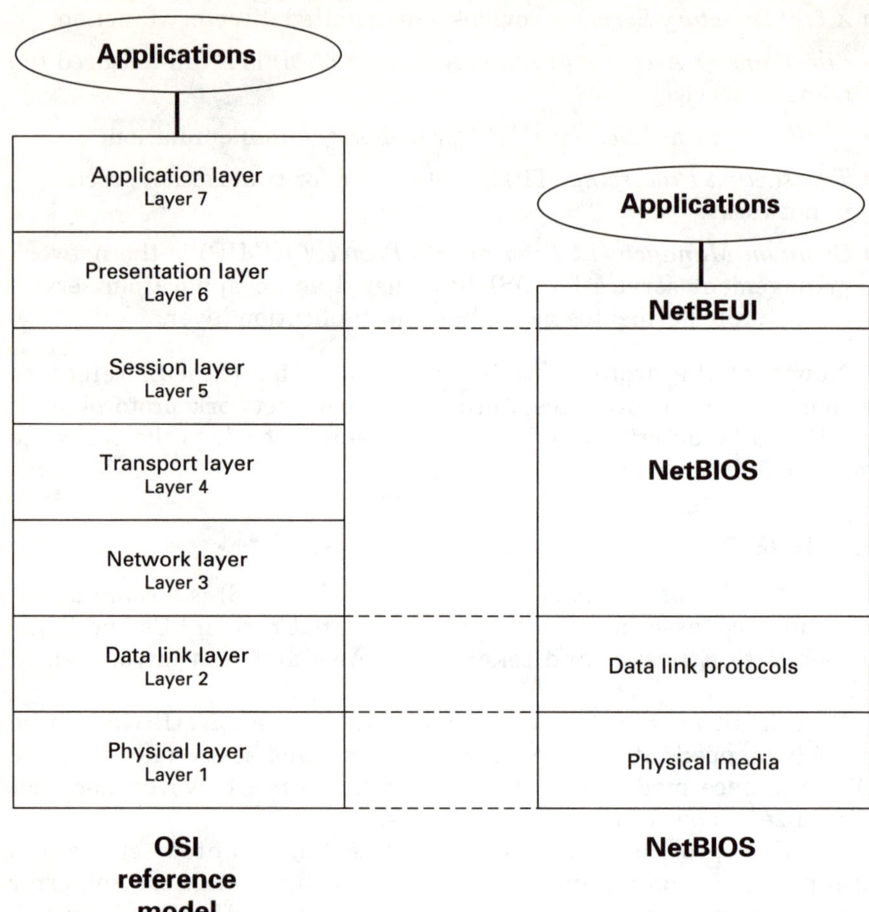

Figure 3.3   The OSI reference model and NetBIOS.

NetBIOS uses a *name service* to locate users in a network. This service employs 16-byte names which are assigned dynamically to individual LAN adapter cards. In order to establish a name, a NetBIOS user issues a NetBEUI ADD NAME command. In order to ensure that a name is unique everywhere in a network, NetBIOS broadcasts the name query to find out if another user is already using the same name. NetBIOS always handles the discovery of names by broadcasting a message to every reachable user, saying "Are you so-and-so?" When the endpoint with the name that is being searched for gets one of these packets, it replies back and a route to that user is then calculated. This use of broadcasting in NetBIOS is one of the weaknesses of the protocol, because it can slow a network down considerably.

A feature of the NetBIOS name service is its ability to create group names. A *group name* is a name that is assigned to more than one LAN adapter. It can be useful if a user wishes to send data to a group of users. Datagrams can be sent to specific user names, multicast to group names, or broadcast to the entire network. Sessions can be created between two users and are initiated when a user issues a NetBEUI LISTEN command using the name by which the user will be known and another name for the other, calling, station. An asterisk (*), however, can be used for the other station's name, in which case, a nonspecified user may connect. The remote session contacts the listening user by issuing a NetBEUI CALL command using the name of the other station.

A list of NetBEUI commands is presented in Table 3.2.

TABLE 3.2   NetBEUI Commands

Name Service Commands	
ADD NAME	Add a name
ADD GROUP NAME	Add a group name
DELETE NAME	Delete a name
FIND NAME	Locate a name

Datagram Service Commands	
SEND DATAGRAM	Send a datagram
SEND BROADCAST DATAGRAM	Send a broadcast datagram
RECEIVE DATAGRAM	Receive a datagram
RECEIVE BROADCAST DATAGRAM	Receive a broadcast datagram

Session Service Commands	
CALL	Establish session
LISTEN	Listen for a session call request
HANG UP	Close a session
SEND	Send data
CHAIN SEND	Send data in chained buffers
RECEIVE	Receive data
RECEIVE ANY	Receive data from anybody
SESSION STATUS	Obtain session status

Other Commands	
RESET	Reset interface
CANCEL	Cancel uncompleted command
ADAPTER STATUS	Obtain interface status
TRACE	Activate command trace

3.4   IPX

The family of communications protocols that is employed in Novell's NetWare is commonly known as IPX or IPX/SPX (and sometimes SPX/IPX). As mentioned in Chap. 1, IPX was derived from the pioneering Xerox Network System (XNS) protocol stack developed at the Xerox Palo Alto Research Center (PARC). Figure 3.4 shows the IPX stack and how it aligns with the OSI reference model.

3.4.1   The IPX network layer

Internetwork Packet eXchange (IPX) is the communications protocol that is used in NetWare's network layer. It is an implementation of

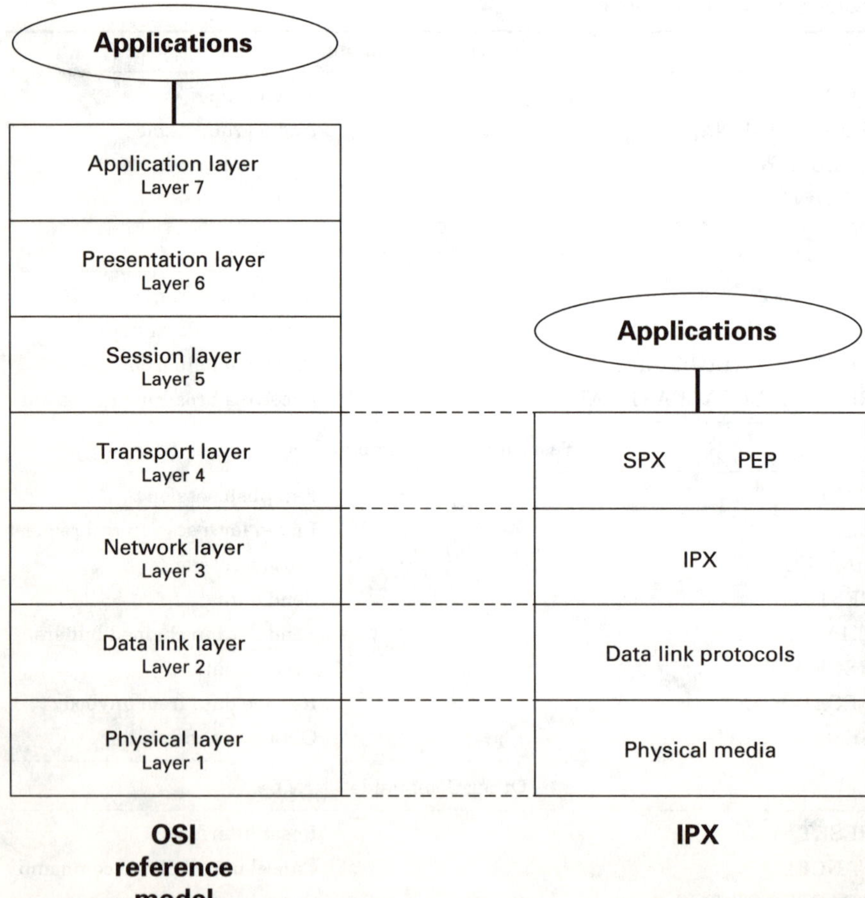

Figure 3.4   The OSI reference model and IPX.

XNS's network layer protocol called the *Internetwork Datagram Protocol* (IDP). IPX provides a connectionless datagram service with best-effort delivery. Additionally, NetWare's network layer also provides routing services using the *Routing Information Protocol* (RIP). Both Novell's RIP and the version of RIP that is used in TCP/IP networks were inspired by the original RIP written for XNS. NetWare's RIP is basically the same as XNS RIP, Novell having only added a 2-byte field to the RIP packet header and changed the algorithm slightly.

IPX combines three different addresses together to create a fully qualified network address. The first address of the fully qualified address is a 4-byte network address, the second is a 6-byte node address, and the third is a 2-byte address called a *socket* address. The network address is the address assigned to the particular network in which an endpoint resides. The node address is the address assigned to a particular node within that network. A socket address pinpoints a location within a computer node that identifies the particular application process that is sending or receiving data within that node. Certain socket addresses are designated as *well known,* which means that they are reserved for use by well-known applications or systems services. These well-known addresses were administered by the Xerox Corporation because they originated in XNS. For example, Xerox has assigned particular socket addresses to be used by Novell NetWare and IPX. *NetWare Core Protocol* (NCP) packets (used for file server commands) are sent to socket 451 (hex) and Novell's RIP uses socket number 453 (hex). Addresses in IPX are notated in hexadecimal format and that is why the number of digits in an address can be up to two times the byte size of the field. Network addresses contain up to 8 hexadecimal digits, being a 4-byte field, and node addresses 12 since they use a 6-byte field.

Figure 3.5 shows the 30-byte network layer header that contains the 6-byte destination node address, the 4-byte destination network address, and the 2-byte destination socket address. It also contains the origination socket, node, and network addresses. The node address in XNS and IPX is always represented by a node's *physical address.* (An IPX node address is the exact size of an Ethernet 48-bit physical address: 6 bytes.) In the case of other protocols that have smaller-sized physical addresses, such as ARCNET which uses a 1-byte physical address, the node address field is padded from the left with zeros. The concept of using the physical address as the node address in the network layer was an idea that occurred to the original designers of XNS, who thought that in this way a computer could move to another network and its 6-byte node address could still remain the same.

The only difference between an IDP and an IPX header is that the checksum field was not used in IPX, except as an optional feature.

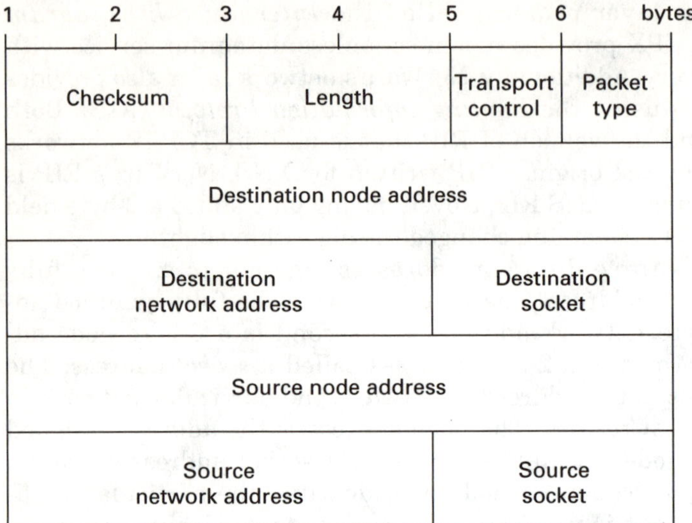

Figure 3.5 The IPX/IDP header.

3.4.2 The IPX transport layer

The connectionless service of IPX in the network layer is the basis for all communication in a NetWare network, but most network services require the use of a connection-oriented protocol to ensure the delivery of packets in their proper sequence. *Sequenced Packet eXchange* (SPX), NetWare's connection-oriented protocol, is an implementation of XNS's *Sequenced Packet Protocol* (SPP) and resides in the transport layer. SPX provides flow control, error recovery, and sequenced packets and has a header that is placed between the data and the IPX header. The SPX header is shown in Fig. 3.6. The 12-byte SPX/SPP header has fields for connection control, data stream type, source and target connection IDs, sequence number, and acknowledgment and allocation numbers. The connection control field contains flags that are used to control the flow of data on a connection. A connection ID identifies a particular connection and, at a destination, is used to demultiplex data belonging to different connections that arrive at the same socket address. The acknowledgment number is used to store the sequence number of the next packet that the receiver is expecting to receive, and the allocation number contains the number of receive buffers that are available. A full-duplex version of SPX, called SPX II, was introduced in NetWare Version 4.0.

The NetWare Core Protocol (NCP) is an important user of the IPX/SPX protocols. The NetWare Core Protocol is the protocol used by

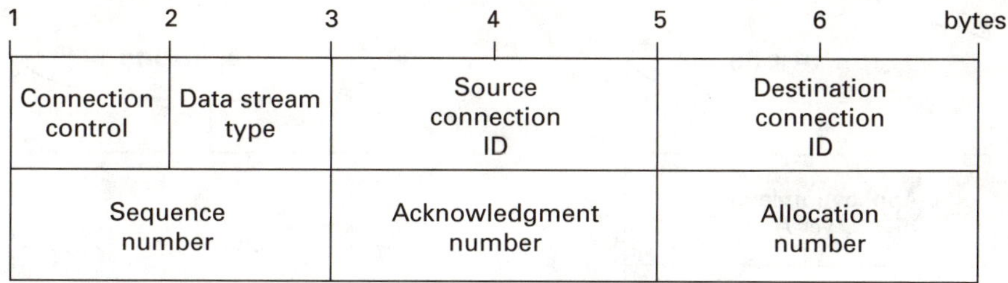

Figure 3.6   The SPX/SPP header.

clients to communicate back and forth with servers. NCP messages are sent by workstations to the file server to request any of the many services available, from reading data to creating queues and assigning trustee rights. Before a workstation can issue NCP requests, however, it must request an SPX connection. If this is granted, a connection ID is assigned. SPX is also used by other NetWare services such as Rconsole, Rprinter, and the SNA Gateway.

In addition to SPP, XNS implemented another transport layer protocol that NetWare uses. This is XNS's *Packet Exchange Protocol* (PEP). Not as full-functioned as SPX, it was designed by XNS for simple request and response transactions. Its header has only three fields: an "ID" field enumerates the request type, "client type" specifies the transport layer user, and a data field contains the actual data being transported in the packet. NetBIOS emulation packets run inside of PEP packets in an IPX network.

The API that is used to access IPX/SPX from user application programs was designed by Novell, and that company provides software development kits to implement it. Function calls allow network user application programs to access any file server service from workstation nodes, assuming that they have proper permissions, as well as to send and receive data using IPX/SPX.

3.5 AppleTalk

AppleTalk was designed in 1983 by Apple Computer Corporation to provide Macintosh computers with an easy-to-use method of local area networking. Figure 3.7 shows the various AppleTalk protocols and their relationship to the OSI reference model.

When AppleTalk was first introduced, it made use of a physical port that was built into Apple computers and printers. This native connection was called LocalTalk. Later, AppleTalk was extended to use token ring and Ethernet networks. Over the years, AppleTalk has

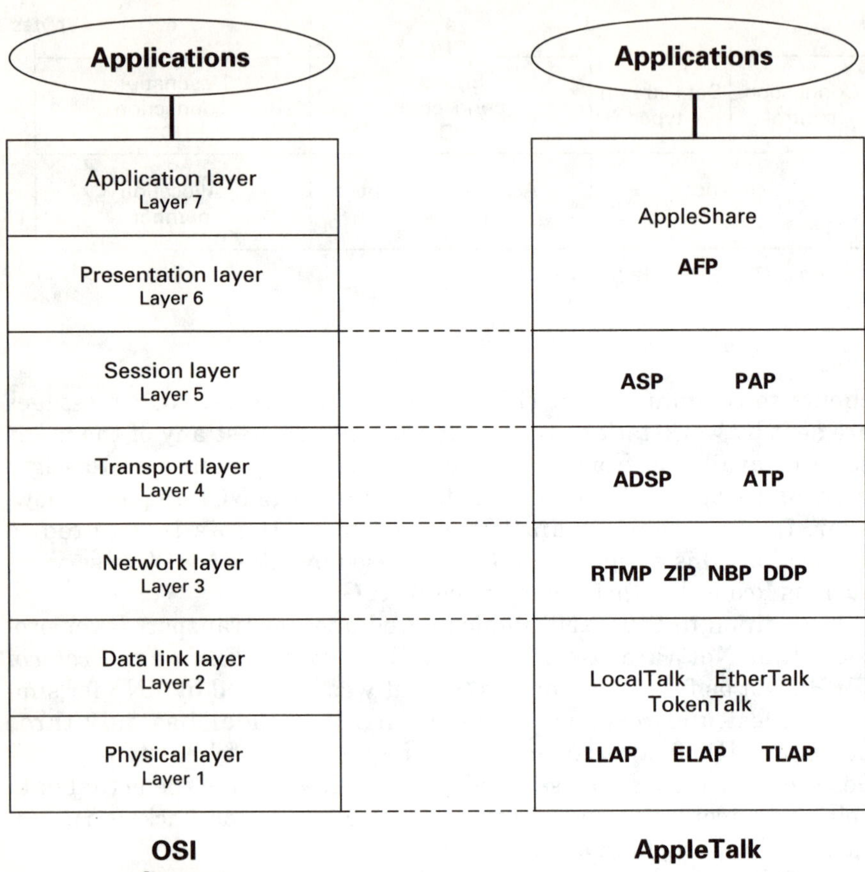

Figure 3.7   The OSI reference model and AppleTalk.

been ported to computers other than those made by Apple, and versions are available for DOS, IBM mainframe, DEC, and Unix platforms.

In the AppleTalk world, physical and data link layers are tied together to become a single layer that has three different implementations: LocalTalk, EtherTalk, and TokenTalk. LocalTalk was the original implementation, EtherTalk provided access to Ethernet, TokenTalk to token rings. Local Talk uses a protocol called the *LocalTalk Link Access Protocol* (LLAP). EtherTalk uses the *EtherTalk Link Access Protocol* (ELAP), and TokenTalk uses the *TokenTalk Link Access Protocol* (TLAP).

3.5.1   The AppleTalk network layer

AppleTalk's network layer implements a protocol called the *Datagram Delivery Protocol* (DDP) that uses socket addresses for user endpoints. The concept of socket addresses is similar to that introduced above in the discussion of IPX. A socket is a subaddress within a computer node that identifies the application process that is sending or receiving data, and in AppleTalk it is identified by a single-byte *socket number*. Socket numbers 1 through 63 are reserved for well-known assignments by Apple for services such as AppleTalk's *Name Binding Protocol* (NBP), to be discussed shortly. The AppleTalk *node ID* is assigned to individual nodes within a network and is just a single byte in length. Networks can be interconnected with the AppleTalk network layer and are identified by a 2-byte network number. An AppleTalk fully qualified network address consists of a network number, node ID, and socket number and is 4 bytes in length.

DDP has a header that comes in two sizes: a 5-byte short header and a 13-byte extended header. The short header is used when internetworking is not involved and data will not go beyond the range of a single network. The DDP header contains a DDP type field to identify the protocol being used inside the packet. There is also a 6-bit *hop count* field in the extended header for routing purposes. Hop count is the number of routing nodes, and hence networks, that can be transversed by the packet of data associated with the header. The hop count is decremented by each routing node the packet traverses. Hop counts limit the amount of networks that a packet of data can travel through, and thus prevent infinite loops.

The *Routing Table Maintenance Protocol* (RTMP) is used to maintain the routing tables used in the routing nodes in AppleTalk. RTMP was based on RIP and uses DDP to send messages and update information about routes. Address translation between data link layer addresses and DDP network layer addresses is provided by the *AppleTalk Address Resolution Protocol* (AARP).

The *Name Binding Protocol* (NBP) is the protocol used in the network layer to map names to network addresses. AppleTalk network nodes can be included in abstractions called *zones*. Zones are used to identify a logical grouping of network nodes and can be given a name. The *Zone Information Protocol* (ZIP) is used to map network addresses into zone names.

3.5.2   The AppleTalk transport layer

The AppleTalk transport layer is implemented with several transport protocols. One, the *AppleTalk Transaction Protocol* (ATP), is a reliable datagram transport protocol used by other higher-layer AppleTalk protocols. ATP is based on a transaction-processing model of making a request, then receiving a response to that request. This style of transaction processing is well suited to the client/server environment. There are three distinct types of ATP packets: *TReq* (transaction request), *TResp* (transaction response), and *TRel* (transaction release). The transactional process works as follows. An end-user socket initiates a transaction with a *TReq,* and a number, called a *Transaction IDentifier* (TID), is assigned to the transaction. When the socket at the other end receives the TReq, a TResp is returned describing the result of the request. The TResp contains the same TID. To complete the transaction, the TRel is sent by the originator of the transaction. ATP uses an 8-byte header with the two high-order bits representing the type of packet: 01 for TReq, 10 for TResp, and 11 for the TRel. Bytes 3 and 4 are the TID.

The *AppleTalk Data Stream Protocol* (ADSP) is a full-duplex, connection-oriented transport layer protocol that sequences its packets and provides flow control. Connections are identified by a unique 2-byte connection identifier that is contained in the 13-byte ADSP header. ADSP is somewhat of a typical connection-oriented transport protocol.

3.5.3   The AppleTalk session layer

AppleTalk has a couple of session layer-like protocols. The *AppleTalk Session Protocol* (ASP) uses ATP packets to create a session between a workstation and a file server. Basically, ASP bundles the client/server transactions of ATP together into a session. ASP does not have a separate header, but makes use of a 4-byte user data field in the ATP header to carry its information. Not a session layer protocol by strict OSI standards, it nevertheless provides the additional features that turn the ATP transport layer datagram protocol into a connection-oriented service.

The *Printer Access Protocol* (PAP) is also a connection-oriented protocol to be used between clients and servers, but it was created as the underlying protocol for communication between a client workstation and LaserWriter printers. It is not limited to use in printing services, however.

3.5.4   Other protocols

One more AppleTalk protocol should be mentioned, and that is the *AppleTalk Filing Protocol* (AFP). AFP is the protocol used in AppleTalk to map the files residing on a file server into the file system residing on individual workstations.

3.6 DECnet

Digital Equipment Corporation (DEC)'s implementation of the Digital Network Architecture (DNA) was introduced in Chap. 1. The DNA architecture uses a layered approach that is similar to that of the OSI reference model and is compared with the model in Fig. 3.8. In DECnet Phase IV, DEC added a full OSI protocol stack to run alongside its traditional DNA stack. This was an attempt to make DECnet more of an open networking platform. It was a brave move—a major statement of Digital's commitment to OSI. Since few vendors have yet placed much emphasis on OSI implementation, interoperability with OSI turned out to be much less an issue than Digital had probably hoped for.

The twin stacks of DECnet Phase V become unique above the transport layer: It is there that OSI and DNA become separate entities. Older DNA applications must use Digital's proprietary *Session Control Protocol,* and the newer OSI applications, such as X.400 and FTAM, must use the OSI presentation and session layer protocols. The OSI transport protocol TP4 can be implemented in the DNA stack, however.

DECnet's data link layer implements the various data link protocols such as LAPB of X.25, HDLC, FDDI, and IEEE 802.2 and 802.3, plus, naturally, DEC's *Digital Data Communications Message Protocol* (DDCMP). DDCMP was DNA's original data link layer protocol.

3.6.1 The DECnet network layer

Originally, DECnet's network layer was called the *routing layer* and implemented proprietary routing protocols. The network layer was enhanced in Phase V by the implementation of the OSI network layer protocols including the OSI IS-IS and ES-IS routing protocols. The Phase V OSI implementation includes both X.25 and the *ConnectionLess-mode Network Protocol* (CLNP). OSI's routing protocols were developed at DEC as a part of Phase V and were based on the routing protocols introduced in DECnet Phase III.

3.6.2 The DECnet transport layer

Originally, the DECnet transport layer was called the *network services layer,* then was renamed the *end communication layer.* The original transport layer protocol implemented in DECnet was called *Network Services Protocol* (NSP). Phase V added the OSI TP0, TP2, and TP4 transport protocols to the layer (TP1 and TP3 were not implemented). The choice of the transport protocol that a Phase V user wishes to use is made during the establishment of a connection.

NSP is connection-oriented and supports segmentation and re-

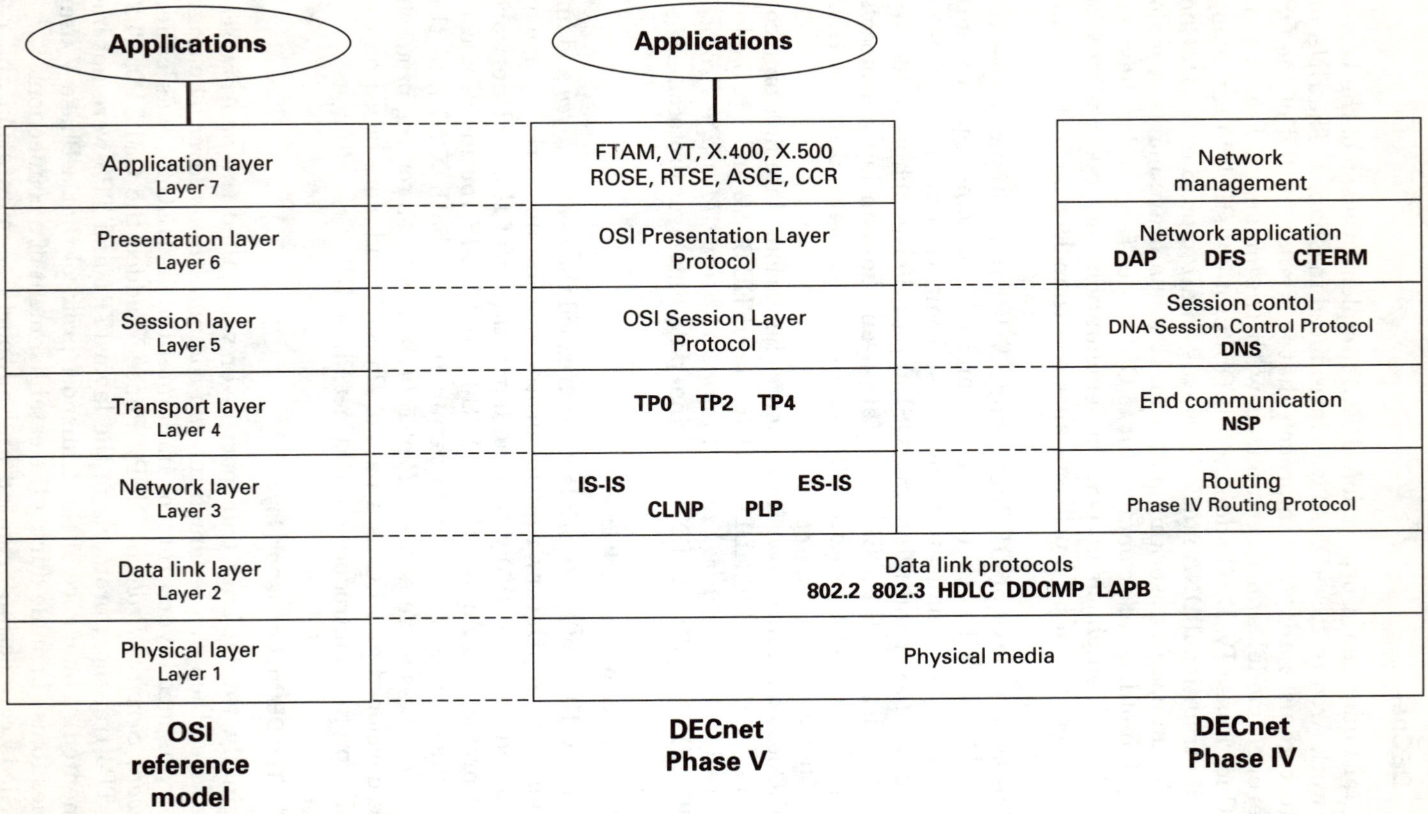

Figure 3.8 The OSI reference model and DECnet Phases IV and V.

assembly. It also has provisions for expedited data and congestion control.

3.6.3 The DECnet session layer

Above the transport layer, a Phase V user has to choose between the services of either the three upper OSI layers or the DECnet session control and network application layer protocols. DNA applications must use DECnet session control; OSI applications must use the OSI application, presentation, and session layers.

The session layer protocol used by DECnet applications is called the *DNA Session Control Protocol* and consists of three parts:

- Connection control
- Address resolution
- Address selection

Connection control governs the establishment and termination of connections. DNA applications use names to specify network users and services, and address resolution is responsible for resolving addresses into names and names into addresses. Address selection selects the protocols below the session layer to be used by the connection.

The original DECnet had static name-to-address mapping. Later a name-to-address mapping service to resolve DNA names, used by DNA applications, into network addresses was introduced. This service is called the *DNA Naming Service* (DNS). DNA Naming Service is an integral part of the session layer and is closely identified with the DNA stack. It provides a distributed and replicated naming service. DNS was adopted by the *Open Software Foundation* (OSF) to become a part of DCE as the *Cell Directory Service* (CDS).

OSI applications use an implementation of the OSI session layer protocol.

3.6.4 DECnet highest layers

DECnet network applications run in the network application layer, which sits on top of the session control layer. OSI applications sit on top of implementations of the OSI application, presentation, and session layers.

Some of the original DNA applications are worth mentioning. The *Data Access Protocol* (DAP) is the original remote file transfer protocol for DNA and runs over the DNA session control layer. DAP makes remote files available on a local computer and has been ported to other, non-VMS systems such as Unix, DOS, and MVS. The *Distributed File*

System (DFS) runs only on LANs of VMS computers and maps remote directories to make them appear local. CTERM is the DNA terminal emulation service.

OSI application layer services include X.400, X.500, FTAM, VT, and CMIP.

3.7 Afterthought

Although the OSI reference model was created as an architectural model for the implementation of the OSI protocol suite, it serves the industry well as a reference for the layered design of modern computer networks. Understanding this layering of network protocols is a necessary prerequisite to understanding today's complex multiprotocol networks.

TCP/IP
and the Internet Suite

4.1 Introduction

The history of the internet suite of communications protocols, also called the internet *stack,* and the Internet's origin as the ARPAnet was presented in Chap. 1. The two major communications protocols belonging to the internet protocol stack are the Transmission Control Protocol (TCP) and the Internet Protocol (IP). These two protocols are used together—TCP in the transport layer and IP in the network layer—and consequently the two together are known as *Transmission Control Protocol/Internet Protocol* (TCP/IP). TCP/IP is also the name commonly applied to the entire internet protocol suite, which includes more protocols than just TCP and IP.

TCP/IP was created by Bob Kahn and Vinton Cerf, who, in 1974, published their historic paper on what would become the TCP/IP communications protocol. By June 1978, IP and TCP had become separated into two layers, one layer for each protocol; then, in September 1981, the fundamental specifications for TCP/IP were released. The basic ARPAnet communications programs telnet, ftp, and sendmail were rewritten to run over TCP/IP, and finally TCP/IP was ported to various local area network platforms.

DARPA contracted Bolt, Beranek, and Newman (BBN) to develop TCP/IP for the Unix operating system, then running on VAX computers, and funded the University of California at Berkeley to enable TCP/IP's inclusion in the BSD version of Unix. In 1983, BSD 4.2 was released and TCP/IP was included. After 1983, TCP/IP was the only communications protocol in use on the Internet, completely replacing the older NCP protocol.

During 1986 and 1987 the Internet was experiencing very serious congestion problems. Van Jacobson of the Lawrence Berkeley Laboratory corrected most of these with his slow start and congestion avoidance algorithms. Since that time, TCP/IP has remained basically the same, while services and applications written to make use of it have increased dramatically.

As a matter of clarification, before beginning our discussion of the internet protocols, a few words about terminology are in order. The large research network that was the outgrowth of the ARPAnet is known as the *Internet*. This is the international network on which more than 4 million computers are attached and which has been doubling in size every year. When this computer network is described in this book, the word *Internet* will be capitalized. That is because there are two generally accepted uses of the word *internet: an* internet, and *the* Internet. "internet" (with a small "i") refers to any series of networks which are tied together, or *internetworked,* using routers and typically using the TCP/IP communications protocol. An internet is a smaller version of *the* Internet and perhaps encompasses only a few nodes. The term *intranet* is sometimes used to describe this kind of network. When TCP/IP is discussed in this book, the principles that are involved usually relate to both the large *I*nternet and to any small *i*nternet, so the term *internet* can be used to describe either. If *the* Internet is inferred, then Internet will be capitalized.

Computers are connected with the Internet using the TCP/IP communications protocol. The term *TCP/IP,* as was mentioned previously, is in common usage today and refers to the *internet suite of protocols* or simply the *internet protocols* or *internet protocol suite*. Even though the label TCP/IP has become a generic title for the internet protocol suite, in reality it refers only to the Transmission Control Protocol (TCP), which is only one of the two available transport layer protocols that run on top of the Internet Protocol (IP). The reader is advised to bear in mind that in addition to TCP, there is also the User Datagram Protocol (UDP), which is used instead of TCP by many of the utilities and services associated with the internet protocols. UDP, like TCP, is a transport layer protocol that runs on top of IP, and this relationship could be described as "UDP/IP." Because of this, to best describe the complete communications protocol stack described in this chapter, the term *internet suite* is perhaps more appropriate than *TCP/IP*. However, the latter is the most prevalent term in use throughout the world today.

TCP/IP was originally associated with the Unix operating system. In fact, it was bundled free with most Unix implementations and is usually considered to be the Unix communications protocol of choice. Because of this, and the fact that it is easy to configure and works well, it was rapidly implemented in networks, especially in the United States.

The utilities and configuration files associated with the internet protocols originally were Unix programs and files. However, now that TCP/IP has spread to many other operating systems, these same utilities and files are a part of many TCP/IP implementations in other systems such as DOS, Windows, NetWare, and MVS. The original concepts used in implementing TCP/IP on Unix systems are usually left intact when TCP/IP is ported to other systems, and many implementations have continued to use the same names, formats, and messages associated with the original Berkeley Unix.

We will begin the discussion of TCP/IP by describing how standards are organized and defined.

4.2   Internet Standards

The protocols in use on the Internet are carefully defined, and standards bodies monitor all Internet activity.

4.2.1   Request For Comments (RFC)

Internet standards are defined in a series of documents called *Request For Comments* (RFC). The RFCs are a series of protocol specifications to which numbers are assigned as they are issued. There are currently many of these, and new RFCs are continually being added to the series. RFCs are the basis of the internet suite of protocols.

The RFC system was started in 1969 at UCLA to coordinate the work of graduate students at the few ARPAnet sites then being placed into operation and was originated by Steve Crocker, who was a student there. The earliest RFCs were specifications for the ARPAnet and NCP (the forefathers of the Internet and TCP/IP) and described the terminal emulation program (telnet) and the file transfer protocol (ftp). Electronic mail was also described in a special section in the RFC for ftp.

RFCs are, and always have been, freely available to the public. They are always "online" and available via internet access. Because these specifications for internet protocols are not, and never have been, produced by any particular vendor and there is no licensing involved, they have been embraced by industry and this helped cause TCP/IP to spread rapidly all over the world.

4.2.2   Internet governing bodies

The Internet Architecture Board (IAB) is a technical body that oversees the development of the internet suite of protocols. It was founded in the early 1980s and includes over a dozen international volunteers from government, research, and industry. The IAB oversees other bodies, including the Internet Research Task Force (IRTF) and the Internet Engineering Task Force (IETF).

Internet standards and the RFCs are developed by the Internet Engineering Task Force, a standards group that is divided into nine areas. Protocol specifications can be submitted to them for consideration for standardization. The IETF holds three week-long meetings a year.

The IRTF researches technical matters that are more *blue sky,* more experimental and not necessarily geared to the immediate future. The IRTF's Privacy and Security Research Group has developed the Privacy Enhanced Mail (PEM) protocols, which were submitted to the IETF for standardization.

In 1992, the IAB became a part of a new organization called the Internet Society.

4.3   The TCP/IP Layers

Figure 4.1 shows a relationship between TCP/IP and the OSI reference model and should aid the reader in understanding the nature of TCP/IP's layers. Basically, TCP/IP consists of just two layers: a network layer and a transport layer. Below the network layer (OSI layer 3) is the data link layer in which a number of data link layer standards are able to run, supporting the two layers of the TCP/IP stack above. Figure 4.2 shows several protocols that belong to the internet stack that are assigned to the data link layer. These are ARP and RARP. These two protocols are a part of TCP/IP, but are not mandatory. They were created to enable the resolution of network layer addresses into data link layer addresses. Therefore, TCP/IP does not really implement a full data link layer; it simply provides for the use of various standard data link protocols.

The network layer in TCP/IP contains the Internet Protocol (IP), the original networking protocol for TCP/IP. Figure 4.2 shows acronyms for two other protocols that are associated with this layer and are mandatory. These two protocols, ICMP and IGMP, will be explained later in this chapter. The transport layer contains the two transport protocols associated with TCP/IP: TCP and UDP.

The transport layer (OSI layer 4) is TCP/IP's top layer. Above the transport layer, however, there usually exists a layer known as the API or socket layer. The socket layer is a part of almost every major TCP/IP implementation and contains the Berkeley socket interface or a similar application programming interface (API) to be used by the applications programs—residing in the layer above the sockets layer—to access the services of TCP/IP.

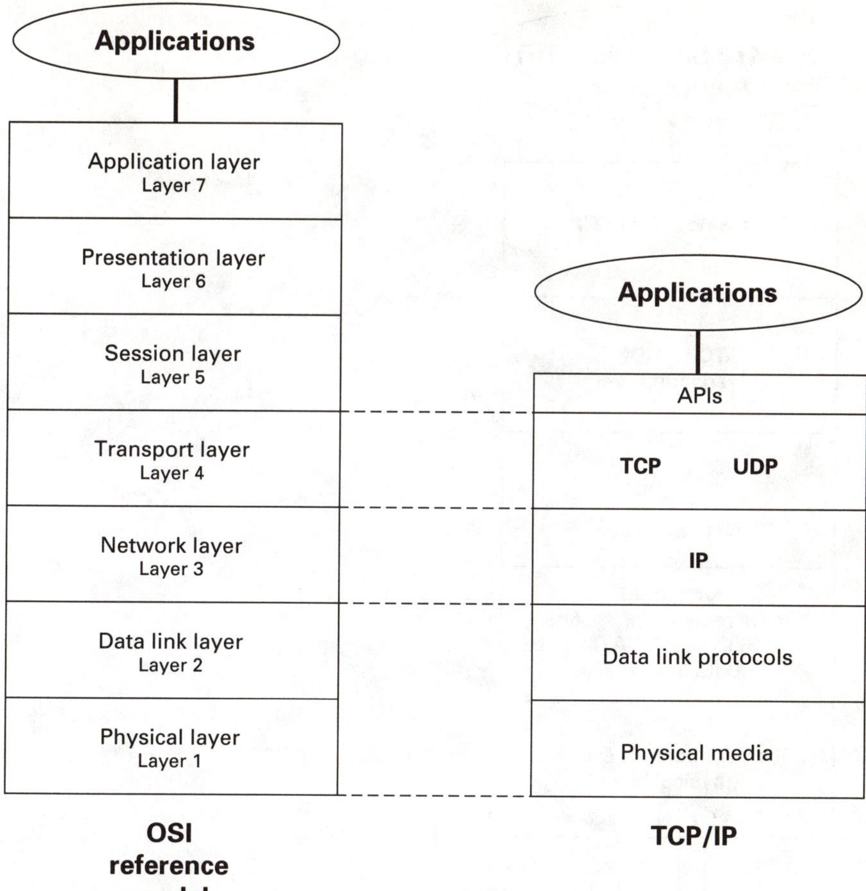

Figure 4.1   The OSI reference model and TCP/IP.

The discussion of TCP/IP layers will continue, beginning with a description of the concepts and protocols of the IP network layer.

4.4   The Network Layer

The network layer of the internet suite of protocols is defined by RFC 791, and its main protocol is the Internet Protocol.

4.4.1   The Internet Protocol

The *Internet Protocol* (IP) is a connectionless network layer protocol. By connectionless, it is contrasted to the network layer of a protocol such as X.25, which sets up virtual circuit connections before data are

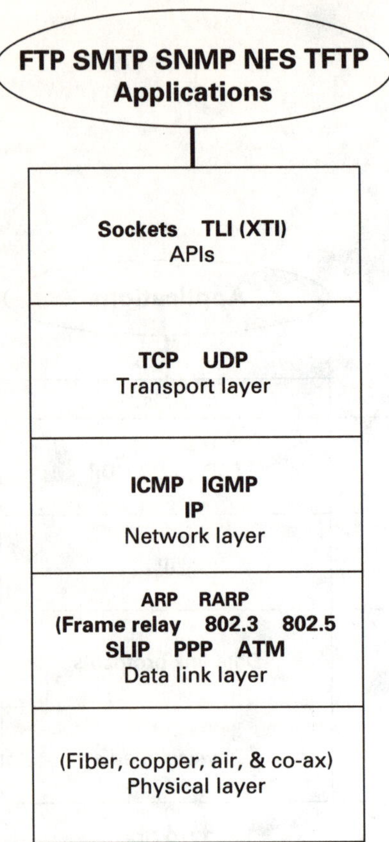

Figure 4.2   The internet protocol suite.

sent to a destination. A connectionless network layer has no predefined path through a network, but sends data a packet at a time according to the addressing information contained in the packet header. These packets, or *datagrams* as connectionless packets are called, can each take a different path to the destination and can arrive at the destination in any order. Additionally, if datagrams are determined to be damaged in transit, or problems, such as network congestion, exist in the network that make it impossible for datagrams to be buffered by intermediary routing nodes, datagrams are simply discarded. Therefore, the service provided by a connectionless network layer such as IP is called an *unreliable,* or *best effort* service: It does the best it can do to deliver the datagrams that are given to it to transport. If *reliable* delivery of datagrams is essential and proper packet ordering is required, routines residing in the higher layers must provide this service.

Datagram packets are not acknowledged and are not associated with any kind of network connection. IP network layer datagrams are called *IP datagrams*. IP datagrams have a header that is always prepended to the data. Figure 4.3 shows the layout of the IP datagram header.

The header contains a 4-bit header length which specifies the number of 32-bit words in the header. It is usually set to five, for 20 bytes. The total length field contains the length in bytes of the entire datagram. The *time-to-live* (TTL) field specifies how long the datagram has to live before it will be discarded. The TTL field is implemented to prevent a datagram from falling into a trap called a *routing loop*, where a network path could cause a packet to pass from one routing node to another in a loop configuration. TTL is initialized to a certain value; then, as the packet passes through routing nodes, the count is decremented by one. When the count in TTL reaches zero, a routing node, rather than decrementing the count, simply discards the packet and notifies the sender.

The protocol field in the header describes the protocol of the data contained within the packet. The header checksum is calculated for the header only and does not include the enclosed data. It is calculated in each routing node to determine if the packet header was modified accidentally during transmission. Headers that do not pass the test for a correct checksum are discarded, and the sender is not notified.

Since many books have been written on the subject of IP and the internet protocols—many of them excellent reference volumes—packet

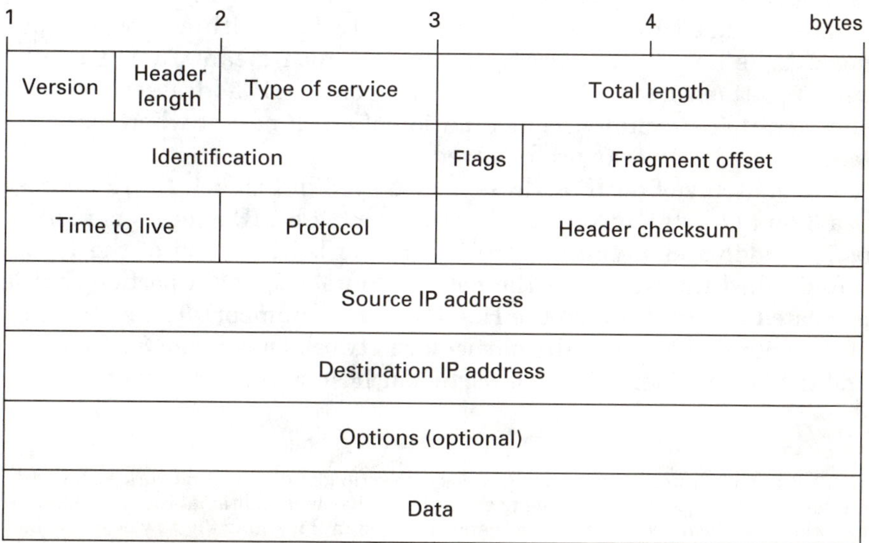

Figure 4.3   The IP header.

headers will not be described in detail. It is suggested that interested readers refer to either the series of books called *TCP/IP Illustrated* by Stevens (1994, 1995, 1996) or *Internetworking with TCP/IP* by Comer (1991, 1993). Both series of books are listed in the Bibliography.

The principal function of a network layer protocol is to route packets of data, and routing of datagrams is what IP is all about. The source and destination network addresses are contained in the IP header and conform to IP address standards, which will be discussed next. In IP datagram routing is accomplished by assigning one of a network's nodes to the purpose of being what was traditionally called a *gateway,* or routing, node. The purpose of a gateway node, in contrast to the other nodes on the network, which were traditionally called *host* nodes, is to interconnect separate networks. The gateway node has more than a single attachment to a network: not only is it attached to a local network, it is also attached, through another network interface, to one or more other networks and/or, perhaps, to the Internet itself. On a gateway machine, routing software examines the IP addresses in incoming datagram headers and determines to what network interface datagrams should be sent. In the original ARPAnet, the computer that was assigned the gateway function was usually a more powerful model of computer, such as a DEC PDP-11. Gateway nodes today are normally called routing nodes, or simply *routers,* if the node is dedicated to the routing function.

4.4.2   IP addresses

IP addresses are the internet protocol's network layer addresses, which are used to pinpoint an exact interface within any network node. IP is an *internetworking* protocol, which means that it can be used to attach networks together. Therefore, IP addresses must be sufficient to determine the destination of an IP packet when many interconnected networks are involved.

The anatomy of an IP address is displayed in Fig. 4.4. An IP address is a 32-bit (4-byte) universal address. Each 32-bit IP address is really a *pair* of addresses because there is a network ID portion of the IP address, called the NetID (or the network number), and a portion that is dedicated to a host, called the HostID (or host number). The NetID part of the address identifies the particular network on which a *host* resides, and the HostID identifies that particular host on that network.*

---

*Traditionally, internet terminology always described individual network nodes with the term *host* and, as was explained earlier, hosts that had additional routing capabilities were called *gateways*. The term "gateway" used in this context is now obsolete, and these nodes are now referred to as *router nodes* or *routers*. This is because the term "gateway" has evolved to describe something entirely different.

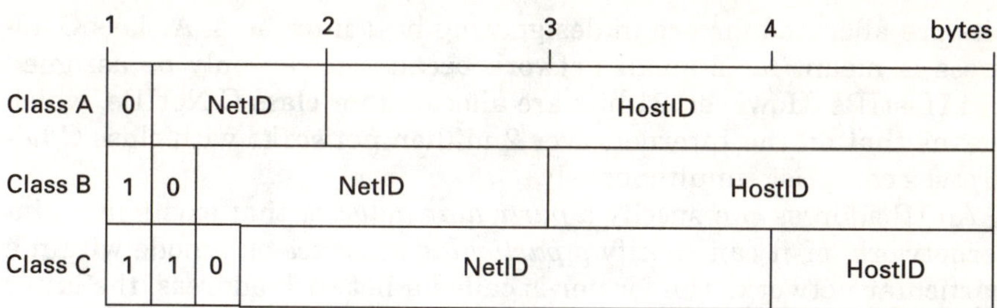

Class A range = 0.0.0.0 to 127.255.255.255
Class B range = 128.0.0.0 to 191.255.255.255
Class C range = 192.0.0.0 to 223.255.255.255

Figure 4.4 The IP address.

4.4.2.1 IP address classes. There are three primary classes of internet addresses: class A, class B, and class C. These three classes are shown as the three types of addresses in Fig. 4.4. The class to which an address belongs is encoded into the address itself. This is accomplished by the use of the high-order bits of the address. If the highest bit in the address is a 0 (and not a 1), then the remaining 31 bits is the actual internet address and it is a class A address. If the high-order bit is instead a 1, then that address is either a class B or a class C address, depending on the state of the next bit. A class B address will always have a 0 following the 1 of the first bit, and the remaining 30 bits contain the internet address. A class C address will always begin with the 3-bit sequence 110, with the remaining 29 bits containing the address.

The best way to conceptualize IP address classes is to study Fig. 4.4. In this figure, the 32 bits of the internet address are shown for each of the three classes. As can be seen, the purpose for the three classes of internet addresses is the length of the NetID, and the HostID portion of each of the classes is different, depending on the high-order bits.

The purpose for having three address classes is to accommodate different networking situations. The NetID portion of the address refers to a particular network in an internet. All the hosts, or nodes, on that network must be addressable by the remaining bits of the address. If the network is identified by a class A address, then, because there is a 24-bit HostID in a class A address, that network can contain as many as 16,777,214 hosts. However, only a limited number of networks can be assigned class A addresses, because the NetID portion of the address contains only 7 bits and the NetID number 127 is reserved. In other words, a class A address should be assigned to the largest networks in the world. A class B address, however, is suited for use by medium-sized networks with up to 65,534 nodes. This is because 16 bits are allocated for use in designating host interfaces. A class C address is meant for a small network because it can only be assigned 254 HostIDs. However, 21 bits are allocated for class C NetIDs, which means that on the Internet, over 2 million networks with class C addresses can exist simultaneously.

An IP address can specify a *particular network* that exists in an internetwork, or it can specify a *particular interface* on a node within a particular network. The former is called a network address, the latter is called a host address. The difference between a network address and an host address is that the HostID portion of a network address will always be set to *zero*. A network address always refers to a specific network, indicated by the NetID. A host address always refers to a specific interface contained within a host and is indicated by the HostID. The network that the host resides in is indicated by the associated NetID.

The usual manner in which internet addresses are represented is called *dotted-decimal notation*. The 32-bit internet address consists of 4 bytes of 8 bits each. Dotted-decimal is a convenient way to notate the bits of the 32-bit address by representing the address as 4 bytes with each byte separated by a *dot:* hence the term "dotted-decimal." For example, the class A address 00000111 00000000 00000000 00000111 would be notated as 7.0.0.7.

In dotted-decimal notation, the range into which the first number falls indicates the class of network into which the address fits. Class A addresses, therefore, fall within a range between 0.0.0.0 and 127.255.255.255, class B between 128.0.0.0 and 191.255.255.255, and class C between 192.0.0.0 and 223.255.255.255.

An IP address must be assigned to every network interface in every node on a network. A router node that interconnects two or more networks will have an address with a different NetID for each network to which it attaches. These nodes are described as *multihomed* because they have more than one interface. Multihomed nodes can also be used to create multiple paths on a network for such use as *load balancing,* which allows two paths to transport data between two nodes, and *high availability,* which provides an alternate path in case of link failure.

Each interface in a node must have a unique address. This is shown in Fig. 4.5, which describes two types of multihomed network nodes. Node A is a router node because it interconnects two networks, net 129 1and net 130, and forwards packets between the two networks. Node B and node C, however, are multihomed, just like node A, but are not functioning as routers. A difference can be seen by the addresses assigned to the network interfaces on the nodes. Node A, the router node, has addresses with different NetIDs (129 and 130), while the NetID (130) for the interfaces for nodes B and C is the same.

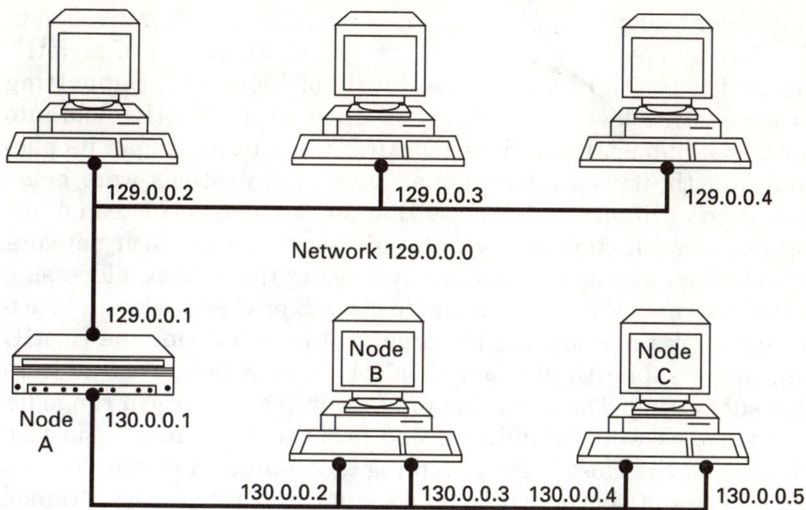

Figure 4.5 Two TCP/IP networks containing multihomed nodes.

It has been mentioned that internet addresses are universal. By that it is meant that the same internet addressing is used throughout the entire Internet. If a person is setting up a simple TCP/IP network in his or her home with three computers attached with Ethernet cable, and this network will never be attached to any other network (never internetworked), then any address class can be used and any network address assigned to this home network.

The situation is different, however, for a company that has decided to become part of the Internet. In this case, the network address must be completely unique from all of the other networks interconnected in the Internet. To achieve this, there is a central authority that assigns internet addresses, called the Internet Network Information Center (InterNIC). The InterNIC only assigns the NetID part of the address. The HostID is always locally administrated.

4.4.2.2 Subnet addressing. The scheme of 32-bit internet addressing was a good method to use in early networking days. However, as the Internet grew in size, it became obvious that so many addresses were being doled out that at some point, the supply of addresses would be depleted. Also, the routing tables on the Internet backbone were becoming too large. It became obvious that the 32-bit address structure needed to be further refined to include another level of networking. With this in mind, a method of *subnet addressing* was devised. Subnet addressing is defined in RFC 950.

Subnet addressing, or *subnetting,* simply makes a further division in the IP address. The three classes, A, B, and C, all consist of a NetID portion and a HostID portion: two levels of hierarchy. Subnetting makes yet another level of hierarchy by dividing the HostID field into two subfields: SubnetID and HostID. After the internet began its phenomenal growth, it was realized that large organizations were being assigned a great number of IP class B and C addresses. Instead of assigning one organization a block of addresses, one for each network the organization has or expects to have, using the subnet addressing feature of internet addressing, a single class B or C address can be assigned to the organization and the organization can divide the HostID portion, using subnetting. Class B is the most widely used address class for subnetting. The class B address contains too large a range for hosts: A network would require 65,535 hosts to max out the HostID. By subdividing the HostID field, making a certain part of it indicate a further division of the network, much more mileage can be attained from the internet addressing structure. Figures 4.6 and 4.7 illustrate the principle of subnetting an internet address.

Figure 4.6 shows two networks with two nodes in each, with a link from one connecting with the Internet using a router. The two class B

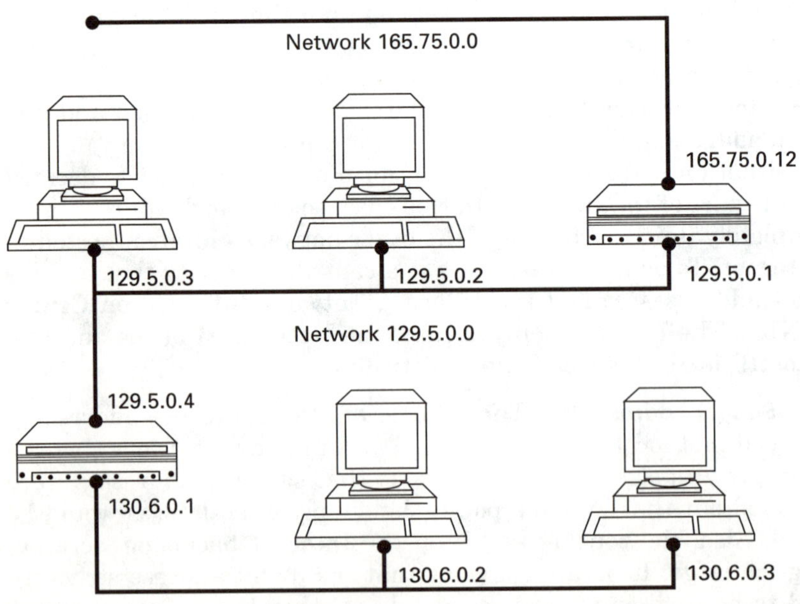

Figure 4.6   Two networks connected to IP network 165.75.0.0.

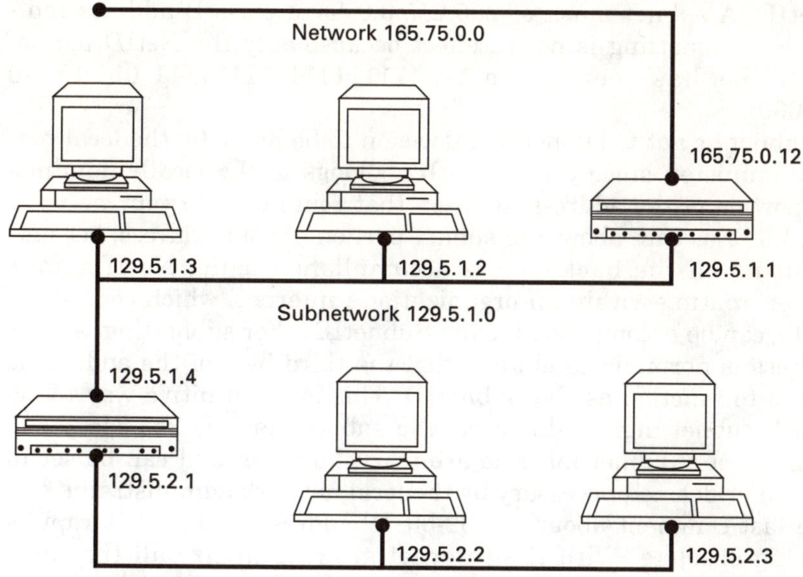

Figure 4.7   Two subnetworks connected to IP network 165.75.0.0.

addresses assigned to the two networks are 129.5.0.0 and 130.6.0.0. Incoming datagrams from the Internet destined for either network come to interface 165.75.0.12 because the router on the 165 network that is connected to our two networks has two additional entries in its routing table, one for each network. In Fig. 4.7 a single class B address has been used and the two networks are separated using subnetting. The NetID for both networks is 129.5.0.0. Using subnetting, one of the two-node networks is 129.5.1.0 and the other is 129.5.2.0. The third byte of the internet address is the subnet number. Using this scheme, 254 subnets can be defined for network 129.5.0.0 (129.5.1.0 through 129.5.254.0) and each subnet can have 254 node interfaces defined (129.0.x.1 through 129.0.x.254).

Subnetting is controlled by a *subnet mask*. A subnet mask is a 32-bit field, just like an internet address, but it is used only to store the pattern that separates the HostID into its host and subnet components. This is accomplished by all the bits that are used for the NetID and the SubnetID being set to 1 in the subnet mask. For example, using dotted-decimal notation, if the NetID is 129.5.0.0 and the subnet mask is set to 255.255.255.0, then the third byte is the subnet portion of the address. We can tell this because we already know that it is a class B address, so we know that the first two bytes constitute the NetID. Therefore, the third byte, since it is all 1s (255 = 11111111), is the

SubnetID. A subnet mask of 255.255.0.0 for a class B address indicates that subnetting is not in effect because only the NetID part of the address has been set to 1s: (11111111 11111111 00000000 00000000).

To subnet or not to subnet is a decision to be made by the local network administer, since the SubnetID belongs to the locally administered portion of the address. Routers that route data to your network do not know or care about the subnet portion of your address, because all routing on the backbone is accomplished using NetIDs only. However, routing within an organization's internet, which consists of subnets, can be accomplished using SubnetIDs. For subnetting, a class B address is normally used and often the third byte of the address is assigned to function as the SubnetID. This is an intuitive way to accomplish subnetting. In this case, the subnet mask is 255.255.255.0. The choice of a subnet mask is arbitrary, however, and can be set in any manner deemed necessary by the local network administrator.

One last comment about the 32-bit IP address is that it is rapidly becoming obsolete. With the Internet growing in size all the time, available addresses are being assigned rapidly. Over half of the class B addresses have already been allocated at the time of this writing. Ways to deal with this problem, such as *classless interdomain routing* (CIDR) and IP version 6 (also called IPng) will not be discussed in this chapter; interested readers are referred to the many TCP/IP books that are currently available.

4.4.2.3 Broadcasting and multicasting.

The Internet Protocol allows both broadcasting and multicasting of datagrams, and both of these services are enabled by using specific forms of IP addressing.

A connectionless network layer provides the ability to transfer single packets of data through the network to an endpoint. Each packet has a header which contains the address of the destination user. Since there is no predefined connection between endpoints and each packet of data contains its destination address, a connectionless network layer can optionally provide the means to deliver a single packet of data to more than one endpoint by using a method of addressing that allows a single address to designate more than one endpoint recipient. This is what broadcasting and multicasting implement. *Multicasting* is the transmission of a datagram to multiple network addresses and *broadcasting* is the transmission of a datagram to an entire network (or subnetwork).

Broadcasting is enabled in IP networks by a *broadcast address,* which uses a reserved feature of IP addressing by which the NetID, SubnetID, and/or HostID portion of the address is set to 1s. A full IP broadcast address is 255.255.255.255. This is an address with every bit set to 1. A datagram using the full broadcast address as the destination should be sent to every interface in every reachable network. However, most routers will not allow these broadcasts to pass through them. Broadcast datagrams can be sent to specific networks by populating the NetID portion of an address with a correct network address, then setting all the bits in the HostID portion to 1s. For example, using a class B network of 129.5.0.0, the broadcast address for every interface on that network would be 129.5.255.255. Routers will forward these datagrams because routers look only at the NetIDs. An optional feature in some routers, however, can be used to disable broadcast messages that may be enabled in other networks.

The principle of broadcasting to specific networks is the same for subnetworks. An example of this could be network 129.5.2.0 and a subnet mask of 255.255.255.0 (subnet 2 on network 129.5.0.0). A destination broadcast address of 129.5.2.255 will send a datagram to every interface on subnet 129.5.2.0.

Multicasting is a subset of broadcasting. Multicasting is similar to broadcasting because it sends a single datagram to multiple locations. However, multicasting does not send the datagram to all interfaces in a network, but to specific IP addresses: addresses which belong to a *multicast group*. Multicasting is discussed further in Sec. 4.4.6.

Multicasting uses an additional address class called the *multicast address*. The multicast address is one of two classes of addresses defined in addition to the three that have already been introduced. These additional classes are class D and E addresses. Class D is the multicast address and class E addresses are reserved for future use. Class D and E addresses are shown in Fig. 4.8. Multicasting has not been widely implemented at the time of this writing, but it could replace broadcasting in cases of, say, a client looking for servers.

Two more reserved address formats need to be mentioned. Two class A addresses are reserved: 127.0.0.0 and 0.0.0.0. The former is the network number for the *loopback* address. The latter is a special address used internally by internet routines, the most notable being bootp. It is also the *default* route. The loopback address is defined in most TCP/IP implementations and is an address that indicates that datagrams sent to it will always loop back to the same node. It is often used by implementors and programmers who are testing TCP/IP applications and wish to retain both communication endpoints on the same machine. Usually the loopback address is defined as 127.0.0.1 and the name *localhost* is assigned to it.

4.4.3 IP fragmentation

The last feature of IP to be described is the use of fragmentation. The IP layer, being a network layer, must provide a seamless network layer across an internet composed of many different data link layers.

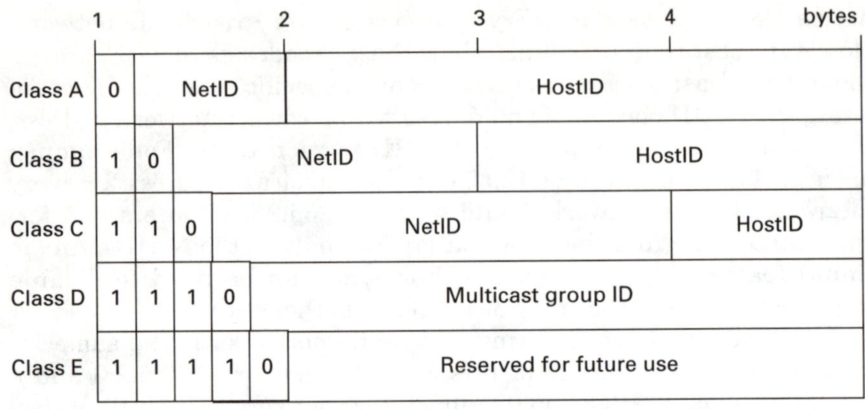

Class A range = 0.0.0.0 to 127.255.255.255
Class B range = 128.0.0.0 to 191.255.255.255
Class C range = 192.0.0.0 to 223.255.255.255
Class D range = 224.0.0.0 to 239.255.255.255
Class E range = 240.0.0.0 to 247.255.255.255

Figure 4.8   IP address classes A through E.

Because different data link layers have different restrictions, different *Maximum Transmission Unit* (MTU) sizes may be imposed on the network layer above. The MTU is the size of the largest frame that a data link layer protocol can accept. If an MTU is encountered that is smaller than the size of the IP datagram being sent, then the IP datagram must be *fragmented,* meaning that it must be cut into two or more smaller pieces, then reassembled at the final host destination. The parameters for fragmentation, should it occur, are stored in the IP header, and each fragment is given a separate header.

The specifics of IP fragmentation will not be dealt with here, and again the reader is referred to one of the excellent books on the subject of TCP/IP.

4.4.4 Routing

Routing is performed in an internet by specifically configuring a node that is common among two or more networks and that routes IP datagram traffic from one to another. In the original ARPAnet, these nodes were called the IMP processors, but later they became known as internet gateways, as we have explained. The gateway, or routing, function can be set up on any node in a TCP/IP network, but pioneering companies such as Cisco Systems, Wellfleet, and Proteon began manufacturing routers as separate, configurable units that could be purchased for use in private networks. These became very popular. The term "gateway" has evolved into the term "router" which, by the early 1990s, has become a very common term to describe the "black box," or a separate, configurable unit sold by manufacturers. When the term "router" is used, however, it does not necessarily refer to a "black box" type of router, because routing is a software function that can be implemented on almost any computer. Commercial routers are computers that are dedicated to the function of routing.

The developers of the original "black box" routers took the idea of the ARPAnet gateway nodes and applied the concept to a specific, configurable unit that was dedicated to a specific purpose. Of course, these routers offer many more features than are found in traditional IP routing software, and they are much more flexible and useful than a simple internet node configured to perform routing. Commercial routers can handle such tasks as dealing with multiple transport and routing protocols, filtering packets by administrator-defined parameters, user authentication, logging, broadcast traffic isolation, encapsulation of data from one network type into network layer packets routable in another type of network, and performing such nonrouter-related functions as data link layer *spoofing,* which terminates data link layer polling at a router in order to prevent needless traffic from being sent across a network.

Routing is a function of the network layer. When datagrams pass through a routing node in an internet, the headers must be checked for the destination network address, then a routing table is consulted to determine to which of the router's interfaces a datagram must be sent and what the IP address of the next *hop* (routing node) in the network is if the destination is not reachable directly. Every host in any internet has a routing table, even if there are only two hosts on the network and no other networks are interconnected. In a routing node, this table is maintained either manually, which is called *static* routing, or by means of special software programs, which is called *dynamic* routing. In the Unix environment, static routing is defined by means of a *route* command, which is used to add or delete routes from the routing table.

Static routes are defined by the network administrator. Dynamic routing is accomplished by using *routing protocols.* These protocols take care of the details of routing, which include building routing tables and adapting to changing network conditions.

Dynamic routing can be performed by installing freely available software, such as the Gateway Routing Daemon (gated) from Cornell or the "routed" program which is usually bundled with Berkeley-flavored Unix systems. There are two types of routing protocols: interior routing protocols and exterior routing protocols.

4.4.4.1   Interior routing protocols.   An *interior,* or *intradomain,* routing protocol is used to route inside an *autonomous system* (AS). An autonomous system is a collection of networks tied together with a particular interior routing protocol. Usually this collection of networks is maintained by a single organization. An example of an AS is a large corporation with many internal networks. Another name for an autonomous system is a *routing domain.* Autonomous systems can be interconnected with each other using *inter*domain routing nodes which implement exterior routing protocols. Figure 4.9 demonstrates this concept. This figure consists of two autonomous systems. The one on the left is two networks (129.5.0.0 and 130.7.0.0) and the one on the right also consists of two networks (162.5.0.0 and 172.6.0.0). Each of the autonomous systems employs an *intra*domain routing protocol to route data between the two networks of which it is comprised. Additionally, the routing nodes on each autonomous system are connected with each other and interdomain routing is performed between the two autonomous systems. Interdomain routing is really a higher tier of routing that ties together autonomous systems similarly to the way intradomain routers tie together computing nodes.

There are two main AS routing protocols in use in the Internet and on TCP/IP networks. The "old standard" is called the Routing Information Protocol (RIP); the other, written to improve on RIP, is called Open Shortest Path First (OSPF).

Routing Information Protocol (RIP).   The *Routing Information Protocol,* introduced in Chap. 3, was developed at Xerox PARC to dynamically route the PARC Universal Packet (PUP) networking protocol. Later it was improved to also route Xerox Network Systems (XNS). Later it became the inspiration for the BSD Unix implementation used in TCP/IP networks.

RIP (defined for IP in RFC 1058) is a very simple routing protocol that uses what is called a *distance vector* algorithm. Using this algorithm, each routing node in an autonomous system sends its routing table to its neighboring AS routing nodes. Each routing node then updates its own routing table with information received from its neighboring routing nodes. This information consists of the addresses of destination networks reachable from that routing node and the distance to that network measured in hops. A routing metric is a figure that describes the cost of a particular route. RIP uses *hops* as its routing metric. The hop metric generally indicates the number of networks that must be traversed in order for a datagram to reach its destination.

Once every routing node in an AS has sent updates to its neighbors and all of the routing tables have been updated using the information received from the updates, each routing node's routing table will point

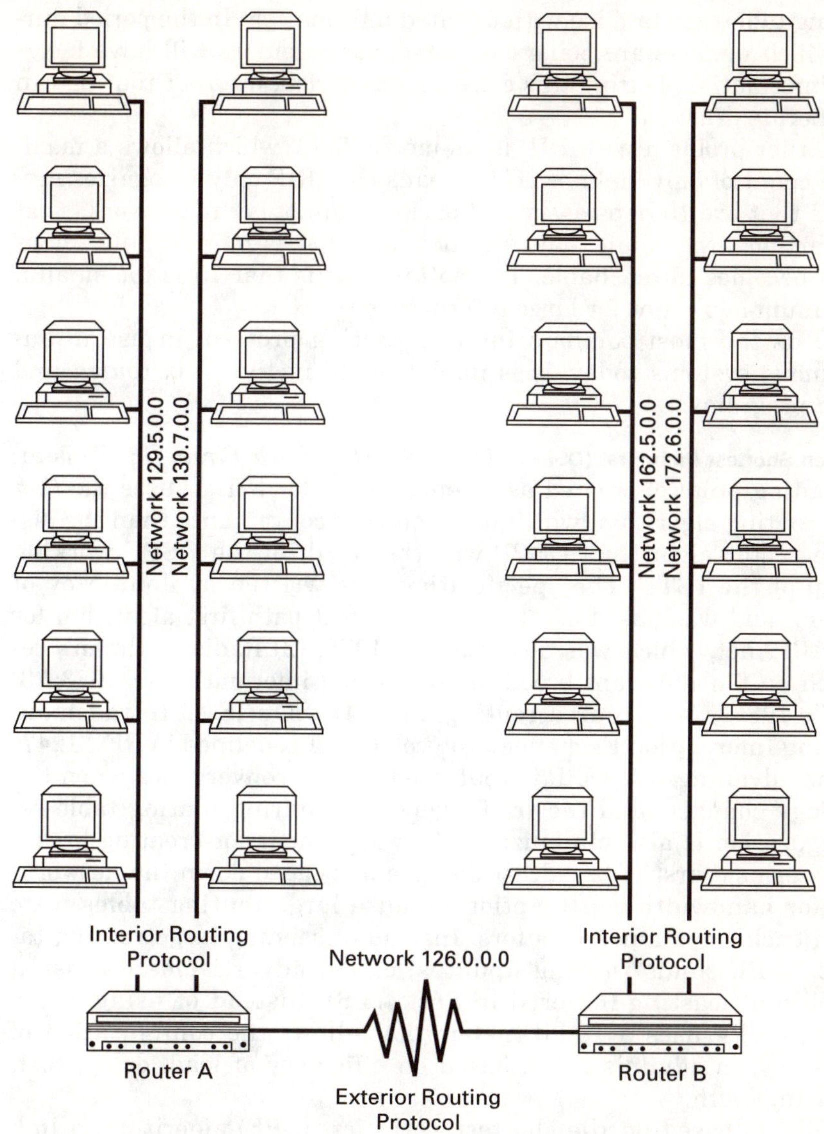

Figure 4.9 Autonomous systems interconnected using an exterior routing protocol.

to all possible reachable networks along with the distance to those networks measured in hops.

Distance vector-based routing protocols have distinct disadvantages. The main problem is their *convergence* time, which is unacceptably long. Convergence is a term used to describe the time that it takes for routing updates to propagate across networks and (thus) for all the routing tables to stabilize with updated information. In the period during which updates are being circulated, some routers will have incorrect information. During this convergence period, internet routing can degenerate drastically.

Another problem with RIP is its metric field, which allows a maximum count of only 15 hops. This means that RIP only recognizes networks that are 15 hops away and packets cannot get to networks that are farther away than that. Any network that is more than 15 hops away becomes unreachable. The bottom line is that 15 is too small a maximum hop count for large internetworks.

RIP is the most common interior routing protocol in use in autonomous systems today. It is implemented in the Unix *routed* and *gated* programs.

Open Shortest Path First (OSPF).   *Open Shortest Path First* (OSPF) is an IP routing protocol created as a replacement for RIP. It uses the *link state* routing algorithm, which has a quicker convergence than the distance vector algorithm. OSPF was the result of the OSPF working group of the IETF. The specification was written by John Moy of Proteon and was based on (1) BBN's shortest path first algorithm for the ARPAnet, which was developed in 1978; (2) Radia Perlman's research on fault-tolerant broadcast of routing information in 1983; (3) BBN's 1986 work on area routing; and (4) ISO's IS-IS Intradomain Routing Information Exchange Protocol. OSPF is defined in RFC 1247.

One advantage of OSPF is that it has a fast convergence when the topology changes, and the traffic generated during routing table reconfiguration is also minimized. RIP was famous for creating broadcast storms (burst of broadcast datagrams bogged down the network) and for bandwidth consumption because large routing tables were being exchanged among routers. Instead of sending large routing tables, OSPF sends routing updates, called advertisements, using IGMP multicasting (covered in Sec. 4.4.6). Instead of using a hop count, OSPF uses a 16-bit metric that allows the configuration of routes by an administrator, based on efficiency of load, delay, cost, and bandwidth.

OSPF is based on the shortest path first (SPF) algorithm, a link state algorithm. Current routing algorithms are based on either the distance vector or the link state algorithm. It has been shown that link state algorithms are better than distance vector algorithms for interior routing protocols because link state converges quickly and distance vector does not.

ES-IS/IS-IS.   There are other intradomain routing protocols. The most important are the OSI protocols developed at DEC for DECnet Phase V called ES-IS and IS-IS. ES-IS and IS-IS were developed to route the

OSI ConectionLess-mode Network Protocol (CLNP), but both have been modified to route TCP/IP (or both TCP/IP and OSI together) as well. *End System to Intermediate System* (ES-IS) is used for end systems to communicate with intermediate systems. An intermediate system is a node with routing abilities (like the IP "gateway"), and an end system is a node without routing intelligence. *Intermediate System to Intermediate System* (IS-IS) is used by routers to communicate with other routers in the same domain. IS-IS employs a link state algorithm and is very similar to OSPF.

Hello. The interior routing protocol known as *hello* uses network delay as the metric for choosing a route instead of hops. Delay is calculated by sending a *hello* datagram to the destination to see how long it takes to get there and back. Hello is not very common and can be considered obsolete. However, it was the interior routing protocol used in the original NSFNET backbone for the internet. It is described in RFC 891.

4.4.4.2 Exterior routing protocols. An exterior, or interdomain, routing protocol is used to route data *between* autonomous systems. Exterior routing is the routing performed on the internet backbone network. Exterior routing protocols run in the nodes that link the autonomous systems to a backbone or to other autonomous systems, and these routing nodes communicate with each other to exchange routing information, the information concerning which networks are reachable inside their autonomous systems. Autonomous systems accomplish their own routing needs by employing RIP or OSPF, then advertise their interior networks to the internet by implementing an exterior routing protocol on the router with which the AS connects to the internet. This makes interior networks reachable and available to internet users.

Exterior Gateway Protocol (EGP). The Internet's most common exterior routing protocol is called the *Exterior Gateway Protocol* (EGP) and is documented in RFC 904. It has a lot of problems, but nevertheless it has tied together the internet routing domains for many years. The way it works is that a router in an autonomous system is designated as an EGP router and it establishes a relationship with an EGP in another autonomous system. The EGP router in each AS has a routing table that lists all the IP addresses of networks in its routing domain. It forwards that list to neighbor EGP routers. These routing updates are similar to distance vector updates, but no metrics are involved. A polling interval controls the interval of time that elapses between transmission of updates. Updates contain network *reachability* information: particular networks are reachable through particular routers.

As the Internet grew, EGP became more unmanageable with its

sending of huge routing tables. Also, the fact that there were no metrics to help determine routes and the fact that EGP nodes had to be configured so that no loops could occur in the topology were big disadvantages. A replacement was looked at.

Border Gateway Protocol (BGP). The proposed replacement for EGP is called the *Border Gateway Protocol* (BGP). BGP is a distance vector protocol defined in RFC 1267. BGP represents an improvement over EGP because it solves the three major problems of EGP: It does not require a loop-free topology, it has metrics, and after all the initial routing information has been sent, BGP routers transmit only the changes, or *deltas,* that occur in the routing tables, rather than retransmitting the entire tables themselves.

BGP routing tables contain paths to destination networks rather than just whether that destination is reachable or not. The paths are sequences of autonomous system numbers. All available paths to a particular network are in the table, but the decision of which route to use is based on policy. This is called *policy-based routing:* A routing policy is considered when determining a route, rather than just a hop count. Policies consist of information that is manually placed in the system to help determine the path to take in the case of multiple routes. Policies are different from metrics. A metric simply states the cost to a destination; a policy is more logical and can become complicated. It will say, for example, "I am willing to go through this route if such-and-such is the case; however, if this-and-such is happening and that-and-this isn't, then I won't." After a policy chooses a route, the route is broadcast to neighbors.

InterDomain Routing Protocol (IDRP). The *InterDomain Routing Protocol* (IDRP) started out as BGP with OSI addressing added by ISO. Once it got to the ISO, however, it started to change and a lot of improvements were made. One change is that IDRP uses metrics instead of policies.

Readers interested in more information about routing protocols are directed to Radia Perlman's *Interconnections: Bridges and Routers* (1992), listed in the Bibliography.

4.4.5 The Internet Control Message Protocol (ICMP)

The *Internet Control Message Protocol* (ICMP), a protocol belonging to the TCP/IP network layer, is used for sending error messages and performing other duties that are associated with routing. ICMP is defined in RFC 792.

ICMP is the error and condition reporting mechanism for the Internet Protocol and provides a way for IP routines in individual nodes to communicate with each other. ICMP uses a defined set of messages, of which there are two types: error notifications and queries. Queries are further divided into two types: requests and replies.

ICMP is similar to a transport layer protocol in that it has its own ICMP header and the entire message is carried inside an IP datagram. Figure 4.10 shows the format for ICMP messages. Following the IP header is the first byte of the ICMP message, *type,* which describes which particular ICMP message is being sent. ICMP consists of 15 different messages, which are listed, along with their message type values, in Table 4.1. The *code* field follows the type field and is used to give additional information about the message described in *type,* if more information is needed. Following the checksum, which is calculated for the ICMP message, is an optional data field that is message-dependent. For example, ICMP messages that report error conditions put the IP header and first 64 bits of the problem-producing datagram in this field.

IP header 20 bytes	Type 1 byte	Code 1 byte	Check- sum 2 bytes	Data variable length

Figure 4.10   The ICMP message.

TABLE 4.1   ICMP Messages

0	Echo reply
3	Destination unreachable
4	Source quench
5	Redirect
8	Echo request
9	Router advertisement
10	Router solicitation
11	Time exceeded
12	Parameter problem
13	Timestamp request
14	Timestamp reply
15	Information request
16	Information reply
17	Address mask request
18	Address mask reply

ICMP message number 8, the echo request, is used to solicit an ICMP echo reply, message 0, from another network node. This ICMP echo request and reply are the basis of the well-known internet *ping* program, which allows a user to "ping" another host to see if it is "alive." Ping, short for Packet InterNet Groper (believe it or not), goes into a loop sending an ICMP echo request then waiting for an ICMP echo reply. If the reply is returned, ping displays a message in the user's window. Another ICMP message is the "destination unreachable" message (type 3) that is returned by a routing node when a destination address cannot be reached. This ICMP message is the source of "destination unreachable" messages that are sometimes displayed in a user's window when a TCP/IP program is trying to establish a connection and network routing is either not set up correctly, or segments of the network are down.

Other important ICMP messages are the "source quench" message (type 4), and "redirect" (type 5). When a node is receiving datagrams too quickly and is forced to discard them, it sends an ICMP "source quench" message to the originator of the datagrams to request that the rate of datagram transmission being sent be slowed down. The "redirect" message is sent by routers to inform a node that a route that it is using is not the best route and requests that the host change its routing table to reflect the better route.

IP routines know if an incoming IP datagram contains an ICMP message by interrogating the IP header *protocol* field (refer to Fig. 4.3). The protocol field will contain a 1 if the data within the datagram are an ICMP message. ICMP can be accessed from application programs by using the raw socket interface, which will be described in Chap. 5.

4.4.6   The Internet Group Management Protocol (IGMP)

The *Internet Group Management Protocol* (IGMP) is the IP protocol used for multicasting. It is defined in RFC 1112.

Multicasting, introduced in Sec. 4.4.2.3, provides the ability to send a single copy of a datagram to multiple nodes at the same time. Multicasting is not yet widely implemented at the time of this writing, but it is a technology with great promise. It provides an ideal means for sending a packet to multiple sites without having to flood the entire network in the way that a broadcast message does.

The internet protocol suite implements multicasting in the network layer using IGMP. Some LAN protocols, such as Ethernet and token ring, support a feature called *hardware multicasting,* and IGMP makes use of the underlying hardware multicast feature if it is available. Multicasting can span more than a single network when networks are interconnected with routers that have the multicast feature installed in them.

Multicasting is accomplished by defining a *multicast group address,* and multicast datagrams are sent to the entire group of IP addresses that are designated by the group address. All addressable units in a network that are to receive a multicast message destined for a group can use IGMP to dynamically *join* the group. The multicast group address is indicated by a specific class of IP address called a class D "multicast" address. It will be recalled that the class D address, as shown in Fig. 4.8, always contains the high-order 4 bits set to 1110. The remaining 28 bits of the 32-bit address contain the multicast group ID. In dotted-decimal notation, multicast addresses fall within the range of 224.0.0.0 and 239.255.255.255.

A multicast group is a group of nodes that listen for a particular multicast group address. Hosts that receive multicast datagrams belong to one or more *multicast groups.* IGMP is the protocol that is used to regulate multicast groups. Like ICMP, IGMP has a message which is enclosed in an IP datagram (Fig. 4.11). There are two IGMP message types: Type 1 is a query, which is sent by routers, and type 2 is a response, sent by hosts. Routers query hosts to determine which hosts belong to which multicast groups.

IP multicasting is, at least at the time of this writing, still not very widely implemented, and not every device or all software supports the multicasting feature or IGMP. The IP demultiplexing routines in individual nodes know if an IP datagram contains an IGMP message by interrogating the IP header *protocol* field (refer to Fig. 4.3). The protocol field will contain a 2 if the data within the datagram are an IGMP message.

4.5 The Transport Layer

As we have seen, the network layer of TCP/IP is implemented using the Internet Protocol (IP) which is a communications protocol that provides "best effort" service where datagrams arrive in any order and can be discarded anywhere along the path to their destination. In order to provide a reliable data delivery service, the transport layer contains a fully reliable transport layer protocol called the *Transmission Control*

IP header 20 bytes	Version 4 bits	Type 4 bits	Reserved 1 byte	Check- sum 2 bytes	Class D address 4 bytes

Figure 4.11 The IGMP message.

Protocol (TCP). TCP uses the datagram services of IP, but before passing packets of data to the network layer, it assigns sequence numbers to individual packets to ensure that they will be delivered to the end user in the correct order. TCP performs error checking when data arrive at a destination to determine if the data have been altered; if packets have been discarded or lost in the network, TCP ensures that the originator of the lost packets retransmits them. Additionally, TCP monitors the flow of data to help prevent network congestion.

The transport layer has an address which is used in addition to the addressing provided by the network layer. The transport layer address adds to the capability of network layer addressing by indicating the endpoint process to which a datagram must be delivered. The transport address is called a *port number.*

If an application program wants to use the reliable transport service, it issues API calls which indicate TCP as the transport service. If an unreliable datagram service is preferred, the transport layer contains another protocol called the *User Datagram Protocol* (UDP), which provides a one-to-one mapping of a transport layer datagram to an IP datagram. UDP, like TCP, has a transport layer header which contains the port number that pinpoints the destination endpoint.

The transport layer endpoints, the UDP and TCP ports, are described internally by a specific number. To make port numbers more user-friendly, specific names are assigned to the numbers. The name-to-number mappings are contained in a TCP/IP file called *services.* On Unix platforms, the services file usually resides in the etc directory and is known as /etc/services. Port numbers in the range from 1 through 1023 are reserved and are called *well-known* ports. They have the distinction of being well known because their numbers are known universally on all machines in which internet protocols reside. These well-known ports belong to the universal services of the internet environment. For example, the telnet server always waits for incoming telnet requests on TCP port 23. The ftp servers always wait on TCP port 21. These well-known port assignments are managed by a body called the Internet Assigned Numbers Authority (IANA). Custom applications can use ports in the 1024–5000 range, which are the "anything goes" ports. The services file will be discussed further in Chap. 5, and an example is shown in Table 5.7.

Our discussion of internet transport layer protocols will begin by introducing TCP.

4.5.1 Transmission Control Protocol (TCP)

The *Transmission Control Protocol* (TCP) is a connection-oriented protocol that provides a reliable transfer of data between two network endpoints. Since reliability cannot be assumed from the IP network layer, TCP, in the transport layer, must provide the reliability itself. Data that are exchanged between endpoints in TCP always follow a specific path through the network between the endpoints. This path is represented by a connection. A connection is established between two endpoints before data are transferred, then data are transferred in this connection following rules imposed by the TCP protocol. Connections are always point-to-point, meaning there are only two users—one at each end of the connection. There is no broadcasting or multicasting using TCP.

TCP is based on the client-server model. One end of the connection is the *server,* which, when in an unconnected state, waits, or *listens,* for incoming connection requests. The other end is the *client,* which sends a connection request to a waiting server. After an initiation exchange, or *handshake,* has taken place, a connection is established. All data that are transferred are transferred on the connection and are in a *byte stream* where records are not delineated. Since a byte stream is simply a chunk of data, all record delineation must take place within an application. TCP is defined in RFC 793.

4.5.1.1 TCP services. TCP offers a number of transport protocol services.

- *Reliable full-duplex data transfer.* Reliability is accomplished in TCP by use of time-outs and retransmissions. After a stream of data is sent in a connection, a timer is set and if an acknowledgment for the data has not been received by the time that the timer has "popped," TCP retransmits it. When a stream of data is received by either end of a connection, TCP routines compare a checksum contained in the TCP header with a checksum that is computed on the received data. If the two do not match, the data are discarded and no acknowledgment is sent. The other end of the connection, when it times-out, will then retransmit the data. If the checksum for the retransmitted data matches the calculated checksum, then the data are accepted and acknowledged. A TCP checksum spans both the header and the data and its compass is end-to-end, meaning that checksums are computed only at the endpoints.

- *Segmentation.* TCP performs segmentation which breaks data up into sizes that are acceptable for the network layer below it. While packets in the IP layer were called datagrams, TCP packets are called *segments.*

- *Sequencing.* Because of the unreliable nature of the IP network layer, which transports segments in datagrams, duplication, and random ordering can occur. TCP ensures that data are delivered to a final destination in correct order and without duplicates by using sequence numbers. Each segment is assigned a sequence number that identifies the byte-offset into a data stream with which the segment begins.

- *Flow control.*   Each end of a connection advertises a window size, which is the size of that endpoint's receive buffer. Each time a connection endpoint receives a stream of data, it sends an acknowledgment back to the sending endpoint. Coupled with the acknowledgment is what is called a *window advertisement,* which specifies the number of bytes the endpoint is willing to receive. In this way, the amount of data that flows from one endpoint to the other is controlled. If an endpoint is receiving data too quickly, it can shrink the size of data that is next sent to it. It can even stop the flow of data by advertising a window size of zero.

- *Urgent mode.*   A special flag/pointer combination in the TCP header delineates data in the stream that has been marked as *urgent* and must be handled with priority.

4.5.1.2   The TCP header.   Before examining the way that TCP establishes and terminates connections, a look at the TCP header is in order. Figure 4.12 shows the position of the header in an IP datagram. The layout of the TCP header is shown in Fig. 4.13.

The header is placed at the front of every TCP segment. The first 4 bytes of the header contain the 16-bit source port number and the 16-bit destination port number. These tell the network routines where the segment is from and where it is going. The exact nodes on which these ports reside, of course, must be determined from the IP addresses in the adjoining IP header. The next field in the header is the 32-bit sequence number assigned to this segment, followed by the 32-bit acknowledgment number. The acknowledgment number is the value of the next sequence number the receiver expects to receive. Following the acknowledgment number is a 4-bit header length that contains the number of 32-bit words in the header, then after six reserved bits a 6-bit flag field follows. These six flags (Table 4.2) are important in the interchange of segments during TCP connection establishment, termination, and data transfer and will be explained

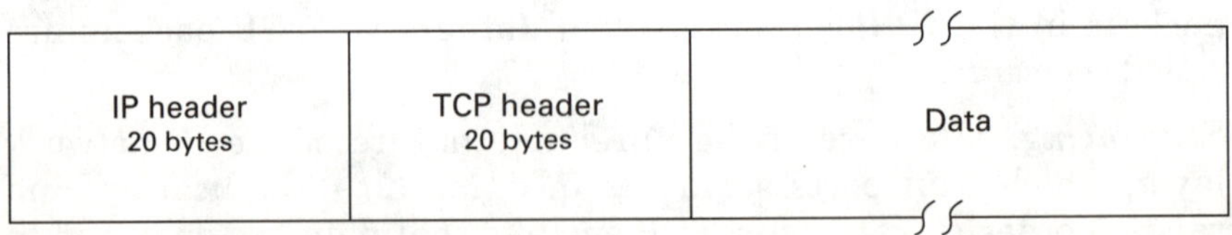

Figure 4.12   TCP data in an IP datagram.

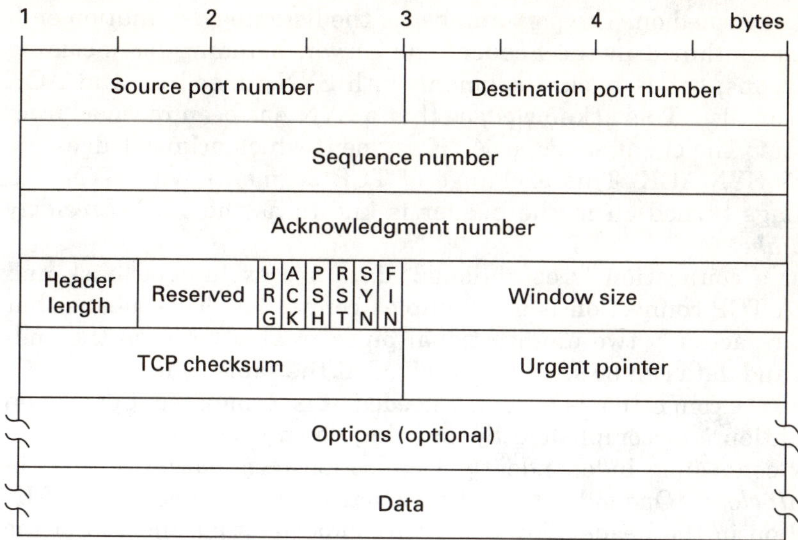

Figure 4.13　The TCP header.

TABLE 4.2　Six Flags over TCP

URG	Urgent
ACK	Acknowledgment
PSH	Push data (flush outgoing data buffer)
RST	Reset
SYN	Synchronize sequence numbers
FIN	Finished

shortly. Following the flags are three 16-bit fields: window size (for window advertisement), checksum, and an urgent pointer that indicates where urgent data ends (the last byte of urgent data in the stream). This field is valid only when the URG flag is set.

Many internet service programs and utilities use the services of TCP. Examples are ftp, rlogin, and telnet. The IP routines know which datagrams contain TCP segments because the IP header's protocol field contains a 6.

4.5.1.3　Connection establishment and termination.　TCP connections are established and a connection state is maintained by segments that have particular flags in the flag field of the header set. When a TCP connection is requested, the client sends a segment with the

SYN flag turned on. The port number of the listening destination endpoint is contained in the header. The server, listening for incoming connections, sends back a segment with SYN turned on and ACK turned on also. This acknowledges that a SYN has been received from the client. The client sends an ACK segment which acknowledges the server's SYN/ACK. This exchange of TCB segments with SYN and ACK flags turned on in the header is known as the TCP *three-way handshake.*

After a connection is established, data are exchanged back and forth. A TCP connection is a full-duplex connection. This means that there are actually two unidirectional pipes created between the endpoints and data can be sent and received at the same time.

When the connection is no longer needed, it is terminated. Connection termination is accomplished by shutting down each side of the full-duplex connection independently. Connection termination consists of two *half-closes.* One side of the connection sends a segment with FIN turned on in the header flag field. This indicates that one end of the connection wishes to stop sending data and is closing down the outgoing side of the connection. This FIN is usually sent when the application performs a close. The recipient of the FIN sends back a segment with ACK turned on. A half-close has been performed and one side of the connection remains active. The active endpoint can continue sending data until it decides to stop. When it has completed sending data, it sends a segment with the FIN flag turned on and waits for a segment with the ACK flag turned on to arrive from the other endpoint. When this ACK segment is received, the full-duplex connection is fully terminated.

4.5.1.4 Additional TCP functions.   Because of space limitations, the description of TCP in this chapter is limited to the very basics. Readers who are interested in learning more about TCP are referred to the series of books mentioned previously: *TCP/IP Illustrated* by Stevens (1994, 1995, 1996), or *Internetworking with TCP/IP* by Comer (1991, 1993). These are listed in the Bibliography. The *TCP/IP Illustrated* series is the more recent of the two series and is highly recommended.

The connection initiation and termination process of TCP described in Sec. 4.5.1.3 is only one example of how the flag field in the segment header is used. Of interest, and importance to those individuals diagnosing problems with and otherwise working with active TCP connections, is the process which TCP continually goes through while a connection is in use. This is defined by what is called a *finite state machine,* which designates the various states that a TCP connection can be in at any time and describes what takes place as communication flow causes a transition from one state to another. Also of interest is the manner in which segment transmission is controlled using the principle of a *sliding window*. Additionally, TCP has many algorithms which were developed to control the flow of data in networks. Of note are the congestion control algorithms such as Van Jacobson's slow start and congestion avoidance algorithms mentioned earlier. These are formulas that help alleviate the conditions that can lead to network congestion. For example, the congestion avoidance algorithm was created on the assumption that when segments are not acknowledged, it is in most cases because congestion has caused routers to discard datagrams (as opposed to datagrams being discarded because of corrupted data). The algorithm causes the number of segments that are sent to decrease when symptoms of congestion are present.

4.5.2   User Datagram Protocol (UDP)

The *User Datagram Protocol* (UDP) is a connectionless transport protocol. Since most of the advantages of a transport layer are contained in connection-oriented services, a connectionless transport layer has little to offer. Basically, UDP is provided in the transport layer for users who wish to send datagrams. UDP simply creates a UDP datagram and then maps it into an IP datagram. The UDP header (Fig. 4.14) contains the destination and source port numbers which are necessary in the transport layer. UDP is defined in RFC 768.

UDP offers the use of the datagram service of the network layer and can be employed when an application itself desires to take care of the details of sequencing and reliability. It can also be used for a service that does not require reliability. Similar to the IP service that it mimics, UDP is unreliable and can only offer the best-effort service of IP.

A number of systems services use UDP. For example, UDP datagrams are used by the Domain Name Service (DNS), Remote Procedure Call (RPC), Network Computing System (NCS), Simple Network Management Protocol (SNMP), and Trivial File Transfer Protocol (TFTP). IP services know that an IP datagram maps to a UDP datagram when the IP header's protocol field contains a 17.

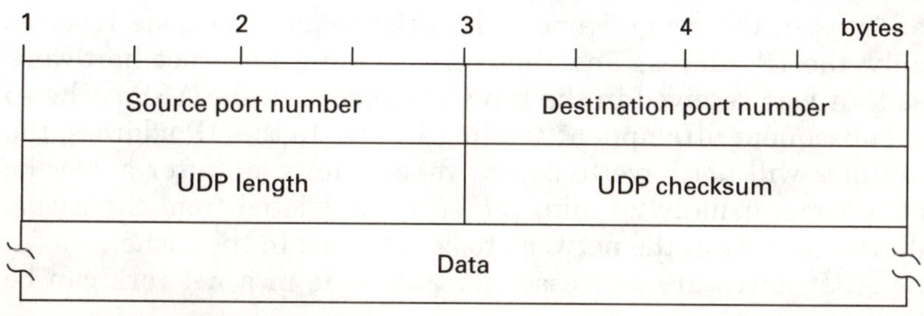

Figure 4.14   The UDP header.

4.6 The Data Link Layer

The internet data link layer contains two optional protocols: the Address Resolution Protocol (ARP) and the Reverse Address Resolution Protocol (RARP).

4.6.1 ARP

The *Address Resolution Protocol* (ARP) works with the protocols of data link layer routines when they need a way to map IP addresses to and from the hardware (also called MAC) addresses of the data link layer. ARP is defined in RFC 826 and was devised in the early 1980s as a way to implement TCP/IP on top of Ethernet LANs. It is used only if it is needed, but it is always present in Ethernet and token ring networks.

Data link layer protocols such as Ethernet get datagrams from the IP layer that are destined to be sent onto the network. The only address the data link layer gets with the packet is the IP address in the IP datagram's header. A table called an *ARP cache* contains mappings of specific IP addresses to their corresponding 48-bit Ethernet *hardware* addresses. Hardware addresses are assigned to Ethernet attachment cards and are the only addresses that Ethernet hardware will acknowledge. The ARP cache is searched, and if an entry with the IP address from the IP datagram header is not found in the table, the 48-bit Ethernet address that will be used to construct a header for an Ethernet frame must be discovered. To accomplish this, the ARP function is called, passing it to the IP address to be resolved. ARP creates a special frame called an *ARP request,* puts the IP address in question in the frame, then sets the destination Ethernet address to *broadcast*. This means that every node on the network will get a copy of this request.

When the individual nodes receive this special ARP broadcast frame, it is passed to their local ARP routines, which check the IP address in the request against the IP address of the node's Ethernet interfaces to see if this is the node that contains the interface that corresponds to the 48-bit Ethernet address. If the addresses match, then the node sends an *ARP reply,* placing the correct Ethernet hardware address in the reply frame. When the requesting node receives this reply, the IP address and the corresponding Ethernet hardware address that was received in the reply are placed in the ARP cache so that on subsequent attempts at sending frames to this IP address, the ARP routines will not have to be reinvoked. However, after a specific amount of time, usually 20 min, the entry is deleted from the cache. This allows changes in the network to be reflected in the cache.

Using ARP, hardware addresses for any node in a network can be retrieved.

4.6.2 RARP

The *Reverse Address Resolution Protocol* (RARP) is similar to ARP but implements IP address resolution for the local node rather than a remote node. It is used by diskless workstations and X terminals to discover their own IP addresses. The service of RARP is needed by these types of units because the IP address for a diskless workstation cannot be retrieved from a configuration file on a local disk drive. RARP is defined in RFC 903.

When it is booted, a diskless workstation can obtain its own IP address by formatting a *RARP request*. This, like the ARP request, is broadcast (the workstation would not know what the address of the node from which to obtain the information would be). The RARP request says: "Help, I am hardware address 'xxx' and will someone please tell me what my IP address is so I can go into normal operation?" A RARP server must be present on the network to respond to these requests. Additionally, it has to know the IP addresses for all potential clients: the X stations and diskless workstations.

4.7   The APIs

Referring back to Fig. 4.2, showing the layers of the internet suite, it can be seen that on top of the transport layer, which contains TCP and UDP, is a thin layer called *APIs*. This layer contains the Application Programming Interfaces (APIs) which allow application programs to access the internet protocol suite. A standard API provides a convenient method of programming network calls, which can be used on many different computer platforms and operating systems. This approach was very successful for TCP/IP.

Two standard APIs are used with the internet stack. The most important is the *sockets* API, which was developed for the C language by the University of California at Berkeley Computer Systems Research Group in 1982. The sockets API provides a set of C function calls which allow full access to the services of not only the transport layer protocols, UDP and TCP, but the network layer protocols such as ICMP as well. This API is described in Chap. 5, so no more will be said about it here.

The other API is the *Transport Layer Interface* (TLI), developed by AT&T and introduced in 1986 in Unix System V, Release 3. TLI provides an interface similar to sockets and uses C-language function calls. TCP/IP was first implemented in the Berkeley version of the Unix operating system, and sockets was the interface provided. TLI provided a retrofit to bring TCP/IP networking capabilities to the original Unix, that of AT&T. TCP/IP was not bundled with AT&T System V, Release 3, so TLI did not have a transport network protocol to work with in the first release. However, TCP and OSI TP4 were included in subsequent releases, and TLI enabled a user to access either one.

TLI is written according to the definition for transport layer services defined in ISO standard 8072, with necessary extensions to provide for non-OSI transport layer standards such as TCP. In recent years, TLI was submitted to X/Open, the vendor consortium that produces standards, and extended by that group. It is now known as the *X/Open Transport Interface* (XTI).

4.8   The Domain Name System

The layers of the internet protocol suite have been described, and the discussion will now turn to other features of TCP/IP that are a part of the overall architecture. The *Domain Name System* (DNS) was created by Paul Mockapetris of the University of Southern California's Information Sciences Institute. DNS was first made available in November 1983 and is defined in RFCs 1034 and 1035.

The purpose of DNS is to provide a database of human-readable names that map to the more abstruse dotted-decimal IP addresses. These DNS names have become commonplace as the ever-present Internet e-mail addresses such as pighed@bork.com or lilly@berkeley.edu. DNS names each represent some specific IP address and must be converted to their IP address equivalents before they can be processed by the IP network layer.

The domain name system is not a centralized repository of names located at some specific site, but is a service that is distributed throughout the Internet. In other words, it is a distributed service, as opposed to a centralized service, and consists of independent *domains,* or sections of the internet.

The structure of DNS is hierarchical, resembling a DOS or Unix file system. At the top is the root domain, similar to a root directory, and underneath are the next levels of domains. There are seven top-level domains, the original seven domains of the internet (Table 4.3). The

TABLE 4.3   The Original Top-Level DNS Domains

com	Commercial organizations
edu	Educational institutions
gov	Governmental bodies
mil	Military organizations
net	Networking organizations, like NSFNET
org	Foundations and related organizations
int	International organizations

hierarchical structure of DNS resembles a tree. Each node in the tree is a domain, and each domain is known by a case-insensitive name of up to 63 characters. Each domain can have any number of users. The *fully qualified name* of any domain consists of the sequence of domain names in a particular branch of the tree, starting from the root with each name separated by a dot (.). The fully qualified name for a domain named "clown," lying directly beneath the top-level domain "com," would be "clown.com." A user named "bozo," located in the clown domain, would be known as "bozo@clown.com" (bozo at clown.com).

At some point in the evolution of DNS, it was felt that the original seven domains were too restrictive, and more top-level domains were added. These newer domains are two-character country names and are described in a document called *ISO 3166: Country Codes*. The two-character name for the United States, "us," is one of them.

Domains are administrated by programs called *name servers*. Name servers contain the information for a part of a domain called a *zone*. A zone consists of all the names for computing nodes within one or more domains administered by the server.

Name servers are accessed by clients called *resolvers*. Resolvers are used by programs that need a name to be resolved into an address. By making a request to a DNS server, the IP address for a host name can be resolved. If the local name server cannot resolve a name, it contacts the name server that can. This is how host names are dynamically resolved into addresses in the Internet.

The most common name server program in use is the *Berkeley Internet Name Domain* (BIND). Written at Berkeley, it is easily and freely available from various internet sources. BIND is the standard program used to implement DNS. It is known in Unix systems as "named," the *name daemon*.

The resolver part of DNS is configured by making entries in the resolv.conf file (/etc/resolv.conf). Resolv.conf can specify the name of a default domain, a list of search domains, and, most important, the IP address of the node in which the local name server is located. Resolvers use this address when sending name queries. The resolver does not exist as a separate program but is implemented as library routines linked into programs that need resolver functionality. Resolver code is accessed by calling the C-language gethostbyname() function, which returns the IP address for a host by passing it the host's DNS name. The gethostbyaddr() function returns a host's name by passing it an IP address.

DNS uses TCP/UDP port 53. UDP is normally used by resolvers for name server queries. TCP is used when data that are more than the maximum length of a UDP datagram need to be transferred.

The "hosts" file plays an important part in DNS. On Unix platforms, it is usually known as /etc/hosts. This file contains static mappings between names and IP addresses and is used by resolvers if a name server cannot be contacted or DNS is not configured. The hosts file can contain name mappings for specific hosts in a network. /etc/networks is used to translate network names into IP addresses.

Interested readers are directed to the somewhat thorough presentation of DNS in Albitz and Liu (1992), *DNS and BIND in a Nutshell,* listed in the Bibliography.

4.9 TCP/IP Utility Programs

A few utility programs associated with TCP/IP on Unix systems have become pretty much synonymous with TCP/IP administration and configuration and appear on many platforms other than Unix. These utilities, ifconfig, netstat, and route, will now be briefly introduced.

4.9.1 Ifconfig

Ifconfig is a BSD Unix utility that is used to configure a network interface. Each network interface attachment card in a Unix system must have an IP address, subnet mask, and broadcast address assigned to it in order to run with TCP/IP. Ifconfig accepts this information, associates it with a particular interface, and adds the information into the IP routing table.

Ifconfig is entered at the command line and has four parameters.

- *Interface.*   This is a name associated with an interface. Typically, in some Unix systems, the name "lan0" is used for a local area network interface. The interface name is an arbitrary name selected by the administrator and is originally created using a system management program such as "sam" in HP/UX or "smit" in AIX. These programs assign the interface name to an actual network interface. Ifconfig makes the interface available to TCP/IP.

- *Address.*   This is the IP address that is assigned to the interface. In the discussion of this chapter, it has been pointed out that IP addresses specify an interface within a computing node. This parameter specifies the IP address for this interface.

- *Subnet mask.*   This parameter is used for specifying the subnet mask used by the interface and associated with the above IP address. The parameter must be coded only if subnetting is in effect; if subnetting is in effect, however, every interface in the subnet must specify the same subnet mask when the interface is configured. The subnet address is entered on the ifconfig command line string using the *netmask* keyword as in the example below.

- *Broadcast address.*   This parameter can be used to set the broadcast address for this interface. The normal broadcast address uses a HostID set to all 1s. The broadcast address is entered in the ifconfig command line string using the *broadcast* keyword as in the following example:

```
ifconfig lan0 129.10.1.4 netmask 255.255.255.0 broadcast 129.10.1.255
```

This example shows ifconfig being used to configure interface "lan0" to be a member of subnet 129.10.1.0 (belonging to network 129.10.0.0). There are four computers in this subnetwork, and each has a single interface. Our computer is the fourth computer, and it is assigned an address of 129.10.1.4. The subnet mask is set to 255.255.255.0 to indicate that subnetting is in effect. Normally, the broadcast address need not be entered using ifconfig; however, some Unix systems are conformant with an old release of Berkeley Unix (BSD 4.2) that used 0s instead of 1s as the broadcast address. In this case, the default broadcast must be changed.

The ifconfig utility can also be used to display the current setting of an interface by entering the ifconfig command along with the interface name. For example,

```
ifconfig lan0
```

4.9.2   Netstat

The *netstat* command is another command line Unix utility developed for the Berkeley version of Unix and modified or rewritten to accommodate other implementations. Netstat is used to display various statistics associated with a network and has a number of options. Some of the various options will be briefly described here, but because of the amount of detail that is displayed, only a very brief description will be given for each option. Additionally, it must be noted that command line options can vary from one Unix platform to the next.

- *Display the status of configured network interfaces (-i).*   This netstat command displays all the defined network interfaces and statistics associated with each.

- *Display the TCP/IP routing table (-r).*   When the netstat command is entered using the -r option, the contents of the local routing table are formatted and displayed. This is useful information for diagnosing network routing problems. Destination IP addresses are displayed along with the gateway (router) used to reach the destination. A flag indicates the characteristics of a route represented by each routing table entry, such as its operational status and if it is a route to a host or to a gateway.

- *Display communication endpoints (-a).*   When the netstat command is entered using the -a option, all the communication endpoints are displayed. These are the TCP and UDP programs that are active in the system. The protocol of the endpoint is indicated along with the number of bytes in the endpoint's data buffer and the local and remote addresses, if they are available. Additionally, the finite state of each active TCP endpoint is also displayed.

- *Display communication buffer statistics (-m).*   This netstat command is used to display the statistics relating to communication buffers. In Berkeley's TCP/IP code, these buffers are called *mbufs,* hence the *m* used in the command. In implementations of TCP/IP that are based on System V, *data blocks* associated with STREAMS are used instead.

- *Display protocol statistics (-s).*   This netstat command is used to display statistics that have been collected by each protocol (IP, ICMP, TCP, and UDP). The statistics gathered and displayed vary from one Unix implementation to the next, but basically show packet and fragment counts and such things as number of bad checksums and other error conditions that were encountered.

4.9.3   Route

The *route* command may be used to add or delete entries in the routing table. The route command constructs a routing table statically. The basic, minimal routing table is first created by the ifconfig utility when the first interface is defined. An entry for the local IP address is placed in the table at that time. Routes can be statically added using the route command. The basic route command has four parameters.

- *Operation.*   This is the keyword *add* or *delete,* which indicates the nature of the operation that is to be performed on the routing table.

- *Destination IP address.*   This is the destination IP address that is reached by this route. The keyword *default* can be entered instead of an address. This keyword indicates that all datagrams have destination addresses that cannot be satisfied using the other entries in the routing table (should they exist) should be sent to the routing node address indicated in the following parameter.

- *Routing node (gateway) address.*   This is the IP address for the node to which all datagrams matching the destination IP address should be forwarded. It is the address of a routing node (previously called an internet *gateway*).

- *Routing metric.*   This is the metric to be associated with this route and is included in the command only on an "add" operation. Basically, the metric (number of hops) is used in static routing only to set this route as being a route to a router (previously called a gateway) or a route to a host node attached to the local network. If the routing metric is 0, then this route is considered to be a route to a host node on the local network. Otherwise, the route is considered to be to a router node (where datagrams can be further routed) and the G flag (*gateway*) is set in the routing table. This flag is displayed when the netstat command is executed with the -r option.

Readers who are interested in more details about the configuration process for TCP/IP are directed to the book *TCP/IP Network Administration* by Craig Hunt (1992), listed in the Bibliography.

4.10 Network Management

The *Simple Network Management Protocol* (SNMP) is the current de facto choice for internet network management. SNMP was the result of work of the IAB.

In February 1988 a committee met at the request of the IAB to discuss network management technology and to make recommendations to the IAB concerning creation of network management standards for the Internet. The IAB then released RFC 1052, which called for the development of an internet management strategy. Most internet professionals were expecting TCP/IP to be phased out and OSI to be implemented in its stead. OSI's *Common Management Information Protocol* (CMIP) would then become the internet network management standard; therefore, a short-term solution would have to be developed. A working group was formed to study the problem, and two tasks were defined: develop a *structure of management information* (SMI), and develop a *management information base* (MIB). The SMI was defined in RFC 1065 and emphasized that the management protocol should be simple and extensible. Managed objects are defined using ASN.1 from OSI's CMIP. The MIB is defined in RFC 1066.

A short-term network management solution needed to be found because CMIP was widely acknowledged to be the long-term solution as soon the then-evolving standard was completed. Because of the need for a short-term solution, the IAB wanted the short-term protocol to be based on existing technology. A working group was put together to modify an extant *simple gateway monitoring protocol* (SGMP), bringing it into alignment with the MIB and SMI. The protocol that was developed was called the *Simple Network Management Protocol* (SNMP) and was first defined in RFC 1098.

SNMP was demonstrated by more than 30 vendors at the 1989 INTEROP internetworking show and quickly won wide acceptance. It continued to be implemented by vendors in many types of network equipment, and on various computing platforms. It was not long before SNMP became *the* accepted network management standard. OSI rapidly fell out of favor during the INTEROP shows in the early 1990s, and discussions turned heated when the subject of network management was brought up. The author was present at several such large discussions at INTEROP conferences. Whenever CMIP or OSI was mentioned, it was to the accompaniment of a great chorus of booing. OSI had in just a few short years changed from the Great White Protocol Knight mounted on its golden steed, to a hated anathema. It had become a faux pax to mention the "O word" in a favorable context. The general feeling was that CMIP was too complicated and the beauty of SNMP was in its great simplicity. Soon, however, arguments of simplicity were abandoned when a new, more complex and complete version of SNMP was announced: SNMP Version Two (SNMPv2).

4.11   Conclusion

TCP/IP is a not-too-difficult-to-understand and easy-to-implement networking protocol that has gained great favor. A knowledge of TCP/IP is essential for today's computer industry specialists as more (but not all) corporate networks convert SNA backbones to TCP/IP, and as Internet access, using SLIP and PPP, moves quickly into a tremendous number of homes and businesses.

The subject of TCP/IP is continued in the next chapter, where the Berkeley socket interface, employed by most TCP/IP applications to access a TCP/IP network, is introduced.

Sockets: Internet's API

5.1 Introduction

The TCP/IP protocols presented in Chap. 4 provide the basis for a transport network. This chapter introduces the most common means of accessing a TCP/IP transport network, the Berkeley socket interface.

5.2 Background

The application programming interface known as *sockets* was developed in 1982 at the University of California at Berkeley as part of a project funded by the Advanced Research Projects Agency (ARPA) to port TCP/IP to the Unix operating system. It is an application-level interface that is programmed by coding a series of function calls supplied as part of the Berkeley version of the Unix operating system.

TCP/IP was first introduced in the Unix release known as BSD Version 4.2 and quickly became a *de facto* standard. Programs written in the C language, Unix's native language, could use function calls from the "sockets library" to communicate with endpoints located on the same or other computers. Today, socket programming is the most important application programming interface for TCP/IP and the internet suite of protocols, and it has been ported not only to other languages, but to other environments, such as Microsoft's Windows, as well.

This chapter introduces the concepts of socket programming, using examples written in the C language. Familiarity with the socket programming interface is valuable not only for programmers in today's network development environment, but also for anyone interested in the workings of internet protocols. Understanding the socket interface will also provide an understanding of communications API basics and a better overall knowledge of how computer networking is accomplished. Finally, for readers of later chapters, this chapter provides the groundwork for understanding how the MPTN architecture enables socket programs to run on top of transport protocols other than TCP/IP.

It is recommended that readers who are not familiar with TCP/IP and internet protocols read Chap. 4 before attempting to understand the concepts presented here.

5.3 Socket Programming

A *socket* is an endpoint established in a computer program that provides access to services that transfer data to another endpoint located in another program. In the network environment, these endpoints are usually in different network nodes, but socket endpoints can actually reside in the same computer, and data can be transferred between two local processes. The socket interface consists of a set of function calls that create a socket endpoint and then perform the various operations which implement the interface. The sockets API embodies the concept of providing a method of transferring data between two *objects,* whatever they may be.

The term *socket* is not clearly defined in the literature and is often used by professionals to describe a number of different concepts. Sometimes the term is used to refer to the sockets API itself, and programmers talk about writing "sockets code." Moreover, the term *socket* is often used to describe the *pipe* between two socket endpoints, and there is often talk of a socket between two programs. However, a socket really is just an endpoint represented by an address called a *socket address.* The socket address, in the internet protocol suite, is a transport layer address.

The concept of the socket originated in the Xerox Network System (XNS) communications protocol which was developed at the Xerox PARC lab in Menlo Park, California (the unsung fount of much of the networking and desktop computer technology of the 1990s), but the concept of providing an API to work with sockets, apparently, was born at Berkeley, with whom PARC had very close ties.

Socket programming, reflecting the nature of the underlying internet protocols, uses the client-server model for defining socket endpoints. One socket endpoint functions as a server waiting for incoming connection requests or datagrams; the other end, the client socket, must initiate either the connection request or the sending of datagrams. This client-server model is passed along to the application programs that use the socket interface and provides the abstraction on which communications in the Unix operating system is built; server programs, in Unix systems, are known as *daemons* and wait on well-known ports for requests from clients.

We begin our discussion of socket programming by introducing the address and protocol families that belong to the socket interface.

5.3.1   Protocol and address families

When a socket is created, the underlying means of transferring data from one endpoint to the other must be selected. For this, the sockets API defines a number of protocol and address *families.*

Protocol families (PF) are an abstraction of socket programming that define the kinds of protocols that are available for the socket interface. *Address families* (AF) are derived from the protocol families and indicate the type of network layer addressing to be used. Since particular types of addresses are normally associated with particular protocols, the two families correspond. Table 5.1 shows the names of the various protocol families that have so far been generally designated. Each family begins with PF_. The address families are the same except that they begin with AF_ instead (Table 5.2).

The designers of the socket interface at Berkeley conceived of the idea of protocol families because they were not only creating an interface for the TCP/IP transport network, they were also creating a generic API that would allow the transfer of data from one endpoint to another using any underlying means of transport. The different

TABLE 5.1   The Protocol Families

PF_UNSPEC	Unspecified	PF_UNIX	Local
PF_INET	Internet	PF_IMPLINK	ARPAnet IMP
PF_PUP	PUP	PF_CHAOS	CHAOSNET
PF_NS	XNS	PF_NBS	NBS
PF_ECMA	European Computer Manufacturers	PF_DATAKIT	Datakit
PF_CCITT	CCITT	PF_SNA	SNA
PF_DECnet	DECnet	PF_DLI	Direct Data Link Interface
PF_LAT	DEC LAT	PF_HYLINK	Hyperchannel
PF_APPLETALK	AppleTalk	PF_NIT	Network Interface Tap
PF_802	IEEE 802.2	PF_OSI	OSI
PF_X25	X.25	PF_OSINET	
PF_GOSIP	GOSIP	PF_NETWARE	NetWare
PF_RIF	Raw Interface	PF_LINK	Link Layer Interface

TABLE 5.2   The Address Families

AF_UNSPEC	Unspecified		AF_UNIX	Local
AF_INET	Internet		AF_IMPLINK	ARPAnet IMP
AF_PUP	PUP		AF_CHAOS	CHAOSNET
AF_NS	XNS		AF_NBS	NBS
AF_ECMA	European Computer Manufacturers		AF_DATAKIT	Datakit
AF_CCITT	CCITT		AF_SNA	SNA
AF_DECnet	DECnet		AF_DLI	Direct Data Link Interface
AF_LAT	DEC LAT		AF_HYLINK	Hyperchannel
AF_APPLETALK	AppleTalk		AF_NIT	Network Interface Tap
AF_802	IEEE 802.2		AF_OSI	OSI
AF_X25	X.25		AF_OSINET	
AF_GOSIP	GOSIP		AF_NETWARE	NetWare
AF_RIF	Raw Interface		AF_LINK	Link Layer Interface

families of underlying protocols which would eventually be provided for the user of the sockets API were defined as the protocol families. This list of protocol families conceived of by the designers at Berkeley was very optimistic, however, as very few of the families were ever actually implemented. The original implementation of sockets in Berkeley Unix (BSD) Version 4.2 provided only two of the protocol and address families: AF_INET (PF_INET) and AF_UNIX (PF_UNIX). The address and protocol families for XNS (AF_NS and PF_NS) and OSI (AF_OSI and PF_OSI) were added in later versions.

AF_INET (Address Family InterNET) is the family used for the internet suite of protocols, and AF_UNIX (Address Family UNIX) is used for interprocess communication in the Unix environment. New address families can be added to the list and implemented. For example, IBM's TCP/IP for the mainframe VM and MVS operating systems support AF_INET and another address family called AF_IUCV. AF_IUCV allows socket programming between address spaces, in the case of MVS, and virtual machines in the case of VM. It is similar to the IPC family of Unix.

To review quickly, the Berkeley sockets API allows programs to create sockets, which are endpoints established within a computer or in a computer network. Sockets have addresses in the form defined by the selected address family. Data are transferred between these endpoints using the underlying services provided by one of the members of the socket interface's protocol family.

TABLE 5.3   Generic Socket Address Structure

```
struct sockaddr {
    u_short              sa_family;       /* The address family      */
    char                 sa_data[14];     /* The address value       */
};
```

TABLE 5.4   IP Socket Address Structure

```
struct sockaddr_in {
    u_short              sin_family;      /* The address family      */
    u_short              sin_port;        /* The port number         */
    u_long               sin_addr;        /* The IP address          */
    char                 sin_zero[8];     /* filler (set to zeros)   */
};
```

5.3.2   Socket addressing

Sockets programs use an addressing technique called *socket addressing*. A socket address is, as was mentioned, the address of a specific endpoint. In order to pinpoint an endpoint within a network, it is necessary to define three separate locations: the particular computer within which the endpoint resides, the network on which the endpoint's computer resides, and the *port* that pinpoints the process that contains the endpoint. The combination of these three things is what constitutes a fully qualified socket address. Table 5.3 shows, in C, the *sockaddr* structure that holds a generic socket address. A socket address will be in a different format for different address families, however. AF_UNIX usually defines its address family to specify a *named pipe* for interprocess communication. Another structure called *sockaddr_in* is shown in Table 5.4, and it specifically defines a socket address to be used in the AF_INET domain. This is the structure that is used to hold an IP address. In this structure, of the 14 bytes set aside for the address, the first two represent the 2-byte port number, which pinpoints the endpoint's software process, the next 4 bytes hold the 32-bit IP address, which provides the address for the specific network and host, and the remainder of the 14-byte field is left unused.

5.3.3   Socket types

The creators of the socket interface at Berkeley designated five different types of sockets. These are shown in Table 5.5. The first three are the only types in common use and provide three different types of interfaces:

TABLE 5.5   Socket Types

1	SOCK_STREAM	Stream socket interface
2	SOCK_DGRAM	Datagram socket interface
3	SOCK_RAW	Raw socket interface
4	SOCK_RDM	Reliably delivered message
5	SOCK_SEQPACKET	Sequenced packet stream

- Stream socket interface
- Datagram socket interface
- Raw socket interface

These three types of sockets represent three different types of interfaces to underlying services. The actual services that are provided by the interface depend on the protocol family that is used. In this chapter, the description will be limited to the services provided by PF_INET, the internet protocol family; other protocol families, such as PF_UNIX or PF_NS, will not be discussed.

5.3.3.1 The datagram socket interface. The datagram socket interface is an interface that is used to send and receive datagrams and is defined as type SOCK_DGRAM. For PF_INET, the datagram interface employs the *User Datagram Protocol* (UDP). The basic services that are provided for the datagram socket interface are very straightforward. Datagrams are simply sent from one endpoint to another, and each datagram contains the IP address of the destination. However, a *pseudo-connected mode* is also available for the continuous sending of datagrams between the same two endpoints. The *Network File System* (NFS) uses datagram sockets.

5.3.3.2 The stream socket interface. The stream socket interface for the internet protocol family uses TCP and is designated as SOCK_STREAM. Connections must be set up between two endpoints before stream data can be transferred.

Common internet application programs that use stream sockets are telnet, ftp, finger, and sendmail.

5.3.3.3 The raw socket interface. The stream and datagram socket interfaces are used by application programs in order to access the two major transport layer protocols of the internet suite: TCP and UDP. There are cases where a program needs to bypass the transport layer altogether and access protocols residing in the network layer directly. The raw socket interface is provided for this purpose and is designated as SOCK_RAW. The raw socket interface is not used except in rare cases and is provided mainly for system-level programs. For example, the *ping* program uses raw sockets to send an ICMP echo request and receive an echo reply.

5.3.4   The client-server model

The two endpoints involved in a transfer of data using the socket interface always conform to the client-server paradigm. One endpoint is the server, the other is the client. The server issues calls which create a socket endpoint and bind the endpoint to an IP address and a port; then, if the type is SOCK_STREAM, the server listens for and accepts incoming connection requests. Once a connection is accepted, data can begin flowing between the endpoints. If the server is of the type SOCK_DGRAM, it has only to create the socket and then bind it to an IP address and a port. It is then ready to accept incoming datagrams. A client, on the other hand, if it is of the SOCK_STREAM type, creates a socket, sets up the IP address of the server it wishes to contact, and then attempts to connect to that server. If a client is of the SOCK_DGRAM type, it has only to create the socket, then begin sending datagrams to the server.

The function calls that do all this are described next.

5.3.5   Socket function calls

So far, the concept of the socket interface and the types of sockets and address/protocol families used with the socket interface have been described. To continue the discussion, the actual function calls of the sockets library are now discussed. Each call is presented with a description of its use and the parameters that are passed along with it. These descriptions show how each call functions. Details such as the types of errors that can result are omitted. More detailed information about the calls of the sockets library can be gleaned from programming manuals associated with the particular platforms and products that are to be implemented.

The basic function calls used in socket programming are shown in Table 5.6. Each of these functions is now described.

5.3.5.1   Basic function calls

rc = socket (int addr_family, int type, int protocol);

The most fundamental socket function call is the *socket()* function call itself. Socket() is issued by programs wishing to create a socket endpoint. After connection-oriented server programs have called socket() and have bound an IP address and port to the newly created socket, they do what is called *listening*—waiting for incoming connection requests. These connection requests are issued by connection-oriented

TABLE 5.6   Socket Function Calls

Setup and Shutdown	
socket()	Create a socket
connect()	Connect with a server
bind()	Bind a local IP address and port number to a socket
listen()	Server wants to listen for incoming connections
accept()	Server will accept the next incoming connection
close()	Close the socket
shutdown()	Shutdown a TCP/IP connection
Send and Receive Data	
read()	Receive data from a connection
write()	Send data on a connection
recv()	Receive a datagram, or data on a connection
send()	Send a datagram, or data on a connection
recvfrom()	Receive a datagram
sendto()	Send a datagram
recvmsg()	Receive a datagram
sendmsg()	Send a datagram

client programs which, after issuing the socket() function call, attempt to connect to a listening server.

It can be seen that a return code, rc, is returned from the function call. Socket() returns a *socket descriptor* in the rc parameter if the socket() call completed successfully. Otherwise, a return code of -1 is returned and the error code that describes which error has occurred is placed in the *errno* system variable. In Unix, a socket descriptor is the same as a file descriptor, a concept familiar to programmers. It is an index into an array of pointers that point to internal control blocks containing the information that pertains to a particular socket.

Socket() opens a socket endpoint but does not transfer data or set up a connection. Other calls, to be described, perform these functions. A socket exists only as long as some process has a descriptor referring to it.

The first parameter passed in the function call specifies the address family, which in our case will always be AF_INET. The second parameter (type) specifies the socket type (Table 5.5). The third parameter (protocol) designates the transport protocol. When it is set to zero, this parameter specifies that the default protocol for the particular protocol family and type combination is to be used. Naturally there is only one protocol, TCP, in use in the PF_INET domain with the SOCK_STREAM type, and similarly, there is only one protocol, UDP, for the SOCK_DGRAM type. Protocols are stored in a file called *protocols* (usually found in the etc directory on Unix systems) and can be retrieved for the socket() call's third parameter using the getprotobyname() function call. The *protocols* file has entries for the protocols, such as TCP, UDP, ICMP, PUP, and IDP, and the protocol number associated with each. It is the protocol number, not the name, that must be passed to the routines that create the socket.

If the call to socket() is unsuccessful, a -1 is placed in the return code (rc) and the global variable *errno* will contain a value which describes the nature of the problem.

For readers who are not familiar with the C language, the term *int* stands for *integer* and specifies that the nature of the parameter is a type of integer. The rc parameter that contains the return code or socket descriptor after the call has completed is also an *int* type.

rc = connect (int sd, *sockaddr_in addr, int addr_len);

Connect() is a function call made by connection-oriented clients. It is called after the client program has received a socket descriptor by calling socket(). The connect() function call is made to establish a connection with a server.

The first parameter in the connect() call is the socket descriptor value that was returned by the socket() function call. The second parameter points to a sockaddr_in structure (Table 5.4) which has been populated with the remote endpoint's IP address and port number. In other words, the second parameter points to the socket address for the destination endpoint. It will be noticed that the type of the second parameter is a type of sockaddr_in rather than a type of int. The * in front of sockaddr_in indicates that the value in the sockaddr_in variable is not passed in the function call, but a pointer to the variable is passed instead. The third parameter specifies the length of the second parameter.

The main purpose of connect() is to create TCP connections. To do this, the program must have issued a socket() call using SOCK_STREAM as the socket type. Connect() then causes a connection to take place using the TCP "three-way handshake" described in Chap. 4. Connect() can also be used for socket type SOCK_DGRAM. Datagrams use the User Datagram Protocol, and, as was detailed in Chap. 4, UDP is connectionless. So why would connect() be associated with a connectionless transport layer protocol? In this case, connect() does not, and *cannot,* actually create a connection; it simply stores the endpoint address specified in the second parameter so that all the following datagrams that are sent on the socket are sent automatically to the same IP address. This is a convenience feature that eliminates the need to specify the remote endpoint address with each call that is made to send a datagram.

If connect() is successful, a 0 is returned in rc. If it is unsuccessful, a −1 is placed in the return code, rc, and the global variable *errno* will contain a value which describes the nature of the problem.

rc = bind (int sd, *sockaddr_in addr, int addr_len);

The *bind()* function call is used mainly by server programs to bind a newly created socket to a well-known port. Server programs, or daemons, wait for connection requests from connection-oriented clients, or incoming datagrams from connectionless clients. Servers wait on ports that have been specified in the *services* file (/etc/services). After a server has issued the socket() call and obtained a socket descriptor, IP kernel routines must be informed of the number for the port on which the newly created socket will be listening. The bind() call performs this function.

Bind() can also be issued by client programs to bind a port to the client's socket, although clients usually let the system issue a random port number. Using a specific port from the services file is not usually necessary for a client.

The first parameter contains the socket descriptor value assigned by the socket() call. The second parameter contains a pointer to a sockaddr_in structure which must be populated before the call is made. The important part of the structure is the port number that must be bound to the socket. This number can be obtained by using the getservbyname() function. The IP address part of the sockaddr_in structure can be set to the IP address of the interface on the local node. If there are multiple interfaces on which incoming connection requests could arrive, the IP address in the sockaddr_in structure can be set to INADDR_ANY, which tells the IP routines to accept connection requests on any of the internet ports.

Table 5.7 shows an example of a typical services file with the names, numbers, and protocols for the *well-known ports*. The well-known ports are the ports with numbers in the range 1 through 1023. These port values were assigned by the Internet Assigned Numbers Authority (IANA) and enable users anywhere in the Internet to issue socket calls for services on any computer, as each computer will contain a services file with the same port service-to-number mappings. It can be seen from Table 5.7, for example, that TCP port 23 has been assigned to the telnet server and that TCP port 21 belongs to ftp. If a user wishes to write his or her own TCP or UDP services, entries can be added to this file. These applications should use ports in the 1024 through 5000 range, outside the range of well-known ports.

If the bind() is successful, a 0 is returned in rc. If it is unsuccessful, a −1 is placed in the return code, rc, and the global variable *errno* will contain a value which describes the nature of the problem.

TABLE 5.7   Services

Service	Port	Alias/Comment	Service	Port	Alias/Comment
echo	7/tcp		echo	7/udp	
discard	9/tcp	sink null	discard	9/udp	sink null
systat	11/tcp	users	daytime	13/tcp	
daytime	13/udp		netstat	15/tcp	
qotd	17/tcp	quote	chargen	19/tcp	ttytst source
chargen	19/udp	ttytst source	ftp-data	20/tcp	
ftp	21/tcp		telnet	23/tcp	
smtp	25/tcp	mail	time	37/tcp	timserver
time	37/udp	timserver	rlp	39/udp	resource location
nameserver	42/udp	name	whois	43/tcp	nicname
domain	53/tcp	DNS	domain	53/udp	DNS
mtp	57/tcp	# deprecated	bootps	67/udp	# bootp server
bootpc	68/udp	# bootp client	tftp	69/udp	
rje	77/tcp	netrjs	finger	79/tcp	
link	87/tcp	ttylink	supdup	95/tcp	
hostnames	101/tcp	hostname #	iso_tsap	102/tcp	
x400	103/tcp		x400-snd	104/tcp	
csnet-ns	105/tcp		pop	109/tcp	postoffice
sunrpc	111/tcp		sunrpc	111/udp	
auth	113/tcp	authentication	sftp	115/tcp	
uucp-path	117/tcp		nntp	119/tcp	USENET News
ntp	123/tcp		NeWS	144/tcp	
snmp	161/udp	# snmp request	snmp-trap	162/udp	# snmp trap port
smux	199/tcp	# snmpd smux	src	200/udp	# SRC
mptn	397/tcp		exec	512/tcp	
biff	512/udp	comsat	login	513/tcp	
who	513/udp	whod	shell	514/tcp	cmd #
syslog	514/udp		printer	515/tcp	spooler #
talk	517/udp		ntalk	518/udp	
efs	520/tcp	# for LucasFilm	route	520/udp	router routed
timed	525/udp	timeserver	tempo	526/tcp	newdate
courier	530/tcp	rpc	conference	531/tcp	chat
netnews	532/tcp	readnews	netwall	533/udp	emergency
uucp	540/tcp	uucp daemon	new-rwho	550/udp	
remotefs	556/tcp	rfs_server	rmonitor	560/udp	
monitor	561/udp				

> **rc = listen (int sd, int queue_len);**

The *listen()* call is issued by connection-oriented servers. The call is made to put the server in the TCP LISTEN state. In this state, the server waits for incoming connection requests destined for the port for which the server has issued a bind() call. The first parameter contains the socket descriptor that was returned from the socket() call. The second parameter is a number that refers to the number of connection requests that can be queued while the server is busy.

If listen() is successful, a 0 is returned in rc. If it is unsuccessful, a -1 is placed in the return code, rc, and the global variable *errno* will contain a value which describes the nature of the problem.

> **rc = accept (int sd, *sockaddr_in addr, *int addr_len);**

Accept() is used by listening servers to accept incoming connection requests from connection-oriented clients. The accept() call is issued only by SOCK_STREAM types of sockets. Listen() has already informed the kernel routines that a socket endpoint is listening for connections that may arrive on the port that was designated by the bind(). Listen() also designated the size of the queue for incoming connection requests in case one arrives while another is being serviced. When the call to accept() is made, the call either *blocks* and waits for a connection request from a client, or it accepts a connection from the queue of waiting connection requests.

The first parameter contains the socket descriptor created by the socket() function. The second parameter contains a pointer to a sockaddr_in structure into which accept() will place the IP address and port number of the remote client once a connection request is received (or removed from the queue). The third parameter contains a pointer to an integer into which the size of the second parameter will be placed when the call completes. A socket is formally completed, end to end, when the client's connect() call is completed with the server's accept(). A connection ID, valid only for the newly accepted connection, is returned in rc if the accept() was successful; otherwise a -1 indicates that an error has occurred and the global variable *errno* will contain a value which describes the nature of the problem. The original socket descriptor can be used for accepting more connections.

> **rc = send (int sd, *char buf, int buflen, int flags);**
> **rc = write (int sd, *char buf, int buflen);**

Send() and *write()* transfer the data contained in the buffer, pointed to by the second parameter, for the length designated in the third parameter, to the other end of a connection. Both calls perform the same function, but the write() call is a Unix system call that is used for writing to files as well as to I/O devices, and send() is a socket interface call only.

Send() and write() are used for connected sockets created with SOCK_STREAM or with the special pseudo-connected version of SOCK_DGRAM. When send() and write() complete, the number of bytes of data that were transferred is placed in the rc return code. If write() or send() was unsuccessful, a -1 is returned in rc and the global variable *errno* will contain a value which describes the nature of the problem.

Send(), being the actual function call associated with the socket interface, has one more parameter than write(), and that is an integer containing flags. The two flags are:

- MSG_OOB.   Send out-of-band data on sockets that support SOCK_STREAM

- MSG_DONTROUTE.   Send without using routing tables

rc = recv (int sd, *char buf, int buflen, int flags);
rc = read (int sd, *char buf, int buflen);

Recv() and *read()* receive data from the other end of a connection and place them in the buffer pointed to by the second parameter. The third parameter contains the size of the data buffer into which the data will be placed. When it completes, the number of bytes of data that were transferred is placed in the rc return code. However, if end-of-file was reached, a 0 is placed in the return code. If the read() or recv() was unsuccessful, a -1 is placed in the return code and the global variable *errno* will contain a value which describes the nature of the problem.

Recv(), being the actual function call associated with the socket interface, has one more parameter than read(), and that is an integer containing flags. The flags are:

- MSG_OOB.   Process out-of-band data on a SOCK_STREAM socket

- MSG_PEEK.   Peek at incoming messages

- MSG_WAITALL.   Block until the full request is satisfied or an error occurs

rc=sendto(int sd,*char buf,int buflen,int flags,*sockaddr_in to,int to_len);
rc=recvfrom(int sd,*char buf,int buflen,int flags,*sockaddr_in from,int from_len);

Sendto() and *recvfrom()* are used with SOCK_DGRAM sockets to send or receive datagrams. They are similar to send() and recv() but additionally provide for IP addresses because a pseudo-connected state may not be in effect. The first parameter contains the socket descriptor issued by the socket() call. The second parameter provides the address of the data buffer. The third parameter contains the length of that buffer. The *flags* parameter is identical to that on the send() and recv() calls. The *to* parameter (in the sendto) contains the IP address and port number for the destination, and the *from* parameter (in the recvfrom) speci-fies the sender's address. The last parameters, *to_len* and *from_len,* contain the length of the address in the sockaddr_in structure.

These calls can be used with either a connection or connectionless socket. However, the purpose of the calls is to provide connectionless service. If an address is not specified, then the socket is assumed to be connected.

If a call to sendto() or recvfrom() was successful, the number of bytes in the message is placed in the return code field rc. If it was un-successful, a -1 is placed in the return code and the global variable *errno* will contain a value which describes the nature of the problem.

rc = sendmsg (int sd, * msghdr msg, int flags)
rc = recvmsg (int sd, * msghdr msg, int flags);

Sendmsg() and *recvmsg()* are used for sending and receiving data-grams and are similar to sendto() and recvfrom(). However, these calls are used to send a specially formatted message which is defined by a structure called *msghdr* (Table 5.8). The first parameter in the call contains the socket descriptor that was assigned to the socket by the socket() call. The second parameter is used to pass the address of the msghdr structure. The message structure contains the address of

TABLE 5.8   Recvmsg() and Sendmsg() Calls

Message Header			
struct msghdr {			
caddr_t	msg_name;	/* Optional address	*/
int	msg_namelen;	/* Size of address	*/
struct iovec	*msg_iov;	/* Scatter/gather array	*/
int	msg_iovlen;	/* Number of elements in msg_iov	*/
caddr_t	msg_control;	/* Ancillary data (see Table 5.9)	*/
int	msg_controllen;	/* Ancillary data buffer len	*/
int	msg_flags;	/* Flags on received message	*/
};			

Message Flags		
MSG_OOB	0x1	Process out-of-band data
MSG_PEEK	0x2	Peek at incoming message
MSG_DONTROUTE	0x4	Send without using routing tables
MSG_EOR	0x8	Data completes record
MSG_TRUNC	0x10	Data discarded before delivery
MSG_CTRUNC	0x20	Control data lost before delivery
MSG_WAITALL	0x40	Wait for full request or error

TABLE 5.9   Ancillary Data Objects Header for Recvmsg() and Sendmsg()

This header is used for ancillary data objects in the msg_control buffer. It is used for additional information with or about a datagram that is not expressible by flags. The format is a sequence of message elements headed by cmsghdr structures.

```
struct cmsghdr {
    u_int       cmsg_len;       /* Byte count, including the header  */
    int         cmsg_level;     /* Originating protocol              */
    int         cmsg_type;      /* Protocol-specific type            */
    u_char      cmsg_data[];    /* Protocol-specific data            */
};
```

the destination socket in the msg_name field. Msg_namelen specifies the size of msg_name. Msg_iovlen specifies the number of elements in the msg_iov array. The msg_control field contains ancillary data. This was implemented by the Berkeley designers for purposes of transferring data needed by applications that use an unconnected socket. For example, connection request data from a higher-layer protocol making use of datagrams as the underlying transport mechanism. Msg_controllen specifies the length of this field. The ancillary data field consists of special headers followed by ancillary data. This header, called cmsghdr, is shown in Table 5.9.

The third parameter of the sendmsg() and recvmsg() calls is a flag field identical to those in the send() and recv() calls.

Sendmsg() and recvmsg() are meant to be used with SOCK_DATAGRAM socket types which do not need a connection. However, they can be used on a connection-oriented socket.

If sendmsg() or recvmsg() was successful, the number of bytes in the message is placed in the return code field. If it was unsuccessful, a −1 is placed in the return code and the global variable *errno* will contain a value which describes the nature of the problem.

rc = close (int sd);

Close() is issued after an applications program has finished using a socket. The only parameter is the socket descriptor returned from socket() when the socket was created. Close() will return a 0 if successful and a −1 if not.

Close() can be issued for any type of socket.

rc = shutdown (int sd, int type);

Shutdown() is issued after an application program has finished using a socket. It serves the same purpose as close(), but shutdown() is provided to give added control over the termination of sockets opened for full-duplex connections (TCP).

In addition to the socket descriptor for the opened socket, which is passed in the first parameter, shutdown() contains a second parameter called *shutdown type*. The values passed in the second parameter are:

- 0. The input side of the full-duplex connection is to be terminated.

- 1. The output side of the full-duplex connection is to be terminated.

- 2. Both sides of the full-duplex connection are to be terminated.

Shutdown() can be used with either SOCK_STREAM or SOCK_DGRAM types of sockets. In the first case, the formal TCP termination process, described in Chap. 4, takes place. In the case of the UDP connected socket, the *type* parameter is not valid and a normal close() for the socket is issued.

If the shutdown() was unsuccessful, a -1 is placed in the return code and the global variable *errno* will contain a value which describes the nature of the problem.

5.3.5.2 Using function calls with stream sockets. Figure 5.1 contains a flow diagram that explains how a very simple connection-oriented client-server socket model works.

1. The server issues a socket() call, then a bind() to establish a port on which to wait. Next the server issues a listen() to inform the IP service routines that the server wishes to be placed in the TCP LISTEN state. An accept() is issued to accept incoming connection requests.

2. Soon, a client desires the services of the server and issues its own socket() call. Once the socket has been established, the client asks to be connected to the server [remember, the server has issued an accept() call]. The three-way handshake for TCP, described in Chap. 4, then takes place to establish a session between the client and the server.

3. When the connection request is received by the server's accept(), the server creates a subtask to handle the new connection, then normally goes back to issue another accept() to handle other asynchronous requests from other clients. The flow of data begins between the two endpoints, sending and receiving data back and forth.

4. When the client has completed its use of the server, it issues a shutdown() for the outward-bound side of the full-duplex TCP connection. This results in a TCP segment being sent to the server with the FIN flag set on. The sockets API returns an end-of-file indicator to the server application program. If no more data remain to be sent from the server side, the server subtask closes the socket and terminates. The kernal IP code sends a TCP segment with the FIN flag set in the header. This is acknowledged by the client's sockets API code, which then completes the client's shutdown() call.

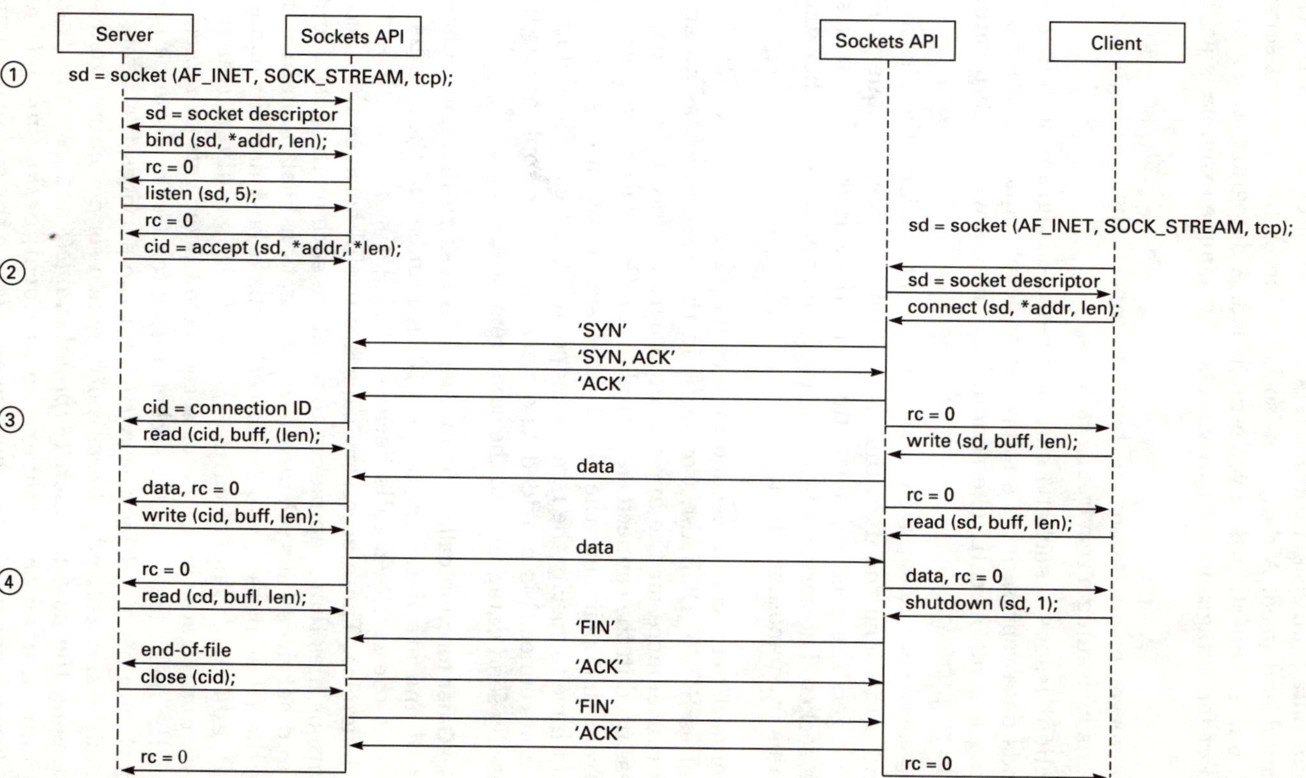

Figure 5.1 A connection-oriented client-server model.

5.3.5.3   Using function calls with datagram sockets.   Figure 5.2 shows one way that datagram sockets, or sockets of the type SOCK_DGRAM, can be created and used. A datagram socket adheres to the client-server model, but a connection is never established. A datagram server waits on a port for datagrams sent by clients. Our simple example is as follows.

1. The server opens its socket, binds to a port, then waits for datagrams by issuing a recvfrom() call.

2. A client issues a socket() call to open a datagram socket, then sends data representing an application-level request to the server using a sendto() call. The sendto() completes with a zero return code.

3. The server receives the request data from the client, then issues a sendto() to send the data that will fulfill the client's request. The client gets the needed information from the server and then closes the socket. The server will issue a rcvfrom and await further datagrams from another client.

A connect() call can be issued by a client after the socket has been opened as SOCK_DGRAM. Connect() in this case provides an additional convenience for the application program. Once it is issued, the address used in the connect() is stored in the IP service routine's memory. From that point on, the client can issue write() and send() calls and not have to specify the remote endpoint IP address. The datagram version of connect() is provided as a convenience for applications that repeatedly send datagrams to the same remote endpoint.

5.3.5.4   Other function calls.   A number of accessory function calls are provided and are listed in Table 5.10. A number of these calls are known as the *getXbyY* calls because they get something based on something else. These accessory calls are useful because they access the various files that map names to numbers such as the hosts, protocols, and services files. *Gethostbyaddr()* gets a host domain name using the IP address; *gethostbyname()* maps a host domain name to an IP address. These calls access DNS resolver routines. *Getpeername()* gets the name of a connected peer; *getsockname()* retrieves the name for a specific socket descriptor. *Getservbyname()* gets the port number used by a service from the services file using the name of the service, and *getservbyport()* gets a service entry (from services) using the port number. *Getprotobyname()* and *getprotobynumber()* can be used to discover the protocol; *gethostname()* and *sethostname()* can be used for getting and setting the node's hostname. *Gethostid()* gets the host's internet address and *sethostid()* sets it.

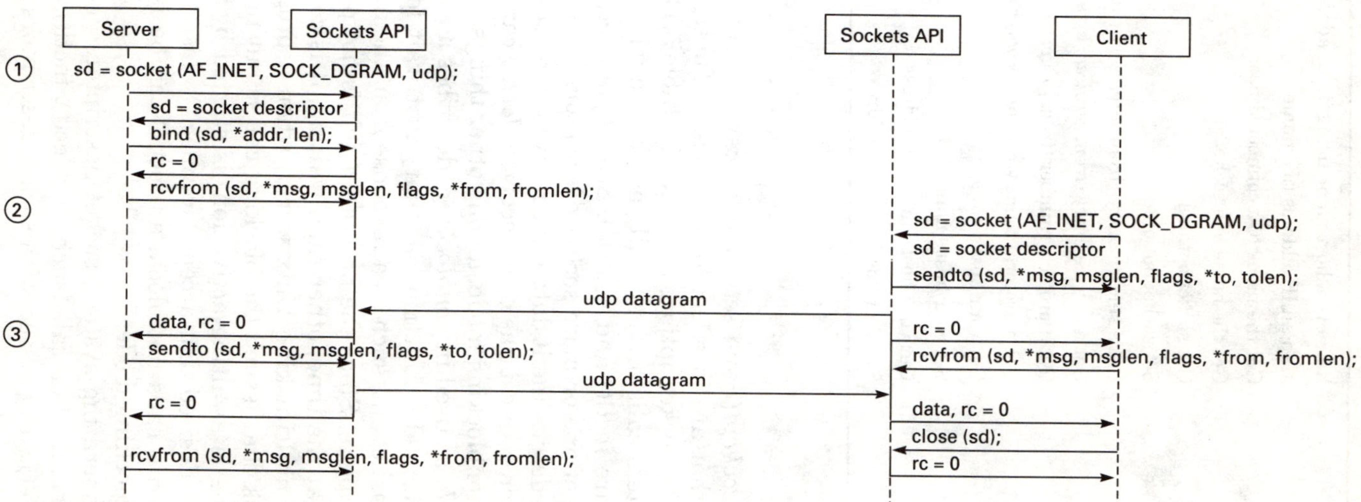

Figure 5.2 A connectionless client-server model.

TABLE 5.10   Accessory Function Calls

gethostbyaddr()	Retrieve a host name using its IP address
gethostbyname()	Map an IP address to a name
getpeername()	Get the name of a connected peer
getsockname()	Get the name of a socket
getsockopt()	Get socket options
setsockopt()	Set socket options
getservbyname()	Get a service entry (from *services*) by its name
getservbyport()	Get a service entry (from *services*) by a port number
getprotobyname()	Get a protocol number (from *protocols*) by its name
getprotobynumber()	Get a protocol name (from *protocols*) by its number
gethostname()	Get your host's name
sethostname()	Set your host's name
gethostid()	Get your host's internet address
sethostid()	Set your host's internet address

Two calls, *getsockopt()* and *setsockopt()*, can be used to retrieve or set the options that are in effect for the socket. These are known as *socket options*. The socket options are listed in Table 5.11.

Two Unix system calls are generally associated with the socket interface. These are ioctl() and select(). *Select()* is used to determine what the status of one or more socket descriptors is. A call to select() can be issued to determine if data have arrived in a socket or if an incoming connection request has been received. *Ioctl()* can be used to set the socket into nonblocking mode, among other things.

The term *block*, as used in *nonblocking*, describes a condition where a program has issued a function call that must wait for the completion of an external event, such as a response from the network, before the call can complete. Since the program itself is not performing any useful function at the time, other than waiting, it is considered to be blocked. In the multitasking Unix world, when a program becomes blocked, the task that issued the blocking call is put to sleep and another task (if one is awaiting activation) is started by the Unix task scheduler. If it is desired that accept(), connect(), close(), and the various read and write calls not block, an ioctl() can be issued to set a socket into nonblocking mode.

In the Unix operating system, socket descriptors and file descriptors are the same. System calls such as select(), fnctl(), ioctl(), close(), read(), and write() can be used with socket descriptors as well as file descriptors.

TABLE 5.11   Option Flags for Getsockopt() and Setsockopt()

SO_DEBUG	0x0001	Debugging information recording
SO_ACCEPTCONN	0x0002	Socket is listening
SO_REUSEADDR	0x0004	Allow local address reuse
SO_KEEPALIVE	0x0008	Keep connections alive
SO_DONTROUTE	0x0010	Just use interface addresses
SO_BROADCAST	0x0020	Permit the sending of broadcast messages
SO_USELOOPBACK	0x0040	Bypass hardware when possible
SO_LINGER	0x0080	Linger on close if data present
SO_OOBINLINE	0x0100	Keep received out-of-band data in band
	Additional Options	
SO_SNDBUF	0x1001	Output buffer size
SO_RCVBUF	0x1002	Input buffer size
SO_SNDLOWAT	0x1003	Output low-water mark
SO_RCVLOWAT	0x1004	Input low-water mark
SO_SNDTIMEO	0x1005	Output time-out
SO_RCVTIMEO	0x1006	Input time-out
SO_ERROR	0x1007	Get error status and clear
SO_TYPE	0x1008	Get socket type

5.3.5.5 Using function calls to create a raw socket. A raw socket is created by issuing a socket() function call and specifying SOCK_RAW as the socket type. The protocol family that is selected for the raw socket is very important because when the network service routines prepend IP headers to the data, they must know what value to place in the protocol field of the IP header. An example of the use of a raw socket is the internet *ping* program, which uses the ICMP protocol to send echo requests and receive echo replies. In order to use ICMP, a raw socket is opened with ICMP specified in the socket() call as the protocol of choice. If ICMP is selected as the protocol, a proper ICMP message must be built by the application program and then sent as a datagram. If XNS's PEP was specified, then PEP messages must be built properly, and so on. Raw sockets are not connected, since they deal only with the IP layer, and IP datagrams are sent and received using the sendto() and rcvfrom() function calls.

5.3.6 Socket program examples

Appendix A contains examples, written in the C language, of two very elementary sockets programs that can communicate with each other using the SOCK_STREAM socket type. The first program is an example of a server; the second is an example of a client.

5.4 WinSock

The Windows Sockets API (WinSock) was developed by a consortium of companies to satisfy the need for a standard internet sockets API for Windows and Windows NT. It was created because TCP/IP had gained tremendous popularity and many different companies offered TCP/IP stacks to run on IBM-compatible personal computing platforms using Windows. However, in order for various applications that used TCP/IP to run over these various TCP/IP implementations, it was necessary to compile the programs separately for use with each separate product. Porting of sockets applications to the various TCP/IP protocol stacks had thus become a major issue for application developers. With the exception of the inevitable instances of misunderstanding the WinSock specification and some occasional bugs, WinSock Version 1.1 solved these porting problems. An application program simply makes all the appropriate socket calls using the formats outlined in the WinSock standard. The program is then dynamically linked with the WinSock library called *winsock.lib* (or *wsock32.lib* when the Win32 API is being used) which is provided by the various TCP/IP vendors.

WinSock is based on the Berkeley socket interface from BSD Unix Version 4.3. However, both WinSock Versions 1.1 and 2.0 have added extensions to the Berkeley interface. The standard WinSock functions are shown in Table 5.12. It can be seen that most of these functions have the same names as the Berkeley functions. Noticeable differences are the closesocket() routine, which replaces Berkeley's close() (actually a Unix system call) and ioctlsocket(), which was added to perform the Unix ioctl() function. It can also be seen that WinSock does not support sendmsg() and recvmsg(). Table 5.13 shows WinSock's implementation of the getXbyY() functions. There are two versions of these, the Berkeley lookalikes and special, nonblocking versions.

Some of the extensions in Version 1.1 were added to compensate for the nonpreemptive task management system employed in Version 3.x of Windows. One of the biggest problems in porting a communications API to Windows Version 3.1 and earlier was the problem created when input and output *blocked*. If a Windows program was waiting for a function to complete, it blocked and Windows could not swap it out to allow another task to make use of the computer's resources. A blocked program caused Windows to stop running entirely. Beginning with Windows 95 and Windows NT, both of which employ the Win32

TABLE 5.12   Standard WinSock Functions

accept()	Accept connections
bind()	Bind socket to a well-known port
closesocket()	Close a socket
connect()	Connect with a server
getsockopt()	Get socket options
getsockname()	Get socket name
getpeername()	Get socket peer's name
gethostname()	Get the host name
ioctlsocket()	Perform a Unix-like ioctl() (to make nonblocking)
listen()	Put server in LISTEN state
recv()	Receive datastream
recvfrom()	Receive a datagram
select()	Perform a Unix-like select() on socket descriptors
send()	Send datastream
sendto()	Send a datagram
setsockopt()	Set socket options
shutdown()	Shut down a connection
socket()	Create a socket

TABLE 5.13   WinSock GetXbyY() Functions

Standard functions	Asynchronous functions
getservbyname()	WSAAsyncGetServByName()
getservbyport()	WSAAsyncGetServByPort()
getprotobyname()	WSAAsyncGetProtoByName()
getprotobynumber()	WSAAsyncGetProtoByNumber()
gethostbyname()	WSAAsyncGetHostByName()
gethostbyaddr()	WSAAsyncGetHostByAddr()

development platform and use separate *threads* for program execution, this is no longer a problem.

The WinSock extensions added because of the problems of blocking that were associated with earlier versions of Windows are called the *WinSock asynchronous functions*. These are so named because they add the feature of asynchronous I/O to the picture more extensively than does the Berkeley socket interface.

The terms *synchronous* and *asynchronous*—used in the context of input and output—should not be confused with synchronous and

TABLE 5.14   WinSock Extension Functions

WSAStartup()	Initialize winsock.dll
WSACleanup()	Terminate use of winsock.dll
WSAGetLastError()	Return the last WinSock error that occurred
WSASetLastError()	Set the value for the last error that occurred
WSAIsBlocking()	Is the current task blocked?
WSAUnhookBlockingHook()	Unhook the default message loop
WSASetBlockingHook()	Substitute for the default message loop
WSACancelBlockingCall()	Cancel the currently blocked call
WSACancelAsyncRequest()	Cancel an executing asynchronous request
WSAAsyncSelect()	Request event notification for a socket

asynchronous communications protocols. Synchronous I/O is a read or write operation that *blocks* or hangs until the operation has completed. An asynchronous function call is different: Once the call has been issued, control is passed back to the program and other instructions in the program can be executed while the I/O operation takes place *asynchronously,* or in its own time, in the background.

The WinSock asynchronous functions begin with a prefix of WSAAsync and are shown in Tables 5.13 and 5.14. Other extensions begin with a WSA prefix and are shown in Table 5.14.

WinSock Version 1.1 supports only the PF_INET protocol family, but Version 2.0 has extensions that allow it to support other protocol families. Additionally, Version 2.0 has added even more extensions. These are shown in Table 5.15.

5.5   TLI and Sockets Compared

For several years, Berkeley and AT&T offered competing versions of Unix. The Transport Layer Interface (TLI), introduced in Chap. 4, was AT&T's version of Berkeley's socket interface. Because it was submitted to X/Open, the vendor consortium that produces standards, and extended by that group, it is now known as the X/Open Transport Interface (XTI). To give the reader some idea of the similarities, the function calls for Berkeley sockets and TLI are compared in Table 5.16.

5.6   Conclusion

The Berkeley AF_INET Sockets API has been used to develop TCP/IP application programs since TCP/IP was added to Berkeley's version of

TABLE 5.15   Extension Functions for WinSock Version 2

WSAAccept()	Conditionally accept a connection
WSAConnect()	Connect and/or join a socket group
WSADuplicateSocket()	Create a shared socket
WSAEnumProtocols()	Get information about available transport protocols
WSAEventSelect()	Specify an event object
WSARecv()	Receive data using overlapped I/O
WSARecvfrom()	Receive datagram using overlapped I/O
WSASend()	Send data using overlapped I/O
WSASendto()	Send datagram using overlapped I/O
WSASocket()	Create a socket for a particular transport provider
WSACreateEvent()	Create an event object
WSACloseEvent()	Close an event object
WSAWaitForMultipleEvents()	Wait for multiple event objects
WSASetEvent()	Set state of event object
WSAResetEvent()	Reset state of event object
WSAGetOverlappedResult()	Return result of overlapped operation
WSAGetQosByName()	Initial quality of service based on a template

TABLE 5.16   TLI and Sockets Calls Compared

Sockets	TLI
socket	t_open
bind	t_bind
connect	t_connect
listen	t_listen
accept	t_accept
read	read
write	write
send	t_snd
recv	t_rcv
sendmsg	
recvmsg	
sendto	t_sndudata
recvfrom	t_rcvudata
select	poll
close & shutdown	t_sndrel, t_snddis, t_close, close
unlink	t_unbind

Unix in the early 1980s. By creating a standard method for coding sockets applications in the Windows environment, the WinSock API has made the socket interface even more popular than it was before. Now that there are many applications using the Berkeley AF_INET socket interface, the ability to run these applications on other than the TCP/IP transport networks for which the programs were originally written has been provided by the MPTN architecture. In later chapters, the reader will be introduced to the methods which allow operation of sockets programs in other types of transport networks.

Systems Network Architecture: SNA

6.1 Introduction

In this chapter, *Systems Network Architecture* (SNA) will be introduced and described. SNA is one of the industry's great success stories. Its historical background was highlighted in Chap. 1. The purpose of this chapter is to present SNA in a way that will enable the reader to understand better the workings of this difficult and complex subject. SNA will first be examined from a horizontal aspect, that is, as a network topology of interconnected nodes. Next, the SNA network will be presented vertically by examining it from the perspective of layers, with an explanation of how the SNA layers relate to the concepts of layered networks presented in Chap. 2.

To accomplish the mission of presenting such a vast subject as SNA in a single chapter, it must be realized that a great many details are omitted. This is because the SNA architecture is comprised of a complex and bewildering array of terms, concepts, algorithms, and protocols.

For many years no books were published on the subject of SNA, and knowledge had to be gleaned from IBM manuals. The complete and definitive reference to the architecture is called the *Systems Network Architecture Format and Protocol Reference Manual: Architectural Logic* (see App. D). This tome is filled with pseudo-code written in a pseudo-programming dialect called *Format and Protocol Language* (FAPL) and overflows with the language of networking architecture: terms such as *finite state machine* and *protocol machine,* which are important concepts to understand, but which can overpower the uninitiated reader looking for simple SNA explanations. Looking through page after page of obscure labels such as TC_OR_BF_TC. DEQUEUE.Q_PAC and FSM_STATION_BIU_ASSEMBLY kept a good many people at a distance. However, this gargantuan work was for years the definitive fount of all SNA knowledge.

Even introductory SNA manuals, such as *Systems Network Architecture General Information,* were no less bewildering. Although containing fewer than 50 pages, this now-obsolete manual overwhelmed the novice with dozens of concepts. Each page unfolded a bewildering array of acronyms: DLC, BLU, NAU, PIU, BTU, LU, PU, DFC, TC, SSCP, PC, NC, SC, RH, RU, FM, DAF, OAF, FID, and CP. These were difficult enough to learn, but coupled with the complexities of normal and expedited flows, TS and FM profiles, half-sessions, intermediate and boundary functions, and virtual route pacing, this manual made the understanding of SNA too much for many people to grapple with.

Finally, in the mid-1980s, hard-cover books explaining SNA began to appear. The scope of SNA is so broad, however, and so much new functionality, such as *Advanced Program-to-Program Communications* (APPC), *Advanced Peer-to-Peer Networking* (APPN), *Dependent LU Requester/Server* (DLUR/S), and *High Performance Routing* (HPR), has been added to the classic architecture that the subject is too detailed and complex to limit to a single book. Limiting the subject to a single chapter, therefore, is really a challenge.

In this chapter, SNA will be presented in a light that we hope will provide the reader with an understanding of how SNA works "under the covers," but the presentation will *purposely* be limited to the "nuts and bolts," staying away from endless enumeration of the many SNA terms.

A *thorough* explanation of the entire subject of SNA, including APPN, could easily be the subject of a multivolume work.

6.2   The SNA Network

A traditional SNA network is centered around software known as the *Virtual Telecommunications Access Method* (VTAM), which provides centralized control of a SNA network. It resides on a mainframe and it, along with satellite communications controllers, provides the traditional, centralized control of an entire SNA network, or *domain.* This domain in a traditional, or *classic,* SNA network consists of a mainframe, attached communications controllers, and terminals and printers attached to cluster controllers, which in turn are attached to the communications controllers or directly to the mainframe. Communications controllers are separate computing units that offload control of communications links, freeing the resources of the mainframe to perform other duties. Cluster controllers are the computing units that control attached terminals and printers.

Before the initial release of VTAM Version 1, the various computer terminals attached to a mainframe were always assigned directly to applications that ran in the mainframe. VTAM changed this by allowing network resources to be shared among applications. VTAM could establish a connection between any VTAM-aware mainframe application and any terminal or printer in a SNA network. VTAM also supported the newest SNA-type devices, such as SNA versions of cluster controllers, as well as older Bisync (BSC) terminals and cluster controllers and ASCII terminals (which IBM originally called start-stop devices).

Along with the introduction of VTAM came the *Network Control Program* (NCP), a communications operating system that worked in conjunction with VTAM but resided in the communications controllers. The communications controllers, such as the IBM 3705, ran the NCP in memory; communicated with the various attached resources, such as terminals and cluster controllers; and exchanged data back and forth with VTAM. Using preconfigured routing tables, it controlled the flow of data in and out of the various attached devices.

From these humble beginnings, SNA networks grew in size and capability to become the prime mover of data in the major corporations of the United States. Today, with the addition of Advanced Program-to-Program Communications (APPC) and Advanced Peer-to-Peer Networking (APPN), SNA has moved outside of its traditional boundaries and VTAM is no longer the center of a SNA world. Instead, the control of SNA networks is being distributed throughout the network.

6.3 SNA Components

A SNA network, like any computer network, is composed of interconnected nodes. The connections between the nodes are made with *links*. There are different types of nodes in an SNA network, but the basis of each is called a *physical unit* or PU.

6.3.1 The physical unit

A simplified model of a SNA network is shown in Fig. 6.1. This figure shows the three basic types of nodes for early SNA networks: a host processor node, a communications controller node, and attached cluster controller nodes, each supporting terminals and one supporting a printer. The communications controller offloads from the host the duties of communications. The cluster controllers control the flow of data to and from the attached 3270 terminals and printer.

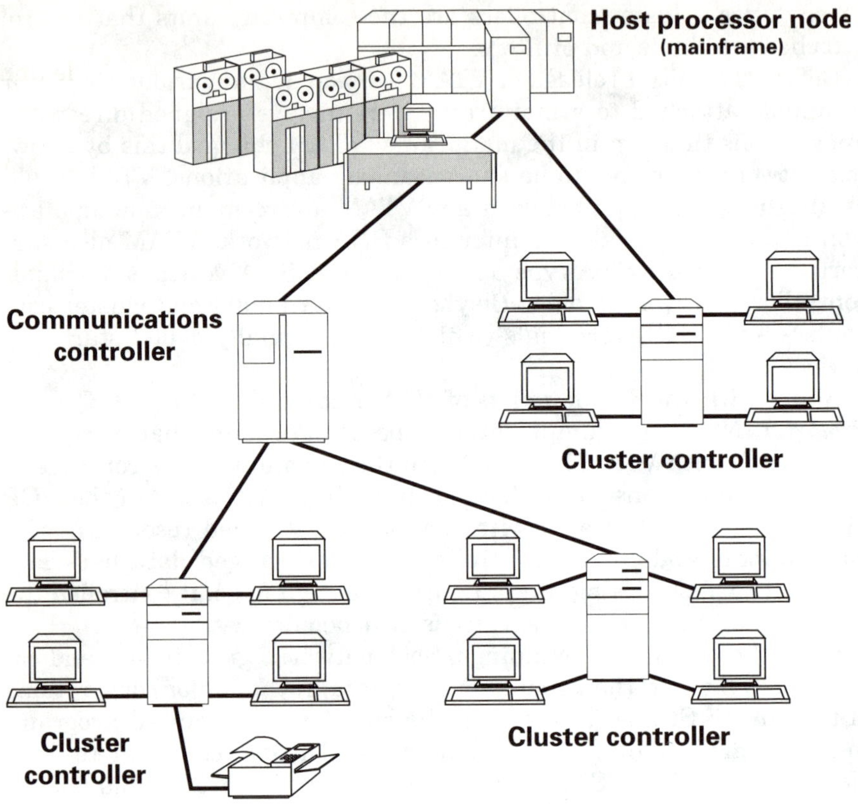

Figure 6.1   A "classic" SNA network.

Our simplified example network consists of five nodes: a host, a communications controller, and three cluster controller units. Of the three cluster controllers, one is link-attached to the communications controller and controls four terminals. The second is also link-attached and controls four terminals and a printer. The third is channel-attached directly to the mainframe and also has four terminals. Cluster controllers are so named because they control a *cluster* of terminals and/or printers. The example shows what is called a *hierarchical* network because its topology is one of a centralized point of control in the mainframe, from which fan out the subservient nodes.

Each host, communications controller, and cluster controller is considered to be a node, or *network addressable unit* (NAU), on the SNA network, and each of these nodes contains a physical unit. A PU is not actually a *physical* device, as the name seems to imply, but is the software program that runs within a physical device and controls that device's communications and attached links. A PU resides in every host, every communications controller, and every cluster controller.

A PU contains a *control point,* software that manages the node and its resources. There are different types of PUs in a SNA network, and the control point types differ for the different types of PUs. Only three PU types, and an offshoot of one of these, are in use in today's SNA networks. These three types are identified by numbers as PU types 2, 4, and 5. The host is represented by PU type 5 and the communications controller by PU type 4; from the PU type 4 radiate links to terminal cluster controllers, PU type 2.

Figure 6.2 again shows our example SNA network with the addition of PU types for each of the nodes. An explanation of the three basic types of PUs follows.

6.3.1.1 PU type 5: The mainframe. PU type 5 resides in a mainframe computer such as an IBM 360, 370, 4300, 3080, 3090, or 9370 series, or a similar product from other manufacturers such as Tandem and

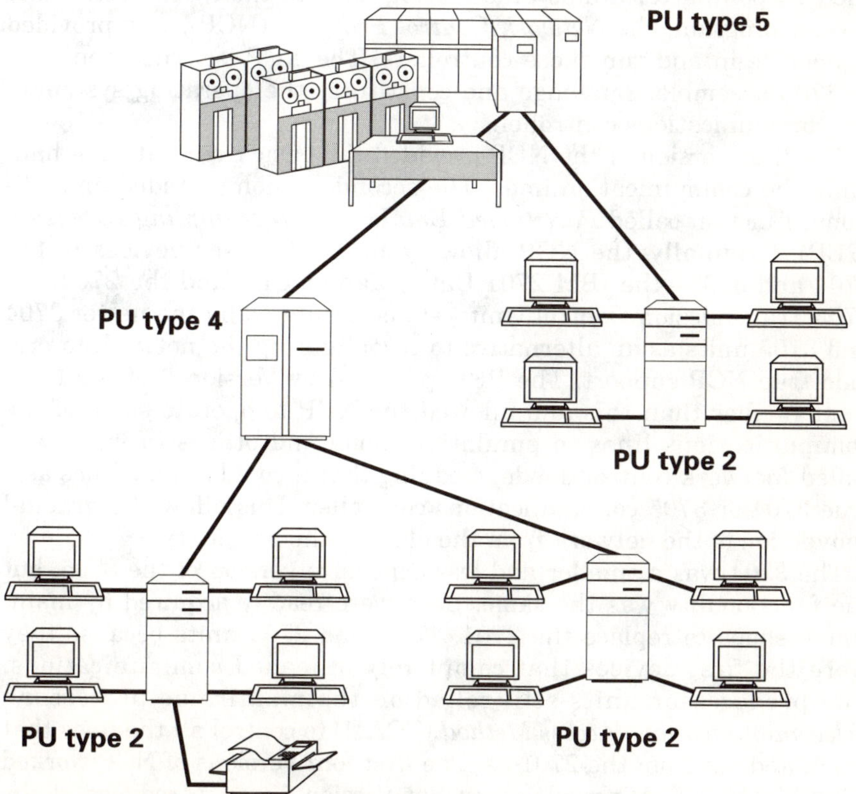

Figure 6.2   A SNA network with three types of PUs.

Amdahl. VTAM runs in the mainframe and contains the host-resident SNA software for PU type 5. In other words, VTAM provides the services of SNA in the mainframe and implements the PU type 5. VTAM/PU type 5 has a special kind of control point called a *system service control point* (SSCP), which controls the activation of the sessions that exist between mainframe applications and the terminals and printers in a SNA network.

The mainframe, PU type 5, was the centerpiece of the corporate network in *classic* SNA. The role of the mainframe in SNA networks, as a PU type 5, is changing, however, as SNA networks become APPN networks.

6.3.1.2   PU type 4: The communications controller.   The concept of a separate computing unit onto which the communications functions being performed by a mainframe computer could be offloaded was embodied by IBM in its 3704 and 3705 communications controllers. These were two models of basically the same device which were attached to the mainframe and performed the communications tasks, such as polling terminals and routing data to their destinations. A special program, the *Network Control Program* (NCP), was provided to operate in and run these controllers. The NCP is written entirely in 3705 assembler language and constitutes the operating system of the communications controller.

The first version of the NCP provided the basic capabilities of handling the communication lines. The second version provided an additional function called *Partitioned Emulation Programming Extension* (PEP). Originally, the NCP allowed the predecessor devices to the 3704 and 3705—the IBM 2701 Data Adapter Unit and the 2702 and 2703 Transmission Control Units—to be emulated by the newer 3704 and 3705 units as an alternative to reconfiguring the network to provide true NCP support. The PEP, provided by Version 2 of the NCP, went further than this and allowed the NCP to operate some of the communications lines in emulation mode and others in what was called "network control" mode, meaning that it could handle lines as a true 3704 or 3705 communications controller. This allowed a gradual conversion of the network from the older to the newer style.

The 3704 was a smaller and less expensive version of the 3705, but the functionality was the same. Both were readily acquired by mainframe shops to replace the 2701, 2702, and 2703 units because they were the first devices that completely offloaded communications. The predecessor units still relied on the mainframe processor's *Telecommunications Access Method* (TCAM) to control all the lines that emanated out from the 2701-3s. The first four versions of NCP worked with TCAM, VTAM's predecessor, but Version 5 was introduced at the same time that SNA, SDLC, and VTAM were introduced.

The 3705 became the flagship of a long line of communications controllers such as IBM models 3720, 3725, and 3745 as well as compatible devices from other vendors such as NCR Compten. For this reason, we will use the term 3705 as a generic term throughout the remainder of this book to refer to the entire line of controllers.

The 3705 can communicate both synchronously and asynchronously with devices attached to its lines, and it supports a number of line speeds. It can be channel-attached to the mainframe or it can be remotely attached by a dedicated line to a locally attached 3705. Corporations began creating complex networks by interconnecting 3705s and hosts. This created what are known as multiple-domain SNA networks (Fig. 6.3).

The control point in a PU type 4 is called a *physical unit control point* (PUCP). A PUCP provides a subset of SSCP functions.

6.3.1.3 PU type 2: The cluster controller. In classic SNA, A PU type 2 was a very important part of a network. PU type 2 is implemented in

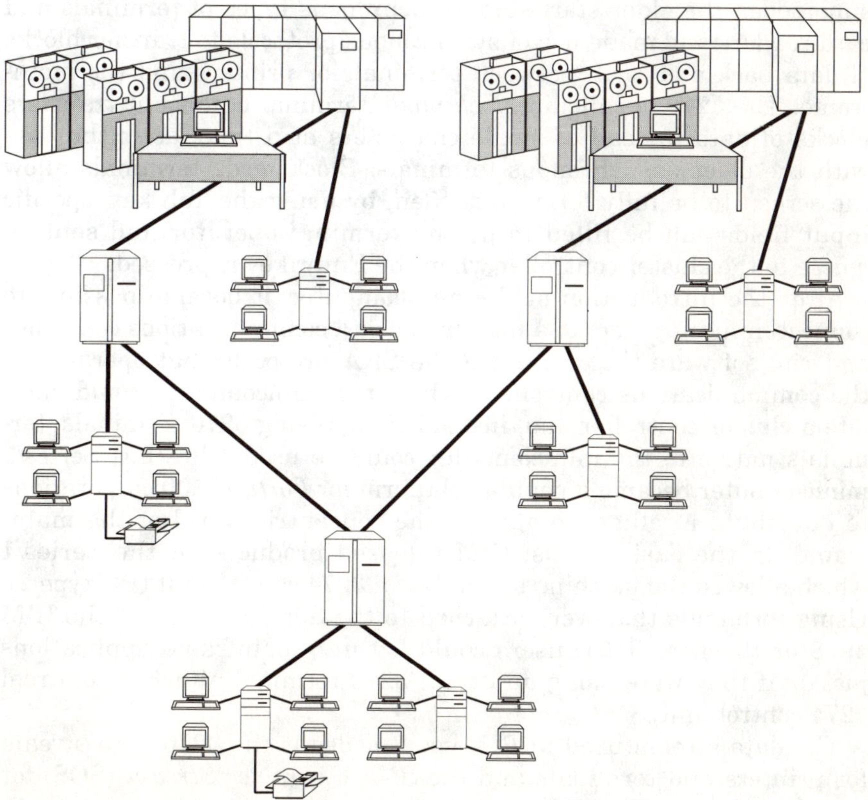

Figure 6.3 A multiple-domain SNA network.

a cluster controller or, precisely, the IBM 3274 control unit. The 3274 is called a cluster controller because it controls a *cluster* of up to 32 terminals or printers. It is the control unit for the classic IBM 3270-type printers and terminals which were the mainstay of SNA networking. These controllers, which resemble small minicomputers, could be found during the 1970s in corporate offices all over the country and throughout Europe. The 3270 terminals and printers in the office were coax-attached to this device. The 3274s, in turn, were either remotely or directly connected with a 3705-type device or in some cases were channel-attached directly to a mainframe.

The original 3274 cluster controller units used the bisync protocol to communicate with the mainframe or the communications controller, but it was an SNA/SDLC version of the 3274 that implemented PU type 2 nodes in a SNA network. The 3274 cluster controller was upgraded by a newer model called the IBM 3174 Subsystem Control Unit, which offered many more features, including token ring attachment.

The 3270 terminal, along with its 3270 communications protocol, superseded the older start-stop asynchronous types of terminals and card readers and made use of synchronous protocols to transfer blocks of data back and forth between terminals or printers and the mainframe. The 3270 is called a *block mode* terminal because it transfers blocks of data instead of single characters at a time, as is the case with the older asynchronous terminals. Block mode terminals allow the screen to be fully formatted; then, by using the Tab key, specific input fields can be filled in by the terminal operator and sent *en masse* to the cluster controller when the Enter key is pressed.

After the introduction of the minicomputer, it became possible to connect minicomputers to a mainframe or a communications controller and run software that *emulated* the SNA protocols that operated in the communications controllers. Thus, the minicomputer could emulate a cluster controller and, instead of supplying 3270 terminals, terminals native to the minicomputer could be used. The IBM Series/1 minicomputer became a popular platform for *Fortune* 500 corporations to distribute intelligence outside the concentric world of the mainframe. In the early 1980s, IBM released products for the Series/1 which allowed the machine to emulate a 3274 control unit (PU type 2). Using terminals that were attached to the Series/1, such as the IBM 4978 or the IBM 3101, users could log into mainframe applications just as if they were using an actual 3270 terminal attached to a real 3274 control unit.

The data stream used in PU type 2 nodes is the 3270 data stream for printers and terminals and the *SNA Character Stream* (SCS) for certain printers. The 3270 data stream employs specific *commands* and *orders* to instruct a 3270-type device what is to be done with data that are sent to it. Data that are sent back to the mainframe when the Enter key, or another special key, is pressed are also specifically formatted. Personal computers, minicomputers, and other devices that provide emulation of PU type 2 terminals must ensure that all data sent to or received from a mainframe conform to the 3270 data stream specification.

PU type 2 nodes contain a PUCP which provides a subset of SSCP functions.

6.3.1.4 PU type 2.1: The peer-to-peer network node.

The introduction of Advanced Program-to-Program Communications (APPC) was the harbinger of the end to traditional SNA. Using APPC, minicomputers, such as the AS/400 and the Series/1, were no longer limited to their networking role of emulating a cluster controller. Two minicomputers could actually communicate directly with each other, using SNA protocols, and transfer data back and forth (Fig. 6.4). In order for the program-to-program networking of APPC to exist in a SNA network, a new type of PU had to be created, and it was decided that this new PU would be an extension to PU type 2. Thus, PU type 2.1 was born.

The PU type 2.1 node was designed for networking. It serves no other purpose other than allowing the node to interoperate with other PU type 2.1 nodes. In other words, it has no specific function, as does a cluster controller node. With the turn of SNA away from a hierarchical network structure to a peer-to-peer structure, where mainframes will eventually abandon the traditional role of network controller and become database servers or other kinds of network nodes, the PU type 2.1 is envisioned as the SNA network node of the future. Once a network is migrated from the hierarchical to the peer-to-peer, all nodes in a SNA network will become PU type 2.1, including any mainframes and communications controllers. Since the enhancements of a PU type 2.1 node are extensions to a PU type 2, PU type 2.1 nodes still maintain backwards compatibility and provide traditional PU type 2 functionality as well. In other words, 3270 ter-

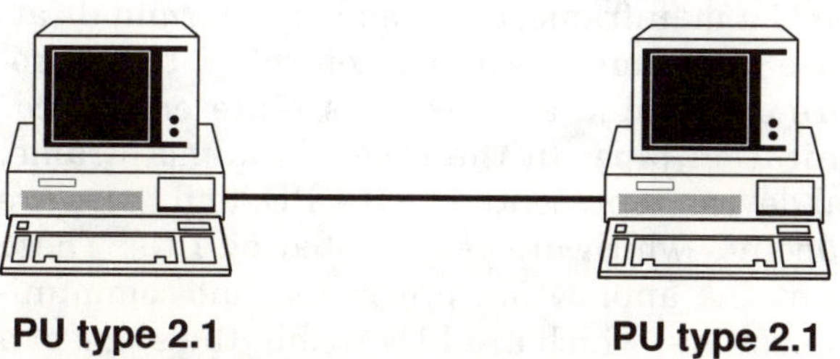

Figure 6.4 Peer-to-peer SNA network nodes.

minal emulation software can run on a PU type 2.1 node because PU type 2.1 is an extension to PU type 2.

There are three kinds of PU type 2.1 nodes:

- Low-entry networking end nodes (LENs)

- APPN end nodes (ENs)

- APPN network nodes (NNs)

The LEN node is the original PU type 2.1 node. It supports APPC in addition to supporting the older PU type 2 protocols. With the introduction of Advanced Peer-to-Peer Networking (APPN), two additional PU type 2.1 nodes evolved. The APPN end node (EN) and network node (NN) will be discussed later in this chapter when APPN concepts are introduced.

There is no specific data stream associated with PU type 2.1 nodes. PU type 2.1 nodes contain a *peripheral node control point* (PNCP) which provides the necessary software to allow SNA nodes to communicate with each other without the aid of the SSCP that is resident in a PU type 5 node.

6.3.1.5   Other PU types.   In the original architecture of SNA, it was thought that there would be a need for another device to fill the place in a network between the communications controller and a cluster controller, but this did not materialize. Hence, there is no such animal as a PU type 3. Additionally, PU type 1 is no longer used. PU type 1 was an older PU type that did not have as many features as PU type 2 and was implemented on IBM System/38, 3640, 3767, 3790, 5250, 6670, and the 3271.

6.3.2   The logical unit

The programs that comprise a physical unit manage the interface to the SNA link and the frames of data that arrive at that node over the link. SNA provides another abstraction called a *logical unit* (LU) that provides the services of a logical endpoint within the scope of a physical unit. Since a PU can contain a number of programs running at the same time, as is the case of a mainframe, or a number of terminals attached to it, as is the case of a communications controller, these programs and terminals are designated as LUs. LUs represent *logical* endpoints of a communication pipe. In the case of the mainframe, there is a single physical device, represented by the PU, and there are a number of *logical* endpoints which are represented by LUs. These mainframe LUs represent the application programs that communicate with terminals and printers, which are LUs within the scope of a communications controller PU.

There are two kinds of LUs: independent LUs and dependent LUs. Dependent LUs are the classic logical units that were originally associated with PU type 2 and PU type 5 nodes: the LUs that provide the older, hierarchical, method of mainframe-resident programs communicating with 3270 terminals and printers. Dependent LUs are dependent on the services of a PU type 5 SSCP for their activation. Independent LUs do not require the services of an SSCP and can be activated independently using the extended resources of a PU type 2.1 node.

LUs communicate with each other by establishing sessions called LU-LU sessions. These SNA sessions will be explained in more detail, but for now assume that a session is similar to a TCP connection. An LU-LU session, like a TCP connection, must first be established between endpoints before any data can be exchanged between the two LUs. An LU-LU session is a logical pipe that is established between LUs through which, for the lifetime of the session, data will travel.

Before an LU-LU session can be established between dependent LUs, two other underlying sessions must be established first: a session between the SSCP and the PU for the node in which the dependent LU resides, and a session between the SSCP and the LU itself. The session between the SSCP and the PU is called an SSCP-PU session and is used as a control session between the physical units. The session between the SSCP and the LU is called an SSCP-LU session and is used for passing control information between the LU and VTAM. After these two sessions are in place, the LU-LU session is established. The SSCP-PU and the SSCP-LU sessions remain active during the lifetime of the LU-LU session.

An independent LU, on the other hand, instead of relying on the SSCP in the mainframe to establish sessions, uses the control point services in the type 2.1 PU to establish an LU-LU session so it has no need of the services of the SSCP. Therefore, there is also no need for SSCP-PU and SSCP-LU sessions. That is why this LU is called independent: It is independent of the SSCP and is not tied to the hierarchical paradigm inherent in legacy SNA. It can operate independently of PU types 5 and 4 or, in other words, it can exist without a mainframe.

Figure 6.5 presents a diagram with three components: a PU type 5, a PU type 4, and a PU type 2 node. LUs are resident within the PU type 5 and 2 nodes. (There is no need for a logical unit within a PU type 4, since it does not act as an endpoint for any communications.) Two LU-LU sessions exist in our example, both dependent. In addition to these two LU-LU sessions, Fig. 6.5 shows the underlying SSCP-LU and SSCP-PU sessions required for these two dependent LUs.

Another distinction that is made with LUs is between primary and secondary LUs. *Primary LU* designates the LU that begins the initiation of a session. *Secondary LU* refers to the other partner LU. The

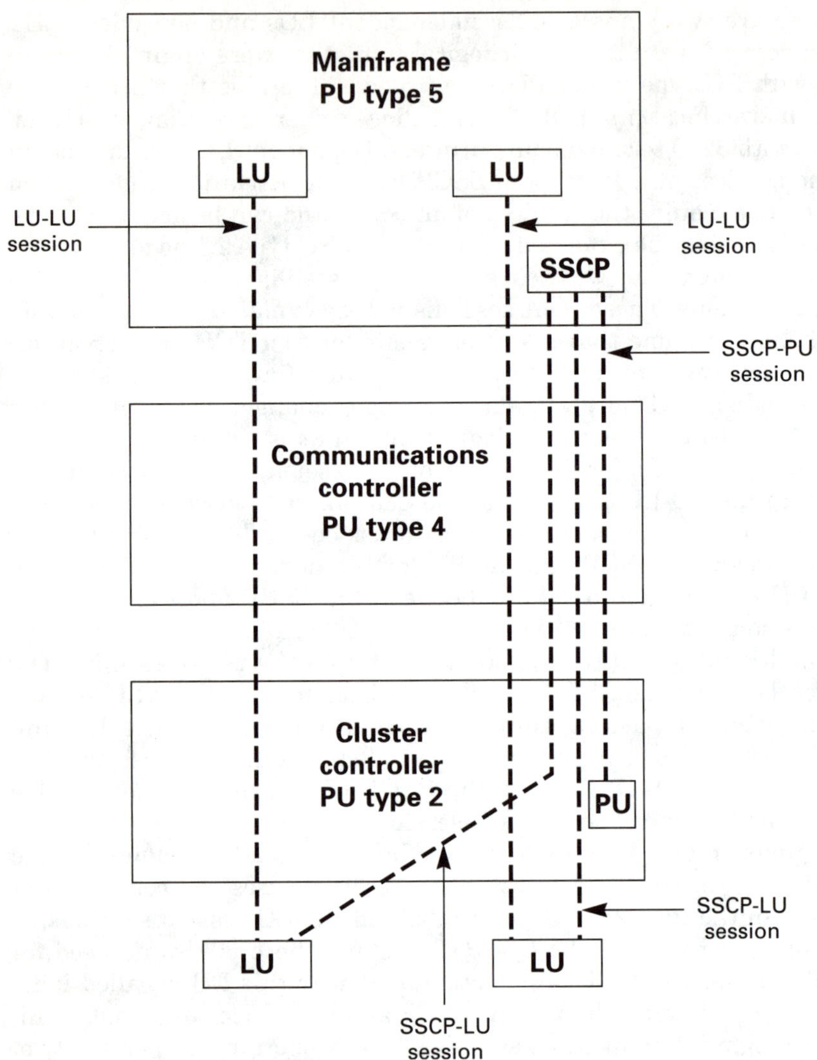

Figure 6.5 A "classic" SNA network with dependent LUs.

primary dependent LU is always resident in the mainframe, and the *secondary dependent LU* represents the 3270 terminal or printer. The primary LU in an independent LU-LU session is the LU that initiates the session.

As is the case with PUs, there are also a number of LU types (Table 6.1).

6.3.2.1 LU type 0. LU type 0, or simply LU 0, is considered to be a *generic* LU type which can implement other than the standard SNA

TABLE 6.1   LU Types

Type	Devices	Data stream
	LU Type 0	
Dependent	IBM 3600 Finance Communication System and 4700 financial terminals; LUA, NetView DM, JES2 Network Job Entry	No specific data stream
	LU Type 1	
Dependent	IBM SCS printers and compatibles; IBM 3767 and 3770 communication terminals, System/32	SNA Character Stream (SCS)
	LU Type 2	
Dependent	3270 terminals	3270
	LU Type 3	
Dependent	3270 printers	3270
	LU Type 4	
Dependent/ independent	IBM 6670 information distributor	SNA Character Stream (SCS) for data processing and Office Information Interchange (OII) Level-2 for word processing
	LU Types 6, 6.1, and 6.2	
Independent	Application programs	User-defined or any others; LU 6.2 uses the General Data Stream (GDS)
	LU Type 7	
Dependent	5250 terminals used on AS/400; System/36 and System/38	5250

protocols. Basically, it is an open interface to the entire LU process. Examples of how LU 0 has been implemented are such system services as the NetView Host Command Facility, which use an LU 0 connection to transport data. IBM used LU 0 before LU 6.2 was created for applications and devices that were not constant with the defined LU types and to provide primitive program-to-program communications. The mainframe database system called IMS and some point-ofsale systems for the banking and retail industries such as the IBM 4680 Store System Operating System used LU 0 in their early versions. Because of the nature of the IBM 3600 Finance Communication System (it is not just a terminal but a system on line with a mainframe IMS database), LU 0 protocols were used to implement communications.

An important implementation of LU 0 is called the *Conventional LU Application Programming Interface* (LUA). LUA is an API that implements an interface to an LU 0. LU 0, being kind of a raw LU, can be used as an API to implement other LU types and is sometimes used for implementing 3270 emulation software (LU type 2).

6.3.2.2 LU type 1. LU type 1 is today generally used to implement SNA Character Stream printers, but it is applicable to many kinds of devices, and function management headers (to be discussed later) can be used to select the device for which LU type 1 data are destined. LU type 1 was implemented as the logical unit type for the IBM 3767 Communications Terminal. Older applications that used LU 1 were often called *remote job entry* (RJE) applications. The SNA Character Stream was used as a replacement for the 3270 data stream in some of IBM's printers, and in today's world, LU type 1 printer emulation is usually available in most SNA software emulation and gateway products.

6.3.2.3 LU type 2. The LU type 2 device, either real or emulated, has been the dominant device in the IBM mainframe world. LU type 2 represents a 3270 terminal attached to a 3270 controller. 3270 terminals populated the branch and home offices of large corporations for many years. Being block mode devices with formatted screens, they served well for interfacing with mainframe applications.

The data stream used for 3270 is a specialized one designed for 3270 terminals. It consists of orders and commands that govern the placement of data on the screen and special formats for data streams that are returned from the terminal.

6.3.2.4 LU type 3. LU type 3 defines a 3270 printer such as the IBM 3284. It uses a 3270 data stream just like the 3270 terminals of LU type 2, but LU type 3 uses a few commands and features of the data stream that are not employed for terminals but are useful for printers, such as the form feed character and a bit that is turned on in the data stream when all the print data have arrived and the data stream is ready to be printed.

6.3.2.5 LU type 4. LU type 4 devices belonged to the older-style IBM 6670 Information Distributors that communicated with each other or with a mainframe. The 6670 was kind of a printer-word processing device and was a PU type 1. The AS/400 used LU type 4 printers attached to 5250 terminal controllers.

6.3.2.6 LU types 6, 6.1, and 6.2. An important aspect of LU type 6 is its use in a transaction-processing environment. It is used where synchronization of resources and update commitment of the phases of the transaction is vitally important. Function management headers, to be explained later, are important to the architecture of this LU type. LU type 6 was developed to provide sessions between transaction processing programs and was originally used in the mainframe environment for communications between IMS and CICS application programs. LU 6 was expanded into LU 6.1 and eventually into LU 6.2, which will be covered in Chap. 7.

6.3.2.7 LU type 7. LU type 7 devices are IBM 5250 terminals that are associated with the AS/400, System/34, and System/38 and use a specific data stream called the 5250 data stream.

6.3.3 SNA nodes

We have just taken a look at the basic types of SNA nodes. Each node in a SNA network has a physical unit designation, and each node may additionally contain logical units. Mainframes, PU type 5, have logical units: the application programs that use the services of VTAM to set up connections with 3270 devices. PU type 2 cluster controllers and emulated cluster controllers contain logical units that represent terminals and printers. PU type 2.1 nodes contain LUs to support communications between applications running in the node with applications running in other nodes.

SNA also describes nodes in a more general manner, and these descriptions will now be presented.

6.3.3.1 Subarea nodes. Classic SNA networks, before APPN and APPC, consisted of only two kinds of nodes: subarea nodes and peripheral nodes. A *subarea node* is a PU type 4 or 5 node, and a *peripheral node* is a PU type 1 or 2 node. Subarea nodes can be interconnected in a mesh topology, but peripheral nodes are simply clusters of terminals and printers. Subarea nodes control peripheral nodes that are connected to it, and the lot taken together is called a *subarea*.

A subarea has its own type of addressing, different from that used in peripheral nodes. The addressing convention for subareas is called a *network addressable unit* (NAU). The NAU is an address that consists of two parts: a subarea address and an element address. The subarea address defines the particular subarea; the element address is unique for every addressable unit within that subarea.

In traditional SNA, subareas are grouped together to form *do-*

mains, with each domain having a controlling SSCP. Domains can be grouped together into multiple-domain networks, with the SSCPs in each domain cooperating with each other to enable LUs that reside in one domain to initiate cross-domain sessions with LUs in another domain.

The subarea node is now, with the advent of APPN, a legacy node. It belongs to the older hierarchical style of SNA. Subarea nodes (PU types 4 and 5) can be phased out of SNA by converting to APPN and PU type 2.1 nodes.

6.3.3.2   Peripheral nodes.   The peripheral nodes, PU types 1 and 2, were called peripheral nodes because of their limited addressing and routing capabilities. They did not participate in subarea network routing and addressing; instead they depended on *boundary function* support within the subareas to transform the larger, global addresses of subareas into a local address. The boundary function is the process that glues subarea nodes to peripheral nodes.

The local address used by peripheral nodes is simply the LU number within the particular PU. For example, a cluster controller that is attached to a PU type 5 communications controller has 32 attached terminals. Each of these has an address, or LU number, in the range of 1 to 32. When data are sent from the mainframe to the communications controller, the transmission header prepended to the data will have a full subarea address consisting of either 16 or 23 bits, depending on whether extended network addressing is in effect or not. When the communications controller sends the data to the cluster controller, its boundary function support program extracts the LU number from the subarea address, creates an appropriate peripheral-node transmission header for the data, and inserts the LU number in the header as the address where the data are going. The cluster controller needs only the LU number to address its attached units.

6.3.3.3   APPN nodes.   Advanced Peer-to-Peer Networking (APPN) is the enhancement to SNA which makes SNA fully and dynamically routable. It provides a facility to locate any remote LU in an internet, and it can select the best route to that remote LU. APPN nodes are based on PU type 2.1 and can be linked together in any kind of mesh configuration, creating any-to-any networking. This is a completely different paradigm from the traditional SNA nodes just described, which were limited to being mainframes, communications controllers, cluster controllers, or some type of emulation of one of these.

APPN makes SNA function more like a TCP/IP network which consists of host and routing nodes. Just as is the case in a TCP/IP internet, with APPN, two SNA networks can be concatenated using a single routing node common between the two networks. With APPN, the internet concept is applied to a SNA network. "Host" nodes are called end nodes (EN), and routing nodes are called network nodes (NN).

The three types of PU type 2.1 nodes were listed in Sec. 6.3.1.4. The LEN node is a basic PU 2.1 node without APPN functionality. The APPN end node is a LEN node with the additional functionality to provide directory, topology, and route selection services to the end users in the node. It participates in the APPN network by invoking the services of an attached APPN network node. The APPN network node is an intelligent network node which provides directory, route selection, and management services to its attached ENs. APPN NNs are actually network node *servers* and have *domains* in which are located end-node clients. End-node clients contact the network node server when they need to locate a remote LU, when they need route selection services, or when they need to make use of the network node's network management services. Without the ability to become an APPN client, a LEN node is limited to initiating or accepting sessions with an LU that is either in an adjacent PU type 2.1 node or is reachable through a subarea boundary node that is PU type 2.1 compliant for independent LU sessions, or a traditional subarea boundary node for dependent LU sessions.

The client-server relationship is established and maintained between EN clients and an NN server through the use of CP-CP sessions, or sessions that are established between the control points of the two PUs. CP-CP sessions use LU 6.2 protocols in order to exchange network information such as directory, topology, route selection, and session establishment services. These CP-CP sessions between APPN nodes are created in pairs to provide a full-duplex pipe between the two endpoint nodes. An end node will have only a single pair of CP-CP sessions with a single network node, its network services server. Network nodes, however, have CP-CP sessions with the client end nodes in their domain as well as with other network nodes.

The CP-CP sessions between end nodes and network nodes are used for registering the resources of end nodes with network nodes, for directory searches requested by an end node, and to send network management alerts from the end nodes to the focal point or relay services function in the network node for network management under IBM's mainframe management tool called NetView. The CP-CP sessions that exist between network nodes are for the purpose of enabling the network nodes to keep track of network topology information. This information is stored in the network node's *topology database*.

PU type 2 nodes must be connected directly to a subarea by means of a boundary function, but PU type 2.1 nodes, since they have the capability to initiate sessions independently of an SSCP, may not be connected directly to a subarea at all. Dependent LU sessions residing in such a PU type 2.1 node, because of the absence of the boundary function support, therefore cannot contact the SSCP and sessions cannot be established. APPN solves this problem. Dependent LU sessions in remote APPN nodes are supported by means of a component called the *Dependent LU Requester/Server* (DLUR/S). DLUR/S consists of two parts:

- *Dependent LU Server* (DLUS)

- *Dependent LU Requester* (DLUR)

The way that DLUR/S works is that a pipe, consisting of two LU 6.2 sessions, is established between the dependent LU requester and the dependent LU server. The server module is loaded in the domain of the SSCP, on a mainframe, and the requester is located in the remote APPN node. The problem with dependent LUs is that the SSCP-PU and SSCP-LU sessions that must be in place before a dependent LU-LU session can be initiated, cannot be created if the LU is in a node that is not connected to a boundary function. The LU 6.2 pipe is used as a path for the SSCP-LU and SSCP-PU sessions, which are encapsulated in LU 6.2 sessions. Once these two sessions have been started, a normal LU-LU session can begin. Only the SSCP-LU and SSCP-PU sessions are encapsulated in the pipe, not the LU-LU session. By using DLUR/S, dependent LU sessions appear to be located within the domain of the controlling SSCP (Fig. 6.6).

6.3.3.4 Node addressing. With the advent of PU type 2.1 nodes, the manner in which nodes are addressed was completely changed. Before the PU type 2.1 node, subarea nodes were addressed using a subarea address; then, in the boundary function, addresses were translated between subarea addresses and local addresses. Local addresses were numbers that designated a particular LU within the PU connected to the boundary function. With the PU type 2.1 node, the term NAU was changed from its original meaning of *network addressable unit* to a new definition of *network accessible unit*. The reason for this is because with the change of the network topology from hierarchical to peer-to-peer, the older network address space represented by the subarea was supplemented by a new scheme (subarea addressing remains in place as a support for legacy systems, however). This new scheme is based on names.

The system of using names to designate the NAUs within a network was added to the SNA architecture by extending existing functions to support the names used in the new scheme. Every SNA network that has migrated to the newer PU 2.1 scheme has a name assigned to it, and this name should be globally unique (IBM main-

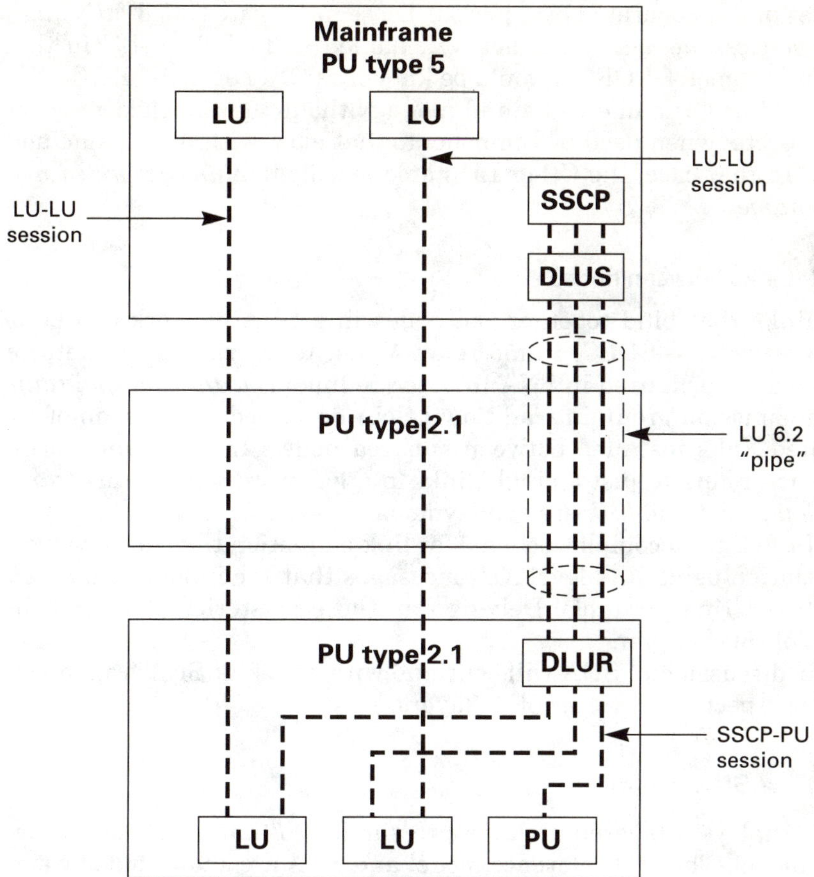

Figure 6.6   Dependent LUs interconnected using DLUR/S.

tains a worldwide registry of these names). The network name is
called the NetID and is eight characters in length. In an APPN network, all the interconnected network nodes belong to the same network and have the same NetID.

NetIDs, like the NetID of IP, identify individual networks. To locate
an individual component within a network, a name is assigned to the
individual components as well. These components, the network accessible units, are the control points and logical units that reside within
each PU. Each control point and every logical unit is assigned an eight-
character name which must be unique, but only within the network.

In order to address any node in any network, the individual name for
the component, which can either be an LU or the CP within a node, is
suffixed to the name assigned to the network in which that component

resides and is separated by a period. These names are called *fully qualified network names*. For a network named OFFNET, an LU in that network named GEORGE would be known as OFFNET.GEORGE.

An LU or CP name can stand alone without the attached network name prefix when used by components that exist within the same network. In that case, the CP or LU name is called an *uninterpreted network name*.

6.3.4   Links between nodes

The links that bind together the nodes in a SNA network can be of many varieties—SDLC, frame relay, WAN, token ring, Ethernet, for example. A term used in SNA to describe links is *transmission group*. A transmission group in traditional SNA described a collection of associated links installed between subarea nodes. In APPN networks, the term refers to just a single link. In other words, the terms *transmission group* and *link* are synonymous.

SNA defines a complex scheme for link activation that can involve a negotiation using link-level *XID* messages that are inherent in SDLC and token ring protocols. Delving into these mysteries is beyond the scope of this chapter.

Our discussion of SNA will continue with a look at SNA from a vertical perspective, in terms of its layers.

6.4   The SNA Model

SNA employs a layered architecture similar to that of the OSI reference model. The OSI reference model and SNA are shown side by side in Fig. 6.7. Even though most of the layers appear to correspond up to a certain point, SNA layers are not as neatly separated functionally as they are in the OSI model. For example, sequence numbers are assigned to SNA data packets in the data flow control layer, checked in the transmission control layer, then finally passed along to the network layer to be inserted into the network layer's header. Interestingly enough, only a single header is created for the top three SNA layers.

The layers of SNA will now be described.

6.4.1   Data link control: The data link layer

The original protocol used in the SNA data link control layer was Synchronous Data Link Control (SDLC), which was first introduced as an integral part of SNA. SDLC will not be described in this chapter because the basic principles of all data link protocols have already been described in Chap. 2.

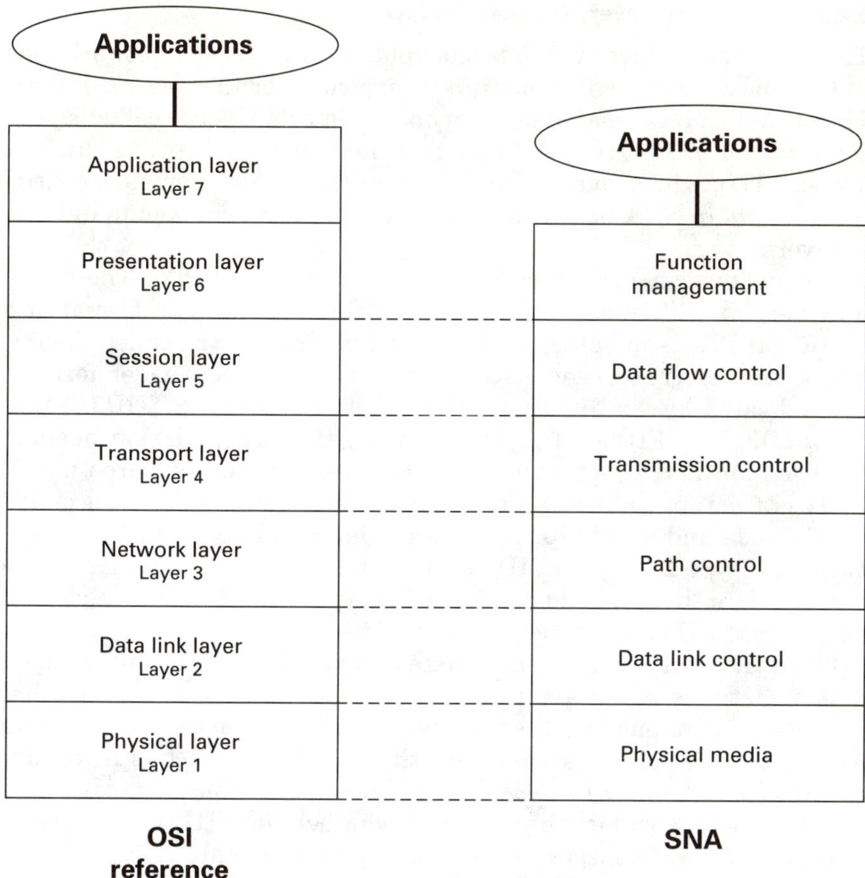

Figure 6.7 The OSI reference model and SNA.

SNA's data link control layer has the same functionality as the OSI data link layer, and this means that other data link layer protocols can be substituted for SDLC in the SNA stack. For this reason, as newer data link layer protocols came into existence, it was easy to make SNA work over them. It is safe to conclude that the protocols that actually belong to SNA begin in the third layer, the path control layer, which is SNA's network layer. In this respect, SNA is similar to other protocols such as IPX and TCP/IP. SNA can be found running over many different data link layer protocols. Examples are SDLC, token ring, Ethernet, PPP, frame relay, ATM, and X.25. SDLC links, which were commonly used for WAN connections, are now being replaced in many installations by frame relay.

6.4.2   Path control layer: The network layer

The path control layer is the bottom of a SNA transport network, and in true network layer fashion, it is responsible for the routing of data. The packet that is created by components in this layer is called a *path information unit* (PIU). A PIU has a header called a *transmission header* (TH), which contains information that is used by path control components in SNA nodes as well as some of the components in higher layers.

A transmission header is found in front of every PIU. There are, however, six different transmission header formats. The format of a particular PIU is indicated by the first 4 bits of the TH, called the *format identifier* (FID). The six different transmission header formats are indicated by six different FIDs: FID0, FID1, FID2, FID3, FID4, and FIDF. The FID0, FID1, FID4, and FIDF transmission headers are used for data being transported between adjacent subarea nodes. FID2 is used for data being transmitted between a PU type 4 or PU type 5 node and a PU type 2.1 or an adjacent PU type 2 node, or between PU type 2.1 nodes. FID3 is obsolete, but was used for transmission headers that flowed between a PU type 4 or PU type 5 node and an adjacent PU type 1 node.

When SNA data packets are passed down to the path control layer, it is sometimes necessary that the data be segmented into smaller packets to accommodate the maximum transmission size of the data link control layer. To accomplish this, path control has a feature called *segmentation and reassembly*. The transmission header has a mapping field with bits that indicate whether the PIU is complete by itself or is part of a larger unit that must be reassembled by path control components in the destination endpoint.

There are basically two styles of path control layer implementations: path control from a boundary function, such as in the NCP of a 3705, to a PU type 1, 2, or 2.1, and path control between subareas. Path control between subareas is complex, and for this reason will not be described in this chapter. The reader is referred to the Bibliography for books and manuals that describe these services.

The network layer addresses used in a transmission header are different for a dependent LU and an independent LU. For a dependent LU, the TH contains a destination and origin address which hold the destination and origin LU numbers. For an SSCP-LU session, the LU number for the origin, the SSCP, is 0. The PU type 2.1 node maintains a table of *local-form session identifiers* (LFSID), which are 17-bit session identifiers. When either a CP or an independent LU in a node decides to activate a session, an LFSID is assigned to the session.

When data are sent on a session, the LFSID is placed in the TH as the address identifier. An LFSID is assigned for each session. The nodes at the respective endpoints of a link use the same LFSID to identify a session and map the LFSID into a FID2 transmission header. Every time a network node is reached (or a hop), each pair of adjacent nodes assigns a distinct LFSID to identify the session. As LU session data flow over the route for that session, network nodes perform *address swapping* of the LFSID in the TH. This occurs as the data flow from one session stage to the next. Each network node along the route replaces the LFSID on the inbound link with the LFSID assigned to the outbound link.

6.4.3 Transmission control:
The transport layer

The transmission control layer is the layer above path control and corresponds to the OSI transport layer. Where the path control layer of the SNA network is responsible for delivering data to the proper location within the network, or to the correct network node, transmission control is responsible for end-to-end delivery. Transmission control controls sessions, checks sequence numbers, and deals with error correction. Two components belong to this layer: the connection point manager and session control. They will be discussed separately.

6.4.3.1 Connection point manager. The connection point manager manages the data that travel through the transmission control layer, handles pacing (sending only the amount of data that the receive buffers can hold), and checks the sequencing of the messages. The connection point manger also performs the important function of creating the basic packet of SNA data called the *basic information unit* (BIU), which consists of a *request/response unit* (RU) and its associated header, the *request/response header* (RH). Even though the responsibility for the creation of the RU belongs to this layer, RUs can be formatted in any of the top three SNA layers.

Basically, an RU consists of either a packet of data, called *function management data* (FMD) because the data originate on the function management layer, or a specially formatted SNA command packet that contains a command code and, in some cases, a variable amount of data. The command RUs originate on the transmission control layer, the data flow control layer, or the function management layer. The particular commands that originate on any particular layer deal with the functions of that layer.

RUs that contain commands are what activate the many services of SNA, and RUs that contain data are the vehicle for transferring data around a network. Every RU, whether it contains data or command, has the 3-byte RH; the packet that results from the combination of request unit with the associated 3-byte RH is a BIU. An RU is called a request unit when it is being sent to a destination LU, but if protocols demand that a response, either negative or positive, be sent back to the originating LU, then the RU is known as a *response unit*. In this case, the RH is called a *response header.*

Figure 6.8 shows the request header and Fig. 6.9 the response header formats. The first bit in the header indicates if the RU is a request or a response. The next 2 bits indicate to which higher layer function the RU belongs: network control (01), session control (11), data flow control (10), or just plain data ("function management data" 00). Byte 1 contains 3 bits of response indicators: Definite Response 1 Indicator, Definite Response 2 Indicator, and Exception Response Indicator. These bits, sparing the details, determine if and how a response will be sent when an RU is received. The Sense Data Included (SDI) indicator is turned on in a response header if the response is a negative response, meaning that the request was not accepted because of an error. The nature of the error is described by a *sense code* included in the RU part of the negative response.

One of the responsibilities of this layer is called session-level pacing. *Session-level pacing* is an option that, when selected, allows transmission control to limit the amount of data that is sent by the partner in a session so that data are not sent faster than expected and buffers are always available. In other words, session-level pacing performs flow control in the transport layer. This pacing is called *session level* because it is independent of pacing that could be taking place in other layers, such as virtual route pacing between subareas in the path control layer and pacing being performed by the data link layer protocol. Pacing in one layer does not necessarily satisfy the needs of pacing in higher layers. For example, the data link control layer can perform pacing of incoming packets yet still deliver the data to the higher layers faster than they were able to process them, for example. Session-level pacing is accomplished by means of a bit in the request header called the *pacing bit*. Tuning pacing in an SNA network and understanding how it works is a subject that will not be dealt with here.

The transmission control layer verifies the sequence numbers in incoming data packets to ensure that packets are sequenced correctly. Sequence numbers are assigned by the data flow control layer, but they are checked by the transmission control layer. When a session is activated, the sequence number is initialized to zero. It is incremented by one by the data flow control layer before a request is sent. When it reaches 65,535, the sequence number wraps back to zero. The only time a zero is ever sent is when the number has wrapped.

SNA has two levels, or classes, of service. These are called *expedited* and *normal flow* in SNA terminology. Normal flow is the normal data that are sent between each of the endpoints of an SNA session.

1 byte

Request/ response indicator (0)	RU category		Reserved	Format indicator	Sense data included indicator	Begin chain indicator	End chain indicator
Definite response type 1 indicator	Reserved	Definite response type 2 indicator	Exception response indicator	Reserved	Request larger window indicator	Queued response indicator	Pacing indicator
Begin bracket indicator	End bracket indicator	Change direction indicator	Reserved	Coded selection indicator	Enciphered data indicator	Padded data indicator	Conditional end of bracket indicator

Figure 6.8 The SNA request header.

1   byte

Request/ response indicator (1)	RU category		Reserved	Format indicator	Sense data indicator	Always set to '1'	Always set to '1'
Definite response type 1 indicator	Reserved	Definite response type 2 indicator	Response type indicator	Reserved		Queued response indicator	Pacing indicator
Reserved							

Figure 6.9   The SNA response header.

The expedited flow is reserved for higher-priority SNA commands that perform such duties as activating and deactivating sessions or requesting a change of direction for the flow of data. Sequence numbers are assigned to normal flow RUs only. In the transmission control header there is an expedited flow indicator that when turned on gives the associated PIU a higher priority, which causes it to be placed ahead of other traffic.

6.4.3.2 Session control. Session control handles the initiation and termination of *sessions*. When comparing the SNA transmission control layer with the transport layer of other protocols, SNA sessions can be compared to transport layer connections. A connection is established between two network endpoints; a session is *bound* between two endpoints called *half-sessions*. Once a session is established, data flow in a controlled manner between the half-sessions. From this point on, connection point management on each end of the session ensures that RUs are sequenced properly and that session-level pacing, or data flow control, is accomplished. The SNA command RUs that are used by the session control component of the transmission control layer are shown in Table 6.2.

Before any user data can flow anywhere in an SNA network, sessions must be created. SNA's transport layer provides connection-oriented services only; there are no datagrams in SNA.

As we have been seeing, there are distinct types of SNA sessions. The session type depends on the half-session components at each end.

TABLE 6.2   Session Control RUs

ACTPU	Activate the PU
ACTLU	Activate an LU
ACTCDRM	Activate cross-domain resource manager
BIND	Bind a session
SDT	Start data traffic
CRV	Cryptography verification
RQR	Request recovery
STSN	Set and test sequence numbers
SWITCH	Change LU-LU session XRF state
DACTPU	Deactivate the PU
DACTLU	Deactivate an LU
DACTCDRM	Deactivate cross-domain resource manager
UNBIND	Unbind a session
CLEAR	Clear data traffic

The following are examples of sessions categorized by their half-session components:

- *SSCP-SSCP sessions* are control sessions between two SSCPs. These sessions are used to manage multidomain networks.

- *CP-CP sessions* are control sessions that are established between control points in APPN nodes.

- *SSCP-PU sessions* must be activated before any dependent LU-LU sessions can be started. The SSCP-PU session is used as a control session on which information such as network management data is transmitted.

- *SSCP-LU sessions* must be activated before a dependent LU-LU session with that LU can take place. The SSCP-LU session is a control session that the LU can use to send out-of-band requests to the SSCP. It is also the session on which the command RUs for starting and terminating an LU-LU session flow. SSCP-LU sessions are also used for transferring character-coded, or non-3270, commands to VTAM.

- *CP-LU sessions* take place between a PU type 2.1 control point and an independent LU. The CP-LU session is the independent LU's version of an SSCP-LU session.

- *LU-LU sessions* are the normal sessions that take place between two LUs. The LU that initiated the session is called the primary LU, and the other is the secondary LU.

The LU-LU session is the session which carries user data from one endpoint to the other and on which all the SNA commands pertaining to the session flow. The LU-LU session constitutes the "pipe" that is created between the two LU half-sessions. LU-LU sessions are established when a BIND request RU is sent by one of the LUs. The LU that sends the bind is designated the *primary LU*. For sessions between dependent LUs, the primary LU must be in a PU type 5 subarea node. Independent primary LUs can reside in a peripheral node. The BIND LU contains the specifications for the requested session. The secondary LU can either reject or accept the terms of the BIND by returning an acknowledgment to the BIND.

The primary LU in a dependent LU-LU session resides in a mainframe because dependent LUs are the LUs of classic SNA. One of the endpoints of a dependent LU-LU session is an application program running in a mainframe (a PU type 5), and the other endpoint is a 3270 terminal or printer (attached to a PU type 2).

It was mentioned above that before dependent LU-LU sessions can be bound, an SSCP-PU session and an SSCP-LU session with the secondary LU must already exist. These sessions are not created by issuing a BIND command as is the case with the LU-LU sessions. The SSCP-PU session is created when an *activate physical unit* (ACTPU) SNA command is sent from the SSCP to the PU and the PU sends back a positive response. Following that, an *activate logical unit* (ACTLU) command is sent on the SSCP-PU session addressed to the LU for which an SSCP-LU session is to be activated. After a positive response is sent back, the SSCP-LU session is in effect. Deactivation of LU-LU sessions is accomplished by an UNBIND command. SSCP-LU sessions are deactivated with a DACTLU and SSCP-PU sessions with a DACTPU.

Session control commands must receive a positive or a negative response. Typically, a 3270 control unit would receive an ACTPU, then send back a positive response. Next an ACTLU would be sent for each LU that was defined in the VTAM or NCP tables for that controller's physical unit. Each of these in turn is responded to. If, for any reason, the controller does not want to activate one of the LUs, a negative response, with the proper sense code loaded into the data area of the RU to explain why, is returned to the SSCP, or a NOTIFY stating that the LU is not yet available is sent.

The *start data traffic* (SDT) command is issued in a dependent LU session to start the flow of traffic. Clear (CLEAR) terminates the flow of data and is used to reset the session.

6.4.4   Data flow control layer: The session layer

The *data flow control layer* (DFC) controls the flow of data transmitted between the LU-LU half-sessions. DFC also is responsible for the session-layer dialog management functions which manage the direction of the flow of data. DFC also assigns the sequence numbers to RUs. The command RUs that are used by this layer are shown in Table 6.3.

6.4.4.1   Chaining.   In order to understand how the data flow control layer deals with data, it is necessary to explain SNA's chaining protocol and the concept of chains. A *chain* is a string of RUs that are bound together to form a single piece of data. This is accomplished by setting the *chaining indicators* in the individual request headers. What this means is that if DFC receives three similar data RUs, if they are to be chained together, they are buffered, then the first RU's chaining indicator is set for "first in chain," the second RU's chaining indicator is set for "middle of chain," and the last RU's chaining indicator is set for (you guessed it) "last in chain." A chain can be segmented by the path control layer and sent in pieces, but at its final

TABLE 6.3   Data Flow Control Layer RUs

BID	Bid
BIS	Bracket initiation stopped
CANCEL	Cancel
CHASE	Chase
LUSTAT	Logical unit status
QC	Quiesce
QEC	Quiesce at end of chain
RELQ	Release the quiesce
RSHUTD	Request shutdown
RTR	Ready to receive
SBI	Stop bracket initiation
SHUTC	Shutdown complete
SHUTD	Shutdown
SIG	Signal

destination it will be put back together into a chain. When RUs are chained together, the chain becomes a single unit and response units apply to the entire chain rather than to the individual RUs of which the chain is made up.

As an example, the function-management data layer routines in a mainframe can format the data for a terminal's screen (consisting of 1920 characters) into three data RUs, splitting the 1920-character screen into three pieces. When these three RUs are processed by the data flow control layer, since the three RUs are related, the data flow control layer can tie the three RUs together into a chain. When this chain gets to the path control layer, the boundary function routines must prepare the data to be sent to the 3270 cluster controller, which requires that the PIUs created by path control be 256 bytes long. The chain is broken up and transmission headers are applied to each piece and are flagged to indicate, in the TH mapping field, which segments are first, middle, and last. When the cluster controller gets the data, it is put back into the original chain and a response is sent to the mainframe indicating that the chain was received.

6.4.4.2 Brackets and the flow of data. The control of the direction in which data flows in a session is governed by the protocols of the data flow control layer. To begin with, there are three *send/receive modes*. These are three different manners in which the direction of data flow is governed in a session in the DFC layer:

- Full-duplex
- Half-duplex contention
- Half-duplex flip-flop

The first, *full-duplex,* is a session condition similar to that of TCP: Data flow simultaneously between two half-sessions in both directions. Full-duplex is a bidirectional pipe. In *half-duplex contention* mode, the session is always in a contention state and either half-session can send chains at any time; however, one side of the session has been designated a contention winner and the other a contention loser, and the contention winner can send a negative response for a chain sent from the other side, forcing the contention loser to wait until the winner has finished sending a chain to attempt transmission again.

Half-duplex flip-flop is the mode used most commonly. In *half-duplex flip-flop* the half-sessions take turns sending data. A flag in the request header, called a *change of direction indicator,* is used to control this flip-flopping of direction. There are two ways this can be handled. One way is to designate one half-session as the first sender. The first sender begins by sending data. When the first sender has finished, it turns the *change of direction indicator* on in the request header and the other half-session sends data. Using the *change of direction indicator,* direction is flip-flopped back and forth.

The other way in which half-duplex flip-flop is implemented is through the use of the data flow control protocol known as the *bracket* protocol. Using half-duplex flip-flop with the bracket protocol is the most common method of exchanging data in the DFC layer.

A *bracket* is kind of a transaction-exchange state that is established for a period of time between the two half-sessions. During this state, called the *in-bracket state,* data flowing between the half-sessions is controlled by the *change of direction indicator.* When the bracket state is terminated, a contention state is entered until one of the two half-sessions begins another bracket state. Either half-session can begin the state of being in-bracket, but one of the half-sessions is considered to be *first speaker* and the other is called the *bidder.* The first speaker always wins a bracket contention, meaning that if both half-sessions try to begin a bracket condition at the same time, the first speaker is the winner. The other half-session is called the bidder because it must bid for the right to begin a bracket.

It must be pointed out that a bracket is *not* similar to a chain. While a chain is a continuous stream of data—a concatenation of request units—a bracket is not. A bracket creates a *state.* A chain is space-oriented, a bracket is time-oriented. Beginning a bracket means that the in-bracket state is entered. Once in the in-bracket state, the two half-sessions know which has the right to send because this is governed by the *change of direction indicator*. The half-session that began the bracket starts by sending data, then turns the direction around by setting change of direction on the last chain it sends. When a bracket is terminated, the *between-bracket state* is entered.

Brackets, as has been said, can be initiated by either half-session. In the case of the common 3270 protocol, LU type 2, the 3270 end of the session is always first speaker; the mainframe application, connected via VTAM, is the bidder. The 3270 LU can start a bracket any time by simply setting the begin bracket indicator in the request header and sending a chain. The mainframe application can do the same thing, but, because it is the bidder, the first speaker can reject the chain by returning a negative response. The mainframe, being the bidder, has another option, and this is common: It can send a *BID* RU, which is an RU with a SNA BID command in it. This command tells the 3270 half-session that the mainframe wishes to *bid* for the right to send data. If a positive response is sent back, then the bidder can send its chain without the possibility of it being rejected.

Brackets can be used wisely, or they can be the cause of many difficult-to-find problems. Some mainframe applications, such as TSO, can enter the in-bracket state as soon as a session is established, then stay in the in-bracket state for the duration of the session. All is orderly. The bracket is not terminated until the session ends. The mainframe CICS application, however, can be very untidy, sending RUs with no data in them to terminate brackets, for example.

6.4.4.3 Other details of data flow control. The commands that are associated with the data flow control layer are listed in Table 6.3. The BID command was mentioned in connection with bracketing. Several of the other commands will be discussed briefly to familiarize the reader with some important SNA concepts.

The SNA CANCEL command is sent at any time by either half-session to terminate a chain that is currently in the process of being sent. LUSTAT is used to send status information concerning an LU to the other half-session. The status information is contained in a 4-byte field in the RU and is used for notifying a mainframe application, for example, that a printer is disconnected or unavailable.

The three shutdown commands, which perform an orderly shutdown of an LU-LU session, work as follows: One of the half-sessions is considered to be the primary logical unit, the other the secondary. The primary logical unit—for example, a mainframe application—can notify the secondary logical unit, the 3270 LU, that it must shut down because the LU-LU session is being terminated. It does this by sending the shutdown command (SHUTD). When the secondary logical unit has completed sending data, it sends the shutdown complete command (SHUTC). If the secondary logical unit needs to initiate a shutdown, it can send an RSHUTD to the primary asking that the session be shut down. The primary logical unit responds by sending an UNBIND, which will be covered in the next section.

SIGNAL is a SNA command meant to *signal* the opposite half-session. It has a 2-byte signal code and a 2-byte extension value that indicate why the signal is being sent. SIGNAL is commonly used for issuing the REQUEST_TO_SEND message by a half-session that is in the receive state. SIGNAL uses the expedited flow. When one half-session has the right to send, but the other half-session wants to send data, it cannot just send data because the other end of the session's SNA routines will return a negative response and will reject the data. It can either wait for the other end to send a chain with the *change of direction indicator* turned on, or wait until a chain is sent with the *end bracket indicator* turned on, or can it send an expedited signal request saying "Please give me the right-to-send." If a positive response is returned, the line has been "turned around," and the direction of the data flow reversed. It will be seen in the following chapter that the change of direction function of SIGNAL is an important part of APPC and the LU 6.2 protocols.

6.4.5 Function management layer

The function management layer is the top layer of the SNA model, although some texts show an application layer residing on top of the function management layer. The function management layer is a complex entity, and we must abbreviate it in order not to risk losing our readers in a sea of acronyms and options. Basically, function management consists of two services: end-user services and network services.

6.4.5.1 End-user services.
End-user services provide services to the end user by transferring end-user data across the network. One example of these services is the use of function management headers. A *function management header* is a specially formatted header that can be carried at the beginning of an RU. Function management headers are used for specific purposes. Table 6.4 describes the ten currently used function management headers. The function management headers used for LU type 6.2 are described in the next chapter.

Another end-user service is a provision for data streams. The data streams used by the various LU types have already been presented in Table 6.1. The two main data streams used in SNA are the 3270 data stream, designed for formatting 3270 terminal screens and print data, and the SNA Character Stream.

The 3270 data stream consists of special commands, orders, and indicators that govern how data are placed on a terminal screen or on a

TABLE 6.4   Function Management Headers

FMH-1	Selects a destination within an LU; i.e., a device or a dataset. Can also indicate that RU data are compressed or compacted.
FMH-2	Used in LU Type 1 and 4 sessions (which use the SNA data stream). Must be used in conjunction with FMH-1, which first indicates the destination. FMH-2 is used to define the data management tasks for that destination (such as creating or deleting a dataset, adding records or scheduling a program).
FMH-3	Defines data management tasks for *all* destinations in the LU-LU session. FMH-3 is almost identical to FMH-2.
FMH-4	Used by LU Type 6 to describe the data stream in the RU.
FMH-5	Used by LU Type 6 and 6.2 to identify the program that the sending LU wishes to attach.
FMH-6	Used by LU Type 6 to send commands and data to the program attached by the other LU.
FMH-7	Used by LU Type 6 and 6.2 after a negative response to provide information about an error.
FMH-8	Used by LU Type 6.1 in IBM/VS logical message services.
FMH-10	Used by LU Type 6 to prepare a session for a sync point.
FMH-12	Used by LU Type 6.2 to transport security information.

printed page. When data are sent to a screen, they are formatted by the mainframe application to include all the special 3270 codes. The way this is accomplished is that the screen is divided into fields. Fields are defined by special characters called *attribute bytes,* which are placed in front of them in the screen's buffer. The attribute byte contains bit settings which define the nature of the field. Fields can have special visual qualities, such as displayable, nondisplayable, and highlighted. They can also be defined as editable fields when they are designated as numeric or character. A bit in the attribute byte is also set when the field has been modified by the terminal operator. Called the *modified data tag,* this bit can be used to determine which fields to send back to the mainframe because they contain the data that were entered by the user. Since all the fields that are returned are marked with coordinates that show where they came from on the screen, it is always clear what parts of the screen the data were associated with. After a terminal operator has typed in all data that needed to be input on the screen, he or she presses the Enter key to send the data back to the mainframe. Either the modified data that were entered by the operator, or the entire screen—depending on the command sent from the mainframe requesting that the screen be read—is formatted along with a byte called an *aid byte* which is set with the type of key (such as the Enter key, a PF key, or the Clear key) that was pressed by the operator, then all of this is sent back to the mainframe.

The 3270 data stream is also used for printers, but the SCS data stream is generally considered to be superior for handling print.

6.4.5.2 Network services. The network services component of the function management layer deals with the work of control points and is divided into three subservices: configuration services, session services, and management services. The control point, it will be recalled, is in charge of the PU. In the traditional mainframe environment, the control point is a part of VTAM and is called the system service control point (SSCP). The control point residing in a 2.1 node is the peripheral node control point (PNCP). The control point deals with all kinds of matters such as the activation of SDLC links, the world of configuration services, the dealing with sessions before they are bound, as in session services, and matters dealing with network management as in management services. These three categories will now be further explained.

Configuration services. Configuration services deal with configuration of the network and with such matters as the activation and deactivation of links. Perusal of Table 6.5, which lists the SNA commands used in configuration services, will indicate to the reader some idea of what these services entail, and no further explanation will be presented. The subject is too complex and not related to the subject of the book.

Session services. Session services RUs deal with matters relating to the establishing and termination of sessions between SNA nodes. Tables 6.6 and 6.7 list the RUs that deal with initialization and termination of sessions, and Table 6.8 shows the RUs that deal with other matters of initialization of sessions.

The subject of session services is an interesting part of the under-the-covers work of a SNA network. However, to describe session services in any detail would require an entire chapter, so only a brief overview will be given.

The network services initialization and termination commands deal with matters of session initialization and termination that take place at a lower level than the session control component of transmission control. Commands are used between the SSCP and primary and secondary LUs to set up a session before the bind flows. Versions of these commands are used for a single-domain environment, others for cross-domain. The INIT-SELF is a common SNA RU that is sent by an LU to a control point to request a BIND, for example. If a control point receives an INIT-SELF, it sends a CINIT to the primary LU informing the session control component in the primary LU to send a BIND RU to the secondary LU. One of the LUs must have been the LU responsible for sending the initial INIT-SELF. INIT-OTHER is

TABLE 6.5 Network Services

Configuration Services RUs

ACTLINK	Activate a link	DACTLINK	Deactivate a link
ACTCONNIN	Activate incoming connections	DACTCONNIN	Deactivate incoming connections
CONNOUT	Initiate a connect-out	ABCONNOUT	Abandon connect-out
REQCONT	Request that a contact be sent	ABCONN	Abandon connection
CONTACT	Contact an adjacent link station	CONTACTED	Contact was performed
DISCONTACT	Deactivate a contact	REQDISCONT	Request a DISCONTACT
IPLINIT	IPL initial: IPL a type 4 PU	IPLTEXT	IPL text for the IPLINIT
IPLFINAL	IPL final completes the IPL		
DUMPINIT	Dump initial: dump a type 4 PU	DUMPTEXT	Dump text from the type 4 PU
DUMPFINAL	Dump final: Dump is finished		
RPO	Remote power-off of a PU type 4		
INOP	Inoperative: connection or contact failure		
INITPROC	Initiate procedure (load operation)	PROCSTAT	Procedure status (of the load)
RSAA	Request network addr assignment		
FNA	Free network addresses		
ADDLINK	Add link (get link network address)	ADDLINKSTA	Add link station (adjacent net addr)
DELETENR	Delete Network Resource		
ESLOW	Entering slowdown state	EXSLOW	Exiting slowdown state
REQFNA	Request free network addresses		
REQACTLU	Request an ACTLU	REQACTPU	Request an ACTPU
SETCV	Set control vector		
ER_INOP	Explicit route inoperative		
LCP	Lost control point		

TABLE 6.6   Network Services

Session Services Initiation RUs

Initiation	
INIT-SELF	Initiate self
INIT-OTHER	Initiate other
CINIT	Control initiate
SESSST	Session started
BINDF	Bind failure
Cross-Domain Initiation	
INIT-OTHER-CD	Cross-domain INIT-OTHER
CDINIT	Cross-domain INITIATE
CDCINIT	Cross-domain CINIT
CDSESSST	Cross-domain SESSST

TABLE 6.7   Network Services

Session Services Termination RUs

Termination	
TERM-SELF	Terminate self
TERM-OTHER	Terminate other
CTERM	Control terminate
CLEANUP	Cleanup session
SESSEND	Session ended
UNBINDF	Unbind failure
Cross-Domain Termination	
DACTCDRM	Deactivate cross-domain resource manager
INIT-OTHER-CD	Cross-domain TERM-OTHER
CDTERM	Cross-domain TERMINATE
CDSESSEND	Cross-domain SESSEND
CDTAKED	Cross-domain takedown
CDTAKEDC	Cross-domain takedown complete

TABLE 6.8   Network Services

Session Services Miscellaneous RUs

NOTIFY	Notify
NSPE	Network services procedure error
DSRLST	Direct search list

sent by an LU to initiate an LU-LU session for two entire different LUs. If these LUs reside in another domain, then the INIT-OTHER-CD is used.

Management services.   Management services RUs are shown in Table 6.9 and give the reader a taste of the complexity of the subject. In order to keep this chapter on SNA at a reasonable length, the details of management services will be left for further perusal on the part of the reader.

6.5   SNA Network Management

When SNA was first introduced in 1974, network management tools for the new architecture were not yet available. Gradually, however, IBM introduced various programs that would aid in the management of SNA networks as they grew in size and complexity. *Network Communications Control Facility* (NCCF), introduced in the late 1970s, returned network management information from controllers and terminals. *Network Problem Determination Application* (NPDA) provided information about network hardware, and the *Network Logical Data Manager* (NLDM), introduced in the early 1980s, presented a logical view of a network and allowed the monitoring of SNA sessions. Two other products were added to the mix: *VTAM Node Control Application* (VNCA) and *Network Management Productivity Facility* (NMPF).

TABLE 6.9   Network Services

Management Services RUs

ACTTRACE	Activate trace
DACTTRACE	Deactivate trace
RECTRD	Record trace data
DISPSTOR	Display storage
RECSTOR	Record storage
EXECTEST	Execute test
RECTD	Record test data
REQMS	Request maintenance statistics
RECFMS	Record formatted maintenance statistics
REQTEST	Request test procedure
TESTMODE	Test mode
RECTR	Record test results
SETCV	Set control vector
ER_TESTED	Explicit route tested

In 1986, IBM bundled these existing management products together and reintroduced them as a single network management product called *NetView*. With all the major existing network management tools under one banner, IBM began a gradual course of improving on the NetView product and NetView became the cornerstone of SNA network management. NetView has three major components:

- A *focal point* resides in a mainframe host and provides centralized network management for all components in a network.

- An *entry point* is a device, such as a 3174 cluster controller or a 3745 communications controller, that concentrates NetView management packets, called *alerts,* that are received from downstream devices, then sends this information to the focal point. The focal point sends management commands to entry points in the performance of its management tasks.

- A *service point* is a device, such as a PC, that concentrates network management information from devices that use management protocols other than NetView, then converts this information to NetView protocols and sends it to the focal point. It also converts commands that are received from the focal point to formats acceptable to the native network management protocol. In other words, a service point is kind of a network management gateway or protocol converter.

Internally, NetView blends into the SNA architecture by using a specific format called a *Network Management Vector Transport* (NMVT) to transport NetView information on an SSCP-PU session. When NetView agents detect problems that occur in a SNA network, they generate a specific NMVT, the *alert.* Alerts are sent to an entry point and from there to a focal point. NetView software in the focal point, the mainframe, displays these errors on a NetView console. The management services component of APPN provides another set of data formats known as *multiple-domain support message units* (MDS-MU) and *control point management services units* (CP-MSU). These packet formats are used to send network management data in an APPN network and flow on LU-LU and CP-CP sessions.

In 1990, IBM unveiled its plan for upgrading its network management strategy with a new network management architecture called *SystemView* and announced NetView Version 2. An important member of the SystemView/NetView family is IBM's NetView for AIX for the RS/6000. An excellent SNMP network management product for TCP/IP networks, NetView for AIX began life in January 1992 as Hewlett-Packard Company's OpenView Network Node Manager. IBM licensed the product from HP and has continuously upgraded it to the point that it has gained a life of its own. NetView for AIX can be used in conjunction with the AIX NetView Service Point program to communicate fully with a mainframe's NetView focal point. NetView for AIX can convert SNMP *traps,* which are generated by SNMP agents when problems occur on the network, into NetView alerts and then display them on the mainframe console. Using this service point implementation, TCP/IP networks managed by NetView for AIX can be managed from a NetView focal point.

6.6 Summary

SNA, a complex communications architecture, can be viewed from two perspectives: the *classic* version, which created an environment that enabled 3270 terminals and printers to access mainframe application programs, and the newer architecture based on APPN, APPC, and HPR. The older, classic SNA, which used the subarea approach, has become largely a legacy system used in modern networks only to support mainframe applications. The newer extensions to the SNA architecture are applicable to modern communications networks. The reader interested in modern SNA networking is referred to the list of IBM publications in App. D for in-depth descriptions of SNA and APPN. APPC, and its associated API CPI-C, are presented in the next chapter. This discussion will provide the reader a better understanding of how modern SNA networks are accessed using a communications programming interface similar in its use to the sockets API (described in Chap. 5), albeit quite different in approach.

APPC and the CPI-C API

7.1 Introduction and Background

Advanced Program-to-Program Communications (APPC) is an extension to traditional Systems Network Architecture. It provides an application protocol boundary that defines the services available to enable communication between programs. It also provides a platform for the development of distributed applications and transaction processing. APPC is implemented mainly with two major extensions to the SNA architecture: logical unit type 6.2, which was a revamping and enlarging of LU type 6.1, and physical unit type 2.1, an extension of PU type 2.

With these new PU and LU types, IBM created a generic PU/LU pair that is both device and data stream independent. The type 2.1 PU itself has evolved into a complex architecture, especially now that it has become the basis of advanced peer-to-peer networking components. At one time, a single IBM manual, the now-obsolete *Type 2.1 Node Reference,* was devoted solely to the subject. Since space is limited, the details of the PU 2.1 architecture will not be discussed, let alone all the intricacies of the LU type 6.2 architecture. What this chapter covers is a general overview of APPC and the application programming interface that was developed for APPC, called CPI-C. APPC and CPI-C provide the means for accessing modern SNA transport networks.

7.2 APPC

APPC was developed by IBM and released in December 1982. It was implemented initially in CICS on the mainframe. In 1983 APPC was introduced for the System/38 and the IBM Displaywriter. APPC gradually migrated to other, smaller computer platforms, such as DOS, the Series/1, and IBM's first RISC machine, the RT, then to the follow-on

RS/6000. By 1990, APPC had been widely implemented and was very visible in IBM mainframe, AS/400, and OS/2 environments. It is also found in all the various 3270 emulation and SNA gateway products available for local area networks, such as Novell NetWare for SAA, Eicon's SNA gateway, Microsoft's SNA Server, and the products from Attachmate (which include DCA's IRMA product line, that Attachmate took over in 1995). APPC is also available for various Unix platforms. One of the most common Unix implementations was created by Data Connection Limited in England. Apertus Technologies (formerly System Strategies Incorporated) has also been a leader in this field, and excellent products are available from TPS Systems and Brixton. All APPC products can interoperate with each other, but because APPC describes a protocol boundary and not an interface, the details of the implementations of the APIs are product dependent and one manufacturer's version of the APPC API cannot necessarily be ported to another platform. This difference in implementation occurs even among IBM products. This portability problem is solved by CPI-C.

Our discussion of APPC will begin with an introduction to the services it offers.

7.2.1   APPC services

APPC provides a peer-to-peer communications "pipe" between computer programs (*peer-to-peer* means that the two communications endpoints are equal in nature). APPC is defined using architectural definitions that represent procedure calls. These are called *verbs*. Verbs are general enough in nature that they can be implemented in various programming languages using the calling mechanism inherent to the language. Programs that require the services of APPC issue procedure calls that provide the services defined in the architecture using verbs.

In addition to the typical send and receive functions of any communications API, APPC includes a transaction-style interface for writing distributed applications and provides a synchronization point, or *syncpoint,* service that uses two-phase commits to ensure consistency in a distributed transaction. APPC also provides the ability to issue negative or positive acknowledgments for data that are received. This service synchronizes the flow of data between endpoints. APPC is a connection-oriented service, and although originally it was implemented only as half-duplex, recent versions enable full-duplex communications as well.

7.2.2   APPC concepts

Communications in APPC is based on a concept called a *conversation.* A conversation takes place between two APPC programs, similar to a telephone conversation. One of the two programs is the initiator of the conversation and is similar to the party that has dialed a phone to contact another party. The other party picks up the phone, and each takes a turn speaking. A conversation in APPC is an orderly, temporary connection between two end users in which data are transferred back and forth.

In APPC, the two endpoints are called *partners.* The terms used to describe partners are *local partner* and *remote partner.* Local and remote partners can reside in the same node or in different computers in the same or different networks. A program can start concurrent conversations with multiple partners at the same time.

7.2.2.1 Conversations.   In APPC, there are two types of conversations: basic conversations and mapped conversations. *Mapped conversations* are designed to be used by application programs under general circumstances. The idea behind the mapped conversation is to provide the ability to engage in a conversation without having to deal with decoding the data stream and worrying about issues of buffering. Because the user of the basic conversation format must deal with buffering and data stream issues, *basic conversations* are intended for use by APPC service programs and applications where more control over the management of data is required.

The basis of a mapped conversation is the *mapped conversation record* (MCR), the basic unit of information that is transferred between two programs in a mapped conversation. MCRs use *general data stream* (GDS) variables which consist of a 4-byte GDS header, called an LLID, and the data. The GDS header has a 2-byte logical length (LL) followed by a 2-byte format identifier (ID) that describes the format of the data. Data belonging to service transaction programs (to be described shortly) and other internal components use GDS variables with special SNA formats. An optional function of mapped conversations allows a program to associate map names with mapped data so that the data can be translated properly by the receiving partner program. These maps are identified by a parameter called MAP_NAME.

Basic conversations use logical records which are prefaced only by the 2-byte LL. The length range for a basic conversation record is an LL value between 0 and 32765. Logical records can be blocked into a buffer and sent all at once.

Conversations exist inside LU 6.2 SNA sessions and begin and end using sessions as a vehicle. The process of beginning and ending conversations is called *allocating* and *deallocating.* Conventional SNA LUs allow only a single concurrent LU-LU session between the same LUs; in LU 6.2, however, there can be multiple sessions. In APPC, these are called *parallel sessions.* Parallel sessions become part of a session pool to be drawn on when conversations are to be allocated.

Session pools are identified by a *mode name* which also defines a set of session characteristics. Session activation is performed by internal LU components, and a session can be used by only one conversation at a time.

The number of parallel sessions assigned to a session pool is indicated by an administrator, a utility program, or the application program itself. The way this is handled depends on the particular implementation. When sessions are initialized by the LU components, a negotiation between components in each endpoint LU takes place to determine the number of contention-winner and contention-loser sessions that will be started for each LU. Contention-winner sessions are LU 6.2 sessions that allow the local partner to begin a conversation when both partners are trying to begin a conversation with each other at the same time. Contention-loser sessions allow the other partner to begin the conversation.

7.2.2.2 Transaction programs.   A term that is common in APPC is the *transaction program* (TP). There are two types:

- Application transaction programs
- Service transaction programs

Application transaction programs are the application programs into which APPC programming calls have been coded. *Service transaction programs* are internal transaction programs that provide specific services belonging to the APPC architecture and are part of the LU itself. For example, the number of sessions created between an LU and its partner is managed by the LU's *control operator.* This component has a service transaction program called the *Control Operator Transaction Program* (COTP), which implements the control operator's interface to the LU.

7.2.2.3 APPC verbs.   As has been mentioned, the APPC API is defined with *verbs.* Verbs are the architectural definition for a specific service of APPC. The conversation protocol of APPC is defined by *conversation verbs.* Table 7.1 shows the APPC conversation verbs.

ALLOCATE is used to allocate a conversation. DEALLOCATE deallocates it when it has completed. SEND_DATA is the verb used to transmit data to a partner LU, and the verbs RECEIVE_IMMEDIATE and RECEIVE_AND_WAIT receive incoming data. CONFIRM can be issued to request a confirmation that data have been received, and CONFIRMED is sent to confirm that data were received successfully. SEND_ERROR informs a partner LU that there was an error. FLUSH will flush the local LU's send buffer, and GET_ATTRIBUTES retrieves information about a conversation.

TABLE 7.1   APPC Verbs

ALLOCATE	Allocate a conversation
CONFIRM	Request confirmation
CONFIRMED	Send confirmation
DEALLOCATE	Deallocate a conversation
FLUSH	Flush local LU's send buffer
GET_ATTRIBUTES	Retrieve information about a conversation
POST_ON_RECEIPT	Notify when data are ready to be received
PREPARE_TO_RECEIVE	Change state from send to receive
RECEIVE_AND_WAIT	Wait for incoming data, then receive it
RECEIVE_IMMEDIATE	Receive data but don't wait for it
REQUEST_TO_SEND	Request change of state to send
SEND_DATA	Send data to partner LU
SEND_ERROR	Inform partner LU that error was detected
TEST	Check for data or RTS received
SYNCPT	Take a synchronization point
BACKOUT	Restore to last syncpoint
GET_TYPE	Find out if mapped or basic conversation
WAIT	Wait for POST_ON_RECEIPT

Two verbs can be used to "turn the line around": PREPARE_TO_RE-CEIVE gives the partner program permission to send data, and RE-QUEST_TO_SEND requests from the partner program permission to send data. POST_ON_RECEIPT can be implemented along with the WAIT verb to tell APPC that the application program wishes to be informed when data arrive in a conversation. TEST can be issued to find out if the partner LU wants to turn the line around.

The SYNCPT verb is used to advance resources to the next syncpoint, BACKOUT restores the resources to the last syncpoint, and GET_TYPE can be called upon to find out if a current conversation is mapped or basic. WAIT is used by a program that has issued a POST_ON_RE-CEIPT and is waiting for data to be received in a conversation.

Table 7.2 lists another category of verbs, the *control-operator verbs.* These are the verbs used by the Control Operator Transaction Program to communicate with the APPC components in the LU. The way that the COTP is programmed is left to the designer of the APPC implementation. For example, it can be a program residing in the background that is called from active application transaction programs to perform services, or it can be activated by specific operator commands—say, at the system console. The control verbs could also be a part of a system-wide network administration service.

TABLE 7.2   APPC Control-Operator Verbs

Change Number of Sessions Verbs	
CHANGE_SESSION_LIMIT	Change the number of sessions limit
INITIALIZE_SESSION_LIMIT	Initialize the number of sessions limit to 0
RESET_SESSION_LIMIT	Reset the number of sessions limit
PROCESS_SESSION_LIMIT	Negotiate number of sessions limit
Session Control Verbs	
ACTIVATE_SESSION	Activate a session
DEACTIVATE_SESSION	Deactivate a session
LU Definition Verbs	
DEFINE_LOCAL_LU	Define local LU name and characteristics
DEFINE_REMOTE_LU	Define remote LU name and characteristics
DEFINE_MODE	Define mode name and characteristics
DEFINE_TP	Define transaction program characteristics
DISPLAY_LOCAL_LU	Display local LU name and characteristics
DISPLAY_REMOTE_LU	Display remote LU name and characteristics
DISPLAY_MODE	Display mode name and characteristics
DISPLAY_TP	Display transaction program characteristics
DELETE	Delete definitions made by DEFINE_ verbs

Four control operator verbs are used with what is called *change number of sessions* (CNOS). CNOS provides the ability in APPC to manipulate the number of parallel sessions provided for a mode. INITIALIZE_SESSION_LIMIT is used to initialize the number of sessions to be used for a particular mode name. CHANGE_SESSION_LIMIT can change that amount. RESET_SESSION_LIMIT will reset the number back to 0, stopping the sessions that were started in INITIALIZE_SESSION_LIMIT. PROCESS_SESSION_LIMIT is used to cause a CNOS negotiation between partner LUs to take place. A CNOS negotiation is enacted between two conversation endpoints to provide a mutually agreed upon number of sessions. When this takes place, GDS variables are exchanged with the CNOS service TP in the partner node to negotiate the limits for the number of parallel sessions.

The ACTIVATE_SESSION and DEACTIVATE_SESSION session control verbs are used to activate and deactivate LU-LU sessions. The LU definition verbs are used to define, modify, display, and delete the local LU operating parameters.

7.2.2.4 APPC states. APPC implements what is called, in communications protocol design, a *finite state machine* (FSM). In an FSM, the current state of a system is always known. Any changes that take place in the state of a system are ordered and methodological. Moving from one state to another is defined as a *transition,* and transitions take place when particular events occur. A simplistic example of a state machine is a man walking to the store. His initial state is "at home," then it is "in transit," and finally it is "at the store." A representation of an FSM can be created using state diagrams that show the transitions between states. Using an FSM in a communications protocol is a clear-cut way to keep track of what the program should be doing in its current processing state. Because transitions from one state to another are clearly defined, it is easy to ensure that correct transitions take place. For example, the man in our example cannot make a transition from "at home" to "at the store" without first going to the state of "in transit" (unless he is magical, of course).

As an application program issues conversation calls, it changes from state to state depending on the nature of the call that was issued and the data or status that was returned when the function call was completed. The FSM of APPC is implemented using the states detailed in Table 7.3. The eight basic states are the normal APPC states, and the

TABLE 7.3 Conversation States

Basic States	
Reset	No conversation in effect
Initialize	Conversation has been initialized
Send	Program can send data
Receive	Program can receive data
Send-Pending	Both data and send control have been received
Confirm	Confirmation has been requested by partner LU
Confirm-Send	Confirmation has been requested and send control has been received
Confirm-Deallocate	Confirmation has been requested and deallocate has been received
Additional States	
Defer-Receive	Enter receive state when synchronization completes
Defer-Deallocate	Deallocate after a commit has completed
Sync-Point	Enter receive state after a commit is performed
Sync-Point-Send	Enter send state after a commit is performed
Sync-Point-Deallocate	Deallocate after a commit is performed

five additional states are extensions that are provided when the sync-point feature is used. The initial state is always set to *Reset.* From there, the state changes to other states depending on the calls that are made and the information that is received back after the calls are complete. The current conversation state restricts the calls a program can issue. From *Reset,* for example, the only state that is acceptable to move to is *Initialize.*

7.2.2.5 Other APPC options. APPC also provides a security option which defines three levels of security:

- Session level security

- Conversation level security

- Session cryptography

APPC defines the architecture for implementing program-to-program communications in a SNA network using LU type 6.2 and PU type 2.1 components. CPI-C provides an API for APPC.

7.3 CPI-C

Common Programming Interface-Communications (CPI-C) was introduced in 1988 to implement a common API across multiple platforms. CPI-C was a part of IBM's effort to standardize issues relating to the implementation of its products. This effort was called *Systems Application Architecture* (SAA).

Because APPC was an architectural specification of a protocol boundary defined by verbs, it was implemented differently by various vendors and even differently by separate divisions within IBM itself. The promise of CPI-C was to rectify this situation by defining an API that implemented the APPC verbs.

CPI-C contains the following features that were not previously included in APPC.

- Two needed functions that were not previously represented by verbs are implemented in CPI-C. These are *Initialize_Conversation,* providing conversation initialization, and *Accept_Conversation,* which implements a way for a passive partner to await incoming conversations.

- A useful feature called *Side Information* has been implemented in CPI-C. Side information is a minidatabase of remote LU names and characteristics that can be referenced by CPI-C calls within programs and changed dynamically without recompiling the program itself.

- The CPI-C call that is used to send data to a partner is functionally the same as the APPC SEND_DATA verb, but it can be combined with other functions, such as flush and deallocate, to make one call perform multiple functions.

- A new conversation state called *send-pending* has been added with CPI-C along with a new conversation characteristic called error_direction. These were added to eliminate the confusion that sometimes occurred when data and a change of direction were both received on a receive call simultaneously.

Additionally, in CPI-C IBM seems to have veered away from using the concept of a "transaction program" and simply calls APPC programs *programs,* but terms that refer to transaction programs, such as *TP_name,* are still used as a holdover. A few of the original functions that are defined in APPC are not implemented in CPI-C. Programs using CPI-C calls can communicate with programs that were written using APPC; that is, as long as any defunct APPC options are not used by APPC programs. CPI-C can be thought of as a layer that sits on top of APPC.

Side information is maintained in an implementation-defined system file that contains the destination information needed when conversations are allocated. Any number of entries can be stored in this file, and each entry is identified by a *symbolic destination name* and consists of:

- *Partner_LU_name:* the name of the Logical Unit (LU) in which the partner resides

- *Mode_name:* the name of the mode to be used

- *TP_name:* the transaction program name in the remote LU

When an application program issues the call to initialize a conversation, which must be done before the conversation can be allocated, a set of default conversation characteristics is placed into effect. Conversation characteristics are parameters that apply to a conversation and are shown along with their default values in Table 7.4. The default values of the conversation characteristics can be changed using CPI-C calls.

7.3.1 CPI-C versions

The first version of CPI-C, CPI-C Version 1.0, was introduced in 1987. Additions were made in 1990 to create CPI-C Version 1.1. These additions included:

- Automatic parameter conversion

- Additional parameter and return code support for syncpoint

TABLE 7.4   Conversation Characteristics

Characteristics	Default values
Conversation_Type	CM_MAPPED_CONVERSATION
Send_Type	CM_BUFFER_DATA
Receive_Type	CM_RECEIVE_AND_WAIT
Deallocate_Type	CM_DEALLOCATE_SYNC_LEVEL
Sync_Level	CM_NONE
Prepare_To_Receive_Type	CM_PREPARE_TO_RECEIVE_SYNC_LEVEL
Return_Control	CM_WHEN_SESSION_ALLOCATED
Error_Direction	CM_RECEIVE_ERROR
Fill	CM_FILL_LL
Log_Data	NULL
Log_Data_Length	0

- Support for communication with programs written using the APPC protocol boundary

- Local/remote transparency

During the same year, X/Open accepted CPI-C 1.1 and added the following features:

- Nonblocking calls

- Ability to accept multiple conversations

- Conversion to and from EBCDIC

- Security parameters

Until 1992, two different versions of CPI-C, Version 1.1 and the X/Open version, existed side by side. This partially defeated the goal of a single, unifying programming interface. Therefore, CPI-C Version 1.2 was soon unveiled. This version unified CPI-C 1.1 and X/Open CPI-C and added these features to Version 1.1:

- Nonblocking calls

- Conversation security parameters

- Multiple conversations

7.3.2   The CPI-C function calls

CPI-C provides actual function calls rather than their architectural equivalents, verbs. These function calls will now be described individually. Each call begins with the letters *cm,* to distinguish it as a CPI-C call. Additional CPI-C calls can be implemented for a particular platform if specific functions are needed for that environment. These calls are prefixed with the letters *xc,* to distinguish them from the regular calls. In cases where calls replace APPC verbs, the verb equivalent is listed in the description. At the time of this writing, the most prevalent version of CPI-C is Version 1.1, and it is that version that we will describe. The CPI-C programming calls available in Version 1.1 are listed in Table 7.5. The calls and conversation characteristics that were added in Version 1.2 are shown in Table 7.6 and Table 7.7.

There are two major groups of calls: *starter set calls* and *advanced function calls.* The starter set contains the bare minimum set of function calls needed to allocate a conversation and exchange data using

TABLE 7.5 CPIC-C Calls

	Starter Set Calls		
CMINIT()	Initialize_Conversation	CM_ACCP()	Accept_Conversation
CMALLC()	Allocate	CMSEND()	Send_Data
CMRCV()	Receive	CMDEAL()	Deallocate
	Advanced Function Calls		
	Synchronization and Control		
CMCFM()	Confirm	CMCFMD()	Confirmed
CMSERR()	Send_Error	CMPTR()	Prepare_To_Receive
CMFLUS()	Flush	CMRTS()	Request_To_Send
CMTRTS()	Test_Request_To_Send_Received		
	Set Conversation Characteristics		
CMSCT()	Set_Conversation_Type	CMSDT()	Set_Deallocate_Type
CMSED()	Set_Error_Direction	CMSF()	Set_Fill
CMSMN()	Set_Mode_Name	CMSPLN()	Set_Partner_LU_Name
CMSLD()	Set_Log_Date	CMSPTR()	Set_Prepare_To_Receive_Type
CMSRT()	Set_Receive_Type	CMSRC()	Set_Return_Control
CMSST()	Set_Send_Type	CMSSL()	Set_Sync_Level
CMSTPN()	Set_TP_Name		
	Extract Conversation Characteristics		
CMEMN()	Extract_Mode_Name	CMECT()	Extract_Conversation_Type
CMESL()	Extract_Sync_Level	CMTPLN()	Extract_Partner_LU_Name
CMECS()	Extract_Conversation_State		

TABLE 7.6   Additional Calls CPIC-C Version 1.2

Synchronization and Control			
CMALLI()	Accept_Incoming	CMCANC()	Cancel_Conversation
CMCNVI()	Convert_Incoming	CMCNVO()	Convert_Outgoing
CMINIC()	Initialize_For_Incoming	CMRLTP()	Release_Local_TP_Name
CMSLTP()	Specify_Local_TP_Name	CMWAIT()	Wait_For_Conversation

Set Conversation Characteristics	
CMSCSP()	Set_Conversation_Security_Password
CMSCST()	Set_Conversation_Security_Type
CMSCSU()	Set_Conversation_Security_User_ID
CMSPM()	Set_Processing_Mode

Extract Conversation Characteristics	
CMECTX()	Extract_Conversation_Context
CMEMBS()	Extract_Maximum_Buffer_Size
CMESUI()	Extract_Security_User_ID
CMETPN()	Extract_TP_Name

TABLE 7.7   Conversation Characteristics Added in CPIC-C Version 1.2

Characteristics	Default valves
Conversation_Security_Type	CM_SECURITY_SAME
Conversation_State	CM_SEND_STATE
Mode_Name	(Supplied from side information)
Partner_LU_Name	(Supplied from side information)
Processing_Mode	CM_BLOCKING
Receive_Type	CM_RECEIVE_AND_WAIT
Security_Password	(Supplied from side information)
Security_User_ID	(Inherited from client)
TP_Name	(Inherited from client)

the default conversation characteristics. The advanced function set provides the means to change states, send confirmations, flush output buffers, and set and extract conversation characteristics. For our explanation, the CPI-C calls we are about to describe have been divided into five sections:

- Conversation initialization, allocation, and deallocation
- Data transfer and acknowledgment

- Control of direction
- Setting of conversation characteristics
- Extraction of conversation characteristics

The first three sections define calls that are virtual replacements for APPC verbs except for the addition of the two new functions cminit() (Initialize_Conversation) and cmaccp() (Accept_Conversation). The verbs RECEIVE_AND_WAIT and RECEIVE_IMMEDIATE have been replaced by a single CPI-C call: cmrcv() (Receive_Data). The APPC verbs that have no equivalent CPI-C function call to replace them are GET_ATTRIBUTES_WAIT, and POST_ON_RECEIPT. SYNCPT and BACKOUT are not provided with CPI-C because CPI-C, being part of SAA, does not implement the two-phase commit and backout functions of APPC but relies instead on the SAA Resource Recovery Interface for these. Table 7.8 shows the relationships between the original APPC verbs and the CPI-C calls.

7.3.2.1 Conversation initialization, allocation, and deallocation. Four programming calls are defined to initialize, allocate, and deallocate conversations.

TABLE 7.8 Comparison between APPC Verbs and CPI-C Calls

Conversation verb	CPI-C call
ALLOCATE	cmallc()
DEALLOCATE	cmdeal()
CONFIRM	cmcfm()
CONFIRMED	cmcfmd()
SEND_DATA	cmsend()
FLUSH	cmflus()
RECEIVE_AND_WAIT	cmrcv()
RECEIVE_IMMEDIATE	cmrcv()
PREPARE_TO_RECEIVE	cmptr()
SEND_ERROR	cmserr()
REQUEST_TO_SEND	cmrts()
TEST	cmtrts()
GET_ATTRIBUTES	NONE
POST_ON_RECEIPT	NONE
SYNCPT	NONE
BACKOUT	NONE
GET_TYPE	cmect()
WAIT	NONE

cminit(convid, system_dest_name, rc)

Full name.   Initialize_Conversation

APPC verb.   None

Parameters

- convid = conversation ID
- system_dest_name = points to an entry in the side information which contains the partner LU name, transaction program name, and mode name
- rc = return code (CM_OK if call was successful)

Cminit() is issued by an active partner before it allocates a conversation. *System_dest_name* contains the name for an entry in the system's side information table and that entry contains three session parameters needed to allocate a conversation: the LU name of the remote partner, called the *partner_LU_name*; the name of the program used at the remote end, called the *TP_name*; and the mode name to be used for the conversation. System_dest_name can be left blank, but the program must initialize the three session parameters using calls to set session characteristics before an allocate can be issued.

If cminit() was successful (CM_OK was returned in rc), an 8-byte conversation ID is returned to the program. This ID is used in all subsequent calls to identify the conversation with which the calls are associated.

Cminit() always assigns the default conversation characteristics listed in Table 7.4 to the conversation. These can be changed, however, by issuing calls to set conversation characteristics.

cmallc(convid, rc)

Full name.   Allocate

APPC verb.   ALLOCATE

Parameters

- convid = conversation ID
- rc = return code (CM_OK if call was successful)

A call to cmallc() is made to establish a conversation with a remote partner. Before cmallc() is issued, the program must first have issued the cminit() call; if any of the default conversation characteristics needed to be changed, calls to set conversation characteristics should have already been made. Cmallc() uses the conversation ID that was assigned to the conversation by the cminit() call. If an LU 6.2 session has not already been activated, internal routines cause a session to be bound before the cmallc() returns.

The conversation state is changed to *send* when the cmallc() completes. This means that if a return code of CM_OK is returned in rc, the program can begin sending data immediately to the remote partner.

The program that issues a cmallc() is the *active partner.*

cmaccp(convid, rc)

Full name.   Accept_Conversation

APPC verb.   None

Parameters
- convid = conversation ID
- rc = return code (CM_OK if call was successful)

The cmaccp() (Accept_Conversation) call is issued by a passive partner to accept an incoming conversation. Accept_Conversation is the passive partner of the conversation because the conversation was initiated at the other end by the cmallc() (Allocate) call. Only a single cmaccp() can be issued by a program: Multiple conversations cannot be accepted in a single program.

When cmaccp() completes successfully, an 8-byte conversation ID, which uniquely identifies the conversation, is returned to the program for use in all subsequent calls and the state is set to *receive.* After cmaccp() is issued, the conversation characteristics are initialized to the values received on the incoming conversation. These values, and the values for *conversation_type, sync_level, mode_name,* and *partner_LU_name* are determined by the active partner's choice of parameters.

cmdeal(convid, rc)

Full name.   Deallocate

APPC verb.   DEALLOCATE

Parameters
- convid = conversation ID
- rc = return code (CM_OK if call was successful)

The cmdeal() call is issued by either partner to terminate an active conversation. There are two types of deallocations. Which one will take place is determined by the setting of the conversation characteristic *deallocate_type.* If deallocate_type is set to *flush,* the communication buffer is flushed before deallocation of a conversation takes place and all outgoing messages in the buffer are sent. This is equivalent to issuing a call to cmflus() before a call to cmdeal(). If *deallocate_type* is set to *confirm,* a confirmation request is sent before deallocation takes place. The deallocate_type conversation characteristic value can

be set before the deallocate call is issued using cmsdt()
(Set_Deallocate_Type).

7.3.2.2 Data transfer and acknowledgment.

The data transfer and acknowledgment calls are used for transferring data back and forth within a conversation. Only two of these calls, cmsend() and cmrcv(), are used for the actual transfer of data; the remainder offer such services as confirmation, error notification, and flushing of the output buffer.

cmsend(convid, buffer, buff_len, rts, rc)

Full name.   Send_Data

APPC verb.   SEND_DATA

Parameters
- convid = conversation ID
- buffer = points to a buffer containing the data to send
- buff_len = length of data to be sent (specifies the number of bytes in the buffer to send)
- rts = if, when the cmsend() completes, this variable is set to CM_REQ_TO_SEND_RECEIVED, then the partner LU has issued a Request_to_Send
- rc = return code (CM_OK if call was successful)

The cmsend() call is issued to send data to the partner LU which will receive the data with a cmrcv(). However, cmsend() may not actually send the data. What cmsend() actually does is transfer the data pointed to by the buffer into a system buffer maintained by the LU. The LU accumulates data in this buffer each time a cmsend() is issued. The LU does not actually send the data until either enough has been accumulated and the LU has determined to send the data, or a command, such as cmflus(), is issued by the program which causes the buffer to be flushed.

For a mapped conversation, a single record is sent; for a basic conversation, however, all the data specified by the *buff_len* field is sent regardless of how many logical records are blocked together in the buffer pointed to by the second parameter.

A call to cmsst() can be made before issuing the cmsend() to affect how cmsend() will behave. Different functions, such as sending, flushing, changing state, confirmation, deallocation, and synchronization, can be incorporated into the send_data function. For a more detailed description, refer to the cmsst() call in Sec. 7.3.2.4.

cmrcv(convid, buffer, buff_len, data_rvc, rcv_len, status, rts, rc)

Full name.   Receive

APPC verb.   RECEIVE_AND_WAIT and RECEIVE_IMMEDIATE

Parameters

- convid = conversation ID
- buffer = points to a buffer into which the data are to be received
- buff_len = maximum size of the input buffer
- data_rcv = specifies if data were received and whether the data were complete
- rvc_len = indicates the amount of data received
- status = if not CM_NO_STATUS_RECEIVED, then contains control information
- rts = if, when the cmrcv() completes, this variable is set to CM_REQ_TO_SEND_RECEIVED, then the partner LU has issued a Request_to_Send
- rc = return code (CM_OK if call was successful)

The cmrcv() call is issued by a program to indicate it wants to receive data from a partner. Before issuing a cmrcv(), calls to cmsf() and cmsrt() can be made to affect the way in which the read will function. Cmsrt() sets the *receive_type* conversation characteristic. Receive_type can be set to either CM_RECEIVE_AND_WAIT or CM_RECEIVE_IMMEDIATE.

The *status* parameter is important for this command and indicates the following conditions:

- CM_SEND_RECEIVED.   Permission to send was received.

- CM_CONFIRM_RECEIVED.   A confirmation request was received.

- CM_CONFIRM_SEND_RECEIVED.   Permission to send and a confirmation request was received.

- CM_DEALLOC_RECEIVED.   Partner has conditionally deallocated the conversation.

cmflus(convid, rc)

Full name.   Flush

APPC verb.   FLUSH

Parameters

- convid = conversation ID
- rc = return code (CM_OK if call was successful)

Cmflus() causes the internal send buffer to be flushed. By using the flush facility, the programmer can make multiple send calls to store the send data in the LU's internal buffers, then issue a call to cmflus() to cause all of the data from the multiple cmsend() calls to go out at one time.

cmcfm(convid, rts, rc)

Full name.   Confirm

APPC verb.   CONFIRM

Parameters
- convid = conversation ID
- rts = if, when the cmcfm() completes, this variable is set to CM_REQ_TO_SEND_RECEIVED, then the partner LU has issued a Request_to_Send
- rc = return code (CM_OK if call was successful)

The cmcfm() call sends a request for a confirmation to the partner LU and then waits for a reply. The remote program replies to this request using cmcfmd() (Confirmed). In order to issue this call, the *sync_level* conversation characteristic must be set to CM_CONFIRM or to CM_SYNC_POINT. A call to cmssl() (Set_Sync_Level) will take care of setting this before the cmcfm() is actually made.

cmcfmd(convid, rc)

Full name.   Confirmed

APPC verb.   CONFIRMED

Parameters
- convid = conversation ID
- rc = return code (CM_OK if call was successful)

Cmcfmd() is used to send a confirmation reply to the partner LU program and is sent in response to a partner's request for confirmation that was made by issuing a cmcfm() (Confirm). A program discovers that a partner has requested confirmation by interrogating the status parameter when data are received from the cmrcv() call. The confirmation reply simply tells the remote partner that the data sent by that partner were received and have been accepted.

cmserr(convid, rts, rc)

Full name.   Send_Error

APPC verb.   SEND_ERROR

Parameters
- convid = conversation ID
- rts = if, when the cmserr() completes, this variable is set to CM_REQ_TO_SEND_RECEIVED, then the partner LU has issued a Request_to_Send
- rc = return code (CM_OK if call was successful)

Cmserr() is sent to a partner program in order to notify the partner that an error has occurred. Cmserr() can be used for a number of functions. It can be sent while in the *send* state to truncate a record that is being sent, in effect canceling it, or it can be issued while in the *receive* state instead of sending a confirmation which, in effect, rejects the data sent by the partner program.

7.3.2.3 Control of direction. Calls to CPI-C routines can be made to control the direction of data flowing on a conversation.

cmptr(convid, rc)

Full name. Prepare_To_Receive

APPC verb. PREPARE_TO_RECEIVE

Parameters
- convid = conversation ID
- rc = return code (CM_OK if call was successful)

The cmptr() call can be issued by a program in *send* state to change to *receive* state. The way the call works depends on the setting of the *prepare_to_receive_type* conversation characteristic. The cmsptr() can be executed before issuing cmptr() to set prepare_to_receive_type.

cmrts(convid, rc)

Full name. Request_To_Send

APPC verb. REQUEST_TO_SEND

Parameters
- convid = conversation ID
- rc = return code (CM_OK if call was successful)

The cmrts() call allows a program to send a *request to send* signal to the partner program. Five calls, cmsend(), cmrcv(), cmserr(), cmcfm() and cmtrts(), have an *rts* parameter, which can be ignored on the cmrcv(). When one of these calls completes, a program should check the state of this parameter to see if it is equal to CM_REQ_TO_SEND_RECEIVED. If it is, the program can honor the request by causing a change of state. Since it is the other partner that holds *send* state, it is the partner holding the cards, so to speak. It is up to the other partner to effect the change of state. This can be done in a number of ways and should be determined by the needs of the application. The remote partner program, for example, can issue a cmptr() (Prepare_To_Receive) call, or it can send data before changing the state by issuing a cmsend (Send_Data) call with *send_type* set to CM_SEND_AND_PREPARE_TO_RECEIVE.

cmtrts(convid, rts, rc)

Full name.   Test_Request_To_Send_Received

APPC verb.   TEST

Parameters
- convid = conversation ID
- rts = if, when the cmtrts() completes, this variable is set to CM_REQ_TO_SEND_RECEIVED, then the partner LU has issued a Request_to_Send
- rc = return code (CM_OK if call was successful)

Cmtrts() can be issued to discover if *request to send* has been issued by the partner program.

7.3.2.4   Setting conversation characteristics.   The set of conversation characteristics, listed in Table 7.4, can be set by specific CPI-C calls.

cmspln(convid, partner_LU_name, partner_LU_name_len, rc)

Full name.   Set_Partner_LU_Name

APPC verb.   None

Parameters
- convid = conversation ID
- partner_LU_name = the name of the partner LU with which a conversation is to be allocated
- partner_LU_name_len = length of the partner LU name
- rc = return code (CM_OK if call was successful)

The cmspln() call can be issued by an active partner program to override the name of the partner LU before a conversation is allocated. The *partner_LU_name* characteristic is used by the local LU to identify the LU with which a conversation is to be allocated. The value in the partner_LU_name field is originally loaded by the cminit() call using the parameter *symbolic destination name* which references the side information table. Cmspln() can be issued after the call to cminit() and before the call to cmallc() to change this value. Additionally, if the symbolic destination name parameter is left blank when cminit() is issued, partner_LU_name must be supplied by cmspln().

cmstpn(convid, TP_name, TP_name_len, rc)

Full name.   Set_TP_Name

APPC verb.   None

Parameters
- convid = conversation ID

- TP_name = the name of the transaction program for the partner LU
- TP_name_len = length of the TP name
- rc = return code (CM_OK if call was successful)

The cmstpn() call can be issued by an active partner program before a conversation is allocated to override the *TP_name* conversation characteristic. TP_name is the name of the transaction program to be used by the partner. The value in the TP_name field is originally loaded by the cminit() call using the parameter *symbolic destination name* which references the side information table. Cmstpn() can be issued after the call to cminit() and before the call to cmallc() to change this value. Additionally, if the symbolic destination name parameter is left blank when cminit() is issued, TP_name must be supplied by cmstpn().

cmsmn(convid, mode_name, mode_name_len, rc)

Full name.   Set_Mode_Name

APPC verb.   None

Parameters
- convid = conversation ID
- mode_name = mode name
- mode_name_len = length of the mode name
- rc = return code (CM_OK if call was successful)

The cmsmn() call can be issued by an active partner program to override the name of the mode to be used when a conversation is allocated. The value of *mode_name* is originally loaded by the cminit() call using the parameter *symbolic destination name* which references the side information table. Cmsmn() can be issued after the call to cminit() and before the call to cmallc() to change this value. Additionally, if the symbolic destination name parameter is left blank when cminit() is issued, mode_name must be supplied by cmsmn().

cmsct(convid, conv_type, rc)

Full name.   Set_Conversation_Type

APPC verb.   None

Parameters
- convid = conversation ID
- conv_type = conversation type
- rc = return code (CM_OK if call was successful)

Cmsct() is issued by a program to set the *conversation_type* characteristic. It is issued after cminit() is called to change the default conversation_type that was set by cminit(). The conversation can be set to:

- **CM_BASIC_CONVERSATION.**   Allocate a basic conversation. Basic conversations are generally used for control programs, not application programs.

- **CM_MAPPED_CONVERSATION.**   Allocate a mapped conversation. Mapped conversations allow one data record per Send_Data, which is recommended for application programming.

cmsdt(convid, dealloc_type, rc)

Full name.   Set_Deallocate_Type

APPC verb.   None

Parameters
- convid = conversation ID
- dealloc_type = type of deallocate desired
- rc = return code (CM_OK if call was successful)

Cmsdt() is issued by a program to set the *deallocate_type* characteristic for a conversation. It can be issued at any time during a good conversation to change the default deallocate_type originally set for the conversation. Setting the deallocate_type affects the way in which a conversation is deallocated. The deallocate_types are as follows.

- **CM_DEALLOCATE_SYNC_LEVEL.**   Deallocate according to the setting of the *sync_level* characteristic.

- **CM_DEALLOCATE_FLUSH.**   Flush the buffer and then deallocate the conversation.

- **CM_DEALLOCATE_CONFIRM.**   Send a confirm message and then, if successfully acknowledged, send a confirm message.

- **CM_DEALLOCATE_ABEND.**   Abnormally terminate the conversation.

cmsed(convid, error_direction, rc)

Full name.   Set_Error_Direction

APPC verb.   None

Parameters
- convid = conversation ID
- error_direction = error_direction characteristic
- rc = return code (CM_OK if call was successful)

Cmsdt() is issued by a program to set the *error_direction* characteristic for a conversation. The error_direction characteristic specifies the direction in which the data were traveling when an error occurred. This call is used to indicate that a cmserr() specifies a record that was received from the partner or a record that is trying to be sent. The error_direction values are as follows.

- CM_SEND_ERROR.   Error occurred sending a record.
- CM_RECEIVE_ERROR.   Error occurred receiving a record.

cmsf(convid, fill, rc)

Full name.   Set_Fill

APPC verb.   None

Parameters
- convid = conversation ID
- fill = the *fill* characteristic
- rc = return code (CM_OK if call was successful)

Cmsf() is issued by a program to set the *fill* characteristic for a conversation. It is issued to change the default fill conversation characteristic. The fill characteristic is used by basic conversations only and can be set to either one of the following.

- CM_FILL_LL.   Specifies that the program is to receive on record at a time based on the LL field.
- CM_FILL_BUFFER.   Specifies that the program is to receive as much data as is available.

cmsld(convid, log_data, log_data_len, rc)

Full name.   Set_Log_Data

APPC verb.   None

Parameters
- convid = conversation ID
- log_data = error information to be logged
- log_data_len = length of the log_data
- rc = return code (CM_OK if call was successful)

Cmsld() is issued by a program to set the *log_data* and *log_data_length* characteristics for a conversation. The log_data characteristic holds error information that will be logged to a system error log. Log_data_length identifies the length of the log_data. This call is used in basic conversations only.

cmsptr(convid, prepare_to_receive_type, rc)

Full name.   Set_Prepare_To_Receive_Type

APPC verb.   None

Parameters

- convid = conversation ID
- prepare_to_receive_type = value to set prepare_to_receive_type
- rc = return code (CM_OK if call was successful)

Cmsptr() is issued by a program to set the *prepare_to_receive_type* characteristic for a conversation. The prepare_to_receive_type characteristic defines the type of Prepare_To_Receive that will take place when cmptr() (Prepare_To_Receive) is issued. Prepare_To_Receive changes the state from *send* to *receive* by sending the permission-to-send to the partner LU. Following are the values that can be set.

- CM_PREP_TO_RECEIVE_SYNC_LEVEL.   Prepare to receive based on the *sync_level* characteristic.

- CM_PREP_TO_RECEIVE_CONFIRM.   Issue a confirmation request before sending a permission-to-send.

- CM_PREP_TO_RECEIVE_FLUSH.   Flush the buffer of any data then grant permission-to-send.

cmsst(convid, send_type, rc)

Full name.   Set_Send_Type

APPC verb.   None

Parameters

- convid = conversation ID
- send_type = type of send that will be performed
- rc = return code (CM_OK if call was successful)

Cmsst() is issued by a program to set the *send_type* characteristic for a conversation. The send_type characteristic defines the type of send that will be performed by cmsend(). There are five possibilities.

- CM_BUFFER_DATA.   Place data into the send buffer.

- CM_SEND_AND_FLUSH.   Place data in buffer then perform a buffer flush. Combines SEND_DATA with FLUSH.

- CM_SEND_AND_CONFIRM.   Send data and then request a confirmation. Combines SEND_DATA with CONFIRM.

- CM_SEND_AND_PREP_TO_RECEIVE.   Send data and then change direction. Combines SEND_DATA with PREPARE_TO_RECEIVE.

- CM_SEND_AND_DEALLOCATE.   Send data and then deallocate the conversation. Combines SEND_DATA with DEALLOCATE.

cmsrt(convid, receive_type, rc)

Full name.   Set_Receive_Type

APPC verb.   None

Parameters

- convid = conversation ID
- receive_type = type of receive that will be performed
- rc = return code (CM_OK if call was successful)

Cmsrt() is issued by a program to set the *receive_type* characteristic for a conversation. The receive_type characteristic defines the type of receive that will be performed by cmrcv(). There are two different receive types: RECEIVE_AND_WAIT and RECEIVE_IMMEDIATE. The first *blocks* until the data arrive, the other does not. In CPI-C a single call, cmrcv(), receives data with the conversation characteristic receive_type set for the type of receive that is to be executed. The settings for receive_type are as follows.

- CM_RECEIVE_AND_WAIT.   Wait until receive completes.

- CM_RECEIVE_IMMEDIATE.   Return from the call immediately with whatever data are available.

cmsrc(convid, return_control, rc)

Full name.   Set_Return_Control

APPC verb.   None

Parameters

- convid = conversation ID
- return_control = type of return on a cmallc() to be performed
- rc = return code (CM_OK if call was successful)

Cmsrc() is issued by a program to set the *return_control* characteristic for a conversation. The return_control characteristic defines whether cmallc() will block or not.

- CM_WHEN_SESSION_ALLOCATED.   Specifies that cmallc() will return when a session is allocated.

- CM_IMMEDIATE.   Specifies that if a session is not immediately available a value of CM_UNSUCCESSFUL is returned in the *rc* (return code) parameter.

cmssl(convid, sync_level, rc)

Full name.   Set_Sync_Level

APPC verb.   None

Parameters
- convid = conversation ID
- sync_level = level of synchronization
- rc = return code (CM_OK if call was successful)

Cmssl() is issued by a program to set the *sync_level* characteristic for a conversation. The sync_level characteristic defines the level of synchronization that will be used between the two transaction programs. The sync_level characteristic must be set while a program is in the *initialize* state. There are three possibilities.

- CM_NONE.   No syncpoint processing or confirmation will be in effect.

- CM_CONFIRM.   Confirmation can be used in the conversation.

- CM_SYNC_POINT.   Syncpoint processing can be used in the conversation.

7.3.2.5 Extracting conversation characteristics.   There are times when a program may need particular information that is unavailable except by issuing a call to retrieve it. The *extract* calls were developed to return to the program needed information. There are five of these calls, and three of them have been supplied for passive partner programs to use to discover information that was determined by the active partner and set by the underlying local LU when the cmaccp() (Accept) was issued. The fifth call can be used at any time by any program to determine the current conversation state.

cmepln(convid, partner_LU_name, partner_LU_name_len, rc)

Full name.   Extract_Partner_LU_Name

APPC verb.   None

Parameters
- convid = conversation ID
- partner_LU_name = the name of the partner LU with which a conversation has been allocated
- partner_LU_name_len = length of the partner LU name
- rc = return code (CM_OK if call was successful)

Cmepln() can be issued by any program to identify the *partner_LU_name* for an active conversation. This call is used mainly

by a passive partner program to determine the partner LU name of
the active partner.

cmemn(convid, mode_name, mode_name_len, rc)

Full name.   Extract_Mode_Name

APPC verb.   None

Parameters
- convid = conversation ID
- mode_name = mode name
- mode_name_len = length of the mode name
- rc = return code (CM_OK if call was successful)

Cmemn() can be issued by any program to identify the *mode_name*
for an active conversation. This call is used mainly by a passive partner program to determine the mode name that the active partner
used in the allocation of the conversation.

cmect(convid, conv_type, rc)

Full name.   Extract_Conversation_Type

APPC verb.   None

Parameters
- convid = conversation ID
- conv_type = conversation type
- rc = return code (CM_OK if call was successful)

Cmect() can be issued by any program to identify the
conversation_type of an active conversation. This call can be issued by
a program to determine if the conversation is basic or mapped.

cmesl(convid, sync_level, rc)

Full name.   Extract_Sync_Level

APPC verb.   None

Parameters
- convid = conversation ID
- sync_level = level of synchronization
- rc = return code (CM_OK if call was successful)

Cmesl() can be issued by any program to identify the *sync_level* for
an active conversation. This call is used mainly by a passive partner
program to determine the synchronization level the active partner
specified in the allocation of the conversation.

cmecs(convid, conversation_state, rc)

Full name.   Extract_Conversation_State

APPC verb.   None

Parameters
- convid = conversation ID
- conversation_state = current state of the active conversation
- rc = return code (CM_OK if call was successful)

The cmecs() can be issued by a program to identify the current state of an active conversation.

7.3.3   CPI-C in action

As an example of the use of the CPI-C calls, setting up and starting a conversation will be described (Fig. 7.1).

1. Before a conversation is established, APPC initializes the state to *reset* in both of the programs of our example. Partner A issues a cminit(). The *symbolic destination name* passed in the cminit() points to an entry in the side information table, which contains the names for the partner LU, the partner LU's transaction program, and the mode. A conversation ID is returned from the call. The conversation ID is used with all calls to identify the conversation because multiple conversations can take place simultaneously within the program. After the cminit() completes, the state becomes *initialize*. In the *initialize* state the program is able to issue calls to change any of the default conversation characteristics that will be active throughout the life of the conversation and that must be set before the conversation is actually allocated. These characteristics, along with the calls that can be used to change them, are shown in Table 7.9. In addition to the six characteristics shown in this table, security parameters introduced in Version 1.2 must also be changed in *initialize* state.

There are two ways in which Partner B can "kick in." As APPC was originally designed, B's application program was loaded by APPC node services when data arrived from the allocating partner. However, beginning in CPI-C Version 1.2, two new calls, cminic() and cmalli(), can be used by a preloaded program to initialize and then accept a request to allocate a conversation. Our diagram will present the *classic* method.

2. Next, partner A allocates the conversation by issuing a cmallc() using the conversation ID obtained from the cminit(). If the call returns with a return code of CM_OK, then all is well and the state has become *send*. Partner A can now send data to the remote partner, and a cmsend() is issued.

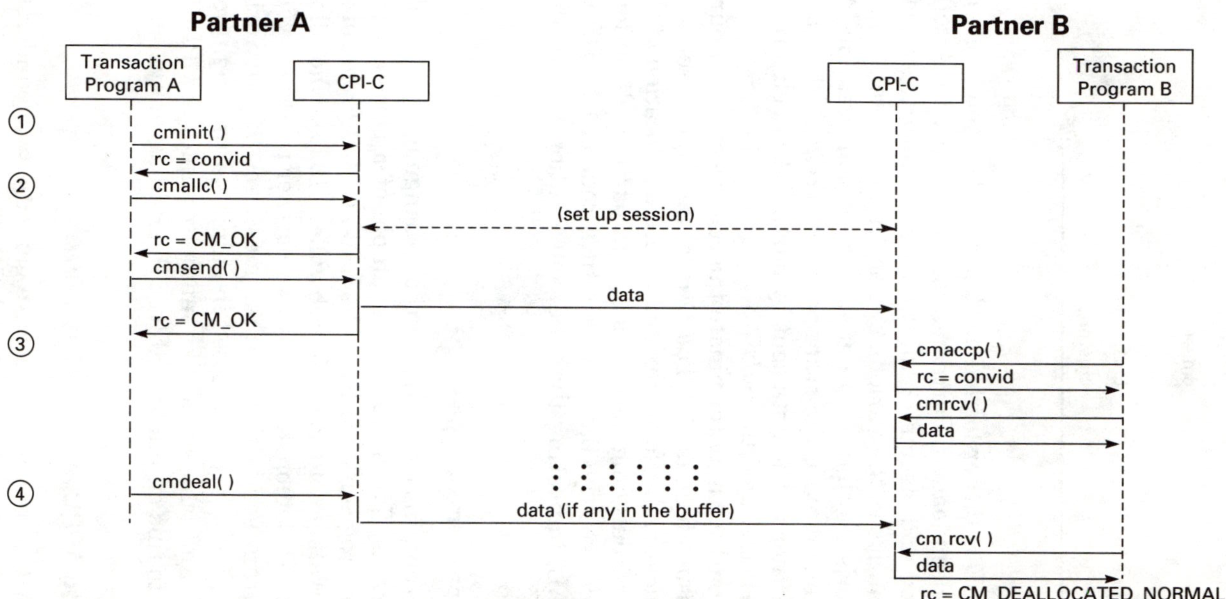

Figure 7.1   Setting up and starting a conversation using CPI-C calls.

TABLE 7.9   Characteristics Set in *Initialize* State

Conversation_Type	cmsct()
Return_Control	cmsrc()
Sync_Level	cmssl()
Mode_Name	cmsmn()
Partner_LU_Name	cmspn()
TP_Name	cmstpn()

3. Partner B is either loaded or, depending on the implementation, has already been loaded. Partner B issues a cmaccp(). A conversation ID is returned and, assuming all went well, a return code of CM_OK. Partner B can issue the various extract calls to obtain the conversation characteristics that are in effect for the conversation. After completion of the cmaccp(), the state becomes *receive*. When a cmrcv() is issued by partner B, the data sent by partner A is delivered and partner B's state is changed to *send*.

4. Either partner may terminate the conversation. In our example, partner A issues a cmdeal(). The *Deallocate_Type* is set to *flush* and the communication buffer is flushed before deallocation of the conversation and any outgoing messages still in partner A's buffer are sent. Partner B receives the data and a return code of CM_DEALLOCATED_NORMAL, indicating that the conversation was deallocated by partner A.

7.3.4   CPI-C program examples

Appendix B contains examples, in the C Language, of two elementary CPI-C programs. The first is an example of a server, the second a client. These programs are from the book, *CPI-C Programming in C*, by John Q. Walker and Peter J. Schwaller (1995), who allowed us to reprint them. To demonstrate how two partner programs work together, one program sends the familiar message, "Hello World," to the other. Readers who are interested in gaining a thorough understanding of CPI-C and who would like many examples of CPI-C programs are referred to this excellent text (see the Bibliography).

7.4   Mapping APPC and CPI-C into SNA

At this point the reader should have gained a basic understanding of how programming with APPC and CPI-C is accomplished. We will now demonstrate how APPC is applied to the SNA architecture presented in Chap. 6.

As we explained in the introduction to this chapter, to place the extension of APPC into the milieu of classic SNA, it was necessary to create a new LU, type 6.2, and a new PU, type 2.1. Another change that was made was to the top layer of the architecture. In the older scheme, detailed in Chap. 6, the top layer was called the function management layer. With the implementation of LU type 6.2, the function management layer is replaced by two layers called the *transaction services layer* and the *presentation services layer.* The details of these two new layers will not be covered here.

All of the features of APPC and CPI-C are mapped into the classic SNA architecture. A conversation is simply the bracket that was described in Sec. 6.4.4.2. All the details of data flow in APPC such as *change of direction* are the same details used in bracket processing that were outlined in Sec. 6.4.4.2. The APPC contention winner is the bracket first speaker; the contention loser is the bidder in the bracket protocol. It can be seen that, once this comparison is made, allocation of a conversation is really the beginning of a bracket, and a conversation is in effect until the bracket is terminated. SNA sessions provide the underlying framework for these conversations and they remain active as brackets (conversations) begin and end within them, just as in traditional SNA. The conversation ID is added to traditional bracketing to keep track of multiple conversations.

CPI-C calls use the principles of SNA outlined in Chap. 6. For example, cmrts() (Request_To_Send) is implemented in the SNA architecture with the Signal (SIG) command, which *signals* the opposite half-session that a REQUEST_TO_SEND is being requested by a half-session that is in *receive* state.

Some of the special needs of APPC are fulfilled by using SNA function management headers that were introduced in Chap. 6. The function management headers used by LU 6.2 are the *attach FM header* (FMH-5), which is used to inform a passive partner to start a transaction program and contains the name of the target TP; the *error-description FM header* (FMH-7), which is used to pass error information; and the *attach failure and security FM header* (FMH-12), which is used to transport security information for LU-LU verification. The first data RU in a bracket always begins with the attach FM header.

If parallel sessions is supported, a separate session for CNOS negotiation must be bound. The reserved mode name for this session is SNASVCMG.

Figure 7.1 presented a simplified example of a CPI-C conversation being allocated, some data being sent, then the conversation being deallocated. Figure 7.2 shows the same example with the underlying SNA commands added. The following describes the flow of data in Fig. 7.2.

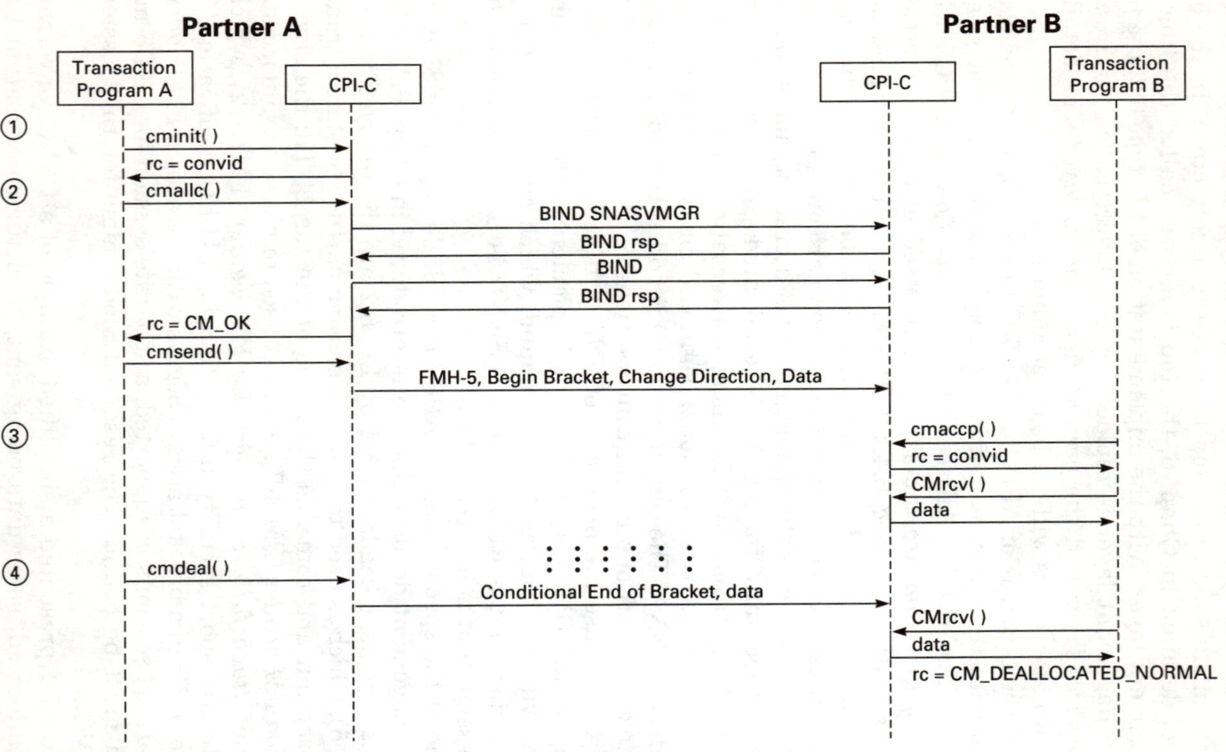

Figure 7.2 Setting up and starting a conversation, showing the underlying SNA details.

1. The cminit() is issued and a conversation ID is returned.

2. When the cmallc() is issued, if a session has not yet been established with partner B, one is established now. Actually, two sessions are established because, for our example, parallel sessions has been selected as an option and a CNOS control session must first be bound. The bind for the CNOS session uses the special reserved mode name SNASVCMG. The second bind is the bind for the session on which our conversation will be allocated. When partner A issues its cmsend() to send data, the data are sent with an FMH-5 attach header placed in front of the data. The FMH-5 specifies the name of the transaction program that is to be loaded. The *begin bracket* (BB) indicator has been turned on in the request header (RH). This is equivalent to the beginning of a conversation. The *change direction* (CD) indicator is also on, which will cause partner B to be placed into the *send* state.

3. Partner B issues a cmaccp() to accept the conversation, receives its conversation ID, then issues a cmrcv(). The data sent from partner A are placed in partner B's buffer.

4. When processing has been completed, partner A issues a cmdeal() with a *deallocate_type* set to *flush*. The SNA RU sent to partner B will contain any data that were left to be sent. The *conditional end of bracket* (CEB) indicator has been turned on to end the bracket and also the conversation. The CEB was not introduced in Chap. 6, and it is used only in LU 6.2 to indicate *end of bracket if the response is positive*. In other words, the CEB is the same as the EB unless a negative response is returned. To demonstrate using our example, if partner B cannot successfully allow the deallocate to take place, it returns a negative response and the bracket is not terminated. In this way, a conversation does not terminate until it is really terminated. In all cases where a positive response is returned, the CEB is exactly the same as the EB.

7.5   CPI-C and APPC for Windows and Windows NT

CPI-C and APPC are both available for the Windows environment. Windows APPC provides the ability to develop APPC applications using either the 16-bit world of classic Windows (Windows 3.1 and earlier) or the Win32 interface first employed in Windows NT and Windows 95. Windows APPC, or WinAPPC, provides the standard APPC calls along with Windows-specific extensions. Like WinSock, discussed in Chap. 5, extensions are included to handle the problems associated with blocking in Windows 3.x (Table 7.10).

TABLE 7.10   Windows APPC Extension Calls

WinAPPCStartup()	Register an application program with Windows APPC. Details about the version of the Windows APPC can be received by this call. Must be called before other calls are issued.
WinAPPCCleanup()	Deregister an application program from Windows APPC.
WinAsyncAPPC()	Provides a nonblocking entry point for all APPC verbs. This is used instead of blocking verbs to run application programs in Windows 3.x.
WinAsyncAPPCEx()	Provides a nonblocking entry point for all APPC verbs. Used instead of blocking verbs to allow multiple sessions to be handled on the same thread. Used only with Win32.
WinAPPCCancelAsyncRequest()	Cancel an outstanding WinAsyncAPPC request.
WinAPPCCancelBlockingCall()	Cancel an outstanding blocking operation.
WinAPPCSetBlockingHook()	Install a function that allows Windows 3.x programs to block.
WinAPPCUnhookBlockingHook()	Remove a previous blocking hook that was installed and reinstall the default blocking hook.
WinAPPCIsBlocking()	Determine if a thread is executing while waiting for a previous blocking call to complete.

Windows CPI-C provides an environment to develop CPI-C applications for Windows using either Win16 or Win32. Windows CPI-C, or WinCPIC, was created in 1993 by a team of PC vendors. It builds on CPI-C Version 1.2 and adds six additional calls to handle extensions for the Windows environment (Table 7.11). WinCPIC provides a standard method of implementing CPI-C that will run in Windows applications and was designed to be consistent with the Windows Open Services Architecture (WOSA) that was employed in the design of WinSock.

7.6 CPI-C Version 2.0

Development of CPI-C Version 2.0 by the CPI-C Implementors Workshop was in progress at the time of this writing and is now available. It includes:

- Support for full-duplex conversations
- Improved support for nonblocking conversations
- Improved diagnostics

TABLE 7.11　Windows CPI-C Extension Calls

WinCPICStartup()	Register an application program with Windows CPI-C. Details about the version of the Windows CPI-C can be received by this call. Must be called before other calls are issued.
WinCPICCleanup()	Deregister the application program from Windows CPI-C.
WinCPICSetBlockingHook()	Install a function that allows Windows 3.x programs to block.
WinCPICUnhookBlockingHook()	Remove a previous blocking hook that was installed and reinstall the default blocking hook.
WinCPICIsBlocking()	Determine if an application program is executing while waiting for a previous blocking call to complete.
xchwnd()	Set the Windows handle to which a message is sent on completion of an operation in non-blocking mode.

7.7　Conclusion

The information presented in this chapter should help the reader gain a general understanding of APPC and the CPI-C application programming interface. It will be seen in later chapters that APPC programs can be implemented on top of transport network protocols other than SNA. Understanding the principles of APPC and CPI-C will aid in the understanding of how APPC and CPIC are implemented in MPTN networks.

Multiprotocol Transport Networking

Multiple Protocols in Transport Networking

8.1 Introduction

Computer networking has grown tremendously during the past several decades. Beginning in the early 1970s, the incorporation of computers into networks was an important contribution to the success of many major corporations. In the 1980s, networking of personal computers became a reality for many small offices and other businesses. In the 1990s, computer networking has reached into our homes.

One result of this phenomenal growth has been the proliferation of many different networking protocols. As computer networks grew, multiplied, and were attached to other computer networks, the result was a polyglot of different computer protocols. The networking picture had become more complex and difficult to handle.

In March 1992, IBM introduced a conceptual framework for structuring modern multivendor, multiprotocol networking called the *Networking Blueprint*. This framework proposed a solution to the problems that had been created by the myriad of computer protocols in use in complex modern networks. *Multiprotocol transport networking* (MPTN) was one of the key components of the Networking Blueprint. Design specifications for MPTN were submitted by IBM to the X/Open consortium for standardization, and were then implemented by IBM in products using the name *AnyNet*. MPTN presents an entirely new way of dealing with multivendor, multiprotocol problems, and this part of the book explores MPTN in detail.

Before introducing MPTN and describing the Networking Blueprint, a brief background of multiprotocol networking will first be presented.

8.2   The Evolution of Multiprotocol Networking

After the introduction of hardware and software products that linked computers into local area networks, the task of defining local area network software standards began. The first and most important standards were created by the Institute of Electrical and Electronics Engineers, Inc. (IEEE). The 802 committee was organized to create standards for LANs. This committee was composed of separate subcommittees. As was noted earlier, Ethernet was standardized by the 802.3 subcommittee and token ring by the 802.5 subcommittee. Other subcommittees worked on other LAN standards, such as 802.2 Logical Link Control, 802.4 Token Bus, and 802.6 Metropolitan Area Networks. One committee was dedicated to standardizing other related work being done with local area networks, and this committee was known as IEEE 802.1, Overview, Interworking, and Systems Management. The major standard issued by 802.1 was for bridges.

8.2.1   Bridges

A *bridge* (also called a MAC bridge) is a device that can connect two or more separate LANs of the same type (and in some cases different types). Bridges operate in the data link layer and, more specifically, in the *medium access control* (MAC) sublayer. By connecting LANs in the data link layer, only the hardware, or MAC, addresses are examined to determine where frames are to be sent. The layers above the data link layer—the network and other higher layers—are transparent to bridges, and bridges do not care which transport protocols flow across them.

In addition to interconnecting LANs, a bridge is a device that can separate a single LAN into two or more separate segments. Each time a bridge is inserted into a LAN, the traffic on each side of the bridge is isolated from the other side unless packets are destined from one LAN segment to another. Bridges can help reduce network congestion by dividing a LAN into two segments. This is because bridges connect two LANs together, then examine each packet that is sent on either LAN to see if the packet is addressed to the other side of the bridge. If it is, it is placed in the other LAN; otherwise it is allowed to continue on the LAN it was originally in. By isolating two LAN segments, the total amount of LAN traffic is not shared as it would be in a single segment. An *intelligent bridge* is one that *listens,* examining all the packet addresses that appear on either LAN and learns which addresses are associated with which LAN. When it first starts up, all the LAN traffic from either side of the bridge is intermixed; however, as the various addresses for nodes on the LANs are learned by the bridge, the total amount of traffic is decreased because the bridge begins filtering the traffic that crosses it. Bridges are also useful for interconnecting LANs with different wiring, say, a twisted pair connected to a coax LAN.

Two types of bridges were agreed upon and standardized by the IEEE 802 committee that standardized LAN protocols in the 1980s. The first type of bridge is called a *transparent bridge*. It was originally developed by Digital Equipment Corporation (DEC) and became part of IEEE Standard 802.1 in 1986. It is called a transparent bridge because it can be installed and run transparently. A transparent bridge is a "plug and play" device that discovers the network topology by itself, without configuration. The second type of bridge, the *source routing bridge,* was developed in the IEEE 802.5 (token ring) committee as a way to interconnect token ring LANs. Source route bridges discover routes through a bridged network by sending discovery packets. The standardization of two vastly different kinds of bridges proved to be a problem in the real world, so it was decided that the transparent bridge would be the main standard, and source routing could be provided as an optional feature. A new type of bridge, called a *source routing transparent bridge* (SRT), resulted from this decision.

Another variety of bridge is a *remote bridge*. This specialized bridge can interconnect local area networks over a wide area connection such as a dedicated telephone line. This application of a bridge is specialized, and the protocols used to convert the bridge traffic to a format acceptable to the wide area link are not standardized; therefore, remote bridges must be procured in pairs.

8.2.2 Gateways

The term *gateway* refers to a device that operates at one of the higher layers in the OSI reference model, higher than either bridges or routers. Gateways convert one protocol stack to another and usually operate in the OSI presentation or application layer. An example of a gateway is a protocol converter.

The most common type of gateway is the *application gateway*. An example of an application gateway is the electronic mail gateway. These gateways convert e-mail from one protocol format to another. Such a gateway, for example, could take mail (called a profs note) from IBM's *profs* system and convert it to the cc:mail format. An example of a presentation layer gateway is terminal emulation. These products take data destined for one type of terminal and convert the data for display on another type of terminal or in a window. Terminal emulation may be as simple a process as converting an ASCII character string designed for a VT200 terminal into a character string for a

TeleVideo 925. In this case, the field positions, designated with escape sequences, must be converted to a different format. In the case of 3270 gateway products—incorporated into LAN servers and used for mainframe terminal access—not only does conversion take place in the presentation layer, including conversion from EBCDIC to ASCII encoding of characters, but the entire protocol stack must be replaced. In the case of the NetWare for SAA gateway, SNA protocols are exchanged for IPX protocols, and in the case of TN3270 gateways, SNA protocols are replaced by TCP/IP protocols which use the telnet presentation layer protocol.

8.2.3 Routers

The concept of routing grew out of the ARPAnet IMPs. These prototype routing nodes provided routing for the ARPAnet and were managed in the early days of ARPAnet by Bolt, Beranek and Newman (BBN), but later they were automated by routing protocols. Routers are smarter than bridges and actually manage the route that data packets take through a network. This is because routers operate in the network layer. Packets of data that arrive in routing nodes have their data link layer headers stripped from them, and routing is determined by examining the network layer headers and routing tables resident in the node. Because of this, routers are designed to work with specific network layer protocols such as IP, IPX, or SNA/APPN path control.

Early routers, such as those from DEC and Novell, were software products that were loaded into a computer. Soon, however, router companies, such as Cisco, Wellfleet, and Proteon, offered *black box* approaches. Cisco's founders apparently learned about routing at Stanford University where they implemented the TCP/IP network while under contract with ARPA.

Early routers handled a single network protocol. For example, the routers in the Internet, the IMPs, routed TCP/IP. However, as the technology of routing became more sophisticated, routers that could concurrently route more than one network protocol were developed.

Bridges, which operate in the data link layer, operate at a lower protocol level than routers, which operate in the network layer, so they inherently handle multiple protocols, meaning that two different communications protocols such as TCP/IP and SNA can run in the same wire and the bridge will not know anything about it. This is because it is the *LAN* that is bridged, not TCP/IP or SNA. Routers, however, work with transport network protocols, such as TCP/IP and SNA, themselves.

As it became apparent that routers needed the same multiprotocol capability that bridges already had, in order to handle the different protocols that were being loaded into networks, multiprotocol features began to be added to routers. The first multiprotocol router was offered by Proteon in 1985. Multiprotocol routers can be attached to a network that contains more than a single network protocol and route each network protocol according to the way the particular protocol should be routed. There are problems associated with this solution, however. One is that not every network protocol can be routed. For example, NetBIOS was designed without considering that packets would travel outside the sphere of the network from which they originated, so an *internetworking* provision was not built into it. Additionally, SNA networks, before the extension provided by APPN, provided the ability to route from one area of a network to another, called *subareas,* but not between peripheral computers that were outside the bounds of a subarea. As has been explained previously, peer-to-peer routing is provided in SNA/APPN networking, but it still does not exist in NetBIOS.

In order to create multiprotocol routers, it was necessary to figure out how to route pre-APPN SNA and NetBIOS. The way that this was accomplished was by a method called *encapsulation* or *tunneling.* The entire SNA and NetBIOS packets were enclosed by the router inside a packet of a routable protocol, usually TCP/IP, then transported over that protocol's network. At first, this method did not work very well because time-outs would occur with SNA, and NetBIOS created a lot of broadcast traffic. Router manufacturers invented methods to fix these problems, and the solution was referred to as *synchronous passthrough, link termination,* or *protocol spoofing.* By terminating a certain amount of the traffic at the router, instead of encapsulating it, the router avoided the pitfalls that were causing problems in the network.

As these solutions were often handled differently by each manufacturer, routers could not interwork, so IBM came up with a method of encapsulation called *Data Link Switching* (DLSw), and this method was standardized as RFC 1434. DLSw transports SNA and NetBIOS over TCP/IP, suppresses NetBIOS broadcasts (which can clog up a network), locally terminates Synchronous Data Link Control (SDLC) and Logical Link Control (LLC) to prevent time-outs, then adds flow control to eliminate packets being discarded when congestion occurs. DLSw is installed in routers that interconnect LANs to make a single, logical LAN. This functionality is similar to that of a bridge.

8.3   Multiprotocol Networking in the 1990s

Multiprotocol networking is a phenomenon of the 1990s. As we have stated previously, the 1970s brought us the basic networking of computers and their devices. The 1980s brought forth ways of connecting more and more computer networks together; however, little attention was paid to what the communications protocols were that linked these computers, as long as it all worked. After LANs began proliferating, the term WAN was born to retrofit the title *wide area network* as a description for networking that took place over dedicated telephone lines. The challenge of the late 1980s was to interconnect LANs over WANs.

There are many reasons why what resulted were multiprotocol networks. The need for reducing costs brought networking decisions down from corporate to divisional and departmental levels. The mainframe "glass house" and its MIS department no longer had a total, enterprise-wide, reign over what was taking place as far as networking decisions were concerned. Therefore, the MIS department no longer decided what networking protocols would ultimately be attached to the enterprise network.

Because of the helter-skelter interconnection of LANs, WANs, and other isolated computer systems and networks, the 1990s inherited a mixture of computer networks and their associated protocols. The 1990s became the era of multiprotocol networks—networks with many communications protocols—implemented mainly with bridges and routers.

By 1994, some of the world's largest companies were faced with immense network nightmares. Hundreds of different local area networks existed in branch offices, remote locations, distribution facilities, and factories. Some were Banyan, some AppleTalk, some Novell, and some TCP/IP.

There are different types of multiprotocol networks because there are different ways that multiprotocol networks can be assembled. Additionally, a multiprotocol network may not be a single type, but can consist of a number of multiprotocol solutions.

8.3.1 Multiprotocol networks using bridges

Bridges were the earliest LAN interconnect solution. Because they are inherently multiprotocol, they can be placed into the mix without considering the proliferation of network protocols that are running on top. It is easy to add more protocols to a bridged network because the bridges and the adapter cards in the individual computers look only at the hardware LAN (also called MAC) addresses. Only after the individual packets of data arrive at their destinations do routines extract the packets destined for particular protocols.

Bridged multiprotocol networks might have begun their life as a single LAN running a single network protocol—say, LAN Manager using NetBIOS. The accounting office next door had its own network, and since the accounting package they wanted to use was a NetWare NLM application, the accounting department purchased Novell

NetWare for their LAN. The two LANs were physically the same: 10BaseT Ethernet. A bridge was purchased to interconnect the two networks. The idea behind buying the bridge was to enable the exchange of e-mail between users on the two LANs. An e-mail package was selected and it used TCP/IP. No problem! Since the workstations on the Novell LAN were already configured with ODI drivers, which allow a user to install more than a one-network protocol on a workstation, and the workstations on the NetBIOS LAN were equipped with NDS drivers, which allowed them to be multiprotocol also, TCP/IP could be added into the mix.

What resulted were two LANs, each running a separate protocol and each also running TCP/IP. Soon, however, one of the workstations on the NetBIOS LAN was reconfigured as a NetWare workstation. It should be clear from this scenario how the network protocols start to add up.

8.3.2 Multiprotocol networks using routers

Multiprotocol routers have replaced many of the bridges in the corporate world. Bridges tend to be a good solution only up to a certain point. As networks become bigger and more sophisticated, the bridge solution is not as effective as it is in a smaller installation. Routers are much smarter and can do a lot more. Network managers realized that they wanted to use some of the features of routers, and started replacing the bridges. Routers can be configured to filter packets, for example. This is a good feature for the network manager who wants to separate parts of the network from other parts, or to create *firewalls* that will provide some security from outside sources, or to isolate *broadcast storms,* a phenomenon that can cripple a network. Routers can also be set up with metrics that define the effectiveness of various links, such as the line speed. Routers can also be used for load splitting, which divides data between two links. These can be powerful tools for the network manager.

But along with the routers come all the various multiprotocol solutions: tunneling, data link switching, and so forth. Now the network might have the added dimension of encapsulation of one protocol within another. Multiprotocol routers also bring another important element to the party, and that is that if dynamic routing is used, each network protocol has its own brand of *routing protocol.*

Routing protocols, discussed in Chap. 4, are another type of communications protocol. Routing protocols are complex and powerful, and some of them very full-featured. They are the protocols that routers use to talk with each other. A whole book can be devoted to just a discussion of these protocols (Perlman, 1992). There are protocols that keep track of the nodes on the immediate network, then contact other routers in other networks to inform them, and keep them informed, of these nodes. In turn, there are protocols routers must use to discover the routes to more distant networks. All the routers in a large network will be busy updating their tables to be fully informed of their network's routes. If a link goes down, all the routers find out about it and a replacement route is determined, if there is one. TCP/IP has its own routing protocols, NetWare has its protocols, SNA has its APPN routing protocol. The more protocols that appear in the network and the bigger the network is, the busier everything will be.

There has been a lot of discussion about the problems of multiprotocol networks and how the multiple routing protocols should be handled. The situation with routing protocols is similar to that which exists with communications protocols: There are those who hope for an OSI-like solution where one single routing protocol will emerge, but meanwhile, routers are being built that handle all of the routing protocols running side by side.

Most likely, this situation will continue as long as multiple protocols persist because, so far, there is no single routing protocol solution that can be used for all of the various communications protocols. It is a very complex situation.

8.3.3 Multiprotocol networks using brouters

Brouters are routers that also bridge. A brouter looks at the individual packets for each protocol, assuming that the brouter also contains multiprotocol routing features. If the packet belongs to a protocol that can be routed, the brouter routes it. If, however, it cannot route the packet, it acts like a bridge. Therefore, for protocols that cannot be routed, a brouter will send the packet on its way as a bridge. In this scenario, it can be seen that this style of multiprotocol network can not only use a number of different protocols, but can also use both bridging *and* routing.

8.3.4 Multiprotocol networks using gateways

Since gateways convert one protocol to another, they can add new communications protocols to a network. For example, in a large network, it is decided to implement a fully interoperable e-mail system. Some of the LANs on the network already have their own proprietary e-mail applications, and it is decided to purchase e-mail gateway software to implement on the nodes that connect the individual LANs to the network backbone. The gateway software runs the X.400 electronic mail protocol on the backbone, then converts the individual LAN e-mail protocols to X.400 on each LAN node that connects with the network backbone. X.400 is an OSI application protocol, so more than likely the e-mail gateway software manufacturer has developed backbone software that uses the full OSI protocol stack (however, some X.400 products use RFC 1006 and TCP/IP—this will be covered later). Since OSI was not installed on the network before, a new network protocol is added.

8.4   What Next?

There is obviously a very strong need to reexamine and redefine networking in order to simplify the jumble of concurrent protocols that exist in many of today's networks. There are just too many problems created when multiple protocols inhabit the network.

One major problem is in the management of the many protocols running together. Network management solutions so far are tied to particular communications protocols, so network management becomes more complicated as the number of protocols increase. IBM's NetView manages SNA, the Simple Network Management Protocol (SNMP) manages TCP/IP, and the Common Management Information Protocol (CMIP) manages OSI. Currently, multiprotocol networks, if they are managed at all (!), must be managed by multiple management tools. So what we have are not only multiprotocol networks, but multimanagement networks!

Another problem is interprotocol congestion management. A very important issue in networking is the detection and management of congestion in a network. SNA has its own methods for handling congestion if it should occur, and so does TCP/IP. But how is congestion handled *between protocols* in a multiprotocol network? This problem has not yet been addressed. There is also the problem of protocol encapsulation. Encapsulating one communications protocol inside another is just not a sound, long-term architectural solution. Some encapsulation techniques are better than others, but encapsulation is obviously a multiprotocol "band aid." Problems have also been associated with encapsulation, such as when connection-oriented protocols are encapsulated in protocols that allow packets to be discarded.

What are the solutions to the multiprotocol problem? Obviously there can be a convergence on a single communications protocol and a single routing protocol. This was the idea behind OSI: it would provide the ultimate solution such that everyone would convert to one, open communications standard and all would be well. Years and years of committee work worked out the intricacies of network communications for a complete package of protocols that would handle all the situations of modern networking. But the big changeover to OSI never took place. It became obvious that networking was not going to be mandated by committees. Besides, who was going to rewrite all the existing network applications to speak OSI? For a convergence to a single protocol to take place, more than a desire by world-class standards organizations with a dream will have to take place.

It is actually very possible that we all will eventually narrow down to a single communications protocol, or at least to a single transport network protocol. But first, one protocol would have to prove itself as being "all things to all computers." This would most likely be a new protocol because, it must be remembered, TCP/IP, XNS and SNA, which are the basis of multiprotocol networking, are already old protocols! If we converge on one of these—say, by the year 2000—a replacement for this protocol may already be waiting in the wings!

If it looks like convergence to a single protocol is not yet in the offing, we can start by converting single protocols, one at a time, to another protocol. There are solutions for this, such as RFC 1006, which allows OSI applications, such as FTAM, X.400, and X.500, to be run on top of TCP/IP; and RFCs 1001 and 1002, which do the same for NetBIOS. However, with this approach, each protocol conversion will have to take place individually. We would need yet another RFC to make SNA or IPX traffic run on TCP/IP.

How about *middleware?* The middleware solution creates a single applications program interface, but runs on many platforms. It can be a pretty good solution if you don't mind rewriting all your old applications. Also, you may end up with a proprietary solution that, if there are problems, depends on the support of the middleware manufacturer. Additionally, there is performance overhead in some middleware solutions.

In the following chapter, we will begin our presentation of the MPTN architecture by introducing the Networking Blueprint, from which MPTN has been derived. MPTN offers a way of simplifying multiprotocol networks without resorting to encapsulation techniques and middleware.

A Blueprint for Networking

9.1 Introduction

The OSI reference model has served the computer industry well over the years, but networking technologies have, in many ways, outgrown it. As has been seen, the OSI model provides an excellent tool with which to describe networks; however, it is well over 15 years old, and networking concepts have changed.

In March 1992, IBM Networking Systems announced a networking model that was targeted for the multivendor, multiprotocol networks of the 1990s. This new model, called the Networking Blueprint, was not intended as a replacement for the OSI reference model. The Networking Blueprint was based on a different concept and approach. The OSI reference model presented a single way to implement networking technologies; the new model presented a way for a number of unlike networking technologies to coexist.

The first version of the Networking Blueprint, shown in Fig. 9.1, consisted of seven layers or sections. The structure of the Networking Blueprint was as follows:

- *Applications*

- *Application programming interfaces (APIs)*
  Common Programming Interface for Communications (CPI-C)
  Remote procedure call (RPC)
  Message queue interface (MQI)

- *Multivendor application support*
  Conversational
  Remote procedure call

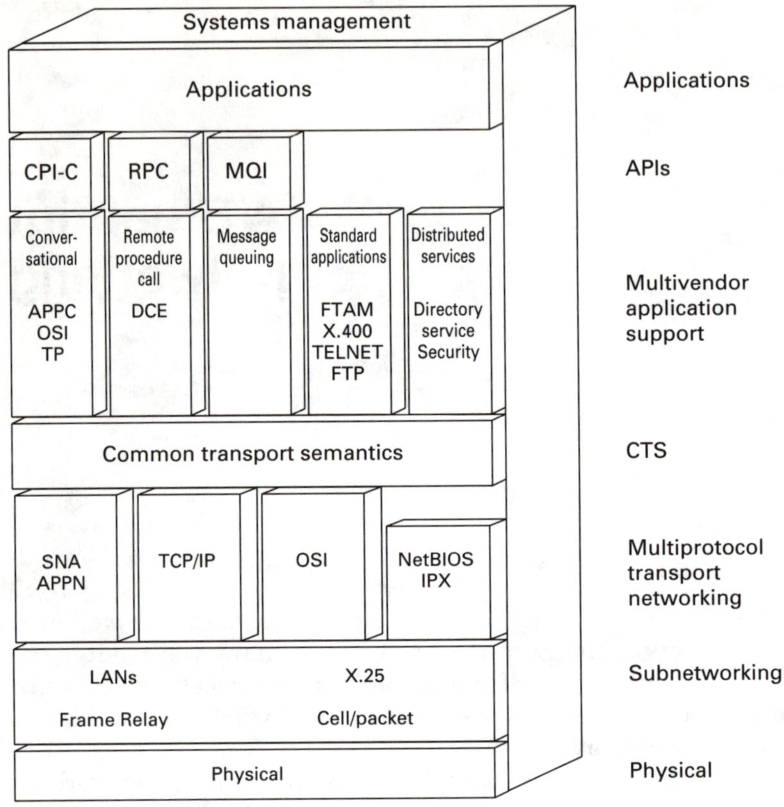

Figure 9.1   The original Networking Blueprint.

Messaging and queuing
Standard applications
Distributed services

■ *Common transport semantics (CTS)*

■ *Multiprotocol transport networking*
SNA and APPN
TCP/IP
OSI
NetBIOS and IPX

■ *Subnetworking*
LANs, frame relay, X.25, and the evolving cell/packet switching
technologies

■ *Physical*

The "backplane" of the model provides another dimension, making the model three-dimensional, and is designated as *systems management:* a requirement for all sections.

The Networking Blueprint was not intended as a replacement for the OSI reference model, but presented a different way to look at networks. A general comparison between the layers of the OSI reference model and the sections of the Networking Blueprint is shown in Fig. 9.2.

In the Networking Blueprint, the topmost section, applications, contains application programs and application services. The next section encompasses the APIs used by the applications to gain access to networking and the distributed services required by application pro-

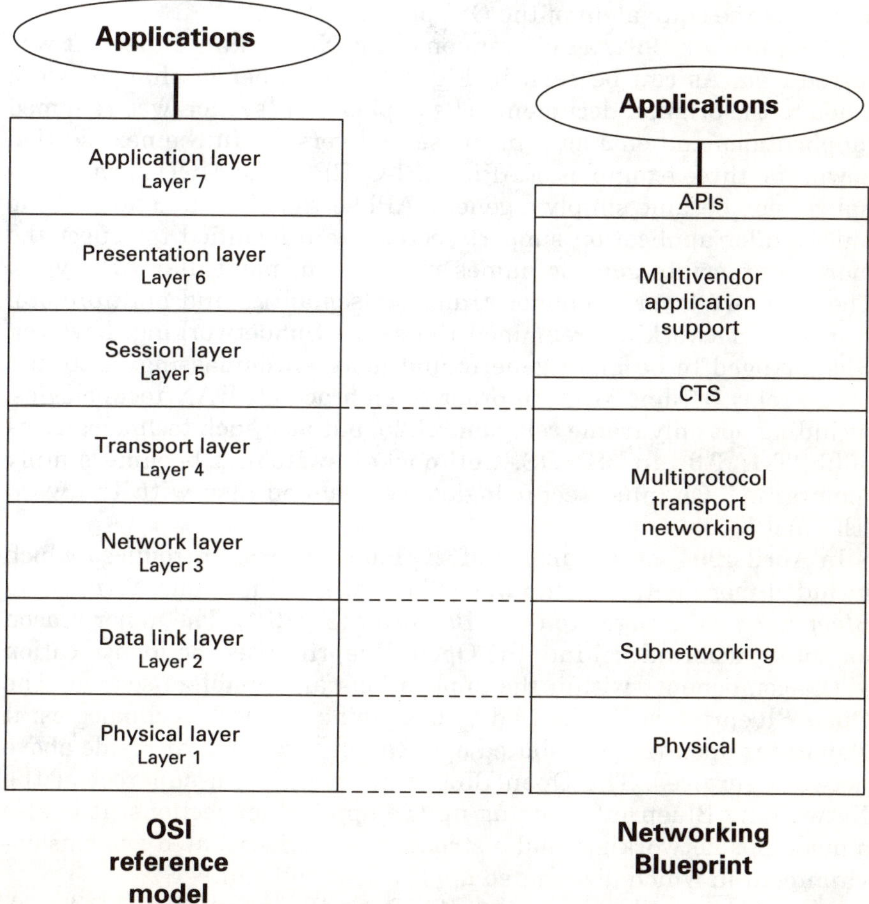

Figure 9.2   The OSI reference model and the Networking Blueprint.

grams. The multivendor application support section makes available the services needed to support what IBM calls the three communication programming *styles:* conversational, RPC, and messaging and queuing. Also in this section are "standard applications," which are well-known networking applications such as the ever-present telnet and ftp programs, and "distributed services," which include services such as directory and security services. "Common transport semantics" embodies a completely new concept for networking. CTS enables the upper sections to make use of the lower sections, regardless of the choice of network communications protocol. The multiprotocol transport networking section contains one or more transport networks such as TCP/IP or SNA. The subnetworking section consists of the various underlying link technologies, which, for the most part, are described by the OSI reference model's data link layer. The "physical" section is the equivalent of the OSI physical layer.

In September 1992, a new version of the Networking Blueprint was introduced. As can be seen in Fig. 9.3, a number of changes were made to the original document. The applications section was renamed "applications and enablers" in the second version. In the next section down, the three examples of APIs (CPI-C, RPC, and MQI) in the original version became simply a generic API section. The functions of the multivendor application support section were modified to reflect the more appropriate generic names rather than particular API types. The next two layers, common transport semantics and multiprotocol transport networking, remained the same. Subnetworking, however, was changed to be more generic and more encompassing: X.25 and frame relay became WAN in order to embrace all WAN technologies, including not only frame relay and X.25, but also such technologies as 56kb, T-1, T-3, and SMDS. Cell/packet switching became simply "emerging." Channel technologies were added also with the word "channel."

In April 1994, an expansion of the blueprint was introduced which included more detail in the upper layers, and the name *Networking Blueprint* was changed to *Open Blueprint* (Fig. 9.4). The major reason for the transformation into the Open Blueprint was the identification of the components within the applications and enablers section. The Open Blueprint is not limited to describing network technologies; it elaborates upon the distributed application services that reside above network services. The Open Blueprint is, hence, a superset of the Networking Blueprint, opening up the application sections. It is also a model for networking, and a structure for a distributed systems environment in which distributed applications can run.

As can be seen by comparing the Open Blueprint of Fig. 9.4 with the previous version of the Networking Blueprint in Fig. 9.3, a num-

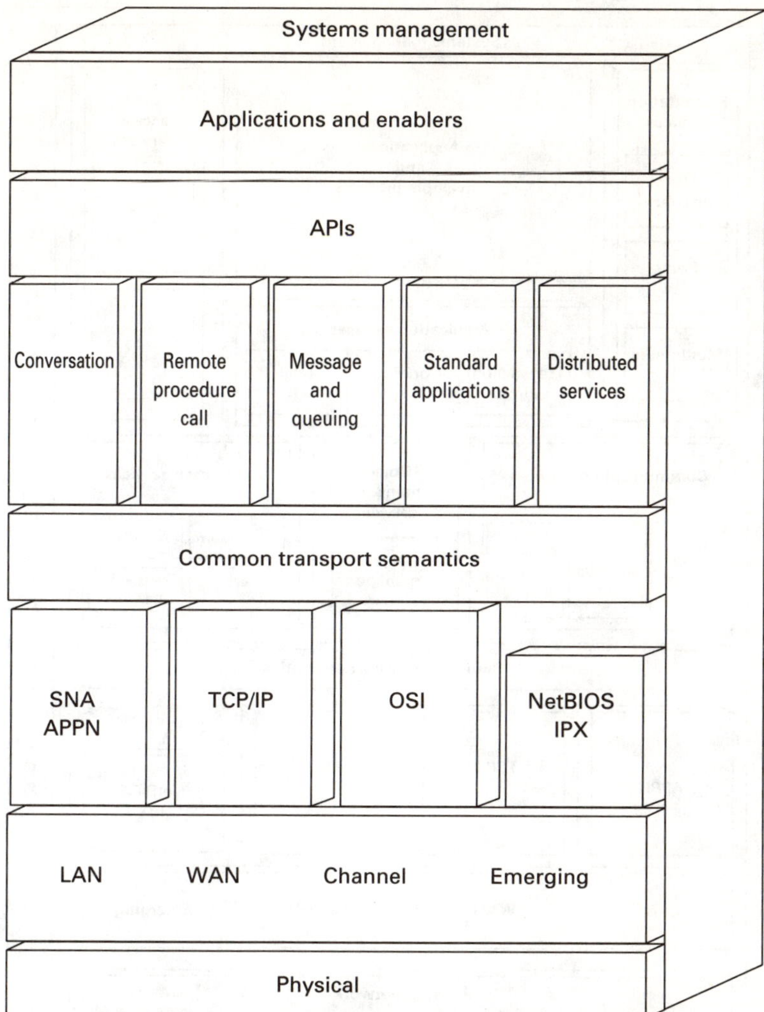

Figure 9.3   The generalized Networking Blueprint of September 1992.

ber of significant changes were made. The Open Blueprint expands the Networking Blueprint in the applications area and defines three basic groups of services:

- Applications and application enabling services
- Distributed systems services
- Network services

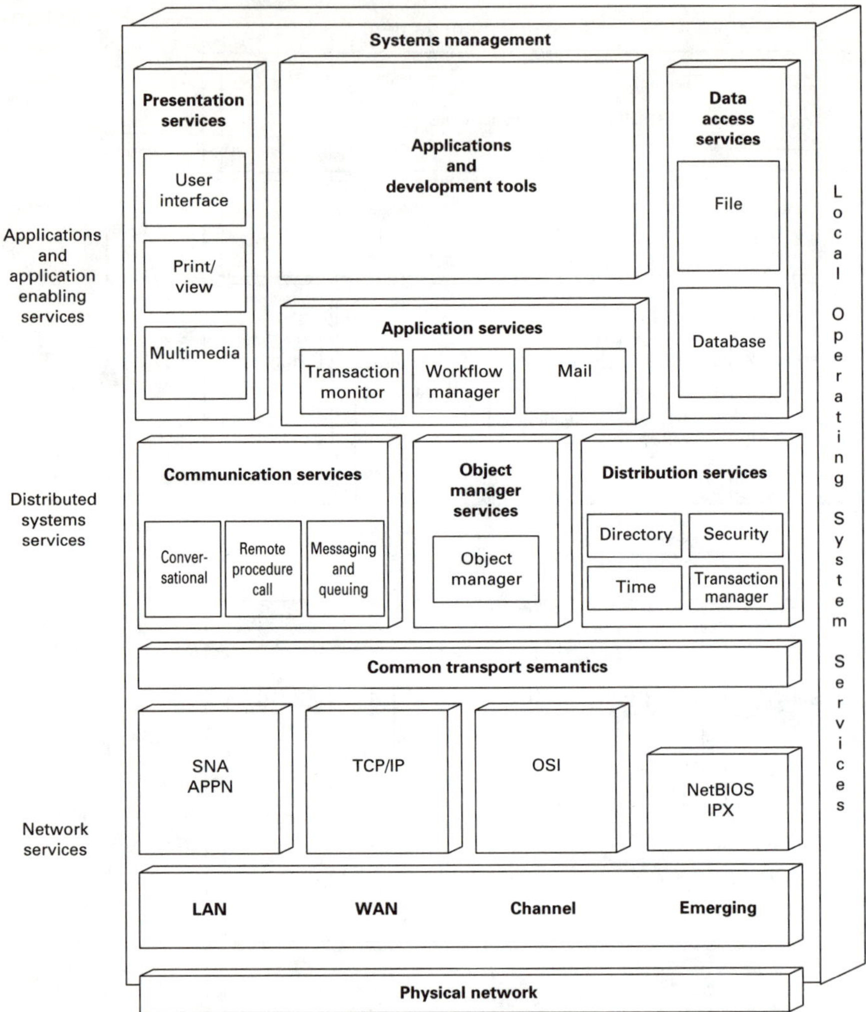

Figure 9.4   The Open Blueprint.

"Applications and application enabling services" consists of what was formerly called "applications and enablers." "Distributed systems services" contains the communications programming APIs and multivendor application support sections, and network services consists of CTS and everything below it.

In transforming the multivendor application support section of the Networking Blueprint into the distributed systems services of the Open Blueprint, a number of changes were made. The first three subcategories in the multivendor application support section are now in a category of their own called "communications services." The "standard applications" of the Networking Blueprint became "applications and application enabling services" in the Open Blueprint and are now a part of "application services" there. "Distributed services" in the Networking Blueprint has retained its identity, but has been expanded with four subcategories. A new category that was not in the Networking Blueprint has been added to distributed systems services, and it is called "object management services." The only other change is the addition of the words "local operating system services" to the side of the Open Blueprint's backplane.

Let us now turn to a specific description of the Open Blueprint.

9.2 The Open Blueprint

The basis of the Open Blueprint is four basic building blocks that are always retained in any particular version of the blueprint (Fig. 9.5). The four building blocks are, from top to bottom:

- Applications
- Application support

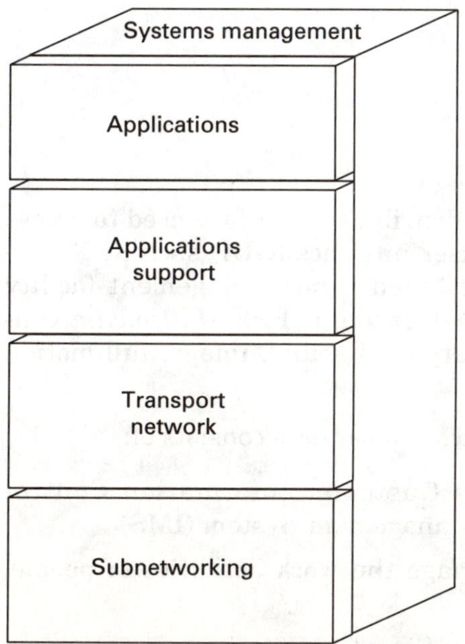

Figure 9.5 The four basic building blocks of the Open Blueprint.

- Transport network

- Subnetworking

The Open Blueprint will now be described, section-by-section.

9.2.1 Applications and application enabling services

Applications and application enabling services is the top section of the Open Blueprint, with applications and development tools in the center and enablers surrounding the applications in a U-shaped formation. This is a realization of the applications building block. Since the focus of this book is on networking, the top of the blueprint will only be briefly described.

"Applications" has no subcategories, but "enablers" has three services:

- Presentation services

- Application services

- Data access services

These will be described briefly.

9.2.1.1 Presentation services. Presentation services consists of three subcategories:

- User interface

- Print/view

- Multimedia

User interface refers to the type of distributed interface used to access applications such as a graphical user interface (GUI) such as X-windows. *Print/view* specifies a distributed print management facility such as IBM's *Advanced Function Printing* (AFP). *Multimedia* consists of application control and output in sound, image, full-motion video, and data.

9.2.1.2 Application services. Application services consists of:

- Transaction monitors, such as Customer Information Control Systems (CICS) or Information Management System (IMS)

- Workflow managers, which manage the work activities of people, devices, and programs

- Mail systems such as X.400 or Simple Mail Transfer Protocol (SMTP)

9.2.1.3 Data access services. Data access services is simply the manner in which applications get data and is divided into:

- File (flat files)
- Database (access to relational databases)

9.2.2 Distributed systems services

The next section of the Open Blueprint, distributed systems services, consists of three services:

- Communication services
- Object management services
- Distribution services

These three services have to do with interconnection of the various parts of the (networked) distributed system. Since they are key to the networking aspect of distributed applications, each will be described.

9.2.2.1 Communication services. The first distributed systems services is *communication services.* These are the services that are made available to application programs so that they may gain access to the network. Communication services provide three ways for a program to access the transport network. These three ways represent the three styles of communication programming prevalent in the industry and mentioned above. The three styles were presented in the original Networking Blueprint by using examples of each: CPI-C, RPC, and MQI. In the Open Blueprint they are called:

- Conversational
- Remote procedure call
- Messaging and queuing

The APIs such as CPI-C, RPC, and MQI that are needed to access these services are included at the top of the communication services component.

Conversational. Conversational communication represents the style of communications used in both sockets and CPI-C programming. Sockets programming, as it applies to communications, was described in detail in Chap. 5 and CPI-C in Chap. 7, so only a cursory explanation of conversational communication need be presented here.

For communications to be conversational, two endpoints must be in conversation with each other, just like a telephone call. These endpoints communicate by sending messages to each other. The conversational style is one of connection-oriented, program-to-program communication and can be used for both peer-to-peer and client-server models of computing.

Remote procedure call.   Remote procedure call (RPC) communication is different from conversational. Instead of being in conversation with another endpoint in the communications session, an application program that uses an RPC interface makes calls to procedures that actually reside and execute in another end node. In other words, the call to the procedure is executed remotely. Data are still transferred back and forth, but the style is much different. An example would be a program that consists of a main section and a subsection. The main section resides in computer A, the program's computer, but the subsection resides in computer B. When the program running in computer A calls a procedure located in the subsection, the parameters that are passed to the procedure are encoded in a format that will make the data network-independent, then it is sent to computer B. While computer A waits, RPC routines in computer B decode the data so that they are recognizable for computer B's architecture, then pass these parameters on to the procedure that is being called. When the procedure is finished executing, a return code, or other data that are returned by the procedure, is sent back to the calling program in computer A.

RPC technology is technology belonging to distributed computing. Distributed applications can be written using RPCs. The procedures in the distributed application that deal with data or routines that reside in a particular computer can be executed in that computer itself.

There are two competing RPC architectures in today's distributed computing technologies. One is the *Distributed Computing Environment* (DCE) RPC from the Open Software Foundation (OSF), and the other is Sun Microsystems' *Open Network Computing* (ONC) RPC. The RPC system that was incorporated into DCE was originally called the *Network Computing System* (NCS) and was developed by The Apollo Corporation. Hewlett-Packard bought Apollo and took over NCS, further developing it. NCS ran over a UDP/IP transport network and the proprietary HP/Apollo Domain DDS. Hewlett-Packard and Digital Equipment Corporation (DEC) jointly submitted NCS Version 2.0 to the Open Software Foundation for inclusion in DCE.

The other RPC architecture, Sun Microsystems' RPC, is a more popular RPC because SUN put the source code into the public domain and it became freely available. It also was the backbone of Sun's well-known and highly visible *Network File System* (NFS). It is basically a *de facto* standard.

A third RPC was developed in Boulder, Colorado, by Netwise, Inc. It has been ported to a number of computer platforms and is a respected product.

Messaging and queuing. The third style of communication defined in the Open Blueprint is called *messaging and queuing.* In this style, each program operates independently of every other. Queues are established between programs instead of connections. By using queues, target programs may be busy or unavailable, but data are queued until such time as they can be received, be that microseconds or seconds. This style of communication is *queue to queue* as opposed to *program to program.* As an implementation of this service, IBM introduced its *Message Queue Interface* (MQI) with the first blueprint, and it has been implemented on more than 15 IBM and non-IBM operating systems using many networking protocols. MQI is explained in *Messaging and Queuing Using the MQI: Concepts and Analysis, Design and Development,* by Blakeley, Harris, and Lewis (1995), listed in the Bibliography and is highly recommended.

9.2.2.2 Object management services. The second set of services belonging to distributed systems services is *object management services.* Object management services implement object-oriented APIs. The Open Blueprint's object manager uses the distributed version of IBM's *Systems Object Model* (SOM) and other technologies that address the issues of interoperability of objects in a distributed environment. Object-oriented programming is a way in which procedures, called objects, perform particular work. Since objects are compiled in particular programming languages, they can be accessed only by programs that have been written in the same language. SOM creates a way with which all objects can be interrelated regardless of the system or language in which they were created. This distributed systems service allows objects to be available to the applications programs residing in the application area above.

9.2.2.3 Distribution services. The third set of services belonging to distributed systems services is *distribution services,* or services to be accessed by distributed applications. These services are an important ingredient in distributed systems. The services available in this category consist mainly of new networking services that have come about as a result of developments in distributed systems. It is assumed that the number of these kinds of services will increase during the coming years. The Open Blueprint includes four examples of distribution services:

- Directory services
- Security services
- Time services
- Transaction manager

Directory services.   The first distributed systems service, *directory services,* is responsible for locating objects anywhere in a network. The term *object* comes from the world of object-oriented programming and is used intentionally here because it defines many network resources: programs, services, servers, files, disk drives, queues, persons, printers, modems, and so on.

The directory concept can be compared with a telephone book. If someone needs to find a dry cleaning service, he or she can look under "Cleaning," find the various cleaning agencies, then compare the *attributes* of each: location, hours of operation, price of services, size of operation, types of services, and so on. The same type of telephone book service is needed in a computer network to locate services such as printers, faxes, modems, files, and even individual users, then look at the attributes associated with each one.

The earliest attempts at creating directory and naming services were locating and making available to users resources such as file systems. Local area networks are typically based on the client-server concept and use a system of *mapping* entire file system directories from a server machine to client machines in order to make the files in these directories available to the clients attached to the server's LAN. As LAN network operating systems became more sophisticated, more objects, such as printers, were made available to clients. In a NetWare LAN, for example, any printer attached to a workstation can be accessed from anywhere in the network by gaining access to a print server queue assigned to that printer. The directory concept, however, is still rudimentary for these kinds of services. The full implementation of directory services has really just begun in the 1990s with object-oriented designs.

There are two styles of directory services: distributed and centralized. A centralized directory resides on a single machine and there is just one directory for everything. It is kind of like a telephone book that all the computers on the network consult in order to locate something. A distributed directory is not located in a single node, but is spread throughout the network. A distributed directory can be compared to a telephone book for a particular town within a state. This telephone book references all of the objects in that town, and all of the towns in the state each have a telephone book for their particular area. A distributed directory service instituted within the state could consult the particular phone book for any particular town to locate an object in that town. In this case, the telephone directories are distributed. Distributed directories separate the total area that is to be covered into domains, and local administrators are responsible for maintaining the directory for their domains. A distributed directory is generally considered to be the only workable global solution.

There were several early directory services for the Unix environment. *Yellow Pages* (YP) was created by Sun Microsystems, but later was renamed *Network Information Service* (NIS) to prevent infringement on a registered trademark. NIS, and its most recent version called NIS+, is a distributed database system which replaces Unix configuration files with centralized files accessible from any machine in a network. Another system, the *Domain Name System* (DNS) (described in Chap. 4), was created in ARPAnet days by Paul Mockapetris of University of Southern California's Information Sciences Institute. He wrote DNS because the method of finding host addresses on the ARPAnet for routing purposes was becoming unmanageable. All of the ARPAnet computers were listed in a single file called hosts.txt. This file had an entry with a name for every host in the ARPAnet and its corresponding address. The file was maintained manually by the Stanford Research Institute's (SRI) Network Information Center (NIC) in Menlo Park. After adoption of TCP/IP on the ARPAnet and the proliferation of many new computing nodes, the distributed services of DNS became an absolute necessity.

YP and DNS are not full-blown directory services. They are referred to as *name services*. The first really advanced directory service was StreetTalk and is a part of Banyan's VINES. First introduced in the mid-1980s, StreetTalk immediately won acclaim as a fine example of a directory service. It has a distributed database which holds name, location, and attributes of everything in the network. StreetTalk allows users to look up network resources in a manner similar to consulting a telephone book.

The first full-fledged standard for a distributed directory service was produced by the ITU-T, which at the time was called the CCITT, and the ISO. It is called X.500 and it is the directory standard for OSI. Work on X.500 began when it was realized that X.400, the OSI standard for electronic mail, would need a directory service in order to locate mail recipients. At the time of this writing, X.500 is not yet widely implemented.

Novell, following the example of StreetTalk and working from the not-yet-completed X.500 standards, released an ambitious directory service with its Version 4.0 of NetWare. It is called *NetWare Directory Services* (NDS).

There are other implementations of X.500. One is incorporated into the *Distributed Computing Environment* (DCE) directory services. DCE has two directory services: One is called *Cell Directory Service* (CDS) and is a fast-response name service that is used within a DCE cell, which is typically a LAN environment. CDS is based on DEC's *DNA Naming Service* (DNS). The other DCE directory service is called the *Global Directory Service* (GDS). GDS uses the X.500 protocols to create a global directory that links the DCE cells. The Open

Software Foundation adopted Siemen's X.500 product for this purpose. CDS exchanges local directory information with GDS.

IBM recommends the DCE directory services and X.500.

Security services.   The second distribution service, *security services*, provides network access control and authentication.

Security functions must be distributed in today's networks. In the days of the hierarchical mainframe environment, systems such as RACF provided security only on the mainframe itself. Since individual nodes on a network are not necessarily secure, distributed security services must be used to ensure that the complete network environment is secure. There is much ongoing work in the area of access control and authentication.

Authentication is the verification of a user's identity. In the past verification was accomplished by prompting the user for a password when he or she logged into a host system or a network. The password was verified by consulting an encrypted, or an access-controlled, password file. Passwords are not a suitable authentication scheme for a network because they can be intercepted by monitoring the network traffic and then used by an unauthorized user to gain access to a host or network.

The most common authentication technology in use today is provided by Kerberos, a distributed authentication system developed in the mid 1980s at MIT. Kerberos verifies the authenticity of a user without sending passwords across a network. It uses messages which contain a checksum and are encrypted with a *Data Encryption Standard* (DES) key to verify that a process belongs to a trusted user. Open Blueprint network authentication is based on the OSF/DCE technology derived from Kerberos.

Access control limits the activities of legitimate users who have perhaps proved their authentication and have logged into a network. By restricting access to specific areas of a network or to particular functions, breaches of security can be prevented. A popular method of access control is in the implementation of *access control lists* (ACLs). Each network object has an ACL which indicates, for every user and program, what that user or program can perform with that object. Access control can be enhanced by *firewalls,* which use packet filters to block out unwanted data packets. A firewall can be placed between two networks to examine all data traveling between them. Only authorized packets are allowed to pass the firewall. The firewall itself must be constructed so that it cannot be penetrated.

The Internet Engineering Task Force (IETF) is working on a standard for securing electronic mail called *Privacy Enhanced Mail* (PEM). PEM encrypts messages using the RSA public-key encryption algorithm and creates a digital signature using the MD5 one-way hash function.

Time services. The third distribution service is *time services.* Time services provides a consistent and relatively accurate time-of-day value across a network.

There are various ways of accomplishing synchronization of time. Generally, each network in an internetwork must have a time server. Clients in the individual networks synchronize their clocks by establishing a relationship with the time server. The time server must get its time aligned with all the other servers in an internet.

In a TCP/IP environment, the *Network Time Protocol* (NTP) is used by time servers to synchronize clocks. It evolved from the *DARPA Time Protocol* (DTP) and the *Internet Control Message Protocol* (ICMP) time-stamp message. It is used to synchronize highly accurate clocks and is very reliable. It is defined in RFC 1305, and a subset called *Simple Network Time Protocol* (SNTP) is defined in RFC 1361. DCE has a time service that consists of distributed time servers with a provider server that gets the standardized time. NetWare 4.01 also provides a time reference server.

IBM recommendation for the Open Blueprint is the distributed time services based on DCE.

Transaction manager. The last service, the *transaction manager,* is a distributed service that includes a resource recovery manager. All the changes made to resources in a distributed system must have completed successfully before a transaction is committed. If there is an error somewhere in the transaction processing, all the other changes that are part of the transaction must then be backed out. Using a banking application as an example, if one account is debited by a transaction that credits the same amount to another account, but the debit part of the transaction fails, then the credit must be backed out or the books will be out of balance. The transaction manager oversees all transactions to ensure that they all have done what they were supposed to do before allowing the final commit of the transaction. Transaction manager is a distributed function because all the transaction managers in every system must cooperate with each other.

The X/Open organization has defined interfaces for transaction managers. These are the TX interface, the XA interface, and the XA+ interface. These three interfaces are recommended by IBM for transaction management.

9.2.3 Network services

Network services consists of two sections from the Networking Blueprint, transport network and subnetworking, and comprises the actual networking portion of the Open Blueprint. Network services is concerned entirely with transporting data in the network and providing the functions that relate to this transfer of data.

Network services consists of

- Common transport semantics (CTS)
- Transport network
- Subnetworking
- Physical

A discussion will now be presented of each of the network services except "physical" which will not be covered. It is the same as the OSI physical layer.

9.2.3.1 Common transport semantics.

Common transport semantics (CTS) is the section that separates distributed services from the transport network. CTS is an important section in the Open Blueprint because it provides the place where the multiprotocol transport networking architecture and IBM's AnyNet products can be implemented. CTS provides a place in the blueprint where a set of transport semantics common to all transport network protocols are provided. This means that the applications in the top section, using their respective APIs and communication programming styles, can select and work with any transport network, regardless of the communications protocol the transport network implements.

Traditionally, APIs were always tied to a particular transport network protocol. For example, if a program used the Berkeley sockets API, the underlying protocol was always TCP/IP. If the program was written using the CPI-C API, the underlying protocol was always SNA. Because of this association, application programs written using a particular API were tied to the transport network with which the API was associated. With CTS in the picture, all of this changes. CTS provides a mechanism that checks to see if the API being used belongs to the same communications protocol provided by the underlying transport network. In other words, CTS checks a sockets program to see if it is running on top of its normal transport network, which is TCP/IP; it checks a CPI-C program to see if it is running over SNA; it checks a NetBEUI program to see if it is running on a NetBIOS transport network, and so on. If the API is not running on its own transport network, then CTS provides a way for the program to run over another transport network instead.

CTS is important because binding application programs to particular kinds of networks is too restrictive. Why not simply pick the applications from any system and run them on top of any available network? Until the introduction of the blueprint and CTS, this was not much of a consideration. Common transport semantics provides the compensations that allow any type of application to run on top of any type of transport network. With a full CTS implementation, the type of transport network is irrelevant to the applications that run in the application part of the blueprint. The choice of transport protocols, be it TCP/IP, IPX, SNA, or even "tin cans with string," is left to the networking gurus and does not rely on the whim of user applications. With CTS, the transport network backbone can be implemented for its own features and is not at the mercy of the applications that run on top of it.

The situation of APIs and their associated transport networks always being connected to each other is a parallel situation to one that existed in the 1970s when transport networks were tied to a particular subnetwork (or data link layer, as it was called then). At that time SNA always ran on top of SDLC, the data link layer for SNA, and TCP/IP ran on top of Ethernet, its usual data link layer protocol. Since SNA's data link layer is a separate, self-contained layer, IBM began implementing data link protocols other than SDLC, such as X.25, token ring, and Ethernet. Similarly, TCP/IP was usually associated with Ethernet, but the *Serial Line Internet Protocol* (SLIP) was built into the Berkeley Software Distribution (BSD)/Unix version of TCP/IP, and it enabled TCP/IP programs to run on serial lines. IBM then offered a version of TCP/IP that would run on token ring networks, and other vendors have ported TCP/IP to other subnetworks.

CTS provides a way to separate the APIs from their original transport networks, allowing them to run on top of other types of transport networks. When the protocols do not match, CTS becomes the glue between them. CTS bridges the gap (if one exists) between the needs of the user of the transport network and the services provided by the underlying transport network itself.

The idea of a common transport semantics is not necessarily new. The concept of providing a method for running applications associated with one transport network protocol over another transport network protocol was defined in RFCs 1001, 1002, and 1006. RFCs 1001 and 1002 describe a way to run the NetBIOS Extended User Interface (NetBEUI) over TCP/IP. RFC 1001 describes the ideas and general methods used to provide NetBEUI over TCP/IP, and RFC 1002 give the detailed specifications including the packet formats and protocols. RFC 1006 describes a method for running OSI application, presentation, and session layers over TCP/IP and UDP/IP (Fig. 9.6). These RFCs present methods that can be used in the implementation of CTS. RFC 1006 was first widely implemented as a part of the *ISO Development Environment* (ISODE, pronounced eyeso-dee-ee), which implements the OSI upper layer on a TCP/IP network. Importantly, RFC 1006 is being used by vendors to implement the OSI X.400 e-mail standard on TCP/IP networks. This demonstrates how impor-

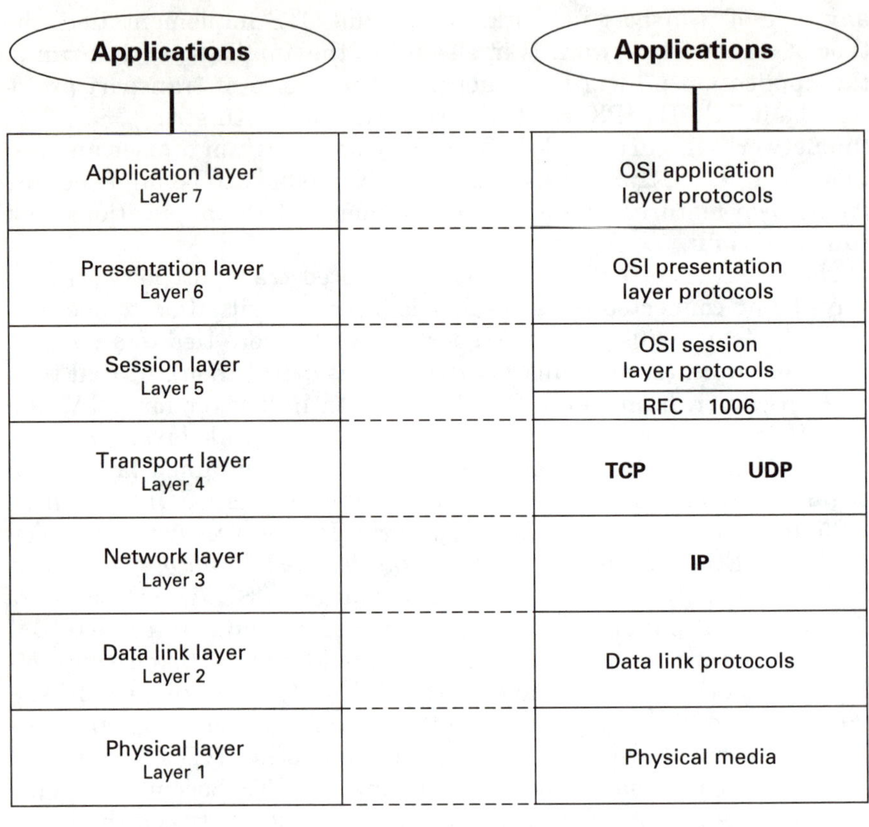

Figure 9.6 The OSI reference model and an OSI-over-TCP/IP network implemented using RFC 1006.

tant the concept of common transport semantics can be in the implementation of modern networking systems.

Figure 9.7 demonstrates what common transport semantics does. If the user of transport services resides on a transport network that is of a dissimilar networking protocol, then either existing standards such as RFC 1001/2 or RFC 1006 are called upon to glue the transport user to the transport provider, or MPTN comes into play. MPTN is the subject of Part 2 of this book, and in the following chapter we will begin its discussion.

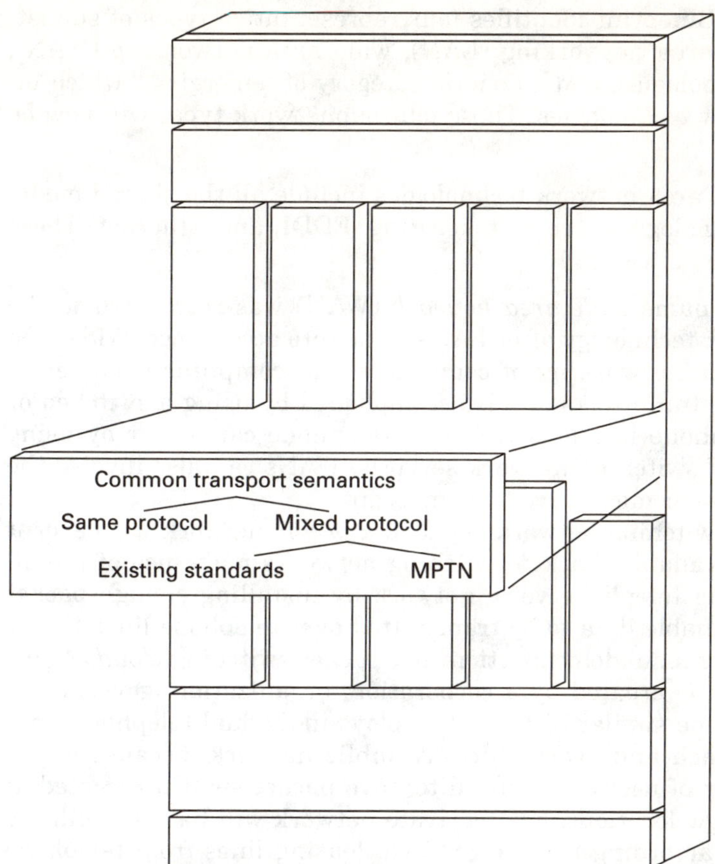

Figure 9.7 Common transport semantics.

9.2.3.2 The transport network. Below the CTS layer is the transport network. This is defined in an IBM publication as "a collection of networking programs that exchange information between and among adjacent and non-adjacent computer systems using a variety of available communications media." The transport network is basically the same as the network and transport layers of the OSI reference model. Examples of transport networks are shown in the Open Blueprint (Fig. 9.4): SNA/APPN, TCP/IP, OSI, NetBIOS, and IPX. These are just five representative examples, and others can be inferred.

9.2.3.3 Subnetworking. Below the transport network is subnetworking, which an IBM publication defines as "a collection of networking programs that exchange information between immediately adjacent (or logically adjacent) physical communications/computing devices."

The Open Blueprint identifies four representative types of subnetworks: local area networking (LAN), wide area networking (WAN), channel technologies, and a general category of "emerging," which includes all new technologies. Those four subnetwork types will now be described.

LAN. Local area network technologies include all the shared media network technologies such as token ring, FDDI, and Ethernet. These were described in Chap. 1.

WAN. The name *wide area network* (WAN) was retrofitted to the older network technology after LANs came into acceptance. Wide area networking is networking of computers and computer peripherals using long-distance links and is accomplished by using a switched or private telephone line leased from a telephone carrier, or by using public packet-switching network services. WANs can also involve the use of satellite or microwave transmission.

A packet switching network is called a *public* network whenever it is publicly available. Packet switching networks make use of the already existing telephone voice network by installing enough packet switches to enable data to be transmitted over telephone lines to any location using a single connection to a packet-switching *cloud*. A *private* network is created by a corporation, organization, government agency, or some similar body, and employs individual telephone lines to connect each and every office. A public network, because of the large number of users, can afford to have packet switches located at many strategic locations, but a private network will have to build up its facilities according to its own need, leasing lines from telephone carriers to run between each site. A private network consisting of two sites will require only a single link, but a private network with four sites, to achieve a full *mesh* topology—where each node can communicate directly with any other node—will require six links (Fig. 9.8). The actual formula for computing the number links is:

$$L = \frac{N \times (N - 1)}{2}$$

where L = number of physical links required to achieve full mesh status

N = number of sites to be interconnected

Plugging a large number of sites into this formula, it can be readily seen why packet switching has become very popular. For the addition of each new interconnected node, the number of links that would have to be installed to support a full mesh topology rises dramatically.

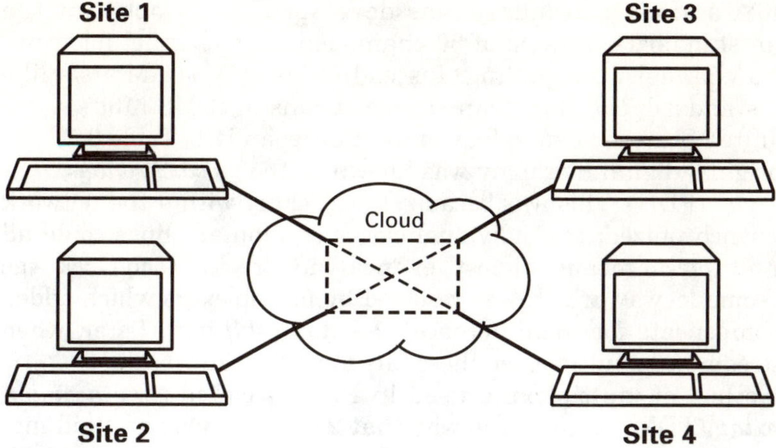

Figure 9.8 A full mesh network with four sites.

The basis for wide area networking is the service provided by the *interexchange carriers* (IXCs) and *local exchange carriers* (LECs). Early wide area network links were achieved using modems to convert digital computer signals into an analog format compatible with the voice-grade telephone network. However, most wide area networking is accomplished today using digital telephone services. With this in mind, a glimpse of wide area networking will begin with a description of what is called the *digital hierarchy*.

The digital hierarchy. In the early 1960s, all telecommunications were analog. Just like stereo records, in which music signals are directly reflected by the shape of the signal etched into the groves of the records, voice signals directly modulated the carrier frequency of the telephone circuit. Because there was not enough room under city streets for all the copper wires needed to carry each of these carrier signals, scientists found a way to digitally encode the voice signals. Digital encoding entails sampling an analog signal at specific time intervals and recording the amplitude of the signal at that point as a numeric value. The result of these scientists' work was *pulse code modulation* (PCM), which converts analog voice signals to digital bit streams. In about 1965, the standard of 24 voice connections, or channels, multiplexed with a framing bit into a 1.544-Mbit/s frame called a DS-1 frame was created at Bell Telephone Labs (BTL) in Holmdel, New Jersey. These 24 connections could be digitally encoded on a single set of copper wires, the same wires that formerly carried a single telephone conversation or a party line. A DS-1 frame consisted of 24 individual time slices each known as DS-0. This was the birth of the *digital hierarchy*.

In 1968, a similar standard was developed in Europe, but the European standard consisted of 30 channels plus a channel for framing and a channel for signaling. Instead of being 1.544 Mbits/s like the U.S. standard, the European standard runs at 2.048 Mbits/s. T-1 in the United States is equivalent to the European E-1 (Table 9.1).

This original digital hierarchy was known as the *plesiochronous digital hierarchy* (PDH). This was because the clocking within the network was not synchronized; the individual clocks of tributary lines could all be different (*plesio* means "almost" or "near" in Greek). Each clock was allowed some leeway, which was resolved by multiplexers which added bits to compensate for the difference (called *bit stuffing*). Later, when the bit stream is demultiplexed, these bits must be thrown away.

The method of multiplexing used in PDH is called *time division multiplexing* (TDM) because the way that 24 connections are laid into the T-1 frame is a time-slice method called *synchronous transfer mode* (STM). Each time slot in the frame is used by a separate channel, or telephone conversation, and each channel is always located in the same place within the frame. T-1 is the name given to the data transmission rate, the carrier system, and the ways that the data are framed. The name for the frame, however, is DS-1.

By looking at Table 9.1, it can be seen how, starting with T-1 and incrementing, higher transmission rates were created: T-2 contains 4

TABLE 9.1 The Digital Hierarchy

Signal	Contains	Rate	No. of voice channels	Carrier system
		United States		
DS-0		64 kbits/s	1	
DS-1	24 DS-0s	1.544 Mbits/s	24	T-1
DS-2	4 DS-1s	6.312 Mbits/s	96	T-2
DS-3	7 DS-2s	44.736 Mbits/s	672	T-3
DS-4	6 DS-3s	274.176 Mbits/s	4032	T-4
		Europe		
E-0		64 kbits/s	1	
E-1		2.048 Mbits/s	30	E-1
E-2	4 E-1s	8.448 Mbits/s	120	E-2
E-3	4 E-2s	34.368 Mbits/s	480	E-3
E-4	4 E-3s	139.264 Mbits/s	1920	E-4
E-5	4 E-4s	565.148 Mbits/s	7680	E-5

T-1s, and T-3 contains 7 T-2s. The T-1 transmission standard became the basic medium of the telephone network after it was converted to digital: T-1 links interconnected the telephone central offices (COs). Carriers then began using higher-speed T-3 links into which T-1 transmissions can be multiplexed. T-3 was originally implemented as a fiber optic link, but now it can also be made of copper.

The first digital private-line communications service was introduced in the mid-1970s by AT&T and was called the *Dataphone Digital Service* (DDS). Because a digital service delivers the data in digital format instead of a voice-grade signal, a modem, which modulates and demodulates digital signals onto an analog carrier signal, was replaced by a *digital service unit* (DSU)/*channel service unit* (CSU). The CSU transforms a signal into something acceptable to transmit and interfaces with the telephone company's signals. The DSU converts a signal to a format compatible with computer standards such as RS-232, V.35, or whatever physical standard is being used. DDS offered a high-speed service at 56 kbits/s. It also offered typical modem-compatible speeds of 2400, 4800, and 9600 bits/s.

Finally, T-1 in the *local loop,* between the CO and customer premises, began to be offered in some locations in the United States. A high-speed local loop was an attractive proposition for some companies because it offered direct high-speed access. T-1 was especially useful for bridging local area networks.

In the 1980s, a new service called *Fractional T-1* (FT-1) arrived. Fractional T-1 was made possible by the advent of a new digital switch called a *digital access and cross connect system* (DACS). The digital cross connect can place a DS-0 in any available T-1 time slot. Before FT-1, there was only a choice between DDS at 56 kbits/s and full T-1 at 1.544 Mbits/s for private digital lines. FT-1 allows the T-1 bandwidth of 24 DS-0 time slices to be divided up allowing a user to select a bandwidth increment between 64 kbits/s and 1.5444 Mbits/s in 64-kbits/s segments without having to pay the full T-1 tariff. Users can combine voice and data streams, then send this combination to the telephone central office, where the data and voice channels can be switched by the DACS to be distributed to different destinations.

Digital hierarchy standards are hard-pressed to fit directly, and snugly, into the OSI reference model. They are partly on the physical layer in that they involve clocking of the signals. They can be partly considered data link layer standards because they define packet formats. However, it will be seen that the digital hierarchy protocols, as well as those of the next generation, the *synchronous digital hierarchy* (which will be discussed later), can allow other data link layer protocols (such as frame relay, which will be discussed in the coming pages) to operate as a layer above them. It is for this reason that the

OSI reference model has become more and more difficult to use in the definition of networking layers.

Three important digital WAN services—ISDN, frame relay, and SMDS—will now be presented.

ISDN.   Integrated Services Digital Network (ISDN) is a digital wide area service that can carry both voice and data in the same connection. Delivered directly to the customer premise as a digital signal, ISDN can be an attractive way for a telephone company customer to mix both voice and data on the same line.

There are two standard ISDN interfaces. *Basic Rate Interface* (BRI) is referred to as containing "2B + D," or two *bearer* channels running at 64 kbits/s plus a *delta* channel of 16 kbits/s. This service is implemented on a standard local loop, a twisted pair of telephone copper wires. You can use the B channel for voice and/or data. The D channel is provided for signaling. It can also carry packetized data or can be used for services such a meter-reading. The *Primary Rate Interface* (PRI) is a "23B + D," or 23 64-kbits/s channels and a 16-kbits/s or 64-kbits/s D channel.

ISDN was very slow in gaining acceptance and became a whipping boy in the trade rags. One reason for its slow acceptance was that it had very scattered availability. All that changed in the early to mid-1990s. ISDN is now becoming a very popular and valuable service.

Frame relay.   Frame relay is a connection-oriented, data link layer, packet switching protocol considered to be a replacement for X.25. It operates with either public (carrier-provided) or private networks. Like X.25, it provides an interface into a network cloud to which user devices (such as bridges, routers, switches, and host computers) can be connected.

The original standards work for frame relay started in the ITU-T in 1984 as an additional packet mode bearer service for ISDN. Work also began in the ANSI-associated T1S1 standards body in the United States. In 1990, Cisco Systems, Stratacom, Northern Telecom, and DEC formed the Frame Relay Forum (FRF) in order to facilitate standardization and interoperability between different products. The first meeting occurred in January 1991. Specifications from the FRF are completely conformant with the ANSI and ITU-T standards, but describe necessary extensions. The Frame Relay Forum extensions describe how frame relay runs on services other than ISDN such as T-1, FT-1, 56 kbits/s, and eventually T-3. A number of interexchange carriers and local exchange carriers currently offer these services.

Frame relay offers a cost-effective, high-speed, bandwidth-on-demand, multiprotocol transport service. It does not perform flow control and error checking at each node of the network like X.25. Instead, bad frames are discarded, so higher-layer protocols in the destination end station must see to it that the discarded frames are retransmitted. X.25 is basically a store-and-forward service; frame relay is not. Today's fiber optic networks do not have the problems of the older analog copper networks, which were noisy and subject to other problems that created errors. The error checking performed by X.25 at each node was important in the old network milieu but not on modern fiber optic lines. Because of its streamlining, frame relay moves data faster through the network. Since frame relay relies on the end user to provide flow control and end-to-end acknowledgment of data, it has no network layer (layer 3). Routing information, instead of being in a third layer, is included in frame relay's frame. Frame relay uses LAP-D, the ISDN link layer standard. Frames are of variable length.

Frame relay was at first envisioned as a packet switching protocol only, but it is now being used for point-to-point links as well, replacing not only X.25, but also SDLC and DEC's Digital Data Communications Message Protocol (DDCMP) links. Frame relay allows many individual logical connections, or virtual circuits, to be multiplexed *statistically* on a single link. This is in contrast to T-1, which uses time division multiplexing—a nonstatistical method. Time division multiplexing is more suited for voice. Statistical multiplexing, which does not reserve bandwidth in preallocated locations in the frame, is generally more suited for data, especially data of a bursty nature such as is found in LAN-to-LAN WAN links. Frame relay was always intended for data traffic only, but products are being sold that support voice as well as data. Cell switching is better suited to this purpose, and frame relay may be an interim technology to be replaced by ATM and cell switching, which we will discuss shortly.

SMDS.　*Switched Multimegabit Data Service* (SMDS) is a packet-switched, high-speed, connectionless, cell-relay public data networking service for WANs. SMDS was developed by Bellcore, the R&D operation of the Regional Bell Holding Companies (RBHCs). Using a connectionless subset of Distributed Queue Dual Bus (DQDB), the MAN technology defined by IEEE 802.6, it is similar to an analog telephone service. SMDS has been employed for LAN-to-LAN interconnection, high-speed remote database access, and packet audio and video. SMDS can run over T-1 or T-3.

In LAN-to-LAN interconnection, a LAN node sends data to a router. The router creates cells, 48-byte packets of data with a 5-byte header. The router's SMDS card is attached to a T-1 or T-3 link and data are sent by the attachment card to a central office SMDS switch. Addresses in the SMDS headers are used by the switch in the CO to route the cells to the correct destination. Multicast is supported, therefore packets can be sent to multiple destinations.

An advantage of SMDS is its connectionless orientation. Frame relay requires a permanent virtual circuit defined between sites. SMDS can communicate with any other SMDS site. SMDS is also cheaper than leasing private lines.

Channel.   A *channel* is a mainframe's "backplane" or bus. Peripherals, such as direct access storage devices (DASD), printers, communications, and cluster controllers, are often attached to mainframe channels. Unlike PC backplanes, channels have their own intelligence which enables I/O processing to be offloaded from the mainframe's central processing unit.

A relatively new feature called a *channel extender* extends the services of a high-speed channel outside the area reachable by traditional channel cabling. By using channel extenders, printers, disk, and tape drives can be located in remote offices. Extenders are attached to the channel and then, through a bridging technology similar to LAN bridging, the high-speed channel signals are converted to a format acceptable to be carried over a WAN link to a remote site, where the signal is converted back to its original, channel-compatible format.

There are two IBM mainframe channel speeds. The older "bus and tag" style channels operated at 4.5 Mbits/s. The newer Enterprise Systems Connection (ESCON) fiber optic channels have a speed of 17 Mbits/s.

Channel networking is a very recent technology. One of its postulates is to combine internetwork traffic with channel traffic on the same WAN link. This means that backplane signals such as those intended for disk drives are carried along with TCP/IP packets! The first generation of such products are being called *channel network controllers*.

Emerging.   The major emerging technologies at the time the Open Blueprint was introduced in 1994 were ATM and SONET, both part of one of the most revolutionizing developments in networking history: the *Broadband Integrated Services Digital Network* (B-ISDN). Because of the importance of broadband networking technology as part of the blueprint, the development of B-ISDN in research laboratories will be explained, then the two most important broadband technologies, ATM and SONET, will be described.

B-ISDN.   The Broadband Integrated Services Digital Network was a development of the ITU-T to create specifications for a technology that would concurrently transport and switch data, voice, and video at very high speeds. The work on B-ISDN was a very ambitious project, and when it was first initiated in January 1985, the high speeds that were being discussed were considered by some to be unattainable and unnecessary. The purpose of the B-ISDN development was to create standardized protocols and specifications for a high-speed integrated-services digital network. The concept of B-ISDN as a high-speed, digital network was in contrast to ISDN, which can now be called N-ISDN, or narrow-band ISDN.

Specifically, it was necessary for B-ISDN to provide these services:

- Interactive and distributed services
- Switched services at very high transmission rates
- Bursty as well as continuous traffic
- Connection-oriented and connectionless services
- Digital signal processing
- Point-to-point as well as complex communications

This was a very tall order and there was no question that B-ISDN represented an entirely new paradigm in technology. N-ISDN was based on the digital hierarchy of today's telephone networks. B-ISDN, it was announced, would be based on a new hierarchy called the *synchronous digital hierarchy*. In 1988, the CCITT, as the ITU-T was then known, decided to use a new method of multiplexing data into fixed-length frames called *cells*. It was called the *asynchronous transfer mode* (ATM). ATM is a new transfer mode, and its concept is different from the traditional *synchronous transfer mode* (STM) of the digital hierarchy. It will be recalled that STM is the time-division method of time slicing the T-series frame. ATM is a statistical method of multiplexing.

The fruits of B-ISDN are the two most important of the emerging technologies: SONET and ATM. Both of these technologies will be introduced, beginning with SONET.

SONET (SDH).   Many forward-looking telecommunications professionals saw that there would be a need for a high-speed, fiber optic, wide area network standard. The protocols used to transfer data over T-3 links were proprietary, so equipment from different manufacturers could not interoperate. The concept of SONET was developed as a replacement for T-3 interoffice trunks.

The ANSI SONET standards work began in the United States and was mostly a joint effort on the part of Bellcore and the Exchange Carriers Standards Association (ECSA), which is associated with the American National Standards Institute (ANSI). In 1984, MCI made a proposal to the Interexchange Carrier Compatibility Forum (ICCF) for a method of interconnecting equipment from different manufacturers over the various fiber optic cable links belonging to the various carriers. This proposal used a system called *mid-fiber meets*. The ICCF went to the ECSA to ask that an optical interface be developed.

Bellcore came up with the basic SONET idea and proposed it to

ECSA's T1X1 committee by February 1985. The Bellcore scheme allowed each resource in the network to be terminated in fiber, while the MCI plan did not. The T1X1 eventually studied hundreds of proposals from more than 50 corporations. As all the proposals were studied, the range was narrowed.

The CCITT, as the ITU-T was then called, had been closely monitoring the U.S. standardization effort, and around 1986 began a standardization process of its own based on the needs of the European community. This work led to the European equivalent of SONET, which is known as the synchronous digital hierarchy (SDH). The major difference between the two is that the U.S. standard is based on multiplexing T-3 signals, while the European is based on E-3.

In late 1988, phase 1 SONET specifications were published and became the North American standard. The CCITT released international standards that were compatible with these.

The hierarchy of SONET transmission rates start at 51.84 Mbits/s and is called *Optical Carrier-1* (OC-1). Higher rates are derived by byte-interleaving multiple frames (Table 9.2).

If all goes according to plan, SONET/SDH will become the universal fiber optic backbone telephone network that will eventually be placed all the way to the customer premises. Frames from other high-speed protocols such as FDDI, ATM, frame relay, and SMDS will simply be mapped into SONET *payloads*.

The new paradigm of SONET is the replacement of the old plesiochronous digital hierarchy with SDH, a new means of multiplexing.

ATM.   Asynchronous transfer mode (ATM) is at the forefront of emerging technologies. ATM was developed as a replacement for STM in B-ISDN and is also called cell relay. ATM operates on either fiber optic or twisted-pair media. It consists of fixed-length 53-byte frames called cells. Each cell includes a 5-byte header, so the data portion of the cell is 48 bytes. ATM was designed specifically to operate at very

TABLE 9.2   SONET Transmission Rates

OC-1	51.84 Mbits/s
OC-3	155.25 Mbits/s
OC-9	466.56 Mbits/s
OC-12	622.08 Mbits/s
OC-18	933.12 Mbits/s
OC-24	1.244 Gbits/s
OC-36	1.866 Gbits/s
OC-48	2.488 Gbits/s

high speeds and to be used for data, voice, and video. The ITU-T, then called the CCITT, adopted ATM as the transfer mode for B-ISDN in 1988. ATM development was restricted for several years to a handful of test beds. However, in 1990 and 1991, a few companies in the United States began thinking about using ATM as a LAN protocol.

In October 1991, four of these companies, Cisco Systems, Network Equipment Technologies (NET), Northern Telecom, and Sprint, founded a consortium called the ATM Forum. The purpose of this new forum was to further the work already done by the ITU-T in standardizing ATM by drafting recommendations that would be needed to deploy the technology more rapidly. By 1993 there were over 300 companies in this forum.

Why all the interest in ATM? Because it is designed for high speeds, and it can be used as a network for multimedia applications. Although it has been demonstrated that multimedia traffic can be run in existing LAN architectures, they were originally designed for data traffic only and are not optimal transports for video and sound. Real-time voice and video really require a constant dedicated bandwidth such as that provided by the digital hierarchy or by a specialized technology that can ensure bandwidth allocation.

ATM is a switched technology. Rather than sharing the media as do traditional LANs, ATM uses a switched star topology. Switching is how the telephone network works: A telecommunications switch takes the data that arrive on a particular port, figures out where they need to go, then routes them to the appropriate output port on the same switch. (This is a simplistic description of the complex technology of switches.) Instead of all the data in the network all sharing the wire and individual stations and routers figuring out who gets what, the switch sends the cells to the correct node by shooting them out the correct port (each port connects with only one node). The difference between switching and sharing a media is similar to the difference between a private phone line and the party lines of days past.

ATM not only operates at a high rate of speed, there is better bandwidth because there is no sharing of the media. Shared media technology has reached its limits in many situations, and switching solutions are being implemented for Ethernet and token ring networks. It must be remembered that even though a LAN operates in the multimegabit-per-second range, the aggregate speed must be divided up among all of the users. Thus, the effective speed for each workstation is actually much less than the specified network speed.

ATM switching technology employs a *star* topology. Each workstation in the network is connected by a single dedicated link to an ATM switch. The switch routes traffic between the dedicated links. Additionally, the ATM switch can be connected into another ATM switch that is hierarchically upstream, and this higher-level ATM switch can provide a collapsed backbone for interconnecting workgroup ATM switches.

ATM is the first technology that is being installed in the local area as well as the wide. Switches are being produced for both environments. Some WAN switching implementations are currently placing ATM cells inside of STM slots, but SONET and SDH will eventually replace the STM technology.

The dream of ATM is that it will be in place everywhere, from the office to the workstation at home, and over the phone lines. This dream is possible because ATM can accommodate differing line speeds. The backbone can run at one speed, the local workgroup at another.

The ATM forum at the time of this writing is still working out the details of ATM protocols, and some things are not yet available at the time of this writing. ATM in B-ISDN was intended to run over SONET: ATM cells bundled up in a SONET *payload*. The ATM Forum, however, has ratified other physical layer standards. Four standards (three of them other than SONET) that were available at the time of the writing are:

- DS-3.

- 4B/5B TAXI. 100 Mbits/s. 4B/5B is the FDDI encoding scheme. This is basically running ATM over an existing FDDI physical structure.

- 8B/10B fiber channel. 155 Mbits/s. The fiber channel encoding scheme. This is basically running ATM over an existing fiber channel physical structure.

- SONET OC-3. 155 Mbits/s.

9.2.4 Systems management services

Systems management services runs across the entire backside of the Open Blueprint description and constitutes a backplane to the blueprint that adds another dimension. The systems management plane is concerned with the management of all the sections on the front part of the drawing. This is easily the topic for an entire, and perhaps multivolume, book and will not be dealt with at length here.

The science and art of network management is really in its infancy. Eventual network management technologies will no doubt involve technologies such as neural networking—which uses very advanced principles of artificial intelligence based on the workings of the human brain, other artificial intelligence technology for problem solving such as expert systems, advanced database technology, object-oriented techniques, and further refinement of management protocols.

Network management should provide system monitoring and control, and fault detection and isolation. As was mentioned in previous chapters, network management is still a young science, and only specific products, based on specific communications protocols, exist at the time of this writing. IBM's NetView is the product that manages mainframe environments. TCP/IP networks use products based on the Simple Network Management Protocol (SNMP), and OSI has a management standard known as the Common Management Information Protocol (CMIP). CMIP has also been tailored to manage other than OSI networks. Modified versions include:

- CMOT: CMIP over TCP/IP

- CMOL: CMIP over IEEE 802.2 LLC. A part of the IEEE 802.1 standards.

- CMOS: CMIP over LU 6.2

Systems management must be all things to everything, as symbolized by the management plane of the Open Blueprint. It is a big task involving not only management of data, but data collection, sampling, recovery, and many other issues.

Our presentation of multiprotocol transport networking will now continue with a discussion of the subject of MPTN itself.

Multiprotocol
Transport Networking: MPTN

10.1 Introduction

Multiprotocol transport networking (MPTN) is an architecture that defines the protocols and data formats that can be used to implement the common transport semantics (CTS) section of the Open Blueprint. CTS can be achieved in many different ways, but MPTN is an open, efficient, uncluttered approach that can be applied to any situation.

MPTN provides a framework that allows applications originally designed to run over a particular transport network to run over other transport networks without employing encapsulation techniques. This is because MPTN provides a switching point in the protocol stack on top of the transport network. With this switching point in place, applications are no longer tied to the underlying transport network.

MPTN provides three important benefits:

- Enterprise networks can be simplified by reducing the number of transport protocols required to support all current and future applications. This will make the enterprise network easier to run, maintain, and manage, resulting in a potential substantial cost savings.

- Applications and protocols can be selected independently of each other. Applications can be purchased based on functions they provide: cost, user friendliness, completeness, and applicability. The transport provider network can be selected based on cost, reliability, functions provided, manageability, and extendibility.

- The reach of applications can be extended so that they run on more networks.

10.2   MPTN Terminology

Table 10.1 provides a list of some of the terminology used to describe MPTN. Before discussing the MPTN architecture, some of these terms should first be defined.

The terms *transport user* and *transport provider* are necessary when discussing MPTN. The transport user is the user of the transport network, and the transport provider is the provider of transport network services. The term *transport network* was introduced in Chap. 9 as a part of the Open Blueprint and consists of transport and network layer protocols. Figure 10.1 shows how the terms *transport user* and *transport provider* relate to networks as a whole and to the Networking Blueprint (shown on the right in the figure) in particular. The transport user is located directly above the CTS section, while the transport provider is directly below it. When using CTS, application programs do not have to be changed to accommodate different transport networks: CTS compensates for any differences between what the applications expect and what the transport network provides. The application program interfaces with the transport user and the transport user interfaces with CTS. The transport provider, which lies below the CTS section, is the transport network that provides transport services to the user.

TABLE 10.1   MPTN Terminology

Transport network	A computer network that consists of transport and network layer protocols
Transport provider	The provider of transport network services
Transport user	The user of transport network services
Native	A condition where the transport user and transport provider are based on the same transport protocols
Nonnative	A condition where the transport user and transport provider are based on different transport protocols
Matching	Transport user/provider endpoints using the same protocol
Nonmatching	Transport user/provider endpoints using different protocols
Access node	An MPTN component that allows transport users to run over a nonnative transport network
Transport gateway	An MPTN component that concatenates dissimilar transport networks
Address mapper	An MPTN component that provides address mapping services
SPTN	Single-protocol transport network: A network that implements a single transport protocol
CMM	The common MPTN manager (CMM) manages MPTN nodes
PMM	The protocol-specific MPTN manager (PMM) performs duties for a CMM that directly involve a transport provider

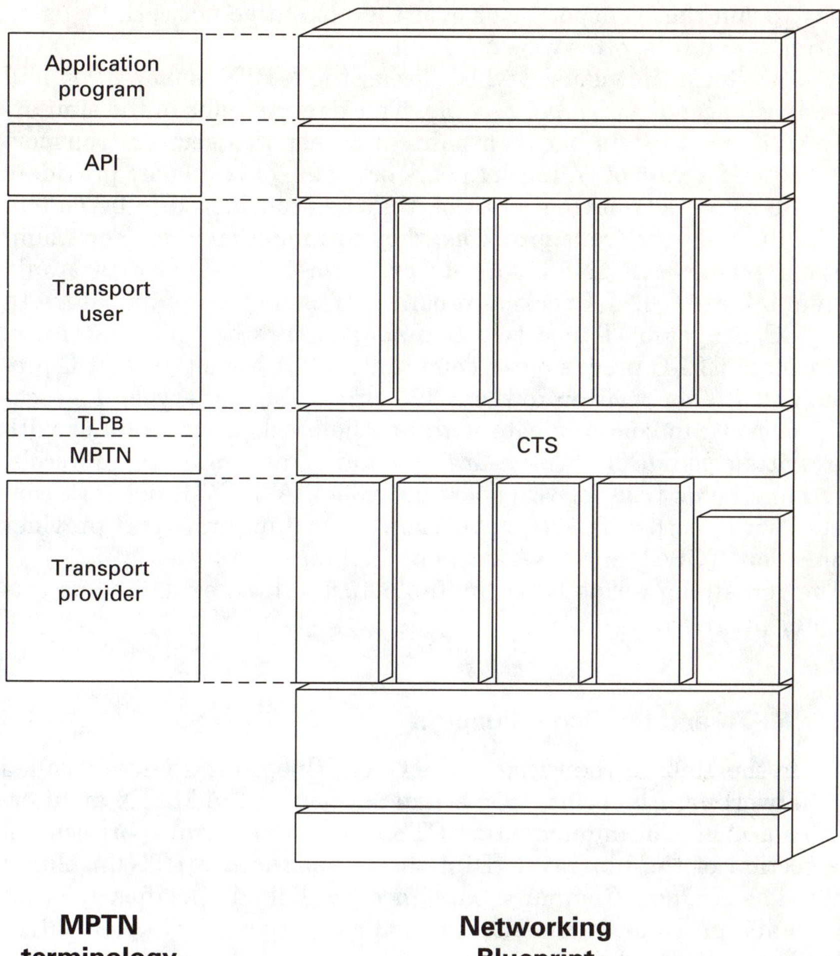

Figure 10.1　MPTN terminology as it relates to the Networking Blueprint.

The term *native* means that the transport provider and transport user belong to the same networking protocol; *nonnative* means that the transport user protocol and the transport provider protocol are incompatible. For example, The Berkeley AF_INET socket interface is native to TCP/IP. Therefore, if a sockets program is running in a TCP/IP network, it is running natively in that network. Nonnative refers to the situation where a transport user's protocol differs from that of the transport provider. This would be the case when a AF_INET sockets program is running in an SNA network. If CTS determines that a transport user is nonnative, it checks to see if there is a way to run the transport user over the nonnative network by using existing standards, otherwise MPTN is invoked.

Another term that is used when discussing MPTN is *matching,* and the opposite condition, *nonmatching.* These terms refer to the similarity of type that exists between pairs of transport users or transport providers. If a pair of transport users or a pair of transport providers uses the same networking protocol, they are considered to be matching. If they use different protocols, they are nonmatching. For example, a Berkeley AF_INET sockets program can communicate only with another AF_INET sockets program; it cannot communicate with a CPI-C program. These two transport users are nonmatching. However, a CPI-C program can communicate with another CPI-C program or with one written to the APPC protocol boundary, and a sockets program can communicate with another sockets program or with one written using XTI. These are matching transport user protocols. The same holds true for transport providers. A TCP/IP network connected with another TCP/IP network is a matching transport provider connection, TCP/IP and SNA are nonmatching.

The remaining terms listed in Table 10.1 will be explained as this chapter progresses.

10.3   MPTN and the Open Blueprint

Prior to the 1992 introduction of the Open Blueprint, originally called the Networking Blueprint, IBM began developing the MPTN architecture as a means of implementing CTS, the common transport semantics section of the blueprint. IBM then announced MPTN in March 1993. The X/Open Company has since published specifications for MPTN and provides documentation that can be used for implementing MPTN-compliant products.

Traditionally, networks employed a single transport network protocol such as SNA, IPX, NetBIOS, or TCP/IP. Application programs gained access to the transport network by using an application programming interface that was associated with that particular type of transport network. The CPI-C API belongs to SNA transport networks, the sockets API with TCP/IP transport networks, and NetBEUI is the interface for NetBIOS. This traditional approach created a situation where application programs were always bound to a particular transport network protocol: CPI-C programs ran only on SNA networks, sockets programs ran exclusively on TCP/IP networks, and programs written with the NetBEUI commands ran only on NetBIOS networks. The choice of applications determined the transport protocol that would be installed in the network. Once a transport protocol was in place, the selection of additional application programs was limited to those that ran on that particular transport protocol. Therefore, if an application had to run on a computer that did not already have the necessary transport protocol installed, this new transport protocol would have to be purchased, installed, and supported on a system that was perhaps already overburdened with multiple transport protocols. This binding between an application and the transport network protocol led to the situation that exists today, where network administrators may be forced to install and support multiple protocols in order to run all the required applications.

Common transport semantics provides a place where a protocol stack can be split between transport users and transport providers and a decision about which transport provider a transport user will use can be made (Fig. 10.2). When a transport user requests the services of a transport provider, CTS checks to see if a native transport provider is available and active (in Fig. 10.2, this is indicated by the "same protocol" path). If it is available and active, the request is passed to the native transport provider and CTS becomes a null function. If not, the "mixed protocol" path is taken. CTS has two ways of providing mixed protocol services, "existing standards" and MPTN. If there is an existing standard, such as RFC 1001 and 1002 (NetBEUI over TCP/IP) or RFC 1006 (OSI over TCP/IP), the request is passed to the existing standard. If one does not exist, the request is handled by MPTN. CTS provides a *switching point* in the networking protocol stack, where the choice of protocol that is used above CTS is independent of the choice of protocol used below CTS.

CTS provides a service at the top of the OSI transport layer (layer 4) that is similar to the service already provided at the top of the data link layer (layer 2). The later service enables transport networks to utilize different data links: Transport network traffic can be routed over various types of subnetworks, including token ring, Ethernet, SDLC, and wide area networks. The former service enables applications to utilize different transport networks. By bringing CTS into the networking picture, networks can now be thought of as having two switching points in the protocol stack: one provided by the network layer and the other provided by CTS.

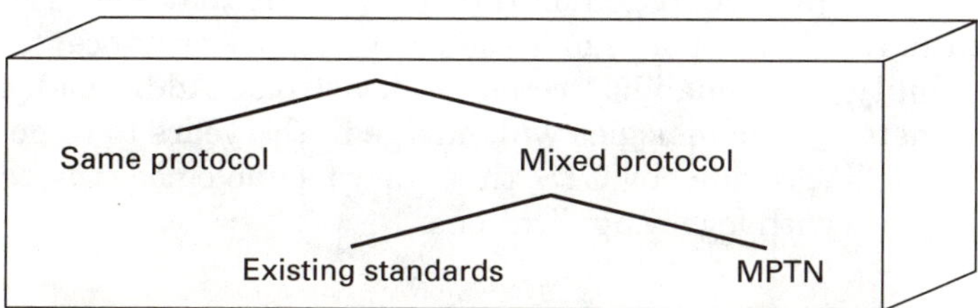

Figure 10.2 Common transport semantics.

There are many programs that are so widely used as networking tools that they have become *de facto* standards. Programs such as ftp, telnet, and X-windows are well known the world over. Because they were written for TCP/IP using the sockets API, they cannot run on other transport networks. Additionally, there is a base of mission-critical legacy applications that use a particular API such as the IPX API, NetBEUI, or APPC for communications. The agencies and corporations that use these programs do not want to rewrite them because of the cost and effort involved and the fact that changes usually introduce new bugs. These programs depend on the transport network protocol for which they were written.

The switching point created by CTS in the protocol stack is a logical next evolutionary step for networking technology. CTS provides a clean separation between application programs and the transport network on which the application is running. Without adding this switching point to the network stack, two situations ensue.

- *Multiprotocol networks proliferate.*   In order to run, for example, TCP/IP applications, NetBIOS applications, and NetWare applications in the same network, workstations must have *all three* protocol stacks installed, network analysts must be familiar with all three protocol stacks (because packets from each will be intermixed "on the wire"), and all three networks and their associated routing protocols will contend for network resources and limit the usefulness of the network.

- *Development of a separate transport network is restricted.*   Network administrators, faced with the daunting task of having to limit the number of transport protocols running in their network, are faced with the decision of having to chose which transport network protocols they wish to run. In other words, it has become necessary to make a critical decision concerning the type of transport network that will be implemented in the network backbone. Since application programs have traditionally been tied to particular transport networks because of the communications API with which they were written, the determining factor in the selection of the protocol for a backbone network is often based on the applications that need to be implemented. To chose a transport network protocol based on the applications that are associated with each, rather than on issues such as price, performance, security, extendibility, and reliability, could be disastrous. Additionally, new transport network technologies will emerge in the years to come, and without the split provided by CTS, these new technologies may be difficult to integrate with legacy applications.

10.4   MPTN Services

In order to provide complete transport provider services for a transport user, MPTN performs two basic functions: compensation and address mapping.

10.4.1   Compensation

Compensation is the MPTN service that fills the gap between what the transport user requires and what the transport provider can actually provide. Whenever a transport user is matched with a native transport provider, expected transport services are automatically available. However, whenever a transport user is matched with a nonnative transport provider, the expected transport services may possibly *not* be available. If they are not, MPTN supplies a compensation to allow missing services to become available.

A set of standard MPTN compensations to be used in all cases was determined by the MPTN architects using a process of examining the transport services provided by four very different transport networks: SNA, TCP/IP, OSI, and NetBIOS. These four protocols include the transport services of most other popular transport protocols. By getting these four protocols to work with MPTN, the architects were confident that MPTN could support every popular protocol. This was substantiated when support for IPX was implemented using the MPTN architecture and no new compensations were needed.

Table 10.2 summarizes the transport services provided among the four selected transport network protocols. Additionally, full-duplex connections, connection outage notification, and a datagram service need to be compensated for in some situations. Each of the four selected protocols supports reliable connections, although the method of establishing and terminating connections varies. MPTN provides compensations for connection establishment and termination, so that even when a given transport user is using a nonnative provider, connection establishment and termination are done in the manner required by the transport user. When a transport user expects notification in the case of a connection outage and the underlying transport provider network has no such service, MPTN must keep track of the status of the connection and provide the necessary notification should the connection terminate unexpectedly.

Examples of some of the compensations that MPTN must support are shown in Table 10.3. However, the subject of MPTN compensations is dealt with in greater detail in Chap. 13.

TABLE 10.2   Transport Services

	SNA	NetBIOS	TCP/IP	OSI
Data type	Record	Record	Stream	Record
Connection data	Not supported*	Not supported	Not supported	Not supported*
Connection reply data	Not supported*	Not supported	Not supported	Not supported*
Close type	Duplex and simplex abortive	Duplex graceful	Simplex graceful	Duplex abortive
Connection termination data	Not supported*	Not supported	Not supported	Not supported*
Maximum record length	No restriction	128 kbytes	Not applicable	Defined by underlying network layer
Maximum expedited data length	86 bytes	Not applicable	Not supported[†]	16 bytes
Expedited data	Supported	Not supported	Not supported[†]	Not supported
Expedited marking	Not supported	Not applicable	Not supported[†]	Not supported
Max. length of data on normal datagram	No restriction	Implementation dependent	Implementation dependent	Defined by underlying network layer
Max. length of data on control datagram	No restriction	Implementation dependent	Implementation dependent	Defined by underlying network layer

*Data in connection establishment/termination requests and replies are formatted. This protocol does not support arbitrary user data.

[†]The TCP/IP urgent data mechanism is not used by MPTN.

10.4.2 Address mapping

In addition to compensations, a method of address resolution called *address mapping* is provided by MPTN. As we have seen, each type of transport network has its own style of addressing: variable-length OSI addresses, 32-bit IP addresses, 1- to 17-byte SNA names, 16-byte NetBIOS names, and fully qualified IPX addresses. When a transport *user* uses a nonnative transport *provider,* the addresses used by the user and the provider are incompatible. Address mapping provides a means for correlating a transport user address to the appropriate

TABLE 10.3   Some MPTN Compensations

Connection establishment	The connection establishment process of the transport user differs from that of the transport provider.
Termination data	The connection termination process of the transport user differs from that of the transport provider.
Full-duplex over half-duplex	The transport user supports a two-way data flow and the transport provider supports only a one-way-at-a-time data flow.
Record delineation	Differences in the delineation of data records.
Expedited data	Expedited data are supported by a transport user, but not by a transport provider.
Datagrams over connections	Datagrams are supported by the transport user, but not by the connection-oriented transport provider.
Connection outage notification	Connection outage notification is unavailable in the transport provider.
Multicasting	Multicasting is supported by a transport user, but not by the transport provider.

transport provider address, thus enabling the transport user's data to be transmitted on the transport provider's network.

The MPTN architecture defines three different methods for mapping addresses.

- *Algorithmic address mapping.*   This method can be used for particular combinations of transport user and transport provider networks that allow the mapping of one address to another using a specific algorithm.

- *Protocol-specific directory.*   A native directory service supplied by the transport provider network may, in some cases, be used to contain transport user-to-transport provider address mappings.

- *Address mapper.*   An optional MPTN component called the address mapper has been designed specifically for mapping addresses and can be used for any combination of transport user and transport provider networks.

10.5   MPTN: A Tale of Two Types

We have discussed some of the services that MPTN must provide. MPTN provides these services using two different types of MPTN nodes. Two different situations led to the development of these two types of MPTN nodes.

- *Mixed-protocol networking.*   Programs originally written to run on top of a particular transport network must run over other transport networks without changing the application.

- *Network interconnection.*   Networks with dissimilar transport protocols must be interconnected so that two programs using matching protocols can communicate with each other across the interconnected networks.

These two situations are represented by two different MPTN node types: the *access node* (for mixed-protocol networking) and the *transport gateway node* (for network interconnection).

When MPTN is installed in a node of a computer network, if it only needs to support the first situation of mixed-protocol networking, then a limited set of functions is provided by an access node. If the second situation of network interconnection is needed, then the full set of MPTN functions must be provided by a transport gateway node.

Both of these MPTN node types will now be discussed, beginning with the access node.

10.5.1   The MPTN access node

An MPTN access node is a network node with MPTN functionality that enables an application program to run over nonnative transport networks. That is, access nodes provide transport users access to nonnative transport providers.

Figure 10.3 presents a very simple example of how an access node works. This example consists of two AIX workstations, which normally use TCP/IP transport networks, interconnected instead with a SNA transport network. One of the machines is running X-windows and is accessing an X-windows client residing on the other machine. X-windows is implemented with the socket interface that normally runs over TCP/IP. In this case, sockets is running on top of SNA, with CTS providing MPTN services.

It can be seen from this example that at least two access nodes need to be installed in order to implement an MPTN service on a single network. The access nodes enable two transport users with matching protocols to communicate over a nonnative transport provider.

Another example is presented in Fig. 10.4. This time an AS/400 computer and an OS/2 PC are running CPI-C applications, one sending data to the other. The link between the two machines is TCP/IP, and in this example, APPC programs (using the CPI-C API) are running over a TCP/IP transport network.

Figure 10.5 shows a multiprotocol network with three IPX access nodes attached to it. The first, access node 1, is connected to two separate nonnative network protocols: one SNA and the other TCP/IP.

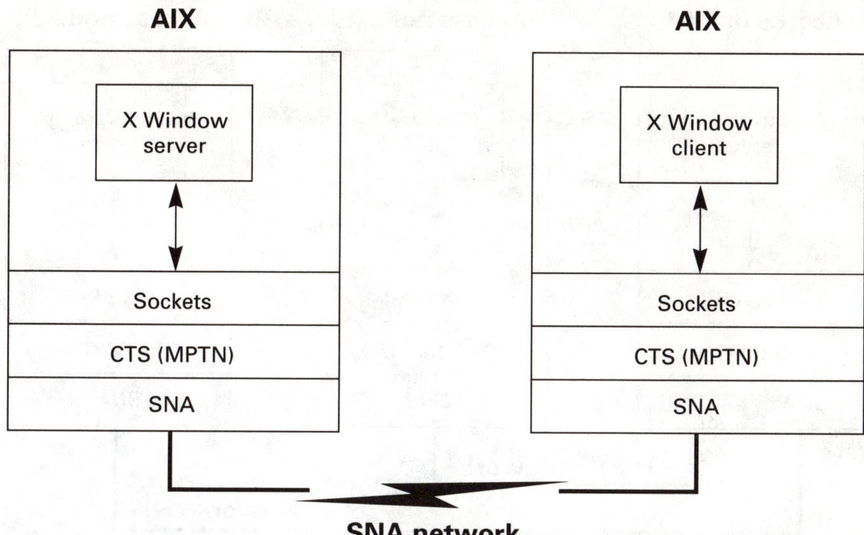

Figure 10.3   "Sockets over SNA" implemented with two access nodes.

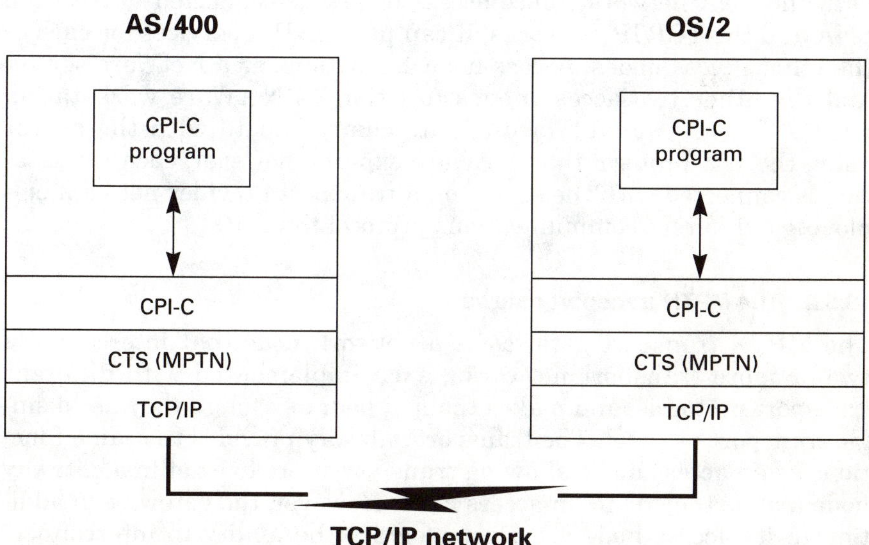

Figure 10.4   "APPC over TCP/IP" implemented with two access nodes.

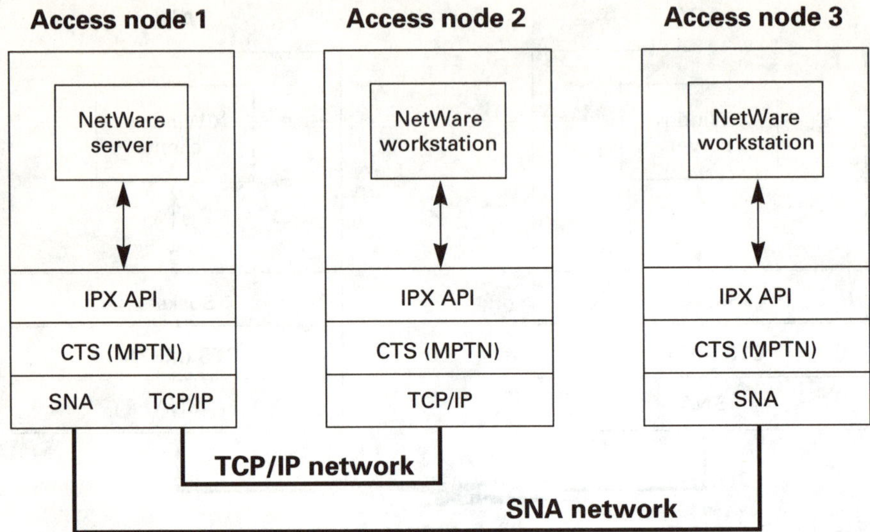

Figure 10.5   NetWare workstations running in access nodes use different underlying transport networks to communicate with a NetWare server.

Access node 2 connects with the TCP/IP network, and access node 3 with the SNA network. Since access node 1 is connected to both the SNA and the TCP/IP networks, it can provide IPX services for each of the other access nodes. Access node 1 functions as a NetWare server, and the other two access nodes function as NetWare workstation clients. These two NetWare clients communicate with the server using the IPX protocol that NetWare expects; however, each workstation is connected with the server on a transport provider network employing a different communications protocol than IPX.

10.5.2   The MPTN transport gateway

The MPTN transport gateway is a network node that interconnects two or more transport networks, each implemented with different transport protocols, and makes them appear as though they use a single transport protocol. The transport gateway provides the same functions as an access node, allowing transport users to exist in a gateway node just as they do in an access node. However, the gateway, in addition to its access node services, provides the ability to interconnect transport networks.

A transport gateway is not the same as the more familiar application gateway. An application gateway works in the OSI application layer. The transport gateway works in the transport layer. The transport gateway provides applications with a seamless transport layer interface in a similar manner to the way routers tie together data link layers to provide a seamless interface to the data link layer.

To make the functions of a transport gateway clearer, we will describe a simple configuration: two networks connected by a transport gateway (Fig. 10.6).

The transport gateway in our example could be designed to work in three different ways.

- *Configuration 1.*   A nonnative user (i.e., in an MPTN access node) in transport network 1 could communicate with a native user (i.e., in a node with no MPTN function) in transport network 2. This requires that the protocol of both transport users be the same (i.e., matching).

- *Configuration 2.*   A nonnative user in transport network 2 could communicate with a native user in transport network 1 if they were both using a matching transport user protocol and the nonnative user is in an MPTN access node.

- *Configuration 3.*   A nonnative user in one of the transport networks could communicate with a matching nonnative user in the other network. Both users would have to be located in an MPTN access node.

The first configuration is shown in Fig. 10.7. Transport network 1 is a SNA network, transport network 2 is a TCP/IP network. The two networks are interconnected by a single common node which func-

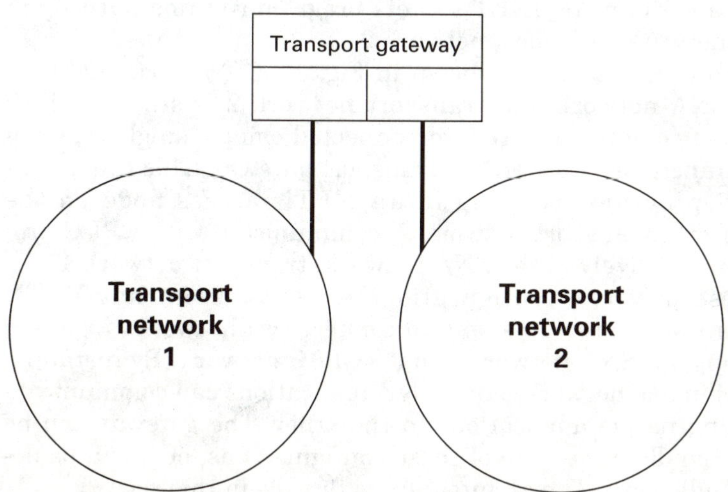

Figure 10.6   An MPTN transport gateway interconnects two transport networks.

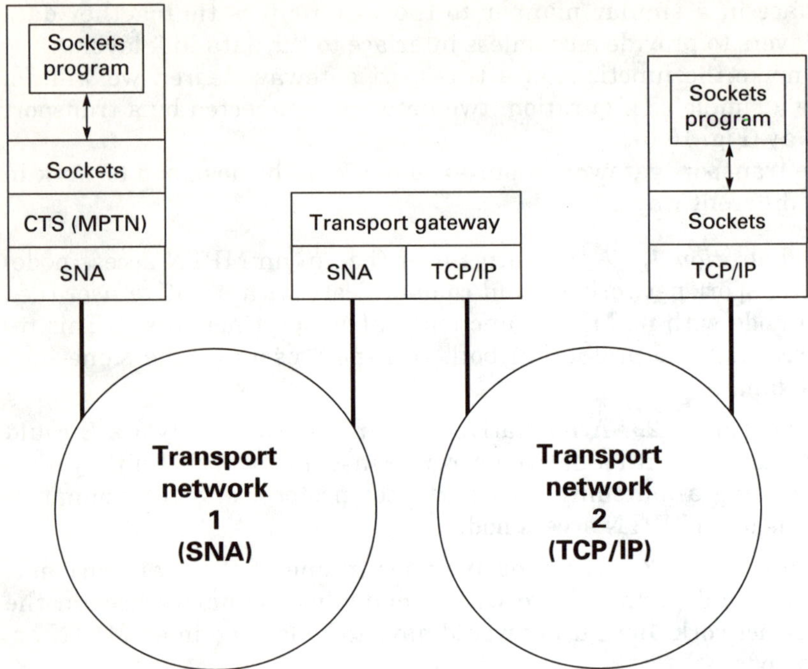

Figure 10.7 A sockets program in a SNA network communicates with a sockets program in a TCP/IP network.

tions as an MPTN gateway. This gateway allows an AF_INET sockets program running in an MPTN access node on the SNA network to communicate with an AF_INET sockets program running natively in the TCP/IP network, transport network 2.

The second configuration is shown in Fig. 10.8. Transport network 1 is still a SNA network and transport network 2 is still a TCP/IP network. The two networks are interconnected using a single common node which functions as an MPTN transport gateway. This time, however, CPI-C programs running in an MPTN access node on the TCP/IP network, transport network 2, communicate with CPI-C programs running natively in the SNA network, transport network 1.

From these first two configurations it can be seen that MPTN transport gateways provide a way to connect two networks together, in our example an SNA network and a TCP/IP network. By installing access nodes in one network, nonnative applications can communicate with matching native applications in the other. The gateway can be designed to handle either one of these configurations, or it can be designed to handle both. The architecture is flexible in this regard.

Figure 10.9 shows our first configuration example again. This time one of the nodes in transport network 2 has been reconfigured as a

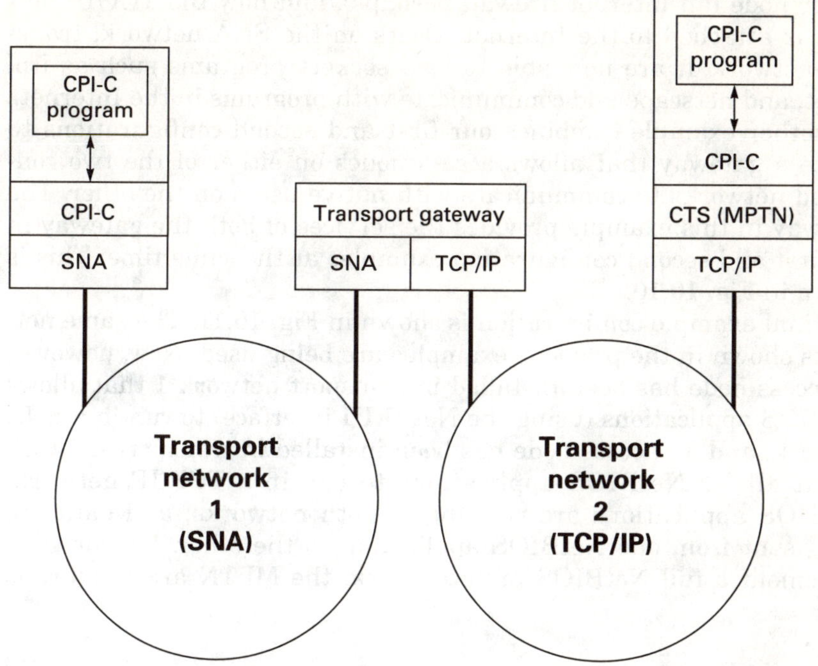

Figure 10.8 A CPI-C program in a TCP/IP network communicates with a CPI-C program in a SNA network.

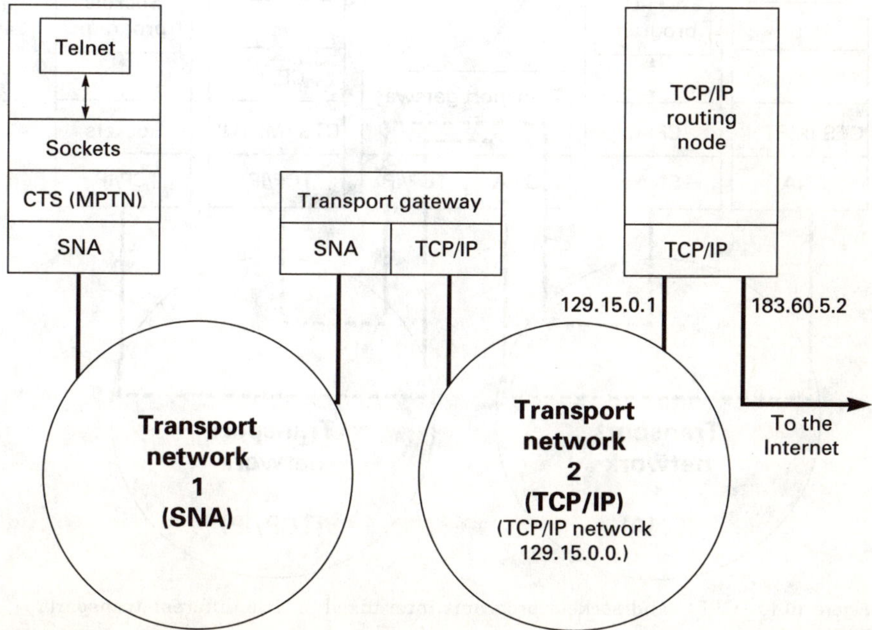

Figure 10.9 A telnet session from a SNA network is established with an Internet host.

router node (an internet firewall perhaps), and now the TCP/IP network is attached to the Internet. Users on the SNA network, transport network 1, are now able to load sockets programs such as ftp, telnet, and netscape and communicate with programs in the Internet.

Another example combines our first and second configurations to create a gateway that allows access nodes on either of the two connected networks to communicate with native users on the other. The gateway in this example provides the services of both the gateway in the first and second configuration examples at the same time. This is shown in Fig. 10.10.

A final example configuration is shown in Fig. 10.11. The same networks shown in the previous examples are being used. Now, however, an access node has been installed in transport network 1 that allows NetBIOS applications (using the NetBEUI interface) to run in a SNA network, and an access node has been installed in transport network 2 that allows NetBIOS applications to run in a TCP/IP network. NetBIOS applications are running in both networks, and data are being sent from one NetBIOS application to the other. Rather than implement a full NetBIOS protocol stack, the MPTN architecture is

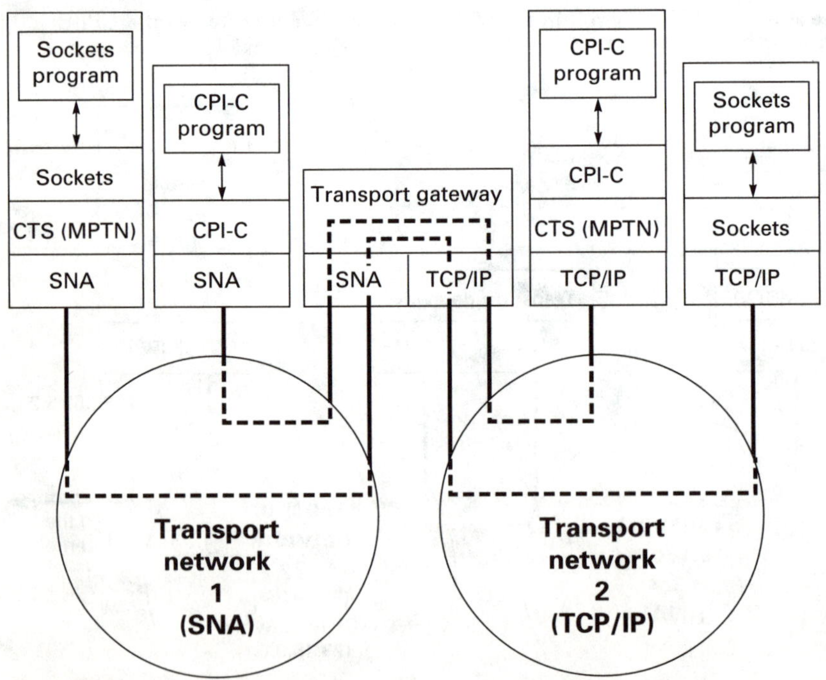

Figure 10.10   CPI-C and sockets programs intermixed on two different transport networks.

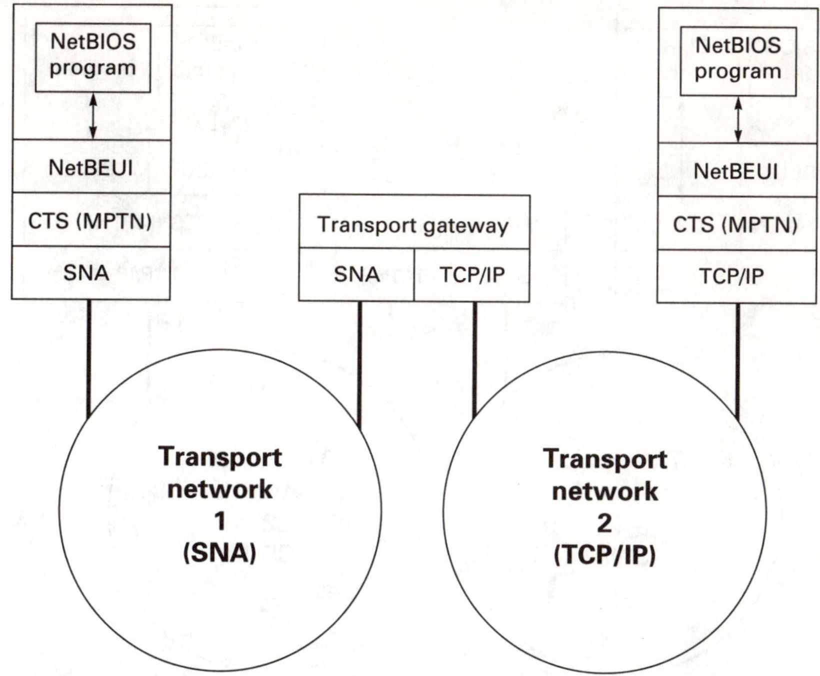

Figure 10.11 NetBIOS programs communicate using SNA and TCP/IP transport providers.

used to implement NetBEUI over SNA in transport network 1, and NetBEUI over TCP/IP in transport network 2. Additionally, AF_INET sockets programs and NetBEUI programs could both use the same access node in transport network 1, and SNA and NetBEUI applications could both use the same access node in transport network 2. This is shown in Fig. 10.12.

MPTN transport gateways can be used in another important configuration. In Fig. 10.13, three transport networks are interconnected using two gateways. All the different methods of using access nodes and gateways that were just presented can be applied to this three-network example, although no access nodes are shown in Figure 10.13. This is an example of two networks that use the same transport protocol being connected through a backbone network which has a different transport protocol. Transport network 1, in this example, is a TCP/IP network, transport network 2 is an SNA network, and transport network 3 is another TCP/IP network. All of the native programs in the TCP/IP networks can communicate with each other using the SNA network as a *backbone* that interconnects the TCP/IP networks. The gateways allow the TCP/IP transport users to use the SNA network as

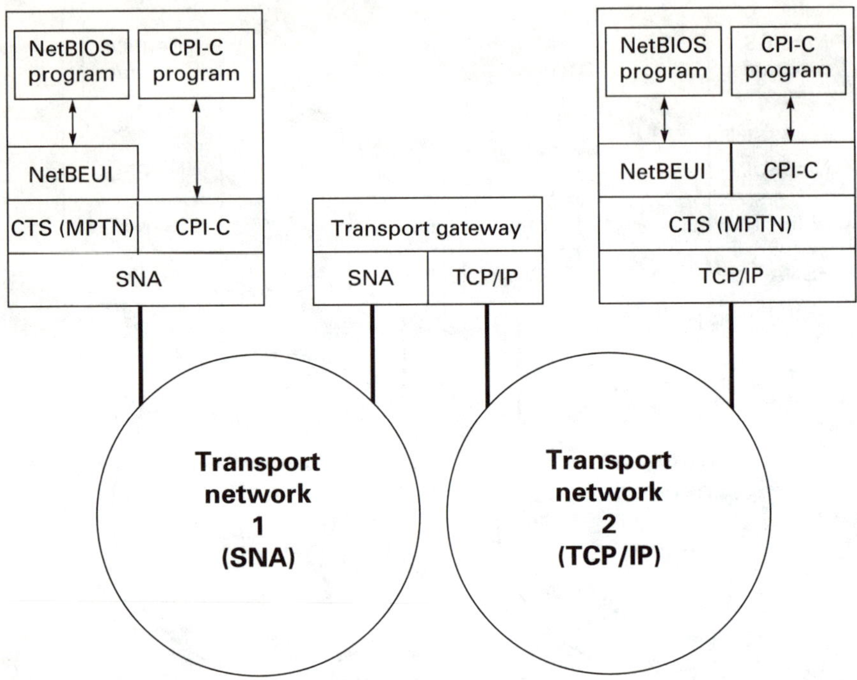

Figure 10.12   NetBIOS and CPI-C programs using the same access node.

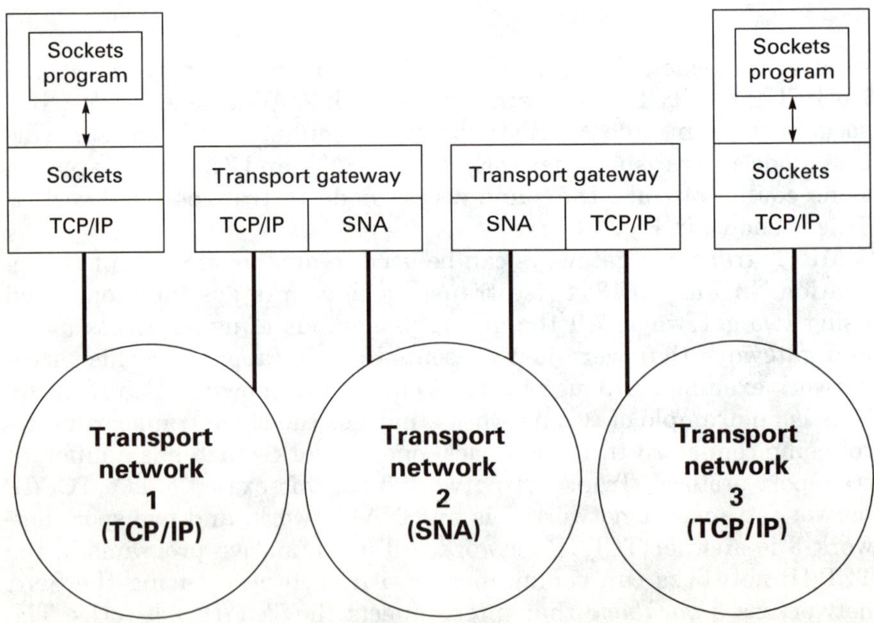

Figure 10.13   Linking two transport networks by means of a third transport network.

a backbone. No access nodes are required for this example. However, access nodes could be installed in the SNA network to enable AF_INET sockets programs to communicate with native programs in either of the TCP/IP networks, and access nodes could be installed in either of the TCP/IP networks to allow SNA programs to communicate with SNA programs running natively in the SNA network.

Naturally, this three-network example could be extended to allow many other combinations. For example, both of the TCP/IP networks could actually be multiprotocol networks with IPX, NetBIOS, and TCP/IP all running together, and the gateways could be designed to allow transport users for all three protocols to communicate with matching users in the opposite network, with all three protocols being transported over the SNA network.

These examples help show the degree to which the MPTN architecture can be extended. For most purposes, however, gateways and access nodes do not need to handle a large number of different situations. An implementation of the MPTN architecture should be based on the particular needs at hand.

10.6   Solving the Multiprotocol Network Puzzle

Chapter 8 described multiprotocol networks and how they came into being. We will now present an overview of some of the various methods that are being used to implement multiprotocol networks, then show how multiprotocol networking can be accomplished using implementations of the MPTN architecture.

10.6.1   Multiple protocols

Three basic situations can cause multiprotocol networks to come into being.

- *Adding new applications.*   A new application is purchased and the networking protocol that it uses is not currently installed in the network.

- *Network interoperability.*   Two independent networks need to be interconnected. This could be the case of company A purchasing company B. Company A has a SNA network and company B has a TCP/IP network. It would be unproductive to convert either the SNA network into a TCP/IP network or the TCP/IP network into a SNA network because the application programs on one of the networks would have to be rewritten to use the new network's protocol.

- *Connecting LANs through a backbone network.* A large company has a SNA network which connects all the branch offices with a central-site mainframe. IPX local area networks have been installed in each of the branch offices, and the branch office managers wish that workstations in their LANs could attach to servers in other branch office LANs. Rather than install a separate IPX network to run between branch offices, MPTN transport gateways can be used to connect the branch office LANs to the SNA network and use SNA as a backbone through which IPX data can travel from one branch office to another.

There are a number of solutions for these problems.

- *Encapsulation (tunneling).* A transport network is used in the capacity of a subnetwork in order to encapsulate another full network stack within it. Encapsulation is a "quick and dirty" solution: It solves the problem of LAN interconnection through a backbone, but not necessarily efficiently and in a manner that is architecturally sound.

- *Protocol server and remote API.* Using a protocol server (a workstation dedicated to the task of protocol conversation) in a local area network to perform needed protocol conversion is one way of solving the problems of multiprotocol networks, but it can add a great deal of traffic to the network and create a bottleneck situation in the protocol server.

- *Multiple protocol stacks.* Supporting multiple protocols means higher costs because each protocol has to be installed in each node that uses the protocol. This may mean more memory, more storage, more CPU power, more network management—plus there will probably be an outlay for installation and software costs, and additional skills will be required to install and maintain each protocol.

- *Middleware.* Middleware can solve multiprotocol problems, but it has two important drawbacks: It is vendor-specific, and applications must be rewritten to use the specific middleware API.

- *Multiprotocol routers.* Multiprotocol routers, discussed in Chap. 8, can be used to route multiple networking protocols over a backbone network. Routers are costly, and they are a network element that is separate from the essential elements of the network and therefore add complexity to network management and maintenance. Additionally, the solutions used by routers are often proprietary and therefore may not interwork. Routers were an important evolution in networking technology, but it is probable that their use will be reduced in the future as networking technologies become simplified. Since routing is simply a software process, as a convergence in the ways that networks are interconnected takes place, the functionality provided by routers will most likely be moved into the computing nodes themselves, or into network interface adapter cards.

10.6.2   The MPTN solution

MPTN can be used to help solve the multiprotocol networking puzzle. Some of the advantages of MPTN are as follows.

- The MPTN access node and address mapper are open architectures. The specifications are available from X/Open. The MPTN architecture is not proprietary, as is the architecture on which middleware products are often based. Because of this, MPTN products from different vendors, if fully conformant, will interoperate. If your middleware manufacturer should discontinue its product line, you could be left "holding the bag."

- MPTN allows applications to be independent of the underlying transport network. The choice of applications and transport network can be decisions that are made independent of each other. This is a very important consideration because it provides the ability to select applications based on the merits of the application and to implement the transport network based on considerations such as cost, performance, usability, and the functions provided. This also allows existing applications to be preserved while changing the network from one type to another.

- MPTN can concatenate networks at the transport layer—a feature not available in routers. Formerly, most networks were concatenated by means of routers, bridges, and application gateways. Now, by using MPTN as the multiprotocol solution, issues such as whether to install IPX, SNA, TCP/IP, or even OSI as a part of the backbone network becomes an issue that can be decided on the merits of the transport network protocol itself rather than on such reasons as "The users want Internet access" or "How am I going to route the LU type 1 print from the mainframe in New Jersey to my printers here in corporate headquarters now that I have converted my SNA network to TCP/IP?"

- MPTN can minimize the use of routers. In cases where routers are being purchased for the sole purpose of encapsulating data, such as LAN traffic over a WAN link, MPTN may be a better solution. However, MPTN can still be implemented in router networks: The two are not mutually exclusive.

- MPTN can help reduce the number of network protocol stacks being loaded in an enterprise network. Multiple protocol stacks often mean multiple vendors, multiple interfaces, multiple setup programs, multiple sets of documentation, multiple kinds of expertise, and increased memory and disk requirements for each workstation.

- MPTN can be used to interconnect LANs over a backbone network. This is an important aspect of the architecture. Additionally, access node users in the backbone network can communicate with matching applications in the LANs.

10.7 MPTN Components

At this point, the reader should have a basic understanding of what the MPTN architecture provides for transport users. Before explaining the access node and transport gateway in greater detail, some of the components of MPTN will first be introduced.

MPTN transport gateways and access nodes contain components that manage and perform MPTN services for the node. Two basic components are fundamental to both the gateway and access nodes:

- The common MPTN manager

- The protocol-specific MPTN manager

How these are used in an MPTN access node is shown in Fig. 10.14.

10.7.1 The common MPTN manager

The *common MPTN manager* (CMM) is the main component of an MPTN transport gateway or access node. The CMM is MPTN's node manager, and one resides in every MPTN transport gateway and access node. The CMM provides MPTN services for all transport users, regardless of protocol. The services provided by the CMM are:

- Connection establishment and termination

- Sending and receiving of data

- Address mapping

- Protocol compensation

- Transport provider selection

- Network management event reporting

- Additional gateway services (in a gateway CMM only)

At the top of Fig. 10.14 are the application programs running in the node. The APIs used by these programs interface with the transport user for the particular protocol. The transport users in turn interface with the CMM through the *transport layer protocol boundary* (TLPB).

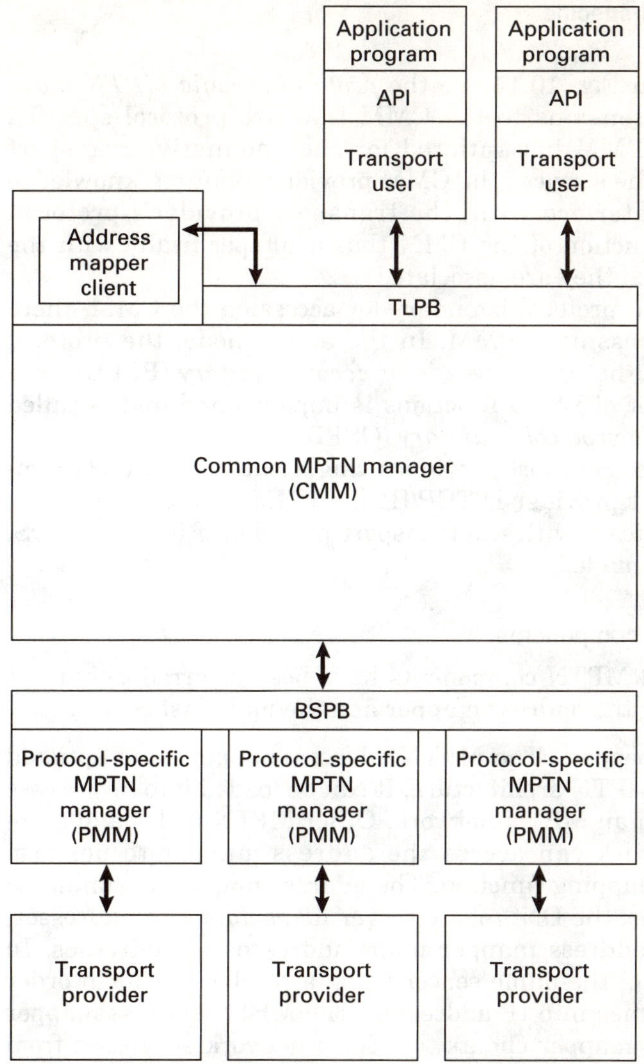

Figure 10.14   MPTN components.

The TLPB is an architecturally defined boundary that separates transport users of various types from the CMM. Specific functions are defined for the TLPB using *verbs,* and these will be described in the next chapter. The TLPB is used not only by transport users that represent specific applications, but by the CMM's own address mapper client. This relationship will be explained as we progress.

10.7.2   The protocol-specific
MPTN managers

Below the CMM in Fig. 10.14 are the *protocol-specific MPTN managers* (PMMs), extensions to the CMM that are protocol-specific. There must be a PMM instantiated for each nonnative transport provider. Some of the services the CMM provides require a knowledge of, and a direct interface with, the transport provider's protocol. PMMs are a subfunction of the CMM that deal specifically with the protocols with which they are associated.

Just as there is a protocol boundary for accessing the CMM, there is also one for accessing a PMM. In the access node, the protocol boundary is called the *below-specific protocol boundary* (BSPB). In a gateway, a superset of BSPB functions is implemented and is called the *gateway-specific protocol boundary* (GSPB).

PMMs access the transport provider using a native API. For example, if the transport provider is TCP/IP, the PMM uses the socket interface to communicate with the transport provider, if it is NetBIOS, NetBEUI calls are made.

10.7.3   Other MPTN components

Two other optional MPTN components have been referred to but not yet been described: the address mapper and the multicast server.

10.7.3.1   Address mapper.   The MPTN address mapper is an optional component in the MPTN architecture. It can be loaded into any access or gateway node in an MPTN network. Other MPTN nodes and gateways in the network can access the address mapper to perform MPTN's address mapping function. The address mapper is similar to a DNS name server; the DNS name server maps *names* to addresses, while the MPTN address mapper maps addresses to addresses. In DNS, clients contact the name server using a resolver client in order to resolve DNS names into IP addresses. The MPTN address mapper is used by address mapper clients to resolve network addresses from one network type into network addresses belonging to another network type. It can be seen in Fig. 10.14 that the address mapper client is part of the CMM. This client is responsible for obtaining address mappings from an address mapper server located somewhere in the network and does so by making requests through the TLPB.

The functions and components of the address mapper are described in detail in Chap. 14.

10.7.3.2   Multicast server.   The MPTN multicast server is another optional component in the MPTN architecture. Like the address mapper, it is—as its name implies—a server. Its purpose is to provide multicast emulation services for transport protocols that do not provide multicasting natively. The functions and components of the multicast server are described in detail in Chap. 14.

10.8 Transport Network Types

One more piece of the terminology must be explained before we wrap up this overview of the MPTN architecture. A *single-protocol transport network* (SPTN) is the designation used to describe a transport network with a single transport provider protocol. In other words, an SPTN is a TCP/IP network, a SNA network, or an IPX network. Since multiprotocol networks can contain more than one transport network protocol running in the same physical medium, two or more SPTNs can exist in the same physical medium. SPTNs can be interconnected with MPTN transport gateways.

10.9 MPTN Network Management

There are no specific provisions yet for network management in the MPTN architecture. MPTN networks must be managed by allowing SPTNs to use their own management protocols. Additionally, vendors can add management functionality directly into transport gateways and access nodes by creating an MPTN MIB for the management of these nodes.

10.10 Summary

Multiprotocol networks are with us. In fact, they may have crept in unannounced (nobody really asked for them). Because of the different networking protocols with which individual networks were created and because applications were written to run exclusively in these networks, various ways of integrating networking protocols came about. This led to the complications of managing a diverse enterprise network. The MPTN architecture provides a solution that will be presented in more detail in the following chapters.

The MPTN Access Node

11.1 Introduction

Multiprotocol transport networking as a function of common transport semantics was presented in Chap. 9, and details of the MPTN architecture were introduced in Chap. 10. This chapter, and the three that follow, will cover the subject in greater detail. In this chapter, the MPTN access node is explained, then Chap. 12 covers the architectural details of the MPTN transport gateway. Chapter 13 presents the formats used in the MPTN architecture, and Chap. 14 explains MPTN address mapping.

11.2 MPTN Access Node Components

Figure 11.1 shows the components of an access node. At the top of the drawing transport users communicate with the common MPTN manager via the transport layer protocol boundary (TLPB) (one of the transport users is the address mapper client). The CMM in turn communicates with a protocol-specific MPTN manager using the below-specific protocol boundary (BSPB). We will now discuss these components, beginning with the transport users themselves.

11.2.1 Transport users

Transport users, as was explained in Chap. 10, are users of the transport network. If they represent an application program, such as a CPI-C or a sockets program, they must provide the interface between the API and the TLPB. This interface is implemented by a *syntax mapper,* which maps the syntax of the API calls used by an application program (such as sockets or CPI-C calls) into appropriate calls

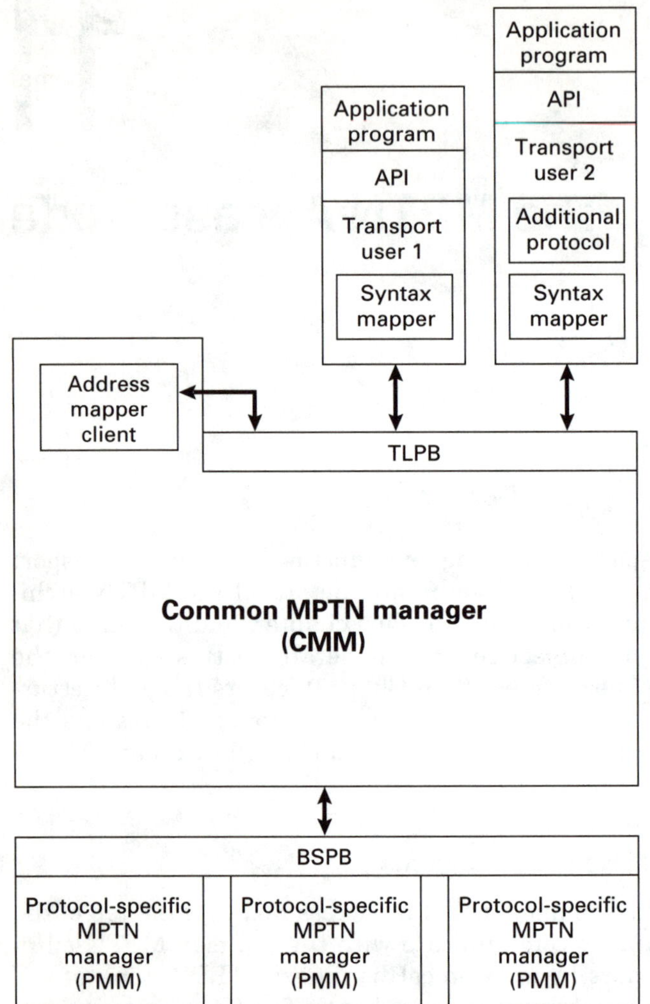

Figure 11.1   The anatomy of an MPTN access node.

that are issued to the TLPB. The architecture does not specify what the nature of a transport user is; this detail depends upon the implementation. Transport users can interface with the APIs of communications protocols, or they can provide entirely different services, such as dealing with address mapping.

There are three types of transport users:

- Direct TLPB users

- Syntax-mapping-only users

- Users that need additional protocol

A direct TLPB user does not perform syntax mapping because it does not perform the function of associating API calls with TLPB calls. A direct TLPB user typically implements an MPTN internal routine such as an address mapper or multicast server. However, it could be any type of function that needs to use the TLPB directly. In Fig. 11.1, the address mapper client is a direct TLPB user.

The second type of transport user performs syntax mapping only. In this case the syntax mapper takes API calls and maps them to TLPB calls. This is the type of transport user that interfaces with APIs such as NetBEUI and sockets. In Fig. 11.1, transport user 1 is a syntax-mapping-only user.

The third type of transport user needs more functionality than just syntax mapping and is best illustrated by example. APPC and the CPI-C interface were explained in detail in Chap. 7. It was shown there that there are features belonging to APPC and CPI-C that are not common to other APIs. These are enhancements such as conversation state management, confirmation of data, and error processing. In CPI-C, for example, if a cmsend() is issued while the conversation state is in RECEIVE, an error must be returned to the application program. There is no equivalent function in the TLPB's vocabulary to which these extra features can be mapped, because they are not transport layer functions. Therefore, additional protocols are required in the transport user to implement these additional features. In Fig. 11.1, transport user 2 has additional protocol support.

11.2.2   The common MPTN manager

The CMM was introduced in Sec. 10.7.1 and is the manager of the MPTN access node. Transport users and the CMM communicate with each other through the transport layer protocol boundary. All the management details of the access node are performed by the CMM except those that directly involve the transport provider's protocol. These details include the selection of transport protocols and the selection of compensations that will be required. The protocol-specific duties, in turn, are handled by the PMMs. The CMM also receives incoming requests and data from the PMMs. These may be responses to commands that the CMM has sent, incoming connection requests, incoming datagrams, or data to be transferred up to a transport user.

11.2.3   The protocol-specific
MPTN manager

The PMM introduced in Sec. 10.7.2 performs protocol-specific MPTN functions. A PMM must exist for each transport provider protocol in a node if nonnative transport users are to be supported over that protocol.

PMMs take care of the protocol-specific duties of CMM management. For example, PMMs send and receive data, and compensations that are determined in the CMM are performed by the PMM. Additionally the PMM must handle some types of address mapping and the protocol-specific elements of connection establishment and termination.

In order for the CMM to perform its duties, it needs the help and cooperation of the transport provider-dependent PMMs. When any of the functions of the CMM involve specifics relating to the transport provider protocol, the specifics are handled by PMMs. PMMs also perform protocol-specific address mapping functions, an example being the use of the domain name system, associated with TCP/IP, which can be used for MPTN address resolution. The PMM communicates with the transport provider using a native communications API.

The way that the CMM and PMM work together to provide a particular function can be illustrated by the way that protocol compensations are performed. Since the CMM knows the characteristics of *both* the transport user and provider, it determines what compensations are needed, but the protocol-specific implementation of the actual compensation is handled by the PMM.

11.2.4   The address mapper client

The address mapper client is a function inside the access node that communicates with the MPTN address mapper (to be discussed in Chap. 14). Even though it is part of the CMM, it uses the TLPB recursively; this is why MPTN access node CMM drawings show the address mapper client in a separate corner, jutting off of the main part of the CMM (Fig. 11.1). The address mapper client is a transport user even though it is part of the CMM, and uses the TLPB to send commands to the address mapper server located somewhere in the SPTN.

The address mapper client is called by the CMM when address resolution or registration is needed and an address mapper, which is an optional feature of the MPTN architecture, is being used. If an address mapper is not being used, address mapping is handled by the PMM instead. The CMM can either call the address mapper client code using a subroutine call, or it can use signals internal to the CMM to contact the address mapper client. These details are implementation-dependent.

11.3   Access Node Services

Now we will turn to a discussion of the services that the access node offers. First we will deal with the services provided by the access node's CMM.

- *Transport user address registration.*   This is a service provided by the CMM that allows the transport user to register its address globally throughout the MPTN network. By registering its address, other matching transport users in the network can communicate with it.

- *Protocol selection.*   The CMM that initiates a connection request, or sends a datagram, is responsible for selecting the transport provider to be used. A connection preference list is an optional local mechanism that lists each installed transport provider type in preferential order. The CMM can use this list sequentially to try to establish a connection with a partner. This list may be based on any number of criteria, such as cost, available bandwidth, and so on. Protocol selection is an implementation-specific detail. For example, selection can be made by comparing protocol mismatches and selecting the transport that minimizes the number of compensations required.

- *Determination of protocol compensation.*   MPTN uses compensation to provide transport services that are required by a transport user but not supported by the selected transport provider. When the transport provider becomes active, it reports the transport characteristics that it supports to the CMM. When a transport user is initialized, it reports what transport characteristics it requires to the CMM. The CMM compares the transport characteristics that are required by the transport user with these supported by the transport provider. Compensation is needed for each mismatch that is found.

- *Connection establishment and termination.*   Connection establishment and termination are functions that the CMM performs in conjunction with other components in the MPTN network. Connection-oriented transport protocols must have a connection in place between the end users before data can be exchanged between them. Connection establishment and termination are the services that put a connection into place and take it down. Since an MPTN connection involves a nonmatching transport user and provider, connections must be established over a nonnative transport protocol. When establishing an MPTN connection, the initiating transport user passes the destination partner's transport user address to the local CMM, which uses address mapping to find the partner's transport provider address. The CMM, working with the PMM, uses the connection establishment protocol of the selected provider along with the MPTN connection establishment protocol to establish an MPTN connection. In the connection termination process, the CMM ensures that the proper close semantics are observed.

- *Nonnative datagram routing.*   The CMM may receive datagrams from a transport user that must be sent using the various transport provider protocols. Since some transport providers, such as SNA, do not provide a datagram service, the CMM, working with the PMM, must provide one. This is accomplished by setting up a connection to be used for datagram delivery only.

11.4   The Transport Layer Protocol Boundary

Transport users communicate with the CMM through the transport layer protocol boundary. The TLPB is architecturally implemented with verbs that represent programming language calls. Transport users must use TLPB calls to communicate with the CMM.

The TLPB defines a protocol boundary at the top of the transport layer. Two transport users located in two different access nodes communicate with each other using the TLPB, as shown in Fig. 11.2.

11.4.1   Format of TLPB calls

The TLPB implements a set of MPTN services that are available to a transport user. Basically, the TLPB represents the top of the common

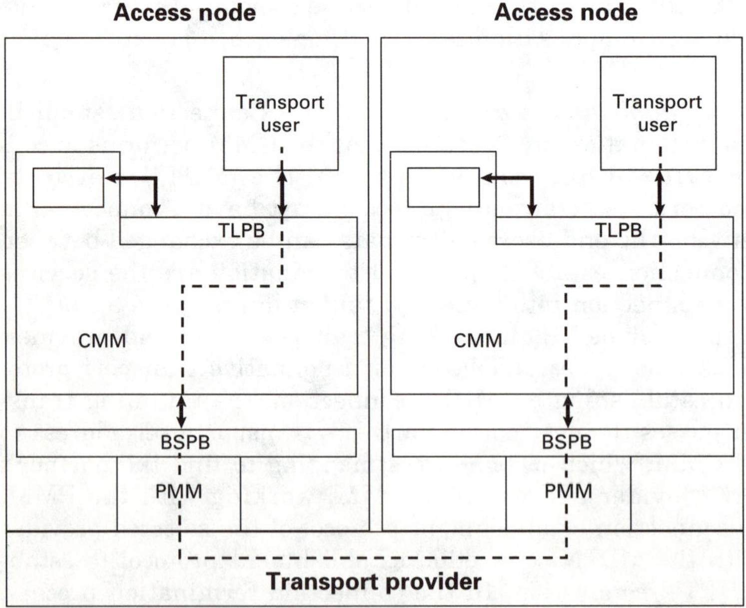

Figure 11.2   Transport users in two different access nodes communicating with each other.

transport semantic section of the Open Blueprint and is defined in the architecture as a set of verbs which represent procedure *calls*. There are two types of calls: *downcalls,* which are calls made by the transport user to the CMM; and *upcalls,* which are calls made by the CMM to the transport user. This distinction will become clear as the individual calls are described. Some of the calls can be used either as upcalls or downcalls. To differentiate between the two, downcalls have a _DC appended to the name of the call and upcalls have _UC appended. All TLPB calls have names that begin with M_ (which stands for MPTN).

TLPB downcalls are nonblocking, meaning that they do not wait, or *block,* for the completion of the call. For example, if a downcall cannot be satisfied quickly, a return code of RC_PENDING is returned and a later upcall is made to inform the user of the completion. This upcall is represented by a verb with the same name as the downcall but appended with _UC instead of _DC.

11.4.2   TLPB calls

The verbs of the TLPB interface will now be presented and each one explained. These verbs, which represent procedure calls that can be implemented in a programming language, are represented by verb names and are grouped into five categories:

- Initialization

- Addressing

- Connection establishment and termination

- Connection-oriented data transfer

- Datagram transfer

The complete set of TLPB verbs is shown in Table 11.1.

Before we begin the discussion, it should be mentioned that this is not a programming reference but an architectural description. Because of this, every return code and all available parameters are *not* described unless a particular point about the call needs to be illustrated. For a more detailed reference, *XMPTN: Access Node* is suggested reading (see App. C).

11.4.2.1   Initialization.   Before a transport user can send or receive datagrams or accept or establish a connection, an endpoint *instance* with its associated *endpoint control block* must be established. Our first verb represents the call that performs this function.

M_CREATE.   A transport user endpoint instance is established by issuing an M_CREATE downcall. M_CREATE_DC tells the CMM what kind of transport user is issuing the call, what kind of service it

TABLE 11.1   TLPB Verbs

Initialization	
M_CREATE_DC	Create an MPTN control block.
Addressing	
M_BIND_DC	Associate a local address with a connection endpoint and register the address with the MPTN network.
M_UNBIND_DC	Remove the association between an MPTN connection endpoint and the transport user name established by an M_BIND_DC and delete any network registration if this is the last endpoint to be associated with an address.
M_CONFLICT_UC	Notify of a conflict that exists between a transport user's address and an address in use by another transport user.
Connection setup and termination	
M_CONNECT_DC	Attempt to establish a connection with another end user. That user must have an outstanding M_LISTEN_DC.
M_LISTEN_DC	A transport user is ready to receive incoming connection requests.
M_ACCEPT_UC	A connection request from a remote user issuing an M_CONNECT_DC has arrived.
M_ACCEPT_DC	Accept or reject a call from a remote user that issued an M_CONNECT_DC.
M_CLOSE_DC	Close an open session.
M_CLOSED_UC	The connection was closed.
Connection-oriented data transfer	
M_SEND_DC	Send data on a connection.
M_RECEIVE_UC	Data have arrived on a connection.
Datagram transfer	
M_SEND_DG_DC	Send a datagram.
M_RCV_DG_UC	A datagram has arrived.
M_RCVDG_INIT_DC	A transport user is willing to receive datagrams.

wants, and what its transport requirements are. A *dom* field specifies if the transport user is a direct user and if not, what protocol it implements. A structure called M_INFO, passed in the M_CREATE_DC call, contains the information that will be used by the CMM to establish a connection or to send datagrams. The fields used in M_INFO are shown in Table 11.2. One of the M_INFO fields is called *conn_chars*. This is a pointer to the connection characteristics described in Table 11.3. These are used when a connection is being established. Another parameter passed in the M_CREATE_DC is the

TABLE 11.2   M_INFO

servtype	Connection (ST_CO) or connectionless (ST_CL)
datatype	If ST_CO, is record (DT_RECORD) or stream (DT_STREAM) required?
conn_chars	Pointer to the connection characteristics
connect	Maximum length of connection data
creplen	Maximum length of connection response data
maxdgm	Maximum length of a datagram that will be sent or received
addr	Maximum length of TLPB user addresses
partial_records	Whether partial records can be sent or received
datagram_segmentation	If connectionless (servtype = ST_CL), datagram segmentation is supported
in_line	Should expedited data be sent in line?
tu_conn_id	Optional TLPB user ID
session_outage_notification	Whether connection outage notification is required
connect_connect	Transport user supports connect/connect
parallel_connections	Supports parallel connections
not_listening_notification	If servtype = ST_CO, notify if trying to connect and partner not listening

TABLE 11.3   Connection Characteristics

tsdu	Maximum record length
etsdu	Maximum expedited record length
discon	Maximum length of connection termination data
close_types	Close type
expedited_marking	Should we mark where expedited data begins?

proto field. This field is set by the transport user to indicate which transport provider protocol the user wants to use. This field can be set to B_MPTN, which tells the CMM that it may use any of the installed transport providers.

The M_CREATE_DC is the only TLPB call in the architecture that implements a parameter that is returned when the call completes. In other words, one of the parameters in the call specifies a local numeric field; when the call completes, that field will have a value in it. The value that the M_CREATE_DC returns is a connection identifier. This unique identifier identifies the particular endpoint control block that was created, and it is passed in all other calls to associate each call with the correct control block. Although it is called a *connection* identifier, it is also used when the *servtype* field in the M_INFO structure has been set to connectionless (ST_CL), meaning that there will be no connection. The reason for this is because an endpoint control block is necessary for the transfer of datagrams as well as the establishment of connections.

11.4.2.2 Addressing. The addressing verbs support the registration of a transport user address throughout an MPTN network, making it known to other transport users.

M_BIND. M_BIND_DC is issued by a transport user to associate a local address with the endpoint control block that was created by the M_CREATE_DC. The endpoint may have been specified in the M_CREATE_DC as either a connection or datagram type. For some types of applications, such as servers, where the address must be made available throughout the network, the address can be registered with MPTN. This is accomplished by setting the *regist* parameter.

MPTN supports multicasting and group addresses, and M_BIND_DC can be used to register a group address as well as an individual address.

M_UNBIND. M_UNBIND_DC removes the association between an MPTN endpoint and the transport user address previously established by a call to M_BIND_DC. It also deletes any network registration for the address if no other endpoints are associated with it.

M_CONFLICT. M_CONFLICT_UC is issued by the CMM to inform a transport user that an address that it is attempting to use has been rejected because the address is being used by another transport user. This call is implemented in the architecture to prevent the disastrous kinds of errors that can result when a programmer, or an administrator, makes a mistake by designating an address which results in more than one transport user trying to bind the same address.

11.4.2.3 Connection establishment and termination. The TLPB verbs that define calls which govern the establishment and termination of connections are important to the access node transport user. The syntax mapper in the transport user code must translate the features of native connection establishment and termination into TLPB calls. Therefore, these verbs contain enough versatility to establish connections for the various types of network protocols.

M_CONNECT. M_CONNECT_DC is issued to establish an MPTN connection with the transport user specified in the destination address parameter. The connection must be established between transport users that have matching protocols: a sockets program connecting with a sockets program, an IPX program with an IPX program. The partner transport user does not have to be using an access node, however; it can be a native user that is accessed through a transport gateway. Before M_CONNECT_DC can be called, M_CREATE_DC and M_BIND_DC must both have been previously issued to set up and bind an endpoint control block.

In an MPTN connection, one transport user is active, the other partner is passive. This creates the typical client–server relationship. The endpoint that issues the M_CONNECT_DC is considered active.

Connection data are passed in the *conn_data* parameter. Connection data are not to be confused with the connection characteristics shown in Table 11.3. Connection data are data that are necessary in some protocols for the establishment of a connection. Connection data must be supplied when using protocols such as SNA, which passes data in the BIND RU. TCP/IP has no data associated with connection establishment, so when a TCP/IP connection is being established over MPTN, the conn_data field is not populated. Other fields passed with the M_CONNECT_DC are *service_mode,* which can be used to set the quality-of-service parameters: a *conn_corr* field, a unique connection correlator used to identify the connection; a *time_to_live* field that indicates how many gateways can be traversed; and a *transport_user_data* field that can be used to transfer data between syntax mappers.

The result of a connection establishment request is returned to the transport user in an M_CONNECT_UC. The status field in the upcall is set to indicate if the connection has been established or if the connection establishment process failed. Typically, the status parameter would indicate:

- M_CONNECT_FAILED: Connect failure

- M_CONNECT_LOC_FAIL: Cannot locate the partner

- M_CONNECT_OK: Success

- M_CONNECT_ERROR: Internal error

If the status of the M_CONNECT_UC indicates that the MPTN connection establishment was successful, the M_CONNECT_UC in some cases will pass to the CMM a *conn_chars* field which contains the connection characteristics that were agreed upon by the remote partner (the original connection characteristics that were set in the M_CREATE downcall can be modified by the passive end of the connection when the transport user protocol has provisions for connection-establishment negotiation). A field called *conn_reply* contains any user-specific connection reply data (an example is the BIND response data in SNA). Also returned in the upcall is the field *prov_id,* which identifies the transport provider that was used in the connection.

M_LISTEN.   The M_LISTEN_DC informs the CMM that the issuing transport user is ready to receive incoming connection requests from other transport users. While an M_CONNECT_DC is issued by an active partner in the connection establishment process, M_LISTEN_DC is issued by a passive partner. After an M_LISTEN_DC has been issued, the transport user listens for an M_ACCEPT_UC to signal an incoming connection request. The M_ACCEPT_UC informs the passive transport user that a connection request has arrived and it then has the option of accepting the request or rejecting it. If the *multiple* parameter is set on an M_LISTEN_DC, the transport user has requested that multiple connection requests be accepted. In this case, the M_LISTEN remains in effect after a connection has been accepted or rejected.

M_ACCEPT.   When a transport user attempts to establish a connection with a partner transport user, it issues an M_CONNECT_DC. The remote partner must be listening for an incoming connection request with an outstanding M_LISTEN_DC. When the connection request is received by the listening transport user's CMM, an M_ACCEPT_UC is issued. The M_ACCEPT_UC informs the passive transport user that a connection request has arrived. The passive transport user has the option of accepting or rejecting the connection request.

The M_ACCEPT_UC, sent to the listening transport user by its CMM, has a *conn_chars* field which contains the connection characteristics requested for the connection by the initiating transport user. Before deciding whether to accept the connection request or not, the transport user can modify some of these connection characteristics, perhaps decreasing some of the limits. The conn_chars fields are listed in Table 11.3. After modifying these fields, if necessary, the connection can be accepted by issuing an M_ACCEPT_DC with the conn_chars field populated with the changed values.

The M_ACCEPT_UC also contains a field called *conn_data* which contains connection data, if any was sent, from the partner transport user. The transport user syntax mapping code can use these data to construct a proper incoming connection request. For example, in SNA, the conn_data field would contain the BIND image which would need to be passed up to the SNA LU. *Prov_id* identifies the transport provider that was used for the connection, *tu_conn_id* contains the connection ID, and *transport_user_data* is used in some cases for transferring data between syntax mappers.

A connection is accepted or rejected by setting the *status* parameter in the M_ACCEPT_DC.

M_CLOSE.   M_CLOSE_DC can be issued by either end of an active connection to terminate the connection.

It is important to mention two of M_CLOSE_DC's parameters. The first is *term_data,* which points to termination data if there are any. Termination data are optional and, like connection data passed during connection establishment, apply only to network protocols that pass data during connection termination. The other parameter, *close_type,* indicates the type of close that should be effected:

- CL_SIMPLEX_ABORT. Simplex abortive

- CL_SIMPLEX_ORD. Simplex orderly

- CL_DUPLEX_ABORT. Duplex abortive

- CL_DUPLEX_ORD. Duplex orderly

A simplex termination closes the connection in the send direction only; a duplex termination closes it in both directions. An abortive close terminates the connection without flushing buffers that could possibly contain data waiting to be sent, or without waiting for data in transit to arrive at their destination. An orderly termination ensures that data either in transit or in send buffers are delivered before the connection is terminated.

M_CLOSED. The M_CLOSED_UC is issued to inform an endpoint that a connection has been closed. The closure could have taken place for either of two reasons: the partner transport user at the other end of a connection has issued an M_CLOSE_DC; or, in the case of a connection failure, M_CLOSED_UC is sent to both endpoint transport users. M_CLOSED_UC contains a *term_data* parameter which includes termination data and a *close_indicator* which shows how the connection was closed. The values set in the close_indicator would typically be:

- CL_SIMPLEX_ABORT. Simplex abortive

- CL_SIMPLEX_ORD. Simplex orderly

- CL_DUPLEX_ABORT. Duplex abortive

- CL_DUPLEX_ORD. Duplex orderly

11.4.2.4 Connection-oriented data transfer. Data are transferred between pairs of connected transport users when one issues an M_SEND downcall to send the data and the other an M_RECEIVE upcall to receive it. The management of buffers in the sending and receiving process is not defined in the architecture and is left as an implementation detail.

M_SEND. M_SEND_DC is the downcall that is issued to send data to the other endpoint in a connection. The transport user places the data that are to be sent into a buffer. If the data are to be sent as expedited, the *expedited_data* parameter is set. The *incomplete_record* parameter is set if only part of the data are in the buffer and more will follow. If the buffer is to be flushed before the M_SEND_DC is completed, the *flush* parameter is set. Setting the flush parameter ensures that data are sent to the PMM by the CMM as quickly as possible.

M_RECEIVE. M_RECEIVE_UC is an upcall issued by the CMM to inform a connection endpoint transport user that data have arrived. The *expedited_data* field will be set in the M_RECEIVE_UC if the data in the receive buffer were marked as expedited. An *expedited_marker* is provided by the CMM for expedited data that begin at an offset into the normal data. Incomplete records can be received for connections that support segmented record-oriented data. An *incomplete_record* parameter indicates whether or not the data constitute a complete record.

11.4.2.5 Datagram transfer. Transport users can set up their endpoint as type connectionless (ST_CL). In this case, a connection is not established, but an endpoint is established from which datagrams can be sent and received. Three TLPB verbs are provided in the architecture to implement programming calls dealing with connectionless data transfer.

M_RCVDG_INIT. A transport user that wishes to receive datagrams must first issue an M_CREATE_DC with M_INFO.servtype set to connectionless (ST_CL). This tells the CMM that a connectionless endpoint for sending and receiving datagrams should be created. The M_RCVDG_INIT_DC is then issued to inform the CMM about what kind of datagrams it wishes to receive. There are two parameters on the M_RCVDG_INIT_DC. The *broadcast* parameter is set if the transport user wants to accept broadcast datagrams. The broadcast parameter has no effect on multicast datagrams which will be received if the transport user has issued an M_BIND_DC downcall for a group address. The *multiple* parameter is set if the transport user wants to receive multiple datagrams. If the multiple parameter is not set, then only a single datagram can be received; after that the CMM will not allow the reception of any more datagrams.

M_SEND_DG. The M_SEND_DG_DC call is issued by the transport user wanting to send a datagram to another user or to a group. (The *targ_user_addr* parameter, which contains the target address, can be either a group or individual address.) A *broadcast* parameter can be set to broadcast the datagram. If the transport user protocol supports datagram segmentation, the *dg_segment* indicator can be set to indicate whether the data being sent in the M_SEND_DG_DC are the first, middle, last, or only segment of a segmented datagram. An

M_SEND_DG_UC is returned to the transport user to indicate the status of the datagram sending operation.

M_RCV_DG. The M_RCV_DG_UC is issued by the CMM to inform the transport user that the CMM has received a datagram. The datagram may be addressed directly to the transport user or, if the transport user has indicated in the M_RCVDG_INIT_DC that it desires to receive broadcast datagrams, the datagram may be an incoming broadcast datagram. The *broadcast* field is set in the M_RCV_DG_UC if the datagram is a broadcast datagram. Segmented datagrams are indicated in a *incomplete_segment* field. In this case, the offset of the segment into the full datagram is placed in a field called *segment_offset*.

11.5   The Below-Specific Protocol Boundary

Just as the MPTN architecture defines the TLPB to provide an interface to be used by the CMM and transport users for communication back and forth, an interface called the below-specific protocol boundary is defined by the architecture to implement an interface between the CMM and the PMMs.

The BSPB is defined by a set of verbs which are shown in Table 11.4.

11.5.1   Format of BSPB calls

The BSPB verbs, like the TLPB verbs, are implemented as programming calls of which there are two kinds: *downcalls,* which are calls made by the CMM to a PMM, and *upcalls* which are the reverse: calls made by a PMM to the CMM. Some of the BSPB calls can be used as upcalls or downcalls. To differentiate between the two, downcalls have a _DC appended to the name of the call and upcalls have _UC appended. BSPB calls have names that begin with a P_, which stands for PMM.

BSPB downcalls are nonblocking, meaning that they do not wait, or *block,* for the completion of the call. If a call cannot be satisfied quickly, a return code of RC_PENDING is returned and a later upcall is made to inform the user of the completion. This upcall is represented by a verb with the same name as the downcall but appended with _UC instead of _DC.

11.5.2   BSPB calls

The BSPB calls will now be presented, and each one will be explained. Calls are grouped into five categories:

- Initialization
- Addressing

TABLE 11.4   BSPB Calls

Initialization	
P_INIT_DC	Initialize a PMM.
P_CREATE_DC	Create a PMM transport endpoint.
Addressing	
P_REGISTER_DC	Register a transport user's address in transport provider-specific name service.
P_DEREGISTER_DC	Deregister a transport user's address.
P_LOCATE_DC	Locate an address mapping in transport provider-specific name service or by algorithm.
P_CONFLICT_UC	An address conflict between two or more transport users has occurred.
P_JOIN_GROUP_DC	Add a transport user's address to a multicast group
P_QUIT_GROUP_DC	Delete a transport user's address from a multicast group
Connection setup and termination	
P_CONNECT_DC	Establish a connection.
P_ACCEPT_UC	An incoming nonnative connection request has arrived.
P_ACCEPT_DC	The transport user has accepted or rejected the incoming connection.
P_CLOSE_DC	Close an established connection.
P_CLOSED_UC	A connection was closed.
Connection-oriented data transfer	
P_SEND_DC	Send data on a connection.
P_RECEIVE_UC	Data have arrived on a connection.
Datagram transfer	
P_SEND_DG_DC	Send a datagram.
P_RCV_DG_UC	A datagram has arrived.

- Connection establishment and termination
- Connection-oriented data transfer
- Datagram transfer

11.5.2.1 Initialization. The PMMs that are associated with an access node must be initialized before they can be used. PMMs also take part in the creation of endpoint instances which are created when transport users issue an M_CREATE_DC.

P_INIT. The P_INIT_DC downcall is issued by a CMM to perform one-time initialization of a PMM. When PMM initialization has completed, the PMM issues a P_INIT_UC. A parameter in the upcall

TABLE 11.5   The PROV_INFO Structure

Characteristics of a Transport Provider

conn_loc_addr	The well-known local address for connections
dg_loc_addr	The well-known local address for datagrams
prov_tsdu	Maximum supported unsegmented record size
prov_etsdu	Maximum supported unsegmented expedited data size
prov_send_maxdgm	Maximum supported unsegmented datagram to send
prov_receive_maxdgm	Maximum supported unsegmented received datagram
prov_protocol_maxdgm	Largest datagram that can be received
addr_service	The address mapping service provided
connect_supported	Connection services are supported
stream_supported	Stream data are supported
record_supported	Record-delineated data are supported
expedited_marking	Expedited marking is supported
datagram_supported	Connectionless transport service is supported
multicast_supported	Multicasting is supported
simplex_abortive	Simplex-abortive termination is supported
simplex_orderly	Simplex-orderly termination is supported
duplex_abortive	Duplex-abortive termination is supported
duplex_orderly	Duplex-orderly termination is supported
prov_id	Transport provider's type of protocol
session_outage_notification	Connection outage notification is supported

points to a PROV_INFO structure which contains the characteristics of the transport provider. It also includes which type of address mapping the transport provider uses. The PROV_INFO structure is presented in Table 11.5 and shows the kind of information that is provided concerning the nature of the transport provider.

P_CREATE.   The P_CREATE_DC downcall is issued by the CMM to tell a PMM to create a connection endpoint control block instance as part of the connection setup initiated by an M_CONNECT_DC that was issued by a transport user. When the CMM receives an M_CONNECT_DC, it selects a transport provider. The CMM then issues a P_CREATE_DC to the particular PMM that represents the selected transport provider. The PMM creates an endpoint connection control block and returns a connection identifier for use by the CMM.

Parameters that are set in the P_CREATE_DC specify options that are supported by the transport user. These are *partial_records,* which indicates if partial records are supported by the transport user; *tsdu,* which defines the maximum unsegmented record size that is support-ed by the transport user; *etsdu,* which defines the maximum unseg-mented expedited data size that is supported by the transport user; *in_line,* which indicates that the transport user's expedited data have to be sent in line; and *expedited_marker,* which indicates whether an expedited marker is required.

11.5.2.2 Addressing. The CMM relies on PMMs to perform some of the functions relating to addressing. One of the important functions that the PMM can perform for the CMM is an optional address map-ping service. The subject of address mapping is covered in Chap. 14 and will not be explained here. However, it should be pointed out that two of the three forms of address mapping that are defined in the ar-chitecture are provided by PMMs: algorithmic mapping and the use of a protocol-specific directory.

P_REGISTER. P_REGISTER_DC is issued by the CMM to register an address. This command is used only when the PMM provides the address mapping service either by algorithmic mapping or a protocol-specific directory. The PROV_INFO structure, passed to the CMM on the P_INIT upcall, contains a parameter *addr_service,* which specifies the type of address mapping service to be used. Therefore, the CMM knows whether to issue a P_REGISTER_DC or to signal the address mapper client to have it register the address. The algorithmic address mapping method is performed quickly, and a response to the P_REG-ISTER_DC completes the command. Use of the protocol-specific direc-tory, however, can be more time-consuming, and it is handled by passing back a return code of RC_PENDING, after which the P_REG-ISTER_UC is issued by the PMM to inform the CMM of the outcome of the registration attempt.

P_DEREGISTER. The P_DEREGISTER_DC is issued by a CMM to tell a PMM to deregister an address that has been registered by a previous P_REGISTER_DC.

P_LOCATE. P_LOCATE_DC is issued by the CMM to locate an ad-dress using a protocol-specific directory or algorithmic address map-ping. The P_LOCATE_DC is issued by the CMM to request that the PMM locate a transport provider address mapping that matches a particular transport user address. P_LOCATE_UC is issued by the PMM to inform the CMM of the outcome of the attempt, to return the status of the P_LOCATE_DC, and, if it was successful, to pass back the address mapping that was obtained.

The P_LOCATE_DC has a field *targ_user_addr,* which contains the transport user address that needs to be located. If the *status* field in the P_LOCATE_UC indicates that the locate request was successful, the *targ_prov_addrs* field contains a list of one or more transport provider addresses that satisfy the request.

P_CONFLICT.   The PMM informs a CMM of an address conflict by issuing a P_CONFLICT_UC. Address conflicts arise when the PMM tries to register an address in the native directory and the address is already registered for another CMM. The conflicting address and the transport provider that discovered the conflict are parameters passed in the call.

P_JOIN_GROUP.   The P_JOIN_GROUP_DC is issued by the CMM to tell the PMM to add a transport user to a multicast group. If the *targ_prov_group* field is null, this is a request for the transport provider to create a group address to add the transport user group address to. A P_JOIN_GROUP_UC is issued by the PMM to inform the CMM of the status of the attempt to join the group. Multicasting is provided either by the transport provider network as a feature native to that network, or by the MPTN multicast server. In either case, the PMM must satisfy the multicast join request. MPTN multicasting is discussed in Chap. 14.

P_QUIT_GROUP.   The P_QUIT_GROUP_DC is issued by the CMM to tell the PMM to delete the transport user from a multicast group.

11.5.2.3   Connection establishment and termination.   The BSPB calls that govern the establishment and termination of connections are similar to the similarly named TLPB calls. Most connection establishment and termination details, however, must be handled in the PMM code.

P_CONNECT.   When a transport user wishes to establish a connection with another user, it issues an M_CONNECT_DC to the TLPB. The CMM, before calling the P_CONNECT_DC, resolves the address mapping for the transport provider address of the target user, and the address is placed in the *targ_prov_addr* parameter of the P_CONNECT_DC. The CMM then issues a P_CONNECT_DC to tell the PMM to establish a connection with the destination represented by the transport provider address. Once a native transport provider connection is established, an MPTN connection request is sent as the first data packet. This is a request for a connection in MPTN format. The actual request that is sent as the first data packet on the transport provider connection is a special packet called an MPTN_Connect and will be discussed in Chap. 13. The MPTN_Connect is fully formatted by the CMM and passed to the PMM in a P_CONNECT_DC field called (appropriately enough) *MPTN_Connect*. The compensation headers that will be used for the connection have been determined by the CMM, and they are passed in the *comp_hdrs* field (compensation headers are also discussed in Chap. 13). A *connect_corr* parameter contains a connection correlator assigned by the CMM that consists of a concatenation of the initiating transport user's address and a correlator that is unique for the connection. It is used to detect loops in connections that traverse MPTN gateways, and is part of the compensation for expedited data.

After the MPTN_Connect message has been processed by the destination node, a response is returned. The PMM examines the response and a P_CONNECT_UC is passed from the PMM to the CMM with the result of the connection request in the *status* parameter. The full response to the MPTN_Connect is passed back in the *mptn_conn_rsp* field. The P_CONNECT_UC also contains a *comp_hdrs* field that is used to pass back the compensation headers returned from the other connection endpoint. Compensation headers are sent to the partner endpoint to examine, because some compensations are negotiable.

P_ACCEPT.   The P_ACCEPT_UC is issued by a PMM to inform a CMM that a nonnative connection request has arrived from another MPTN node. The CMM in turn sends an M_ACCEPT_UC to the transport user that is listening for incoming connection requests. If the transport user decides to accept the request, it issues a M_ACCEPT_DC and the CMM issues a P_ACCEPT_DC with a *status* parameter set to indicate that the transport user has accepted the request. The status parameter can also be set to reject the request.

When a CMM sends a P_ACCEPT_DC to accept a connection request, compensation headers are placed by the CMM in the *comp_hdrs* field. These headers represent the compensations the CMM has decided need to be provided for the connection. These are sent back to the active endpoint's CMM in the MPTN_Connect response message. Compensation headers and the MPTN_Connect message are described in Chap. 13.

P_CLOSE.   The P_CLOSE_DC verb is issued by a CMM to terminate a connection. P_CLOSE_UC is issued by the PMM when the close has completed. P_CLOSE_DC pretty much echos the M_CLOSE_DC call that invokes it.

Two of P_CLOSE_DC's parameters are particularly important. The first is *term_data,* which points to termination data if there are any. Termination data are optional and, like connection data passed during connection establishment, apply only to network protocols that pass data during connection termination. The other parameter, *close_type,* indicates the type of close that should be effected:

- CL_SIMPLEX_ABORT. Simplex abortive
- CL_SIMPLEX_ORD. Simplex orderly

- CL_DUPLEX_ABORT. Duplex abortive

- CL_DUPLEX_ORD. Duplex orderly

A simplex termination closes the connection in the send direction only; a duplex termination closes it in both directions. An abortive close terminates the connection without flushing buffers that could possibly contain data waiting to be sent, or without waiting for data in transit to arrive at their destination. An orderly termination ensures that data either in transit or in send buffers are delivered before the connection is terminated.

P_CLOSED.   The P_CLOSED_UC is issued to inform an endpoint that a connection has been closed. The closure could have taken place for either of two reasons: The partner transport user at the other end of a connection has issued an M_CLOSE_DC and its CMM has issued a P_CLOSE_DC; or, in the case of a connection failure, P_CLOSED_UC is sent to both partner CMMs. P_CLOSED_UC contains a *term_data* parameter which includes termination data if applicable and a *close_indicator* which shows how the connection was closed. The values set in the close_indicator would typically be:

- CL_SIMPLEX_ABORT. Simplex abortive

- CL_SIMPLEX_ORD. Simplex orderly

- CL_DUPLEX_ABORT. Duplex abortive

- CL_DUPLEX_ORD. Duplex orderly

11.5.2.4 Connection-oriented data transfer.

Once a connection has been established, data flow freely back and forth between transport users. Two verbs show how calls can receive and send data on a connection.

P_RECEIVE.   The P_RECEIVE_UC is issued by a PMM to inform a CMM that data have arrived on a connection. Four parameters arrive on the P_RECEIVE_UC. The first is a *status*, which reflects the status of the receive. Two more parameters deal with expedited data: *Expedited_data* indicates if data received are marked as expedited data and, *expedited_marker* indicates whether a marker is used to correlate the position of expedited data in the normal data stream. An *incomplete_record* indicator is used to indicate whether the record being passed to the PMM in the data part of this call is a complete record or not.

P_SEND.   The P_SEND_DC is issued by a CMM to send data on a connection. Parameters can be set by the CMM. *Expedited_data* indicates if the data should be marked as being expedited data. An *incom-*

plete_record indicator is used to indicate whether the record being sent is a complete record or not. The *flush* parameter is set on the last of a set of P_SEND_DC calls. The CMM can segment an M_SEND_DC into multiple P_SEND_DC calls and use the flush parameter to control the building of a complete record in the PMM's buffer.

11.5.2.5 Datagram transfer. Two BSPB verbs deal with connectionless data transfer.

P_RCV_DG. The P_RCV_DG_UC is issued by a PMM to inform a CMM that a datagram has been received. A flag is returned in this upcall to indicate if the datagram was a broadcast datagram.

P_SEND_DG. The P_SEND_DG_DC is issued by a CMM to send a datagram.

11.6 Access Nodes in an SPTN

The manner in which TLPB and BSPB calls are used will be illustrated using a connection establishment sequence between two access nodes in an SPTN. Figure 11.3 shows the command flow that illustrates our discussion.

1. Transport users in access node 1 and access node 2 both issue an M_CREATE_DC. The CMMs receive these calls and CMM endpoint control blocks are created. The CMMs pass control back to the transport users, completing the M_CREATE_DC calls and passing the connection identifiers to the transport users. Next, the transport users in access nodes 1 and 2 each issue an M_BIND_DC to bind their transport user address to the just-created CMM control block. The CMM in access node 2 places the address into its internal table and then, since the *regist* parameter was set in the M_BIND_DC, issues a P_REGISTER_DC to register the address. The CMM receives an immediate response and does not have to wait for a P_REGISTER_UC.* Responses are issued for the M_BIND_DC calls.

2. The transport user in access node 2 sets up a passive endpoint by issuing an M_LISTEN_DC. This tells the CMM that the transport user is ready to accept an incoming connection request. The CMM responds to the M_LISTEN_DC. The transport user in access node 1 now starts the ball rolling when it receives a connection request such as a SNA

---

*Algorithmic address mapping is instantaneous and does not require the use of a P_REGISTER_UC. However, the use of a protocol-specific directory does. Further discussion of address mapping techniques appears in Chap. 14.

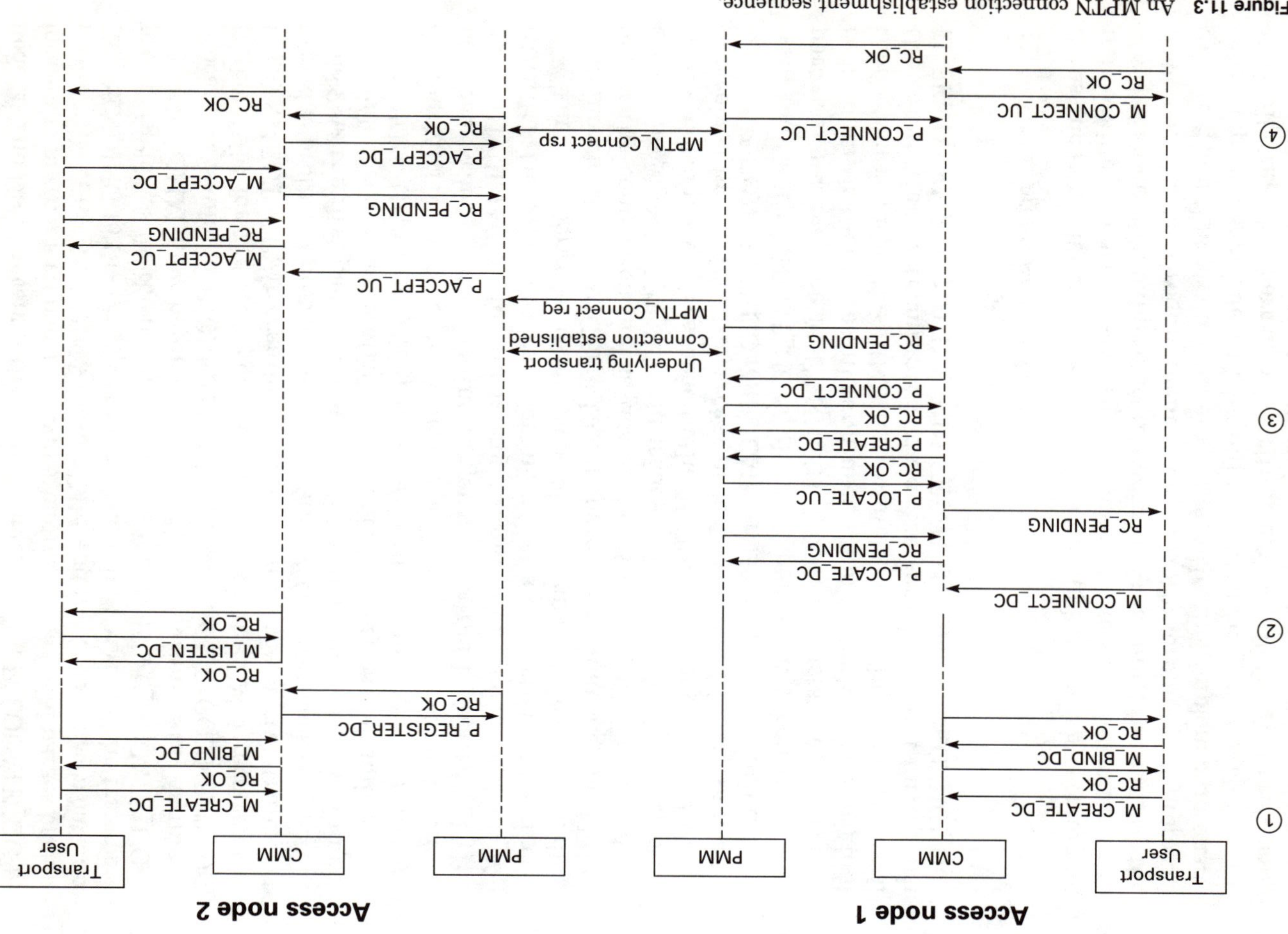

Figure 11.3 An MPTN connection establishment sequence.

BIND or a socket connect call. It issues an M_CONNECT_DC, providing the transport user address for the partner transport user in access node 2. The CMM receives the request and issues a P_LOCATE_DC to locate the partner's transport provider address. The PMM passes back a return code of RC_PENDING to the CMM and the CMM passes back an RC_PENDING to the transport user. When the PMM has the transport provider address for the partner, it passes it back in a P_LOCATE_UC.

3. The CMM now begins the MPTN connection establishment process by issuing a P_CREATE_DC followed by a P_CONNECT_DC to the PMM for the transport provider. When the PMM receives the P_CONNECT_DC, it creates a connection in the native transport provider protocol and then sends an MPTN_Connect packet to access node 2 as the first packet of data on that connection. The PMM in access node 2 receives the MPTN connection request packet and sends a P_ACCEPT_UC to the CMM in access node 2, notifying it of the incoming MPTN connection request. The CMM knows that the transport user whose address is the target user in the P_ACCEPT_UC is currently listening for incoming connections and issues an M_ACCEPT_UC to tell the transport user that a connection has arrived.

4. The transport user in access node 2 examines the connection data contained in the M_ACCEPT_UC, if there is any, and then decides to accept the connection and issues an M_ACCEPT_DC. The CMM receives the M_ACCEPT_DC and issues a P_ACCEPT_DC. The PMM then sends a positive response to the MPTN_Connect command which is received by the PMM in access node 1. The PMM in access node 1 sends a P_CONNECT_UC to the CMM in access node 1, which in turn issues an M_CONNECT_UC to the transport user. When the transport user receives the M_CONNECT_UC, it extracts the connection reply data, if there are any, and uses them to reply to the original connection request, the BIND for example. From this point on, until the connection is terminated, data are sent back and forth with M_SEND_DC, P_SEND_DC, P_RECEIVE_UC, and M_RECEIVE_UC.

11.7   Creating an Access Node

Access node products can be designed and implemented by vendors of networking or network-aware software. The design, flexibility, and scope of any individual product are decisions that must be made by the designer. The only requirement is that MPTN formats and protocols are used, and that products interoperate with other implementations.

Transport user code can be implemented in a number of ways. Basically, the transport user is written as a part of the API processing layer. API calls from the application programs can be passed to the MPTN transport user if a nonnative transport network is to be used.

TLPB calls can be implemented as function calls that pass information to the CMM.

A full-blown CMM, or a paired-down version, can be written. The CMM/PMM model that we have been describing is not a requirement for protocol compatibility. A full CMM/PMM implementation may be called for when a number of transport users and/or providers are to be supported. However, if just a single transport provider protocol is all that is being implemented, TLPB calls can be replaced by calling the API for the transport provider directly. Address mapping can be implemented by any means devised by the product implementor, unless conformity to existing standards or implementations (such as the address mapper) is desired.

A PMM can be implemented as a program or task that is separate from the CMM process and the transport provider network can be accessed using its native API. For SNA networks, the CPI-C API can be used to create the LU 6.2 sessions necessary to carry the MPTN formats to other access or gateway nodes. For a TCP/IP transport provider network, the socket interface is all that is required. NetBEUI commands can be used to access a NetBIOS network, and the IPX calls available as a runtime library from Novell can be implemented in an IPX network. In this way, the transport provider network does not have to be modified; the access node implementor can simply make a choice of a transport network protocol stack, then implement the PMM using API calls to that stack.

MPTN access nodes can be placed directly into products as an option, or even included as a transparent, "under-the-covers" feature. For example, if a product offers a TCP/IP stack as a part of the product, an option can be included that offers an additional function for running sockets programs, normally associated with the TCP/IP stack, over other protocol stacks, such as IPX or NetBIOS. Since IBM is bundling its AnyNet products with its system software, it should be an attractive feature for third-party vendors to be able to interoperate with IBM transport gateways and access nodes. For a full-blown implementation, the provider of the TCP/IP stack must design the MPTN access node feature into the transport user code, then design a syntax mapper to map the sockets calls to TLPB calls, create a CMM, then create PMMs for each transport provider. Since the PMMs use API calls, transport provider networks can belong to other vendors: There is no need to modify the transport provider stacks at all. The PMM is just a user application program as far as the transport provider network is concerned, and it can be implemented as either a *.dll* or *.exe.*

MPTN can be implemented as a transparent feature. When a sockets application program is loaded and the initial *connect()* call is made, the underlying routines in the socket layer can determine what actual transport provider networks are available. If native TCP/IP is not available to the destination but another transport network is, an MPTN connection can be made using an alternate transport network instead. This would be transparent to users. The partner user would have to be running in a node that has access node software installed (such as an AnyNet feature), or running in a native network connected via an MPTN gateway. A discovery process can be used to determine if MPTN is available in a partner's node, or if the partner is available through an MPTN gateway. Discovery can start by attempting to establish a connection to the MPTN well-known port, to be discussed in Chap. 13.

A CMM, or equivalent function, can be designed to operate over numerous transport provider networks using numerous transport users, or can simply provide a one-for-one service that allows a single transport user protocol to operate over another single transport provider protocol. As long as the formats and protocols of MPTN are employed correctly, an MPTN product will interoperate with products from other manufacturers, including the AnyNet products from IBM, and will interoperate with MPTN transport gateways that may be located in an enterprise network. By incorporating MPTN, a product is assured that it will work in enterprise networks that rely on MPTN to provide network interconnection.

11.8 Conclusion

The access node provides MPTN services that enable transport users to access nonnative transport providers. The MPTN architecture defines the format and protocols that must be employed. The architectural model—represented by the CMM, the PMM, TLPB, and BSPB—is presented in the architecture as a design foundation that can be used to implement MPTN; it is not a required part of the architecture, however, and thus is not required in an implementation of MTPN. System architects and implementors can design access nodes that will interwork with products from IBM and other vendors by using the format specifications that are available from the X/Open Company in England. X/Open information and document names and product numbers are listed in App. C.

The MPTN
Transport Gateway

12.1   Introduction

Because of its ability to interconnect transport networks, the MPTN transport gateway plays a major role in the MPTN architecture. The transport gateway will be examined in terms of its components, focusing on how they work together. The transport gateway has additional functionality beyond the capability of the access node in that it must interface directly with a native transport network. This interfacing is accomplished using the gateway-specific protocol boundary (GSPB). The GSPB will be presented, and the verb formats used by gateways to deal directly with native networks will be introduced. Following this description, gateway configurations will describe how data flow internally through the network. The chapter ends with a short discussion about creating a full-function MPTN gateway.

12.2   The MPTN Transport Gateway

The MPTN transport gateway has the same capabilities as an access node, described in Chap. 11, but includes the additional ability to interconnect networks at the transport layer. When networks are interconnected with MPTN gateways, matching application programs can access this MPTN internetwork to communicate with each other. MPTN gateways create a seamless transport internetwork by interconnecting TCP/IP, SNA, IPX, NetBIOS, or OSI networks so that application programs can communicate regardless of the nature of the underlying transport protocol. The only requirement is that nonnative programs access the MPTN network using an MPTN access node.

12.3   MPTN Transport Gateway Components

Figure 12.1 shows the MPTN transport gateway in terms of its components. Like the access node, it has a single common MPTN manager and two or more protocol-specific MPTN managers. These managers provide more functionality than the corresponding managers in an access node. Transport users in a gateway communicate with the CMM using the same TLPB interface defined for an access node. In fact, at this level, the gateway is just the same as an access node.

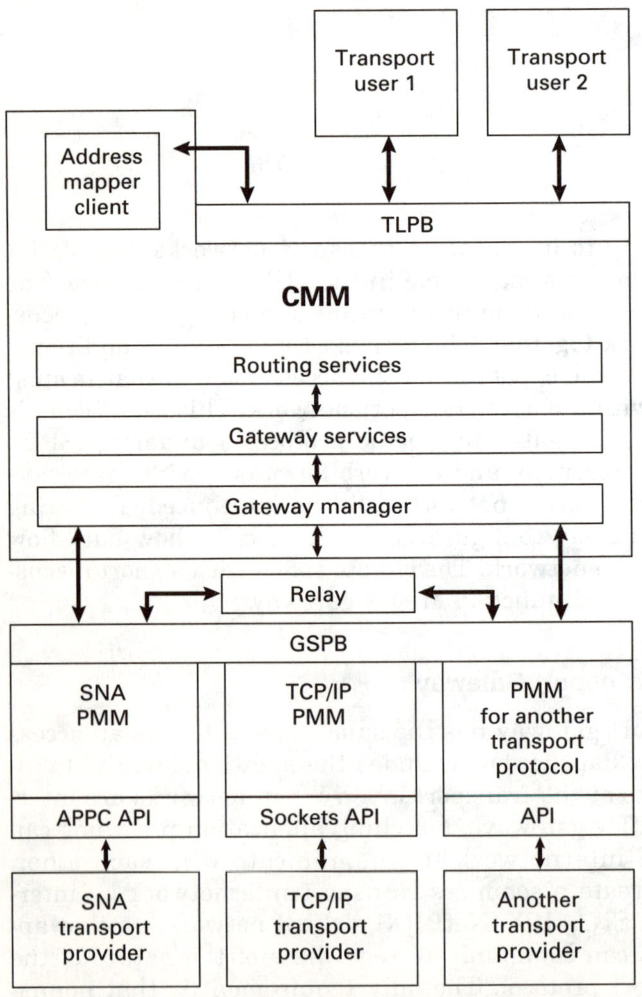

Figure 12.1   The anatomy of an MPTN transport gateway.

The gateway CMM has a component called the *gateway manager*, which has similar functionality to an access node CMM. This component manages the gateway node just as an access node CMM manages the access node. Any functionality that is specific to a gateway, however, is provided by two additional components: *gateway services* and *routing services*. Anything that the gateway manager receives that is specific to a gateway is passed by the gateway manager to gateway services. Gateway services, in turn, passes anything pertaining to routing in an MPTN network to routing services.

The gateway CMM, like the access node CMM, contains an address mapper client component to provide address mapping services when an address mapper server is used. An address mapper server can be loaded in the MPTN gateway node or can reside in any of its connected SPTNs.

The gateway has a protocol-specific MPTN manager for each SPTN that is connected to the gateway. Since the gateway interconnects at least two networks, the minimum number of PMMs is two. The gateway PMMs, similar to the PMMs in an access node, handle the protocol-specific duties related to the transport provider to which the PMM is associated. PMMs, therefore, access the transport provider network directly. A PMM appears to the transport provider network as just another component running in that network and uses a standard API to access network services. A TCP/IP PMM uses the AF_INET sockets interface; an IPX PMM uses an IPX API; and so on. The gateway CMM uses a superset of the below-specific protocol boundary (BSPB) called the gateway-specific protocol boundary (GSPB) to communicate with its PMMs.

The gateway also contains another important component called the *gateway relay*. This component is created when a connection is established between users across the gateway. Once the connection is established, a relay component instance is created by gateway services to be used by the session as a pipe for passing data from one PMM to the other; it remains in place until the connection is terminated.

Each component in the MPTN gateway will now be discussed.

12.3.1   The common MPTN manager

The gateway CMM contains four components:

- The gateway manager
- Gateway services
- Routing services
- The gateway relay component

12.3.1.1 The gateway manager. The gateway manager is the main component in a gateway CMM. Basically, the gateway manager is similar to an access node CMM except that it detects requests and responses that deal specifically with details relating to the functioning of the gateway. These are handed off to the gateway services component to be dealt with. The gateway manager interacts with PMMs via the GSPB.

12.3.1.2 Gateway services. Gateway services is a component of the gateway CMM that assists in the establishment of MPTN connections and the forwarding of datagrams that travel across the gateway.

When a user located in an access node wishes to establish a connection with another user that resides in an SPTN with a native protocol, it issues an M_CONNECT_DC. The CMM receives this request and resolves the destination address using address mapping. The connection needs to pass through a gateway to reach the destination, so address mapping returns the transport provider address for a gateway. The CMM creates an MPTN connection request message, called an MPTN_Connect, and passes this message along with the gateway's transport provider address to the PMM. The PMM establishes an underlying transport connection using the transport provider address, then sends the MPTN_Connect request to the gateway. The gateway PMM passes the request up to the gateway manager, which determines that the connection request is not for a local transport user and then passes the request to gateway services. Gateway services requests a resolution of the destination transport user address from routing services. Routing services passes back a transport provider address for the destination node (or another gateway, if the destination is not on an attached SPTN). Gateway services compares the transport user address of the destination with the transport provider address received from routing services. When the transport user and provider addresses are the same, gateway services knows that the network connection will be native. Otherwise, the connection will be an MPTN connection. The CMM uses the MPTN qualifier in the MPTN-qualified transport provider address to determine which SPTN to use. The qualifier is a field that identifies the protocol type for which the address is formated and is discussed further in Chap. 13.

MPTN protocols are not used between a gateway and a native destination node. To handle the situation of establishing a native connection, the GSPB superset commands come into play and a GSPB native connect request is issued by gateway services. This request, the G_NATIVE_CONNECT_DC, is described in Sec. 12.4. The PMM receives the G_NATIVE_CONNECT_DC and establishes a native connection with the destination user.

Once the connection is created, gateway services creates an instance of a gateway relay to handle traffic that will be transported on the connection. This relay is simply a pipe through which data coming and going on the connection will pass. The gateway services component is not invoked again for this connection until the connection is terminated.

Connections can be established by gateway services in three ways.

- *Incoming MPTN connection to outgoing native connection.* An incoming connection request in the form of an MPTN_Connect is received by a gateway PMM from an access or gateway node in an SPTN. The destination transport user is running natively in an SPTN that is connected to the gateway. Gateway services requests that the appropriate PMM establish a native connection with the destination user.

- *Incoming native connection to outgoing MPTN connection.* A native connection request is received by a gateway PMM from a native user in an SPTN. The destination user is running in an access node in another SPTN that is either connected to the gateway or an SPTN that is reachable through the gateway. Gateway services requests that the outgoing PMM establish an MPTN connection with the destination user.

- *Incoming MPTN connection to outgoing MPTN connection.* A connection request in the form of an MPTN_Connect is received by a gateway PMM from an access or gateway node in an SPTN. The destination user is running in an access node in another SPTN that is either connected to the gateway or reachable from an SPTN that is connected to the gateway, or is a native user connected to a gateway that is reachable from the connected SPTN. Gateway services requests that the outgoing PMM establish an MPTN connection with the destination.

A fourth combination, "native connection to native connection," naturally will never be found in an MPTN gateway.

Gateway services also handles datagrams. When either MPTN or native datagrams are received by a gateway's PMM, they are handed to gateway services. Gateway services resolves the destination address by calling routing services, then forwards the datagram to the PMM representing the SPTN on which the datagram must be sent. If the user on that SPTN is a native user (the transport user address matches the transport provider address), a P_SEND_DG_DC is issued with a null MPTN header (MPTN header formats are covered in Chap. 13).

12.3.1.3 Routing services. The routing services component of a gateway CMM maintains the gateway's MPTN routing table (or a routing cache). When connection requests and datagrams are received by gateway services, a request is made to routing services to determine the transport provider address to which these datagrams and connection requests must be sent in order to reach their final destination. The MPTN gateway routing table is where routing services stores fully qualified MPTN network address pairs that have already been determined. Routing services uses address mapping services to determine the transport provider address(es) associated with each transport user address. Addresses are always stored in MPTN-qualified address format (MPTN-qualified addresses are explained in Chap. 13). If an address mapper is to be used, routing services interfaces directly with the address mapper client to resolve address mappings.

When gateway services needs an address resolved, it passes the transport user address to routing services. Routing services maps the transport user address to a transport provider address. When the transport provider address is determined, the gateway knows which SPTN to use by examining the MPTN qualifier of the transport provider address. If the MPTN qualifier indicates NetBIOS, the attached NetBIOS SPTN is used. If the MPTN qualifier is TCP/IP, the TCP/IP SPTN is used.

In order for transport users located in a native SPTN to be reachable from nodes elsewhere in the MPTN network, routing information about these native nodes must be advertised throughout the MPTN network. Likewise, for transport users in the MPTN network to be reachable by nodes in a native SPTN, MPTN routing information must be advertised inside the native network. MPTN gateways function as routers in each connected SPTN network. In other words, if one of the SPTNs is a TCP/IP network, then the TCP/IP PMM in the gateway functions as a router node in the TCP/IP network, using RIP or possibly OSPF to participate as an intradomain router. If another PMM is connected to an APPN SNA network, that PMM functions as a *network node* (NN)—the APPN node that performs routing—in the SNA network. In IPX networks, the gateway functions as an IPX router, and in an OSI SPTN, the gateway participates in level 2 IS-IS routing.

By participating in native routing, the MPTN network can be integrated into any internetwork. Native routing protocols maintain the routing tables in the router nodes of an autonomous system. These tables contain the addresses of networks that are reachable from that routing node and the cost information, or metric, associated with the route. Routing updates are sent incrementally to keep all the tables up to date.

To participate in routing protocols, each PMM must have a hook into the router code for its network. For example, if RIP is implemented for TCP/IP on a Unix computer, then the routed program must be modified so that when the IP routing table updates arrive at the node, they are forwarded to the PMM. The PMM passes this native routing information to the gateway manager in a GSPB G_NATIVE_ROUTEINFO_UC. The gateway manager passes the information to gateway services, and gateway services passes it to the routing services component.

Routing services gathers native routing information from all connected SPTNs. Each PMM in each SPTN acts as a router on that network, maintains a routing table for that network, and receives routing updates from neighboring routers. All this information is used by routing services to build the MPTN gateway routing table.

Routing information for a particular protocol is also passed by routing services to native SPTNs that support that protocol. When routing services receives routing updates, the G_ROUTEINFO_DC is issued to tell the PMM to use its hook into the native router code to distribute the native routing information on that network. Naturally, this native routing information is passed only to the PMM that supports the protocol of the routing information. TCP/IP routing information is passed to TCP/IP PMMs, not to SNA PMMs or NetBIOS PMMs.

An example is shown in Fig. 12.2. A user called "Bill" resides in a TCP/IP SPTN called "net1.com." Bill wants to establish a connection with another user, called "Pam," on another TCP/IP SPTN called "net3.com." Both Bill and Pam are running natively in their own networks, and both networks have the same transport protocol. However, both net1.com and net3.com are connected across another SPTN using MPTN transport gateways. This intervening network is a SNA network. It must be remembered that net1.com and net3.com have

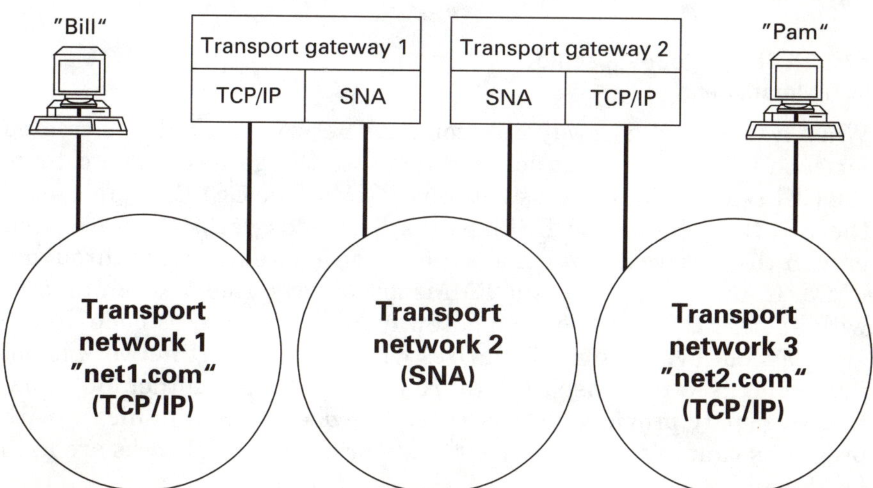

Figure 12.2 MPTN gateways perform the routing functions necessary when similar transport networks are interconnected by a third transport network.

the same TCP/IP transport protocol. If they had been attached directly to each other, there would have been a common node between them that functioned as a router to route traffic between them. An entry for net3.com would have been in this router's routing table and when Bill tried to establish the connection to Pam, his own routing table would have pointed to the router. Since the two networks are interconnected by two MPTN gateways and an intervening network instead of a router, the MPTN gateways have to participate in native routing protocols and perform actual routing functions.

The way this works is as follows: When Bill establishes the connection to Pam, the entry for Pam in Bill's routing table is the address of the TCP/IP PMM for gateway 1. How did Pam's address get into Bill's routing table? Gateway 2 knows about Pam and the other nodes on net3.com to which gateway 2's TCP/IP PMM has access. This routing information is sent to the CMM in gateway 2 in a G_NATIVE_ROUTE_INFO_UC and is stored in an MPTN address mapper. Since net3.com is a TCP/IP network, gateway 1 will take the information about net3.com from the address mapper and cause it to be advertised in net1.com by issuing a G_NATIVE_ROUTEINFO_DC.

The gateway routing component was designed to eventually implement a gateway-to-gateway protocol which will cause routing table updates to be exchanged between gateways. Metrics indicate the cost of various routes. IBM will probably choose the InterDomain Routing Protocol (IDRP), introduced in Sec. 4.4.4.2, for this purpose. Some of the early MPTN documents show the gateway-to-gateway routing as an already-established feature of the architecture, but IBM has chosen to define it at a later date.

12.3.2 The protocol-specific MPTN manager

When a transport gateway interconnects networks, a PMM is created for each SPTN that is attached directly to the gateway. The calls of the GSPB are used to access gateway PMMs. The GSPB, a superset of the BSPB, includes the BSPB verbs, but adds verbs that are used only in the gateway, to provide support for native networks through a PMM. In the access node, the PMMs are always used to communicate with another PMM, either in a gateway in another access node. In the gateway, however, a situation arises where a transport network is not just being used to transport data from one PMM to another, but a native transport provider network itself is used to communicate with programs running natively in that network. The GSPB verbs are used for this native access.

From the viewpoint of a gateway, or a gateway PMM, there are two ways to view an SPTN.

- *Native access.*   A connection is established with, or a datagram sent directly to, a native user, and native routing protocols are hooked into.

- *MPTN access.*   An MPTN connection is established with, or an MPTN datagram sent directly to, another PMM residing in either a gateway or an access node.

A gateway PMM must support both of these situations.

An example of this is a gateway that has two SPTNs: a SNA SPTN and a TCP/IP SPTN. The SNA PMM communicates with the SNA network, and in our example it will always be nonnative because sockets applications run on it. The TCP/IP PMM will operate as a native PMM for the sockets applications. If NetBIOS applications are able to pass through the gateway over the SNA and TCP/IP networks, then the TCP/IP PMM will need to provide both MPTN and native access. It will need to provide native services for sockets programs as well as establish MPTN connections to another gateway or access node for NetBIOS programs.

12.3.3   The gateway relay component

A gateway relay component is created when a connection is established through the gateway. The CMM creates an instance of a relay component to be used exclusively by the connection as long as it is alive. The relay interconnects the two PMMs involved in the connection, and after it is established, the gateway CMM has nothing more to do with the connection until termination time: All data are passed through the relay. An instance of the relay component exists for every established connection in a gateway.

The gateway relay, in conjunction with the PMMs, uses a process called *header substitution* to perform its duties. When data are received, the PMM removes the transport provider protocol headers and the MPTN headers from the user data, then gives the user data, along with some parameters, to the relay. The relay performs the necessary compensations and then sends the user data, and parameters, to the other PMM. The second PMM prepends new headers for the second transport provider protocol to the front of the transport user data packet. Figure 12.3 shows an example of data coming from an SNA network and going to a TCP/IP network. The TH and RH headers will be removed from the data, and IP and TCP headers will be prepended. The transport user's data are never touched.

Segmentation of packets of data is another important duty of the relay because the transport network onto which the data packets are being placed may have a maximum transmission unit (MTU) that is smaller than the proceeding transport network; in that case, packets that are too large must be separated into two or more segments.

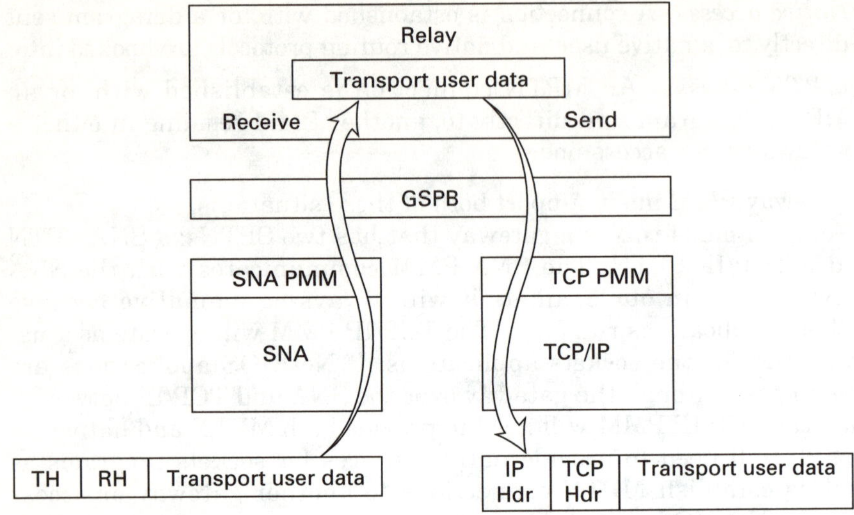

Figure 12.3   Data traveling from a SNA network to a TCP/IP network.

12.4   The Gateway-Specific Protocol Boundary

The gateway's CMM, including the gateway relay component, communicates with PMMs using the GSPB. The GSPB contains all the calls of the BSPB, which were described in Chap. 11, plus additional calls that are specific to the gateway function. Access node PMMs always establish connections with and send datagrams to either a gateway PMM or the PMM in another access node. Gateway PMMs, however, must also establish connections with and send datagrams to native destinations in the SPTN and interact with native routing code. To provide this additional functionality, special GSPB verbs are defined.

12.4.1   Format of GSPB calls

The GSPB verbs that represent the additional calls used in a gateway to access native network services are prefixed with G_. Upcalls to the CMM or gateway relay component have a _UC suffix, and downcalls from the CMM or relay are suffixed with _DC. All of the BSPB calls that were described in Chap. 11 are included in the GSPB and are differentiated from the additional calls added in the GSPB by their prefix, P_.

12.4.2   GSPB calls

Like the BSPB verbs, the GSPB verbs represent function call prototypes that would be coded in the programming language used to build the gateway. The term "verb" is used to describe an architectural description of the programming call, but the actual calls are implemented as runtime library routines called within a computer program to provide the interface between the gateway CMM component and the gateway PMMs, and between the gateway relay component and the PMMs.

The GSPB calls occupy two categories:

- Addressing

- Connection establishment and termination

12.4.2.1 Addressing. The addressing GSPB calls are important for the gateway, which, in addition to the normal MPTN registering and locating functions, must also interoperate with native routing protocols.

G_NATIVE_LOCATE. When a native search for an address is initiated in a transport provider network, the gateway is queried because the address may be located in a network that can be reached by the gateway. For example, an APPN locate is intercepted and passed to the PMM, which issues a G_ NATIVE_LOCATE_UC to the gateway manager in the CMM. The manager passes the request to routing services, which resolves it and sends the resolution back in a G_NATIVE_ LOCATE_DC. The G_NATIVE_LOCATE verb is used only in search-based networks such as NetBIOS and SNA.

G_NATIVE_SEARCH. A G_NATIVE_SEARCH_DC is issued by the gateway's CMM to ask a PMM to initiate a native search of the SPTN for an address. A native search request is initiated by the PMM in the native network. The hook into the transport provider's routing code captures the result of the search and transfers it to the PMM. The response is sent back to the CMM in the gateway in a G_ NATIVE_SEARCH_UC. The G_NATIVE_SEARCH verb is used only in search-based networks such as NetBIOS and SNA.

G_NATIVE_ROUTEINFO. G_NATIVE_ROUTEINFO is the verb used by the gateway to interface with native routing protocols. The PMM issues a G_NATIVE_ROUTEINFO_UC to make native routing updates available to MPTN routing services in the gateway.

G_NATIVE_ROUTEINFO_DC is used by the CMM to give routing information to a PMM to distribute in the native network using the native routing protocols.

12.4.2.2 Connection establishment and termination. Two means of transporting data are supported by the transport gateway: datagrams and connections. Datagrams are passed to routing services to determine where they need to be sent. The initial connection request is passed to routing services for the same reason, but once the connection is established, the gateway relay handles the transfer of the data that is passed back and forth between the two PMMs in the gateway. The CMM does not get involved again until it is time to terminate the connection.

Two GSPB calls deal with the establishing of native connections.

G_NATIVE_CONNECT.   The G_NATIVE_CONNECT_DC is issued by the gateway CMM to request that a PMM initiate a native connection. A G_NATIVE_CONNECT_UC is issued by the PMM to inform the CMM that the connection request has been completed.

G_NATIVE_ACCEPT.   The G_NATIVE_ACCEPT_UC is issued by a gateway PMM to inform the gateway's CMM that an incoming connection request has arrived from a native user. The CMM issues a G_NATIVE_ACCEPT_DC to accept the incoming native connection request.

12.5   Interconnecting SPTNs with Transport Gateways

Now that the components of the MPTN transport gateway have been presented and the GSPB introduced, the actual function and configuration of gateway topologies can be presented.

Figure 12.4 shows the flow of a connection request in a gateway. In our example, transport provider 1 is a TCP/IP network and transport provider 2 is a SNA network. The gateway in our example is one that concatenates a *native* SNA network with a TCP/IP network.

1. An APPN locate request arrives at the gateway on the SNA network. The address that is being looked for is not within the SNA network's directory. The hook into APPN directory services captures the locate request and passes it to transport provider 2's PMM to be resolved. This PMM issues a G_NATIVE_LOCATE_UC to the CMM. The gateway manager sees that the requested destination is not a local transport user, so it passes this request to gateway services, which in turn hands it to routing services. Routing services determines that the requested destination can be reached through the TCP/IP network. The next hop information is returned to gateway services, which then passes it to the gateway manager. The gateway manager issues a G_NATIVE_LOCATE_DC to the SNA PMM. The SNA PMM receives the downcall, and a response to the original APPN locate is returned via the hook code into APPN's directory services. This APPN locate response will show that the requested destination can be reached through the MPTN gateway.

2. Now that it has been determined that the destination can be reached through the MPTN gateway, the native node on transport

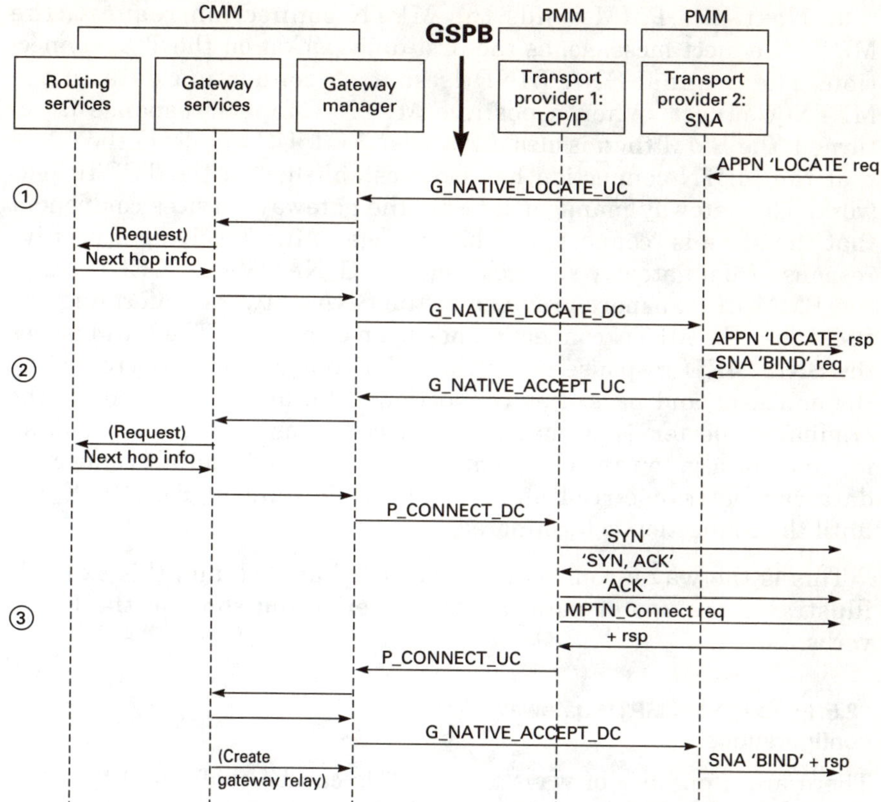

Figure 12.4   A native-to-nonnative connection request through an MPTN gateway.

provider 2, the SNA network, issues a BIND to bind an LU 6.2 session. This BIND is sent to the gateway and is received by the PMM in the SNA network, transport provider 2. The PMM creates a G_NATIVE_ACCEPT_UC and sends that to the CMM. This upcall tells the CMM that a native connection request, in our case an SNA BIND, has arrived at the SNA network's PMM. The CMM manager component checks to see if this connection request is for a local transport user. When it is determined that it is not, the manager passes the G_NATIVE_ACCEPT_UC data to gateway services. Gateway services asks routing services to return an address and again, routing services provides the destination transport provider address. Now that a transport provider address for the eventual connection endpoint has been determined, the gateway manager issues a P_CONNECT_DC, this time for transport provider 1's PMM, and a TCP connection with the destination node's PMM is established using the three-way handshake (SYN, SYN-ACK, ACK) described in Chap. 4.

3. Next, the PMM sends the MPTN connection request, the MPTN_Connect message, as the first data packet on the TCP connection. The original SNA BIND is sent as connection data in the MPTN_Connect. When a positive MPTN_Connect response is returned, the PMM then issues a P_CONNECT_UC to inform the CMM that the MPTN connection has been established in the TCP/IP network. The gateway manager informs the gateway services component that the state is "connected." The manager, after receiving a positive response from gateway services, sends a G_NATIVE_ACCEPT_DC to the PMM in transport provider 2, the SNA network, informing the PMM that the MPTN connection has been completed. The PMM issues the SNA BIND response using the BIND image that was created by the end user and passed as connection data, and this is sent to the original requester. Now that the connection has been established, an instance of a gateway relay component is created and all connection data can be transferred using P_SEND_DC and P_RECEIVE_UC until the connection is terminated.

This is the way a connection request is handled, and this example illustrates the use of gateway components and some of the GSPB verbs.

12.5.1   Extended MPTN gateway configurations

There are a number of ways that SPTNs can be configured by interconnecting them with gateways, and various topologies can be created. The point of using MPTN is to solve particular networking problems. For that reason, the following example configurations present solutions to different problems. It is very important to realize, however, that the architecture establishes no limits on how SPTNs can be interconnected using MPTN gateways.

12.5.1.1   Gateways connect two SPTNs through a backbone.   As has been stated, MPTN can be used to connect similar LANs across a backbone network. Figure 12.5 illustrates two IPX networks connected over a SNA backbone network. Perhaps a large corporation with many regional offices already has a SNA backbone network in place and wishes to interconnect LANs located in remote offices using the existing SNA network as an interconnection medium, and then upgrade the SNA network by installing APPN *High Performance Routing* (HPR). This MPTN solution is accomplished using two MPTN transport gateways.

IPX traffic in office 1 has been confined to the local area network, which consists of a number of workstations. Now that the MPTN gateways have been installed, the NetWare workstations in office 1

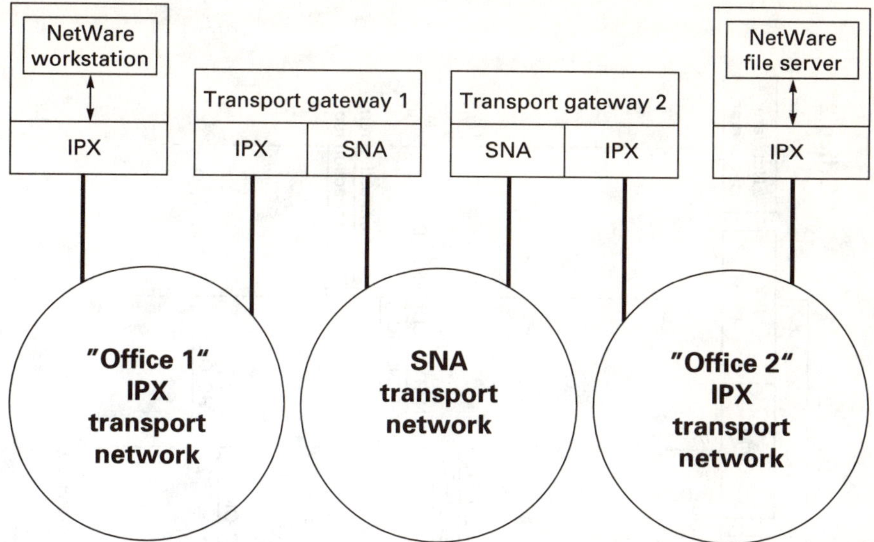

Figure 12.5 A NetWare workstation on an IPX LAN communicates with a NetWare file server on another IPX LAN. These are interconnected by a SNA network.

can attach to an NetWare file server located in office 2. How this is accomplished is illustrated in the flow diagram of Fig. 12.6.

1. An SPX connection request is sent to gateway 1's IPX PMM. The PMM issues a G_NATIVE_ACCEPT_UC and the CMM issues a P_CONNECT_DC to the SNA PMM after resolving the address using routing services. The SNA PMM creates a SNA LU 6.2 session with the other gateway, then sends an MPTN_Connect request message on that session. When the SNA PMM in gateway 2 receives the MPTN_Connect request, it issues a P_ACCEPT_UC. The CMM in gateway 2 issues a G_NATIVE_CONNECT_DC and the IPX PMM establishes an SPX connection with the NetWare file server in office 2's IPX network.

2. Gateway 2's IPX PMM receives a response to the IPX connection request and issues a G_NATIVE_CONNECT_UC. The CMM issues a P_ACCEPT_DC to the SNA PMM, which sends an MPTN_Connect positive response on the LU 6.2 session to gateway 1. Gateway 1's SNA PMM receives the MPTN_Connect response and issues a P_CONNECT_UC. The CMM issues a G_NATIVE_ACCEPT_DC to the IPX PMM, saying that the original session that was requested from the workstation in the office 1 network has been accepted. The PMM sends a positive response to the IPX workstation, and a connection has been established from the workstation in the office 1 network with the NetWare file server in office 2.

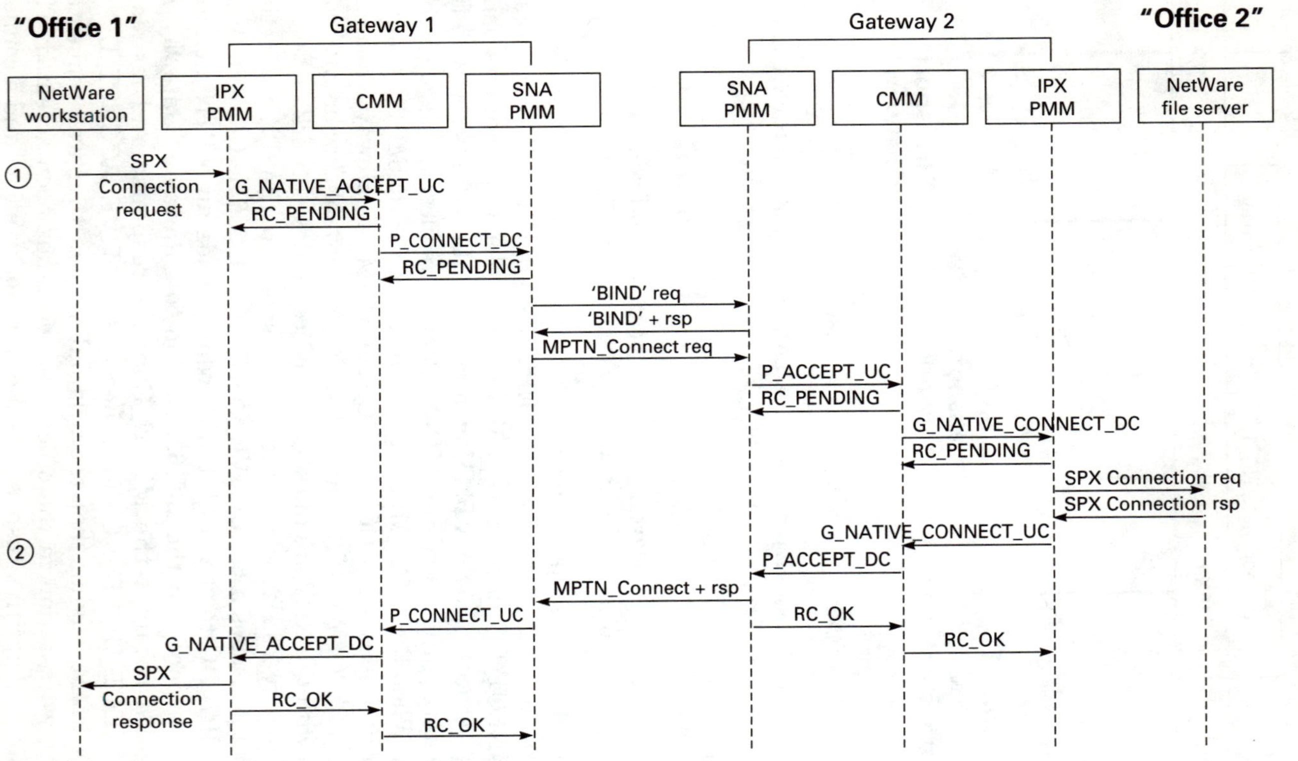

Figure 12.6   A NetWare workstation connects with a file server across an interconnecting SNA transport network.

From this point on, data flow effortlessly between the workstation on the LAN in office 1 and the server on the LAN in office 2 using the services of relay components in both gateways. It is interesting to point out that both endpoints are native; the only nonnative traffic flows over the SNA network that interconnects the two gateways. If the middle network is used only as a backbone, then no access nodes need to be installed.

12.5.1.2 Three SPTNs using different protocols connected by two gateways.

The network shown in Fig. 12.7 has three SPTNs, each with a different network protocol, interconnected by two gateways. In this example, SPTN 1 is a TCP/IP network, SPTN 2 is a SNA network, and SPTN 3 is IPX. This configuration is not the same as the preceding example, where the middle network provides a backbone for the other two networks. This example presents three distinct networks interconnected with MPTN gateways.

This type of MPTN network, in contrast to the previous example, relies heavily on access nodes and demonstrates some of the possibilities that can be implemented with the MPTN architecture. In SPTN 1, there are two access nodes: One provides support for IPX transport users, another provides support for CPI-C users. In SPTN 2 there is just one access node, which provides access for sockets programs. SPTN 3 also has only one access node and it provides support for CPI-C programs. Access node 1 in SPTN 1 provides NetWare workstation access in the TCP/IP network, and a workstation in SPTN 1 can be attached to a NetWare file server running natively in SPTN 3. Access node 2 in SPTN 1 provides access for CPI-C programs, which can converse with CPI-C programs running natively in SPTN 2 or running in the CPI-C access node 4 in SPTN 3. Sockets programs running in the access node located in SPTN 2 can converse with sockets programs running natively in SPTN 1.

To provide an example of the gateway workings for our drawing, we will describe the flows that take place when access node 2 in SPTN 1 connects with access node 4 in SPTN 3. These flows are shown in a sequence of figures (Figs. 12.8 through 12.12) which illustrate the flow that takes place when a single CPI-C command, a cmallc(), is issued by access node 2.

Figure 12.8 shows the flow of data and commands that move between access node 2 and gateway 1.

1. A user in access node 2 in SPTN 1 loads a CPI-C program and issues a cmallc() to allocate a conversation with a user in access node 4 in SPTN 3. If no sessions already exist, the SNA software in access node 2 must start one. A BIND is issued for a session, which causes the SNA transport user to issue an M_CONNECT_DC to the CMM.

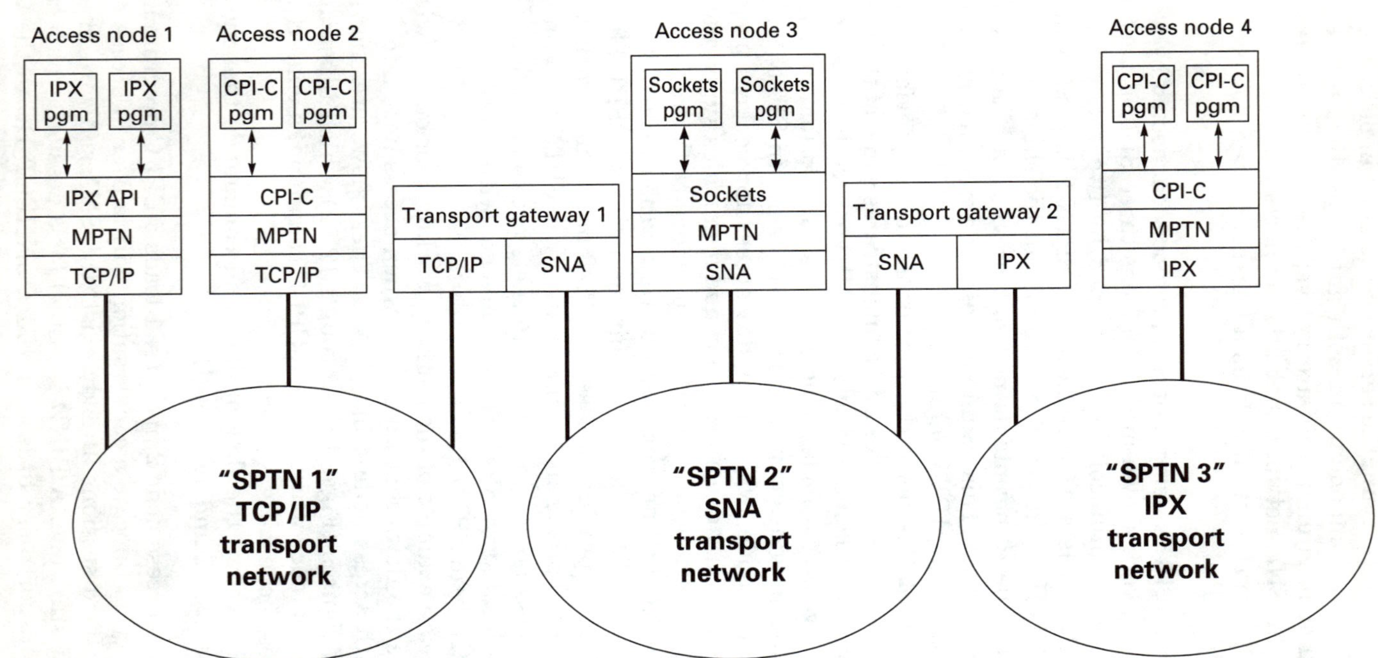

Figure 12.7 Three different transport networks interconnected by means of MPTN transport gateways.

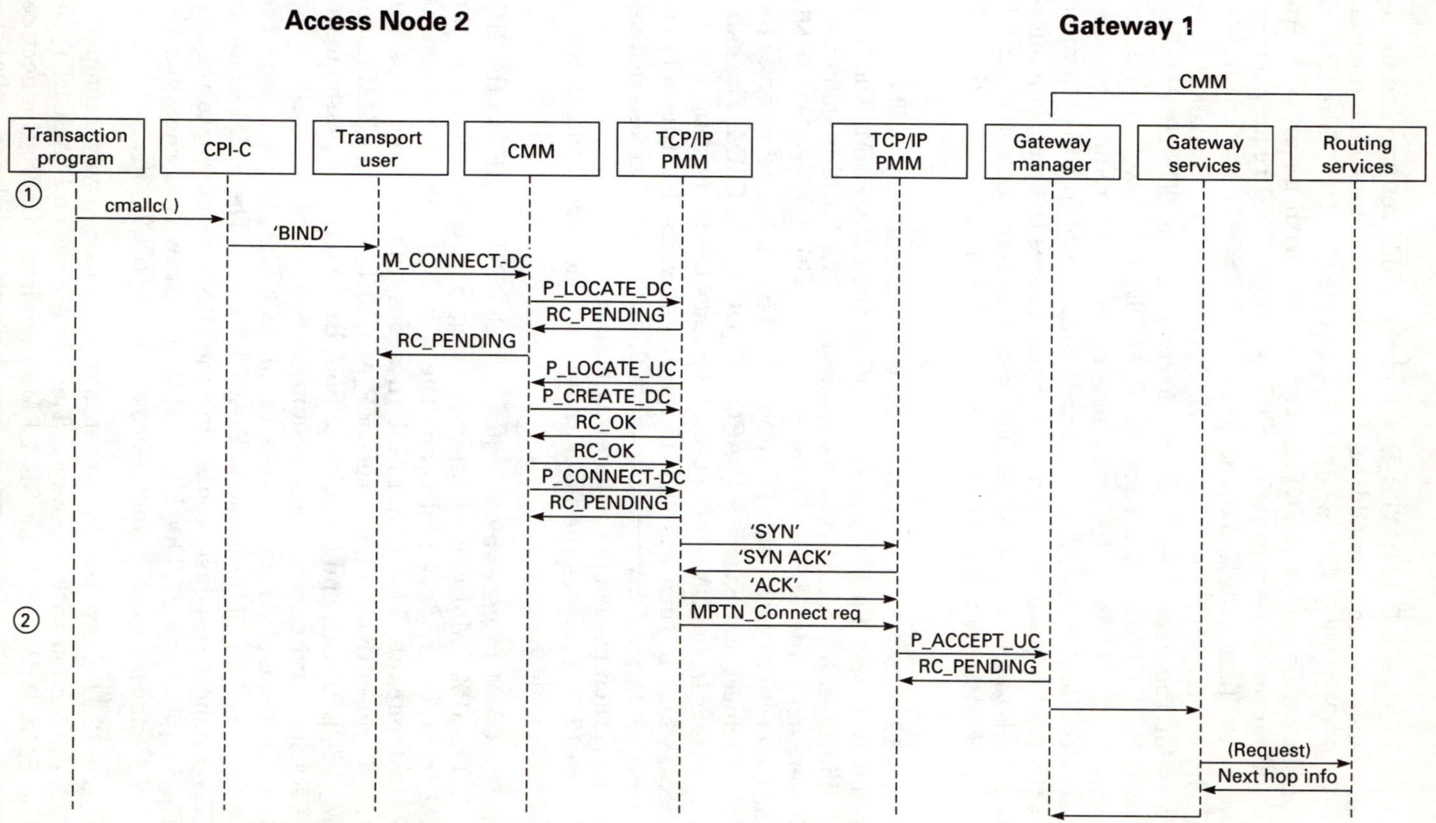

Figure 12.8 Access node 2 connects with gateway 1.

The CMM issues a P_LOCATE_DC, and the PMM returns the destination transport provider address for gateway 1. The CMM then issues a P_CREATE_DC and a P_CONNECT_DC. The PMM establishes a underlying TCP/IP connection with gateway 1. An MPTN_Connect request containing the original BIND request image is sent as the first TCP/IP data packet.

2. The MPTN_Connect request, which contains the transport user address for the actual destination, arrives in the TCP/IP PMM in gateway 1. The PMM then passes a P_ACCEPT_UC to the CMM in gateway 1. The CMM gateway manager passes the request to gateway services, and gateway services calls routing services to determine what the next hop will be. Routing services passes the next hop information back to gateway services. The next hop transport provider address is for gateway 2, which connects the SNA network with the IPX network.

Figure 12.9 shows the flow from gateway 1 to gateway 2. The CMM in gateway 1 issues a P_CONNECT_DC to the SNA PMM. The SNA PMM binds an LU 6.2 SNA session with the SNA PMM in gateway 2 and then sends the MPTN_Connect request with the original BIND in the connection_data field. The SNA PMM in gateway 2 receives the MPTN_Connect and passes a P_ACCEPT_UC to the CMM. The gateway manager in the CMM of gateway 2 passes the request to gateway services, which in turn passes it to routing services. Routing services passes back to gateway services the IPX address for access node 4, and this is then passed to the gateway manager.

Figure 12.10 provides the flows that take place between gateway 2 and access node 4.

1. The CMM in gateway 2 issues a P_CONNECT_DC to the IPX PMM. The IPX PMM creates an underlying SPX connection with the PMM in access node 4 and sends the MPTN_Connect request as the first packet. The IPX PMM in access node 4 receives the MPTN_Connect request and issues a P_ACCEPT_UC. The CMM issues an M_ACCEPT_UC, and the original SNA BIND image is passed to the SNA session services component residing in access node 4.

2. SNA session services issues an M_ACCEPT_DC to accept the SNA session. The CMM issues a P_ACCEPT_DC. The PMM sends an MPTN_Connect response, containing the BIND response, to the IPX PMM in gateway 2. The IPX PMM in gateway 2 receives the MPTN_Connect response and issues a P_CONNECT_UC.

Figure 12.11 shows the flows that take place as gateway 2 completes MPTN connection with gateway 1. The CMM issues a P_ACCEPT_DC to the SNA PMM, and the SNA PMM sends a MPTN_Connect response to the SNA PMM in gateway 1 using the already-allocated

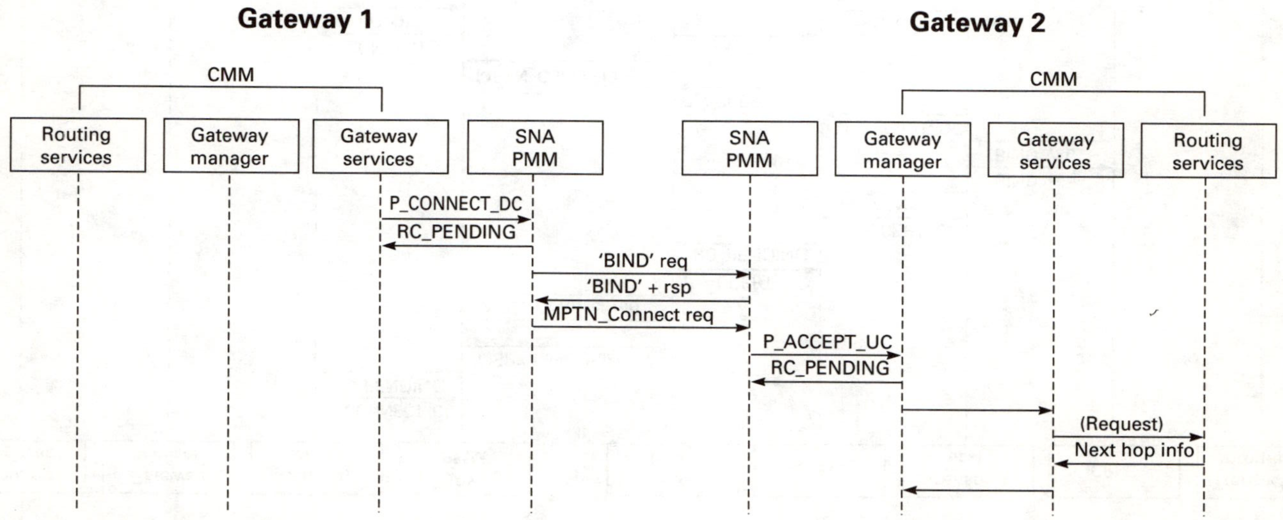

Figure 12.9 Gateway 1 connects with gateway 2.

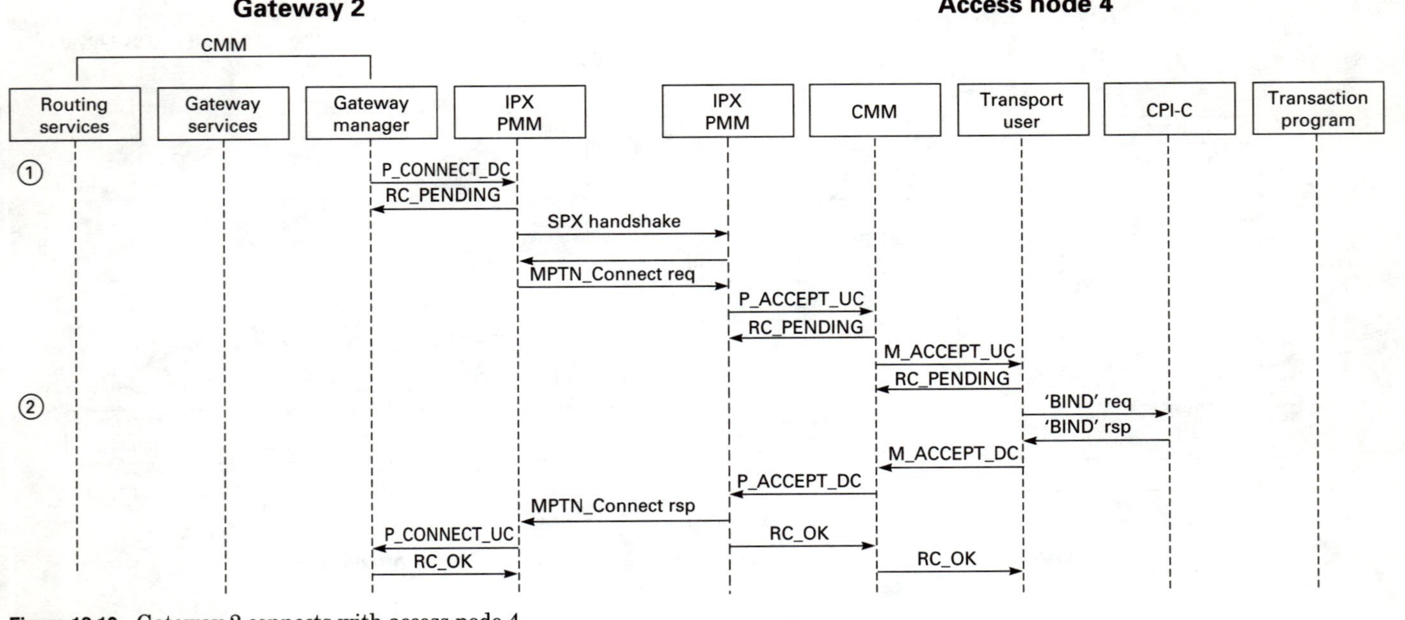

Figure 12.10 Gateway 2 connects with access node 4.

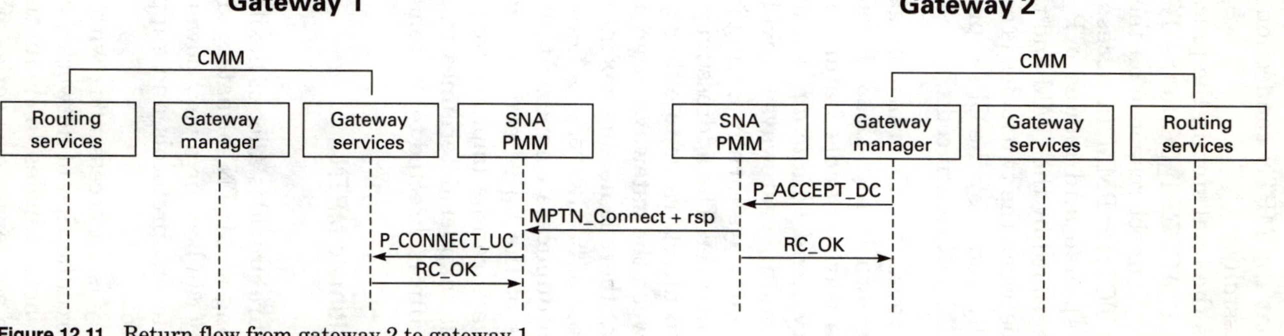

Figure 12.11   Return flow from gateway 2 to gateway 1.

SNA LU 6.2 session. When the PMM in gateway 1 receives the MPTN_Connect response, it issues a P_CONNECT_UC to inform the gateway manager that the MPTN connection that it requested has been completed successfully.

Figure 12.12 shows the final step in the process. Gateway manager in gateway 1 sends a P_ACCEPT_DC to the TCP/IP PMM. The PMM then sends an MPTN_Connect response on the TCP/IP connection to access node 2. The TCP/IP PMM in access node 2 receives the MPTN_Connect response and issues a P_CONNECT_UC. An M_CONNECT_UC is issued by the CMM and the BIND is completed. Now that the BIND between the two nodes is established, the cmallc() call that was originally issued by the CPI-C program in access node 2 is completed with a CM_OK return code.

12.5.1.3 Parallel gateways. MPTN transport gateways can be configured in parallel as shown in Fig. 12.13. Parallel gateways between two SPTNs provide a way to handle features such as load balancing and high availability. *Load balancing* is a method of distributing throughput between multiple gateways to divide a load evenly. This is accomplished by the gateways each reporting information about their loads to the address mapper. The address mapper, which is described in Chap. 14, can then direct traffic to either gateway and effectively balance the load between the gateways. *High availability* is a method that helps ensure that there is no single point of failure in a network. When a system, a piece of hardware, or a network element fails, high availability causes a duplicate component or path to "kick in" and take over the duties of the failed component until the problem is fixed. Parallel gateways can be implemented to provide high availability. If the address mapper determines that one of the gateways has gone down, all traffic is directed to the remaining gateways.

12.6 Building the Ultimate MPTN Transport Gateway

The MPTN architecture provides a lot of flexibility for product implementation, and as long as MPTN formats and protocols are adhered to, an MPTN gateway can become a very powerful tool, perhaps interconnecting many different protocols and supporting any number of transport user protocols.

The MPTN gateway is an access node with additional capabilities that enables the interconnection of networks. Applications running in native SPTNs, or in access nodes in nonnative SPTNs, are able to communicate through a gateway, or a series of gateways, with matching native applications running in a native SPTN, and matching nonnative applications running in access nodes in nonnative SPTNs. The

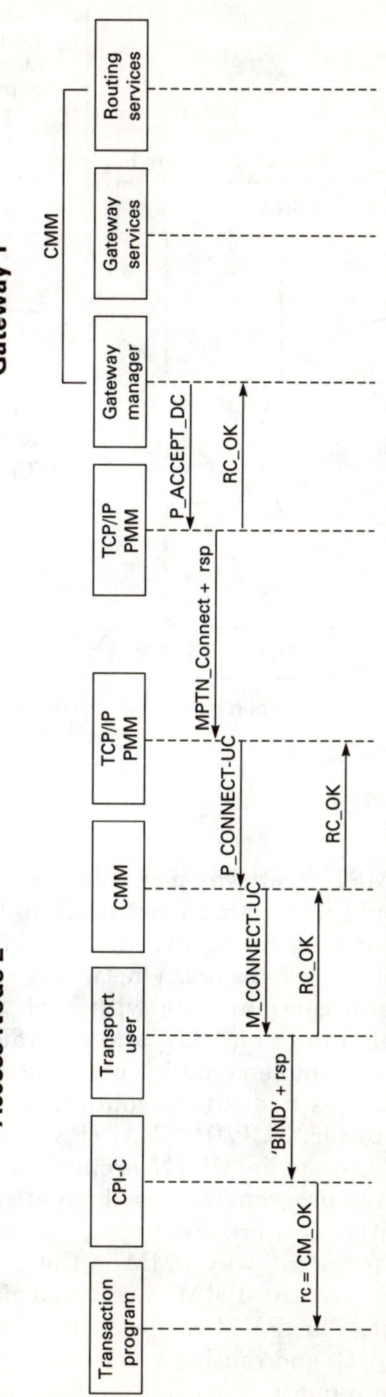

Figure 12.12 Return flow from gateway 1 to access node 2.

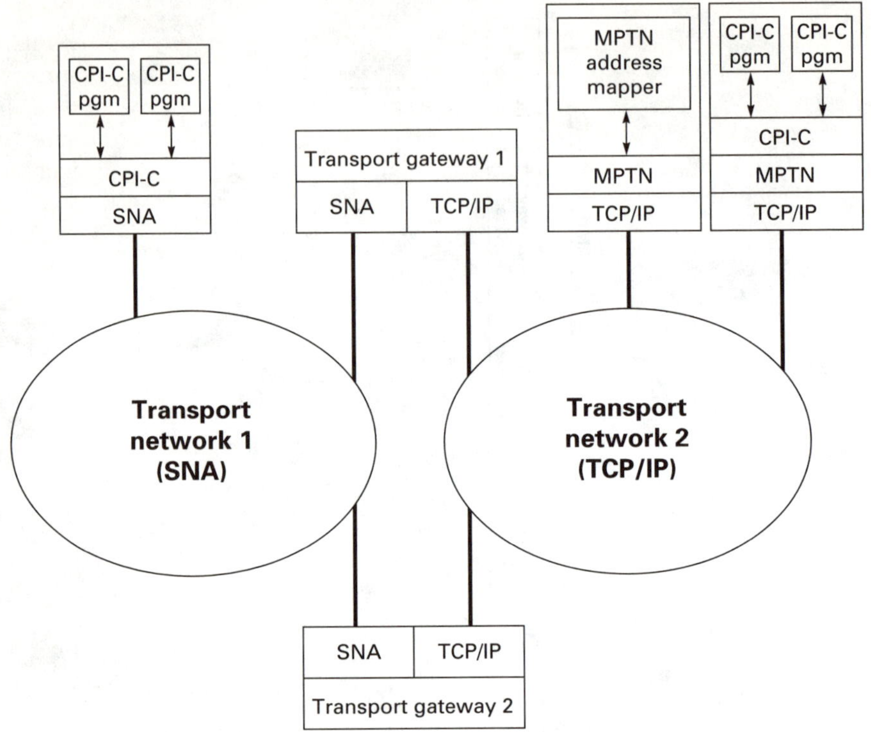

Figure 12.13   Parallel MPTN transport gateways.

architecture of an MPTN gateway can potentially be used to build a component that would interconnect networks to the extent that any *like* applications running anywhere in an entire MPTN network (which could consist of perhaps *many* networks interconnected using MPTN gateways) can communicate with each other regardless of where they are located in the MPTN, and regardless of the transport protocol that has been implemented. This ultimate MPTN internetwork would have access nodes that could accept any of the major transport user protocols: TCP/IP, SNA, IPX, NetBIOS, AppleTalk, DECnet, and OSI. Using the MPTN architecture, programs would communicate with any program that used a matching protocol located anywhere in the MPTN network.

The bottom line for a gateway PMM is that, to establish connections across a gateway, the PMM receives a native or nonnative connection request. The PMM issues a P_ACCEPT_UC or a G_NATIVE_ACCEPT_UC, and routing services decides where to further route the connection request. The eventual destination for the request may be located in an SPTN that is many hops away. The gateway manager issues a P_CONNECT_DC to establish a connection with the next hop, or a G_NATIVE_CONNECT_DC to establish a connection with the destination user. The ultimate MPTN gateway would allow all the different transport user protocols provided by the access nodes to pass through the gateway, and the gateway would connect to any of the major types of transport networks: TCP/IP, SNA, IPX, NetBIOS, AppleTalk, DECnet (and OSI). With this ultimate implementation, a truly seamless MPTN transport network would allow complete application independence without having to implement multiple transport protocols in the same network.

12.7 Conclusion

Routers, operating in the network layer, came quietly into the global networking picture in the 1980s and revolutionized networking. Routers and bridges were the first devices that could be plugged into networks to make dissimilar protocols interwork. With the ability to strip off the data link layer headers of incoming packets and attach data link layer headers to outgoing packets, routers could tie together networks that had dissimilar data link layers. That was a revolution in networking. With one black box, two or more networks could be tied together, if both ran the same transport network protocol.

As router vendors added more and more functionality to their products, routers became more than just "routers": They became network interconnection devices that provided encapsulation of one network protocol within another, for example, or made available such functionalities as data link layer *poll spoofing*.

MPTN transport gateways provide the same sort of network "splicing" as routers, only higher in the protocol stack. MPTN gateways cannot tie together a token ring and an Ethernet network like a router or a bridge; the intention of the MPTN gateway is not to provide the same functionality as routers, but to provide new functionality that can further liberate networking in the 1990s as routers and bridges did in the 1980s.

By examining the sample configurations that have been provided in this chapter, it can be seen that MPTN gateways can be implemented by manufacturers to handle many real-world needs. Even though routers have helped patch networks together, the issue of dissimilar transport layers in SPTNs can be solved only by a solution that operates on top of the transport layer, just as routers provide a solution by operating on top of the OSI data link layer. Multiprotocol transport networking is a way to integrate networks further, and it could provide the means for the next evolution in network integration.

MPTN Formats

13.1   Introduction

Discussion of the multiprotocol transport network architecture continues in this chapter by introducing and describing the various data structure formats that are used by MPTN components. The MPTN architecture specifies formatted messages and other structures to contain the information needed by the components that provide MPTN services. Discussion of MPTN formats begins with the MPTN address, after which the various formats used to create MPTN messages are introduced. The remainder of the chapter is devoted to the subject of protocol compensation and the use of another format: the MPTN header.

13.2   MPTN Network Addressing

Formats that represent a network address are different for every transport network protocol. SNA networks employ a fully qualified name, TCP/IP networks use a 32-bit IP address (with an associated socket number), and NetBIOS networks employ 16-byte names. OSI networks use a variable-length NSAP/Tselector, and the IPX protocol uses IPX socket addresses. Because these network address formats are each different in both content and size, a common method of address representation has been created as part of the MPTN architecture.

13.2.1   The MPTN-qualified address

To create addresses that are completely unique in MPTN networks, an *MPTN-qualified transport address* (or simply an MPTN-qualified address) is employed throughout the MPTN architecture. This address format is used to identify all addressable units in an MPTN network—transport users, transport providers, address mappers, multi-cast servers—and provides a basis for routing data in an MPTN network. An MPTN-qualified address contains the actual native transport protocol address plus other relevant information.

The MPTN-qualified address (Table 13.1) has a variable length and is made up of four fields. The first field is a 1-byte *MPTN qualifier* (listed in Table 13.2) which describes the particular networking protocol with which the address is associated. The MPTN qualifier not only informs MPTN components of the manner in which the address is formatted, it also ensures that a unique address is always specified (it is possible for identical network addresses to be created by two different transport networks).

The next field is a 1-byte *address mode*. This field indicates if the address is an individual or group address, and if it is a datagram or not. Additionally, the address mode field tells whether the address belongs to an MPTN address mapper server or an MPTN address mapper client.

TABLE 13.1   The MPTN-Qualified Transport Address

MPTN qualifier (1 byte)	X'02' IP address and port number X'07' OSI TSAP address X'0B' SNA fully qualified LU name in EBCDIC X'12' NetBIOS name X'16' IPX address X'7C' Old-style SNA address (subarea style) X'7F' Local-form address X'FF' An MPTN component
Address mode (1 byte)	X'01' Individual address X'02' Group address X'03' Datagram: group or individual status not known X'04' Address mapper client X'05' Address mapper server X'06' Multicast server
Node address	■ Length (1 byte) Range 2–255 bytes ■ Node address (variable length) A specific network address
Local address	■ Length (1 byte) Range 1–255 bytes ■ Local address (variable length) The transport layer part of an address OSI: the TSAP IP: the port number SNA: null NetBIOS: null IPX: socket number

TABLE 13.2   MPTN Qualifiers

IP address	X'02'	A 32-bit IP address
OSI TSAP address	X'07'	A variable-length OSI address
SNA fully qualified LU name	X'0B'	A SNA LU name in the format "NETNAME.LUNAME"
NetBIOS address	X'12'	A 16-character name
IPX/SPX address	X'16'	An IPX 4-byte network and 6-byte node address
Old SNA address	X'7C'	Older-style FID2 LU number address
Local form address	X'7F'	A free-form address defined by a local node
MPTN specific family address	X'FF'	An MPTN component (such as an address mapper)

The third field, *node address,* contains the network address in the format native to the transport network to which it belongs. If the transport network is a (new-style) SNA network, the node address contains a fully qualified LU name*; node addresses for a NetBIOS network contain a NetBIOS name; IPX node addresses contain a 4-byte IPX network address and a 6-byte IPX node address. The node address for an OSI address consists of an OSI NSAP; TCP/IP network addresses have an IP address in the node address field. The node address field begins with a 1-byte subfield that includes the length of the address. The range for this length is 2 to 255 bytes (the minimum value that can be specified in the length subfield of the node address is 2: the length of the length field itself plus at least a 1-byte network address).

The fourth, and final, field is called the *local address.* It is constructed in a similar manner to the node address, with a 1-byte subfield (containing the address's length) followed by an address. The local address field contains the address specific to the endpoint within a node. The difference between a node address and a local address is that the node address contains the address of the node in which the endpoint process resides, and the local address identifies the specific endpoint within the node.

For an IP address, the local address is either a TCP or a UDP port number. For an OSI address, it is a Tselector. The local address field is not used in SNA and NetBIOS. In SNA, the LU name identifies the specific endpoint; in NetBIOS, the NetBIOS name identifies the end-

---

*The LU name in a new-style SNA address must always be fully qualified in an MPTN address. Refer to Sec. 6.3.3.4 in for more information about fully qualified LU names.

point. Therefore, the local address in these cases is zero. For an IPX address, the local address is a 2-byte IPX socket number followed by a 2-byte connection ID. The 1-byte length field of the local address contains a number in the range 1–255 bytes. The local address length field always contains at least a 1, because the length field itself has a length of 1 byte.

13.2.2 Wildcard addresses

MPTN transport gateways use a specific function of MPTN addressing called a *wildcard address.* A wildcard address contains a part that is defined, and a part that is not defined.

The concept of a wildcard is perhaps best explained by illustration. Readers may be familiar with Unix and MS-DOS wildcards. In these operating systems a file name can be designated by including a certain number of constant characters followed by the wildcard character, *, indicating that the remaining characters in a filename may be substituted by anything. For example, a filename of LRS* describes all files that begin with the three letters LRS. Included are files such as LRS, LRSXXX, and LRSTTTTT. Another example that demonstrates a concept similar to the wildcard is the use of the subnet mask in TCP/IP networks (described in Chap. 4). MPTN's use of the wildcard is similar to a subnet mask in relationship to an IP address. The subnet mask indicates which part of an address is constant and which part is variable.

The MPTN wildcard address is an address with a particular portion that is static. Associated with each wildcard address is a mask that defines which part of the complete address is the static portion. The mask shows which bits are included in the static part of the address. This static part represents the network portion of an address. The rest of the address is represented by the "wildcard," and is the part of the address that normally holds the endpoint and node information. MPTN gateway routing is based on MPTN wildcard addresses. When gateway routing services registers an address of a network, it registers a wildcard address plus a mask. Like a wildcard in a card game, one card can represent any other card. In other words, if a gateway connects two networks, the gateway registers the address of each network. Since it is a network address that it is registering and not a single user endpoint address, as would be registered by an access node, the local and node parts of the address are not registered, only the network portion is—the address for a specific network. When supplying a wildcard address and a mask along with a registration request, the address that is registered is a network address.

If the address AAA with a mask of three characters (24 bits) is registered, then all requests to locate addresses such as AAA000, AAA0, AAAAAAA, and AAA are satisfied by the wildcard entry, unless specific addresses that are not wildcard addresses and that completely match these address are also registered. If the address AA0A with a mask of AA0A is registered, then all requests to locate addresses such as AA0A, AAAA, AA4AAAAA, and AA4A are satisfied by the wildcard entry, unless specific addresses that are not wildcard addresses and that completely match these address are also registered.

The wildcard feature enables the network addresses from various transport protocols to be registered by the routing services component in MPTN gateways. The mask associated with the wildcard entry indicates which part of the address is the NetID portion of an IP address, the network qualifier for a (new-style) SNA address, or the network portion of an IPX address, for example.

Additionally, using wildcard addressing, configurations such as *split networks* can be realized, in which two SPTNs, interconnected by another SPTN, are configured as belonging to the same logical network by assigning the same wildcard mask and name to both networks. Split networks can only be created over SNA and NetBIOS transport providers.

13.2.3 Well-known MTPN addresses

Another addressing feature that is used in MPTN networks is the *well-known address*. The concept of a well-known address was introduced in Chap. 3 in the discussion of IPX networks and was described later, in Chap. 4, in relationship to TCP/IP networking protocols. A well-known address in an MPTN network is a transport address that is unique and used only for one purpose: specifying the transport address of an MPTN service within an SPTN. It is called *well known* because the same transport address is unique for each specific transport networking protocol and always remains the same.

MPTN's well-known address is the transport-layer address of the PMM component that receives data from an MPTN network.

If packets of data that are being transported in an MPTN network have been sent by an MPTN transport gateway to an endpoint user in a native transport network, the transport address for that user is the same as the destination transport address. In other words, if the packet being sent from the gateway is a segment of data belonging to a TCP telnet connection, then the packet's transport address is port number 23 (the telnet server). However, if the same packet of data is traveling in a nonnative network and the end user is a telnet server in an access node, then the packet of data instead will be addressed to the MPTN well-known port address. In this way, packets containing nonnative data sent by MPTN components are sent to an MPTN component to be dealt with. The MPTN component for any node is the PMM that is assigned to that particular transport provider network.

Well-known port numbers have been established for MPTN in the various transport provider networks. For TCP/IP, the well-known port is TCP/UDP port number 397, assigned for use by MPTN components by the *Internet Activities Board* (IAB). In a SNA network, the well-known MPTN address is a reserved transaction program name of X'28F0F0F1' (a hex 28 followed by EBCDIC '001'). In a SNA transport provider network, when LU 6.2 sessions are bound, the transaction program name that is sent in the FM-5 attach header is this special, reserved name. For OSI transport provider networks, a reserved Tselector is used. In NetBIOS, the well-known MPTN address is a generated name. For IPX networks, Novell has assigned MPTN socket 8795 for SPX, and 8796 for IPX.

13.3   MPTN Messages

An *MPTN message* is a structure that is used for formatting MPTN datagrams and connection establishment packets. Datagrams are employed in the MPTN architecture to send *MPTN command requests* and *responses* between MPTN components.

The description of MPTN message formats begins with the basic MPTN message structure.

13.3.1   The MPTN message structure

MPTN messages begin with an *MPTN message header,* which consists of one to four separate parts (Fig. 13.1):

- A common prefix
- A routing prefix
- Required fields
- Optional fields

The *common prefix* is a 4-byte field that contains information that is common to every message. The *routing prefix* is a variable-length field that identifies the source and destination transport user address. It is used for routing datagrams and MPTN connection requests in an MPTN network. *Required fields* can be variable or fixed in length and are required for any particular message type that uses

Common prefix	Routing prefix	Required fields	Optional fields

Figure 13.1   The MPTN message header.

required fields. *Optional fields* are included in messages only if needed. They are identified by a 4-byte prefix.

The common prefix is always present in messages. However, the other parts are not always included, depending on the particular message format. Table 13.3 shows the message header and its four parts.

TABLE 13.3   MPTN Message Header

Common Prefix (4 bytes)

Command type (1 byte): The command ID for this particular message
Flag (1 byte: bits 0–7)
  Request: Bit 0 is 0
    Bit 4: 1 = gateway must reject if unrecognized command
        0 = gateway must forward if unrecognized command
    Bit 6: 1 = destination must reject if unrecognized command
        0 = destination must discard if unrecognized command
  Response: Bit 0 is 1
    Bit 1: 1 = negative response
        0 = positive response
    Bit 2: 1 = command is a valid command but was rejected (neg. response only)
    Bit 5: 1 = gateway did not recognize this command
    Bit 7: 1 = destination did not recognize this command
Command length (2 bytes)

Routing Prefix (variable length)
Time to live (1 byte) Destination user address (5–512 bytes): MPTN-qualified format Source user address (5–512 bytes): MPTN-qualified format Correlator suffix (2–9 bytes: length (1 byte), value (1–8 bytes))
Required Fields (fixed or variable length)
Fields that are required in specific messages
Optional Fields (fields are identified by prefix)

Prefix
  ■ ID (1 byte): The prefix ID for the optional field
  ■ Processing specification (1 byte)
    Request
      Bit 4: 1 = gateway must reject if unrecognized command
         0 = gateway must forward if unrecognized command
      Bit 6: 1 = destination must reject if unrecognized command
         0 = destination must discard if unrecognized command
    Response
      Bit 5: 1 = gateway did not recognize this command
      Bit 7: 1 = destination did not recognize this command
  ■ Field length (2 bytes)

Messages that are sent in stream-oriented transport providers, such as TCP/IP, always contain a 4-byte length field attached to the front of each message. This is necessary because stream-oriented protocols do not have record delineations. Since this length field is not always included, it is not shown in any of the accompanying diagrams, nor is it described below.

The four parts of the MPTN message header will now be presented.

13.3.1.1 Common prefix.   The common prefix is a 4-byte field common to each message. It is used to identify the message and contains three subfields: command type, flag, and command length.

Command type is a 1-byte indicator that specifies the message format that is being used. The next subfield, the *flag,* is a 1-byte field that contains flag bits that, when set, indicate particular conditions relating to the message. For example, the first bit in the field, when set, indicates that the message format is a response; otherwise it is a request. The use of the other seven flag bits is shown in Table 13.3. The last two bytes of the common prefix is the *command length* that is used to specify the total length of the message.

13.3.1.2 Routing prefix.   The routing prefix is used to route messages from one SPTN to another and are required, for example, in MPTN_Connect and MPTN_Datagram messages. It consists of four subfields.

The first subfield of the routing prefix is a 1-byte field called the *time to live* field, which is implemented to prevent routing loops that can occur when a destination address is never reached and a message continues to be routed through the same MPTN gateways in a loop. At each transport gateway hop in an MPTN network, the "time to live" field is decremented. When the field becomes zero, the packet is discarded or a negative response is returned.

The second and third subfields are the *destination* and *source addresses.* These MPTN-qualified addresses show where the message came from and where it is going.

The fourth and last subfield is called the *correlator suffix.* It has a variable length between 2 and 9 bytes including a 1-byte length and is used differently for datagrams and connection requests. In a datagram, it is used to correlate datagram segments (datagrams may be segmented to accommodate maximum lengths). The correlator suffix is used to rebuild the original datagram from its segments. In a connection request, the correlator suffix is used to correlate a request with its response.

13.3.1.3 Required fields.   *Required fields* are fields that are mandatory for some message formats and can be either fixed or variable in length. They are identified by the position of the field within a message. A variable-length required field has a length value associated with it, which is used to step over the field when locating fields that are placed after it in the message.

13.3.1.4 Optional fields. Optional fields are not required for *each* particular message format and are included at the end of the MPTN message header. The number of optional fields included depends on the message, and each is identifiable by the first byte of a 4-byte *prefix* called the field identifier. A number of different optional fields are defined in the architecture, and each has its own identifier. Some of these fields, such as *Diagnostics* (X'F0'), are used in most MPTN messages, but most of the optional fields pertain to particular message formats. As an example, Table 13.4 shows optional fields that can be associated with two message formats, MPTN_Connect and MPTN_Datagram.

The second byte of an optional field's prefix is the *processing specification*. This byte is used to indicate to the receiver of the message what to do if it fails to recognize the optional field. The bit settings in this subfield are described in Table 13.3.

The last two bytes of the prefix contain the optional field's length, which includes the length of the 4-byte prefix itself.

13.3.2 Message formats

Six different message formats are defined in the architecture. The first message format is used to establish connections in MPTN net-

TABLE 13.4 MPTN_Connect and MPTN_Datagram: Optional Fields

Name	Value	MPTN_Connect	MPTN_Datagram
Direct TLPB user type	X'04'	X	X
Service mode	X'05'	X	X
Connection data	X'0A'	X	
Retry	X'12'		X
User characteristics	X'18'	X	
Compensations required	X'19'	X	
Optional compensations	X'1A'	X	
Node initialization ID	X'1C'	X	X
Source provider	X'28'		X
Destination provider	X'2B'		X
Segment specification	X'2D'		X
Maximum datagram size	X'2E'		X
User data	X'AF'	X	
Diagnostics	X'F0'	X	X

works, and the remaining five are variations on a basic MPTN datagram message format:

- MPTN_Connect
- MPTN_Datagram
- MPTN_DG_OOB_Data
- MPTN_Cntrl_Datagram
- MPTN_Syntax_Mapper_Signal_Datagram
- MPTN_DG_KEEPALIVE_Hdr

These message formats will be divided into two classes for purposes of discussion: the connection request message and the datagram messages. The discussion will begin with a description of the connection request message.

13.3.2.1 The connection request message.

Connection establishment and termination in MPTN can be viewed as a form of compensation, because establishing and terminating connections in the various transport networking protocols is accomplished differently by each protocol. In order to provide a standardized format to handle establishment and termination regardless of the underlying transport provider network, a standard manner of dealing with connection issues is part of the architecture.

MPTN connections are established using a message called the MPTN_Connect. Reference to this command has been made throughout the last three chapters; now we will look at the actual format of the command.

MPTN_Connect. MPTN_Connect request and response messages are used in the process of establishing MPTN connections. The request is sent from an initiating endpoint to a terminating endpoint, and can pass through multiple SPTNs. An MPTN_Connect response is returned by the destination endpoint to the initiating endpoint and reflects the outcome of the connection request: whether connection establishment succeeded or failed. The structure of MPTN_Connect is shown in Table 13.5.

The common prefix for MPTN_Connect contains a command type of X'80' to identify it as an MPTN_Connect. Bits 4 and 6 of the processing specification field are always set, and the routing prefix is always used. The correlator suffix is employed to correlate MPTN_Connect requests with associated responses. The first byte of the correlator suffix contains the length of the entire correlator suffix field, and the following byte(s) contain a unique value.

The required fields for an MPTN_Connect are called *user transport*

TABLE 13.5 MPTN_Connect

Common Prefix		
Command type	X'80'	1 byte
Processing specification		1 byte
Command length		2 bytes
Routing Prefix		
Time to live		1 byte
Destination user address	MPTN-qualified transport address	5–512 bytes
Source user address	MPTN-qualified transport address	5–512 bytes
Correlator suffix		2–9 bytes
Required Fields		
User transport requirements		(15 bytes)
User transport requirements length		1 byte
Maximum record length		4 bytes
Maximum expedited data length		4 bytes
Maximum termination data length		4 bytes
Termination type		1 byte
Expedited marking		1 byte
Optional Fields		
Direct TLPB user type		(6–12 bytes)
Direct TLPB user prefix	X'04'	4 bytes
Direct TLPB user type		2–8 bytes
Service mode		(6–260 bytes)
Service mode prefix	X'05'	4 bytes
MPTN service mode		1 byte
User-defined service mode		(1–255 bytes)
Connection data		$(4-(2^{16}-1)$ bytes)
Connection data prefix	X'0A'	4 bytes
Connection data		$0-(2^{16}-5)$ bytes
User characteristics		(5–36 bytes)
User characteristics prefix	X'18'	4 bytes
User characteristics		1–32 bytes
Compensations required		(4–23 bytes)
Compensations prefix	X'19'	4 bytes
Compensations		0–19 bytes
Optional compensations		(5–36 bytes)
Optional compensations prefix	X'1A'	4 bytes
Optional compensations		1–32 bytes
Node initialization ID		(12 bytes)
Node initialization ID prefix	X'1C'	4 bytes
Node initialization ID		8 bytes
Diagnostics (for negative responses only)		(18–799 bytes)
Diagnostics prefix	X'F0'	4 bytes
Primary return code		4 bytes
Secondary return code		4 bytes
Error detector address	MPTN-qualified transport address	5–512 bytes
Error detector data		1–255 bytes
User data		$(5-(2^{16}-1)$ bytes)
User data prefix	X'AF'	4 bytes
User data		$1-(2^{16}-5)$ bytes

requirements. These are the characteristics requested by the source transport user.

- *User transport requirements length.*   The length of the user transport requirements.

- *Maximum record length.*   The maximum size of a record that can be sent on a connection. This field is used only for transport providers that are record-oriented. For stream-oriented transport users, the field is not used and is set to 0.

- *Maximum expedited data length.*   The maximum size of an expedited data record that can be sent on a connection. If expedited data are not supported by the transport user, this field is set to 0.

- *Maximum termination data length.*   The maximum length of termination data for a connection. This field is used only for transport providers that support termination data, and it is set to 0 if it is not used.

- *Termination type.*   The type of termination used to close a connection. It is indicated by the bit settings in this 1-byte field:
  Bit 0.   Simplex-abortive
  Bit 1.   Simplex-orderly
  Bit 2.   Duplex-abortive
  Bit 3.   Duplex-orderly
  Bits 4–7.   Reserved

- *Expedited marking.*   If the transport user requires the ability to mark the position in the normal data where expedited data begin, this field is set to 1; otherwise it is set to 0.
  A number of optional fields are used in MPTN_Connect.

- *Direct TLPB user type.*   This field is present when the transport user is a direct TLPB user (such as an address mapper client). The "direct TLPB user type" consists of a string of 2 to 8 bytes that is used to identify the direct TLPB user.

- *Service mode.*   This optional field specifies the level of service that is needed by the transport user. The service mode field is inserted into the MPTN_Connect when the transport user requires a class of service definition; otherwise it is left out. There are two service mode subfields: an MPTN service mode and a user-defined service mode. The MPTN service mode consists of a byte set to one of the MPTN service mode values listed in Table 13.6. The user-defined service mode subfield can be set to a user-defined service mode value.

- *Connection data.*   Some transport protocols associate data with a connection. In SNA this is the BIND image. Since these data are needed to establish a connection, they must be transported to the

TABLE 13.6   Service Modes

X'00'	User-defined service mode is applied
X'01'	No specific service mode is required
X'02'	High bandwidth is required
X'03'	Fast response time is required
X'04'	Secure service with high bandwidth is required
X'05'	Secure service with fast response time is required

TABLE 13.7   User Characteristics

Connection outage notification	X'01'
Nonqueued responses sent as expedited data	X'02'

remote endport; for this reason, the connection data optional field is made available. Connection data can be sent with the request and can be returned with a positive or negative response.

- *User characteristics.*   This is a list of 1-byte user characteristic values. At the time of writing, there are two values—*connection outage notification* and *nonqueued responses sent as expedited data*—shown in Table 13.7. User characteristics are characteristics of a user that must be supported in a connection. User characteristics can be negotiable, and if the passive partner in the connection cannot support a characteristic, then that value is set to X'00' in the MPTN_Connect response. The number of elements in the list is determined from the length subfield.

- *Compensations required.*   This optional field is included if compensations are to be used in a connection. They are specified by a string of headers that represent each of the compensations. Compensations are valid only for a particular SPTN and must be redetermined if the MPTN_Connect enters another nonnative SPTN through a transport gateway. Compensation headers are discussed later in this chapter.

- *Optional compensations.*   This optional field is specified if compensations are to be used that are considered to be optional (not required). They are specified by a string of 1-byte headers. Compensations are valid only for a particular SPTN and must be redetermined if the MPTN_Connect enters another nonnative SPTN through a transport gateway.

- *Node initialization ID.*   The node initialization ID is a number (such as a time stamp) that indicates when the node was initialized.

This number is used by the keep-alive process to determine if the session was reinitialized.

- *User data.* This field can be used to transfer data between syntax mappers residing in the two endpoints during connection setup. It is also known as *transport user data.*

- *Diagnostics.* This field is used in the MPTN_Connect negative response to describe why a connection was rejected. Bits 4 and 6 in the processing specification, the second byte of the prefix, are both 0, because negative responses are not sent for what is already a negative response. The primary return code value contains a 1-byte hexadecimal code for the command type that was found to be in error. This is followed by a diagnostic value. The diagnostic values are shown in Table 13.8. The secondary return code field provides additional information associated with a given primary return code.

TABLE 13.8   Diagnositic Values

X'0001'	Connection limits exceeded
X'0002'	User not found
X'0003'	User not reachable
X'0006'	Service mode not supported
X'0007'	Rejected by user
X'0008'	User not listening
X'0009'	Time-to-live counter expired
X'0014'	User characteristics mismatch
X'0015'	Compensation unrecognized
X'0016'	Compensation mismatch
X'0017'	Error in user data
X'001E'	Connection data unexpected
X'001F'	Connection data missing
X'0020'	Expected optional field missing
X'0029'	Error in destination address
X'002A'	Error in source address
X'002B'	Optional fields out of sequence
X'002C'	Error in correlator
X'002D'	Length error: field too long
X'002E'	Length error: field too short
X'002F'	Error in receiver connection alias
X'0032'	Format error
X'0033'	Invalid header in MPTN_DG_OOB_Data
X'003C'	Internal processing error

13.3.2.2 MPTN datagrams. Datagrams, individual packets of data that are not associated with a connection, were described in Chap. 4 in the discussion of the Internet Protocol. MPTN has a datagram service that provides the underlying support for a transport-user datagram service. Additionally, datagrams are used by MPTN itself for sending command requests and responses among its components, and to provide other internal features such as session outage notification. This section describes the datagram message formats that are part of the MPTN architecture. MPTN supports three types of datagrams:

- Unicast datagrams: Datagrams exchanged between partners

- Multicast datagrams: Datagrams sent to a group of transport users

- Broadcast datagrams: Datagrams sent to all transport users

A number of datagram message formats are used in the MPTN architecture. Each of these datagram message formats will now be explained.

MPTN_Datagram. The basic datagram format for the MPTN architecture is the MPTN_Datagram. It provides the vehicle for carrying datagrams that belong to a transport user protocol. The original user's datagram is placed inside the MPTN_Datagram as *user data*. The format of the MPTN_Datagram is shown in Table 13.9.

The command code for MPTN_Datagram is X'81'. Bits 4 and 6 of the processing specification field are always set to 0, indicating that a negative response is not sent if the message is not recognized by a gateway or destination node. This is fully consistent with the discardable nature of a datagram. Positive responses are not sent for MPTN_Datagrams either: The only response is a negative one.

A routing prefix is always used in an MPTN_Datagram. Since datagrams are sent as individual packets and they can travel across more than one SPTN, the routing information contained in the routing prefix is absolutely necessary. As datagrams traverse various SPTNs interconnected by transport gateways, they may need to be segmented if the maximum datagram size for a transport provider is smaller than the size of the datagram. The correlator suffix is used to correlate these datagram segments. It consists of a 1-byte length and the correlator suffix value which is the number assigned to the segment. This number must be unique for a long enough period of time to ensure that all segments of the datagram arrive at their destination.

The MPTN_Datagram has no required fields. A number of optional fields, however, may be used.

- *Direct TLPB user type.* This optional field is present when the transport user establishing the connection is a direct TLPB user,

TABLE 13.9   MPTN_Datagram, MPTN_Cntrl_Datagram, and MPTN_Syntax_Mapper_Signal_Datagram

Common Prefix		
Command type:		1 byte
MPTN_Datagram	X'81'	
MPTN_Syntax_Mapper_Signal_Datagram	X'8E'	
MPTN_Cntrl_Datagram	X'8F'	
Processing specification		1 byte
Command length		2 bytes

Routing Prefix		
Time to live		1 byte
Destination user address	MPTN-qualified transport address	5–512 bytes
Source user address	MPTN-qualified transport address	5–512 bytes
Correlator suffix		2–9 bytes

Required Fields		
Not used		

Optional Fields		
Direct TLPB user type		(6–12 bytes)
Direct TLPB user prefix	X'04'	4 bytes
Direct TLPB user type		2–8 bytes
Service mode		(6–260 bytes)
Service mode prefix	X'05'	4 bytes
MPTN service mode		1 byte
User-defined service mode		1–255 bytes
Sequence number		(10–12 bytes)
Sequence number prefix	X'07'	4 bytes
Sequence number		6–8 bytes
Retry		(5 bytes)
Retry prefix	X'12'	4 bytes
Retry value		1 bytes
Node initialization ID		(12 bytes)
Node initialization ID prefix	X'1C'	4 bytes
Node initialization ID		8 bytes
Source provider		(9–516 bytes)
Source provider prefix	X'28'	4 bytes
Source provider address		5–512 bytes
Destination provider		(9–516 bytes)
Destination provider prefix	X'2B'	4 bytes
Destination provider address		5–512 bytes
Segment specification		(12 bytes)
Segment specification prefix	X'2D'	4 bytes
Segment specification		8 bytes
Maximum datagram size		(8 bytes)
Maximum datagram size prefix	X'2E'	4 bytes
Maximum datagram value		4 bytes
Diagnostics (for responses only)		(18–799 bytes)
Diagnostics prefix	X'F0'	4 bytes
Primary return code		4 bytes
Secondary return code		4 bytes
Error detector address	MPTN-qualified transport address	5–512 bytes
Error detector data		1–255 bytes
User data (optional in a response)		$0-(2^{32}-28)$ bytes

such as the address mapper client. The direct TLPB user type is a string of 2 to 8 bytes that is used to identify the direct TLPB user.

- *Service mode.* This optional field specifies the level of service that is needed by the transport user. The service mode field is inserted into the MPTN_Datagram when the transport user requires a class of service definition; otherwise, it is left out. The MPTN service mode is defined using one of the MPTN service mode values listed in Table 13.6. A user-defined service mode can be specified also.

- *Sequence number.* This optional field gives the transport user the ability to assign sequence numbers to datagrams.

- *Retry.* "Retry" is a true-or-false value which tells MPTN nodes to flush their caches in order to recalculate the routing of a datagram.

- *Node initialization ID.* The node initialization ID is a number, such as a time stamp, that indicates when the node was initialized.

- *Source provider.* This optional field changes the address of the source. When a datagram is sent, the sender may want return datagrams to be sent to another address—one that is different from the source of the datagram. The optional source provider field is provided for this reason.

- *Destination provider.* This optional field is used to store a *preferred* destination address. This is an address that will be used by the last gateway in a path to a destination to replace the MPTN well-known local address. The optional destination provider field can be used to direct an MPTN datagram to a destination at the destination node other than the PMM represented by the well-known address.

- *Segment specification.* This field is included in a datagram when the datagram has been segmented and is used in the reassembly of the original datagram. It consists of a 4-byte subfield that contains the length of the original datagram, and a 4-byte subfield that contains an offset value used as a pointer into the original datagram to determine where this datagram segment is located.

- *Maximum datagram size.* When a transport provider is able to receive a datagram which has a length that is greater than the already-established maximum datagram size for the transport provider, this optional field is used to tell the destination it can use the new maximum datagram size. The value is coded as a 4-byte binary number.

- *Diagnostics.* This field is used in a negative response to describe why a datagram was rejected. The primary return code value contains a 1-byte hexadecimal code for the command type that was found to be in error. This is followed by a diagnostic value. Diagnostic values are shown in Table 13.8. The secondary return code field provides additional information associated with a given primary return code.

- *User data.*   This is the actual data supplied by the transport user. All that precedes this field is system-related information.

MPTN_DG_OOB_Data.   MPTN_DG_OOB_Data is a datagram format used for sending data that are "out of band" from a connection. In other words, if data must be sent separately, outside the flow of data that has been established as a connection, this datagram format is used. It is needed in "expedited data" compensation, for example. If a PMM has sent expedited data in-band in a connection, but the data have not reached the destination, the data are sent separately as an MPTN_DG_OOB_Data datagram. MPTN_DG_OOB_Data makes use of both positive and negative responses, and its format is shown in Table 13.10.

The command code for the MPTN_DG_OOB_Data is X'83'. Bits 4 and 6 of the processing specification field are always set to 0 and 1, respectively, indicating that a negative response is not sent if the message is not recognized by a gateway, but must be sent if the message is unrecognized by a destination node. A routing prefix is not used in MPTN_DG_OOB_Data.

The required fields of the MPTN_DG_OOB_Data message consist of a connection sequence number and a connection correlator. These fields are used to correlate the datagram with the connection with which it is associated. The connection correlator field consists of two subfields: the correlator address and the correlator suffix. The address is the address for the transport user that initiated the connection with which the out-of-band data are associated. The correlator identifies the particular connection with which the datagram is associated and was originally assigned by the CMM that originated an MPTN_Connect for the connection.

A number of optional fields are associated with MPTN_DG_OOB_Data.

- *Sender connection alias.*   The sender connection alias field can be used to provide an *alias* for the sender to help locate the transport user's connection. This alias would typically be an index into a table of connection control blocks, or a value to be used in a "hash" function to provide an index into the table.

- *Receiver connection alias.*   The receiver connection alias field can be used to provide an *alias* for the receiver to help locate the transport user's connection. This alias would typically be an index into a table of connection control blocks, or a value to be used in a "hash" function to provide an index into the table.

TABLE 13.10   MPTN_DG_OOB_Data

	Common Prefix	
Command type	X'83'	1 byte
Processing specification		1 byte
Command length		2 bytes
	Routing Prefix	
Not used		
	Required Fields	
Connection sequence number		2 bytes
Connection correlator		(7–521 bytes)
Correlator address	MPTN-qualified transport address	5–512 bytes
Correlator suffix		2–9 bytes
	Optional Fields	
Sender connection alias		(9–516 bytes)
Sender alias prefix	X'28'	4 bytes
Sender alias address	MPTN-qualified transport address	5–512 bytes
Receiver connection alias		(9–516 bytes)
Receiver alias prefix	X'29'	4 bytes
Receiver alias address	MPTN-qualified transport address	5–512 bytes
Maximum datagram size		(8 bytes)
Maximum datagram size prefix	X'2E'	4 bytes
Maximum datagram value		4 bytes
Diagnostics (for responses only)		(18–799 bytes)
Diagnostics prefix	X'F0'	4 bytes
Primary return code		4 bytes
Secondary return code		4 bytes
Error detector address	MPTN-qualified transport address	5–512 bytes
Error detector data		1–255 bytes
MPTN header (on requests only)		
User data (on requests only)		

■ *Maximum datagram size.*   When a transport provider is able to receive a datagram which has a length that is greater than the already-established maximum datagram size for the transport provider, this optional field is used to provide the new maximum datagram size. The value is coded as a 4-byte binary number.

- *Diagnostics.*   This field is used in a negative response to describe why an out-of-band datagram was rejected. The primary return code value contains a 1-byte hexadecimal code for the command type that was found to be in error. This is followed by one of the diagnostic values as shown in Table 13.8. The secondary return code field is valid for certain diagnostic values and provides additional information.

- *MPTN header.*   At the end of the optional fields in an MPTN_DG_OOB_Data request (not in a response), the header representing the compensation that is associated with this message must be included (compensation headers are discussed in the next section). The headers that can be associated with the MPTN_DG_OOB_Data request are

  X'01'. Expedited message
  X'10'. Duplex-abortive termination
  X'18'. Simplex-abortive termination

- *User data.*   This is the out-of-band data being sent with this datagram.

MPTN_Cntrl_Datagram.   MPTN_Cntrl_Datagram is used to send a transport user control datagram over a nonnative transport provider. Its format is identical to the MPTN_Datagram, but it uses a command type of X'8F' (Table 13.9). It is used to supply information to a transport user that would normally be supplied by the native transport provider. Examples of the use of an MPTN control datagram are as follows.

- The NetBIOS *status* command returns, along with status and configuration information, a field called *local name table information.* When a NetBIOS syntax mapper processes the NetBIOS status command, it must first send an MPTN_Cntrl_Datagram to the remote node to retrieve the local name table information.

- The TCP/IP raw socket interface relies on the IP header being passed back to the application so that it can identify its own packets. Since the IP header is not available on a nonnative network, the MPTN_Cntrl_Datagram carries an IP header (which was supplied by the sending syntax mapper) in addition to the contents of the IP packet.

MPTN_Syntax_Mapper_Signal_Datagram.   The datagram MPTN_-Syntax_Mapper_Signal_Datagram is used for sending signals between syntax mappers. Its format is identical to that of the MPTN_Datagram, but it has a command type of X'8E' (Table 13.9). MPTN_Syntax_Mapper_Signal_Datagram is similar to the

MPTN_Cntrl_Datagram in that it supplies a feature that is available in a native transport protocol. Instead of passing an existing transport user data format to a syntax mapper, however, the signal datagram taps a syntax mapper on the shoulder and asks it to do something. An example of the use of the MPTN signal datagram is in the support for dependent LUs in a SNA transport network using DLUR/S. When SSCP-PU and SSCP-LU sessions need to be deactivated, the signal datagram is sent by the syntax mapper in an access node where the dependent LU is located across a nonnative network to the syntax mapper for the Dependent LU Requester to tell it to send the DACTPU and DACTLU commands. This will cause deactivation of the sessions.

MPTN_DG_KEEPALIVE_Hdr. MPTN_DG_KEEPALIVE_Hdr is used exclusively in the MPTN "keepalive" protocol. The format is shown in Table 13.11, and the command code is X'84'. Bits 4 and 6 of the processing specification field are always set to 0, indicating that a negative response is not sent if the message is not recognized by a gateway or destination node.

The routing prefix is not used in the MPTN_DG_KEEPALIVE_Hdr because MPTN_DG_KEEPALIVE_Hdr is valid only within a single

TABLE 13.11   MPTN_DG_KEEPALIVE_Hdr

	Common Prefix	
Command type	X'84'	1 byte
Processing specification		1 byte
Command length		2 bytes
	Routing Prefix	
Not used		
	Required Fields	
Source address	MPTN-qualified transport address	5–512 bytes
Destination address	MPTN-qualified transport address	5–512 bytes
	Optional Fields	
Diagnostics (for responses only)		18–799 bytes
Diagnostics prefix	X'F0'	4 bytes
Primary return code		4 bytes
Secondary return code		4 bytes
Error detector address	MPTN-qualified transport address	5–512 bytes
Error detector data		1–255 bytes

SPTN. The required fields used for the keepalive datagram header are source and destination transport provider addresses. The destination address specifies the address to which the MPTN_DG_KEEPALIVE_Hdr request is being sent. The source address specifies the address to which the MPTN_DG_KEEPALIVE_Hdr response is to be sent.

These datagrams are sent periodically when MPTN needs to implement a keepalive protocol in a transport provider that is consistent with a keepalive protocol expected by a transport user.

13.4   MPTN Headers and Compensation in MPTN Networks

In addition to the message formats for connection requests and datagrams, another format, called the MPTN *header,* is also employed in MPTN. An MPTN header is a simple 1-byte field that is placed in front of a data packet to specify a compensation that must be provided by MPTN. The list of MPTN headers and the associated compensation for each is shown in Table 13.12.

Since headers are used for compensation in MPTN networks, the subject of compensation will now be discussed, showing the use of headers as well as describing other methods that provide compensation. Compensation in the MPTN architecture is necessary to make up for services that are provided in a transport user's native protocol but that are unavailable in a nonnative networking protocol. Most protocol compensation is accomplished by using an MPTN header.

TABLE 13.12   MPTN Headers

X'00'	Record: no compensation with this message. Stream: record boundary marker
X'01'	Expedited message
X'03'	Expedited message acknowledgment
X'10'	Duplex-abortive termination
X'12'	Duplex-abortive termination acknowledgment
X'14'	Duplex-orderly termination
X'16'	Duplex-orderly termination acknowledgment
X'18'	Simplex-abortive termination
X'1A'	Simplex-abortive termination acknowledgment
X'1C'	Simplex-orderly termination
X'1E'	Simplex-orderly termination acknowledgment
X'20'	Segmented message
X'21'	Segmented expedited message

The 1-byte header that is added to the front of data identifies the compensation that is in effect for that particular data. Only one header is ever used at a time. When compensations are to be used in MPTN connections, the complete set of compensations must be identified at connect time. Compensations that are provided by datagrams, such as the MPTN_DG_OOB_Data and MPTN_DG_KEEPALIVE_Hdr messages, are identified at connect time as 1-byte fields containing the command type for that message. Some compensations, such as connection keepalive, are negotiable, and for that reason the following takes place during connection establishment.

The active transport endpoint user of the connection initiates the connection establishment process by issuing an M_CONNECT_DC call. Its CMM, knowing the characteristics of both the transport user and the transport provider, determines the compensations that will be required on the connection and issues a P_CONNECT_DC containing, in the *comp_hdrs* field, a string of compensation headers for the connection. These headers are sent to the partner node in the MPTN_Connect message. When the MPTN_Connect arrives at its destination, a P_ACCEPT_UC is issued by the receiving PMM, informing the CMM of the incoming connection request. The headers are passed up to the CMM, which in turn issues an M_ACCEPT_UC to the transport user, informing it of the incoming connection request. If the transport user accepts the connection, the CMM determines the compensations that will be required on the connection. The headers sent in the MPTN_Connect are examined, and if there are any inconsistencies in any of the negotiable compensations, the compensation headers selected by the local CMM are sent to the PMM in the P_ACCEPT_DC. The PMM sends these headers in the response to the MPTN_Connect. When the response is received by the originating PMM, the headers are delivered to the CMM in a P_CONNECT_UC. The CMM compares the headers for the negotiable compensations that were received with those that were sent originally and makes any adjustments.

When compensations are required in a connection, a header is added to every packet that is sent on the connection: Every packet of data has an extra byte prepended to it. The value in the header indicates the compensation that is required for that packet. Packets of data that do not require compensation carry the *no compensation required* (X'00') header. Thus, a compensation header is always the first byte of data in every packet, except in cases of a stream transport network, where data are always proceeded by a 4-byte record length.

The individual compensations that are provided in the MPTN architecture will now be discussed, including compensations that are provided without the use of headers. The first compensation that will be described is called "connection data."

13.4.1   Connection data

Connection data describes a data structure that is transported between endpoints when a connection is being established. Some transport protocols require an exchange of information concerning the connection that is being established; others do not. Both OSI and SNA, for example, require that a data structure be transferred between endpoints when a connection is being established, but TCP/IP does not.

The compensation for connection data is not handled by headers. Instead the CMM on the active end of the connection sends the connection data in the *connection_data* optional field of the MPTN_Connect request. In the MPTN_Connect response, the CMM on the other end of the connection puts connection response data into the *connection_data* field of the MPTN_Connect response if there is any, otherwise it echoes back the original connection data. A negative MPTN_Connect *response* can contain connection response data relating to the reason the connection was rejected. In other words, any data that are exchanged between endpoints during connection establishment are included in the connection data field of the MPTN_Connect request and response.

13.4.2   Termination data

Termination data are similar to connection data. Termination data are sent during the connection termination process. The data might simply contain a code that represents the reason for the termination. Termination data, if required, are sent as *user data* following any of the four MPTN termination headers:

- Duplex-abortive termination
- Duplex-orderly termination
- Simplex-abortive termination
- Simplex-orderly termination

The CMM at the receiving end extracts termination data and sends it to the transport user. For an abortive termination, since orderly shutdown is not being provided, the termination data are sent as expedited data.

13.4.3   Full-duplex over half-duplex

Full-duplex over half-duplex compensation is necessary because the data flow in the transport or session layer of a transport provider network may work differently than is required by an associated transport user. Some transport protocols provide a half-duplex flow of data on a connection: One endpoint waits while the other transmits, and only one end at a time sends data. This is the case for SNA 3270 traffic, for example. TCP connections, however, are full-duplex: data are able to flow both ways at the same time.

The compensation that allows a full-duplex transport user, such as TCP/IP, to use a transport provider that transfers data in half-duplex mode, such as SNA, is handled by the PMM, which establishes *two* half-duplex native connections: one for sending data, the other for receiving.

13.4.4   Record over stream

Some transport users, such as SNA, OSI, and NetBEUI, send data as distinct records; TCP/IP, does not. TCP/IP is called a *stream-oriented* protocol because it transmits a stream of bytes without consideration of record format. In order to delineate records that are sent over TCP/IP, there must be a way to delimit records so the destination PMM will know where they begin and end. Since records can be variable in length, each record must be recognized individually.

As will be recalled, a 4-byte length field is always inserted before data in a stream-oriented transport network. The 1-byte MPTN *record* header (X'00') is then inserted after the length field, to identify the beginning of a record. The 4-byte length field provides the length of the record. If another type of compensation is needed for the record, then the appropriate header is used instead of the X'00' record compensation header. X'00' headers therefore actually state that no other compensation is present.

13.4.5   Expedited data over normal data

Expedited data must be sent ahead of any normal data being transmitted on a connection. Expedited data are given first priority. When expedited data are received, the data are usually bumped to the front of the incoming data queue. The concept of expedited data is not supported in all transport network protocols and must therefore be compensated for if required by a transport user. Additionally, expedited data—if provided by a transport provider network—are not always handled similarly to the method used by the transport user.

Expedited data are compensated for by sending the expedited data along with an MPTN *expedited data* header (X'01'). After the expedited data and the header have been transmitted, the sending endpoint waits for an *expedited data acknowledgment* (X'03') to be returned from the partner PMM. If the acknowledgment does not arrive, the expedited data is sent in an MPTN_DG_OOB_Data datagram. Since the datagram travels outside the connection, it should circumvent the limits that have been imposed on the normal flow and a stalled or otherwise dysfunctional connection should not interfere with the datagram's arrival.

OSI and SNA transport networking protocols both support an expedited data service; NetBIOS does not. TCP/IP provides an URG (urgent) flag to signal that data being sent are more urgent than normal data, but during congestion, when the TCP window size has been reduced to 0, the transmission of data marked URG is not guaranteed. Therefore, in a TCP/IP network, MPTN *always* sends expedited data with an expedited data header rather than using the URG flag. If this fails, a UDP datagram (carrying the MPTN_DG_OOB_Data message) is sent, retransmitting the expedited data.

An example of sending expedited data over TCP/IP takes place when the SNA SIG (signal) command (designating Request-To-Send) is transmitted by a SNA transport user. If it is sent over a TCP/IP network, it is sent as expedited data with an expedited data MPTN header in the front of the RU packet and SNA data. The PMM sets a timer to wait for an expedited data acknowledgment. If the timer pops, the acknowledgment was not received. In that case, the source PMM sends a UDP datagram with an MPTN_DG_OOB_Data format containing the full packet—consisting of SNA sequence numbers, request header, and request unit—along with the expedited data header. Another timer is set for the receipt of the MPTN_DG_OOB_Data response. The target LU may end up receiving both SIG commands (the original one and the retransmitted version), but it only responds to one. (SNA has always worked this way; subsequent signals are rejected, either because the sequence number for both signals is the same, or because the first one was satisfied and the target's state subsequently changed.)

If the expedited data must be segmented, a *segmented expedited message* header (X'21') is appended to the front of the data.

13.4.6   Correlation of expedited data with normal data

Compensation is necessary for protocols that support expedited data and normal data that are packaged together. The stream-oriented protocol TCP/IP provides an example of this. A stream-oriented protocol sends data in chunks and has no regard for record boundaries. To support expedited data, TCP/IP identifies the place in a normal data stream where expedited data [marked with the URG (urgent) flag] begin. Compensation is required when TCP/IP is the transport user protocol and the transport provider protocol has support for out-of-band expedited data, but is not stream-oriented. Data must be separated into separate packets with the expedited data in a packet of their own.

If the expedited data must be segmented, a *segmented expedited message* header (X'21') is appended to the front of the data.

13.4.7 Differences in length

The maximum lengths supported by a transport user may be greater than those supported by the transport provider; in this case, compensation must be made. A difference in the maximum allowed length can occur for different reasons, and each case will be discussed separately.

13.4.7.1 Datagrams. When the maximum length allowed for datagrams differs between a transport user and the underlying transport provider, and the datagram being sent is longer than is allowed in the transport provider's network, the datagram must be segmented. Each of these segments becomes a segmented MPTN_Datagram in the transport provider network. The datagram can be reassembled based on the information in the header.

13.4.7.2 Expedited data. If expedited data are supported by a transport provider, but the expedited data are of greater length than that allowed by the provider, then the expedited data are segmented into packets that are not longer than the maximum expedited packet size. The first packet contains the *segmented expedited message* header (X'21'), and the last contains the *expedited message* header (X'01'), so the transport protocol must guarantee that the packets of segmented expedited data are delivered in the order in which they were sent.

For example, an OSI transport provider network can send expedited data using the T-EXPEDITED-DATA request, but only 16 bytes of data can be transferred by most OSI transport networks. A nonnative transport user, such as SNA, that can send larger amounts of expedited data may perhaps wish to transmit 40 bytes of expedited data. This can be divided into three OSI expedited packets. The first OSI packet contains the *segmented expedited message* header (X'21') plus 11 bytes of data. The next packet contains the X'21' header and the next 16 bytes; the last packet contains an *expedited message* header (X'01') and the remaining 13 bytes.

If the underlying transport protocol operates in such a manner that the above scenario cannot be enacted because the expedited packets may arrive out of order, then another method is used for mapping larger amounts of expedited data onto smaller maximum amounts. In this case, a length field and header is placed in front of the data as before, then as much data as can be sent in a single expedited packet is transmitted and the remaining data are sent in the normal data stream.

13.4.7.3 Records. If a record is too large for a transport network to handle, then the record must be segmented. Each of the resultant segments of the record contains a *segmented message* header (X'20'). The last segment contains a field (X'00') that identifies the segment as the final one. In this way the target transport user knows when the record is complete.

13.4.8 Datagrams over connections

In some cases, the transport user may have the ability to send datagrams, yet the underlying transport provider may not provide a datagram service. This is the case when SNA is the transport provider, because SNA is a connection-oriented networking protocol. In order to provide a datagram service using a networking protocol like SNA, a special connection (or in the case of SNA, a special conversation) must be created and dedicated to the exclusive purpose of sending datagrams between two endpoints. To ensure that such connections do not proliferate needlessly, a timer is associated with each one; after a designated period of inactivity, the connection is terminated.

13.4.9 Connection termination differences

The various networking protocols provide different ways in which connections are terminated. Since a transport user may require a different method of termination than can be provided by a nonnative transport provider, MPTN compensations must be provided. Three termination differences are compensated for:

- Graceful termination over abortive termination
- Simplex termination over duplex termination
- Duplex termination over simplex termination

13.4.9.1 Graceful termination over abortive termination. If the transport provider closes its connections without ensuring that any data that are still in transit or in buffers awaiting delivery are sent to the destination before the connection is terminated, this is called an *abortive* termination. A *graceful* termination is a termination that will not close a connection until all data that are still sitting in buffers, or in transit, are delivered properly. If the transport user requires that a graceful termination take place, and a nonnative transport provider provides only an abortive termination, then compensation is required.

To perform the compensation, the PMM performing the termination sends a packet with an MPTN header of either *duplex-orderly termination* (X'14') or *simplex-orderly termination* (X'1C'). The packet contains the termination data, if there are any; otherwise, just the MPTN header itself is sent. When the receiving PMM receives the packet, it issues a *simplex-orderly termination acknowledgment* (X'1E') for a simplex termination. For a duplex termination, when the CMM receives the duplex-orderly termination header, it sends back the *duplex-orderly termination acknowledgment* (X'16') along with any data that remain to be sent.

SNA and OSI both have abortive termination, whereas TCP/IP and NetBIOS provide graceful termination.

13.4.9.2 Simplex termination over duplex termination. Some network protocols only allow a full-duplex connection to be closed in a single direction at a time. This is called a simplex termination. Other protocols close both sides of a full-duplex connection at the same time. This is a duplex termination. A simplex termination is terminated from the initiator of the request to the other endpoint (the *send* direction). SNA supports both simplex and duplex termination. TCP/IP supports simplex termination only. OSI and NetBIOS both support duplex termination and do not support simplex termination.

MPTN compensates for a simplex-over-duplex termination in the following way. One of the two transport endpoints issues a termination of an open connection. Since the transport user supports simplex termination of a connection, the connection must be closed in a single direction only. Since the transport provider supports a duplex close only, compensation must take place. To provide this, the issuing PMM sends a packet with either the *simplex-abortive termination* (X'18') or *simplex-orderly termination* (X'1C') header. The receiving PMM sets a flag noting that one-half of the session has been terminated and data can flow in only one direction. When the other transport user issues its simplex termination, the PMM can effect a full duplex termination, shutting down the entire connection.

13.4.9.3 Duplex termination over simplex termination. The reverse of the above situation takes place when the transport user requests a duplex termination and the transport provider can provide only a simplex termination. In this case, MPTN handles the compensation in the following way. The originating PMM, after receiving the request for a duplex termination, sends a *duplex-abortive termination* (X'10') or *duplex-orderly termination* (X'14') header and closes the send direction of the connection. After the other end of the connection receives the duplex termination header, it issues a duplex termination acknowledgment. Following this, the transport provider connection is closed from the other direction. Thus what amounts to a duplex termination has taken place.

13.4.10   Connection outage notification

Some transport network protocols, such as SNA, provide a service called *connection outage notification,* a method of informing users of network or link failures, should they occur. Other network protocols (NetBIOS, for example) do not perform this function. TCP/IP provides connection outage notification with a timer that is set when the SO_KEEPALIVE socket option has been selected. This timer typically "pops" after two hours of connection inactivity and sends a probe to the other endpoint to determine if that system is still active. Two hours is too long an interval to be used as a compensation by other transport protocols, such as SNA, and connection outage notification must be provided for in a TCP/IP network.

MPTN provides compensation for connection outage notification by exchanging *keepalive* messages to ensure that the other endpoint is still available. Two CMMs execute this MPTN keepalive compensation protocol if at least one of the connections between the two CMMs has a need for connection outage notification. An installation-defined setting defines a timer value. After inactivity between the nodes is detected for the amount of the timer value, the CMM's PMM sends a keepalive datagram. A maximum of five datagrams are sent. If the other node does not send a response and no other data are received from that node, the PMM terminates all connections that have requested connection outage notification.

13.5   Conclusion

The MPTN architecture provides a number of message formats. One of these, the MPTN_Datagram, is used not only for sending transport user datagrams across an MPTN network, but also for sending requests and responses to MPTN components such as an address mapper and multicast server. The formats for these commands are presented in the next chapter.

MPTN Address Mapping

14.1 Introduction

The topic of address mapping has been introduced up numerous times in the past four chapters. Now the subject will be discussed thoroughly. In fact, this entire chapter is dedicated to the subject.

Address mapping is a term that is perhaps unique to the MPTN architecture. In order to associate a transport user address with a nonnative transport provider address(es), an association, or a *mapping,* must be provided that links transport user and provider addresses.

The MPTN address mapper, the most significant provider of address mapping services in an MPTN network, will be described, and the ways that it can be configured will be covered. The command formats that are used by gateways and access nodes to communicate with the address mapper will then be detailed. The chapter concludes with an explanation of the MPTN multicast server.

14.2 Address Mapping

Because a transport user address and its associated nonnative transport provider address(es) can have different formats, a method of associating transport user and provider addresses was devised that enables transport users to continue to use their own address formats while, under the covers, the transport provider network performs routing and delivery of data using the address format native to the transport provider's networking protocol.

The transport user might be, for example, a SNA application program, and the transport provider an OSI network. In order to send data on the OSI network, the OSI address of the destination node must be determined (the destination transport user's SNA address would be useless in the OSI network). *Address mapping* deals with the issue of resolving one transport network address format into another.

The technique of address mapping is similar to the technique used by the ARP protocol described in Sec. 4.6.1. The similarity is that the ARP protocol maps a network address to a MAC address. In MPTN, a transport user address is mapped to a transport provider address.

Address mapping produces a set of addresses: a transport user address and the transport provider address(es) associated with the transport user address. Why can there be multiple transport provider addresses associated with a single transport user address? Because it is possible for more than one SPTN to connect a user to a destination node. For example, in a multiprotocol network with MPTN implemented for each protocol, any of the multiple protocols are potential transport provider candidates.

14.3   Address Mapping Services

MPTN transport gateways and access nodes provide two types of *address mapping services:*

- *Address registration.*   A transport user address and its associated transport provider address(es) are made available to other transport users in the MPTN network.

- *Address resolution.*   A transport user address is resolved to one or more transport provider addresses.

14.3.1   Address registration

One of the functions of address mapping services in the MPTN architecture is the registration of transport user addresses. When access node transport users "sign on" to an MPTN network, their addresses are registered using MPTN address-mapping services. The M_BIND_DC downcall triggers the actual registration (if the transport user has set the *regist* parameter). Either individual or group addresses can be registered. Registering a transport user address causes that address to be known and provides a way for the transport user to be located anywhere within an MPTN network. Stored along with transport user address are the transport provider address(es) that can be used to access that user.

14.3.2   Address resolution

Before a transport user can communicate with another transport user, it must acquire a transport provider address for that user. Transport user addresses that have been registered can be accessed by users of the MPTN network, and the transport provider addresses associated with that address can be retrieved. This is called *address resolution.* Address resolution is performed automatically when a transport user issues an M_CONNECT_DC or an M_SEND_DG_DC. In order for the CMM to determine the transport provider address of the destination, it must resolve the destination transport user's address into an appropriate transport provider address. This resolution of the partner address is performed by one of MPTN's three address mapping techniques.

14.4 Address Mapping Techniques

The MPTN architecture provides three different address mapping techniques:

- Algorithmic address mapping
- Protocol-specific directory
- The MPTN address mapper

These three techniques represent three possible ways that address mapping can be accomplished in an MPTN network. The first two techniques, if they are used, are implemented within a PMM. The third technique, the MPTN address mapper, is an optional MPTN component. Three techniques have been designated because each has advantages and disadvantages; by offering three different ways to implement address mapping services, the designer of an MPTN implementation is free to select the best fit. In actuality, a PMM can implement *any* type of address mapping technique.

Basically, the CMM understands two ways that address mapping can be performed: either by a PMM or by the address mapper client. When the CMM issues the P_INIT_DC to initialize the PMM before any processing takes place, the P_INIT_UC that the PMM sends back to the CMM as a response includes a field called *prov_info* which contains a pointer to a PROV_INFO structure. This structure contains the characteristics of the transport provider, among which is a characteristic called *addr_service.* Addr_service specifies the type of address mapping service provided by the transport provider—the address mapper or a PMM service.

If the CMM needs to access an address mapper for address mapping services, it uses the address mapper client, resident in access node and transport gateway CMMs, to request address mapping from the address mapper, known as the *address mapper server.* If the CMM needs to register or locate addresses using the PMM, it issues a P_REGISTER_DC or a P_LOCATE_DC. The relationship between the address mapper client and address mapper server will be covered later in this chapter.

We will now turn to a description of the three address mapping techniques specified in the MPTN architecture. We will begin with the two methods employed by the PMM.

14.4.1 Algorithmic address mapping

The first method of address mapping defined by MPTN is called *algorithmic address mapping*. Algorithmic address mapping simply uses an algorithm to map a transport user address into a nonnative transport provider address. The idea is very simple. An algorithm is a specific formula that can be used to translate an address belonging to one networking protocol into an address belonging to another. By applying this algorithm each time address mapping is required, a correct result is always attained.

An example of algorithmic address mapping could be the mapping of SNA addresses into TCP/IP addresses. If each address in a SNA network has been defined with an LU name in a range of LU001 to LU254, this range of SNA addresses could be mapped to corresponding TCP/IP addresses by taking the last three digits, the numbers from 1 to 254, and using them to create IP addresses in the range of, for example, 129.1.1.1 through 129.1.1.254.

The advantage to using the algorithmic address mapping technique is that an additional database is not required to store pairs of addresses for each transport user. Instead of consulting a database, the transport user address is crunched through the algorithm to generate a corresponding transport provider address dynamically. Also, since there is no database, an address database does not have to be modified when new addresses are added to the network. The algorithmic method, however, is limited in its use, and it is not very flexible.

14.4.2 Use of a protocol-specific directory

The second method of address mapping is the use of a *protocol-specific directory*. A protocol-specific directory is a directory service inherent to the native transport protocol. In other words, if the underlying transport provider network already has a service that can be used to contain MPTN address mappings, then this service can be used by MPTN.

An example of a protocol-specific directory is well illustrated by the Domain Name Service (DNS) used in TCP/IP networks and introduced in Chap. 4. DNS provides a name-to-IP address service. If the address mapping that is required has transport user addresses that consist of alphanumeric names, and the transport provider is a TCP/IP network, then DNS can be used.

For example, a SNA transport user might be used in conjunction with a TCP/IP transport provider. In this case, DNS can be used to store SNA LU names along with their IP address counterparts. In order to accomplish this, a domain name server must be configured with a subdomain name such as net1.dbr.com and a DNS resource record must be created for each LU name. Using DNS, NET1.LU1 becomes lu1.net1.dbr.com and the IP address obtained from DNS is the corresponding IP address for NET1.LU1. To implement a protocol-specific directory, the TCP/IP PMM implements the necessary code to resolve domain names.

The disadvantage of a protocol-specific directory, besides the fact that it cannot be implemented in every transport protocol, is that it will only be applicable to a single SPTN. If a transport user attempts to send a datagram or establish a connection with an end user in another SPTN, the address will not be in the protocol-specific directory, and a gateway must be contacted. In this case an address mapper may be required.

14.4.3 The MPTN address mapper

The most flexible way to map addresses in MPTN is to use an address mapper. The address mapper is a separate MPTN component that employs a database to store transport user-to-provider address mappings. Some protocol combinations, such as NetBIOS over SNA, require the use of an address mapper because 16-character NetBIOS names cannot be easily mapped to 8-character SNA LU names using the algorithmic method, nor does a SNA directory exist that can be used for protocol-specific directory mapping.

The address mapper employs a client/server model. The client part of the address mapper is resident in all MPTN CMMs, but the server part, which is the actual address mapper, is an entirely separate component. Only one address mapper needs to be loaded in an SPTN, although there are configurations, which will be discussed shortly, where more than one can be made available. The address mapper can be installed in either an MPTN transport gateway node or in an access node.

The address mapper is the only one of the three address mapping methods that is fully suitable for the MPTN architecture. The other two methods, algorithmic and protocol-specific directories, can be used when MPTN address resolution is confined to a single SPTN (they can be extended to more than one SPTN with some limitations by hardcoding addresses in transport gateways). The address mapper server provides address mapping services for all MPTN nodes in an SPTN. It also provides address mapping services for multiple SPTNs if they all share the same media. In other words, if two or more SPTNs run on the same physical media—a local area network that runs multiple protocols, for example—all nodes can access a single address mapper through different PMMs. Each of these transport network protocols is an SPTN, but since they all exist on the same LAN, they can use the same address mapper, each communicating with the mapper using their own native protocols. If the address mapper server resides in a gateway node, it can serve all of the SPTNs to which the gateway is attached.

14.5   About the Address Mapper

The address mapper server is a separate component in an MPTN network. It requires the services of a CMM, however, so it must be loaded in a gateway or access node. It has its own set of commands with which it communicates with other MPTN components.

14.5.1   Address mapper components

The address mapper, as we mentioned before, is designed using a client–server architecture. Figure 14.1 shows the relationship between the address mapper client and server. It can be seen from the figure that both the server and client components must communicate with CMMs. The client uses the TLPB of the CMM of which it is a part, and the server relies on the CMM in the node into which it has been loaded.

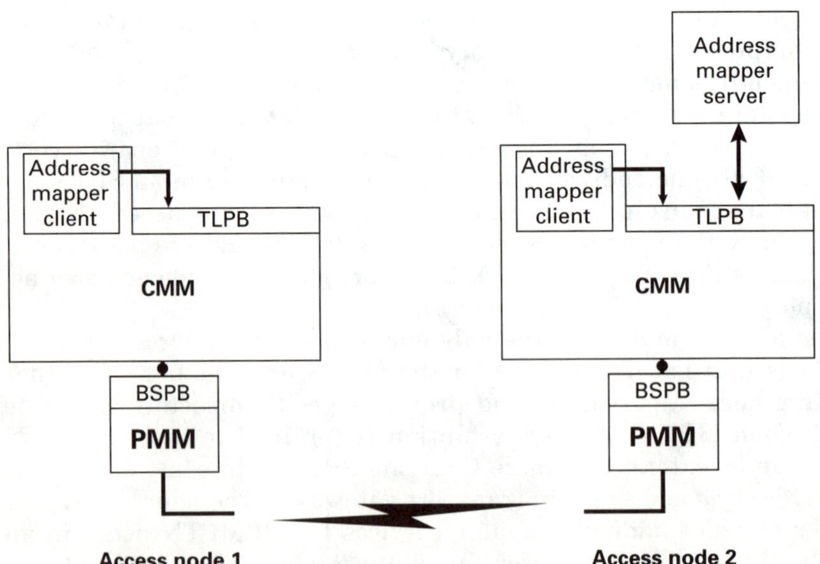

Figure 14.1 The relationship between an MPTN address mapper client and an MPTN address mapper server.

The address mapper client communicates with the TLPB of the CMM using datagram calls. It must first issue an M_RCVDG_INIT_DC, then it uses the M_SEND_DG_DC call to send messages and the M_RCV_DG_UC to receive messages. These messages are address mapper commands, to be discussed shortly. The address mapper server communicates with its TLPB using the same calls as the address mapper client to send and receive datagrams.

The address mapper has a database that is used to store address mappings. The database can be either *volatile,* meaning it is memory-resident, or *nonvolatile,* which means that it is disk-resident. The address mapper database is built dynamically as transport users enter the MPTN network and their addresses are registered.

The addresses that a CMM gets, either from an address mapper client or a PMM service, can be stored in an address *cache*. This ensures that repeated requests for address mappings are not performed unnecessarily. When an address mapping is needed, the CMM can simply check the cache, located in memory, to see if the address is already available before sending a locate request to either the address mapper client or a PMM. Suitable cache management routines can be implemented to ensure that cache entries are updated at certain intervals to remain current.

14.5.2 Address mapper commands

The MPTN architecture defines a set of commands that are used by an address mapper to communicate with transport gateway and access nodes. These commands will now be presented (Table 14.1).

TABLE 14.1   Address Mapper Commands

ABM_AM_LOCATE_REQUEST	Request to retrieve an address mapping
ABM_MA_LOCATE_REPLY	Reply to a locate request
ABM_AM_REGISTER_REQUEST	Request an address be registered with the address mapper
ABM_MA_REGISTER_REPLY	Reply to a register request
ABM_AM_DEREGISTER_REQUEST	Request address be deregistered with the address mapper
ABM_MA_DEREGISTER_REPLY	Reply to a deregister request
ABM_MA_I_AM_BACK_REQUEST	Address mapper is back after a network node failure
ABM_AM_NOT_FOUND_REQUEST	An address obtained from the address mapper was not valid
ABM_MA_R_U_THERE_REQUEST	Will a node at a specific address respond?

Address mapper commands are placed in the *user datagram* field of MPTN_Datagrams. In other words, the address mapper commands are wholly contained within an MPTN_Datagram. The MPTN_Datagram fields specified in Chap. 13, and shown in Table 13.9, will all be present. It is in the user datagram field (shown at the bottom of Table 13.9) that the address mapper command begins.

At the beginning of each address mapper command is an *address mapper header.* This header resembles the MPTN message format in its layout. The address mapper header has a prefix that resembles the common prefix of the datagram header. Since the address mapper header follows the MPTN_Datagram message fields, there is no routing prefix; however, there are required and optional fields that are specific to the address mapper header. The address mapper header is shown in Table 14.2. The *address mapper command type* contains the hexadecimal value for the particular address mapper command. Each command has a different command type.

Address mapper commands are prefixed with ABM, the acronym that is used for the address mapper, for easy identification. Following the ABM prefix is another prefix. This second prefix indicates the direction of the command, to or from the address mapper, and it is set according to the following codes:

- _AM_: Access node (or gateway) to address mapper

- _MA_: Address mapper to access node (or gateway)

Commands that are sent to the address mapper from a gateway or access node begin with ABM_AM, and commands sent from an address mapper to an access node or gateway begin with ABM_MA.

If a command can be executed without incurring too much delay, the results are placed in the response to the command (the MPTN_Datagram response). Otherwise, the response is sent back with the return code set to RC_PENDING, which informs the sender of the command that the data will be forthcoming. The data are then returned in a REPLY version of the original REQUEST (and the reply must be responded to). If the command received an error, a negative response is returned with a *diagnostics* optional field.

The required fields for address mapper commands are as follows.

- *Command modifier.* This field is used to identify certain options in some of the commands.

- *Transaction identifier.* This field is used to correlate address mapper transactions. If a response is not received within the allotted time, a request is resent using the same transaction identifier. In this way, responses and requests are all grouped within the same transactions. The transaction identifier is also used to relate replies

TABLE 14.2   Address Mapper Header

Address Mapper Header Prefix		
Command type:		1 byte
ABM_AM_REGISTER_REQUEST	X'A1'	
ABM_AM_DEREGISTER_REQUEST	X'A2'	
ABM_AM_LOCATE_REQUEST	X'A5'	
ABM_MA_I_AM_BACK_REQUEST	X'A8'	
ABM_MA_REGISTER_REPLY	X'B1'	
ABM_MA_DEREGISTER_REPLY	X'B2'	
ABM_MA_LOCATE_REPLY	X'B5'	
ABM_AM_NOT_FOUND_REQUEST	X'B8'	
ABM_MA_R_U_THERE_REQUEST	X'E0'	
Processing specification		1 byte
Command length		2 bytes
Required Fields		
Command modifier		1 byte
Transaction identifier		2–9 bytes
Return code		3 bytes
Optional Fields		
Source CMM routing		(9–262 bytes)
Source CMM routing prefix	X'A1'	4 bytes
Source CMM address	MPTN-qualified transport address	5–258 bytes
Address mapper's alias		(9–262 bytes)
Address mapper's alias prefix	X'A3'	4 bytes
Address mapper's alias	MPTN-qualified transport address	5–258 bytes
Diagnostics (for responses only)		(18–799 bytes)
Diagnostics prefix	X'F0'	4 bytes
Primary return code		4 bytes
Secondary return code		4 bytes
Error detector address	MPTN-qualified transport address	5–512 bytes
Error detector data		1–255 bytes

to an original request. This is necessary when a request is responded to with an RC_PENDING.

■ *Return code.*   The possible return codes for address mapper commands are shown in Table 14.3.

Two optional fields are always present in address mapper commands.

■ *Source CMM routing.*   This optional field is identified by its prefix, A1. It contains the address of the CMM from which the address mapper command was issued.

TABLE 14.3   Address Mapper Command Return Codes

OK	X'00'	Success
USER_NOT_FOUND	X'02'	Transport user address not in the address tables
USER_NOT_REACHABLE	X'03'	The network of the transport user cannot be reached
ADDRESS_CONFLICT	X'04'	Multiple registrations found for transport user address
DUPLICATE ADDRESS	X'05'	Transport user address already in use
CONFLICT_WITH_INDIVIDUAL_ADDRESS	X'06'	Multicast group name conflicts with individual user address
PENDING	X'07'	Result of request will arrive in a reply
UNAUTHORIZED_ACTION	X'08'	The action was not authorized
MULTICAST_GROUP_ALREADY_EXISTS	X'09'	The multicast group name already exists

■ *Address mappers alias.*   This optional field is identified by its prefix, A3, and contains the address mapper's *alias address,* a local-form address used by the address mapper. A local-form address (MPTN qualifier 7F) is a free-form address that a transport user can use any way it wants. CMMs and PMMs sometimes use free-form addresses to create an *alias* for an MPTN address to be used as a fast index into control blocks.

A number of optional fields are used for individual commands. These are shown in Table 14.4.

The address mapper commands will now be presented.

ABM_AM_LOCATE_REQUEST.   The ABM_AM_LOCATE_REQUEST command is sent by an address mapper client to an address mapper server when an access node or transport gateway wishes to obtain an address mapping. The command type for this command is X'A5'. The fields associated with this command are numerous.

The command modifier is set to indicate the type of locate the address mapper client is requesting.

Type 1 (X'01').   Obtain the transport provider address(es) associated with a transport user address.

Type 2 (X'02').   Obtain the transport user address(es) associated with a transport provider address.

TABLE 14.4   Optional Fields: Address Mapper Commands

Optional field name	Prefix	Command(s) that use the field
Count of registered pairs	X'15'	ABM_MA_I_AM_BACK_REQUEST
Volatility flag	X'16'	ABM_MA_I_AM_BACK_REQUEST
Alias address	X'A3'	ABM_MA_I_AM_BACK_REQUEST
Requester's supported providers	X'A6'	ABM_AM_LOCATE_REQUEST
Transport user's address	X'A7'	ABM_MA_NOT_FOUND_REQUEST
		ABM_AM_REGISTER_REQUEST
		ABM_AM_DEREGISTER_REQUEST
		ABM_AM_LOCATE_REQUEST
Transport provider's address	X'A8'	ABM_AM_NOT_FOUND_REQUEST
		ABM_AM_DEREGISTER_REQUEST
		ABM_AM_LOCATE_REQUEST
Transport user's address list	X'A9'	ABM_MA_LOCATE_REPLY
Transport provider's address list	X'AA'	ABM_MA_LOCATE_REPLY
		ABM_AM_REGISTER_REQUEST
Transport provider information field	X'AB'	ABM_MA_LOCATE_REPLY
Requester's user address	X'AC'	ABM_AM_LOCATE_REQUEST
Registrant/requested MPTN type	X'AD'	ABM_AM_REGISTER_REQUEST
		ABM_AM_LOCATE_REQUEST
Transport user information list	X'AE'	ABM_MA_LOCATE_REPLY
User data	X'AF'	ABM_AM_REGISTER_REQUEST
		ABM_MA_LOCATE_REPLY
Transport user's address mask	X'BO'	ABM_AM_REGISTER_REQUEST
		ABM_AM_LOCATE_REQUEST
		ABM_MA_LOCATE_REPLY
Load level	X'B1'	ABM_AM_REGISTER_REPLY
Dubious validity flag	X'B2'	ABM_MA_LOCATE_REPLY
Limited-use cache	X'B3'	ABM_MA_LOCATE_REPLY
		ABM_MA_REGISTER_REPLY

Type 3 (X'03').   Obtain the transport provider address(es) based on an MPTN type. MPTN types, listed in Table 14.5, enumerate the various MPTN components.

The type 1 ABM_AM_LOCATE_REQUEST command is issued by a CMM's address mapper client. When a transport user issues an M_CONNECT_DC or an M_SEND_DG_DC, the CMM signals the address mapper client to obtain transport provider address(es) associated with a transport user address. The address mapper client sends

TABLE 14.5   MPTN Types

Non-MPTN node	X'01'
MPTN access node	X'02'
MPTN gateway node	X'04'
Address mapper	X'08'
Multicast server	X'16'

the type 1 ABM_AM_LOCATE_REQUEST by issuing an M_SEND_DG_DC to the CMM's TLPB.

The response is either sent directly, as part of the response to the command (an MPTN_Datagram response), or is sent in an ABM_MA_LOCATE_REPLY. If the data are not sent in the response, the return code in the response is set to RC_PENDING to inform the address mapper client that the data will be forthcoming. See the ABM_MA_LOCATE_REPLY for a description of the data that is returned to the access node.

The type 2 ABM_AM_LOCATE_REQUEST command is reserved for future use. It can be used for retrieving network management information, for example.

The type 3 ABM_AM_LOCATE_REQUEST command is issued to discover all transport provider addresses of a certain type, for example, all non-MPTN nodes, all transport gateways, or all address mappers. Using a wildcard with a type 3 request, one could locate, say, all SNA MPTN gateways.

A number of optional fields are necessary for this command.

- *Service mode.*   This optional field, with an ID of X'05', specifies the level of service needed by a transport user. The MPTN service mode is defined in a byte using one of the MPTN service mode values listed in Table 13.6. This field can have a size of up to 255 ASCII bytes, preceded by a 1-byte length, to be used with user-defined values. The service mode optional field was described in Chap. 13.

- *Requester's user address field.*   Optional field X'AC' defines the requester's address. This is the address of the originator of the locate command.

- *Requester's supported providers.*   Optional field X'A6' contains a list of the transport providers supported by the CMM of the requester. The list consists of a string of MPTN qualifiers. The qualifiers were presented in Chap. 13 as the first byte in an MPTN-qualified address, and are shown in Table 13.2. The qualifiers specify the type of protocol to which the transport user's address belongs. This field is used only in a type 1 locate.

- *Transport user's address field.* Optional field X'A7' contains the transport user address that is needed for a type 1 locate, or a wildcard address for a type 3 locate when the scope of the search is to be limited.

- *Transport provider's address field.* Optional field X'A8' is used to store a transport provider address for a type 2 locate.

- *Requested MPTN type field.* This optional field has a prefix value of X'AD' and contains a 1-byte MPTN type and a 1-byte qualifier. The MPTN types are shown in Table 14.5. These are hex values that represent an MPTN component. The qualifiers were presented in Chap. 13 as the first byte in an MPTN-qualified address and are shown in Table 13.2. They specify the type of protocol to which the transport user's address belongs. The requested MPTN type field is used by the address mapper to identify the type and protocol for the address it is locating.

- *Transport user's address mask.* This optional field has a prefix value of X'B0' and contains a wildcard mask. The wildcard mask is a form of MPTN-qualified address with only the significant bits that represent the static positions in the transport user's address turned on. In other words, if a bit is on in the mask, then it is significant in the transport user address; otherwise it is considered to be "wild". The wildcard mask optional field is included only in type 3 locates when the transport user's address represents a wildcard address.

ABM_MA_LOCATE_REPLY. After an ABM_AM_LOCATE_REQUEST is sent to an address mapper server, the resolution of the request is returned either as the datagram response or as an ABM_MA_LO-CATE_REPLY. Either way, the same fields are returned. The following optional fields are returned.

- *Transport provider's address list.* Optional field X'AA' contains a count, then a list of transport provider addresses associated with a transport user. This field is used only in a type 1 locate response.

- *Transport provider information field.* Optional field X'AB' contains the transport provider address, dubious validity flag, and optional user data field for each transport provider found in a type 1 locate.

- *Dubious validity flag.* Optional field X'B2' contains the dubious validity flag that can be returned on a type 1 locate response. This flag is maintained by the address mapper and indicates that the validity of a transport user/provider mapping is dubious because a previous transport user was unable to contact the transport user successfully using the transport provider address.

- *User data field.*   This optional field has a prefix value of X'AF'. User data is a string of bytes that is to be associated with the transport user's address in the address mapper database. Transport user syntax mappers can make use of this field to store relevant data.

- *Limited-use cache field.*   This optional field has a prefix value of X'B3'. The limited-use cache field contains a cache count from the address mapping cache located in the address mapper. This count tells the CMM that issued the locate that this address mapping information may be valid for an indefinite length of time. Gateways use the limited-use cache field in an address mapper for load balancing.

- *Transport user's address mask.*   This optional field has a prefix value of X'B0' and contains the wildcard mask. The wildcard mask is a form of MPTN-qualified address with only the significant bits that represent the static positions in the transport user's address turned on. This wildcard mask optional field is included only when the transport user address is actually a wildcard address.

- *Transport user's address list.*   This optional field has a prefix value of X'A9' and contains all the registered transport user addresses that are associated with the transport provider address specified in a type 2 or 3 locate.

- *Transport user information field.*   This optional field has a prefix value of X'AE' and is used on a type 2 locate response to return optional user data for each transport user associated with the requested transport provider address.

ABM_AM_REGISTER_REQUEST. The ABM_AM_REGISTER_REQUEST command is sent by an address mapper client to an address mapper server to register a transport user address and its associated transport provider address(es). This process of registering an address takes place when a transport user issues an M_BIND_DC with the *regist* parameter set. If the address mapper is to be used, the CMM, when it receives the M_BIND_DC, signals the address mapper client component located in the CMM. The client then sends the ABM_AM_REGISTER_REQUEST command by issuing an M_SEND_DG_DC to the CMM's TLPB. The list of transport provider addresses sent along with the ABM_AM_REGISTER_REQUEST is derived from the endpoint control block that was originally set up by the M_CREATE_DC.

The ABM_AM_REGISTER_REQUEST can also be used to register a group address if the transport provider supports multicasting. In this case, the ABM_AM_REGISTER_REQUEST asks the address mapper for a transport provider group name that corresponds with the transport user's group name. If none is available, the address mapper requests that a transport provider group name be created.

The response to the command can carry the appropriate reply data, or the data can be sent back as an ABM_MA_REGISTER_REPLY. In the later case, the response for the ABM_AM_REGISTER_REQUEST contains a return code of RC_PENDING.

The command type for this command is X'A1'. The address mapper header command modifier field, although not used in every other address mapper command, is used in a few commands, and here it is set to indicate one of three conditions concerning the transport user address that is being registered.

X'00': The transport user address is unique.

X'01': The transport user address requires verification.

X'02': The transport user address is a multicast group.

A number of optional fields are used with this command.

- *Transport user's address.*   Optional field X'A7' contains the transport user address to be registered. The mode byte in the address indicates if the address belongs to a group or not.

- *Transport provider's address list.*   Optional field X'AA' contains a count and a list of transport providers that are associated with the transport user address being registered.

- *Registrant's MPTN type field.*   This optional field has a prefix value of X'AD' and contains a 1-byte registrant's MPTN type and a 1-byte registrant's qualifier. The MPTN types (Table 14.5) are hex values that represent an MPTN component. The qualifiers were presented in Chap. 13 (Table 13.2) and specify the type of protocol to which the transport user's address belongs. The registrant's MPTN type field is used by the address mapper to identify what type of transport user address it is registering.

- *User data field.*   This optional field has a prefix value of X'AF". User data is a string of bytes that can be associated with the transport user's address in the address mapper. The string is returned in any subsequent locate requests for this transport user.

- *Transport user's address mask.*   This optional field has a prefix value of X'B0' and contains the wildcard mask. The wildcard mask is a form of MPTN-qualified address with only the significant bits that represent the static positions in the transport user's address turned on. This wildcard mask optional field is included only when the transport user address is actually a wildcard address.

ABM_MA_REGISTER_REPLY.   The ABM_MA_REGISTER_REPLY is sent in reply to the ABM_AM_REGISTER_REQUEST if the data were not returned in the response to the ABM_AM_REGISTER_REQUEST. A return code indicates if the registration was successful or not, and an *address conflict* parameter is set if the address was already registered (which can happen if a user did not verify a previous registration). *Duplicate* is returned if the transport user address was already registered by another access node. Gateways can register duplicate transport user addresses, since the address can be available through more than a single gateway. A *multicast group already exists* condition is returned if a multicast group address is already registered. In this case, the transport provider address(es) that are registered for this group address are returned in the ABM_MA_REGISTER_REPLY so that the requester can use the address(es) to issue group joins in the transport provider(s) to which it has access.

A number of optional fields are necessary for this command.

- *Load level field.*   This optional field has a prefix value of X'B1'. When there are multiple paths to a destination through parallel MPTN gateways, this field allows the gateways to balance the load between them more effectively.

- *Limited-use cache field.*   This optional field has a prefix value of X'B3'. The limited-use cache field is used in conjunction with the load-level field. It contains a count that applies to the address mapping cache, and tells the access node that address mapping information is based on something that may change over time.

ABM_AM_DEREGISTER_REQUEST.   The ABM_AM_DEREGISTER_RE-QUEST command is issued by an address mapper client to delete one or more registered transport user/provider pairs. The command type for this command is X'A2'. The address mapper header command modifier field, although it is not used in all other address mapper commands, is used here and is set to indicate one of four types of deregistration.

X'00': Delete all address pairs associated with this client except those that are associated with the requester itself.

X'01': Delete all transport users associated with a particular transport provider address.

X'02': Delete a single transport user and all of its associated transport provider addresses.

X'03': Delete a single transport user/provider.

Two optional fields are sometimes required in this command.

- *Transport user's address.*   Optional field X'A7' is included in the command if the command modifier is set to either X'02' or X'03'. It contains the transport user address that is to be deregistered.

- *Transport provider's address.*   Optional field X'A8' is included in the command if the command modifier is set to either X'01' or X'03'. It contains the transport provider address that is to be used when a deregistration based on a transport provider address is requested.

ABM_MA_DEREGISTER_REPLY.   The ABM_MA_DEREGISTER_REPLY is sent if ABM_AM_DEREGISTER_REQUEST could not be processed within a short time (the REPLY commands are used to prevent ABM_AM_ commands from blocking for too long). A return code indicates if the deregister request was successful or not, or if an unauthorized deregister request was issued (an access node tried to deregister addresses belonging to another access node).

The command type for this command is X'B2'.

ABM_MA_I_AM_BACK_REQUEST.   The ABM_MA_I_AM_BACK_RE-QUEST message is sent by the address mapper server to all of its clients each time it is loaded. The address mapper clients are located in CMMs whose addresses have been stored in the address mapper's database. This command also includes a indicator to specify if address mappings have been preserved since the last load of the address mapper, a count of the address mappings that have been retained for each of the address mapper's clients, and the time the last command was received from each client. These data can be examined by the CMMs to determine if recovery proceedings should be initiated or not.

The command type for this command is X'A8', and three optional fields are defined.

- *Alias address.*   Optional field X'A3' contains the address mapper's alias address. This address is used for reference in all subsequent commands sent to and from the address mapper.

- *Count of registered pairs.*   This 2-byte optional field, with an identifier of X'15', contains the number of transport user/provider address pairs stored in the address mapper's database for this client and is present only if the following optional field, the volatility flag, is present (if registrations were stored in volatile memory, they were not retained through a reloading process).

- *Volatility flag.*   The volatility flag optional field is assigned an ID of X'16' and indicates whether the address mapper's database is stored in volatile memory or on a nonvolatile hard disk. The presence of this optional field means that the address mapper uses nonvolatile storage to contain its address pairs.

ABM_AM_NOT_FOUND_REQUEST.   The ABM_AM_NOT_FOUND_RE-QUEST is sent to an address mapper server by an address mapper client to notify the address mapper server that an address that had been previously retrieved from the address mapper server has proven to be unusable. The CMM that issues this command has found that the node (or the network) represented by the address was unreachable when the CMM issued a datagram or connection request destined for it.

The ABM_AM_NOT_FOUND_REQUEST has a command type of X'B8'. Two optional fields are necessary for this command.

- *Transport user's address.*   Optional field X'A7' contains the transport user address that the node was attempting to reach.

- *Transport provider's address.*   Optional field X'A8' contains the transport provider address which was previously obtained from the address mapper server.

ABM_MA_R_U_THERE_REQUEST. The address mapper server sends the ABM_MA_R_U_THERE_REQUEST command to determine if an access node or gateway is active or not. This command is usually sent by the address mapper because an ABM_AM_NOT_FOUND was sent to the address mapper, indicating that a node was unreachable (nodes that were formerly active can become nonavailable due to system or network failures). The ABM_MA_R_U_THERE_REQUEST verifies that an ABM_AM_NOT_FOUND message was valid. When an access node receives an ABM_MA_R_U_THERE_REQUEST command, it simply returns an immediate positive response. For this reason there is no need for a special reply format for this command. The address mapper command type for ABM_MA_R_U_THERE_REQUEST is 'E0'.

14.5.3   Address mapper functions

The address mapper server has five basic functions:

- Initialization
- Termination
- Synchronization
- Registration
- Resolution

Each of these functions will be described individually.

14.5.3.1   Initialization.   The address mapper server's initialization function takes place when an access node or gateway is loaded either normally or after a network or system failure. When an access or gateway node is first loaded, the address mapper client's initialization routine locates an address mapper server, if one is in use. The method of doing this is implementation-dependent. It can be accomplished by the access node's PMMs using a technique of broadcasting, or multicasting. There are a number of other ways that an access node CMM's address mapper client can be written to find the address of an address mapper server. In fact, its address could be hard-coded in a configuration file. The address mapper server, as a transport user, will have issued an M_CREATE_DC and an M_BIND_DC, and its CMM will recognize the address as one belonging to address mapper server because the *address mode* is set to indicate that fact. It will be up to the PMMs in the node in which the address mapper server is loaded to receive commands that are broadcast from address mapper clients looking for an address mapper server and pass these requests in M_RCV_DG_UCs to the address mapper server. Again, this process of address mapper clients discovering a server is implementation-dependent.

The net result of the above is that a PMM in the node in which an address mapper server is loaded will, in whichever way the task has been implemented, inform any nodes looking for an address mapper server that it in fact has an address mapper server. If the network in which an address mapper server is loaded is a multiprotocol network and the access or gateway node that has been looking for the address mapper has performed the search using more than one of the transport protocols of the multiprotocol network, it will receive back more than one transport provider address for the address mapper. It will have to determine if these multiple addresses are for the same address mapper by examining the CMM source address returned by both replies.

After one or more transport provider addresses for an address mapper server have been located, the initialization function actually takes place. When the first command is sent from an access or gateway node to an address mapper server, it creates a relationship between client and server. The first command registers the particular node's transport provider address along with the transport user address for the address mapper client. This registration *must* take place before any other transport user addresses are registered. Next, an ABM_AM_DEREGISTER_REQUEST type X'00' is sent by the CMM's address mapper client to deregister all the addresses currently assigned to it. This command causes the address mapper server to delete all address pairs that the access node registered previously, except the pair of addresses just registered, for the address mapper client in the access or gateway node. This function is performed so that any out-of-date address registrations inadvertently left over from the CMM's last use of the address mapper will not be used.

14.5.3.2 Termination. The termination function takes place when an access or gateway node closes down gracefully. At that time it must issue an ABM_AM_DEREGISTER_REQUEST type X'00' to deregister all the addresses currently assigned to it. This command causes the address mapper server to delete all address pairs that the access node registered except the pair of addresses that designate the access or gateway node itself and its address mapper client.

14.5.3.3 Synchronization. The synchronization function in the address mapper server is used to ensure integrity between access and gateway node clients and the address mapper server. A system or network failure can cause a loss of synchronization between clients and server, and resynchronization must then be performed.

Synchronization in the address mapper server begins when the address mapper server is loaded. It first sends an ABM_MA_I_AM_BACK_REQUEST message to all clients in the active client list that it maintains. This message has an indicator to specify if address mappings have been preserved since the last load of the address mapper, a count of the address mappings that have been retained for each of the address mapper's clients, and the time the last command was received from each client. The address mapper clients in the various CMMs will be able to examine these data to determine if recovery proceedings should be initiated or not. If it appears that the address mapper is out of synchronization with the node, the node can issue a ABM_AM_DEREGISTER_REQUEST type X'00' to deregister all the addresses currently assigned to it. This command causes the address mapper server to delete all address pairs that the node registered, except the pair of addresses that designate the access or gateway node itself. Transport users belonging to the node that just deregistered all of its addresses have to reregister their addresses with the address mapper to build the database back up.

Another feature of address mapper synchronization is performed when a gateway or access node reports that an address held by the address mapper has been found to be unreachable. This is accomplished by the node sending an ABM_AM_NOT_FOUND_REQUEST. When the address mapper receives one of these requests, it marks the entry that was not found as of "dubious validity," then sends an ABM_MA_R_U_THERE_REQUEST to that address to determine if the node is really alive or not. If the node is alive, the "dubious" flag is turned off. The ABM_MA_R_U_THERE_REQUEST can be scheduled to be resent at intervals. Every 2 hours, the mapper goes through the list of clients; if there are any "dubious validity" flags that are over 2 hours old, the entries are removed.

14.5.3.4 Registration. The registration process is essential for an address mapper server, because it must create a database of address mappings to be used for satisfying address resolution requests. As has been explained, CMMs in access and gateway nodes register addresses of new transport users with an address mapper server if one is used in the MPTN network. This is accomplished by the CMM when the M_BIND_DC is issued by a transport user. All the transport provider addresses associated with the CMM are stored in the endpoint control block created by the M_CREATE_DC and are registered along with the transport user address. These can be placed in an order of preference.

The registration is performed by the address mapper client in a CMM which issues an MPTN_Datagram containing an ABM_AM_ REGISTER_REQUEST. If the command modifier field is set to a X'01', the address mapper verifies that the transport user address has not already been registered by another node. In the case of a gateway, however, duplicate entries are allowed because two gateways can register the same address.

Gateway nodes can register addresses for entire networks that are accessible to them using a wildcard address to represent that network. For example, one gateway could register network address NETAxxxx, another NETBxxxx. Network NETAxxxx could contain LU names in the range of NETA.LU1 through NETA.LU9 and NETBxxxx could contain LU names in the range of NETB.LU1 through NETB.LU9. When wildcards are registered, the address mapper stores the wildcard address and the mask along with the associated transport provider address.

Another feature of registration is the use of the *user data* field in the ABM_AM_REGISTER_REQUEST. This field can be used to pass user-specific data to the address mapper server to be stored along with the registration for the address. The data can be retrieved later using an ABM_AM_LOCATE_REQUEST.

Multicast group addresses are registered with an address mapper server. This feature allows multicast group addresses to be mapped to various transport providers. Group registration is performed by a CMM's address mapper client sending an ABM_AM_REGISTER_ REQUEST to the address mapper server with the group address and a null value for the transport provider address. If the group has already been registered, the address mapper sends back the transport provider address(es) that are associated with that group entry and increments a count associated with the group that keeps track of the number of users contained within it. When the node that has requested the multicast group registration receives the reply containing the transport provider addresses, it can use any of the addresses that match a transport provider protocol with which it has an active association and join groups in those networks either natively or using an MPTN multicast server that is active for that protocol.

14.5.3.5 Resolution. The resolution of transport user addresses is the primary function of the address mapper server. When a gateway or access node needs to resolve a transport user address to a corresponding transport provider address, the address mapper client formats an MPTN_Datagram containing an ABM_AM_LOCATE_REQUEST and sends this to the address mapper server to resolve.

The address mapper server resolves the request by checking its memory cache (which contains the most recently used registration pairs). If the address is not located in the memory cache, the non-volatile database (if one exists) is searched. If a match is found, the transport provider address(es) that is registered for the matching transport user address is returned either in the response to the request or in a reply. If more than one address pair is returned, the requester has to select which transport provider to use.

If the address mapper server cannot find an address, wildcard addresses are compared for a match. Each wildcard entry is checked, and the one with the longest match is picked. If there are more than one with the longest match, then all matches are sent back in the reply. If the destination address is located in the same SPTN, the destination's transport provider address(es) is returned, otherwise the transport gateway transport provider addresses for the next hop is returned to the requesting CMM.

14.5.4   Address mapper configurations

Address mapper servers can be configured in an MPTN network in a number of ways. Four basic configurations will be presented:

- One address mapper server in an SPTN

- Multiple address mapper servers in an SPTN

- One address mapper server shared by multiple SPTNs

- Multiple address mapper servers shared by multiple SPTNs

The four basic configurations will now each be discussed.

14.5.4.1   One address mapper server for each SPTN.   A single address mapper server can be configured for an SPTN. This configuration provides no backup in case of a failure. Figure 14.2 shows an SPTN with a single address mapper server.

14.5.4.2   Multiple address mapper servers in an SPTN.   Figure 14.3 shows an SPTN with two address mapper servers. One of the address mapper servers is the active address mapper, and the other is called a *virgin backup address mapper.* The term *virgin* is used to show that the backup address mapper contains no history of the registrations that the active address mapper has kept. In this case, clients have to reregister all of their addresses if the active address mapper server should fail and the virgin address mapper server take over. The

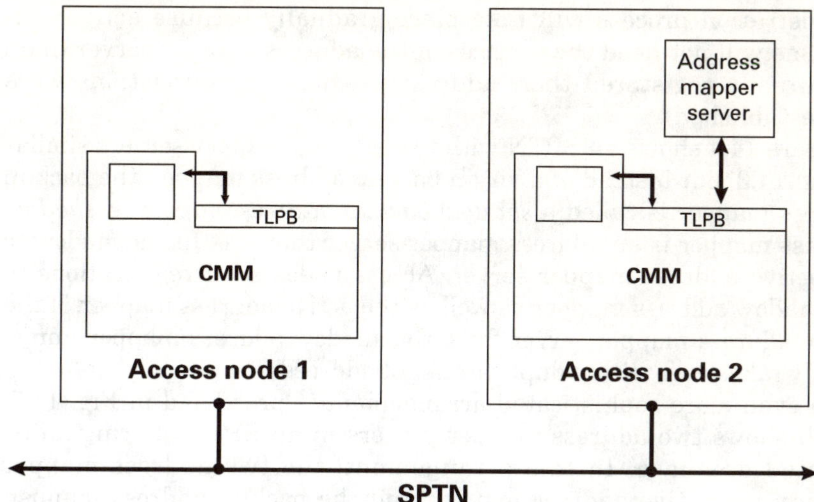

Figure 14.2   An SPTN containing a single address mapper.

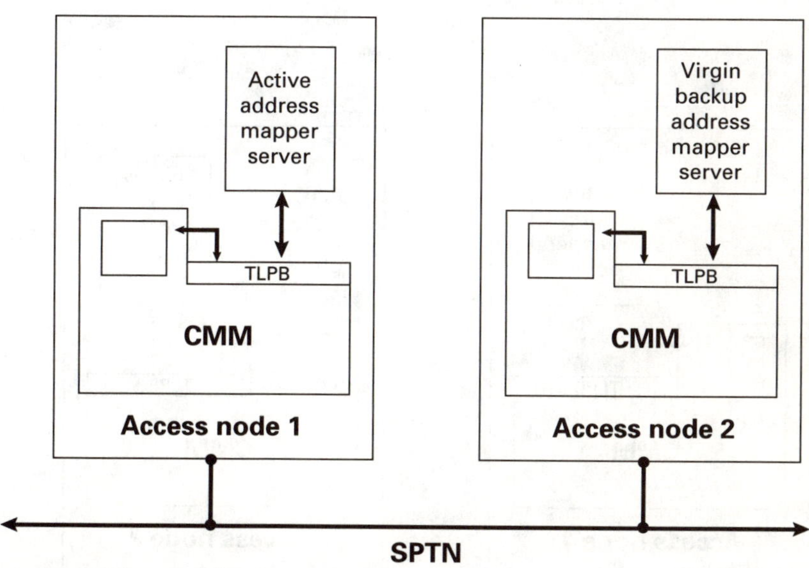

Figure 14.3   An SPTN with an active address mapper and a virgin backup address mapper.

reregistration process will take place gradually because active connections will not need the services of the address mapper server (having already registered their addresses when the connections were first established).

Figure 14.4 shows an SPTN with two address mapper servers similar to Fig. 14.3, but instead of a virgin backup address mapper, the backup address mapper is called a *shadow backup address mapper.* A *shadow* address mapper is an address mapper server that acts like a shadow to the active address mapper server. Access nodes send registrations to the shadow address mapper as well as the active address mapper. If the active address mapper server fails, the shadow address mapper immediately takes over with a duplicate set of address mappings.

An even more sophisticated arrangement is presented in Fig. 14.5, which shows two address mapper servers in an SPTN sharing a distributed database. In this arrangement, the two address mapper servers, the active address mapper and the backup address mapper, both share a common (distributed) database. If the active address mapper fails, the backup address mapper takes over. Since they are both accessing the same database, there is seamless consistency from one mapper to the other.

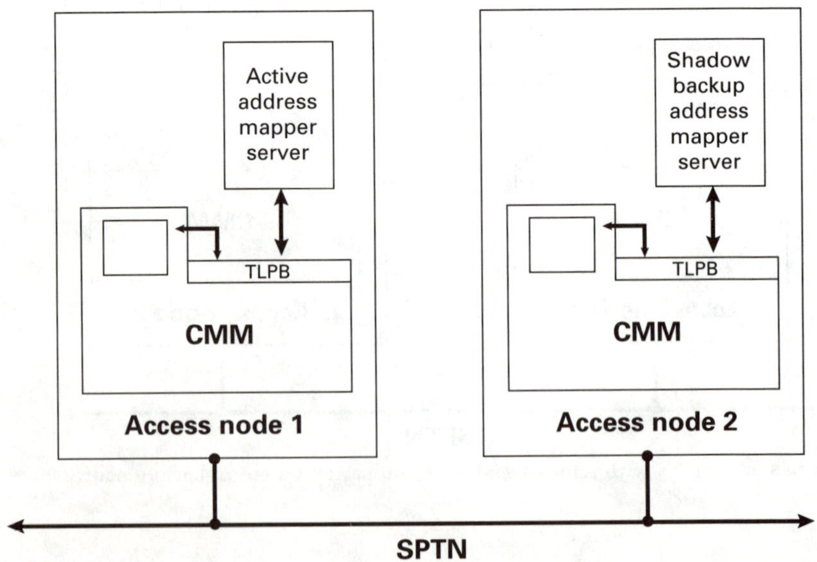

Figure 14.4 An SPTN with an active address mapper and a shadow backup address mapper.

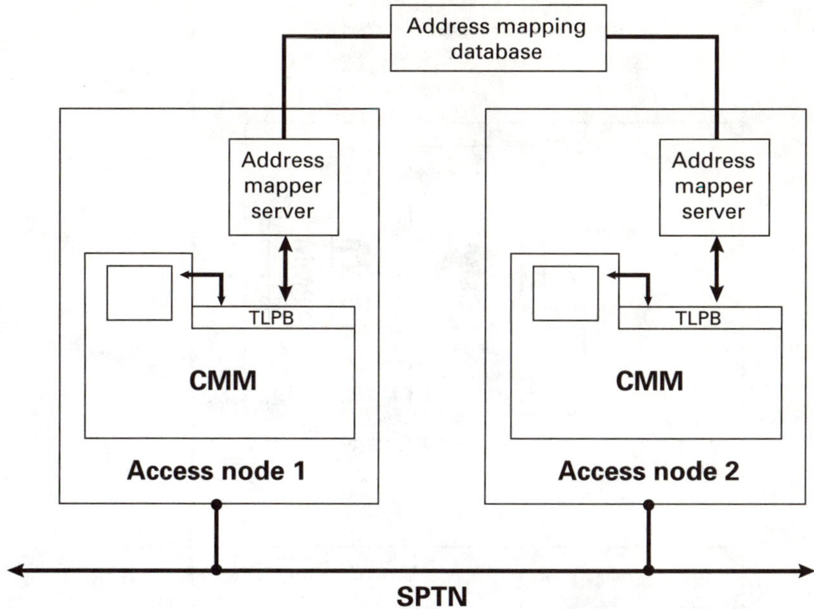

Figure 14.5 An SPTN with two address mappers that share a common address mapping database.

14.5.4.3 One address mapper server shared by multiple SPTNs. A single address mapper server can provide its services to any number of SPTNs (Fig. 14.6). An exposure exists with this configuration as it did when only one address mapper was employed in an SPTN. If the address mapper server goes down, address mapping comes to a screeching halt.

14.5.4.4 Multiple address mapper servers shared by multiple SPTNs. Multiple address mapper servers can provide services to any number of SPTNs. A single address mapper server can be employed as the active address mapper with another address mapper standing by as either a virgin or a shadow address mapper (Fig. 14.7), or two address mappers can share a distributed database (Fig. 14.8).

14.6 MPTN Multicasting

The last feature of address mapping that will be discussed is *multicasting* in MPTN networks. The MPTN architecture defines a way to implement multicast compensation. Multicasting was explained in Sec. 4.4.2.3 and provides a way to send datagrams to a group of transport users, rather than to just one.

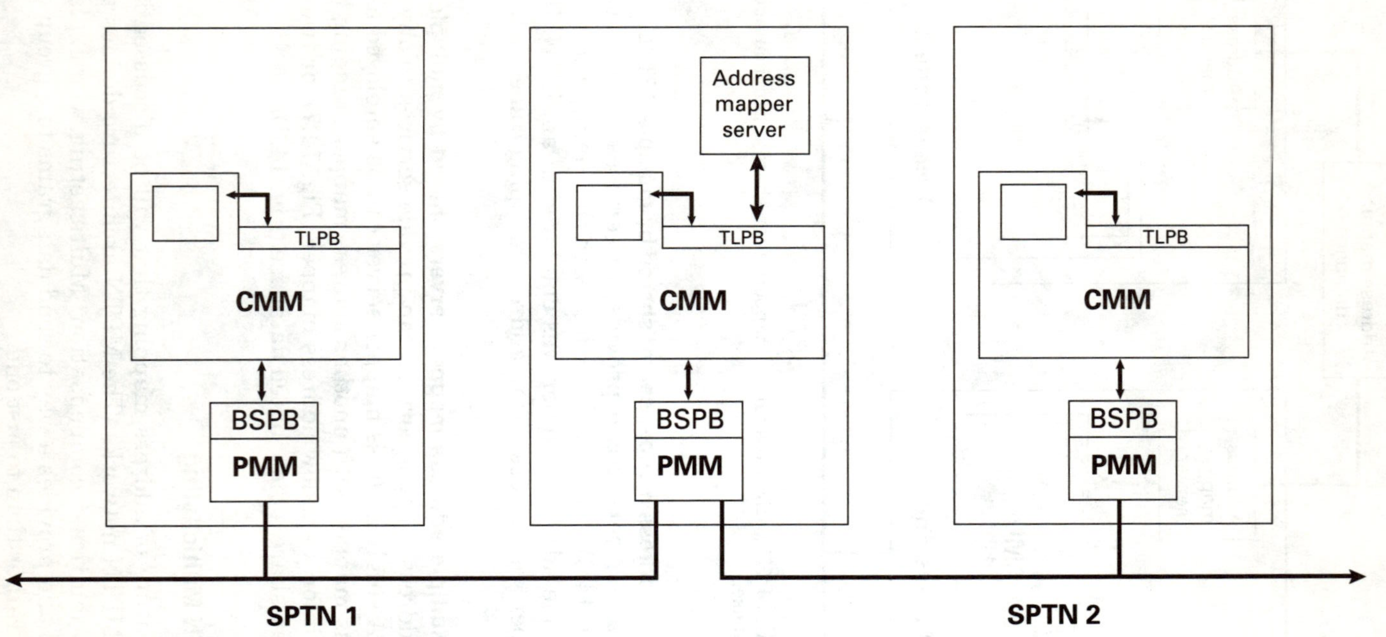

Figure 14.6 Two SPTNs using a single address mapper.

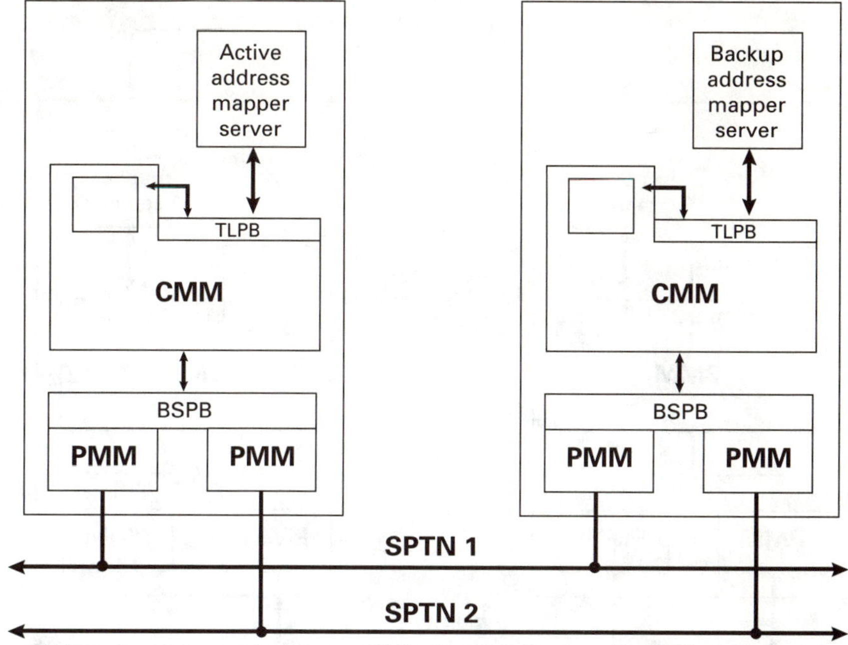

Figure 14.7   An active and a backup MPTN address mapper serving two SPTNs.

MPTN multicast datagrams can be sent to any SPTN, and can use any transport provider protocol. Recipients belong to a multicast group which they previously joined when they issued an M_BIND_DC call.

14.6.1   The MPTN multicast server

Compensation for multicasting is needed when the transport user network supports multicasting, but the underlying transport provider network does not. If the transport provider network provides multicasting, then the native multicasting feature is used to implement the multicasting required by the transport user; otherwise, MPTN must compensate for multicasting through the use of an optional component called the *MPTN multicast server.*

The multicast server implements multicasting simply: It unicasts the datagram to all recipients of the multicast group. The multicast server provides *multicast emulation,* and the domain of the multicast server is a single SPTN.

When an M_BIND_DC is issued by a transport user to register a group address, the CMM in the access node either issues a P_JOIN_GROUP_DC to join a multicasting group in a native protocol, or signals the address mapper client to register the group address in

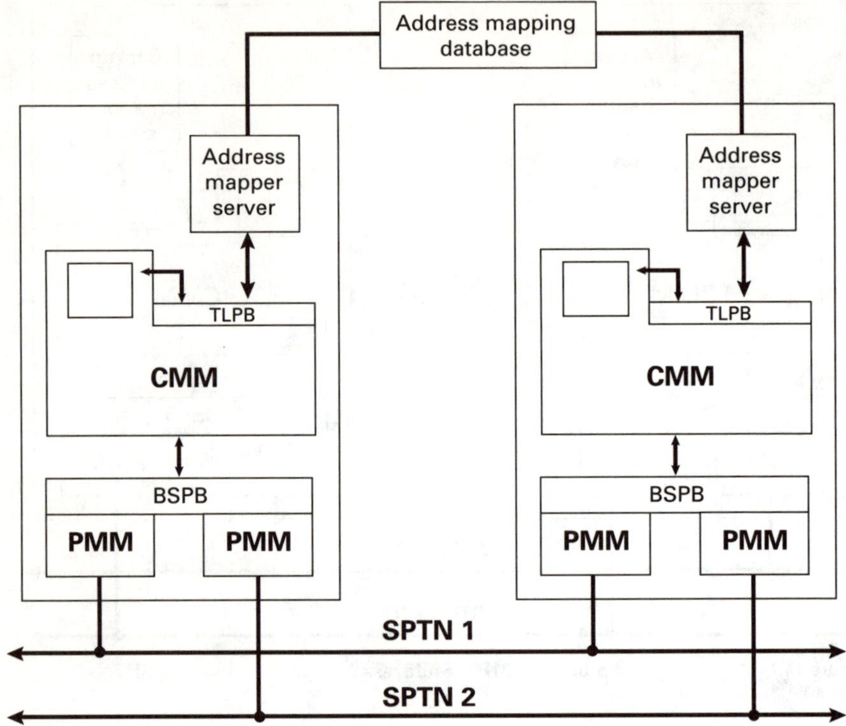

Figure 14.8 Two MPTN address mappers sharing a common address mapping database serving two SPTNs.

the address mapper server, if present, and sends a command to the multicast server. The first M_BIND_DC for a group creates that group's entry in the address mapper and the multicast server. After this, any new users issuing M_BIND_DC calls for the group are just entered as members in that group's membership list. The CMM in an access node sends an MCS_AC_JOIN_REQUEST to a multicast server to enter a user into a multicast group.

14.6.1.1 Multicast server commands.

The MPTN architecture defines a set of commands that are used by transport gateway and access nodes to communicate with a multicast server. These commands will now be presented (Table 14.6).

Multicast server commands are sent in MPTN_Datagrams in the *user datagram* field. In other words, the multicast server commands are wholly contained within a MPTN_Datagram. The MPTN_Datagram fields specified in Chap. 13 will all be present. At the beginning of each multicast server command is a multicast server header. This header resembles the MPTN message formats in its layout. Instead of a common

TABLE 14.6   Multicast Server Commands

MCS_MC_R_U_THERE_REQUEST	Address mapper wants to know if the multicast server is there
MCS_CM_REGISTER_REQUEST	Multicast server requests that the address mapper register an address
MCS_MC_REGISTER_REPLY	Reply from the address mapper
MCS_AC_JOIN_REQUEST	Access node requests that a transport user join a multicast group
MCS_AC_QUIT_REQUEST	Access node requests that a transport user quit a multicast group
MCS_AC_DISTRIBUTE_REQUEST	Access node sends a datagram to the multicast server to distribute to members of a group

prefix, however, it has a multicast server header prefix, which has the same format as the common prefix. Since the multicast server header follows the MPTN_Datagram message fields, there is no routing prefix. There are, however, required and optional fields specific to the multicast server header. The multicast server header is shown in Table 14.7. The multicast server command type contains the hexadecimal value for the particular multicast server command. Each command has a different command type.

For easy identification, multicast server commands are prefixed with MCS, the acronym for the multicast server. Following the MCS prefix is another section. This second section of the command indicates the direction of the command, to or from the multicast server.

Three letters are used:

A = access node (or transport gateway)

M = address mapper

C = multicast server

The second section of multicast server commands can be:

- _CM_: Multicast server to address mapper server
- _MC_: Address mapper server to multicast server
- _AC_: Access node to multicast server

Commands that are sent to the multicast server from an access node begin with MCS_AC. Commands sent from an address mapper server begin with MCS_MC. Commands sent from a multicast server to an address mapper server begin with MCS_CM.

If a command can be executed without incurring too much delay, the results are placed in the response to the command. Otherwise, the re-

TABLE 14.7   Multicast Server Header

Multicast Server Header Prefix		
Command type:		1 byte
MCS_CM_REGISTER_REQUEST	X'C0'	
MCS_MC_REGISTER_REPLY	X'C1'	
MCS_AC_JOIN_REQUEST	X'C8'	
MCS_AC_QUIT_REQUEST	X'CA'	
MCS_AC_DISTRIBUTE_REQUEST	X'CC'	
MCS_MC_R_U_THERE_REQUEST	X'E1'	
Processing specification		1 byte
Command length		2 bytes
Required Fields		
Command modifier		1 byte
Transaction identifier		2–9 bytes
Return code		3 bytes
Return code value		1 byte
Return code modifier		2 bytes
Optional Fields		
Source CMM routing		(9–262 bytes)
Source CMM routing prefix	X'A1'	4 bytes
Source CMM address	MPTN-qualified transport address	5–258 bytes
Diagnostics (for responses only)		(18–799 bytes)
Diagnostics prefix	X'F0'	4 bytes
Primary return code		4 bytes
Secondary return code		4 bytes
Error detector address	MPTN-qualified transport address	5–512 bytes
Error detector data		1–255 bytes

sponse is sent back with the return code set to RC_PENDING. This informs the sender of the command that the reply data will be forthcoming. The data are then returned in a REPLY version of the original REQUEST. If the command receives an error, it is sent back as a negative response with an optional diagnostics field placed on the end.

The required fields for multicast server commands are as follows.

- *Command modifier.*   This field is used in only some of the multicast server commands.

- *Transaction identifier.*   This field is used to correlate multicast server transactions. Since the multicast server uses datagrams, if a response is not received within the allotted time, a request is resent using the same transaction identifier. Responses and requests are all grouped within the same transactions.

- *Return code.*   The return code field is used to reflect the result of a command. There are two subfields: *return code value* and *return code modifier.* The latter field is not used at the time of this writing.

The return codes are the following.

- *OK (X'00').*   Successful completion of the command.

- *NEW_GROUP (X'01').*   The multicast group did not exist and was created.

- *SERVER_ALREADY_EXISTS (X'05').*   The address mapper server found that the multicast server was already registered.

- *PENDING (X'07').*   The command will not be completed immediately, so completion will be reflected in a forthcoming REPLY message.

- *UNSUCCESSFUL (X'08').*   Unsuccessful completion of the command.

The only optional fields used in multicast server commands are source CMM routing and diagnostics. The diagnostics optional field was discussed earlier.

- *Source CMM routing.*   This optional field has a prefix value of X'A1' and contains the source CMM address which is needed for routing.

The optional field X'A7' is used in individual multicast server commands to represent a transport user address. The use of this optional field in various commands is shown in Table 14.8.

MCS_CM_REGISTER_REQUEST.   The MCS_CM_REGISTER_REQUEST command is issued by a multicast server to register its transport provider address with an address mapper server. This command must be issued when the multicast server is loaded so that the address mapper server can communicate with it. The command is also issued when the multicast server has a group name to register with the address mapper.

The command type for MCS_CM_REGISTER_REQUEST is X'C0'. The command modifier field is set to indicate the type of transport

TABLE 14.8   Optional Fields: Multicast Server Commands

Optional field name	Prefix	Command(s) that use the field
Address to register	X'A7'	MCS_CM_REGISTER_REQUEST
Multicast group name	X'A7'	MCS_AC_JOIN_REQUEST
		MCS_CM_QUIT_REQUEST
		MCS_CM_DISTRIBUTE_REQUEST

provider that is supported by the multicast server. The values for this field are

IP: X'02'

OSI: X'07'

SNA: X'0B'

NetBIOS: X'12'

IPX: X'16'

An optional field is included in the command to provide a transport user address:

- *Address to register.* The optional field X'A7' contains the transport user address that is to be registered with the address mapper server. The mode byte in the address is set to X'02' when the transport user address represents a group name that is to be registered, or to X'06' when the multicast server itself is to be registered.

MCS_MC_REGISTER_REPLY. The MCS_MC_REGISTER_REPLY is sent by an address mapper server to the multicast server if the reply data were not included in the response to the MCS_CM_REGIS-TER_REQUEST and the return code was specified as RC_PENDING.

The command type for MCS_MC_REGISTER_REPLY is X'C1'. The command modifier field is set to indicate the type of transport provider that is supported by the multicast server. The values for this field are

IP: X'02'

OSI: X'07'

SNA: X'0B'

NetBIOS: X'12'

IPX: X'16'

The reply informs the multicast server of the outcome of the request.

MCS_MC_R_U_THERE_REQUEST. The MCS_MC_R_U_THERE_RE-QUEST is issued by the address mapper server to the multicast serv-er to see if it is operational. The command type is X'E1'.

MCS_AC_JOIN_REQUEST. The MCS_AC_JOIN_REQUEST command is sent from an access or transport gateway node to the multicast server when the node has a user that requests to join a multicast group. The command type is X'C8'.

The command modifier field is set to indicate the type of transport provider the requester access node requires. The values for this field are

IP: X'02'

OSI: X'07'

SNA: X'0B'

NetBIOS: X'12'

IPX: X'16'

An optional field is included:

- *Multicast group name.*   Optional field X'A7' contains the multicast group name.

MCS_AC_QUIT_REQUEST.   The MCS_AC_QUIT_REQUEST command is sent from an access node or gateway to the multicast server when a user wishes to quit a multicast group. The command code is X'CA', and there is an optional field provided for the multicast group name:

- *Multicast group name.*   Optional field X'A7' contains the multicast group name.

MCS_AC_DISTRIBUTE_REQUEST.   The MCS_AC_DISTRIBUTE_RE-QUEST command is sent from an access node or gateway to the multicast server to provide a datagram to be unicast to all the addresses registered for the multicast group. The command type is X'CC'. The datagram is included at the end of the command.
There is an optional field provided for the multicast group name:

- *Multicast group name.*   Optional field X'A7' contains the multicast group name that is associated with the addresses to which the datagram will be sent.

14.6.2   MPTN broadcasting

Broadcasting in networks that do not support broadcasting natively, such as SNA, is handled as a type of multicasting where the multicast group is a single network. If broadcasting is supported by a transport user protocol and multicasting is functional in a transport provider SPTN, ether inherently or by the use of an MPTN multicast server, then MPTN automatically enters each user in the broadcast group.

AnyNet

Chapter

15

IBM's AnyNet Products

15.1 The AnyNet Story

This chapter provides an introduction to IBM's AnyNet products. These products, first announced in 1993, use the MPTN architecture to provide access nodes and transport gateways for such platforms as Windows, AS/400, RS/6000, OS/2, and the MVS mainframe operating system. The AnyNet products were the first products to implement the MPTN architecture. Before continuing, a chronology of MPTN and AnyNet is first presented.

15.1.1 The beginnings

MPTN was born in the summer of 1989, when IBM Fellows Larry Loucks and Jim Gray were discussing the fact that IBM had created two networking protocols—SNA and NetBIOS—and that they did not interact in any way. This conversation led them to begin considering ways that a NetBIOS interface could be supported in a SNA network, allowing NetBIOS programs to run over SNA. The irony of this work was that NetBIOS was originally created because the LAN version of SNA's APPC interface was not ready in time.

The technical work of implementing a NetBIOS interface for a SNA network was begun by a joint Austin-Raleigh team led by another IBM Fellow, Diane Pozefsky. The original name given the new interface was the Transport Layer Protocol Boundary (TLPB) (affectionately known as Terribly Large Peanut Butter cookies). The TLPB name was chosen because of the similarity of the new interface to the transport layer interface (TLI) (discussed in Chaps. 4 and 5). Once work had began, however, the designers began considering a larger, more general, problem: the support of applications over nonnative transport networks. Soon the larger problem, not just a NetBIOS interface for a SNA transport network, became the focus of the project.

While the team was pondering the dilemma of applications running on nonnative transport networks, IBM's corporate design council was working with distributed computing. The council recognized that they had a problem making the Distributed Computing Environment (DCE), developed for TCP/IP, run in a SNA network. The TLPB concept was brought forward as a potential solution and was endorsed, not just as a solution to the problem of running DCE over SNA, but also as a solution for running any internet sockets program in a SNA network. A project was funded to develop a Sockets-Over-SNA product. Prototype work on the project began in the summer of 1991.

The new Sockets-Over-SNA product was built on the TLPB concept, although its early versions did not use any architected flows or structures. A prototype was developed and testing began (the first byte of test data sent was an X'42', in honor of the *Hitchhiker's Guide to the Galaxy*). Soon, the prototype was implemented as MVS and OS/2 products and the name *SNAckets* was adopted. SNAckets was tested on various machines and was gradually refined. Meanwhile, a team began working on a generalized architecture that could be used to implement applications on nonnative transport networks. This team decided that a networking architecture should not be called a protocol boundary, as was the case with the TLPB name, so the architecture was renamed Multiprotocol Transport Networking (MPTN).

After an MPTN architecture had been designed, the team decided to build a prototype from the ground up, using the architecture. This prototype would allow APPC programs to run in TCP/IP networks (APPC-Over-TCP/IP). Work on this prototype began in December 1991. Just as the work began, the Boeing Co. informed IBM that it had a problem. The company had planned to migrate its corporate network from SNA to OSI, using CPI-C as the primary programming interface. With the demise of OSI, however, Boeing was looking for a way to run CPI-C applications in a TCP/IP network. The prototyping effort soon became a product.

The incorporation of MPTN into the Networking Blueprint evolved during 1991. The Networking Blueprint was already being used as a tool within IBM, and was being included in various presentations. During the course of preparations for the announcement of APPN, outside consultants encouraged IBM to make the Networking Blueprint official. Therefore, in March 1992, the Networking Blueprint was announced together with APPN. The centerpiece of the blueprint was the capability to run applications over nonnative transport networks.

By the end of the year IBM was demonstrating SNAckets to the public, and in February 1993, IBM demonstrated both products, SNAckets and APPC-Over-TCP/IP (implemented for both MVS and OS/2 platforms), at the Washington, D.C., ComNet show. By March, IBM felt that both products were ready to be announced. The name *SNAckets* was changed to the more formal VTAM MultiProtocol Transport Feature (MPTF). The name *SNAckets,* however, as will be seen, still lingers in various places in the Sockets-Over-SNA product.

15.1.2 MPTN announced

The announcement of the multiprotocol transport networking architecture occurred on March 9, 1993, at the Spring Interop Show in Washington, D.C., and included two access node products,

- Sockets-Over-SNA
- APPC-Over-TCP/IP

These were included in VTAM Version 3 Release 4.2 for MVS/ESA. There were two versions of each combination: one ran on the MVS platform, the other with OS/2. Once MPTF was installed on the mainframe, the OS/2 modules could be downloaded from MVS.

The announcement also mentioned an MPTN product that was being developed jointly by IBM and Ki Networks of Columbia, Maryland: a DECnet-over-SNA transport gateway that would enable Ki's DECnet applications to communicate over a SNA backbone network.

15.1.3 AnyNet is born

On April 27, 1993, IBM announced the availability of the new MPTF products. At this time, the name was changed from MPTF to AnyNet/MVS. This would be the first in a new family of AnyNet products. (The name *AnyNet* stands for "any application over any network.") AnyNet/MVS was basically a repackaging and renaming of MPTF. An APPC-Over-TCP/IP MPTN transport gateway for MVS was also included in the announcement.

AnyNet/2 for the OS/2 platform was introduced by IBM on August 17, 1993. The APPC-Over-TCP/IP and Sockets-Over-SNA OS/2 products that were formerly available only by an MVS download were now available as separate products. Also announced was the AnyNet/2 Sockets-Over-SNA gateway for OS/2. This was an MPTN transport gateway that interconnected SNA with TCP/IP networks to allow sockets programs running in Sockets-Over-SNA nodes in a SNA network to communicate with native sockets programs running in TCP/IP networks. Six days later, on August 23, 1993, there was an announcement by PeerLogic of San Francisco of support for MPTN; then on the following day ProTools of Beaverton, Oregon, announced that its OS/2

Communications Manager network analysis products would use MPTN to transport SNMP management data over SNA networks.

Availability for the AnyNet/2 Sockets-Over-SNA gateway was announced on October 19, 1993. Also at this time, a beta test program was unveiled for a NetBEUI-Over-SNA product for OS/2. The beta test period ended in 1994, and the product became generally available in July of that year.

15.1.4 The big mainframe release: VTAM Version 4 Release 2

VTAM Version 4 Release 2, announced January 17, 1994, was the first VTAM release that contained both AnyNet and APPN together. The new AnyNet/2 Sockets-Over-SNA gateway for OS/2 was added as a downloadable feature. Also, because APPN and DLUR/S support was now available, APPC-Over-TCP/IP became SNA-Over-TCP/IP. The difference between the two is that SNA-Over-TCP/IP supports classic SNA 3270 applications as well as applications based on CPI-C and APPC.

15.1.5 X/OPEN and new platforms

The January 17, 1994, announcement for VTAM Version 4 Release 2 also included notification that X/Open Company Limited, the British standards organization, would publish specifications for the MPTN architecture beginning with a guide called the *X/Open Guide: Multiprotocol Transport Networking Architecture,* to be released later that month.

An announcement made on June 21, 1994, was important because it contained three new platforms for AnyNet products. They were the AS/400, the RS/6000, and PCs running Windows. AnyNet/6000 APPC-Over-TCP/IP was announced for the RS/6000 along with a Sockets-Over-SNA beta test program for that platform. AnyNet/400 contained two products built into the AS/400's OS/400 operating system: APPC-Over-TCP/IP and Sockets-Over-SNA. AnyNet for Windows contained an APPC-Over-TCP/IP that would be available for beta testing.

Also on June 21, another transport gateway product was announced: the AnyNet SNA-Over-TCP/IP gateway for OS/2. The product name had been changed from "AnyNet/2" to "AnyNet for OS/2." (The product names AnyNet/2, AnyNet/400, AnyNet/6000, and AnyNet/MVS were gradually all retired in favor of the "AnyNet for..." style as time progressed.)

In October 1994, the X/Open MPTN specifications became available. These were contained in three publications: *XMPTN Access*

Node, XMPTN Address Mapper, and *XMPTN Data Formats* (see App. C for details).

On November 9, 1994, the AnyNet SNA-Over-TCP/IP gateway for OS/2 and an AnyNet IPX-Over-SNA gateway for OS/2 were announced.

15.1.6   New announcements in 1995

On March 21, 1995, IBM announced a new hardware product, the IBM 2217 Nways Multiprotocol Concentrator. This device could be used in enterprise networks to provide interconnection of multiprotocol LANs across a single SNA or APPN High Performance Routing (HPR) backbone.

15.2   The AnyNet Platforms

At the time of this writing, AnyNet products are available for five different platforms: MVS/ESA, OS/2, AS/400, AIX (RS/6000), and Windows. The number and type of products that are available for each platform vary, and some combinations and types are available on more platforms than on others. The first products introduced by IBM for the AnyNet product family were based on the TCP/IP and SNA protocols. The next protocol to be introduced was NetBIOS, then IPX came along. As can be seen from the details presented above, products have been designed to run particular protocols on top of others exclusively. MPTN transport gateway products are available for only two platforms at the time of this writing.

The various AnyNet platforms and the products available at the time of this writing will now be discussed.

15.2.1   AnyNet for MVS

Three AnyNet MVS products are available for IBM mainframes:

- Sockets-Over-SNA

- SNA-Over-TCP/IP

- SNA-Over-TCP/IP gateway

All three are included in VTAM Version 4 Release 2 and later.

15.2.1.1   AnyNet Sockets-Over-SNA for MVS.   Sockets-Over-SNA enables MVS programs that use the AF_INET socket interface to communicate with other AF_INET sockets programs running in a SNA network, or to communicate with AF_INET sockets programs running in a TCP/IP network connected to the SNA network by means of an

AnyNet Sockets-Over-SNA gateway for OS/2. Figure 15.1 presents an example of how Sockets-Over-SNA can be used. In this example, three application programs are loaded in MVS, and each uses AF_INET sockets to communicate with three programs loaded in three other nodes. The Sockets-Over-SNA component of VTAM in the MVS node uses MPTN formats and protocols to map the data exchanged between the sockets programs and their partners into SNA packets. Program 1 is connected with a program located in an OS/2 that is running AnyNet Sockets-Over-SNA for OS/2. Program 2 is connected with an AF_INET sockets program running in the AS/400 that is using Sockets-Over-SNA for the AS/400. The third MVS program is connected with an AF_INET sockets application running in the AIX node. The program running in the AIX machine is communicating over a TCP/IP network that is connected to the SNA network by means of an AnyNet Sockets-Over-SNA gateway for OS/2.

The necessary software required to support Sockets-Over-SNA for MVS is

- MVS/ESA System Product Version 3 Release 1.3 or later

- IBM C for System/370 Version 2 (at PUT level 9107) or later

- VTAM Version 4 Release 2 with AnyNet host feature or later

15.2.1.2   AnyNet SNA-Over-TCP/IP for MVS.   SNA-Over-TCP/IP for MVS allows SNA applications to communicate with other SNA applications that are running either in an MPTN access node on a TCP/IP network or running natively in a SNA network that is connected to the TCP/IP network by means of a SNA-Over-TCP/IP gateway for OS/2. Figure 15.2 shows an example of how a SNA-Over-TCP/IP for MVS can be used. In this example, three CPI-C programs are running in the MVS mainframe. The first program communicates with a CPI-C program running on a Windows platform running APPC-Over-TCP/IP, and the second communicates with a CPI-C program running on an AS/400 running APPC-Over-TCP/IP. An OS/2 running the SNA-Over-TCP/IP gateway interconnects the TCP/IP network with a SNA network, and the third mainframe CPI-C program is in conversation with a CPI-C program running on an AIX RS/6000 machine connected to the SNA network.

It can be seen from the drawing that in addition to the CPI-C programs, conventional SNA programs are running on the MVS mainframe and are able to use printers and emulated terminals that are attached to the OS/2 machine. The support for these dependent LUs is made possible by the DLUR/S feature introduced in VTAM Version 4 Release 2.

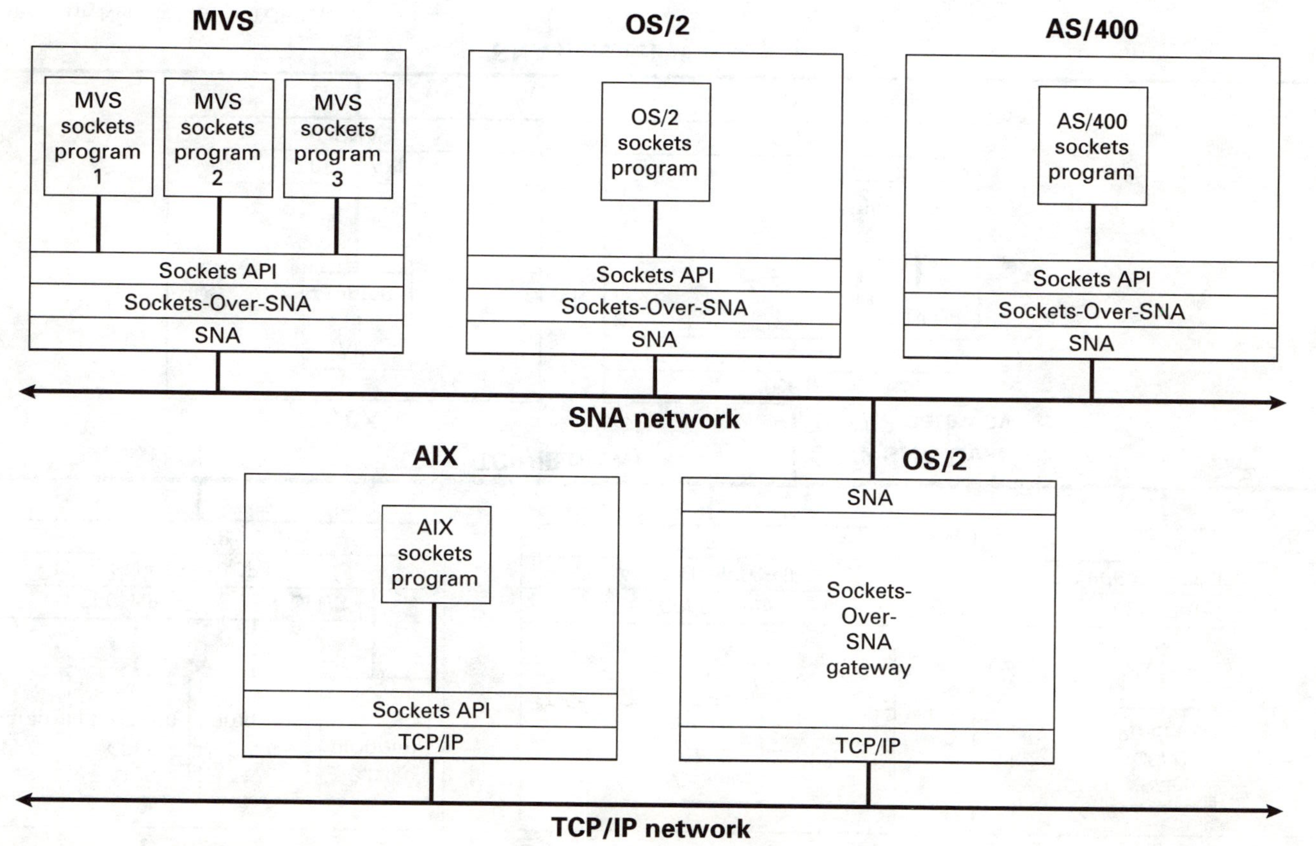

Figure 15.1   AnyNet Sockets-Over-SNA.

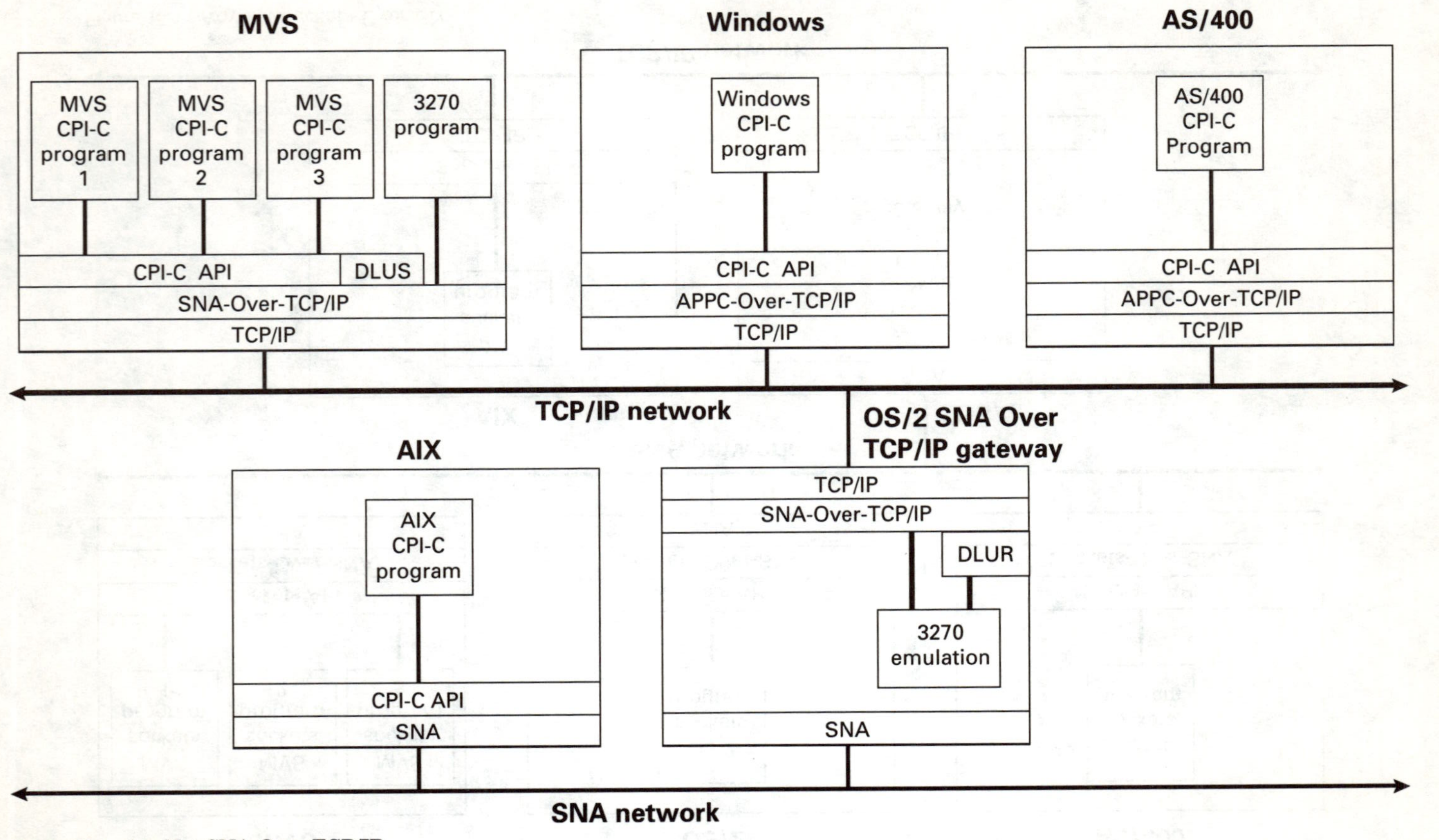

Figure 15.2 AnyNet SNA-Over-TCP/IP.

The software requirements for SNA-Over-TCP/IP for MVS are

- MVS/ESA System Product Version 3 Release 1.3 or later
- MVS/ESA System Modification Program/Extended Release 5 or later
- IBM TCP/IP Version 2 Release 2.1 for MVS or later
- IBM C for System/370 Version 2 (at PUT level 9107) or later
- VTAM Version 4 Release 2 with AnyNet host feature or later

15.2.1.3 AnyNet SNA-Over-TCP/IP gateway for MVS.   The AnyNet SNA-Over-TCP/IP gateway for MVS enables a mainframe to become a gateway to interconnect a TCP/IP and a SNA network. Using this gateway, CPI-C and APPC programs running in nodes in the TCP/IP network, on which AnyNet SNA-Over-TCP/IP or APPC-Over-TCP/IP has been installed, are able to communicate with native CPI-C, APPC (and SNA) programs that are running in the SNA network. Figure 15.3 shows how the AnyNet SNA-Over-TCP/IP gateway for MVS can be used. The MVS host interconnects two networks: a SNA network and a TCP/IP network. In this figure, an AIX RS/6000 is running AnyNet APPC-Over-TCP/IP and a CPI-C program is in conversation with a CPI-C program running natively on an AS/400 connected to a SNA network. The path between the RS/6000 and the MVS gateway is a TCP/IP network. Between the MVS gateway and the AS/400 the path is a SNA network.

The software requirements for this gateway are the same as SNA-Over-TCP/IP for MVS.

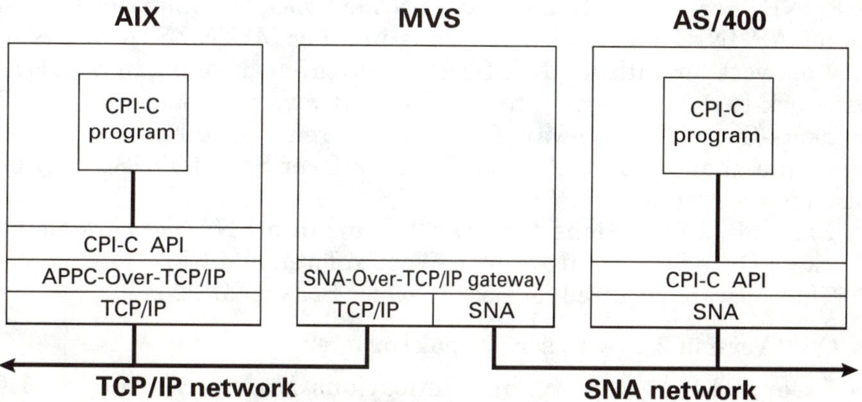

Figure 15.3   The AnyNet SNA-Over-TCP/IP gateway for MVS.

15.2.2   AnyNet for OS/2

The OS/2 operating system is the platform on which the most AnyNet options are available at the time of this writing. Five access nodes and two MPTN gateways have been released for OS/2. Additionally, there are two AnyNet LAN to LAN wide area network (LTLW) gateways available for OS/2. These gateways do not use the MPTN architecture and will be described in Sec. 15.3.

The following are the AnyNet MPTN products available for OS/2 at the time of this writing:

- OS/2 MPTN access nodes
  Sockets-Over-SNA
  Sockets-Over-NetBIOS
  Sockets-Over-IPX
  SNA-Over-TCP/IP
  NetBIOS-Over-SNA

- OS/2 MPTN gateways
  Sockets-Over-SNA gateway
  SNA-Over-TCP/IP gateway

In July 1995, AnyNet for OS/2 was enhanced to include four access nodes (the first four above) in a single product. This is perhaps an indication of where IBM is going with their AnyNet products: into a tighter integration with each other and other products such as operating systems and communications products.

Each of the AnyNet access nodes and MPTN gateway products available for the OS/2 platform will now be introduced.

15.2.2.1   AnyNet Sockets-Over-SNA for OS/2.   Sockets-Over-SNA for OS/2 enables C-language application programs using the IBM TCP/IP AF_INET socket interface to use a SNA network to communicate with other AF_INET applications running in other MPTN access nodes in the network, or with AF_INET sockets programs running in a TCP/IP network that is connected to the SNA network by means of an OS/2 Sockets-Over-SNA gateway. The reader is referred to Fig. 15.1 for an example showing how AnyNet Sockets-Over-SNA for OS/2 can be used in a network.

Example applications that can be run in a SNA network using Sockets-Over-SNA are ftp, telnet, WebExplorer, and NFS.

The software required for Sockets-Over-SNA for OS/2 is

- OS/2 Version 2.0 (with service pak) or later

- Extended Services or Communications Manager/2 Version 1.0 (Version 1.11 for full-duplex APPC support) or later

The hardware requirements are

- 386SX or later, 8 Mbytes RAM (12 Mbytes recommended), 1.5 Mbytes disk space

15.2.2.2 AnyNet NetBEUI-Over-SNA for OS/2. AnyNet NetBEUI-Over-SNA enables an OS/2 workstation to run NetBIOS programs over a SNA network to communicate with programs running in other OS/2 workstations running AnyNet NetBEUI-Over-SNA. Examples of NetBIOS applications that can run in a SNA network using NetBEUI-Over-SNA are the IBM Distributed Console Access Facility (DCAF), LAN NetView Management Utilities (LMU), LAN Server and LAN Requester, Time and Place/2, Person to Person/2, Lotus Notes, and cc:Mail.

Figure 15.4 shows two OS/2 PCs connected to a SNA network. Each machine has AnyNet NetBEUI-Over-SNA installed, and NetBIOS programs are running in each and can communicate with each other.

The software requirements for NetBEUI-Over-SNA are

- OS/2 Version 2.0 or 2.1 (with service pak) or later

- Communications Manager/2 Version 1.01 or 1.11 (with service pak) or later; Version 1.11 recommended

- IBM OS/2 LAN Adapter and Protocol Support Version 2.14 (with service pak) or later

The hardware requirements are

- 386SX or later, 8 Mbytes RAM, 4 Mbytes disk space

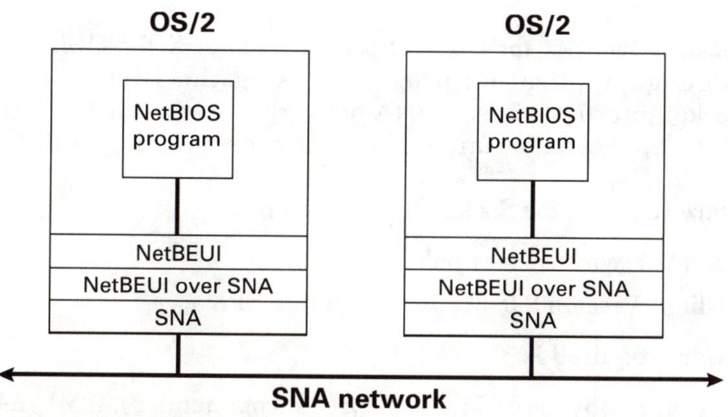

Figure 15.4 AnyNet NetBEUI-Over-SNA.

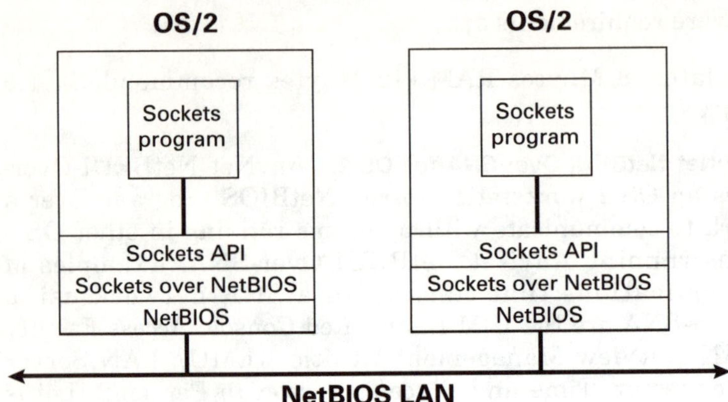

Figure 15.5   AnyNet Sockets-Over-NetBIOS.

15.2.2.3   AnyNet Sockets-Over-NetBIOS for OS/2.   AnyNet Sockets-Over-NetBIOS allows AF_INET sockets programs to use a NetBIOS network to communicate with other AF_INET sockets programs running in other AnyNet Sockets-Over-NetBIOS nodes. Figure 15.5 shows two OS/2 workstations connected to a NetBIOS network. Each machine has Sockets-Over-NetBIOS installed, and AF_INET sockets programs running in each are able to communicate with each other.

The software requirements for Sockets-Over-NetBIOS are

- OS/2 Version 2.0 (with service pak) or later

- Network Transport Services (NTS/2) Version 1.1 or later

  The hardware required is

- 386SX or later, 8 Mbytes RAM (12 Mbytes recommended), 2 Mbytes disk space

15.2.2.4   Sockets-Over-IPX for OS/2.   Sockets-Over-IPX for OS/2 enables C-language application programs using the IBM TCP/IP AF_INET socket interface to use a SNA network to communicate with other AF_INET applications running in other nodes running Sockets-Over-IPX for OS/2.

The software required for Sockets-Over-SNA is

- OS/2 Version 2.0 (with service pak) or later

- NetWare Client Version 2.0 or later, including SPX

  The hardware required is

- 386SX or later, 8 Mbytes RAM (12 Mbytes recommended), 2 Mbytes disk space

15.2.2.5 AnyNet SNA-Over-TCP/IP for OS/2.

SNA-Over-TCP/IP for OS/2 enables CPI-C and APPC programs to use a TCP/IP network to communicate with CPI-C and APPC programs running in other APPC-Over-TCP/IP and SNA-Over-TCP/IP nodes. Additionally, CPI-C and APPC programs can communicate with native CPI-C and APPC applications running in a SNA network if it is connected with the TCP/IP network by means of a SNA-Over-TCP/IP gateway for OS/2 or a SNA-Over-TCP/IP gateway for MVS. Additionally, support is provided to allow access to legacy 3270-based SNA programs. The 3270 gateway feature of Communications Manager/2 is fully functional, and a TCP/IP network can be used between the gateway and a (mainframe) host or between the gateway and downstream LUs.

Figure 15.6 presents an example of the use of AnyNet SNA-Over-TCP/IP for OS/2. Programs running on the MVS host are in session with emulated 3270 terminals on the OS/2 machine, and the path between them is TCP/IP. Dependent LU sessions can be established over the TCP/IP network because SNA-Over-TCP/IP (as opposed to APPC-Over-TCP/IP) is installed in both machines and the DLUR/S support of VTAM is active. In addition to the dependent LUs, the OS/2 platform also has two active CPI-C programs. One of these programs is in conversation with a CPI-C program in the node running AnyNet APPC-Over-TCP/IP for Windows, and another is in conversation with a CPI-C program running in the AS/400. The AS/400 is attached to a SNA network, and the SNA network is connected with the TCP/IP network by means of an OS/2 SNA-Over-TCP/IP gateway.

The software requirements for SNA-Over-TCP/IP are

- OS/2 Version 2.0 (with service pak) or later

- Communications Manager/2 Version 1.11 (with service pak) for dependent LU support or later; Communications Manager/2 Version 1.0 supports only APPC-Over-TCP/IP

- IBM TCP/IP Version 2 for OS/2 or later

The hardware requirements are

- 386SX or later, 8 Mbytes RAM (12 Mbytes recommended), 1.5 Mbytes disk space

15.2.2.6 AnyNet Sockets-Over-SNA gateway for OS/2.

The Sockets-Over-SNA gateway for OS/2 is an MPTN transport gateway that interconnects a SNA network and a TCP/IP network. AF_INET sockets programs running in Sockets-Over-SNA nodes can communicate with native TCP/IP programs running in a TCP/IP network when the TCP/IP network and the SNA network are interconnected by means of an AnyNet Sockets-Over-SNA gateway for OS/2. Additionally, two

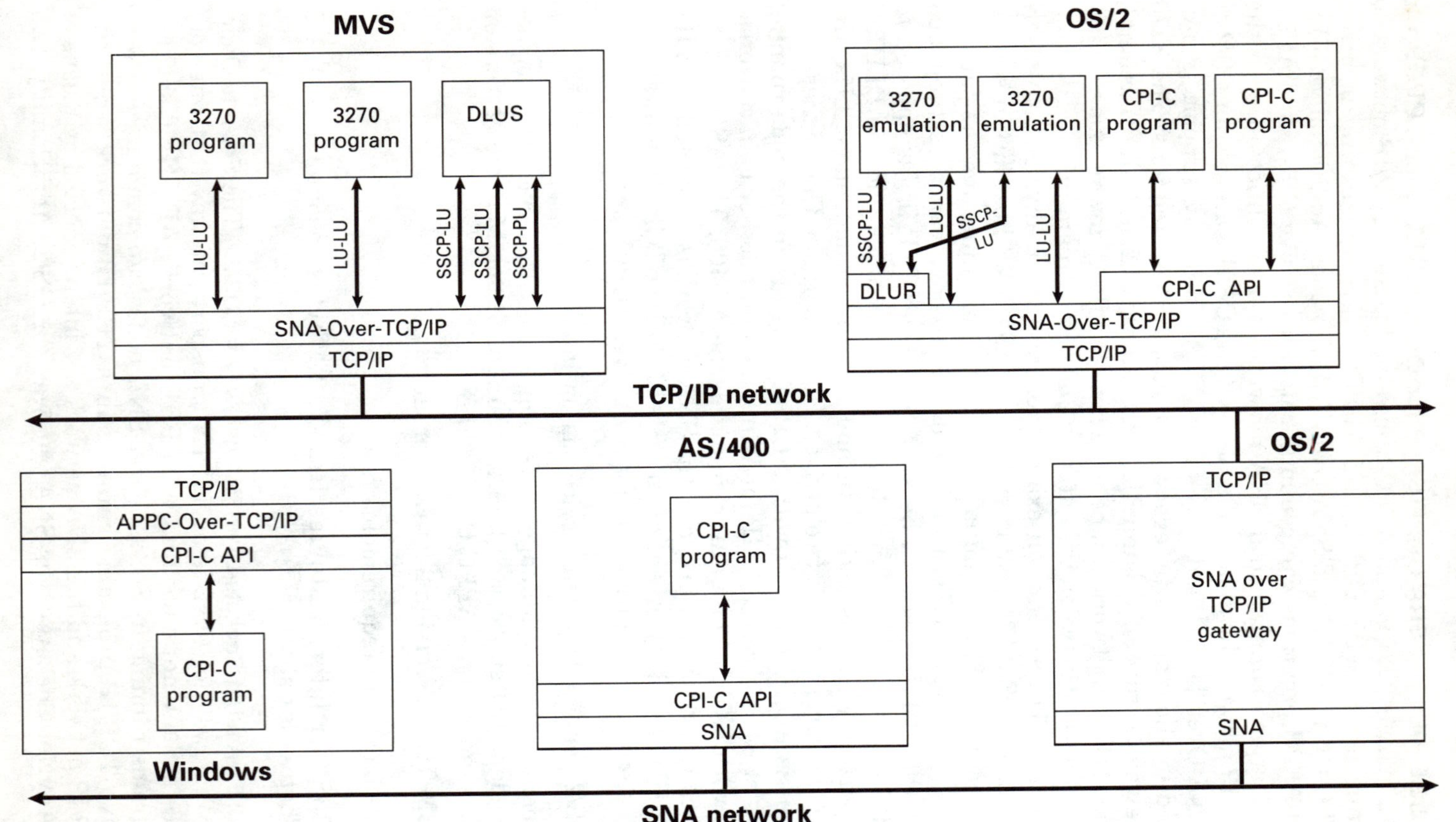

Figure 15.6 AnyNet SNA-Over-TCP/IP configuration showing dependent LU sessions.

AnyNet Sockets-Over-SNA gateways can be used in conjunction with each other to form a *double gateway* configuration that allows two TCP/IP networks to be interconnected over a SNA backbone network. Figure 15.1 shows an example use of the Sockets-Over-SNA gateway for OS/2.

The software requirements for the Sockets-Over-SNA OS/2 gateway are

- OS/2 Version 2.0 (with service pak) or later

- TCP/IP Version 1.2.1 for OS/2 (with corrective service diskette) or later or TCP/IP Version 2.0 or later

- Extended Services (ES) or Communication Manager/2 Version 1.0 or later

The hardware requirements are

- 386SX, 8 Mbytes RAM (12 Mbytes recommended), 820 kbytes disk space

15.2.2.7 AnyNet SNA-Over-TCP/IP gateway for OS/2. The SNA-Over-TCP/IP gateway for OS/2 is an MPTN transport gateway that, like the Sockets-Over-SNA gateway, interconnects a SNA network and a TCP/IP network at the OSI transport layer. The SNA-Over-TCP/IP gateway, however, interconnects the networks in such a way that SNA programs running in mainframes or OS/2 workstations that have SNA-Over-TCP/IP installed, or in AS/400s and RS/6000s running APPC-Over-TCP/IP, can communicate over a TCP/IP network with native SNA programs running in a SNA network. Additionally, two AnyNet SNA-Over-TCP/IP gateways can be used in conjunction with each other to form a double gateway configuration that allows two SNA networks to be interconnected over a TCP/IP backbone network. Figure 15.2 shows an example use of the SNA-Over-TCP/IP gateway for OS/2. In this example, a CPI-C program running in the MVS mainframe is in conversation with another CPI-C program running in an AIX RS/6000. The AnyNet SNA-over-TCP/IP gateway interconnects the SNA and TCP/IP networks so that the CPI-C conversation can use the TCP/IP network between the OS/2 gateway and the MVS mainframe. Additionally, in this drawing, dependent LUs are supported using the DLUR/S feature of VTAM, which allows the 3270 applications running in the mainframe to communicate with emulated 3270 terminals in the OS/2 AnyNet gateway. This is an example of using this node not only as an AnyNet gateway to interconnect TCP/IP and SNA networks, but also to support dependent LUs. These dependent LUs are not confined to the gateway machine, but may additionally reside *downstream* in other SNA/APPN nodes. The details of DLUR/S, which allows 3270 access over a nonnative transport network, are covered in more detail in Chap. 17.

The software requirements for the gateway are

- OS/2 Version 2.0 (with service pak) or later
- Communications Manager/2, Version 1.11 (with service pak and apar) or later
- VTAM-provided OS/2 DLUR support (if dependent LUs are used)
- TCP/IP, Version 1.2.1, for OS/2 or later

The hardware requirements are

- 386SX or later (486 is recommended), at least 16 Mbytes RAM (more is needed for higher-volume gateways), 2 Mbytes disk space

Figures 15.2 and 15.6 show configurations using the SNA-Over-TCP/IP gateway.

15.2.3 AnyNet for AIX

AnyNet for AIX was developed for IBM's line of RS/6000 workstations and is a feature of SNA Server for AIX. SNA Server for AIX is an IBM product for the RS/6000 that provides SNA services including support for APPC, CPI-C, and LU types 0, 1, 2, 3 (and 6.2). The AnyNet feature provide additional flexibility and opportunities for the SNA user on this platform by offering the ability to run CPI-C and APPC programs over a TCP/IP network, and sockets programs over a SNA network.

The name originally applied to this product was AnyNet/6000. It has been changed to *AnyNet for AIX*.

15.2.3.1 AnyNet Sockets-Over-SNA for AIX.

The AnyNet Sockets-Over-SNA for AIX is an implementation of an MPTN access node that enables AF_INET sockets programs to operate over a SNA network. Sockets-Over-SNA can be used in several configurations. It can be used in a purely SNA network to provide a way for AF_INET sockets programs to communicate with AF_INET sockets programs running in other Sockets-Over-SNA nodes in a SNA network. Additionally, AF_INET sockets programs can communicate with other AF_INET sockets programs running in a TCP/IP network that is connected to the SNA network using an AnyNet Sockets-Over-SNA gateway for OS/2.

The software requirements for Sockets-Over-SNA for AIX are

- AIX Version 4.1 or later
- SNA Server for AIX Version 3.1 or later

The hardware requirements are

- RISC System/6000 POWERstation or POWERserver
- 2 Mbytes disk space

15.2.3.2   AnyNet APPC-Over-TCP/IP for AIX.   AnyNet APPC-Over-TCP/IP for AIX is an implementation of an MPTN access node and is a feature of SNA Server for AIX. It provides the ability for CPI-C and APPC programs to communicate with other CPI-C and APPC programs running in other APPC-Over-TCP/IP and SNA-Over-TCP/IP nodes using a TCP/IP network. Additionally, CPI-C and APPC programs running in an AIX workstation with APPC-Over-TCP/IP installed can communicate with other CPI-C and APPC programs running in SNA networks that are connected to the TCP/IP network by means of an AnyNet SNA-Over-TCP/IP gateway for OS/2 or an AnyNet SNA-Over-TCP/IP gateway for MVS.

The software requirements for APPC-Over-TCP/IP for AIX are

- AIX Version 4.1 or later
- SNA Server for AIX Version 3.1 or later

The hardware requirements are

- A minimum of a POWERstation or POWERserver workstation
- 2 Mbytes disk space

15.2.4   AnyNet for the AS/400

The AS/400 is IBM's popular midrange platform, and can be found in both SNA and TCP/IP networks. Two AnyNet implementations are bundled with Version 3 Release 1 of the OS/400 operating system: APPC-Over-TCP/IP and Sockets-Over-SNA. At the time of this writing, IBM has issued statements of direction for two additional products: Sockets-Over-IPX and APPC-Over-IPX.

15.2.4.1   AnyNet Sockets-Over-SNA for the AS/400.   The AnyNet Sockets-Over-SNA for the AS/400 is an implementation of the MPTN access node for the AS/400 that allows AF_INET sockets programs to operate unchanged over a SNA network. This feature of the OS/400 operating system can be used in several ways. It can be used in a purely SNA network to provide a way for AF_INET sockets programs to communicate with AF_INET sockets programs running in other Sockets-Over-SNA nodes, or it can be used to provide a way for AF_INET sockets programs to communicate with AF_INET sockets programs running natively in a TCP/IP network that is connected to the SNA network by means of an AnyNet Sockets-Over-SNA gateway for OS/2.

The software requirement for Sockets-Over-SNA for the AS/400 is

- OS/400 Version 3 Release 1 or later

The hardware requirement is

- AS/400

15.2.4.2   AnyNet APPC-Over-TCP/IP for the AS/400.   AnyNet APPC-Over-TCP/IP for the AS/400 is an implementation of the MPTN access node that provides the ability for CPI-C, Intersystems Communications Function (ICF), and Customer Information Control System/400 (CICS/400) APPC programs to communicate not only over a native SNA network, but also on a TCP/IP network, either with other programs running in other APPC-Over-TCP/IP nodes in the SNA network or with programs running natively in SNA networks that are connected to the TCP/IP network using the AnyNet SNA-Over-TCP/IP gateway for OS/2 or the AnyNet SNA-Over-TCP/IP gateway for MVS.

The software requirement for APPC-Over-TCP/IP for the AS/400 is

- OS/400 Version 3 Release 1

The hardware requirement is

- AS/400

**15.2.5   AnyNet APPC-Over-TCP/IP
for Windows**

The Windows platform is important in the overall networking picture, and IBM has begun addressing this platform with at least one AnyNet product at the time of this writing: APPC-Over-TCP/IP for Windows. It is expected that other access node products will emerge from IBM, including Sockets-Over-SNA for Windows.

With APPC-Over-TCP/IP for Windows installed, CPI-C and APPC programs can communicate with other CPI-C and APPC programs running in other APPC-Over-TCP/IP and SNA-Over-TCP/IP nodes over a TCP/IP network. Additionally, CPI-C and APPC programs running in Windows can communicate with other CPI-C or APPC programs running in a native SNA network if the SNA network is connected to the TCP/IP network by means of an AnyNet SNA-Over-TCP/IP gateway for OS/2. Figure 15.2 shows a Windows PC running a CPI-C program on a TCP/IP network.

The software requirements for AnyNet APPC-Over-TCP/IP for Windows are

- Windows 3.1, Windows for Workgroups 3.11, or later

- IBM APPC Networking Services for Windows, Version 1.0 or later

- A TCP/IP protocol stack. At the time of this writing, seven products are supported:

  IBM TCP/IP for DOS, Version 2.1.1 (with CSD UB10718) or later
  FTP Software PC/TCP for DOS/Windows, Version 3.0 or later
  FTP Software PC/TCP OnNet for DOS/Windows, Version 1.1 or later
  Microsoft TCP/IP-32 for Windows for Workgroups, Version 3.11
  NetManage Chameleon TCP/IP for Windows, Version 4.1 or later
  Novell LAN WorkPlace for DOS, Version 4.2 or later
  Walker, Richer, Quinn (WRQ) TCP Connection for Windows Version 4.01 or later

The hardware requirements are

- 386SX or later, 4 Mbytes RAM (8 Mbytes recommended), 1 Mbyte disk space

15.3   LAN to LAN over WAN

LAN to LAN Wide Area Network (LTLW) is a technology developed by IBM to interconnect local area networks over a wide area network. The principle of LTLW is that of a *double gateway* and is illustrated in Fig. 15.7. This figure shows two IPX LANs connected with each other over a SNA wide area network accessed by two LTLW gateways. Because the two gateways work in conjunction with each other, they are called a double gateway configuration. The gateways encapsulate the data from the LANs into SNA LU 6.2 sessions that are established over the WAN.

The LTLW technology had its beginnings in 1989 when a large retailer submitted a requirement to run NetBIOS-Over-SNA to the IBM PC Bridge Division, where NetBIOS had been written. The LTLW NetBIOS-Over-SNA double gateway product became available in 1991.

Three double gateways have been developed using LTLW technology: IPX-Over-SNA, TCP/IP-Over-SNA, and NetBIOS-Over-SNA. In 1995, these products were integrated into the AnyNet product line. Even though they now belong to the AnyNet product family, they are not compatible with MPTN because the protocols that are used for gateway-to-gateway communications are not based on the MPTN architecture.

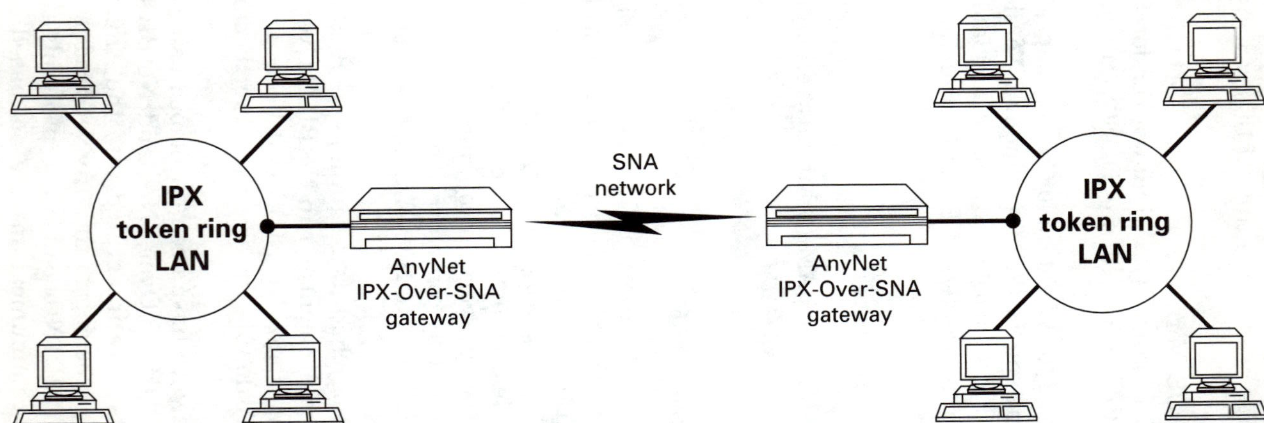

Figure 15.7 Two IPX token ring LANs interconnected over a SNA network.

15.3.1   AnyNet IPX-Over-SNA
gateway for OS/2

The AnyNet IPX-Over-SNA gateway for OS/2 uses the LTLW technology to interconnect two IPX token ring LANs over a SNA network (Fig. 15.7). The IPX-Over-SNA gateways encapsulate IPX sessions within SNA LU 6.2 sessions.

In the IPX networks, the IPX-Over-SNA gateways appear as IPX routers, and the gateways implement both NetWare "SAP" and "RIP" protocols. The NetWare *Service Advertisement Protocol* (SAP) is a standard feature of NetWare servers. Servers broadcast advertisements for their services throughout an IPX network every 60 seconds. Large networks can experience a great deal of SAP broadcasts, and NetWare routers always filter this traffic. The AnyNet gateways use a link-state algorithm to inform the other gateway of router and server changes that take place rather than letting RIP and SAP broadcasts travel over the WAN. The *Routing Information Protocol* (RIP) for IPX was described in Chap. 3.

The software requirements for the AnyNet IPX-Over-SNA gateway are

- OS/2 Version 2.0 or later

- Communications Manager/2 Version 1.0 or later

- If VTAM is installed in the backbone network: Version 3.2 or later

   The hardware requirements are

- 386SX or later, 8 Mbytes memory (12 Mbytes recommended), 1.2+ Mbytes disk space

15.3.2   LTLW NetBIOS-Over-SNA
gateway for OS/2

The NetBIOS*-Over-SNA Gateway for OS/2 is based on the LTLW technology and allows the interconnection of NetBIOS LANs over a SNA backbone. NetBIOS traffic is encapsulated within SNA LU 6.2 sessions. The use of the NetBIOS-Over-SNA gateways is the same as that of the IPX-Over-SNA gateways as shown in Fig. 15.7.

---

*Because this gateway product was developed separately from the "NetBEUI over SNA" MPTN products, it carries a different name. Instead of "NetBEUI over SNA," it is called "NetBIOS over SNA." The use of the name "NetBEUI" is very confusing. For example, Microsoft uses the terms "NetBEUI" and "NetBIOS" in the opposite way they are used in the AnyNet products. In Microsoft literature, NetBEUI refers to the protocol stack and NetBIOS to the user interface.

The software requirements are

- OS/2 Version 2.0 or later
- Communications Manager/2 Version 1.0 or later

The hardware requirements are

- 386SX or later, 8 Mbytes memory, 1.2+ Mbytes disk space

15.3.3   The 2217 Nways Multiprotocol Concentrator

The IBM 2217 Nways Multiprotocol Concentrator is a standalone hardware device that was announced by IBM on March 21, 1995. It provides interconnection of multiprotocol LANs across a single SNA, APPN, or High Performance Routing (HPR) backbone. TCP/IP, IPX, NetBIOS, and SNA datastreams are concentrated onto a single SNA backbone and flow freely between geographically dispersed LANs. Using these devices, LANs can be connected to an already-existing SNA backbone network and make use of its reliability, and take advantage of the HPR feature associated with APPN. Figure 15.8 presents an example configuration showing LANs connected over a WAN using 2217 Nways Multiprotocol Concentrators. LAN 1 contains a node with a NetBIOS LAN Requester communicating with a NetBIOS LAN Server on a node in LAN 2. LAN 2 also contains a NetWare client workstation in session with a NetWare file server located in LAN 3. Also in LAN 3 is an X-Window Server that is communicating with an X-Window Client located in a node in LAN 1.

The 2217 consists of a dedicated PC running OS/2 and three different AnyNet gateways: the AnyNet NetBIOS-Over-SNA gateway, the AnyNet IPX-Over-SNA gateway, and the AnyNet (MPTN) Sockets-Over-SNA gateway. A SNA-Over-TCP/IP gateway is also included in the unit, and will allow SNA programs to run on the LAN. In the SNA network, the 2217 appears as an APPN network node (NN), and dependent LUs running 3270 emulation or terminal concentrators and printers can be accessed from mainframe applications using the Dependent LU Requester/Server (DLUR/S).

The 50-MHz, 486-based 2217 Nways Multiprotocol Concentrator model 200 supports either a token ring or an Ethernet adapter and an X.21, V.35, RS-422, or RS-232 adapter for the synchronous WAN interface. The WAN adapter can run SDLC, frame relay, or X.25. Frame relay can be employed at T-1 speeds. An optional interface for the WAN adapter allows a second WAN port to be installed. The device is shipped with a preloaded hard disk and a 14.4-kbits/s internal modem for remote servicing and software upgrades. It is configurable

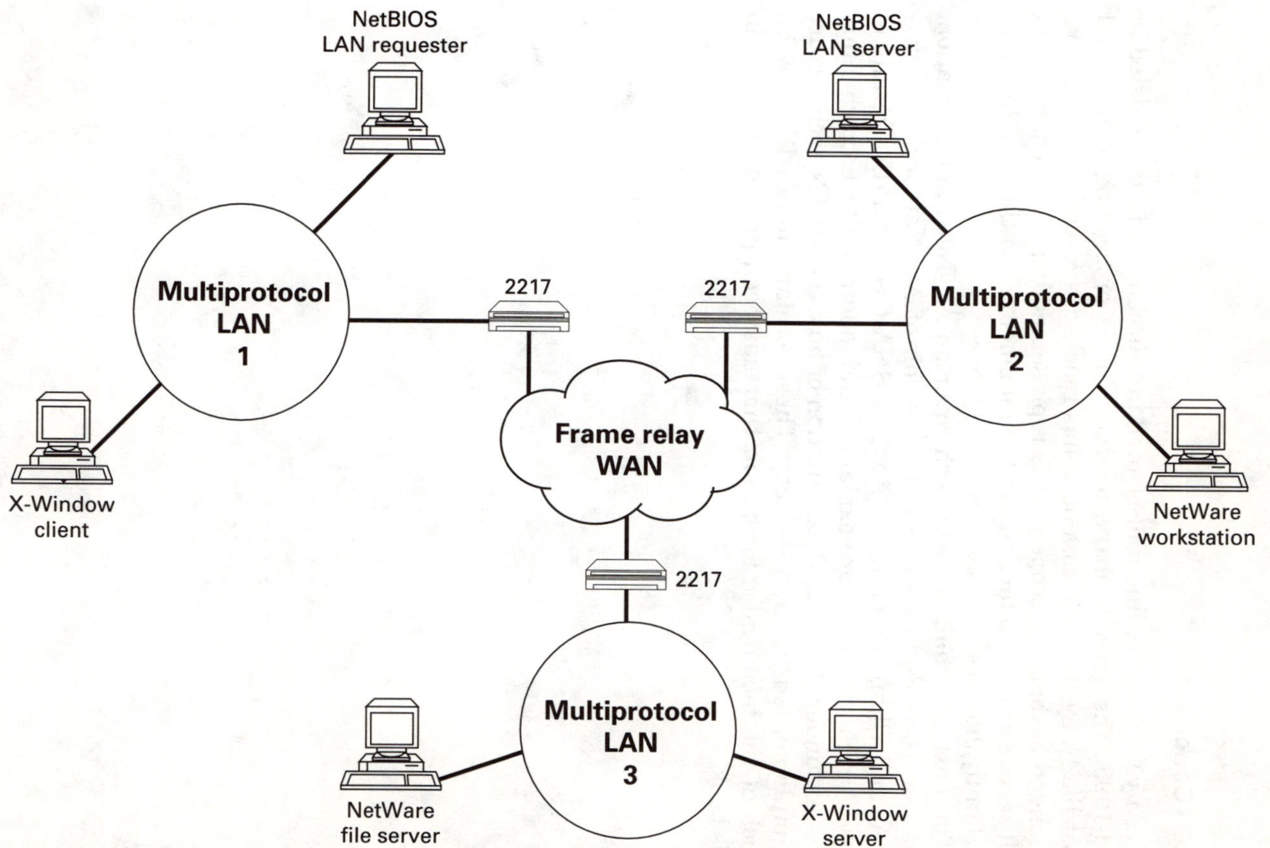

Figure 15.8 Multiprotocol LANs interconnected with 2217 Nways Multiprotocol Concentrators.

using a remote configuration utility that is shipped on a diskette. This utility can be loaded on a workstation to configure the 2217 remotely.

15.4   Conclusion

The AnyNet product line represented in this chapter is as it existed in mid-1995. The growth of the product line is proceeding swiftly, and most likely, by the time this book has reached the reader, it will have expanded beyond the scope that is represented here. The chapter will still serve as an introduction to the fundamentals of the AnyNet product family, however.

The next two chapters will each cover an AnyNet implementation. Chapter 16 is dedicated to a description of AnyNet Sockets-Over-SNA, and Chap. 17 is about AnyNet SNA-Over-TCP/IP. Details of these AnyNet products are explained and, additionally, both chapters give an "under the covers" explanation of how the MPTN architecture is implemented in the products. These explanations will draw on much of the technical information that has been presented so far in this book.

AnyNet Sockets-Over-SNA

16.1   Introduction to AnyNet Sockets-Over-SNA

Chapter 15 presented IBM's AnyNet product line. Chapter 16 is devoted to a single AnyNet product: Sockets-Over-SNA.

Sockets-Over-SNA enables AF_INET sockets applications such as ftp, X-Windows, NFS, telnet, and DCE that normally run in a TCP/IP network, to communicate, without change, in a SNA network. Additionally, the Sockets-Over-SNA gateway interconnects SNA and TCP/IP networks in such a way that sockets applications running in Sockets-Over-SNA nodes in a SNA network can communicate with native sockets applications running in a TCP/IP network. Using two gateways, a SNA network can become a backbone through which two TCP/IP networks can be interconnected.

We will begin our discussion of Sockets-Over-SNA by describing its features and some of the details of its configuration. These details are presented not as a workbook for use by implementors, but as a way for the reader to gain familiarity with the way IBM has implemented the products. Configuration setups are presented for different platforms, and readers familiar with these specific platforms may use these descriptions to advantage. However, none of the configuration details are so specific that the uninitiated cannot understand them.

The discussion of configuration begins with a nonspecific description that is applicable to several platforms. This discussion sheds light on the manner in which IBM designers have implemented the MPTN architecture and also gives the interested reader insights into the ease of use and adaptability of the AnyNet products.

16.2   Configuring Sockets-Over-SNA

The Sockets-Over-SNA product is implemented similarly on several platforms, and our discussion of the Sockets-Over-SNA configuration will begin with general product details and then proceed to configuration details for specific platforms.

16.2.1   Sockets-Over-SNA utility programs

A set of utility programs is provided for some of the Sockets-Over-SNA products:

- *Sxmap* is a utility that can be used to maintain the IP-LU address mapping table.

- *Gwstat* is a gateway utility that displays the status and statistics of connections.

- *Sxtrace* is a trace utility that is used in problem determination.

- *Ifconfig, netstat,* and *route* are TCP/IP utilities used for configuring and displaying the Sockets-Over-SNA interface and routing table.

16.2.2   Defining a local IP address

The first step in the Sockets-Over-SNA configuration process is defining a *local IP address.* The local address is the IP address assigned to the Sockets-Over-SNA interface. It will be recalled from the discussion of TCP/IP in Chap. 4 that IP host addresses represent an *interface:* the point where a computing node attaches to an IP network. Configuring the local interface is accomplished in Sockets-Over-SNA the same way that a native TCP/IP interface is configured on a Unix host. Sockets-Over-SNA uses the same routing table as native TCP/IP and uses the same three basic TCP/IP utilities that were described in Chap. 4 to maintain and display the routing table: ifconfig, netstat, and route.

In a Sockets-Over-SNA network, the local address is an IP address that is configured for an interface called *sna0.* The interface name "sna0" is similar to the "lan0" label that is often used on Unix hosts as the interface name for a single IP interface, but sna0 always indicates that an interface belongs to a Sockets-Over-SNA network. As described in Chap. 4, the *ifconfig* utility program is used to relate an interface name, such as lan0, to an IP address and subnet mask, and to build a minimal routing table. It is also used to display the characteristics of an already-configured interface. In Sockets-Over-SNA, ifconfig is used not only to configure an IP interface, if one exists, but also to configure the sna0 interface as well. If an access node has two interfaces for two separate networks, a TCP/IP network and a

Sockets-Over-SNA network, ifconfig will be used to configure two interfaces: lan0 and sna0.

After the sna0 interface is configured, the *route* utility can be used to add and delete entries from the routing table, and *netstat,* using the -r option, can be used to display the routing table.

16.2.3   Address mapping in Sockets-Over-SNA

The second step in configuring Sockets-Over-SNA is preparing the system for address mapping. It will be recalled from the previous discussions of MPTN address mapping techniques in Chap. 14 that the MPTN architecture defines three ways to implement address mapping: algorithmic, a protocol-specific directory, and an address mapper. Address mapping in Sockets-Over-SNA is accomplished either by using the algorithmic method or by entering address pairs manually for specific Sockets-Over-SNA nodes.

The algorithmic method was selected as the primary method of address mapping in Sockets-Over-SNA because it allows transport provider LU names to be generated automatically from given transport user IP addresses. In large networks, in which many IP address/LU combinations may otherwise have to be entered manually, this is a time-saving measure. Additionally, an MPTN address mapper does not have to be loaded and configured.

16.2.3.1   Algorithmic address mapping.
The algorithmic address mapping method that is used to map transport user addresses into transport provider addresses employs a specific *formula* to translate a particular address belonging to one networking protocol into an address belonging to another. Thus, by applying the algorithm each time address mapping is required, the same result will always be attained. In Sockets-Over-SNA, algorithmic mapping is accomplished by applying a formula to the parameters supplied in specific entries in a table called the *IP-LU mapping table.*

16.2.3.2   The IP-LU mapping table.
The IP-LU mapping table is used in Sockets-Over-SNA to hold all address mapping information for the node. This information has two varieties: (1) table entries that describe a single IP-LU one-to-one mapping and (2) table entries that contain patterns to be used for algorithmic mapping.

The IP-LU mapping table is loaded into memory when Sockets-Over-SNA is first started. It can contain any number of entries, and each entry has four fields, as follows.

- *IP address.*   This is the IP address of a specific remote node, network, or subnetwork.

- *Address mask.*   This is the mask used for algorithmic mapping or 255.255.255.255 to indicate a static one-to-one mapping.

- *SNA network ID.*   This is the name of the SNA network in which a remote node resides, or the SNA network name that corresponds to an IP network or subnetwork.

- *LU name template.*   This field either contains the template that is used for creating LU names, or it contains a specific LU name for a one-to-one mapping.

16.2.3.3 Algorithmic mapping in Sockets-Over-SNA. Algorithmic mapping takes the transport user IP address and maps it to the corresponding SNA transport provider address. It performs this mapping by comparing the transport user IP address that needs to be mapped with each IP address in the IP-LU table. The two IP addresses are compared using the *address mask,* which determines which bits in the IP addresses are to be compared. When an IP address in a table entry, with the mask applied to it, matches the IP address that needs to be mapped, the address mask and *LU name template* fields are used to create the final transport provider LU name, and the SNA network ID provides the final transport provider network name.

For example, if the Sockets-Over-SNA network is defined to TCP/IP as an IP network using the network address 129.10.0.0 and the subnet mask in the IP-LU mapping table is 255.255.0.0, then any IP address belonging to network 129.10.0.0 will cause a match. However, if more than one match is found, the match using the address mask with the most bits turned on is the entry that is used. To create a transport provider LU name, the value in the IP address represented by the remaining bits of the mask, those bits that are not set to 1 in the mask (the IP "host" address), are fed into the algorithm, which generates characters to be appended to the LU name template. The resulting LU name is then connected to the *SNA Network ID* using a period. This creates a fully qualified LU name of the familiar SNA format *NetID.LUname.*

16.2.3.4 How Sockets-Over-SNA uses the IP-LU mapping table. When a Sockets-Over-SNA CMM has an address that needs to be mapped, it issues a P_LOCATE_DC. The PMM searches the IP-LU mapping table, finds the entry that satisfies best the criteria for a match, and then performs the algorithmic address mapping function. If the entry that satisfies the match is a one-for-one entry that specifies a particular remote address, the address mask in the table entry will contain all 1s (255.255.255.255), which will cause the algorithmic address mapping function to use what is in the LU name template as the final LU name.

The PMM searches the IP-LU mapping table by comparing the transport user IP address that is to be resolved with each IP address in the table, while applying the address mask. In other words, the IP address in each table entry is compared to the address that must be resolved, but only the same bits that are 1s in the mask are turned on in the table entry IP address when performing the compare function. Any matches that are made from the various table entries are recorded, and the match that was made using the mask with the most bits turned on is used.

This can be illustrated with an example. Table 16.1 shows an IP-LU mapping table with two entries. The first entry contains an IP address of 129.1.0.0 with a mask of 255.255.0.0. This is a class B IP address with no subnetting in effect. The second entry contains an address of 129.1.1.0 with a mask value of 255.255.255.0. This is a class B address with a subnet of 1. If the destination address is 129.1.1.1, then the second entry is used even though the first entry also matches. The mask for the second entry has more bits turned on. If the second entry contained a different IP address—say, 129.1.2.0 (a subnet of 2), then the first entry would be used to satisfy the request. The IP-LU mapping table can be set up to create an IP subnet to the SNA network one-for-one mapping.

Continuing with our example, after the entry in the IP-LU table has been determined, the address mask field is used again, this time to determine the LU name. The bits that were turned off in the address mask correspond to the numbers of the IP address that will be added to the end of the LU name template to create an LU name. If the address mask contains all 1s, or 255.255.255.255, the LU name template field in the entry contains an exact LU name just as the IP address contains an exact host address. The LU name is combined with the SNA network ID to become the fully qualified LU name of the type NetID.LU-name. Since our address mask is not all 1s, the SNA network ID in the example is NETB, and the LU name is LU, the SNA transport provider address for 129.1.1.1 will be NETB.LU000001. The transport provider address for 129.1.1.2 will be NETB.LU000002, and so on.

Using the algorithmic method, hosts in specific IP networks and subnetworks can be mapped into corresponding LUs in SNA net-

TABLE 16.1 IP-LU Mapping Table: Example 1

IP address	Address mask	SNA NetID	LU name
129.1.0.0	255.255.0.0	NETA	LU
129.1.1.0	255.255.255.0	NETB	LU

TABLE 16.2   IP-LU Mapping Table: Example 2

IP address	Address mask	SNA NetID	LU name
129.1.1.0	255.255.255.0	NETA	LU
129.1.2.0	255.255.255.0	NETB	LU
129.1.3.0	255.255.255.0	NETC	LU

works. Table 16.2 shows an IP-LU table containing three entries. The first entry contains an IP address for network 129.1.1.0 with a mask of 255.255.255.0. This is subnet 1 on IP network 129.1.0.0. The next entry has an IP address of 129.1.2.0 with a mask of 255.255.255.0. This is subnet 2 in the same IP network. The first entry's SNA network ID is NETA; the second is NETB. Clearly, IP subnetworks are mapped to SNA networks. The third entry, 129.1.3.0 with a mask of 255.255.255.0 and a SNA network ID of NETC, will cause IP 129.1.3.0 subnetwork addresses to be mapped to SNA network NETC. Using the IP-LU mapping table of Table 16.2, nodes can be added to any of three SNA networks and the corresponding Sockets-Over-SNA IP addresses will automatically map IP subnetworks to these SNA networks.

It has been mentioned that entries in the mapping table that are specific and not meant to be used for algorithmic address mapping are indicated by setting the mask to all 1s (255.255.255.255). Basically, this says that the entire destination IP address must match the entire IP address in the table (a specific host), and since there are no bits that are *not* turned on in the address mask field of the table entry, no suffix to the LU name template will be added, and just the LU name template itself will be used to create the fully qualified LU name. For example, if the destination IP address of 129.1.1.5 is matched with the entry in Table 16.3, the resulting fully qualified LU name to be used for the destination transport provider will be NETC.LU.

For simplicity, the administrator is urged to use a single entry in the mapping table: A single template to create all LUs. This not only simplifies the table and limits the look-ups on the table, it also ensures that the IP-LU mapping table does not have to be reconfigured when new nodes are added to the Sockets-Over-SNA network.

TABLE 16.3   IP-LU Mapping Table: Example 3

IP address	Address mask	SNA NetID	LU name
129.1.1.5	255.255.255.255	NETC	LU

TABLE 16.4   Sxmap Parameters

ADD	*Add a new entry to the IP-LU mapping table*
	    Arguments: ip_address,
	                   subnet_mask,
	                   sna_netname,
	                   lu_template

DELETE	*Delete an entry from the IP-LU table*
	    Arguments: ip_address_begin_range,
	                   ip_address_end_range,
	                   subnet_mask,
	                   lu_template

FLUSH	*Delete all entries from the IP-LU table*
GET	*Display the entire IP-LU table*
QMAP	*Display the LU name for an entry in the table* Argument: ip_address

CONVERT	*Convert a specified IP address into an LU name*
	    Arguments: ip_address,
	                   subnet_mask,
	                   lu_template

16.2.3.5   The sxmap utility. The sxmap utility is used for configuring the IP-LU mapping table and is available on several AnyNet platforms. The commands used with sxmap are shown in Table 16.4. The sxmap *add* command adds new entries to the table. *Delete* deletes entries from the table. Since there is no update command to change an entry, the entry must first be deleted, then added back. The *get* command displays the table, and *flush* clears it. Two commands are used to show what a resultant LU name will be after the address mapping algorithm has been applied: *Qmap* displays the resultant LU name for the current table entry, and *convert* shows what the resultant LU name would be for any given IP address. *Convert* has been included in sxmap so that LU names that must be defined manually can be determined before their actual entries are added to the table. This option is needed in networks that do not have the dynamic allocation capabilities of APPN. In these networks, the LU names need to be defined statically before they are added to the IP-LU mapping table. The *convert* option can be used to determine what an LU name will be after algorithmic mapping eventually converts the IP address.

16.2.4   Mode assignments

One feature that has been built into the AnyNet Sockets-Over-SNA products takes advantage of the ability to define different levels of service in a SNA network using the *mode name* facility. It will be recalled from Chap. 7 that a mode name is used in SNA networks to define a set of session characteristics. Sockets-Over-SNA allows the network administrator to associate a particular TCP port number, as defined in the */etc/services* (or SERVICES) file, to a particular SNA mode name. This feature enables the network administrator to associate specific TCP/IP services, such as telnet, ftp, or Xwindows (or any sockets application, for that matter) with a mode name that has been defined for the service level required by that service. For specific services not configured this way, a general default is in effect.

16.2.5 Configuring the domain name system

Sockets programs running in a Sockets-Over-SNA network may use the services of the Domain Name System (DNS) associated with TCP/IP networks and described in Chap. 4. Translation of IP host and network names to IP addresses is a necessity for most sockets programs, because most call the *gethostbyname()* sockets function. *Gethostbyname()* uses domain name resolution to convert a name to an IP address.

The DNS name server is not available as part of Sockets-Over-SNA, but it can be used with Sockets-Over-SNA for resolving names if it is otherwise available. In other words, any name server that is reachable from a Sockets-Over-SNA program can be used by that program to resolve domain names as long as a RESOLV file has been correctly configured. The RESOLV file, or */etc/resolv.conf,* is a file used by domain name resolution to locate a name server. If a RESOLV file is not already set up, it can be created to identify a name server.

The */etc/hosts* (HOSTS) and */etc/network* (NETWORKS) files can also be set up in a Sockets-Over-SNA network to resolve host and network names. If TCP/IP is already installed in the node, these files will already be available. If not, they can be created.

16.3 Configuration for the Individual AnyNet Platforms

The various platforms on which Sockets-Over-SNA has been implemented will each be presented from a configuration perspective, to show how the features of Sockets-Over-SNA are provided on individual network nodes.

16.3.1 Configuring AnyNet Sockets-Over-SNA for OS/2

Sockets-Over-SNA is configured on the OS/2 platform from within the AnyNet *configuration notebook*. This notebook is accessed by clicking on the "AnyNet Sockets-Over-SNA" folder, then choosing the

"Configure AnyNet Sockets-Over-SNA" object. The configuration notebook contains a set of five configuration screens, or pages, that can be used to set up the local address and IP-LU mapping table, and to specify the SNA service modes and other parameters.

16.3.1.1 AnyNet configuration notebook page 1. Configuration page 1 is used for configuring the local IP address for the *sna0* interface. It prompts the operator for the following information.

- *Start Sockets-Over-SNA automatically.*   Check "Yes" or "No."

- *IP address for SNA.*   This is the local IP address to be used by Sockets-Over-SNA. This address will be associated with the *sna0* interface.

- *Address mask.*   This is the subnet mask associated with *sna0*.

- *LU template.*   This is the LU name template used to create the LU name for the local IP address.

- *SNA network name.*   This is the SNA network name to be used for the local node.

For gateway nodes, an additional parameter is requested.

- *Gateway connection limit password.*   This is a password supplied by IBM that allows the number of connections that can be supported by the gateway (20, 100, or 250 connections) to be configured.

If the user responds affirmatively to "Start Sockets-Over-SNA automatically," an icon for SXSTART.CMD is added to the system startup folder. SXSTART.CMD is the script that starts Sockets-Over-SNA. It is created from the information supplied on this first page. The IP address for SNA, address mask, LU template, and SNA network name are used to create the sxmap and ifconfig commands that SXSTART.CMD will issue.

16.3.1.2 AnyNet configuration notebook page 2. Configuration page 2 is used to configure the IP-LU mapping table. On this screen, the following fields are entered.

- *IP network ID.*   This is the IP network, subnetwork, or host address.

- *Address mask.*   This field contains an address mask or "255.255.255.255" for a one-to-one mapping.

- *LU template.*   This field contains the LU name template or the LU name for a one-to-one mapping.

- *SNA network name.*   This is the SNA network in which the LU is located.

A "next" button is clicked on to reset the screen in order to create more entries. The data from each screen are used to create an sxmap command in the SXSTART.CMD shell script file.

16.3.1.3   AnyNet configuration notebook page 3.   Configuration page 3, along with page 4, is used to set the following Sockets-Over-SNA start options (Table 16.5).

- *Maximum numbers of sessions per destination.*   The number of SNA sessions needed to support all Sockets-Over-SNA connections.

- *Log file name.*   This entry contains the path and file name for the Sockets-Over-SNA trace output. The default is SNACKETS.LOG.

- *Maximum log file size.*   The size for the log file in bytes is entered here. The default is set at 100 kbytes.

- *Sockets-Over-SNA tracing—current trace options.*   Pressing the "change options" button will cause another panel to be presented. This panel contains options related to tracing.

16.3.1.4   AnyNet configuration notebook page 4.   Configuration page 4 is used to set the following Sockets-Over-SNA start options.

- *SNA data buffer size.*   This field must contain the maximum number of bytes that Sockets-Over-SNA sends at one time. The default is 8300 bytes.

- *Number of idle seconds (time-out for the datagram conversation).* This field designates the time-out value for the datagram conversation. A conversation is allocated when a datagram is sent to a node with which a datagram conversation is not currently allocated. When this conversation is unused for the amount of time specified in this field, it is deallocated. The default setting is 90 seconds. The effect of setting this field depends on the nature of the sockets applications using the network and the frequency of datagram usage.

TABLE 16.5   AnyNet Start Options for OS/2

Option	Default	Range or choice
Maximum sessions per SNA destination	30	Range: 0–32,767
Log file name	SNACKETS.LOG	Any file name
Maximum log file size	100,000 bytes	Range: 1,000 bytes to 2 Gbytes
Tracing	Off	Off or On
SNA buffer size	8,300 bytes	Range: 55–32,767 bytes
Datagram session time-out value	90 seconds	Range: 0–65,536 seconds
Data chaining	MPTN	Choice of MPTN or LL

■ *Use data chaining.*   This field specifies the method to be used in
the segmentation of a datagram if segmentation is required because
of size constraints in the network. "Yes" indicates that the architected MPTN method is to be used; "No" is entered if APPC segmentation, performed using LL values in the buffer, is to be used instead.
The default is "No." "Yes" may need to be specified for interoperability with other MPTN implementations.

The settings from pages 3 and 4 are reflected in the *start snackets*
command generated by the SXSTART.CMD.

16.3.1.5   AnyNet configuration notebook page 5.   Configuration page 5
is used to specify the SNA mode names. The fields on this screen can
also be set as environment variables (Table 16.6).

■ *Default mode for all ports.*   The default mode name is to be used
for all underlying SNA sessions except those representing TCP services that have had SXMODEn variables set for them. This option
sets the environment variable SXMODE_DEFAULT. The default
mode name is SNACKETS.

■ *Modes for individual ports.*   The entry in this field sets the environment variable SXMODEn. This variable relates individual TCP
port numbers to specific SNA mode names. As an example, to cause
all connections destined for TCP port 99 to use the SNA mode name
TSTMODE, set the following environment variable: SXMODE99 =
TSTMODE.

**16.3.2   Configuring the AnyNet Sockets-
Over-SNA gateway for OS/2**

Configuring the AnyNet Sockets-Over-SNA gateway is the same as
configuring Sockets-Over-SNA with the exception of the *gateway connection limit password* that is entered on page 1 of the AnyNet configuration notebook. The gateway, however, has an additional command
that is used to display gateway status and statistics. Called *gwstat,* it
is executed at the command line (Table 16.7).

**16.3.3   Configuring AnyNet Sockets-
Over-SNA for MVS**

AnyNet Sockets-Over-SNA for MVS is installed on an IBM mainframe using the *System Modification Program* (SMP). The datasets

TABLE 16.6   AnyNet Environment Variables for OS/2

SXMODE_DEFAULT	The default mode name for Sockets-Over-SNA; default is *SNACKETS*
SXMODEn	Mode name for port *n*

TABLE 16.7   Gwstat Command

gwstat -c	Displays the status of all active connections.
gwstat -d gwID	Displays the status of a single active connection. gwID is the ID of the entry to be displayed.
gwstat	Displays statistics relating to all active connections.

that are updated or created during the installation process are shown in Table 16.8. Sockets-Over-SNA utilities are available on the MVS platform and are stored in the *sys1.vtamlib* dataset. The actual names used for the utility programs have been created to conform with MVS standards and are shown in Table 16.9.

16.3.3.1 Defining Sockets-Over-SNA to VTAM. Because it operates as an LU 6.2 application program, Sockets-Over-SNA must be defined to VTAM. A VTAM APPL major node definition is included in VTAMLST for each copy of Sockets-Over-SNA, and the ACBNAME parameter in the APPL definition must contain the local LU name.

TABLE 16.8   Datasets Used by AnyNet for MVS

SYS1.LPALIB:	Cross-memory code
SYS1.LINKLIB:	Cross-memory code
SYS1.VTAMLIB:	Most of the product load modules
SYS1.SAMPLIB:	Samples of HOST, NETWORKS, PROTOCOL, SERVICES, RESOLV files
SYS1.SISTLMD1:	API code needed by applications at runtime
SYS1.SISTDAT2:	Message source
SYS1.SISDAT3:	API stubs to be link-edited with application programs
SYS1.SISDAT4:	Downloadable OS/2 code
SYS1.SISTMAC2:	C header files to be included in application programs

TABLE 16.9   Sockets-Over-SNA for MVS Utility Programs

Name	Load module name
sxmap	istskmap
sxtrace	istsktrc
ifconfig	istskifc
netstat	istsknst
route	istskrte
ping	istskpng

The local LU name is the transport provider LU name associated with the local IP transport user address and is obtained by running sxmap with the address mask and LU name template that will be used by ifconfig to configure the sna0 interface.

It is necessary to ensure that the following APPL parameters are set thus: APPC = YES and AUTOSESS = 0. The MODETAB parameter can be set to point to a logon mode table that contains the mode names used by Sockets-Over-SNA. At least one MODEENT macro entry is necessary for the logon mode for the LU 6.2 sessions that are established by Sockets-Over-SNA. The default logon mode name is SNACK-ETS for all the conversations that are allocated by Sockets-Over-SNA.

If VTAM is not configured for APPN, all destination nodes to which connections will be established must be defined as independent LUs, a task that is accomplished by defining *Cross-Domain Resource* (CDRSC) major nodes. CDRSCs are necessary only when a mainframe sockets program attempts to initiate a connection which is not locatable via APPN. The *convert* option of sxmap can be used to determine the LU names that must be defined.

16.3.3.2 Defining a local IP address. Defining the local IP address and subnet mask for the Sockets-Over-SNA sna0 interface is accomplished by using the *ifconfig* utility. Ifconfig is member ISTSKIFC in the vtamlib partitioned dataset. The ifconfig command can be issued either from a batch JCL dataset or using TSO. As an example, the following command could be entered on the TSO command line:

```
call 'sys1.vtamlib(istskifc)' 'sna0 129.10.10.10 netmask 255.255.255.0'
```

16.3.3.3 Using the route utility. Routes can be configured using the *route* utility, which can be run interactively using TSO, or in a JCL batch file. The parameters used for the route utility are add/delete, net/host, destination/default, and gateway/metric. As an example, the following command could be entered at the TSO command line:

```
call 'sys1.vtamlib(istskrte)' 'add net 129.10.0.0 129.10.0.1 1'
```

16.3.3.4 Configuring the IP-LU mapping table. Sxmap is used to configure the IP-LU mapping table. Sxmap is member ISTSKMAP in the sys1.vtamlib partitioned dataset and may be invoked from either TSO or batch JCL. From the TSO command line, an example call to sxmap would look like this:

```
call 'sys1.vtamlib(istskmap)' 'add 129.10.1.0 255.255.255.0 NET1 LU'
```

16.3.3.5 Defining environment variables. A number of configuration parameters can be set and, because they are similar to those in OS/2, they are called *environment variables*. Since the concept of an envi-

TABLE 16.10   AnyNet ENVVAR Parameters for MVS

ADDRINFO	Dataset name of the HOSTS.ADDRINFO dataset
COMMENT	Character to be used for a comment character other than '#'
DG_CONV_IDLE_TIMEOUT	Amount of time-out for an unused datagram conversation
DG_SEGMENTATION	Type of datagram segmentation: LL or MPTN
DNS_XLATE_TABLE	Dataset name for the ASCII-to-EBCDIC translate table
ETC_HOSTS	Dataset name for the HOSTS dataset
ETC_NETWORKS	Dataset name for the NETWORKS dataset
ETC_PROTOCOLS	Dataset name for the PROTOCOLS dataset
ETC_RESOLV	Dataset name for the RESOLV dataset
ETC_SERVICES	Dataset name for the SERVICES dataset
GROUP_NAME	Group name (instead of *SNACKETS*)
HOSTS_FILE_FORMAT	Format of HOST and NETWORK files: BSD or MVSTCP
HOSTNAME	Host name to be returned by gethostname()
MAX_DG_CONVS	Maximum number of datagram conversations allocated at once
MAX_SENDBUF	Maximum size in bytes of the outbound send buffer
NUMBER_OF_SERVERS	Maximum number of server tasks in the address space
SITEINFO	Name of the SITEINFO dataset
SXMODE_DEFAULT	Mode name to use as the default (instead of *SNACKETS*)
SXMODEn	Mode name to use for TCP port n instead of the default
USE_TCPIP_FORMAT	Obsolete

ronment variable is foreign to MVS, these configuration parameters are stored in a flat file called the ENVVAR dataset. The ENVVAR DD JCL statement can be coded in the job used to start Sockets-Over-SNA with a "DSN =" that points to an EBCDIC dataset containing the Sockets-Over-SNA configuration parameters listed in Table 16.10.

16.3.3.6   Defining mode names.   Both the default mode name and the mode names used to represent TCP services can be set using "environment variables."

- *Default mode for all ports.*   This is the default mode name used for all SNA LU 6.2 sessions except those that represent TCP services and have SXMODEn variables defined for them. The default mode environment variable is called SXMODE_DEFAULT. If this variable is not set, the *default* default mode name *SNACKETS* is used.

- *Modes for individual ports.*   The environment variable SXMODEn relates individual TCP port numbers to specific SNA mode names. To cause all connections destined for TCP port 99 to use the SNA mode name TSTMODE, set the following environment variable: SXMODE99 = TSTMODE.

16.3.3.7 Running Sockets-Over-SNA. Sockets-Over-SNA is started either as a job or as a "proc." Operation parameters come from the dataset pointed to by an ENVVAR DD statement on the job JCL, or by execution of one of the utility programs. A setup job is run in MVS when Sockets-Over-SNA starts that is functionally equivalent to the EXSTARTN.CMD script that is run in OS/2 workstations. The IP-LU mapping table and the local address are configured by this job, which issues *sxmap, ifconfig,* and *route* commands to set up the environment.

A sample JCL dataset that runs *sxmap, ifconfig, netstat, route,* and *sxtrace* is shown in Table 16.11.

16.3.4 Configuring AnyNet Sockets-Over-SNA for AIX

Configuring Sockets-Over-SNA for AIX on the RS/6000 is accomplished by using the *System Management Interface Tool* (SMIT). Configuration for any IBM RS/6000 product is accomplished using SMIT, and this interface should be familiar to RS/6000 administrators. SMIT is a system of menus and screens that display the parameters available in the configuration or installation process. In order to access specific screens within this menu hierarchy quickly, SMIT provides a *fast path name* for screens. This allows a user to get quickly to a particular screen without having to traverse an entire menu tree.

To invoke the Sockets-Over-SNA menu, the fast path command that is entered at the AIX command prompt is

```
smit _snackets
```

This command loads SMIT and a menu called "AnyNet Sockets-Over-SNA." The first entry from this menu is a screen called "Minimum Configuration (required)." From this menu, select "Add/Change/Show a Profile." (A SMIT profile can be thought of as a configuration record.) For each Sockets-Over-SNA screen, a configuration record/profile with a specific name is created. Using the profile concept, multiple sets of configurations can be stored, and each can be evoked using a specific name.

16.3.4.1 SMIT *minimum configuration* screen. The "Add Minimum Configuration Profile" SMIT screen prompts the administrator for the following information. The first set of parameters on the screen is called "local information":

TABLE 16.11   MVS Configuration JCL

//SETUP	JOB CLASS = A,MSGCLASS = A,MSGLEVEL = (1,1)
//SXMAP	EXEC PGM = ISTSKMAP,
//	PARM = ('add 129.1.1.0 255.255.255.0 USIBMNR LUNUM')
//STEPLIB	DD DSN = SYS1.VTAMLIB,DISP = SHR
//	DD DSN = SISTLMD1,DISP = SHR
//	DD DSN = EDC.V2R1M0,SEDCLINK,DISP = SHR
//	DD DSN = PLI.V2R3M0,SIBMLINK,DISP = SHR
//SYSABEND	DD SYSOUT = A
//SYSPRINT	DD SYSOUT = A
//LOCONFIG	EXEC PGM = ISTSKIFC,PARM = ('lo localhost')
//STEPLIB	DD DSN = SYS1.VTAMLIB,DISP = SHR
//	DD DSN = SISTLMD1,DISP = SHR
//	DD DSN = EDC.V2R1M0,SEDCLINK,DISP = SHR
//	DD DSN = PLI.V2R3M0,SIBMLINK,DISP = SHR
//SYSABEND	DD SYSOUT = A
//SYSPRINT	DD SYSOUT = A
//IFCONFIG	EXEC PGM = ISTSKIFC,PARM = ('sna0 129.1.1.1')
//STEPLIB	DD DSN = SYS1.VTAMLIB,DISP = SHR
//	DD DSN = SISTLMD1,DISP = SHR
//	DD DSN = EDC.V2R1M0,SEDCLINK,DISP = SHR
//	DD DSN = PLI.V2R3M0,SIBMLINK,DISP = SHR
//SYSABEND	DD SYSOUT = A
//SYSPRINT	DD SYSOUT = A
//ROUTE	EXEC PGM = ISTSKRTE,PARM = ('add default 129.1.1.2 1')
//STEPLIB	DD DSN = SYS1.VTAMLIB,DISP = SHR
//	DD DSN = SISTLMD1,DISP = SHR
//	DD DSN = EDC.V2R1M0,SEDCLINK,DISP = SHR
//	DD DSN = PLI.V2R3M0,SIBMLINK,DISP = SHR
//SYSABEND	DD SYSOUT = A
//SYSPRINT	DD SYSOUT = A
//NETSTAT	EXEC PGM = ISTSKNST,PARM = ('sna0 129.1.1.1')
//STEPLIB	DD DSN = SYS1.VTAMLIB,DISP = SHR
//	DD DSN = SISTLMD1,DISP = SHR
//	DD DSN = EDC.V2R1M0,SEDCLINK,DISP = SHR
//	DD DSN = PLI.V2R3M0,SIBMLINK,DISP = SHR
//SYSABEND	DD SYSOUT = A
//SYSPRINT	DD SYSOUT = A
//SXTRACE	EXEC PGM = ISTSKTRC,PARM = ('on all')
//STEPLIB	DD DSN = SYS1.VTAMLIB,DISP = SHR
//	DD DSN = SISTLMD1,DISP = SHR
//	DD DSN = EDC.V2R1M0,SEDCLINK,DISP = SHR
//	DD DSN = PLI.V2R3M0,SIBMLINK,DISP = SHR
//SYSABEND	DD SYSOUT = A
//SYSPRINT	DD SYSOUT = A

- *Profile name.*   This is the name assigned to this profile.

- *IP address.*   This is the local IP address to be associated with the sna0 interface.

- *Subnet mask.*   This is the subnet mask associated with the sna0 interface.

- *Mode name.*   The default mode name is used for all sessions initiated from this platform that do not have specific mode names set for them. The default is SNACKETS.

- *Maximum send buffer size.*   This sets the maximum size of the SNA buffer that is used to build and contain outgoing data packets. The range for this field is 1,024–32,767 bytes, and the default setting is 8,300 bytes.

- *Datagram conversation time-out.*   This field specifies the amount of time, in seconds, before an unused datagram conversation is automatically deallocated. A datagram conversation is allocated by Sockets-Over-SNA for datagrams that are sent to a particular destination. When these conversations are unused for the time-out period, they are deallocated. The default setting is 90 seconds.

- *Connection start time-out.*   This field sets the amount of time, in seconds, that Sockets-Over-SNA waits for a response from a partner node when a conversation is being allocated. The default setting is 90 seconds.

The second set of parameters on the screen is called "LU mapping information":

- *LU name template.*   This field contains the template to be used to generate the local SNA-LU name or the LU name itself. The default setting is "s."

- *LU mapping field.*   This field contains the subnet mask used for the local IP address and to create the local LU name algorithmically. A value of all 1's (255.255.255.255) indicates that the LU name template (above) contains the actual LU name.

16.3.4.2 SMIT *remote address mapping* screen.   The "Remote Address Mapping" screen is used to build the IP-LU mapping table. The following fields are entered:

- *Profile name.*   This is the name assigned to this profile.

- *Remote IP address.*   This is a network, subnetwork, or host IP address.

- *LU mapping mask.*   This field contains the algorithmic mapping mask or 255.255.255.255 to indicate one-for-one mapping. The default setting is "s."

- *LU name template.* This field contains the template for algorithmic LU name mapping or an explicit LU name.

- *Network name.* This is the SNA network name associated with the remote node.

16.3.4.3 SMIT *SNA mode to socket port assignment* screen. The next SMIT screen is "SNA Mode to Socket Port Assignment." This profile contains the mode assignments. The screen contains the following fields:

- *Profile name.* This is the name assigned to this profile.

- *Mode name.* This is the mode that is to be used for sessions that are established with a partner using the TCP port number in the following field. The mode that is specified must also be defined in a SNA Server/6000 mode profile.

- *TCP/IP port number.* This is the TCP/IP port number.

16.3.4.4 SMIT *static route to Sockets-Over-SNA gateway* screen. The next SMIT screen, "Static Route to Sockets-Over-SNA Gateway," is provided for adding a gateway entry in the routing table, using the *route* command. This screen can be used to place a route to an AnyNet Sockets-Over-SNA gateway for OS/2 in the table. AnyNet gateways are marked in the routing table as IP routers. The screen contains the following fields:

- *Profile name.* This field sets the name assigned to this profile.

- *Destination type.* Select *net* or *host* to indicate whether the destination is for a network or a host. *Net* is the default.

- *Destination address.* This field specifies the IP address of the host or network that can be reached through the gateway.

- *Gateway address.* The gateway address entered with the route command is the IP address of the gateway.

16.3.4.5 Other AIX configuration details. AnyNet for AIX is started and stopped using these commands:

```
sna -start anynet
sna -stop anynet
```

The active connections can be displayed using

```
sna -display anynet
```

The sxmap utility is available as a command-line option. ifconfig, netstat, and route are available to be used for both TCP/IP and Sockets-

Over-SNA networks. The sxtrace utility is not available. Tracing is performed by other means documented in SNA Server for AIX manuals.

16.3.5 Configuring AnyNet
Sockets-Over-SNA for the AS/400

There are no special installation requirements for Sockets-Over-SNA for the AS/400, because the product is already part of the base OS/400 operating system. In order to configure Sockets-Over-SNA, two prerequisites are necessary.

- An underlying APPC configuration must be established between end systems before any other configuration can take place.

- The network attribute ALWANYNET must be set to *YES using the CHGNETA command. By setting this AS/400 network attribute, all AnyNet products are allowed for use in the node. AS/400 network attributes can be displayed with the DSPNETA command.

Following these prerequisites, use the CFGIPS command to display the "Configure IP over SNA" menu. Use option 1, "Work with IP over SNA Interfaces," to enter the local IP address(es) and subnet mask(s); option 2, "Work with IP over SNA Routes," to define routes; option 3, "Work with IP over SNA Locations," to enter the IP-LU mappings for the local and remote nodes; and option 4, "Work with IP over SNA Type of Service," to enter mode names associated with particular services. Option 20, "Convert IP Address Into Location Name," provides the AS/400 with the sxmap convert option that was explained in Sec. 16.2.3.5. Option 21 is "Convert Location Name Into IP Address."

16.3.5.1 Screen 1: *work with IP over SNA interface.* Screen 1, "Work with IP over SNA Interface," is used to enter the local IP address. The administrator is prompted for the following information.

- *Opt.*   1 = Add, 2 = Change, 4 = Remove, 9 = Start, 10 = End.

- *Internet address.*   This is the local IP address.

- *Subnet mask.*   This field contains the subnet mask to be associated with the interface.

The IP address(es) and subnet mask(s) that are used by the local system for Sockets-Over-SNA are specified using this screen. The first field on all of the configuration screens is "Opt," and it is used for specifying the option. An option must be chosen from among those indicated as being available. For this screen, the Add, Change, Remove, Start, and End options can be used.

After the interface is created with this screen, it is automatically started and is shown as *active* on the screen. Up to eight Sockets-Over-SNA interfaces can be configured and started.

16.3.5.2 Screen 2: *work with IP over SNA routes.* Screen 2, "Work with IP over SNA Routes," implements the TCP/IP route command and adds routes to the AS/400's IP routing table. Entries in the routing table are necessary for destinations outside the local network. IP hosts and gateways located on a TCP/IP network that is attached to an AnyNet Sockets-Over-SNA gateway for OS/2 must be specified with this screen.

- *Opt.*   1 = Add, 4 = Remove.

- *Route destination.*   This field contains the destination network, subnetwork, or host IP address.

- *Subnet mask.*   This is the subnet mask associated with the IP address, if it represents a network. A value of *HOST is entered if the destination is a host.

- *Next hop.*   This is the IP address of a gateway through which the destination is reached.

    Entries in this screen can be added or removed as indicated in the Opt field.

16.3.5.3 Screen 3: *work with IP over SNA locations.* Screen 3, "Work with IP over SNA Locations," is used to create IP-LU table entries. Entries can be one-for-one IP-LU entries, or an entry that specifies the parameters that enable algorithmic mapping to take place. The fields in this panel are as follows.

- *Opt.*   1 = Add, 2 = Change, 4 = Remove.

- *Remote destination.*   This field contains the IP address of a specific remote node or for a network or subnetwork.

- *Subnet mask.*   This field contains the subnet mask. A value of *HOST sets this field to 255.255.255.255, which indicates a one-to-one IP-LU mapping.

- *Remote network ID.*   This is the SNA network name for the remote destination network. A value of *NETATR indicates that the value specified in the AS/400 network attributes should be used.

- *Location template.*   This is the LU name template for algorithmic mapping or an explicit LU name.

16.3.5.4 Screen 4: *work with IP over SNA type of service.* Screen 4, "Work with IP over SNA Type of Service," is used to change the SNA mode name that is associated with a particular type of service. The fields in this panel are as follows.

- *Opt.*   2 = Change.

- *Type of service.*   These types of service are available: MINDELAY, MAXTHRPUT, MAXRLB, MINCOST, NORMAL.

- *SNA mode.*   This field contains mode names that have been previously defined.

Modes are created using the CRTMODD (Create Mode Description) command. A SNACKETS mode may be created using CRTMODD.

16.3.5.5   Other AS/400 configuration details.   *Netstat* is executed by entering the NETSTAT command. Option 1 from the main menu yields a "Work with TCP/IP Interface Status" panel. This panel shows the routing table and the interface status.

16.4   Components of Sockets-Over-SNA

The remainder of this chapter discusses more technical details of Sockets-Over-SNA. It is suggested that the reader be familiar with the material presented in Chap. 11 before attempting to understand the components to be described.

For this discussion of Sockets-Over-SNA components, the AIX implementation will be described. The product is implemented differently for the OS/2, MVS, and AS/400 platforms. The components of the AnyNet Sockets-Over-SNA access node used in our example are shown in Fig. 16.1. At the top of this figure is an application program that has implemented the Berkeley AF_INET sockets API. Below the application program is the *socket layer,* which contains the actual socket functions such as *socket(), bind(), listen(),* and so forth. When a socket function is called, the socket layer performs syntax checking of the function's arguments, retrieving of socket information, and other protocol-*independent* duties, then calls a function called pr_usrreq() to handle the protocol-*dependent* work of the function call. In the Sockets-Over-SNA access node, pr_usrreq() resides in the syntax mapper component of the transport user.

The syntax mapper must perform the task of determining whether the request is for an endpoint located in the Sockets-Over-SNA network, or an endpoint located on a native TCP/IP network. Sockets-Over-SNA requests are mapped by the syntax mapper into TLPB downcalls for the CMM. The CMM uses the BSPB to issue calls to the PMM, and the PMM issues APPC calls to the transport provider.

Each Sockets-Over-SNA component will now be described.

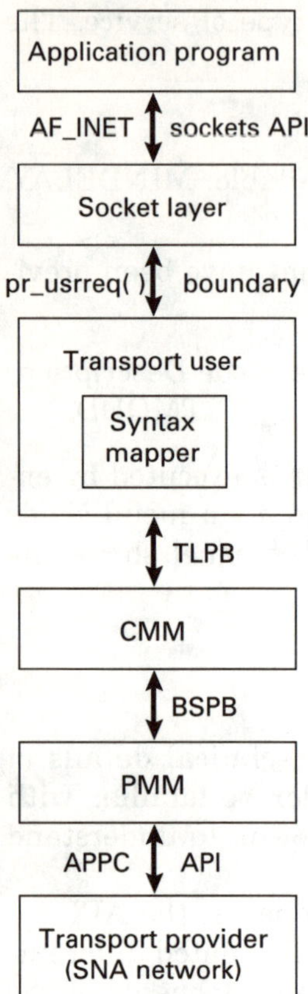

Figure 16.1   Sockets-Over-SNA components.

16.4.1   The socket layer

The *socket layer* resides between the application programs that are using the sockets API and the Sockets-Over-SNA transport user. The actual sockets API functions themselves reside in the socket layer. In Sockets-Over-SNA, only the internet address family AF_INET (described in Chap. 5) is supported. Other address families, such as AF_UNIX and AF_NS, are not. In other words, only sockets programs intended for use with the internet protocols (TCP, UDP, and raw sockets) are supported. Therefore, any normal TCP/IP socket program, such as ftp, ping, rlogin, telnet, rcp, SNMP, and X-Windows programs, can run in a Sockets-Over-SNA network.

When an application program makes a sockets API call, the actual function that is called is located in the socket layer. This function parses the request parameters and calls another routine to perform protocol-dependent processing. The pr_usrreq() function that is called

TABLE 16.12   Pr_usrreq Requests

PRU_ABORT	Abort a connection	PRU_ACCEPT	Accept a connection
PRU_ATTACH	Create a new socket	PRU_BIND	Bind address to socket
PRU_CONNECT	Connect with remote user	PRU_CONNECT2	Connect sockets in AF_UNIX
PRU_DETACH	Close socket	PRU_DISCONNECT	Break socket connection
PRU_LISTEN	Listen for connection	PRU_PEERADDR	Return peer address
PRU_RCVD	Data were received	PRU_RCVOOB	Receive out-of-band data
PRU_SEND	Send data	PRU_SENDOOB	Send out-of-band data
PRU_SHUTDOWN	Shut down connection	PRU_SOCKADDR	Return local address

to process the protocol-specific parts of the socket request is formatted in the C language as follows:

```
int pr_usrreq( struct socket *so, int request, struct mbuf *m0, *m1, *m2);
```

where *so* points to a socket structure which contains information about the socket, *request* contains the type of request represented by the socket function call, and *m0, m1, m2* are the parameters that are passed in the call. The parameters m0, m1, and m2 have a unique type for each use of the pr_userreq call (in other words, for each request type). They are specified in the function prototype as pointers to *mbuf* structures, however. The socket request types represented by the *request* parameter are listed in Table 16.12, and the observant reader will see that they correspond to the various calls of the sockets API. Normally, the pr_usrreq() function resides in the TCP, UPD, or raw sockets protocol-specific routines, but in a Sockets-Over-SNA implementation, the pr_usrreq() function is located in the syntax mapper of the transport user. This feat is accomplished by Sockets-Over-SNA replacing the original pointers to pr_usrreq() routines with new pointers pointing to the appropriate syntax mapper pr_usrreq() function. The original pointers are saved by the syntax mapper so that it can pass requests to the native functions if it determines that they are not destined for the Sockets-Over-SNA network.

16.4.2   The transport user

The *transport user* is the code that lies between the routines of the socket layer and the CMM. Its principal component is the *syntax mapper,* which is responsible for mapping sockets calls to TLPB downcalls. Most of the sockets calls map directly to TLPB downcalls, but some do not. Code in the transport user handles nonmappable requests such as the getsockname(), getpeername(), and select() function calls.

16.4.2.1   The syntax mapper.   When a pr_usrreq() function is called, the first task performed by the syntax mapper is to determine whether the underlying transport provider network is native or nonnative. If the transport provider is a native network, the syntax mapper forwards the request to the original pr_usrreq() function located in the native TCP/IP stack, the pointer to which was saved by the transport user's initialization code. Otherwise the syntax mapper maps the request into a TLPB call. How mapping between pr_usrreq() requests and TLPB calls is performed will be explained in Sec. 16.5.

16.4.3   The CMM

The Sockets-Over-SNA *CMM* receives TLPB downcalls from, and sends TLPB upcalls to, transport users, and implements an MPTN access node. There is no address mapper client in the Sockets-Over-SNA CMM. The address mapper is not implemented in the Sockets-Over-SNA for AIX product.

16.4.4   The PMM

The *PMM* handles protocol-dependent functions for the CMM, such as maintaining the IP-LU mapping table. The PMM establishes APPC conversations in which MPTN messages, TCP/IP connection data, and UDP datagrams are transported. Conversations that are to be used exclusively for datagrams sent to any single IP address are called *datagram conversations.* These conversations are allocated when the first P_SEND_DG_DC is issued for a particular destination address, and are deallocated after an inactivity timer for datagram sessions, designated by the network administrator, expires.

When a P_CONNECT_DC is received by the PMM, it attempts to allocate a full-duplex APPC conversation to provide a two-way path for full-duplex TCP traffic. If the remote SNA implementation does not support the full-duplex feature of APPC, two sessions—which provide two conversations—are established instead, and TCP traffic is divided so that the two conversations are used bidirectionally. These conversations are deallocated when the MPTN connection is closed. The PMM maps all BSPB requests from the CMM into appropriate APPC basic conversation calls, which are issued to the SNA transport provider network.

16.4.5 The transport provider

The *transport provider* is the SNA network that the PMM uses. The PMM appears to the SNA network as an APPC transaction program with a *TP_name* of X'28F0F0F1'. Obviously, this name was chosen by Sockets-Over-SNA designers because of its uniqueness. All conversations allocated by the PMM have a conversation_type of *basic*.

16.5 Connection Establishment in the Sockets-Over-SNA Access Node

To demonstrate how all the AnyNet Sockets-Over-SNA components work in conjunction with each other, an example will show what happens when a TCP/IP socket is established over a SNA network using Sockets-Over-SNA access nodes (Fig. 16.2). The example will draw on information already presented in this book. The sockets API was presented in Chap. 5, and SNA in Chap. 6. Chapter 11 presented the TLPB and BSPB calls used in our example, Chap. 13 explained the MPTN formats used for establishing a connection, and Chap. 14 explained how address mapping works. All of this information is required to understand the sequence of events in this example.

Our example presents a SNA network that contains two access nodes: access node 1 and access node 2. Application program 1 is the client and application program 2 provides the server side of the connection. Application program 2, residing in access node 2, issues a socket() call with AF_INET and SOCK_STREAM parameters to establish a TCP/IP socket endpoint, then issues bind(), listen(), and accept() calls. Application program 1, located in access node 1, issues a socket() and a connect(). The whole sequence of events that takes place in establishing the Sockets-Over-SNA connection is illustrated in the flow diagram of Fig. 16.2.

The flow diagram shows five components in each access node:

- Application program
- Socket layer
- Transport user syntax mapper
- CMM
- PMM

In the interests of keeping the diagram as uncluttered as possible, a sixth component, the transport provider, has not been included in the figure.

The following dialog explains Fig. 16.2.

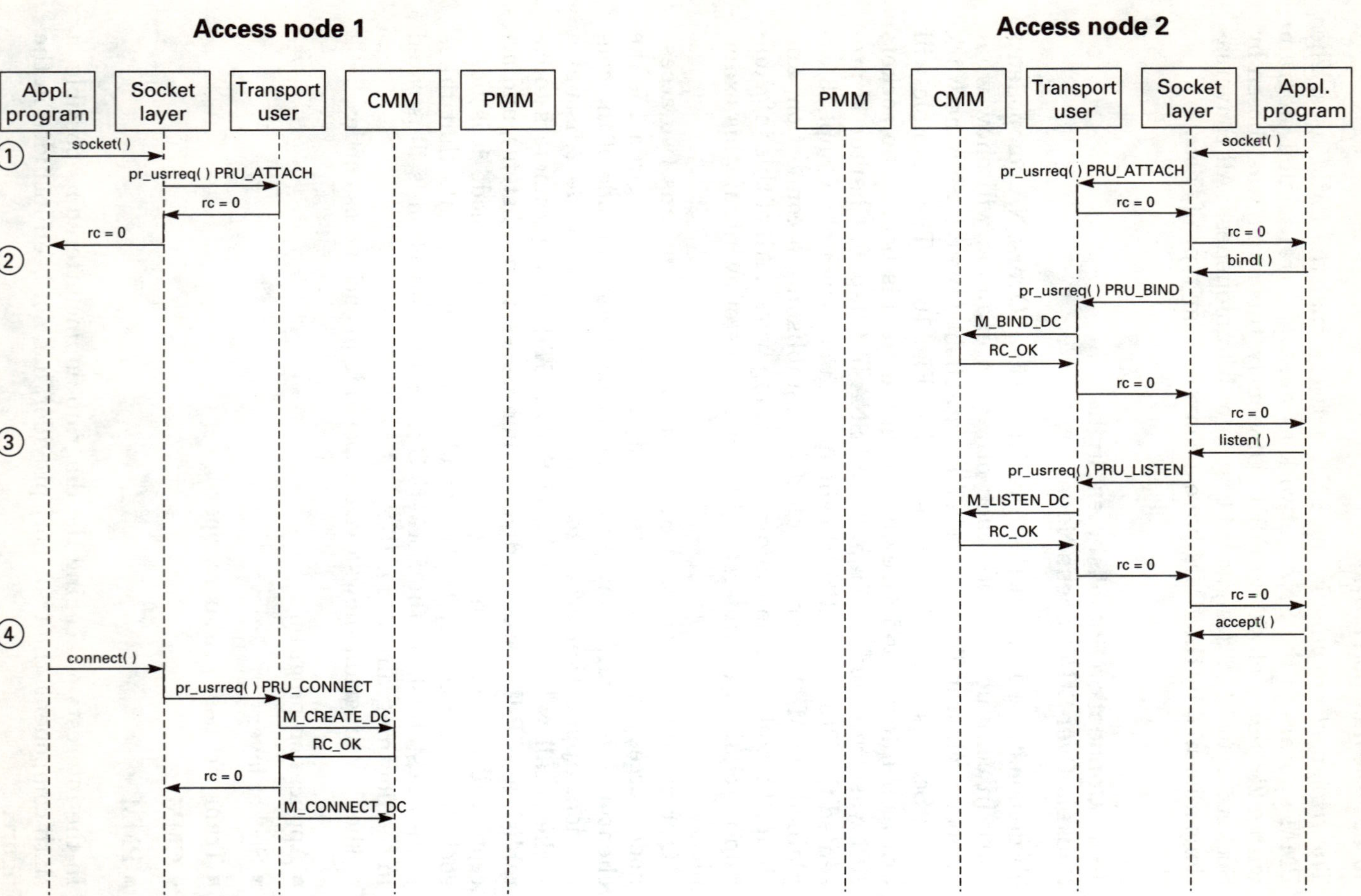

Access node 1
Appl. program
Socket layer
Transport user
CMM
PMM
socket( )
pr_usrreq( ) PRU_ATTACH
rc = 0
rc = 0
connect( )
pr_usrreq( ) PRU_CONNECT_DC
M_CREATE_DC
RC_OK
rc = 0
M_CONNECT_DC
Access node 2
PMM
CMM
Transport user
Socket layer
Appl. program
socket( )
pr_usrreq( ) PRU_ATTACH
rc = 0
rc = 0
bind( )
pr_usrreq( ) PRU_BIND
M_BIND_DC
RC_OK
rc = 0
rc = 0
listen( )
pr_usrreq( ) PRU_LISTEN
M_LISTEN_DC
RC_OK
rc = 0
rc = 0
accept( )

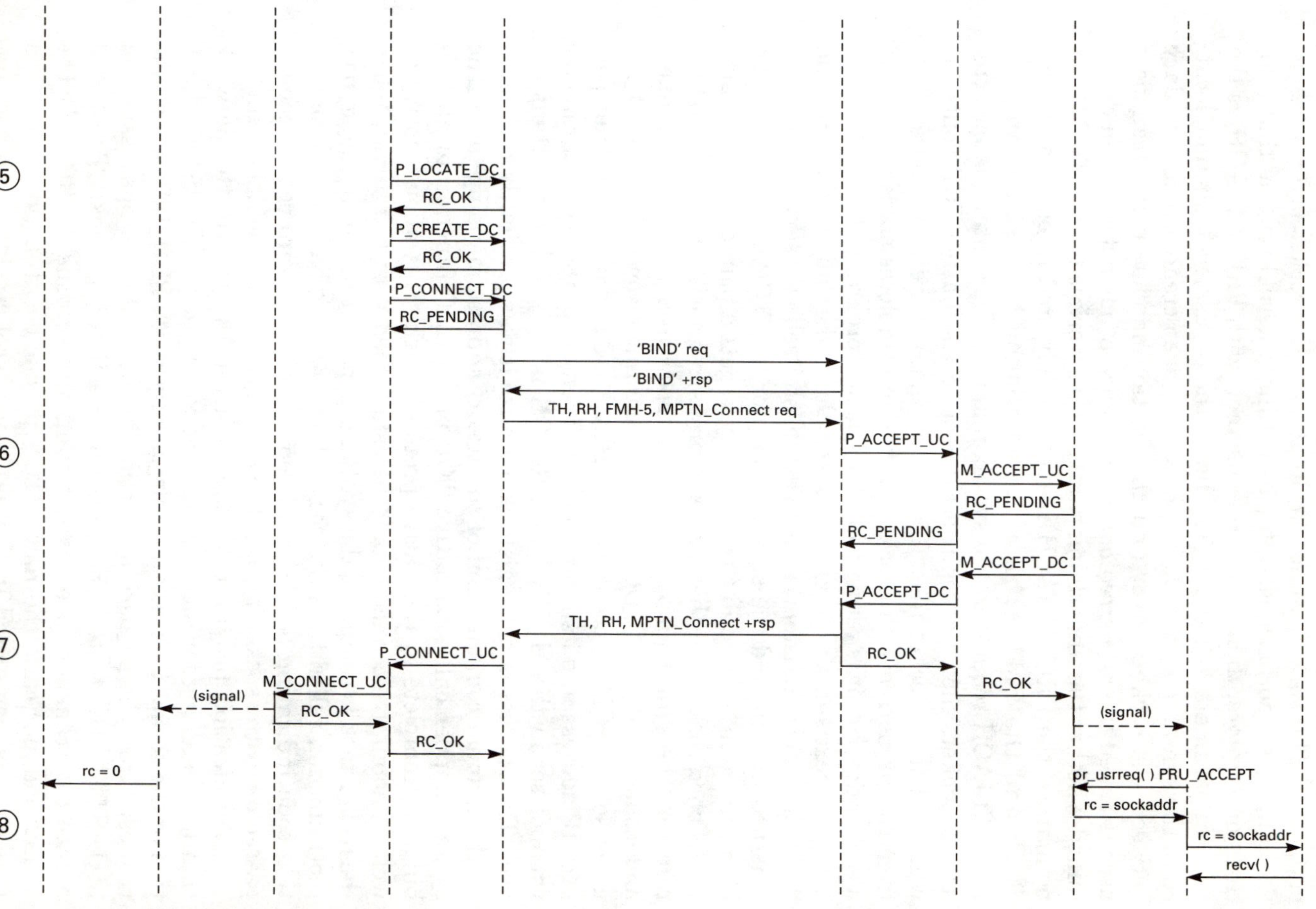

Figure 16.2 Establishing a Sockets-Over-SNA connection.

1. Application programs 1 and 2 both issue a SOCK_STREAM socket() call for the AF_INET address family. These calls establish socket endpoints. The socket() function, located in the socket layer, receives the call, gets a socket descriptor by calling a kernel routine that allocates descriptors, then issues a pr_usrreq() with PRU_ATTACH as the request parameter. PRU_ATTACH tells the pr_usrreq() function, located in the syntax mapper, that a socket has been created. The boundary between the sockets layer and the syntax mapper in the transport user is called the *pr_usrreq boundary*. Since it has not yet been determined whether the underlying transport network is native (TCP/IP) or nonnative, the PRU_ATTACH request is delivered to both the native stack and the CMM. This is accomplished by first passing the PRU_ATTACH request to the syntax mapper. The syntax mapper creates a socket, then passes the request to the native TCP routines, which create a socket also. The syntax mapper returns successfully from the pr_usrreq(), the socket() function completes successfully, and a socket descriptor is returned to application programs 1 and 2.

2. The next step in the process takes place when application program 2 issues bind() and listen() calls to establish itself as a server. The bind() is issued first to bind the socket descriptor to a TCP port number. The bind() function, located in the socket layer, gets a pointer to its already-established socket and then issues a pr_usrreq() with a PRU_BIND parameter. The syntax mapper in the transport user receives the request and issues an M_BIND_DC. The *regist* parameter on this M_BIND_DC is not set. The CMM receives the M_BIND_DC and places the transport user IP address into its internal table. Then, since the *regist* parameter was not set in the M_BIND_DC, RC_OK is returned to the transport user. The address is not registered because it was previously registered by the manual configuration of the IP-LU address mapping table. The syntax mapper calls the native TCP pr_usrreq() function to allow a bind() to complete in the native protocol stack. This allows native as well as nonnative connections to be established with the server. When the native task is complete, the syntax mapper returns from the pr_usrreq() function called from the socket layer, passing back a zero completion code indicating a successful completion. The zero return code is passed on by the socket layer as the return code from the bind() call.

3. Application program 2 issues a listen() to inform the network that it is listening for incoming connection requests. The listen() function in the socket layer issues a pr_usrreq() with PRU_LISTEN as the request type. The pr_usrreq function in the syntax mapper issues an M_LISTEN_DC to tell the CMM of the listen request. The CMM marks the transport user as listening and returns an RC_OK. The syntax mapper calls the native TCP pr_usrreq() function to allow a listen() to be completed in the native protocol stack. This allows native as well as nonnative connections to be established with the serv-

er. When the native task is complete, the syntax mapper returns from the pr_usrreq() function that was called from the socket layer, passing back a zero completion code to indicate success. The syntax mapper completes the pr_usrreq() with a return code of zero, and the listen() call completes successfully.

4. Application program 2 now issues an accept() to accept any incoming connection requests. The accept() function in the sockets layer validates the parameters that were passed in the call, then calls a system function that allows the task to go to sleep while waiting for a connection request to arrive. Application program 1 issues a connect() to connect with application program 2. The connect() function in the socket layer issues a pr_usrreq() with PRU_CONNECT as the request. The syntax mapper must determine whether the underlying transport network is a native or nonnative transport provider by examining the interface name associated with the IP address in the node's routing table. If the interface is not sna0, then the syntax mapper passes the request to the native TCP pr_usrreq() function to be processed. In our case, the request contains an IP address that has been configured for the sna0 interface. The syntax mapper issues an M_CREATE_DC to create an MPTN endpoint. The CMM receives the M_CREATE_DC, stores the necessary information, and then returns a successful-completion code to the syntax mapper (RC_OK). The syntax mapper issues an M_CONNECT_DC and returns to the connect() function in the socket layer. The connect() function calls a system function that allows the task to go to sleep while waiting for a connection request to be completed.

5. Meanwhile, the CMM receives the M_CONNECT_DC and issues a P_LOCATE_DC to resolve the IP address for application program 2. The PMM interrogates the IP-LU table to get the next hop address and maps that IP address into an LU name specified in the NetID.LUNAME format. The PMM returns the NetID.LUNAME and an RC_OK response, and the CMM issues a P_CREATE_DC to ask the PMM to create a connection endpoint. The PMM performs this function and returns an RC_OK. Finally, the CMM issues a P_CONNECT_DC. The PMM takes the fully qualified LU name that is passed in the P_CONNECT_DC *targ_prov_addr* field and issues an APPC *allocate_conversation* to allocate a full-duplex conversation with the PMM in access node 2. If no SNA sessions were previously bound for these endpoints, they are bound now. Next, the PMM sends a data packet consisting of the MPTN_Connect. Once the transport provider has packetized the data, it consists of a transmission header (TH), a request header (RH), a SNA attach header (FMH-5), and an MPTN_Connect message. The *begin bracket indicator* is turned on in the request header to indicate the beginning of a conversation.

6. When the PMM in access node 2 receives this data packet, it issues a P_ACCEPT_UC to inform its CMM of the incoming connection

request. The CMM examines the incoming address for the port number that is stored in the local node section of the fully qualified MPTN address. Next, it interrogates its list of tasks for a process that is listening on that port number. Application program 2 has issued the listen() for that port, so the CMM issues an M_ACCEPT_UC. The syntax mapper in access node 2's transport user must signal the sleeping task residing in the socket layer. This is the accept() function waiting for incoming connection requests. The syntax mapper issues an M_ACCEPT_DC to accept the incoming connection request, and the CMM issues a P_AC-CEPT_DC to the PMM. An MPTN_Connect response is sent back to the originator. SNA transmission and request headers and an MPTN_Connect response message are sent to the other endpoint.

7. In access node 1, the MPTN_Connect response is received and the PMM issues a P_CONNECT_UC to tell the CMM that the connection has completed. The CMM issues an M_CONNECT_UC to tell the syntax mapper about this. The syntax mapper issues a Unix signal, and the connect() call, which has blocked waiting for the connection, wakes up to complete successfully.

8. Application program 2's accept(), waiting for an incoming connection in the socket layer, wakes up and issues a pr_usrreq() with PRU_ACCEPT as the request type. The syntax mapper in the transport user returns application program 1's full socket address (the IP address and port number). Application program 2's accept() is completed, and a new socket descriptor for the connected socket is returned to the application program. Application program 2 moves on to the next socket call, a recv(), and waits for data to arrive on the new connection.

Now that the connection is complete, data can be sent using send() calls.

16.6   Conclusion

This chapter has presented the AnyNet Sockets-Over-SNA access node and gateway products, showing how IBM has made use of the MPTN architecture in its implementations. The algorithmic mapping method was chosen by AnyNet designers to provide an effortless means of mapping transport-user IP addresses to transport-provider SNA addresses. The ability of the underlying SNA network to provide varying levels of service is used to provide a way to prioritize various types of TCP/IP connections.

The chapter concludes by examining the internals of Sockets-Over-SNA with an example of a typical connection setup, and material that was presented earlier in the book is brought into play.

The following chapter examines the AnyNet SNA-Over-TCP/IP product transposing our networking protocols to show how SNA is provided over a TCP/IP network.

AnyNet SNA-Over-TCP/IP

17.1   Introduction to AnyNet
SNA-Over-TCP/IP

Chapter 16 presented IBM's AnyNet product called Sockets-Over-SNA. Sockets-Over-SNA allows AF_INET sockets application programs to run in a SNA network. This chapter is devoted to a discussion of the IBM AnyNet SNA-Over-TCP/IP product, which allows SNA application programs to run in a TCP/IP network. The AnyNet SNA-Over-TCP/IP gateway also interconnects SNA and TCP/IP networks in such a manner that SNA applications running in SNA-Over-TCP/IP nodes in a TCP/IP network can communicate with native sockets applications running in a SNA network. Additionally, when two gateways are used, a TCP/IP network can become a backbone over which two SNA networks are interconnected.

There are two versions of AnyNet SNA-Over-TCP/IP. One is called APPC-Over-TCP/IP and the other is called SNA-Over-TCP/IP. Both products allow SNA programs to run without change in a TCP/IP network. However, APPC-Over-TCP/IP supports only APPC and CPI-C programs—which use independent LUs (LU 6.2)—while SNA-Over-TCP/IP supports traditional SNA programs that use dependent LUs (LU 0, 1, 2, and 3) as well. Throughout this chapter, the name "SNA-Over-TCP/IP" will be used to describe both products, unless APPC-Over-TCP/IP is being specifically referred to.*

There are two types of AnyNet SNA-Over-TCP/IP products: the ac-

---

*In order for SNA-Over-TCP/IP to be implemented on a platform, Dependent LU Requester (DLUR), which provides one end of a pipe for dependent LU activation, must be available. At the time of this writing, DLUR had not yet been implemented on all of the APPC-Over-TCP/IP platforms.

cess node, which enables SNA application programs to communicate with other SNA programs running in other access nodes on a TCP/IP network, and the gateway node, which enables TCP/IP and SNA networks to be interconnected.

We will begin our discussion of AnyNet SNA-Over-TCP/IP by describing its features and the configuration process for various platforms. The various platforms for which AnyNet SNA-Over-TCP/IP gateways and access nodes and APPC-Over-TCP/IP access nodes are available are described in Chap. 15.

17.2 Configuring SNA-Over-TCP/IP

SNA-Over-TCP/IP (and APPC-Over-TCP/IP) has been implemented in a similar manner on various platforms. Our discussion of configuration will begin with general details, then proceed to specific details for the various platforms.

17.2.1 SNA-Over-TCP/IP LU preference table

Several of the AnyNet SNA-Over-TCP/IP products implement a feature called an *LU preference table*. The purpose of this feature is to provide a transparent method of determining, in cases where parallel TCP/IP and SNA are available, whether specific SNA programs should be routed over the native SNA network or over the TCP/IP network using SNA-Over-TCP/IP. Presumably, IBM implemented the LU preference table to provide a means for customers converting their SNA networks to TCP/IP networks to operate the old and new networks in parallel during the conversion process. LU preference allows users to fall back on the SNA network if the new TCP/IP network fails. Also, during a network migration phase, some SNA applications may need to run in the SNA network, and others not.

Routing preference takes place when a SNA session is bound. At this time, SNA-Over-TCP/IP consults the LU preference table to decide which underlying transport network to use. If TCP/IP and SNA networks are both available, the SNA session can be established over either network, the SNA network using native SNA, or the TCP/IP network using SNA-Over-TCP/IP. Defining LU preferences gives the network administrator the ability to tell SNA-Over-TCP/IP how to decide which network to use.

The LU preference table is arranged according to LU names. Each possible destination LU name is entered in the table, along with a preference for that LU. In MVS and OS/2 implementations, there are four possible preference settings:

- *Native.*   Attempt to use the SNA network; if that fails, use the TCP/IP network.

- *Nonnative.*   Attempt to use the TCP/IP network; if that fails, use the SNA network.

- *Native only.*   Use the SNA network only.

- *Nonnative only.*   Use the TCP/IP network only.

SNA-Over-TCP uses a default setting of *native* if there is no entry for an LU in the table. This default setting can be changed, however.

17.2.2 Environment variables

The SNA-Over-TCP/IP and APPC-Over-TCP/IP products use a standard set of parameters that are available as *environment variables* on most platforms. These can be used for fine-tuning or customizing a system. The tuning parameters have been preconfigured to IBM-recommended values and are generally best left alone. Under certain conditions, however, one or more of the parameters may need to be changed to correct a specific problem. The various tuning parameters will be described when the configuration details for individual platforms are presented.

Parameters that have been made available for customizing a system are *domain name suffix* and *MPTN well-known port*. The domain name suffix is used in SNA-Over-TCP/IP address mapping and is described in detail in the next section. The MPTN well-known port (described in Sec. 13.2.3) defines the port number to be used by PMMs for communicating in the underlying TCP/IP network and defaults to port number 397. This parameter should not be changed except under very unusual conditions. The purpose for providing a way to change the port number is twofold: (1) It can be changed to provide a version of SNA-Over-TCP/IP to be used for testing that will not interfere with a production system, and (2) it can be changed if the default value of 397 conflicts with a preexisting port number assignment. The latter should never occur, because port values that fall within the range 1–1023 are reserved. Custom applications normally use only ports in the 1024–5000 range. The MPTN well-known port must be assigned the same value everywhere in the SNA-Over-TCP/IP network in order for SNA-Over-TCP/IP to operate. It should be noted that the MPTN well-known port cannot be changed in the Windows version of APPC-Over-TCP/IP, and this option will not be available in future releases of all AnyNet products.

17.2.3 Address mapping in SNA-Over-TCP/IP

It will be recalled from previous discussions of MPTN address mapping techniques that the MPTN architecture defines three implementations: algorithmic, protocol-specific directory, and use of an address mapper. In SNA-Over-TCP/IP, address mapping is accomplished by using a combination of algorithmic address mapping and a protocol-specific directory. Use of a protocol-specific directory was chosen for the SNA-Over-TCP/IP products because of the availability of the Domain Name System (DNS) in the underlying TCP/IP network. DNS, the protocol-specific directory service of TCP/IP discussed in Chap. 4, provides a convenient database in which address mappings can be stored, and it is easily accessible.

DNS is used by TCP/IP to map IP domain names to IP addresses (domain names, it will be recalled from Chap. 4, are created using a hierarchy of subdomains). DNS is used by SNA-Over-TCP/IP to map transport user LU names to IP addresses. Two methods are provided by DNS for storing address mappings. The first involves the use of the HOSTS file (*/etc/hosts*). The second employs a domain name server.

SNA-Over-TCP/IP address mapping is accomplished in the following manner. The host name that is submitted to DNS for resolution to an IP address must be in a specific format: *LUname.NetID.SNAsuffix*. This is a format of LU name followed by SNA network name followed by a domain name suffix. The *domain name suffix* is an agreed-upon character string that conforms to DNS standards. It is represented by a configurable *environment variable* set to a default of *sna.ibm.com*. This suffix is automatically attached by SNA-Over-TCP/IP to the end of the LUname.NetID combination to create a name that is in DNS format. Use of the suffix provides a way for a fully qualified LU name to be resolved by the domain name system into an IP address. The network administrator's choice of suffix ensures that duplicate names will not be encountered when querying DNS. The following example illustrates how SNA-Over-TCP/IP domain names are constructed.

1. A fully qualified SNA transport user address of SNANET.LU1 is converted to an LUname.NetID format.
   - LUname: lu1
   - NetID: snanet

2. Added to that is the SNAsuffix environment variable.
   - SNAsuffix: sna.ibm.com

3. The resultant domain name is
   - lu1.snanet.sna.ibm.com

The resultant name, *lu1.snanet.sna.ibm.com,* can be registered with a name server, or hard-coded in HOSTS files for all active SNA-Over-TCP/IP nodes.

17.2.3.1 Configuring a HOSTS file for address mapping. Remote LU addresses in a SNA-Over-TCP/IP network must be defined to DNS either by adding them to the name server database or to the HOSTS file. It will be recalled that the HOSTS file contains sets of domain names with their corresponding IP addresses. In the AIX environment, this file is located in the *etc* directory and is often referred to as */etc/hosts.* In the OS/2 world, the file is called HOSTS and is found in the directory specified in the ETC environment variable. In other environments it is sometimes referred to simply as HOSTS, or HOSTS.LOCAL. It will be referred to as HOSTS in our discussions.

If a domain name server has not been installed in the TCP/IP network and the administrator does not want to set one up, the HOSTS file can be used instead. However, the administrator will be responsible for the maintenance of every copy of the file in each node of the network. By implementing a name server or defining the LU names to a currently implemented server, only a single server has to be maintained for an entire network instead of having to maintain HOSTS files for every active SNA-Over-TCP/IP node.

HOSTS file entries contain an IP address, a domain name, and domain name aliases. An example entry, using the LU name from the above example, is

```
129.10.0.1 lu1.snanet.sna.ibm.com lu1
```

The first parameter in this example HOST file entry is the transport provider IP address for the access node where LU1 resides. The second parameter is the name, and the third entry is an alias which, in the case of SNA-Over-TCP/IP, is not needed. Alias names are names that can be used in lieu of the full name. SNA-Over-TCP/IP, however, always uses full names.

17.2.3.2 Configuring a name server for address mapping. If a name server is to be used for SNA-Over-TCP/IP address mapping, a RESOLV file must be created (if one does not already exist on the system). The RESOLV, or */etc/resolv.conf,* file is provided in TCP/IP to identify the domain name server that can resolve LU names. It is required if the name server program, called *named,* is not running in the system, or if the domain name for the server is not derivable from the local host name. RESOLV is read by the resolver routine used by functions such as *gethostbyname()* to locate a name server. The RESOLV file usually contains two entries: *nameserver* and *domain.*

Name server entries are of the format

```
nameserver address
```

Nameserver identifies the entry as a name server entry, and *address* specifies the IP address for the domain name server. Any number of name server entries may be entered in the file. An example entry is

```
nameserver 129.10.2.1
```

This entry tells us that there is a name server at IP address 129.10.2.1.

Domain entries are of the format

```
domain name
```

Domain identifies the entry as a domain entry, and *name* is the default domain name. The default domain name is the string that the resolver affixes to a host name that does not end with a dot. Names can be used in TCP/IP that are internal to a domain, such as the name *sam*. Since this name does not end with a period, it is assumed that it represents a name in the local domain. The default domain name contains the string that must be added to the local name to make it globally recognizable. Only one default domain name can be defined for a domain.

It is recommended that a name server be used for address mapping in all cases except the smallest of networks. The name server can be located anywhere in a network, as long as it is reachable via TCP/IP. The name server is configured by adding resource records (RRs). Each LU that will be mapped by SNA-Over-TCP/IP must have a corresponding *address resource record* defined in a DNS resource set.

17.3   Configuration on the Individual AnyNet Platforms

The various platforms on which SNA-Over-TCP/IP has been implemented use different methods in their configuration process, but the basics vary little from what has just been presented. Configuration is usually tied to the standard configuration process that belongs to a platform itself.

17.3.1   Configuring AnyNet SNA-Over-TCP/IP for OS/2

At the time of this writing, OS/2 and MVS have the most complete implementations of SNA-Over-TCP/IP because they include not only support for dependent LUs, but also an MPTN transport gateway.

TABLE 17.1   SNA-Over-TCP/IP Files for OS/2

\ANYNET	anycfg.ico
	anyfldr.ico
	anynet.ico
	anynetcf.exe
	anynetcf.hlp
	checkcm.exe
	istskkey.pkg
	snip2.pkg
	syslevel.any
\ANYNET\BIN	abinfo.exe
	anmb.exe
	getipint.exe
\ANYNET\DLL	anutil.dll
	mptncmm.dll
	tcppmm.dll
\ANYNET\MISC	any.msg
	anyh.msg
	anynet.cfn

Before SNA-Over-TCP/IP can be configured, OS/2 TCP/IP should first be installed. The configuration process can be accomplished using the AnyNet/2 SNA-Over-TCP/IP configuration notebook which is loaded during installation. The configuration notebook can also be loaded at any time by clicking on its icon in the AnyNet/2 folder or by entering the ANYNETCF command at the command line. SNA-Over-TCP/IP for OS/2's major files and programs are shown in Table 17.1.

AnyNet SNA-Over-TCP/IP for OS/2 configuration consists of setting up an LU preference table, configuring address mapping, and assigning values to the environment variables. This will be presented using the screens of the configuration notebook.

17.3.1.1 AnyNet configuration notebook page 1. Configuration notebook page 1 is used for setting the SNA domain name suffix and the status of the workstation.

- *SNA domain name suffix.* This field sets the domain name suffix in the SNAsuffix environment variable used for address mapping. The default is *sna.ibm.com.*

- *Is this a critical workstation?* This field determines if this workstation will send both conditional and unconditional alerts. Click "Yes" to send both, or "No" to send only unconditional alerts. The environment variable associated with this field is CRITICAL_WS, and the default is "No."

17.3.1.2 AnyNet configuration notebook page 2. Configuration notebook page 2 is used to specify the well-known MPTN port and three timer values.

- *Well-known port for MPTN.*   This field sets the well-known port used by MPTN. The environment variable that is set by this field is MPTN_WELL_KNOWN_PORT, and the default is 397.

- *Maximum number of minutes to wait for TCP/IP to start.*   If Communications Manager/2 is started before OS/2 TCP/IP, this value is used to determine how long to wait for TCP/IP to start before giving up. The environment variable that corresponds with this field is TCPWAIT_MINS, and the default is 15 minutes.

- *Maximum number of seconds to wait for a connection setup.*   When a SNA session is started for a transport user, an underlying TCP/IP connection must be established to carry session data. The time-out value specified in this field, and the corresponding CONNWAIT_SECS environment variable, designates the amount of time that SNA-Over-TCP/IP will wait (after the TCP/IP session has been established) for an MPTN connection to complete before giving up. The default value is 30 seconds.

- *Maximum number of seconds to retry a connection.*   This field sets the maximum time in seconds that SNA-Over-TCP/IP will attempt to create an MPTN connection. If an attempt fails, each transport provider address associated with the transport user address is tried until the time specified by this environment variable is exhausted. The environment variable represented by this field is CONN_RETRY_SECS, and the default value is 300 seconds.

17.3.1.3 AnyNet configuration notebook page 3. The third page of the configuration notebook contains three more timer values.

- *Maximum number of minutes to retry unacknowledged datagrams.* This is the time interval that will pass before out-of-band datagrams, representing SNA expedited data, and MPTN KEEPALIVE datagrams are resent if they are not acknowledged. The environment variable that corresponds to this is UNACKED_DG_RETRY_SECS, and the default is 30 seconds.

- *Maximum number of seconds to retry unsent datagrams.*   This timer represents the amount of time that SNA-Over-TCP/IP will wait for an acknowledgment for expedited data sent in the normal datastream with the expedited data MPTN header, before resend-

TABLE 17.2   SNA-Over-TCP/IP Environment Variables for OS/2

ANYNETPATH	Directory path name where SNA-Over-TCP/IP lives
CONN_RETRY_SECS	Length of time to wait for an MPTN connection
CONNWAIT_SECS	Length of time to wait for a TCP/IP connection
CRITICAL_WS	Send critical error alerts for critical workstations
INACTIVITY_TIMER_SECS	Time IP address remains inactive before keepalive sent
MPTN_WELL_KNOWN_PORT	TCP and UDP port used by PMMs (397 is the default)
SNASUFFIX	The domain name suffix
TCPWAIT_MINS	Interval PMM waits for TCP/IP to be started
UNSENT_DG_RETRY_SECS	Interval after which an OOB datagram is sent
UNACKED_DG_RETRY_SECS	Length of time between retries sending datagrams

ing the data in an MPTN_DG_OOB_Data datagram. The environment variable that corresponds to this is UNSENT_DG_RETRY_SECS, and the default is 3 seconds.

- *Maximum number of idle seconds before SNA-Over-TCP/IP queries the remote node to see if it is still active.* This is the KEEPALIVE timer. SNA-Over-TCP/IP will wait INACTIVITY_TIMER_SECS seconds, specified by this field, for a data packet from a remote host before sending it an MPTN_DG_KEEPALIVE_Hdr datagram.

The parameters specified in all three screens are represented by environment variables. The entire list of environment variables is shown in Table 17.2.

17.3.1.4 Configuring the LU preference table.

The LU preference table can be configured in various ways.

- LULIST is the command line interface for configuring the preference table. It has the following arguments:

  A: ADD LUNAME
  R: REMOVE LUNAME
  L: LOOKUP LUNAME
  P: PRINT TABLE
  C: CHANGE LUNAME
  D: PRINT OR SET DEFAULT
  U: UPDATE TABLE
  H: HELP

  A numeric value is used to identify the state of an entry: 0 = native, 1 = nonnative, 2 = native only, 3 = nonnative only. Entries to the LU preference table can be added, removed, changed, and displayed using this very basic utility.

- LUTPM is an OS/2 Presentation Manager utility that can be used to modify the LU preference table. It has the same commands, but has a friendlier user interface. LUTPM presents a menu with Add, Delete, Change, Find, and Delete All options. The purpose of this utility is to specify how SNA-Over-TCP/IP should establish a connection for a particular partner LU. Use the Add command to add partner LU names to the LU preference table. Enter the fully qualified LU name and then specify one of the following four options.
  NATIVE: Attempt to use SNA first, then TCP/IP.
  NONNATIVE: Attempt to use TCP/IP first, then SNA.
  NATIVE ONLY: Use SNA only.
  NONNATIVE ONLY: Use TCP/IP only.

- The table itself is stored on disk as \CMLIB\LUTAB.LST and is created by SNA-Over-TCP/IP during installation with one entry: NATIVE. It can be modified manually, but this is not recommended.

- An APPC program can be written to access the table by using the *lutabvb* structure.

17.3.1.5 Configuring address mapping. Address mapping is configured by (1) setting the SNAsuffix environment variable and (2) entering the LU names for the hosts with which sessions will be established in a name server or in a HOSTS file.

A utility, ABINFO, is supplied with SNA-Over-TCP/IP to display remote IP address/LU name combinations that are associated with an active LU-LU session and the local LU names of associated active sessions for a local IP address. ABINFO has the following arguments.

- A2B *protocol_name attribute*

- B2A *protocol_name attribute*

ABINFO gives information about "A," a transport user address, and "B," the associated transport provider address. There are two possible commands.

- ABINFO A2B SNA [*PCID*] causes a display of the SNA LU names and their associated IP addresses for a particular session, indicated by the PCID attribute. The PCID is obtained by using the OS/2 PMDSPLAY command.

- ABINFO B2A INET [*IP_ADDRESS*] displays the LU names that are associated with a specific IP address.

17.3.1.6 Configuring the AnyNet SNA-Over-TCP/IP gateway for OS/2. Configuring the AnyNet SNA-Over-TCP/IP gateway for OS/2 is similar to configuring SNA-Over-TCP/IP, except that a *gateway connection limit password* must be entered on the first configuration notebook screen. This password tells the gateway the maximum number of LU-LU sessions it is licensed to support. Another difference is that in an APPN SNA network, the SNA-Over-TCP/IP gateway must be configured as an APPN network node. The SNA-Over-TCP/IP gateway provides all the services of an access node except that NONNATIVE or NONNATIVE ONLY cannot be selected when specifying the default routing preference. Individual logical units, however, can have routing preferences of NONNATIVE.

The main considerations for configuring a gateway have to do with setting up address mapping. Wildcard addresses can be used when configuring the gateway if a SNA network has a unique SNA network name that corresponds exactly to an IP network. For example, an IP network might be 129.10.10.0 with a subnet mask of 255.255.255.0 (subnetwork 10 on IP network 129.10.0.0). This network could be represented by a single SNA network, for example, NETA. A single domain name is coded for the SNA network name (NETA), and a wildcard entry (*) is specified as the LU name. Through use of this technique, a single domain name server entry can be used to represent every LU in that network.

In a configuration where two or more gateways interconnect two or more IP networks through a SNA network backbone, a unique SNA *control point* (CP) name and a unique SNA connection network name for each IP network must be defined. The CP name defines a control point for an entire TCP/IP network, which makes all the LUs, in all of the access nodes, appear to exist within a single SNA node. All SNA-Over-TCP/IP gateways and all access nodes in the TCP/IP network appear to be attached to the connection network. The DNS reverse data file should be used to define the CP name and the connection network name for a given IP network. This file maps IP addresses to domain names.

Dependent LUs that can be reached through a SNA-Over-TCP/IP gateway require an extra step when configuring address mapping, because dependent LUs must be mapped using two DNS entries. One of the two entries maps the dependent LU to its IP address—just as is the case with an independent LU—and the other entry specifies the same LUname.NetID.SNAsuffix name but maps to a reserve IP address of 127.0.0.2. This additional entry is used to indicate to the gateway that the specified LU is a dependent LU.

17.3.2   Configuring AnyNet
SNA-Over-TCP/IP for MVS

The MVS platform can be implemented with either an AnyNet SNA-Over-TCP/IP access node or a gateway. Both products require IBM's TCP/IP Version 2 Release 2.1 for MVS or later and VTAM Version 4 Release 2 with the AnyNet host feature.

17.3.2.1 Defining SNA-Over-TCP/IP to VTAM. Defining SNA-Over-TCP/IP to VTAM is a three-step process. The first step is to define a TCP/IP major node. A TCP/IP major node is how the SNA-Over-TCP/IP network is represented to VTAM, and it is defined with the VTAM VBUILD macro using a new *TYPE* for SNA-Over-TCP/IP, "TYPE = TCP." An example VBUILD statement is shown in Table 17.3, and the operands are explained in Table 17.4. A number of these operands are similar to the environment variables belonging to SNA-Over-TCP/IP for OS/2. The VBUILD TYPE = TCP is where the various timers and configuration values are defined through VTAM to MVS. Because of the similarity of these parameters to those explained in the section on OS/2 configuration, they will not be further explained here. At least one GROUP, LINE, or PU statement must be coded for each VBUILD.

The MVS implementation of SNA-Over-TCP/IP has no routing preference feature.

17.3.2.2 Defining independent LUs. The second step in defining SNA-Over-TCP/IP to VTAM is defining independent LUs. Independent LUs, it will be recalled, are SNA type 6.2 logical units that can communicate with each other in a peer-to-peer fashion without relying on a VTAM SSCP to initiate sessions as do the dependent (types 0, 1, 2, 3, 4, and 7) LUs of classic SNA (independent and dependent LUs were discussed in Chap. 6).

A remote independent LU is defined to VTAM as a *cross-domain resource* (CDRSC) major node. If the remote independent logical unit initiates the sessions, VTAM can define the LU dynamically if DYNLU = YES was specified in the VTAM start options. If sessions with remote independent LUs are initiated by VTAM, the CDRSC can

TABLE 17.3   VTAM VBUILD for SNA-Over-TCP/IP

SNAOVRIP VBUILD TYPE = TCP			
	CONTIMER = 30,	TIMER FOR MPTN TO START	X
	DGTIMER = 30,	TIMER FOR RETRIES	X
	DNSUFX = IBM.COM,	DOMAIN NAME SUFFIX	X
	EXTIMER = 3,	EXPEDITED DATA TIMER	X
	IATIMER = 120,	KEEPALIVE TIMER	X
	PORT = 397,	MPTN WELL-KNOWN PORT	X
	TCB = 50,	# OF MVS TASK CNTL BLKS	X
	TCPIPJOB = T11ATCP,	TCP/IP JOBNAME	X
SNAOIPGR GROUP	ISTATUS = ACTIVE		
SNAOIPLN LINE	ISTATUS = ACTIVE		
SNAOIPPU PU	ISTATUS = ACTIVE		

TABLE 17.4   VTAM Operands

VBUILD	
CONTIMER	Length of time VTAM waits for an MPTN connection to be established
DGTIMER	Length of time between retries sending control datagrams
DNSUFX	Domain Name System suffix used for address mapping
EXTIMER	Length of time between sending expedited data and using a datagram
IATIMER	Length of time for IP address to remain inactive before keepalive sent
PORT	TCP and UDP port used by PMMs (397 is the default)
TCB	Number of MVS subtasks that can be used to access TCP/IP
TCPIPJOB	1- to 8-character job name used to start the TCP/IP address space
TYPE = TCP	This major node is a TCP/IP major node
GROUP, LINE, PU	
ISTATUS	Is this minor node to be activated after major node is first activated?
SPAN	Span of control for VTAM minor node resources
NETID	1- to 8-character network ID coded on the PU statement

be defined dynamically using the ALS selection function of the session management exit routine. Otherwise, a CDRSC for the remote independent LUs must be defined, and the name of the cross-domain resource must be the same as the independent LU name.

17.3.2.3   Defining dependent LUs.   The third step in defining SNA-Over-TCP/IP to VTAM is to define dependent LUs. Dependent LUs are defined to VTAM in a switched major node. This major node is typical, and no new parameters are used.

Dependent LUs are enabled in a SNA-Over-TCP/IP network by the Dependent LU Server (DLUS) and Dependent LU Requester (DLUR) functions which were introduced in Chap. 6 and will be explained later in this chapter. The DLUR must be defined to VTAM as a cross-domain resource.

17.3.2.4   Mapping LU names to IP addresses.   SNA-Over-TCP/IP for MVS has a HOSTS file named *HOSTS.LOCAL* that can be used either exclusively or in conjunction with a domain name server to contain the LU-to-IP mappings needed for the SNA-Over-TCP/IP network. The names used in the file must agree with the domain suffix specified in the DNSUFX operand on the VBUILD macro. A domain name server can be located anywhere in the IP network, and the DNS RESOLVER file must be coded to find it. HOSTS.LOCAL is searched if a name server cannot find a name. Each LU must have a resource record (RR) defined in a DNS resource set, if a name server is used.

17.3.3   Configuring AnyNet
APPC-Over-TCP/IP for AIX

The APPC-Over-TCP/IP feature of SNA Server for AIX supports only independent LUs at the time of writing because of the absence of Dependent LU Requester/Server (DLUR/S) support on that platform. Most of the configuration that is necessary is performed using the System Management Interface Tool (SMIT). Address mapping must be defined by entering LU names in either the */etc/hosts* dataset or in a domain name server, or both.

The various settings defined in the OS/2 product as environment variables, and in MVS as options for the VBUILD macro, are implemented in AIX using SMIT, the administrative tool used for all IBM configurations. The APPC-Over-TCP/IP SMIT screen is displayed by entering the following command-line fast path:

```
smit _snasnaip
```

"APPC/IP Environment Settings" is selected, then "Change/Show the Profile." Table 17.5 lists these variables. To modify the routing tables entries, select "APPC/IP Routing Protocol Preference," then "Add a Profile" or "Change/Show a Profile."

17.3.3.1   SMIT APPC/IP environment settings.   The SMIT "APPC/IP Environment Settings" screen prompts the administrator for the following information.

TABLE 17.5   Environment Variables for AIX and Windows

SNA domain name suffix	The domain name suffix used for address mapping
Connection retry duration	The length of time APPC-Over-TCP/IP waits for MPTN connection establishment
Connection wait time limit	The length of time APPC-Over-TCP/IP waits for a TCP/IP connection to complete
Remote node inactivity poll interval	The length of time a partner node can remain inactive before a keepalive datagram is sent
Well-known port for MPTN	The TCP and UDP port used by MPTN (397 is the default)
Unacknowledged datagram retry interval	The length of time APPC-Over-TCP/IP waits before resending an unacknowledged out-of-band or keepalive datagram
Unsent datagram retry interval	The length of time APPC-Over-TCP/IP waits for acknowledgment after sending expedited data on a connection before sending an out-of-band datagram

- *Profile name.*   This is the name assigned to this profile.

- *SNA domain name suffix.*   This is the domain name suffix to be used for address mapping. This default is sna.ibm.com.

- *Connection retry duration.*   This is the maximum time in seconds that APPC-Over-TCP/IP attempts to create an MPTN connection. If an attempt fails, each transport provider address associated with the transport user address is tried until the time specified by this environment variable is exhausted. The default is set for 300 seconds.

- *Connection wait time limit.*   This is the length of time APPC-Over-TCP/IP will wait for a TCP/IP connection to be established. The default value is 30 seconds.

- *Remote node inactivity poll interval.*   This is the number of seconds APPC-Over-TCP/IP waits during a period of inactivity between two partners before sending a keepalive datagram. The default is 120 seconds.

- *Well-known port for MPTN.*   This is the well-known port used by MPTN. The default is 397.

- *Unacknowledged datagram retry interval.*   This is the number of seconds that will elapse before APPC-Over-TCP/IP resends out-of-band and keepalive datagrams. The default is 30 seconds.

- *Unsent datagram retry interval.*   This is the length of time APPC over SNA waits for an acknowledgment of expedited data before sending an out-of-band datagram. The default is 3 seconds.

17.3.3.2   SMIT APPC/IP routing protocol preference.   The SMIT "APPC/IP Routing Protocol Preference" screen prompts the administrator for the following routing preference information.

- *Profile name.*   This is the name assigned to this profile.

- *Partner LU name.*   This is the name of the partner LU (or wildcard).

- *Protocol.*   This is the protocol to be selected.

For each partner LU name, a native (SNA) or nonnative (TCP-IP) transport network can be selected. If a session is to use TCP/IP, a profile must be defined for that session. A wildcard character can be used to indicate that a set of partner LUs will all use the same transport protocol. The wildcard character, *, can be entered by itself to indicate that all partner LUs should use the selected protocol, or it can be entered after part of an LU name to indicate that all LUs beginning with those characters are to use the selected protocol.

17.3.3.3   Other AIX configuration details.   AnyNet for AIX is started and stopped using these commands:

```
sna -start anynet
sna -stop anynet
```

17.3.4   Configuring AnyNet APPC-Over-TCP/IP for the AS/400

There are no special installation requirements for APPC-Over-TCP/IP on the AS/400. The product comes with the base OS/400 operating system. In order to configure APPC-Over-TCP/IP, two prerequisites are necessary.

- An underlying TCP/IP configuration must be established between end systems before any other configuration can take place.

- The network attribute ALWANYNET must be set to *YES using the CHGNETA command. By setting this AS/400 network attribute, all AnyNet products are allowed. AS/400 network attributes can be displayed with the DSPNETA command.

Following these prerequisites, it is necessary to create an APPC controller with LINKTYPE(*ANYNW). The controller description on the AS/400 defines the remote system. A new LINKTYPE called *ANYNW has been added to the system for APPC-Over-TCP/IP. The CRTCT-LAPPC command is used to create the APPC controller.

Next, an APPN remote location list entry for every remote system to which APPC-Over-TCP/IP will communicate must be created. To update the APPN remote location list, the CHGCFGL command with the *APPNRMT parameter is used. The remote control point name in the remote location list must match the remote control point in the APPC controller. Since this is not an APPN session, the remote control point has no meaning other than mapping the APPC controller to the correct entry in the remote configuration list.

The CFGTCP command is executed next to display the "Configure TCP/IP" menu. Select Option 10 for the "Work with TCP/IP Host Table Entries" panel. This screen is used for entering the remote systems with which APPC-Over-TCP/IP will communicate. The user is prompted for:

- *Opt.*   1 = Add, 2 = Change, 4 = Remove, 5 = Display, 7 = Rename.

- *Internet address.*   This is the internet address of the remote system.

- *Host name.*   This is the LU name and NetID for the remote system.

17.3.5   Configuring AnyNet APPC-Over-TCP/IP for Windows

The AnyNet APPC-Over-TCP/IP product for Windows provides a way to run CPI-C and APPC application programs in a TCP/IP network.

Before APPC-Over-TCP/IP can be configured, IBM APPC Networking Services for Windows and TCP/IP for DOS must be installed.

17.3.5.1 Configuring address mapping. The first step in configuring AnyNet APPC-Over-TCP/IP for Windows is to set up the HOSTS file or a domain name server to be used for address mapping. The HOSTS file is all that needs to be configured for smaller APPC-Over-TCP/IP networks; for larger ones, however, a name server is recommended. The location of the HOSTS file is determined by setting the ETC environment variable in the AUTOEXEC.BAT file. The default is in the \TCPDOS\ETC directory. To use a domain name server, set up a RESOLV file in the same directory to point to the DNS name server that will handle the mapping. Any domain name server can be used.

17.3.5.2 Setting environment variables. The AnyNet configuration tool is used for setting environment variables. To access this tool, click on the "AnyNet Configuration Tool" icon located in the AnyNet group.

- *SNA domain name suffix.* This is the domain name suffix to be used for address mapping. The SNAsuffix environment variable is equivalent to this field. This default is sna.ibm.com.

- *Connection retry duration.* This is the maximum time in seconds during which APPC-Over-TCP/IP attempts to create an MPTN connection. If an attempt fails, each transport provider address associated with the transport user address is tried until the time specified by this environment variable is exhausted. The environment variable is called CONN_RETRY_SECS. The default is 300 seconds.

- *Connection wait time limit.* This is the length of time APPC-Over-TCP/IP will wait for an MPTN connection to be finalized after the TCP/IP connection has been established. The default value is 30 seconds.

- *Remote node inactivity poll interval.* This is the interval in seconds that APPC-Over-TCP/IP will wait during a period of inactivity between two partners before sending a keepalive datagram. The environment variable set by this field is INACTIVITY_TIMER_SECS, and the default is 60 seconds.

- *Unacknowledged datagram retry interval.* This is the number of seconds that must elapse before APPC-Over-TCP/IP resends out-of-band and keepalive datagrams that have not been acknowledged. The environment variable is UNACKED_DG_RETRY_SECS, and the default is 30 seconds.

- *Unsent datagram retry interval.* This is the length of time that APPC-over-TCP/IP waits for an acknowledgment of expedited data—sent on the normal data stream—before sending an out-of-band datagram. The environment variable is UNSENT_DG_RETRY_SECS. The default value is 3 seconds.

17.3.5.3 Starting APPC-Over-TCP/IP for Windows. The following steps show how to start APPC-Over-TCP/IP for Windows.

- Start TCP/IP for DOS.

- Start Windows.

- Start APPC Networking Services for Windows.

- In the "IBM APPC Networking Services" window, click on the "Advanced Operations" icon. The "Networking Services Advanced Operations" window will be displayed.

- Select "Operation" on the menu bar and click on the "LU Control" option. The "Local LU Control" window will be displayed.

- Click on the "Initialize LU" button.

The abinfo utility, described in Sec. 17.3.1.5, is included in the Windows APPC-Over-TCP/IP product. This utility displays the mapping between APPC and TCP/IP. Click on the "ABINFO Mapping Utility" icon in the AnyNet group.

17.4   Components of SNA-Over-TCP/IP

The remainder of this chapter discusses more technical details of SNA-Over-TCP/IP. It is suggested that the reader be familiar with the material presented in Chap. 11 before attempting to understand the components about to be described.

The components of the AnyNet SNA-Over-TCP/IP access node are shown in Fig. 17.1. At the top of this figure is a SNA application program using either a traditional SNA interface, such as provided by LU 0, 1, 2, 3, or 7, or the APPC protocol boundary, as provided by LU 6.2, and the CPI-C API. The application communicates directly with the transport user.

Also communicating with the transport user is the DLUR component of DLUR/S. DLUR, because it uses LU 6.2 protocols, is simply another application program. However, it is not present in the APPC-Over-TCP/IP implementation of the access node. This is because AnyNet SNA-Over-TCP/IP products provide support for dependent LUs; APPC-Over-TCP/IP products do not. SNA-Over-TCP/IP uses *Dependent LU Requester/Servers* (DLUR/S), introduced in Chap. 6, to support dependent LUs. Except in the case of downstream LUs, which will be described shortly, the DLUR component is used when dependent LU sessions need to be established over a nonnative network.

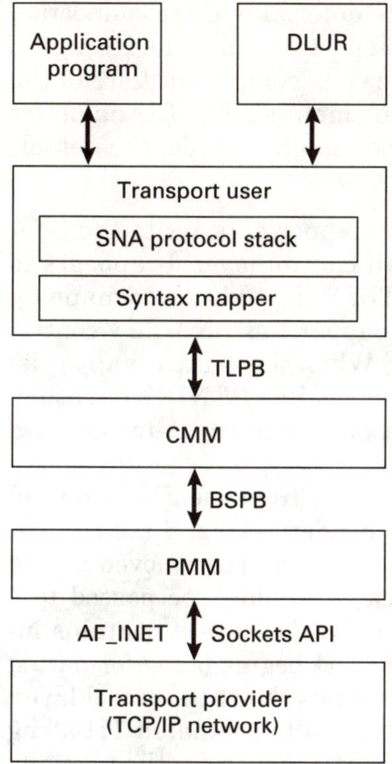

Figure 17.1   SNA-Over-TCP/IP components.

The transport user section of Fig. 17.1 contains two components, a SNA protocol stack and the syntax mapper. It communicates with the CMM via the TLPB. The CMM uses the BSPB to communicate with the PMM, and the PMM uses the AF_INET sockets API to communicate with the TCP/IP transport user.

17.4.1   The transport user

The SNA transport user consists of two components:

- The SNA protocol stack

- The syntax mapper

The relationship of these components is shown in Fig. 17.1.

17.4.1.1   The SNA protocol stack.   In SNA-Over-TCP/IP, most of the SNA protocol stack above the path control layer is included in the product. This is because functions such as sequence numbering are implemented in the lower layers of SNA. The SNA session services component described in Chap. 6 is changed slightly so that when a session is requested, a table is accessed to determine if the connection should be over a native or nonnative transport provider. To determine this, a routine is built into the session services component to read the LU preference table, if onc has been implemented. The LU name for the connection target is searched for; if no match is made, the default value is used.

17.4.1.2 The syntax mapper.

The syntax mapper appears to the SNA protocol stack as a component of the path control layer. It appears to the CMM as a transport user using the TLPB. In addition to mapping SNA syntax to TLPB calls, the syntax mapper ties SNA flow control to that of TCP/IP, the transport provider. When the syntax mapper issues M_SEND_DC calls that pass back an RC_PENDING return code, the syntax mapper uses pacing responses to regulate the data arriving from the SNA components.

The syntax mapper receives packets of data from the SNA protocol stack that contain both the transmission header (TH) and the request header (RH). The TH is the header that is added and removed by the path control layer. Normally layer 3 packets wouldn't be passed to a syntax mapper from other protocols. However, because it contains information that applies to other layers, the TH begins being formatted by SNA routines before the data packet reaches the path control layer. Therefore, the syntax mapper receives a partially populated TH along with the RH and RU. Information must be extracted from the partially filled TH; then, since the path control layer of SNA is not used, the TH is discarded.

Three fields are extracted from the transmission header: the 2-byte sequence number, the *expedited flow indicator,* and the mapping field. These data are used to set M_SEND_DC parameters. The mapping field of the TH must be set in the M_SEND_DC because segmenting of PIUs is performed by path control layer components, but reassembly is done by the LU component. SNA session data that pass through an MPTN gateway may end up being segmented and must be reassembled by the LU component. The *expedited flow indicator* must be checked to determine if the packet contains expedited data which must be compensated for. The sequence number from the TH is placed in front of the RH, as it is necessary that it be sent (sequence numbers functionally belong to the higher layers in a protocol stack, and in SNA they are rather ill-placed in the transmission header).

17.4.2 The CMM

The CMM used in SNA-Over-TCP/IP is a normal access node CMM as described in Chap. 11. It does not contain an address mapper client

because the address mapper has not been implemented in any
AnyNet SNA-Over-TCP/IP products as of this writing.

17.4.3   The PMM

The PMM appears to the transport provider to be just another sockets
program. All interaction with the TCP/IP network involves using the
socket calls of the Berkeley AF_INET interface. A socket is opened for
the MPTN well-known port 397. The PMM also performs address
mapping functions by converting LU names to ASCII, formatting a
string consisting of the LU name, network ID, and SNA domain name
suffix, then issuing a *gethostbyname*() call to resolve the resultant
string into an IP address.

Since data use a TCP/IP connection, they are sent with a 4-byte
length prefix in addition to the 1-byte compensation header. Figure 17.2
shows the format of data once they are sent onto the TCP/IP "wire."
Packets begin with a 20-byte IP header followed by a 20-byte TCP
header. Next in the stream is a 4-byte length prefix that identifies the
data length. Following the length prefix is a 1-byte compensation header, which will have a value of X'00' whenever some compensation is not
in effect. Following this is the 2-byte sequence number from the SNA
FID2 TH, the 3-byte SNA RH, and the SNA RU.

When a P_INIT_DC is issued by the CMM to initialize the PMM, the
PMM must initialize an AF_INET socket to wait for incoming connection requests. First, a *socket*() is issued to set up the socket endpoint on
the TCP/IP network. Then a *bind*() for TCP port 397, or the port specified in the MPTN well-known port environment variable, is issued,
and a *listen*() call is made to inform the TCP/IP network that it will be
listening for incoming connection requests on that port. The PMM creates subtasks to accept individual incoming connection requests.

17.4.4   The transport provider

The transport provider for SNA-Over-TCP/IP is the TCP/IP protocol
stack (presented in Chap. 4) through the Berkeley AF_INET socket
interface (presented in Chap. 5).

IP header 20 bytes	TCP header 20 bytes	Length 4 bytes	MPTN header 1 byte	Seq. no. 2 bytes	Request header 3 bytes	Request unit variable length

Figure 17.2   A SNA-Over-TCP/IP packet.

17.5   Independent LUs in SNA-Over-TCP/IP

To demonstrate how all the AnyNet SNA-Over-TCP/IP components work in conjunction with each other, an example will show what happens when a CPI-C conversation is allocated using SNA-Over-TCP/IP. The example will draw on information already presented in this book. CPI-C was presented in Chap. 7, and SNA in Chap. 6. TCP/IP was presented in Chap. 4, and the sockets API in Chap. 5. Chapter 11 presented the TLPB and BSPB calls used in this example, Chap. 13 explained the MPTN formats for establishing a connection. Chapter 14 explained address mapping. All of this information is required to understand the sequence of events in this example.

17.5.1   Establishing a SNA-Over-TCP/IP independent LU session

To demonstrate how AnyNet SNA-Over-TCP/IP components interact, an example will show a CPI-C conversation being allocated with a partner in an AnyNet SNA-Over-TCP/IP network. Transaction program 1, residing in access node 1, will be the client in the conversation, and transaction program 2, residing in access node 2, will be the server. The example will demonstrate the flows that take place when a *cmallc()* is issued by access node 1 and a *cmaccp()* by access node 2.

The flow diagram of Fig. 17.3 has six components for each access node:

- Transaction program
- SNA protocol stack
- Syntax mapper
- CMM
- PMM
- Socket layer of the transport provider

During the initialization process, when local LUs are defined or SNA-Over-TCP/IP is loaded, the syntax mapper performs initialization for passive LUs. The passive LU is the endpoint that will issue a *cmaccp()*. In this example, the passive LU resides in access node 2. Also, as part of the SNA-Over-TCP/IP initialization process, a P_INIT_DC is issued by the CMM. The PMM, upon receiving the P_INIT, issues *socket()*, *bind()* (for MPTN port 397), *listen()*, and *select()* calls to create a listening socket waiting for incoming connection requests for the various SNA-Over-TCP/IP users in access node 2.

1. The syntax mapper in access node 2 issues an M_CREATE_DC downcall to create an MPTN endpoint instance. The CMM receives

the M_CREATE_DC, stores information in the endpoint control block, and then returns a successful completion code (RC_OK) to the syntax mapper. The syntax mapper issues an M_BIND_DC to associate transaction program 2's local LU name with the endpoint that was established with the M_CREATE_DC, and to register the address. The M_BIND_DC includes SNA transport user data in the local_user_data field. Transport user data are formatted similarly to MPTN optional fields discussed in Chap. 13. These transport user data are formatted as type X'07', which are known as *SNA Transport User, LU Type/CP Name* and contain

- LU type (1 byte)
  0 = Independent LU
  1 = Dependent LU
  2 = Node ID/block number (downstream LUs)
- CP name length (1 byte)
- CP name (0–17 bytes)

(The various types of transport user data are shown in Table 17.7.)

The CMM receives the M_BIND_DC and responds with an RC_OK. The syntax mapper now issues an M_LISTEN_DC to put the endpoint into the passive state required of a server. The CMM receives the M_LISTEN_DC request, and returns an RC_OK. Transaction program 2 issues a *cmaccp*() to accept the conversation that will be allocated by transaction program 1.

2. Transaction program 1 allocates a conversation with transaction program 2 by issuing a *cmallc*(). Session services in the transport user checks to see if a session to the partner LU is available for use. If a session does not exist or is not available, the session services component of SNA checks the LU preference table to determine if a native or nonnative connection must be established. In this case, it will be a nonnative connection, and because no sessions already exist, session services sends a SNA BIND to the syntax mapper to set up the LU 6.2 session. The syntax mapper issues an M_CREATE_DC and the CMM returns a successful completion code (RC_OK). Next, the syntax mapper issues an M_CONNECT_DC.

3. The CMM issues a P_LOCATE_DC to get the IP address of the access node where the partner LU resides. The PMM receives the P_LOCATE_DC, then responds with an RC_PENDING. The transport user address passed in the P_LOCATE_DC is an MPTN-qualified address with a node address consisting of a fully qualified LU name in the format "NetID.LUname." The PMM translates and reformats the address and attaches the SNAsuffix environment variable to get a

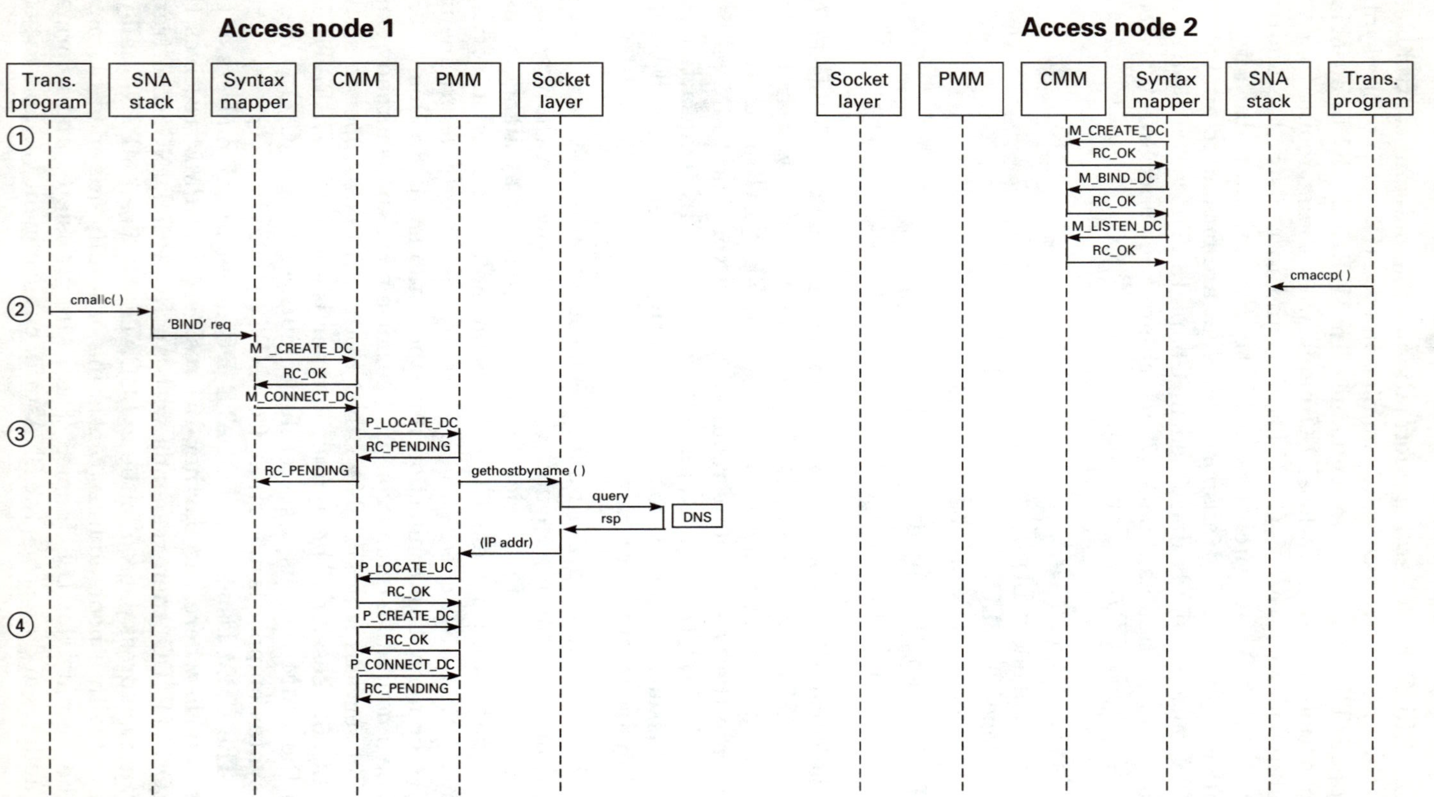

Access node 1
Trans. program
SNA stack
Syntax mapper
CMM
PMM
Socket layer
Access node 2
Socket layer
PMM
CMM
Syntax mapper
SNA stack
Trans. program
1
M_CREATE_DC
RC_OK
M_BIND_DC
RC_OK
M_LISTEN_DC
RC_OK
cmaccp( )
2
cmallc( )
'BIND' req
M _CREATE_DC
RC_OK
M_CONNECT_DC
3
P_LOCATE_DC
RC_PENDING
RC_PENDING
gethostbyname ( )
query
rsp
DNS
(IP addr)
4
P_LOCATE_UC
RC_OK
P_CREATE_DC
RC_OK
P_CONNECT_DC
RC_PENDING

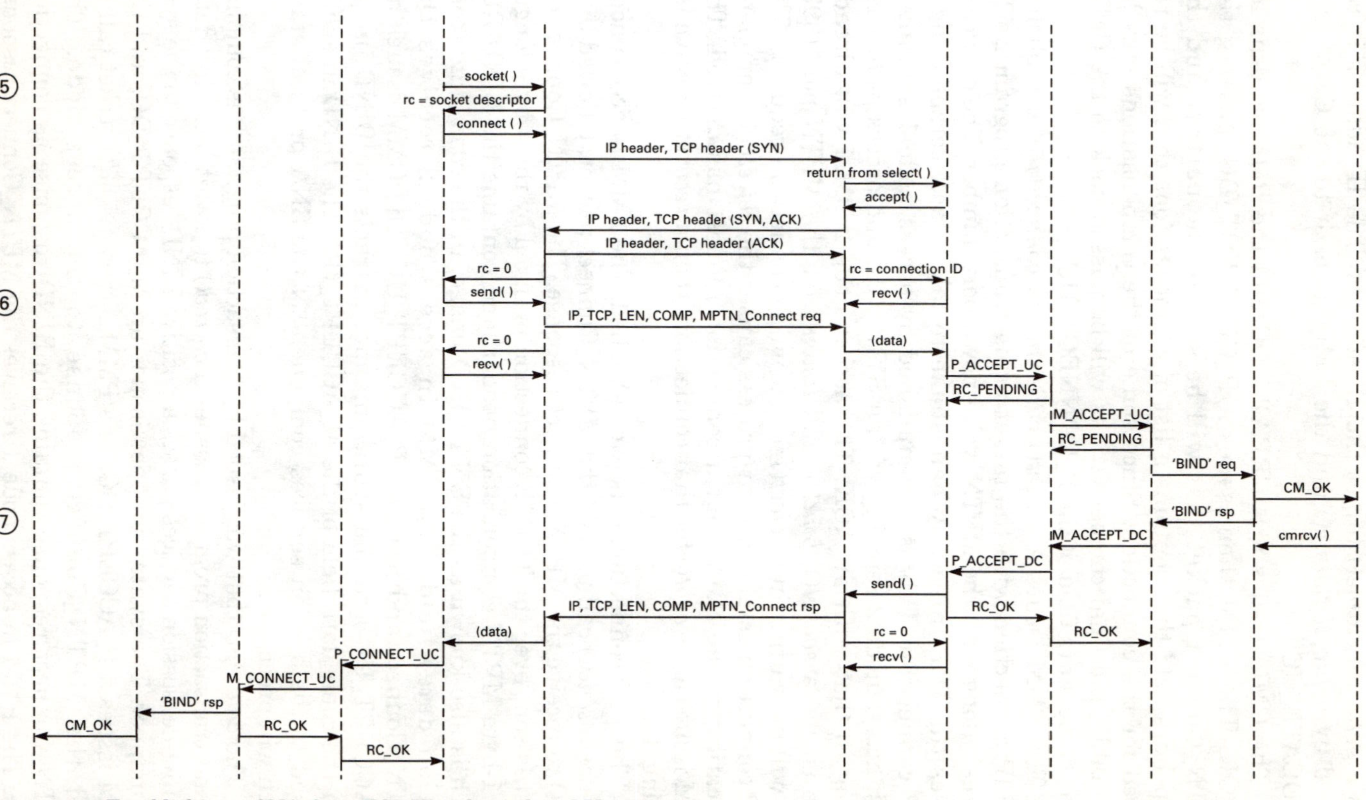

Figure 17.3 Establishing a SNA-Over-TCP/IP independent LU session.

string in the form of "LUname.NetID.SNAsuffix." The PMM then issues a *gethostbyname*() to get the IP address. The IP address is returned by *gethostbyname*() and the PMM gives it to the CMM in a P_LOCATE_UC.

4. The CMM issues a P_CREATE_DC and the PMM returns an RC_OK. The CMM then issues a P_CONNECT_DC, passing the MPTN_Connect packet that will be sent to the partner and the comp_hdrs field that contains a list of compensations that will be required for the connection. Since some of the compensations may be negotiable, the final compensations will be passed back to the CMM in the comp_hdrs field of the P_CONNECT_UC.

5. The PMM issues a *socket*() call, then a *connect*() to establish a TCP/IP connection with the target using transaction program 2's IP address along with the MPTN well-known port number. The *connect*() causes the TCP three-way handshake to take place, establishing a TCP connection. This is accomplished by access node 1 sending a SYN, access node 2 replying with a SYN ACK, and access node 1 replying to that with an ACK. The access node 2 PMM will already have issued a *socket*(), *bind*(), and *listen*() for the MPTN port (397) and will be waiting in a *select*() for incoming connection requests. The TCP connection establishment process causes the *select*() to complete, indicating to the PMM that a connection request has arrived. The PMM issues an *accept*() for that connection, then a *recv*() to receive incoming data.

6. The TCP connection is now established. The PMM in access node 1 issues a *send*() call to send the MPTN_Connect packet, followed by a *recv*() to receive the MPTN_Connect response. The MPTN_Connect request is sent over the TCP/IP connection prefixed by the 4-byte length and 1-byte MPTN compensation header, and contains the BIND RU, which is also known as the SNA BIND image, in the *conn_data* (connection data) field. The PMM in access node 2 receives the MPTN_Connect and issues a P_ACCEPT_UC. The CMM issues an M_ACCEPT_UC and the syntax mapper extracts the BIND image from the conn_data field of the M_ACCEPT_UC. The BIND image is passed to the session services component of the SNA protocol stack which will process it.

7. The *cmaccp*() that was issued by transaction program 2 is completed, and transaction program 2 issues a *cmrcv*() to await incoming data. Meanwhile, session services passes a positive BIND response to the syntax mapper. The syntax mapper issues an M_ACCEPT_DC, and the CMM issues a P_ACCEPT_DC. The PMM issues a *send*() socket call to send the MPTN_Connect response to the access node. The MPTN_Connect response contains the BIND response as connection data. The PMM in access node 1 receives the MPTN_Connect response

and issues a P_CONNECT_UC. The CMM issues an M_CONNECT_UC. The syntax mapper extracts the BIND response from the M_CONNECT_UC and hands it to the SNA session services component. Now that the BIND has taken place, the outstanding *cmallc()*, originally issued by transaction program 1, can be completed with a CM_OK.

17.6   Dependent LUs in SNA-Over-TCP/IP

Dependent LUs require special treatment in SNA-Over-TCP/IP because of the additional SSCP-PU and SSCP-LU sessions that must be established before an LU-LU session can be bound. The LU-LU session can be established over a nonnative transport network, but the two SSCP sessions cannot be established without extra provisions.

Two problems must be solved when AnyNet is brought into the picture to replace a SNA network with a SNA-Over-TCP/IP network. One is created when the SNA network between a PU type 2.1 node and an MVS mainframe is replaced by a TCP/IP network. The other is created when the SNA network between an OS/2 Communications Manager/2 gateway, which will be explained shortly, and its associated downstream PUs is replaced with a TCP/IP network.

In the first case, the dependent LU problem is solved by using the Dependent LU Server (DLUS) and Dependent LU Requester (DLUR) (Fig. 17.4). In this case, DLUR/S encapsulates the SSCP-PU and SSCP-LU sessions required for dependent LU activation within LU type 6.2 sessions. An LU 6.2 pipe is created between the DLUS in the mainframe and the DLUR in the OS/2 Communications Manager/2 gateway. This gateway node also must be an AnyNet SNA-Over-TCP/IP gateway, because the SNA LAN network connects with the TCP/IP network.

In the second case, the dependent LU problem is solved using datagrams belonging to the MPTN architecture and an extended MPTN_Connect command (Fig. 17.5). The OS/2 Communications Manager/2 gateway must also be an AnyNet SNA-Over-TCP/IP gateway in this case also, because it connects a SNA with a TCP/IP network.*

Both of the above cases can be combined to create only a TCP/IP network (Fig. 17.6). In this case, both the network that attaches the OS/2 Communications Manager/2 gateway to the mainframe and the LAN are TCP/IP networks. In this case, the Communications

---

*DLUR/S can still be used to solve the second case. DLUR can be loaded in each downstream workstation on the TCP/IP LAN or wherever the dependent LU is needed. This is not the recommended method, however.

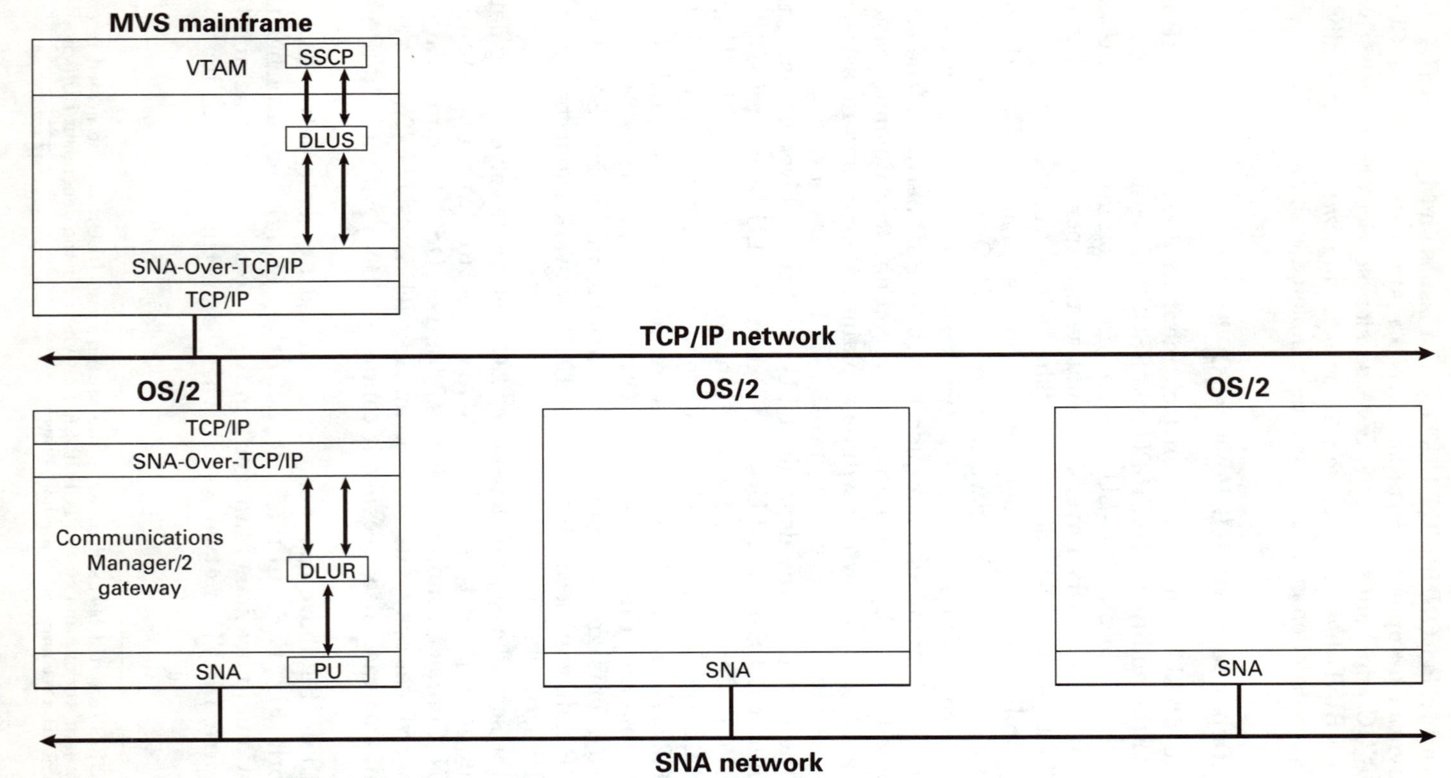

Figure 17.4   Using DLUR/S to provide dependent LU support over a TCP/IP network.

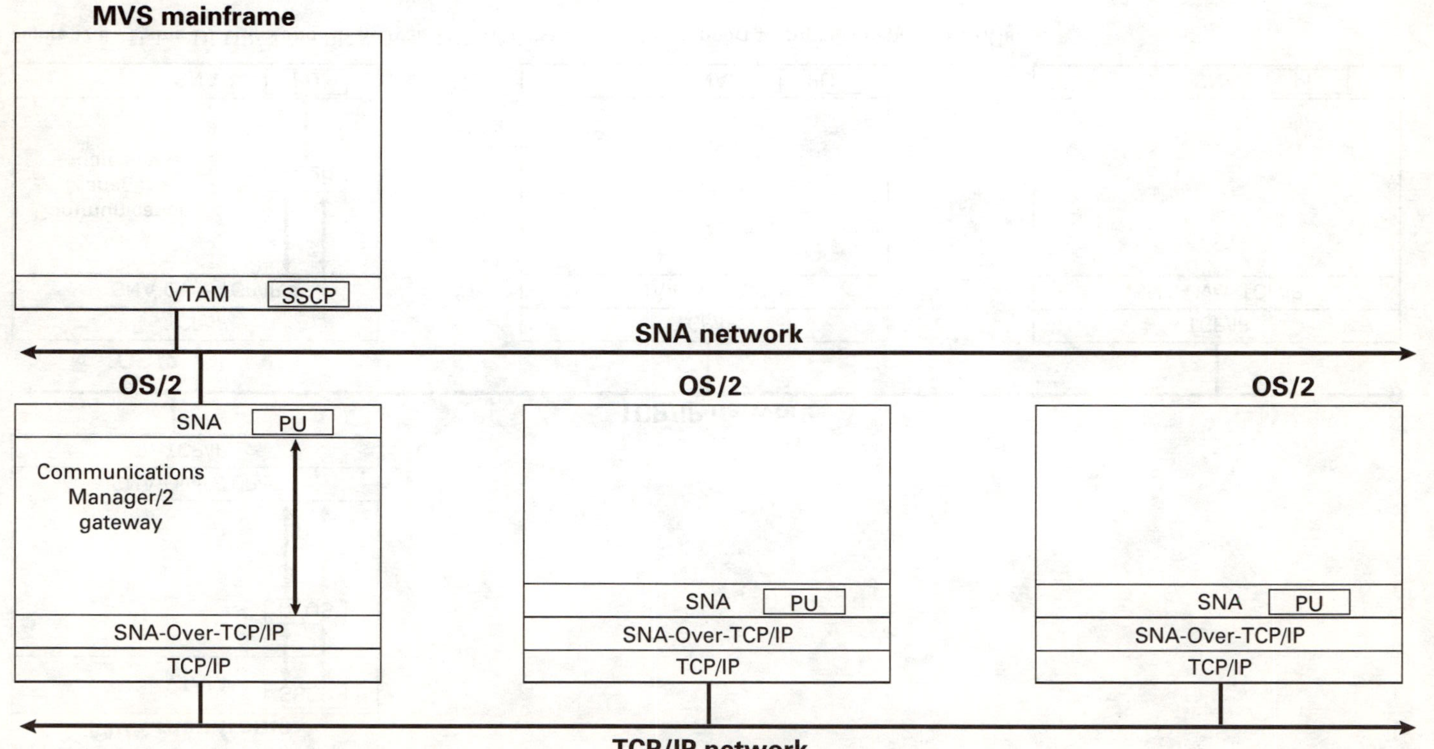

Figure 17.5   Using SNA-Over-TCP/IP downstream PU support to support dependent LUs.

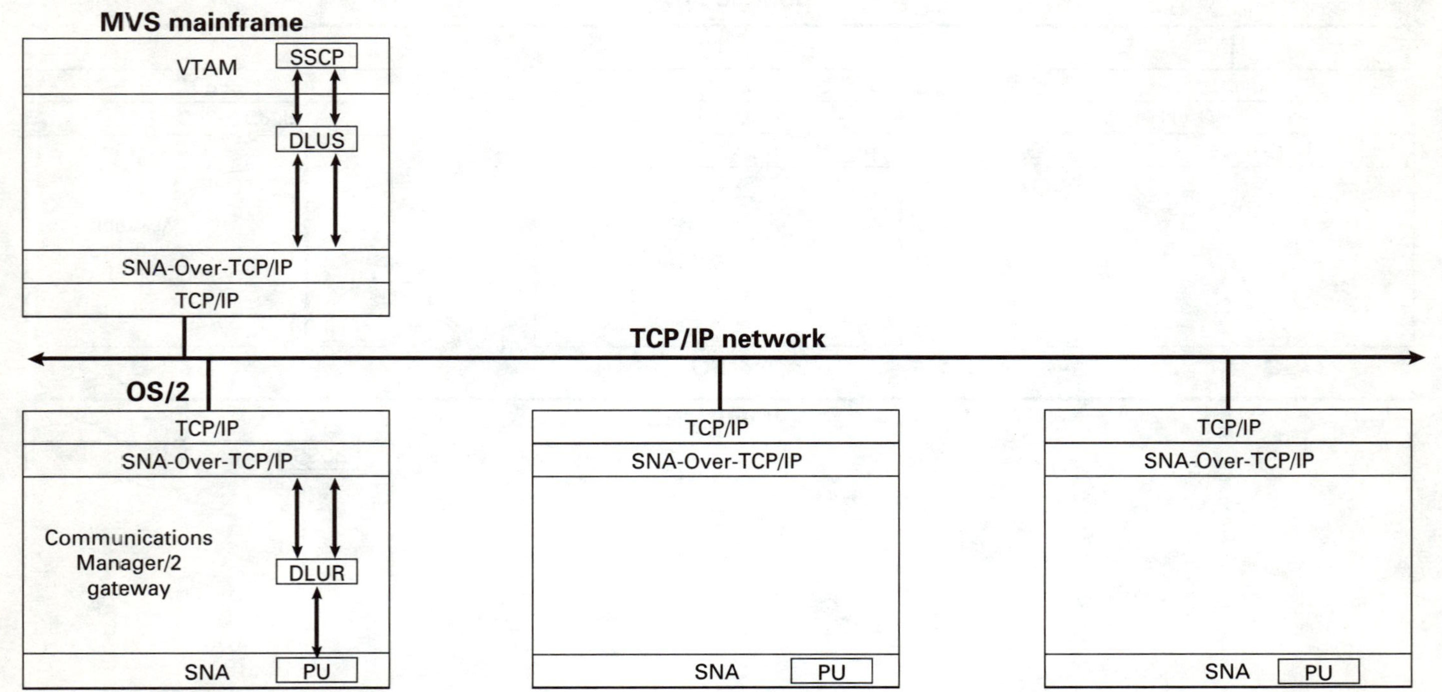

Figure 17.6 Using DLUR/S and SNA-Over-TCP/IP downstream PU support to support dependent LUs.

Manager/2 gateway is still required to interconnect the LAN with the WAN, but an AnyNet SNA-Over-TCP/IP gateway is not required because two transport networks are now no longer being interconnected.

The implementation of dependent LUs will now be discussed. The MVS mainframe supplies the platform on which classic SNA applications written for 3270 terminals (LU type 2), 3270 printers (LU type 3), and SCS printers (LU type 1) make their home. The terminals and printers are emulated on the OS/2 platform using the emulation capabilities of Communications Manager/2.

Normally, one OS/2 node connects to the SNA subarea network boundary node. This node is the Communications Manager/2 gateway. The Communications Manager/2 gateway is an application gateway that provides the capability for OS/2 machines on a SNA LAN to access the services of SNA on a mainframe and should not be confused with an AnyNet gateway (which is a transport gateway). Because it connects directly to the SNA network at the boundary node, the SSCP-PU and SSCP-LU sessions for the dependent LUs are established with the gateway machine. Since the SSCP-PU and SSCP-LU sessions cannot be carried to the other LUs in the LAN over the native SNA flow (these sessions cannot be carried from node to node), the Communications Manager/2 gateway sends its own ACTPUs and ACTLUs to the other PUs and LUs in the network, just as if they came from the mainframe. Each LU appears, therefore, to be attached directly to the boundary function. The gateway, in turn, associates the SSCP-PU and SSCP-LU sessions from the other LUs on the LAN with the SSCP-PU and SSCP-LU sessions between the gateway and VTAM in the mainframe. The non-gateway PUs in the LAN are called *downstream PUs,* and the LUs associated with these PUs are called *downstream LUs.*

17.6.1   Dependent LU Requester/Server

The Dependent LU Requester/Server (DLUR/S), developed for APPN and first available in VTAM Version 4 Release 2 (and described in Chap. 6), provides a way to transport the SSCP-PU and SSCP-LU sessions needed for dependent LU activation across APPN networks to nodes that are not adjacent to the mainframe's boundary function. It must be remembered that in classic SNA subarea networks, dependent LUs have to be located in nodes attached directly to the mainframe. The boundary function component translates subarea packet and address formats to and from the formats used by the 3274 controllers that control the terminals and printers used by mainframe applications. If a network segment is placed between the boundary function component and the dependent LU's node, there must be a way to transport the SSCP-PU and SSCP-LU sessions needed to activate the PU and LUs across the intervening network or network segment. DLUR/S provides the means to extend SSCP-PU and SSCP-LU sessions across an APPN network to bring the boundary function support across the network to the node in which the dependent LU resides. DLUR/S uses LU 6.2 sessions to encapsulate SSCP-PU and SSCP-LU flows. DLUR/S can also be used in MPTN networks because AnyNet solutions allow LU 6.2 sessions to be set up nonnatively.

The control sessions that are required before dependent LU-LU sessions can be established are created by the SSCP when it sends an ACTPU, creating an SSCP-PU session, and one or more ACTLUs, which create an SSCP-LU session for each dependent LU. Because these sessions can only be established with devices that are attached directly to the boundary function of a subarea, and are not transportable across an APPN network, the DLUR/S provides an LU 6.2 *pipe* in which these sessions are encapsulated. This pipe connects dependent LU requesters that reside in PU 2.1 workstations with a dependent LU server in a mainframe.

The DLUR/S pipe consists of two LU 6.2 sessions—a contention-winner and a contention-loser session—and is called a *CP-SVR pipe*. CP-SVR sessions are activated by an ACTPU or REQACTPU request, and remain active throughout the life of associated LU-LU sessions. The pipe can be activated from either the DLUR or DLUS end. The SNA mode name used by the CP-SVR pipe is *CPSVRMGR*.

17.6.2   Downstream LUs

When a LAN is attached to a mainframe-centric SNA network, one node on the LAN performs the function of a gateway node, transferring data between the mainframe and the LAN. One important function of the gateway is performing peripheral node services for dependent LUs. In classic SNA, a 3274 cluster controller is attached directly to a mainframe boundary node function. By *attached directly,* we mean that there are no intervening nodes. The gateway node, which is also attached directly to a mainframe boundary function, is only one workstation on a LAN that contains many workstations. In order for the remaining LAN workstations, which also have PUs with associated LUs, to appear to be directly attached as well, there must be a scheme in place to connect the downstream PUs with the boundary function support.

Downstream PUs belong to other workstations on the LAN that are located downstream from the gateway. Downstream LUs are the LUs belonging to the downstream PUs. Downstream PUs with their associated LUs must appear to the SSCP (which is in the mainframe) as if they are located in the Communications Manager/2 gateway node (which is either attached directly as a peripheral node to the boundary function of VTAM, or connected through a DLUR/S CP-SVR pipe which emulates a direct connection).

The Communications Manager/2 gateway handles its downstream PUs in the following manner. When the Communications Manager/2 gateway receives an ACTPU and the ACTLUs for a downstream node, it accepts these as if they relate to the local PU and the local LUs. The actual communication on the SNA network to these downstream PUs with their associated downstream LUs is performed by the gateway, however, which sends its own ACTPU and ACTLUs in emulation of a boundary node. The gateway makes its own association between the SSCP and the downstream PUs. Figure 17.7 shows this relationship.

When the link between the Communications Manager/2 gateway and the downstream nodes is no longer provided by a SNA transport network, but has been replaced by TCP/IP (or any other transport provider, for that matter), there must be a way to deal with the downstream PU link activation. It could be handled by DLUR/S if a DLUR was loaded in each node. That way, the DLUR/S pipe would extend all the way from the mainframe to each downstream PU. This is not necessary, however, because when the Communications Manager/2 gateway is attached directly to the mainframe's SNA network, and the

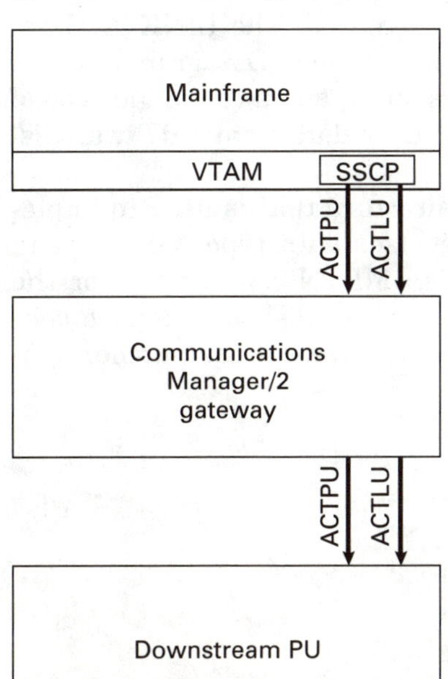

Figure 17.7 The Communications Manager/2 gateway handles SSCP-PU and SSCP-LU session establishment for downstream PUs.

LAN is running TCP/IP, so there is no need to run DLUR/S to solve the downstream PU dilemma. AnyNet takes care of it.

17.6.2.1 Establishing downstream LU control sessions.

AnyNet SNA-Over-TCP/IP uses formats available in the MTPN architecture to provide the downstream PUs with the SSCP-PU and SSCP-LU sessions that were formerly provided by the Communications Manager/2 gateway.

When downstream PUs are linked to the Communications Manager/2 gateway by a non-SNA network, the manner in which SSCP-PU and SSCP-LU sessions are extended from the gateway to the downstream workstations can no longer be used because ACTPU and ACTLU flows are not supported in SNA-Over-TCP/IP. AnyNet SNA-Over-TCP/IP OS/2 workstations use two formats in the MPTN architecture to enable SSCP support for downstream PUs. The first is the MPTN_Syntax_Mapper_Signal_Datagram with a *LINK_ACT* request. This MPTN datagram is issued by AnyNet components in the downstream PUs to notify the Communications Manager/2 gateway that SSCP services are required. The LINK_ACT request is formatted as transport user data similar to the optional fields that were described in Chap. 13. These fields have a 4-byte common prefix consisting of a command type, processing specification, and command length. Table 17.6 shows the format of transport user data, and Table 17.7 shows the various types of transport user data. The command type for LINK_ACT is X'01'. There is no other specific transport user data enclosed in the datagram; the LINK_ACT command type is all that is required. The LINK_ACT response is sent in an MPTN_Syntax_Mapper_Signal_Datagram and has a command type of X'02' for a positive response, and a command type of X'03' for a negative response. Transport user data type X'07' was discussed in Sec. 17.5.1.

The second format of the MPTN architecture that is used to implement the SSCP extensions is transport user data type X'08' sent in the MPTN_Connect message to establish MPTN connections for the SSCP-PU and each of the SSCP-LU sessions. Called the *extended connection data indicator*, this format is used to inform the partner syn-

TABLE 17.6   Transport User Data Format

Field name	Identifier size
Command type	1
Processing specification	1
Command length	2
Transport user data	Variable

TABLE 17.7   Transport User Data Types

Name	Type	Data length	Purpose
Link Activation	X'01'	0	Request ACTPU/ACTLU
Link Activation Positive Response	X'02'	0	Request ACTPU/ACTLU positive response
Link Activation Negative Response	X'03'	0	Request ACTPU/ACTLU negative response
Link Deactivation	X'04'	0	Request DEACTPU/DEACTLU
Link Deactivation Response	X'05'	0	Request DEACTPU/DEACTLU response
Diagnostics	X'06'	2	Included in negative responses
LU Type/CP Name	X'07'	2–19	Set LU type and CP name
Extended Connection Indicator	X'08'	1	Indicate an extended MPTN_Connect
Non-Queued Response Indicator	X'09'	1	Non-queued responses are sent as expedited data

tax mapper that the connection data in the MPTN_Connect include fields required for establishing SSCP sessions.

The flow diagram in Fig. 17.8 and the following description explain how the SSCP-PU session extension with the downstream PU is accomplished. Activation of the SSCP-LU sessions is not described, but they are activated in the same manner.

The flow diagram shows three components for each node:

- Syntax mapper

- CMM

- PMM

The sockets and SNA layers (which were previously included in flow diagram Fig. 17.3) are not included in this diagram, but are implied.

1. When a downstream PU requires link activation, the syntax mapper in the downstream PU's access node issues an M_SEND_DG_DC to send an MPTN_Syntax_Mapper_Signal_Datagram with a LINK_ACT request placed in it. The CMM locates the transport provider address for the Communications Manager/2 gateway by issuing a P_LOCATE_DC. The PMM passes back a return code of RC_PENDING, then obtains the address by assembling the domain name and issuing a *gethostbyname*() function call. The transport provider address for the Comm Manager gateway is passed back to the CMM in a P_LOCATE_UC.

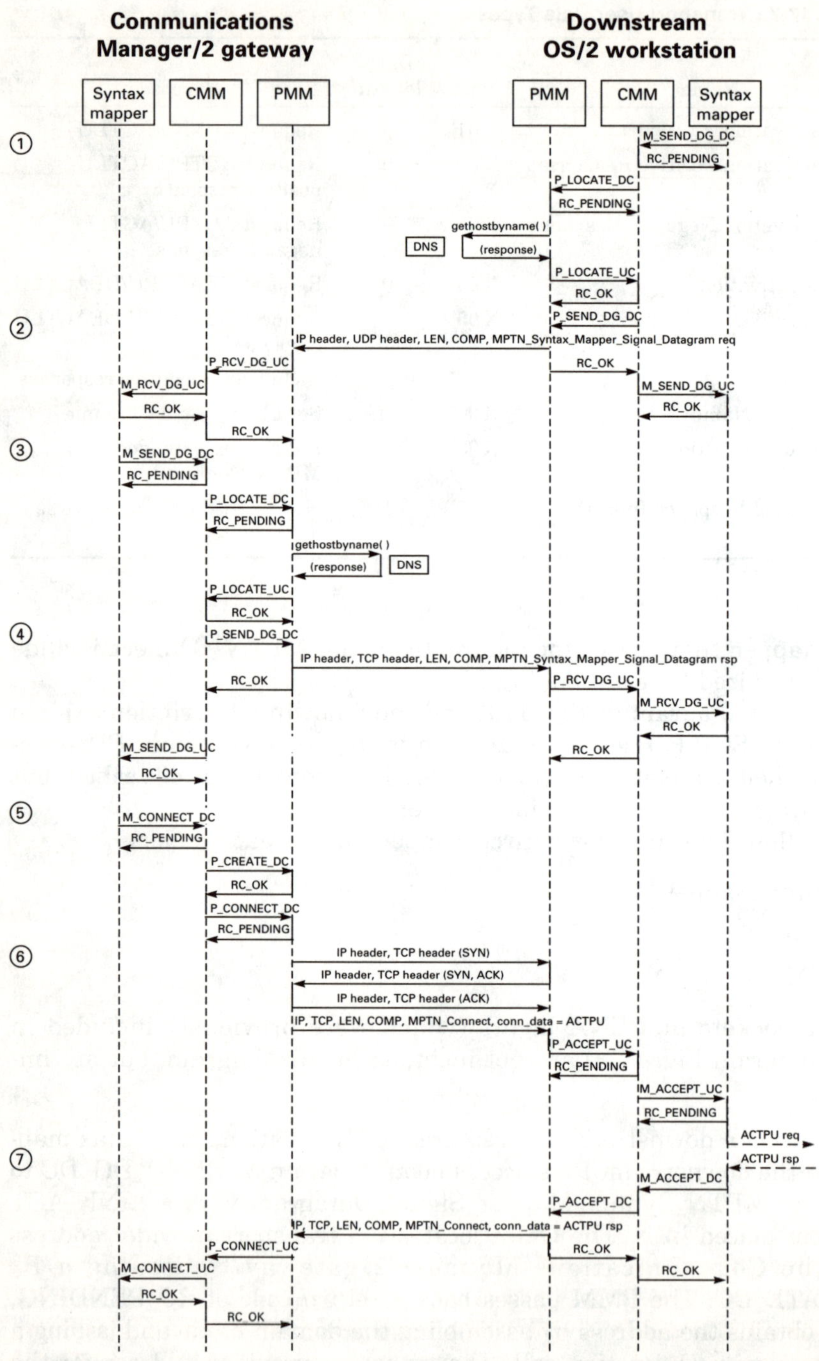

Figure 17.8 SNA-Over-TCP/IP SSCP-PU session establishment with a downstream PU.

2. The CMM in the downstream PU passes the MPTN_Syntax_Mapper_Signal_Datagram to the PMM in a P_SEND_DG_DC. The PMM sends this MPTN datagram in a UDP datagram to the Communications Manager/2 gateway. The Communications Manager/2 gateway's PMM receives the UDP datagram and passes the MPTN_Syntax_Mapper_Signal_Datagram to the CMM in a P_RCV_DG_UC. The CMM passes the datagram to the syntax mapper in an M_RCV_DG_UC.

3. The syntax mapper in the gateway places an MPTN_Syntax_Mapper_Signal_Datagram response in an M_SEND_DG_DC. The CMM gets the transport user address of the node that is requesting the LINK_ACT from the datagram, then issues a P_LOCATE_DC to obtain the transport provider address mapping. The PMM passes back a return code of RC_PENDING, then obtains the transport user address by issuing a *gethostbyname*() function call. The address is passed back to the CMM in a P_LOCATE_UC.

4. The gateway's CMM now passes the MPTN_Syntax_Mapper_Signal_Datagram response to the PMM in a P_SEND_DG_DC. The PMM sends the MPTN datagram as a UDP datagram to the workstation. The PMM in the workstation receives the UDP datagram, extracts the MPTN_Syntax_Mapper_Signal_Datagram response, and passes it to the CMM in a P_RCV_DG_UC. The CMM passes the datagram to the syntax mapper in an M_RCV_DG_UC.

5. The Communications Manager/2 gateway's syntax mapper issues an M_CONNECT_DC for each session: one for the SSCP-PU, and one for each SSCP-LU session to be established with the downstream node (our example, however, will only describe the SSCP-PU session). The CMM receives the M_CONNECT_DC request for the SSCP-PU session and formats an MPTN_Connect message with an *extended connection data indicator* as transport user data. The command type for this format is X'08' (see Table 17.7). The data part of the transport user data field is set to a value of X'01', and the connection_data field is loaded with the *origin address field* (OAF) and *destination address field* (DAF) from the transmission header of the ACTPU. These values are the endpoint addresses for the SSCP-PU and SSCP-LU sessions. The CMM issues a P_CREATE_DC, followed by a P_CONNECT_DC, passing the MPTN_Connect message as a parameter to the PMM. (P_LOCATE_DC is not issued by the CMM to resolve the workstation's transport user address because the address was already resolved when the datagram was sent and resides in the CMM's address cache.)

6. The PMM sends the MPTN_Connect request to the downstream workstation. The PMM in the downstream workstation receives the MPTN_Connect and gives it to the CMM in a P_ACCEPT_UC. The

CMM passes the transport user data from the request to the syntax mapper in an M_ACCEPT_UC. The syntax mapper issues an ACTPU to the SNA protocol stack.

7. When the syntax mapper receives a positive response for the ACTPU, it formats an M_ACCEPT_DC. The CMM then issues a P_ACCEPT_DC and the PMM sends an MPTN_Connect response with the ACTPU response in the connection_data field. The PMM in the Communications Manager/2 gateway receives the MPTN_Connect response and passes it to the CMM in a P_CONNECT_UC. The CMM issues an M_CONNECT_UC.

This process is reiterated for each ACTLU that is sent to activate an LU in the downstream node, using the same method as defined for the ACTPU. When these MPTN connections have been established, the downstream LUs are ready for BINDs that will be sent from the host, and LU-LU sessions to be established.

When the access node is ready to be brought down, it sends an MPTN_Syntax_Mapper_Signal_Datagram formatted with a *LINK_DEACT* to the Communications Manager/2 gateway. The LINK_DEACT uses transport user data with a command type of X'04'. The gateway responds with an MPTN_Syntax_Mapper_Signal_ Datagram with a transport user data field containing a command type of X'05', which is the response for the deactivation request.

17.7 Conclusion

This chapter described the configuration of the AnyNet SNA-Over-TCP/IP and APPC-Over-TCP/IP access node and gateway products, showing how IBM has chosen to make use of the MPTN architecture in its implementations. Chapter 18 presents a brief overview of several AnyNet implementations.

AnyNet in the Enterprise

18.1   Introduction

The MPTN architecture and IBM's AnyNet products have been described. This final chapter presents a very brief summing up of MPTN and the AnyNet products by showing their use in actual networks.

18.2   The U.S. Postal Service

The U.S. Postal Service has maintained a very large SNA network across the United States for many years. Originally, this SNA network provided mainframe access for 3270 terminals connected to 3174 control units in offices all over the United States. Over the years, these offices began installing Ethernet LANs with Windows-based workstations. The LANs were connected to the Postal Service's two mainframes by means of Eicon SNA gateways, which allowed mainframe 3270 programs to be accessed from individual PCs running in the LANs. In addition to needing to access 3270 programs running in the mainframes, a file transfer program called Legent XCOM was also in use. This program ran on an OS/2 machine that was attached to a mainframe by an SDLC link.

In 1992, the Postal Service decided to interconnect all of its 300 LANs. A large router network was designed and installed by the Postal Service's National Network Service Center in Raleigh, North Carolina. This large TCP/IP network consists of three tiers. The top-level tier is the backbone of the network and consists of 15 routers interconnected with frame relay WAN links. These routers are located in area offices. The next tier consists of 86 routers located in district offices. Two IBM mainframes are connected to routers in this second tier using channel-attached IBM 3172 Interconnect Controllers. The mainframes run MVS and use the IBM TCP/IP product. The third tier of the network consists of the 300 Ethernet LANs located in plants scattered throughout the United States. These LANs are connected to the 86 second-tier routers.

Once the LANs were interconnected by means of the TCP/IP network, the Postal Service began looking at ways to use this network to provide mainframe SNA access for the LANs. This would eliminate operating a TCP/IP and a SNA network in parallel. This consolidation of the two networks would provide financial savings because of the cost of maintaining hardware and software associated with the SNA network. Additionally, applications that formerly used the SNA network would benefit from the higher bandwidth provided by the TCP/IP network which used newer technology.

To accomplish the conversion from SNA to TCP/IP, TN3270 was installed to provide 3270 emulation services for the LAN-attached PCs. The Legent XCOM file transfer application running in the OS/2 server did not use 3270 protocols, using APPC instead, and could not take advantage of TN3270. The Postal Service wanted to continue running the XCOM application instead of purchasing a different application just to accommodate the transport network. A method for running APPC applications on the TCP/IP network was needed, so AnyNet SNA-Over-TCP/IP was installed in the OS/2 machines as well as in the mainframes. AnyNet provides the ability not only to continue running the APPC-based Legent XCOM file transfer program, it will also enable other APPC programs that may be considered for future implementation to run over the TCP/IP network as well.

The TCP/IP and SNA networks continue to operate simultaneously while SNA sites are migrated to TCP/IP one by one. To accomplish the migration, TCP/IP stacks and TN3270 are installed in all workstations requiring 3270 access, and AnyNet SNA-Over-TCP/IP for OS/2 is configured in the OS/2 server located in each network.

18.3 Pacific Bell

Pacific Bell is the California arm of Pacific Telesis—the regional phone company for Nevada and California—and has a network that spans thousands of miles. Pacific Bell had a dilemma similar to that of the U.S. Postal Service: it had converted its SNA network to TCP/IP, but there remained a need to run APPC programs. Pacific Bell originally looked for a billing application for its business offices written for TCP/IP that would replace the legacy APPC application, but could not find a TCP/IP application that met their requirments. The application that best suited Pacific Bell's needs was the original APPC application that was already being used. Pacific Bell was not sure what to do until AnyNet was announced in March 1993. The company decided to give SNA-Over-TCP/IP and APPC-Over-TCP/IP a try.

Pacific Bell business offices access the DB2 databases located in Pacific Bell MVS mainframes using either of two server platforms: DB2/6000 running on RS/6000s, or XDB running on Intel-based OS/2s. The SQL-based communications with the mainframe uses LU 6.2 sessions. AnyNet APPC-Over-TCP/IP for AIX and SNA-Over-TCP/IP for OS/2 allow the offices to continue using DB2 as they had before, while swapping out their SNA transport network.

Charles Hights, senior systems analyst at Pacific Bell, who oversaw the installation of AnyNet and continues to work with the network, reports that the company is very happy with the AnyNet products, and that they were easy to install and configure. APPC programs operate in the TCP/IP network without a hitch.

18.4   Future Directions

MPTN is not just another interim solution to the problems brought on by multiprotocol networks, but represents, in this author's opinion, a breakthrough. Perhaps the best sales pitch for the MPTN architecture and the associated AnyNet products is seeing and working with MPTN in actual implementations.

The acceptance of MPTN by the computer industry will help create a seamless internetworking among the various networking protocols. MPTN could be built into third-party products such as the network operating systems of Banyan Vines, NetWare, and LAN Manager, to enable the LANs on which these systems operate to be interconnected over SNA and TCP/IP networks. SNA gateway products, such as NetWare for SNA and Windows NT SNA Server, for example, could be fitted with a configuration option that would allow the network between the SNA gateway and the mainframe to use MPTN formats and protocols to enable SNA programs to run over other than SNA networks. These products would interface directly with AnyNet SNA-Over-TCP/IP for MVS in the mainframe.

As AnyNet is incorporated more and more into enterprise networks, MPTN compatibility will become a desirable feature to be introduced into popular networking products—not only in network operating systems, but also into other products and the various PC-based TCP/IP protocol stacks.

For example, the WinSock interface is a standardized approach for implementing sockets applications in the Windows environment. At the time of this publication, the WinSock API is being expanded to enable it to access transport protocols other than TCP/IP. This will be accomplished by specifying the transport protocol of choice directly in the *socket*() programming call. However, using MPTN, applications programs would not have to be written to use a specific networking protocol, and an AF_INET sockets application could run on any potential transport network. Using MPTN, the choice of transport networks is not left to the application programmer to decide.

The socket layer in WinSock is contained in a dynamically loaded module called *winsock.dll*. A version of winsock.dll can be supplied by software vendors that implements an MPTN access node. This module would not only allow sockets programs to run over other networks besides the traditional TCP/IP network, it would also be compatible with AnyNet products and with MPTN products from other manufacturers. This would be an asset for vendors whose products are targeted for large enterprise networks where AnyNet gateways are likely to appear. WinSock could provide a winsock.dll module that consulted a configuration file (or a routing preference table) to decide if it should operate as a regular TCP/IP winsock.dll or use some other transport network instead.

Client-Server Programming Examples Using the Sockets API

Two basic example programs, written in the C language, are presented to demonstrate the use of the Berkeley sockets API described in Chap. 5.

A.1   The Server

The server program implements a very basic example of a server module using the AF_INET sockets interface.

```
/***********************************************************************
*                            SERVER
***********************************************************************/
#include              <errno.h>
#include              <sys/types.h>
#include              <sys/socket.h>
#include              <netinet/in.h>
#include              <netdb.h>
main()
{
   int      Connection;                /* the tcp connection socket number */
   char     ServerName[] =    "test";
   int      sd;                        /* Socket Descriptor */
   int      RemainLen;
   int      offset = 0;
   int      readlen = 0;
   int      buff_lng;
   int      addrsize;
   char     buffer[1920];
   extern int  errno;
   struct   servent      *Server;   /* server info */
   struct   sockaddr_in  sockaddr;
   struct   hostent      *Host;
   struct   sockaddr_in  SockAddr;
   printf("Server: Welcome to the Server Module\n");
```

```c
/***********************************************************************
Service is called 'test'. Here we ensure there is a port in etc/services.
Its port number is placed in the 'servent' structure pointed to by 'Server'
***********************************************************************/

    if ( !(Server = getservbyname( ServerName,"tcp" )) )
    {
        printf("Server: server %s not found in /etc/services\n",ServerName);
        return;
    }
    printf("Server: The port number is: %d\n",Server->s_port);
    printf("Server: The service name is: %s\n",Server->s_name);

/*********************************************
Set up the server socket address structure
*********************************************/

    bzero( &SockAddr,sizeof(SockAddr) );
    SockAddr.sin_family = AF_INET;
    SockAddr.sin_addr.s_addr = INADDR_ANY;
    SockAddr.sin_port = htons(ntohs((u_short)Server->s_port));

/*************************
Create the server's socket
*************************/

    if ( (sd = socket(AF_INET, SOCK_STREAM, 0) ) < 0)
    {
        printf("Server: cannot create socket\n");
        return;
    }
    printf("Server: socket created\n");

/***************
Bind our socket
***************/

    if ( bind(sd,(struct sockaddr*) &SockAddr, sizeof(SockAddr) ) == -1)
    {
        if (errno == EADDRINUSE)
            printf("Server: server already loaded\n");
        else
            printf("Server: socket bind failed %d\n",errno);
        close(sd);
        return;
    }
    printf("Server: socket bound\n");

/****************************************************
Listen on our server socket for incoming connections
****************************************************/

    if ( listen(sd,3) == -1 )
    {
        printf("Server: listen failed with errno %d\n",errno);
        close (sd);
        return;
    }
/******************
Accept a connection
******************/
    addrsize = sizeof(sockaddr);
    if (( Connection = accept( sd, &sockaddr, &addrsize)) == -1)
    {
        printf("Server: accept failed with errno %d\n",errno);
        close (sd);
        return;
```

```
    }
    printf("Server: new connection!\n");
    buff_lng = sizeof(buffer);
    RemainLen = buff_lng;
    while (offset < buff_lng) {        /* data can arrive in pieces */
        readlen = read( Connection, buffer + offset, RemainLen);
        if (readlen == -1)
        {
            if ( errno == ECONNRESET )
                printf("Server: connection terminated by peer\n");
            else
                printf("Server: read error. errno = %d\n",errno);
            close(Connection);
            close(sd);
            return;
        }
        if (readlen == 0)
        {
            printf("Server: read was terminated\n");
            close(Connection);
            close(sd);
            return;
        }
        offset += readlen;             /* increment count of data received */
        RemainLen = buff_lng - readlen;
        printf("Server: read %d bytes sent from client\n",readlen);
    }    /* end of while loop */
/******************************************************************
Since this is a very basic sample program, we will close after reading
in the data sent by the client program
******************************************************************/

    printf("Server: closing connected socket\n");
    close(Connection);
    printf("Server: closing listening socket\n");
    close(sd);
    return;
}
```

A.2 The Client

The client program implements a program that communicates with the
above server program example.

```
/******************************************************************
*                          CLIENT
******************************************************************/
#include         <errno.h>
#include         <sys/types.h>
#include         <sys/socket.h>
#include         <netinet/in.h>
#include         <netdb.h>
main()
{
    char    Host[]      = "Curly";  /* Hostname where server lives  */
    char    Server[]    = "test";   /* Server name                  */
    int     sd;
    char    buffer[] = "ABCDE";
extern  int     errno;
```

```c
        struct  servent      *sp;                    /* server info */
        struct  hostent      *hp;
        struct  sockaddr_in  sockaddr;
/*****************************************************************************
Locate our server. It must first have been entered into the IP file
"etc/services" on this machine with the port number the actual server
listens on
*****************************************************************************/
        if ( (!sp = getservbyname( Server,"tcp" ) ))
        {
                printf("Client: server %s not located. Check etc/services\n",
                Server);
                return;
        }
        printf("Client: just found server %s\n",Server);

/***********************************************************************
Get the IP address of the host on which the server resides
***********************************************************************/
        if (!(hp = gethostbyname(Host)) )
        {
                printf( "Client: host %s not found\n", Host );
                return;
        }
        printf( "Client: Host %s found\n", Host);

        bzero( &sockaddr, sizeof(sockaddr) );   /* clear the sockaddr_in
                                                   structure */
        sockaddr.sin_family = AF_INET;           /* set family to 'internet'   */
        bcopy((char *)hp->h_addr,(char *) &sockaddr.sin_addr, hp->h_length);
        /* IP address */
        sockaddr.sin_port = sp->s_port;        /* port */
        if ( (sd = socket( sockaddr.sin_family, SOCK_STREAM, 0)) == -1)
        {
                printf("Client: socket() Error; errno = %d\n",errno);
                return;
        }
        printf("Client: Socket created\n");

/*****************************************************
    Attempt to connect to the server
*****************************************************/
        if ( connect(sd,&sockaddr,sizeof(struct sockaddr_in) ) == -1 )
        {
                printf("Client: connect() failed\n");
                close(sd);
                return;
        }
        printf("Client: connected!\n");


/***********************************************************
    Write data to the newly connected socket
***********************************************************/

        if ( write( sd, buffer, strlen(buffer) ) == -1 )
                printf("Client: write error: %d\n",errno);

        printf("Client: closing socket\n");
        close(sd);
        return;
}
```

Client-Server Programming Examples Using the CPI-C API

Two very basic example programs, written in the C language, are presented to demonstrate the use of the CPI-C API described in Chap. 7.

B.1 The Server

This example program shows how a server program can be written using the CPI-C API.

```
/*---------------------------------------------------------------------
 * CPI-C "Hello, world" program
 * Server side (file HELLO1D.C) from
 * CPI-C Programming in C by John Q. Walker II and Peter J. Schwaller
 * used by permission
 *---------------------------------------------------------------------*/
#include <cpic.h>                /* conversation API library    */
#include <stdio.h>               /* file I/O                     */
#include <stdlib.h>              /* standard library            */

int main(void)
{
    unsigned char conversation_ID[CM_CID_SIZE];
    unsigned char data_buffer[100 + 1];
    CM_INT32 requested_length = (CM_INT32)sizeof(data_buffer)-1;
    CM_INT32 received_length = 0;
    CM_RETURN_CODE cpic_return_code;

    CM_DATA_RECEIVED_TYPE data_received;
    CM_STATUS_RECEIVED status_received;
    CM_REQUEST_TO_SEND_RECEIVED rts_received;

    cmaccp(                       /* Accept_Conversation          */
      conversation_ID,            /* O: returned conversation ID  */
      &cpic_return_code);         /* O: return code from this call */
```

```
  cmrcv(                              /* Receive                        */
    conversation_ID,                  /* I: conversation ID            */
    data_buffer,                      /* I: where to put received data */
    &requested_length,                /* I: maximum length to receive  */
    &data_received,                   /* O: data complete or not?      */
    &received_length,                 /* O: length of received data    */
    &status_received,                 /* O: has status changed?        */
    &rts_received,                    /* O: was RTS received?          */
    &cpic_return_code);               /* O: return code from this call */

  data_buffer[received_length]='\0';   /* insert the null              */
  (void)printf("%s\nPress a key to end the program...\n",
    data_buffer);
  (void)getchar();                          /* pause for any keystroke */
  return(EXIT_SUCCESS);
}
```

B.2   The Client

This example of a CPI-C client program sends data to the server program listed above.

```
/*---------------------------------------------------------------------
 * CPI-C "Hello, world" program
 * Client side (file HELLO1.C) from
 * CPI-C Programming in C by John Q. Walker II and Peter J. Schwaller
 * used by permission
 *--------------------------------------------------------------------*/

#include <cpic.h>                /* conversation API library      */
#include <string.h>              /* strings and memory            */
#include <stdlib.h>              /* standard library              */

/* this hardcoded sym_dest_name is 8 chars long & blank padded      */
#define SYM_DEST_NAME (unsigned char*)"HELLO1S "

/* this is the string we're sending to the partner                  */
#define SEND_THIS (unsigned char*)"Hello, world"

int main(void)
{
    unsigned char conversation_ID[CM_CID_SIZE];
    unsigned char * data_buffer = SEND_THIS;
    CM_INT32 send_length = (CM_INT32)strlen(SEND_THIS);
    CM_RETURN_CODE cpic_return_code;

    CM_REQUEST_TO_SEND_RECEIVED rts_received;

  cminit(                             /* Initialize_Conversation       */
    conversation_ID,                  /* O: returned conversation ID   */
    SYM_DEST_NAME,                    /* I: symbolic destination name  */
    &cpic_return_code);               /* O: return code from this call */

  cmallc(                             /* Allocate                      */
    conversation_ID,                  /* I: conversation ID            */
    &cpic_return_code);               /* O: return code from this call */

  cmsend(                             /* Send_Data                     */
    conversation_ID,                  /* I: conversation ID            */
    data_buffer,                      /* I: send this buffer           */
```

```
    &send_length,              /* I: length to send            */
    &rts_received,             /* O: was RTS received?         */
    &cpic_return_code);        /* O: return code from this call */

  cmdeal(                      /* Deallocate                   */
    conversation_ID,           /* I: conversation ID           */
    &cpic_return_code);        /* O: return code from this call */

  return(EXIT_SUCCESS);
}
```

X/Open MPTN Documents

The following four MPTN documents are available from the X/Open Company in England. This standards publishing company refers to MPTN as XMPTN, to distinguish IBM from X/Open materials. Information for ordering XMPTN documents can be obtained using the X/Open Home Page at http://www.xopen.co.uk/.

C.1   XMPTN Documents

XMPTN Architecture Guide

X/Open Guide, December 1995. Multiprotocol Transport Networking (XMPTN) Architecture. ISBN 1-85912-116-0, C506.

XMPTN Access Node

X/Open CAE Specification. Multiprotocol Transport Networking (XMPTN): Access Node. ISBN 1-85912-106-3, P521.

XMPTN Data Formats

X/Open Guide. Multiprotocol Transport Networking (XMPTN): Data Formats. ISBN 1-85912-111-X, C522.

XMPTN Address Mapper

X/Open Guide. Multiprotocol Transport Networking (XMPTN): Address Mapper. ISBN 1-85912-101-2, C520.

D.1 Networking Manuals

GG24-4338. *Introduction to Networking Technologies.*
G326-0395. *Introduction to the Open Blueprint.*
SBOF-8702. *Open Blueprint Technical Reference.*
GC31-7057. *Networking Blueprint Executive Overview.*
GC23-3808. *Open Blueprint: Technical Overview.*
SC31-7123. *Planning for Integrated Networks.*

D.2 SNA Manuals

SC30-3112. *Systems Network Architecture Format and Protocol Reference Manual: Architectural Logic.*
GC30-3073. *Systems Network Architecture: Technical Overview.*
GC20-1868. *Systems Network Architecture: Sessions between Logical Units.*
LY43-0081. *Systems Network Architecture: Network Products Formats.*
SV40-1010. *APPN Dependent LU Requester Architecture Reference.*
GA23-0061. *IBM 3270 Information Display System: 3274 Control Unit Description and Programmer's Guide.*
SC31-6180. *Common Programming Interface Communications Specification: CPI-C 2.0.*
GC30-3084. *Systems Network Architecture: Transaction Programmer's Reference Manual for LU Type 6.2.*

D.3 MPTN Manuals

GC31-7073. *Multiprotocol Transport Networking (MPTN): Technical Overview.*
GC31-7074. *Multiprotocol Transport Networking (MPTN) Architecture: Formats.*
SG24-4170. *Multiprotocol Transport Networking (MPTN) Architecture: Tutorial and Product Implementations.*

D.4 AnyNet Manuals

MVS

SC31-6526. *VTAM AnyNet Feature for V4R2: Guide to Sockets over SNA.*
SC31-6527. *VTAM AnyNet Feature for V4R2: Guide to SNA over TCP/IP.*
SC31-6559. *VTAM AnyNet Feature for V4R3: Guide to Sockets over SNA for MVS.*
SC31-6560. *VTAM AnyNet Feature for V4R3: Guide to SNA over TCP/IP for MVS.*

OS/2

GV40-0402. *IBM AnyNet/2: NetBEUI over SNA Administrator's Guide.*
GV40-0405. *IBM AnyNet: Guide to AnyNet IPX over SNA Gateway for OS/2.*
GV40-0374. *IBM AnyNet/2: Guide to Sockets over SNA Gateway.*
GV40-0216. *IBM AnyNet/2: Guide to SNA over TCP/IP Gateway for OS/2.*
GV40-0377. *IBM AnyNet/2: NetBEUI over SNA User's Guide.*
GV40-0375. *IBM AnyNet/2: Guide to SNA over TCP/IP.*
SV40-0111. *IBM AnyNet/2: Guide to Sockets over NetBIOS.*
SV40-0112. *IBM AnyNet/2: Guide to Sockets over IPX.*
SV40-0376. *IBM AnyNet/2: Guide to Sockets over SNA.*
GC31-8190. *IBM Communications Server Guide to Sockets over SNA.*
GC31-8191. *IBM Communications Server Guide to Sockets over SNA Gateway.*
GC31-8192. *IBM Communications Server Guide to SNA over TCP/IP.*
GC31-8193. *IBM Communications Server Guide to SNA over TCP/IP Gateway.*

Windows

SV40-0215. *IBM AnyNet: Guide to APPC over TCP/IP for Windows.*
GV40-0113. *IBM AnyNet: Guide to SNA over TCP/IP for Windows.*

AIX

SV40-0212. *AIX SNA Server/6000 AnyNet Feature: Guide to APPC over TCP/IP.*
SC31-8065. *AIX SNA Server/6000 AnyNet Feature: Guide to Sockets over SNA.*
SC31-8217. *SNA Server for AIX AnyNet Guide to Sockets over SNA V3R1.*
SC31-8221. *SNA Server for AIX AnyNet Guide to APPC over TCP/IP V3R1.*

Other products

GC30-3706. *2217 Nways Multiprotocol Concentrator User's Guide.*

Redbooks

GG24-4066. *VTAM V3R4.2 AnyNet/MVS Implementation.*
GG24-4395. *AnyNet: SNA over TCP/IP Installation and Interoperability.*
GG24-4396. *AnyNet: Sockets over SNA and NetBIOS over SNA Installation and Interoperability.*
GG24-2531. *AS/400 AnyNet Scenarios.*

Bibliography

Albitz, P., and C. Liu, 1992. *DNS and BIND in a Nutshell*. O'Reilly & Associates, Sebastopol, Calif.

Ali, M. I., 1992. "Frame Relay in Public Networks," *IEEE Communications Magazine*, vol. 30, no. 3, pp. 72–78 (Mar.).

Barnett, R., and S. Maynard-Smith, 1988. *Packet Switched Networks*. John Wiley, New York.

Bellovin, S. M., and W. R. Cheswick, 1994. "Network Firewalls," *IEEE Communications Magazine*, vol. 32, no. 9, pp. 50–57 (Sept.).

Black, U., 1991. *OSI: A Model for Computer Communications Standards*. Prentice-Hall, Englewood Cliffs, N.J.

Black, U., 1991. *X.25 and Related Protocols*. IEEE Computer Society Press, Los Alamitos, Calif.

Black, U., 1994. *Frame Relay Networks*. McGraw-Hill, New York.

Black, U., *Physical Level Interfaces and Protocols*. IEEE Computer Society Press, Los Alamitos, Calif.

Blakeley, B., H. Harris, and R. Lewis, 1995. *Messaging and Queuing Using the MQI: Concepts and Analysis, Design and Development*, McGraw-Hill, New York.

Bloomer, J. 1991. *Power Programming with RPC*. O'Reilly & Associates, Sebastopol, Calif.

Britton, K., W. E. Chen, T. D. Chung, A. Edward, J. Mathew, D. Pozefsky, S. Sarkar, R. Turner, W. Boeringer, and D. Dykeman, 1993. "Multiprotocol Transport Networking: A General Internetworking Solution," *Proceedings of the 1993 International Conference on Network Protocols*, IEEE Computer Society Press, Los Alamitos, Calif.

Brodd, W. D., 1983. "HDLC, ADCCP, and SDLC: What's the Difference?," *Data Communications*, pp. 115–122 (Aug.).

Chappell, D., 1987. "Guide to Transport-Layer Interfaces for Unix Users," *Data Communications*, pp. 139–144 (July).

Chappell, L. A., and D. E. Hakes, 1994. *Novell's Guide to NetWare LAN Analysis*, 2d ed. Sybex, Alameda, Calif.

Cheswick, W. R., and S. M. Bellovin, 1994. *Firewalls and Internet Security*. Addison-Wesley, Reading, Mass.

Ching, Y., and H. S. Say, 1993. "SONET Implementation," *IEEE Communications Magazine*, vol. 31, no. 19, pp. 34–40 (Sept.).

Chorafas, D. N., 1984. *Designing and Implementing Local Area Networks*. McGraw-Hill, New York.

Cole, G. D., 1990. *Implementing OSI Networks*, John Wiley, New York.

Coltun, R., 1989. "OSPF: An Internet Routing Protocol," *ConneXions: The Interoperability Report*, vol. 3, no. 8, pp. 19–25 (Aug.).

Comer, D. E., 1991, 1993. *Internetworking with TCP/IP,* vols. I–III. Prentice-Hall, Englewood Cliffs, N.J. A great set of books on TCP/IP: A must for anyone wanting to learn TCP/IP at the C programming level. Every aspect of the internet protocols is presented and illustrated with C programming examples. Volume I deals with the IP network layer and IP applications, Volume II with TCP, RIP, and SNMP, and Volume III with API issues such as sockets or TLI, depending on which version of the book you buy.

Cooney, M., 1994. "Aging SNA Faces a Fight for Its Survival," *Network World,* vol. 11, no. 36, pp. 1, 12–13 (Sept.). This article has "20 years of SNA highlights." The title is typical of the trade rags.

Cypser, R. J., 1991. *Communications for Cooperating Systems: OSI, SNA, and TCP/IP.* Addison-Wesley, Reading, Mass.

Davis, R., 1993. *Windows Network Programming.* Addison-Wesley, Reading, Mass.

Day, A., 1991. "International Standardization of BISDN," *IEEE LTS: The Magazine of Lightwave Telecommunications Systems,* vol. 2, no. 3, pp. 13–20 (Aug.).

Delisle, D., and L. Pelamourgues, 1991. "B-ISDN and How It Works," *IEEE Spectrum,* pp. 39–42 (Aug.).

Dumas, A., 1995. *Programming WinSock.* Sams Publishing, Indianapolis, Ind.

Durr, M., 1994. "ISDN Reemerges," *LAN Magazine,* pp. 103–112 (Jan.).

Edmunds, J. J., 1992. *SAA/LU 6.2 Distributed Networks and Applications.* McGraw-Hill, New York.

Gohring, H., and F. Kauffels, 1992. *Token Ring: Principles, Perspectives and Strategies.* Addison-Wesley, Reading, Mass.

Gray, J. P., P. J. Hansen, P. Homan, M. A. Lerner, and M. Pozefsky, 1983. "Advanced Program-to-Program Communication in SNA," *IBM Systems Journal,* vol. 22, no. 4, pp. 298–318.

Herman, J., 1994. "The Rebirth of CMIP," *Business Communications Review,* pp. 56–57 (Feb.).

Hunt, C., 1992. *TCP/IP Network Administration.* O'Reilly & Associates, Sebastopol, Calif. An excellent book: A must for anyone wanting to learn TCP/IP configuration.

Karels, M., 1994. "How TCP Became Smarter," *Unix Review,* p. 43 (May).

King, S. S., 1992. "Middleware! Making the Network Safe for Application Software," *Data Communications,* pp. 58–67 (March).

Lini, K. F., and J. Y. Moore, 1990. *GOSIP Made Easy: The Complete Procurement Guide.* Computing Unlimited, Fort Collins, Colo.

Lisowski, B., 1991. "Frame Relay: What It Is and How It Works," *Supplement to Business Communications Review,* pp. 3–12 (Oct.).

Lynch, D. C., and M. T. Rose, 1993. *Internet System Handbook.* Addison-Wesley, Reading, Mass.

Malamud, C., 1991. *Analyzing DECnet/OSI Phase V.* Van Nostrand Reinhold, New York.

Martin, J., and K. K. Chapman, 1987. *SNA: IBM's Networking Solution.* Prentice-Hall, Englewood Cliffs, N.J. A dated, but excellent, introduction to SNA.

Martin, J., and K. K. Chapman, 1989. *Local Area Networks: Architectures and Implementations.* Prentice-Hall, Englewood Cliffs, N.J.

McQuillan, J. M., 1989. "Routers as Building Blocks for Robust Internetworks," *Data Communications,* pp. 28–33 (Sept.).

Meijer, A., 1987. *Systems Network Architecture: A Tutorial.* Pitman Publishing, London, and John Wiley, New York. This book is old, but explains many SNA concepts in a short amount of space.

Meijer, E. E., 1989. "LAN Gateways: Paths to Corporate Connectivity," *Data Communications,* pp. 72–84 (Aug.).

Mier, E. E., 1992. "IBM's SNMP Management System Performs Well in Lab," *Communications Week,* p. 100 (Oct.).

Miller, M. A., 1991. *Lan Protocol Handbook.* M&T Books, San Mateo, Calif. All of Mark Miller's books are recommended: They are excellent sources of information.

Miller, M. A., 1991. *Troubleshooting Internetworks: Tools, Techniques, and Protocols.* M&T Books, San Mateo, Calif.

Mills, D. L., 1994. "Precision Synchronization of Computer Network Clocks," *ACM Computer Communication Review,* vol. 24, no. 2, pp. 28–43 (Apr.).

Minoli, D., 1993. *Enterprise Networking: Fractional T1 to SONET, Frame Relay to BISDN*. Artech House, Boston.

Minzer, S., 1989. "Broadband ISDN and Asynchronous Transfer Mode (ATM)," *IEEE Communications Magazine*, pp. 17–24 (Sept.).

Mogul, J., 1989. "Subnetting: A Brief Guide," *ConnecXions: The Interoperability Report*, vol. 3, no. 1, pp. 2–9 (Jan.).

Muller, N. J., and R. P. Davidson, 1991. *The Guide to Frame Relay*. Telecom Library, New York.

Muller, N. J., and R. P. Davidson, 1991. *The Guide to Sonet*. Telecom Library, New York.

Neibaur, D., 1989. "Understanding XNS: The Prototypical Internetwork Protocol," *Data Communications*, pp. 43–51 (Sept.). Here is the "skinny" on XNS by a co-author of IPX/SPX.

Nemeth, E., G. Snyder, and S. Seebass, 1989. *Unix System Administration Handbook*. Prentice-Hall, Englewood Cliffs, N.J.

Neuman, C., and T. Ts'o, 1994. "Kerberos: An Authentication Service for Computer Networks," *IEEE Communications Magazine*, vol. 32, no. 9, pp. 33–38 (Sept.).

Ogle, D. M., K. M. Tracey, R. A. Floyd, and G. Bollella, 1993. "Dynamically Selecting Protocols for Socket Applications," *IEEE Network*, pp. 48–57 (May).

Omidyar, C. G., and A. Aldridge, 1993. "Introduction to SDH/SONET," *IEEE Communications Magazine*, vol. 31, no. 19, pp. 30–33 (Sept.).

Paulak, E., 1994. "Why Use Private Lines When You've Got SMDS?," *Network World*, p. 52 (Sept. 12).

Perlman, R., 1992. *Interconnections: Bridges and Routers*. Addison-Wesley, Reading, Mass. Radia Perlman is a *pearl* of the data communications industry. This is the book to read if you want to know how routers and bridges work.

Powers, J. T., and H. H. Stair, 1990. *Megabit Data Communications*. Prentice-Hall, Englewood Cliffs, N.J.

Pozefsky, D. P., Daniel A. Pitt, and J. P. Gray, 1989. "IBM's Systems Network Architecture," in *Computer Network Architectures and Protocols*, 2d ed., edited by Carl A. Sunshine, pp. 449–509. Plenum, New York.

Pozefsky, D., R. Turner, A. Edwards, S. Sarkar, J. Mathew, G. Bollella, K. Tracey, D. Poirier, J. Fetvedt, and W. S. Hobgood, 1995. "Multiprotocol Transport Networking: A Software Declaration of Application Independence," *IBM Systems Journal*. Date unknown.

Ranade, J., and G. C. Sacket, 1989. *Introduction to SNA Networking: A Guide for Using VTAM/NCP*. McGraw-Hill, New York.

Ranade, J., and G. C. Sacket, 1991. *Advanced SNA Networking: A Professional's Guide to NCP/VTAP*. McGraw-Hill, New York.

Rekhter, Y., 1991. "The Border Gateway Protocol," *ConneXions: The Interoperability Report*, vol. 5, no. 1, pp. 24–29 (Jan.).

Robertson, D., 1993. "OSI: Boondoggle or Network Standards of the Future?," *IBM Internet Journal*, vol. 1, no. 2, pp. 20–26 (Feb.).

Robertson, D., 1993. "ATM: Technology for Tomorrow," *STACKS: The Network Journal*, vol. 1, no. 4, pp. 41–48 (Aug.).

Rose, M. T., 1990. "A Brief History of Network Management," *ConneXions: The Interoperability Report*, vol. 4, no. 8, pp. 18–27 (Aug.).

Rose, M. T., 1990. *The Open Book: A Practical Perspective on OSI*. Prentice-Hall, Englewood Cliffs, N.J.

Routt, T. J., 1988. "SNA Network Management: What Makes IBM's NetView Tick?," *Data Communications*, pp. 203–227 (June).

Routt, T. J., and L. H. Wells, 1995. *Supporting SNA Dependent LUs: A Primer*. Vedacom Corporation, Seattle, Wash.

Sacket, G. C., 1993. *IBM's Token-Ring Networking Handbook*. McGraw-Hill, New York.

Sanders, J. P., M. R. Jones, J. E. Fetvedt, and M. E. Ferree, 1989. "A Communications Interface for Systems Application Architecture," *IEEE Journal on Selected Areas in Communications*, vol. 7, no. 7, pp. 1073–1081 (Sept.).

Sandhu, R. S., and P. Samarati, 1994. "Access Control: Principles and Practice," *IEEE Communications Magazine*, vol. 32, no. 9, pp. 40–48 (Sept.).

Schriftgiesser, D., 1992. "SMDS: A Phone Service for Computers," *Business Communications Review Supplement,* pp. 4–7.

Schwaderer, W. D., 1988. *C Programmer's Guide to NetBIOS.* Howard W. Sams, Indianapolis, Ind.

Schwaderer, W. D., 1989. *IBM's Local Area Networks: Power Networking and Systems Connectivity.* Van Nostrand Reinhold, New York.

Sidhu, G. S., R. F. Andrews, and A. B. Oppenheimer, 1990. *Inside AppleTalk,* 2d ed., Addison-Wesley, Reading, Mass.

Stallings, W., 1987. *Handbook of Computer-Communications Standards: The Open Systems Interconnection (OSI) Model and OSI-Related Standards.* Howard W. Sams, Indianapolis, Ind.

Stallings, W., 1987. *Handbook of Computer-Communications Standards: Local Network Standards.* Howard W. Sams, Indianapolis, Ind.

Stallings, W., 1993. *SNMP, SNMPv2, and CMIP.* Addison-Wesley, Reading, Mass.

Stallings, W., 1994. "Confidentially Speaking," *Lan Magazine,* pp. 49–54 (Aug.).

Steedman, D., 1990. *Abstract Syntax Notation One.* Technology Appraisals, Great Britain.

Steedman, D., 1993. *X.500: The Directory Standard and Its Application.* Technology Appraisals, Great Britain.

Stevens, W. R., 1990. *Unix Network Programming.* Prentice-Hall, Englewood Cliffs, N.J.

Stevens, W. R., 1994, 1995, 1996. *TCP/IP Illustrated,* vols. I–III. Addison-Wesley, Reading, Mass. This is a fabulous set of books about TCP/IP. It is well written, concise, well organized, carefully illustrated, and written in a manner that clarifies the subject.

Tanenbaum, A. S., 1981. *Computer Networks.* Prentice-Hall, Englewood Cliffs, N.J.

Teja, E. R., 1989. "Router Roundup: Tools for Network Segmentation Come of Age," *Data Communications,* pp. 35–40 (Sept.).

Toigo, J. W., 1993. "Channel Networking: The Holy Grail of Channel and LAN Integration," *IBM Internet Journal,* pp. 16–20, p. 50 (Aug.).

Toigo, J. W., 1993. "Channel Networking: Clouds in the Forecast," *IBM Internet Journal,* pp. 20–22 (Dec.).

Trindell, L. D., 1993. *NetView: A Professional's Guide to SNA Network Management.* McGraw-Hill, New York.

Trulove, J. E., 1992. *A Guide to Fractional T1.* Artech House, Norwood, Mass.

Tsuchiya, P. F., 1991. "Inter-Domain Routing in the Internet," *ConneXions: The Interoperability Report,* vol. 5, no. 1, pp. 1–9 (Jan.).

Vereen, L., 1991. "Finding Your Way," *Interoperability Supplement to LAN Magazine,* pp. 43–48 (Fall). This is an article about directory standards.

Walker, J. Q., and P. J. Schwaller, 1995. *CPI-C Programming in C.* McGraw-Hill, New York. This is the book for those of you who want to learn CPI-C in the C language. It was written very carefully to ensure a clear and thorough presentation of the subject matter.

White, J. E., 1989. "ASN.1 and ROS: The Impact of X.400 on OSI," *Selected Areas in Communications,* vol. 7, no. 7, pp. 1060–1072.

Woodburn, R., 1991. "Issues in Inter-Domain Routing," *ConneXions: The Interoperability Report,* vol. 5, no. 1, pp. 10–17 (Jan.).

The Lessons of Internet History, 1992. Tape, Interop.

Windows Sockets 2: Application Programming Interface. Revision 2.0 (Winsock 2).

IEEE Network: The Magazine of Computer Communications, Jan. 1988, vol. 2, no. 1. This is the definitive set of router/bridge articles.

"Building Multiprotocol Networks with MPTN," *SNA Perspective on Internetworking,* July 1994, vol. 15, no. 7. The Saratoga Group.

Supporting SNA Dependent LUs: A Primer: A Guide to the Many Varieties of Support for Dependent LUs across APPN and TCP/IP. Vedacom Corp.

ABOUT THE AUTHOR

Don Robertson has over 20 years of systems programming
and networking experience. He has designed and implemented data communications and systems software on a
wide variety of operating systems using assembler, C, C++,
and (most recently) Java languages. He founded DBR
Network Systems, Inc. in 1984 and has consulted and contracted over the years with major corporations such as IBM,
Hewlett-Packard, Aetna Life & Casualty, Norwest Banks,
and several state and municipal government agencies.
He has written articles in key journals on OSI, ATM, and
MPTN.

Mr. Robertson is also a well-known musician and
composer with seven albums to his credit. He was one of the
founders of the New Age Music genre and his music is
played on national radio in North America, Europe, and the
Far East.

Readers interested in Don Robertson's music can visit his
home page at:

http://home.earthlink.net/~dbrmusic